CATHOLIC MISSAL F(

CATHOLIC SUNDAY AND DAILY MASS READINGS FOR 2023 WITH THE PRINCIPAL CELEBRATIONS OF THE LITURGICAL YEAR A, 2023

By

Catholic Lectionary Publishers

CONTENTS

Section A

Section B

SECTION A

PRINCIPAL CELEBRATIONS OF THE LITURGICAL YEAR A, 2023

CELEBRATIONS	DATE
First Sunday of Advent, Year A	November 27, 2022
Ash Wednesday	February 22, 2023
Easter Sunday	April 9, 2023
The Ascension of the Lord	May 21, 2023
Pentecost Sunday	May 28, 2023
The Most Holy Body and Blood of Christ (*Corpus Christi*)	June 11, 2023
First Sunday of Advent, Year A	December 3, 2023

SECTION B

SUNDAY AND DAILY MASS READINGS FOR 2023

JANUARY 2023

Sunday January 1, 2023

Solemnity of Blessed Virgin Mary, Mother of God

First Reading – Numbers 6:22-27

22The LORD said to Moses: 23 "Speak to Aaron and his sons
and tell them: This is how you shall bless the Israelites. Say to
them: 24The LORD bless you and keep you! 25The LORD let
his face shine upon you, and be gracious to you! 26The LORD
look upon you kindly and give you peace! 27So shall they
invoke my name upon the Israelites, and I will bless them."

Responsorial Psalm – Psalms 67:2-3, 5, 6, 8.

R. (2a) May God bless us in his mercy.

2 May God have pity on us and bless us;

may he let his face shine upon us.

3 So may your way be known upon earth;

among all nations, your salvation.

R. May God bless us in his mercy.

5 May the nations be glad and exult

because you rule the peoples in equity;

the nations on the earth you guide.

R. May God bless us in his mercy.

6 May the peoples praise you, O God;

may all the peoples praise you!

8 May God bless us,

and may all the ends of the earth fear him!

R. May God bless us in his mercy.

Second Reading – Galatians 4:4-7

Brothers and sisters: [4]When the fullness of time had come,
God sent his Son, born of a woman, born under the law, [5] to
ransom those under the law, so that we might receive
adoption as sons. [6]As proof that you are sons, God sent the
Spirit of his Son into our hearts, crying out, “Abba, Father!” [7]So
you are no longer a slave but a son, and if a son then also an
heir, through God.

Alleluia – Hebrews 1:1-2

R. Alleluia, alleluia.

[1]In the past God spoke to our ancestors through the prophets;[2]
in these last days, he has spoken to us through the Son.

R. Alleluia, alleluia.

Gospel – Luke 2:16-21

[16] The shepherds went in haste to Bethlehem and found Mary
and Joseph, and the infant lying in the manger. [17] When they
saw this, they made known the message that had been told
them about this child. [18]All who heard it were amazed by what
had been told them by the shepherds. [19]And Mary kept all
these things, reflecting on them in her heart. [20]Then the
shepherds returned, glorifying and praising God for all they
had heard and seen, just as it had been told to them. [21]When
eight days were completed for his circumcision, he was named
Jesus, the name given him by the angel before he was
conceived in the womb.

Monday January 2, 2023

Memorial of Saints Basil the Great and Gregory Nazianzen, Bishops & Doctors

First Reading – 1 John 2:22-28

Beloved: [22]Who is the liar? Whoever denies that Jesus is the
Christ. Whoever denies the Father and the Son, this is the
antichrist. [23]Anyone who denies the Son does not have the
Father, but whoever confesses the Son has the Father as well.
[24]Let what you heard from the beginning remain in you. If what
you heard from the beginning remains in you, then you will
remain in the Son and in the Father. [25]And this is the promise

that he made us: eternal life. [26]I write you these things about
those who would deceive you. [27]As for you, the anointing that
you received from him remains in you, so that you do not need
anyone to teach you. But his anointing teaches you about
everything and is true and not false; just as it taught you,
remain in him. [28]And now, children, remain in him, so that
when he appears we may have confidence and not be put to
shame by him at his coming.

Responsorial Psalm – Psalms 98:1, 2-3AB, 3CD-4

R. (3cd) All the ends of the earth have seen the saving power of God.

1 Sing to the LORD a new song,

for he has done wondrous deeds;

His right hand has won victory for him,

his holy arm.

R. All the ends of the earth have seen the saving power of God.

2 The LORD has made his salvation known:

in the sight of the nations he has revealed his justice.

3AB He has remembered his kindness and his faithfulness

toward the house of Israel.

R. All the ends of the earth have seen the saving power of God.

3CD All the ends of the earth have seen

the salvation by our God.

4 Sing joyfully to the LORD, all you lands;

break into song; sing praise.

R. All the ends of the earth have seen the saving power of God.

Alleluia – Hebrews 1:1-2

R. Alleluia, alleluia.

1 In the past God spoke to our ancestors through the prophets;
2 in these last days, he has spoken to us through the Son.

R. Alleluia, alleluia.

Gospel – John 1:19-28

19This is the testimony of John. When the Jews from Jerusalem sent priests and Levites to him to ask him, "Who are you?" 20He admitted and did not deny it, but admitted, "I am not the Christ." 21So they asked him, "What are you then? Are you Elijah?" And he said, "I am not." "Are you the Prophet?" He answered, "No." 22So they said to him, "Who are you, so we can give an answer to those who sent us? What do you have to say for yourself?" 23He said: "I am the voice of one crying out in the desert, 'Make straight the way of the Lord,' as Isaiah the prophet said." 24Some Pharisees were also sent. 25They asked him, "Why then do you baptize if you are not the Christ or Elijah or the Prophet?" 26John answered them, "I baptize with water; but there is one among you whom you do not recognize, 27the one who is coming after me, whose sandal strap I am not worthy to untie." 28This happened in Bethany across the Jordan, where John was baptizing.

Tuesday January 3, 2023

Tuesday of the Christmas Weekday

First Reading – 1 John 2:29-3:6

29If you consider that God is righteous, you also know that everyone who acts in righteousness is begotten by him. 1See what love the Father has bestowed on us that we may be called the children of God. Yet so we are. The reason the world does not know us is that it did not know him. 2Beloved, we are God's children now; what we shall be has not yet been revealed. We do know that when it is revealed we shall be like him, for we shall see him as he is. 3Everyone who has this hope based on him makes himself pure, as he is pure. 4Everyone who commits sin commits lawlessness, for sin is lawlessness. 5You know that he was revealed to take away sins, and in him there is no sin. 6No one who remains in him sins; no one who sins has seen him or known him.

Responsorial Psalm – Psalms 98:1, 3CD-4, 5-6

R. (3cd) All the ends of the earth have seen the saving power of God.

1 Sing to the LORD a new song,

for he has done wondrous deeds;

His right hand has won victory for him, his holy arm.

R. All the ends of the earth have seen the saving power of God.

3CD All the ends of the earth have seen

the salvation by our God.

4 Sing joyfully to the LORD, all you lands;

break into song; sing praise.

R. All the ends of the earth have seen the saving power of God.

5 Sing praise to the LORD with the harp,

with the harp and melodious song.

6 With trumpets and the sound of the horn

sing joyfully before the King, the LORD.

R. All the ends of the earth have seen the saving power of God.

Alleluia – John 1:14A, 12A

R. Alleluia, alleluia.

14A The Word of God became flesh and dwelt among us. 12ATo those who accepted him he gave power to become the children of God.

R. Alleluia, alleluia.

Gospel – John 1:29-34

29John the Baptist saw Jesus coming toward him and said, "Behold, the Lamb of God, who takes away the sin of the
world. 30He is the one of whom I said, 'A man is coming after
me who ranks ahead of me because he existed before me.' 31I
did not know him, but the reason why I came baptizing with

water was that he might be made known to Israel." 32John testified further, saying, "I saw the Spirit come down like a dove from the sky and remain upon him. 33I did not know him, but the one who sent me to baptize with water told me, 'On whomever you see the Spirit come down and remain, he is the one who will baptize with the Holy Spirit.' 34Now I have seen and testified that he is the Son of God."

Wednesday January 4, 2023

Memorial of Saint Elizabeth Ann Seton, Religious

First Reading – 1 John 3:7-10

7Children, let no one deceive you. The person who acts in righteousness is righteous, just as he is righteous. 8Whoever sins belongs to the Devil, because the Devil has sinned from the beginning. Indeed, the Son of God was revealed to destroy the works of the Devil. 9No one who is begotten by God commits sin, because God's seed remains in him; he cannot sin because he is begotten by God. 10In this way, the children of God and the children of the Devil are made plain; no one who fails to act in righteousness belongs to God, nor anyone who does not love his brother.

Responsorial Psalm – Psalms 98:1, 7-8, 9

R. (3cd) All the ends of the earth have seen the saving power of God.

1 Sing to the LORD a new song,

for he has done wondrous deeds;

His right hand has won victory for him,

his holy arm.

R. All the ends of the earth have seen the saving power of God.

7 Let the sea and what fills it resound,

the world and those who dwell in it;

8 Let the rivers clap their hands,

the mountains shout with them for joy before the LORD.

R. All the ends of the earth have seen the saving power of God.

[9] The LORD comes;

he comes to rule the earth;

He will rule the world with justice

and the peoples with equity.

R. All the ends of the earth have seen the saving power of God.

Alleluia – Hebrews 1:1-2

R. Alleluia, alleluia.

[1] In the past God spoke to our ancestors through the prophets;
[2] in these last days, he has spoken to us through the Son.

R. Alleluia, alleluia.

Gospel – John 1:35-42

[35]John was standing with two of his disciples, [36]and as he
watched Jesus walk by, he said, "Behold, the Lamb of God."
[37]The two disciples heard what he said and followed Jesus.
[38]Jesus turned and saw them following him and said to them,
"What are you looking for?" They said to him, "Rabbi" (which
translated means Teacher), "where are you staying?" [39]He
said to them, "Come, and you will see." So they went and saw
where he was staying, and they stayed with him that day. It
was about four in the afternoon. [40]Andrew, the brother of
Simon Peter, was one of the two who heard John and followed
Jesus. [41]He first found his own brother Simon and told him,
"We have found the Messiah," which is translated Christ.
[42]Then he brought him to Jesus. Jesus looked at him and said,
"You are Simon the son of John; you will be called Cephas,"
which is translated Peter.

Thursday January 5, 2023

Memorial of Saint John Neumann, Bishop

First Reading – 1 John 3:11-21

Beloved: [11]This is the message you have heard from the
beginning: we should love one another, [12]unlike Cain who

belonged to the Evil One and slaughtered his brother. Why did
he slaughter him? Because his own works were evil, and
those of his brother righteous. [13]Do not be amazed, then,
brothers and sisters, if the world hates you. [14]We know that we
have passed from death to life because we love our brothers.
Whoever does not love remains in death. [15]Everyone who
hates his brother is a murderer, and you know that no
murderer has eternal life remaining in him. [16]The way we
came to know love was that he laid down his life for us; so we
ought to lay down our lives for our brothers. [17]If someone who
has worldly means sees a brother in need and refuses him
compassion, how can the love of God remain in him?
[18]Children, let us love not in word or speech but indeed and
truth. [19]Now this is how we shall know that we belong to the
truth and reassure our hearts before him [20]in whatever our
hearts condemn, for God is greater than our hearts and knows
everything. [21]Beloved, if our hearts do not condemn us, we
have confidence in God.

Responsorial Psalm – Psalms 100:1B-2, 3, 4, 5

R. (2a) Let all the earth cry out to God with joy.

1B Sing joyfully to the LORD, all you lands;

2 serve the LORD with gladness;

come before him with joyful song.

R. Let all the earth cry out to God with joy.

3 Know that the LORD is God;

he made us, his we are;

his people, the flock he tends.

R. Let all the earth cry out to God with joy.

4 Enter his gates with thanksgiving,

his courts with praise;

Give thanks to him; bless his name.

R. Let all the earth cry out to God with joy.

5 The LORD is good:

the LORD, whose kindness endures forever,

and his faithfulness, to all generations.

R. Let all the earth cry out to God with joy.

Alleluia

R. Alleluia, alleluia.

A holy day has dawned upon us. Come, you nations, and adore the Lord. Today a great light has come upon the earth.

R. Alleluia, alleluia.

Gospel – John 1:43-51

[43]Jesus decided to go to Galilee, and he found Philip. And Jesus said to him, "Follow me." [44]Now Philip was from Bethsaida, the town of Andrew and Peter. [45]Philip found Nathanael and told him, "We have found the one about whom Moses wrote in the law, and also the prophets, Jesus, son of Joseph, from Nazareth." [46]But Nathanael said to him, "Can anything good come from Nazareth?" Philip said to him, "Come and see." [47]Jesus saw Nathanael coming toward him and said of him, "Here is a true child of Israel. There is no duplicity in him." [48]Nathanael said to him, "How do you know me?" Jesus answered and said to him, "Before Philip called you, I saw you under the fig tree." [49]Nathanael answered him, "Rabbi, you are the Son of God; you are the King of Israel." [50]Jesus answered and said to him, "Do you believe because I told you that I saw you under the fig tree? You will see greater things than this." [51]And he said to him, "Amen, amen, I say to you, you will see the sky opened and the angels of God ascending and descending on the Son of Man."

Friday January 6, 2023

Memorial of Saint Andre Bessette

First Reading – 1 John 5:5-13

Beloved: [5]Who indeed is the victor over the world but the one who believes that Jesus is the Son of God? [6]This is the one who came through water and Blood, Jesus Christ, not by water alone, but by water and Blood. [7]The Spirit is the one who testifies, and the Spirit is truth. So there are three that testify, [8]the Spirit, the water, and the Blood, and the three are of one accord. [9]If we accept human testimony, the testimony

of God is surely greater. Now the testimony of God is this, that
he has testified on behalf of his Son. 10Whoever believes in
the Son of God has this testimony within himself. Whoever
does not believe God has made him a liar by not believing the
testimony God has given about his Son. 11And this is the
testimony: God gave us eternal life, and this life is in his Son.
12Whoever possesses the Son has life; whoever does not
possess the Son of God does not have life. 13I write these
things to you so that you may know that you have eternal life,
you who believe in the name of the Son of God.

Responsorial Psalm – Psalms 147:12-13, 14-15, 19-20

R. (12a) **Praise the Lord, Jerusalem.** or: **R. Alleluia.**

12 Glorify the LORD, O Jerusalem;

praise your God, O Zion.

13 For he has strengthened the bars of your gates;

he has blessed your children within you.

R. Praise the Lord, Jerusalem. or: **R. Alleluia.**

14 He has granted peace in your borders;

with the best of wheat he fills you.

15 He sends forth his command to the earth;

swiftly runs his word!

R. Praise the Lord, Jerusalem. or: **R. Alleluia.**

19 He has proclaimed his word to Jacob,

his statutes and his ordinances to Israel.

20 He has not done thus for any other nation;

his ordinances he has not made known to them. Alleluia.

R. Praise the Lord, Jerusalem. or: **R. Alleluia.**

Alleluia – Mark 9:6

R. Alleluia, alleluia.

6 The heavens were opened and the voice of the Father thundered: This is my beloved Son. Listen to him.

R. Alleluia, alleluia.

Gospel – Mark 1:7-11

[7]This is what John the Baptist proclaimed: "One mightier than I
is coming after me. I am not worthy to stoop and loosen the
thongs of his sandals. [8]I have baptized you with water; he will
baptize you with the Holy Spirit." [9]It happened in those days
that Jesus came from Nazareth of Galilee and was baptized in
the Jordan by John. [10]On coming up out of the water he saw
the heavens being torn open and the Spirit, like a dove,
descending upon him. [11]And a voice came from the heavens,
"You are my beloved Son; with you I am well pleased."

or Luke 3:23-38

[23]When Jesus began his ministry he was about thirty years of
age. He was the son, as was thought, of Joseph, the son of
Heli, [24]the son of Matthat, the son of Levi, the son of Melchi,
the son of Jannai, the son of Joseph, [25]the son of Mattathias,
the son of Amos, the son of Nahum, the son of Esli, the son of
Naggai, [26]the son of Maath, the son of Mattathias, the son of
Semein, the son of Josech, the son of Joda, [27]the son of
Joanan, the son of Rhesa, the son of Zerubbabel, the son of
Shealtiel, the son of Neri, [28]the son of Melchi, the son of Addi,
the son of Cosam, the son of Elmadam, the son of Er, [29]the
son of Joshua, the son of Eliezer, the son of Jorim, the son of
Matthat, the son of Levi, [30]the son of Simeon, the son of
Judah, the son of Joseph, the son of Jonam, the son of
Eliakim, [31]the son of Melea, the son of Menna, the son of
Mattatha, the son of Nathan, the son of David, [32]the son of
Jesse, the son of Obed, the son of Boaz, the son of Sala, the
son of Nahshon, [33]the son of Amminadab, the son of Admin,
the son of Arni, the son of Hezron, the son of Perez, the son of
Judah, [34]the son of Jacob, the son of Isaac, the son of
Abraham, the son of Terah, the son of Nahor, [35]the son of
Serug, the son of Reu, the son of Peleg, the son of Eber, the
son of Shelah, [36]the son of Cainan, the son of Arphaxad, the
son of Shem, the son of Noah, the son of Lamech, [37]the son of
Methuselah, the son of Enoch, the son of Jared, the son of
Mahalaleel, the son of Cainan, [38]the son of Enos, the son of
Seth, the son of Adam, the son of God.

OR Luke 3:23, 31-34, 36, 38

23When Jesus began his ministry he was about thirty years of
age. He was the son, as was thought, of Joseph, the son of
Heli, 31the son of Melea, the son of Menna, the son of
Mattatha, the son of Nathan, the son of David, 32the son of
Jesse, the son of Obed, the son of Boaz, the son of Sala, the
son of Nahshon, 33the son of Amminadab, the son of Admin,
the son of Arni, the son of Hezron, the son of Perez, the son of
Judah, 34the son of Jacob, the son of Isaac, the son of
Abraham, the son of Terah, the son of Nahor, 36the son of
Cainan, the son of Arphaxad, the son of Shem, the son of
Noah, the son of Lamech, 38the son of Enos, the son of Seth,
the son of Adam, the son of God.

Saturday January 7, 2023

Memorial of Saint Raymond of Penyfort - Priest

First Reading - First John 5: 14-21

14And this is the confidence which we have towards him: That,
whatsoever we shall ask according to his will, he heareth us.
15And we know that he heareth us whatsoever we ask: we
know that we have the petitions which we request of him. 16He
that knoweth his brother to sin a sin which is not to death, let
him ask, and life shall be given to him, who sinneth not to
death. There is a sin unto death: for that I say not that any
man ask. 17All iniquity is sin. And there is a sin unto death.
18We know that whosoever is born of God, sinneth not: but the
generation of God preserveth him, and the wicked one
toucheth him not. 19We know that we are of God, and the
whole world is seated in wickedness. 20And we know that the
Son of God is come: and he hath given us understanding that
we may know the true God, and may be in his true Son. This
is the true God and life eternal. 21Little children, keep
yourselves from idols. Amen.

Responsorial Psalm - Psalms 149: 1-2, 3-4, 5 and 6a and 9b

R. (4a) **The Lord takes delight in his people.** or **R. Alleluia.**

1 Sing ye to the Lord a new canticle: let his praise be in the
church of the saints.

[2] Let Israel rejoice in him that made him: and let the children of Sion be joyful in their king.

R. The Lord takes delight in his people. or **R. Alleluia.**

[3] Let them praise his name in choir: let them sing to him with the timbrel and the psaltery.

[4] For the Lord is well pleased with his people: and he will exalt the meek unto salvation.

R. The Lord takes delight in his people. or **R. Alleluia.**

[5] The saints shall rejoice in glory: they shall be joyful in their beds.

[6a] The high praise of God shall be in their mouth.

[9b] This glory is to all his saints. Alleluia.

R. The Lord takes delight in his people. or **R. Alleluia.**

Alleluia - Luke 7: 16

R. Alleluia, alleluia.

[16] A great prophet has arisen in our midst and God has visited his people.

R. Alleluia, alleluia.

Gospel - John 2: 1-11

[1]And the third day, there was a marriage in Cana of Galilee:
and the mother of Jesus was there. [2]And Jesus also was
invited, and his disciples, to the marriage. [3]And the wine
failing, the mother of Jesus saith to him: They have no wine.
[4]And Jesus saith to her: Woman, what is that to me and to
thee? my hour is not yet come. [5]His mother saith to the
waiters: Whatsoever he shall say to you, do ye. [6]Now there
were set there six waterpots of stone, according to the manner
of the purifying of the Jews, containing two or three measures
apiece. [7]Jesus saith to them: Fill the waterpots with water. And
they filled them up to the brim. [8]And Jesus saith to them: Draw
out now, and carry to the chief steward of the feast. And they
carried it. [9]And when the chief steward had tasted the water
made wine, and knew not whence it was, but the waiters knew
who had drawn the water; the chief steward calleth the
bridegroom, [10]And saith to him: Every man at first setteth forth
good wine, and when men have well drunk, then that which is

worse. But thou hast kept the good wine until now. [11]This
beginning of miracles did Jesus in Cana of Galilee; and
manifested his glory, and his disciples believed in him.

Sunday January 8 2023

Solemnity of the Epiphany of the Lord

First Reading – Isaiah 60:1-6

[1]Rise up in splendor, Jerusalem! Your light has come, the
glory of the Lord shines upon you. [2]See, darkness covers the
earth, and thick clouds cover the peoples; but upon you the
LORD shines, and over you appears his glory. [3]Nations shall
walk by your light, and kings by your shining radiance. [4]Raise
your eyes and look about; they all gather and come to you:
your sons come from afar, and your daughters in the arms of
their nurses. [5]Then you shall be radiant at what you see, your
heart shall throb and overflow, for the riches of the sea shall
be emptied out before you, the wealth of nations shall be
brought to you. [6]Caravans of camels shall fill you, dromedaries
from Midian and Ephah; all from Sheba shall come bearing
gold and frankincense, and proclaiming the praises of the
LORD.

Responsorial Psalm – Psalms 72:1-2, 7-8, 10-11, 12-13.

R. (cf. 11) **Lord, every nation on earth will adore you.**

[1] O God, with your judgment endow the king,

and with your justice, the king's son;

[2] He shall govern your people with justice

and your afflicted ones with judgment.

R. Lord, every nation on earth will adore you.

[7] Justice shall flower in his days,

and profound peace, till the moon be no more.

[8] May he rule from sea to sea,

and from the River to the ends of the earth.

R. Lord, every nation on earth will adore you.

10 The kings of Tarshish and the Isles shall offer gifts;

the kings of Arabia and Seba shall bring tribute.

11 All kings shall pay him homage,

all nations shall serve him.

R. Lord, every nation on earth will adore you.

12 For he shall rescue the poor when he cries out,

and the afflicted when he has no one to help him.

13 He shall have pity for the lowly and the poor;

the lives of the poor he shall save.

R. Lord, every nation on earth will adore you.

Second Reading – Ephesians 3:2-3A, 5-6

Brothers and sisters: 2You have heard of the stewardship of
God's grace that was given to me for your benefit, 3Anamely,
that the mystery was made known to me by revelation. 5It was
not made known to people in other generations as it has now
been revealed to his holy apostles and prophets by the Spirit:
6that the Gentiles are coheirs, members of the same body, and
copartners in the promise in Christ Jesus through the gospel.

Alleluia – Matthew 2:2

R. Alleluia, alleluia.

2We saw his star at its rising and have come to do him homage.

R. Alleluia, alleluia.

Gospel – Matthew 2:1-12

1When Jesus was born in Bethlehem of Judea, in the days of
King Herod, behold, magi from the east arrived in Jerusalem,
2saying, "Where is the newborn king of the Jews? We saw his
star at its rising and have come to do him homage." 3When
King Herod heard this, he was greatly troubled, and all
Jerusalem with him. 4Assembling all the chief priests and the
scribes of the people, He inquired of them where the Christ
was to be born. 5They said to him, "In Bethlehem of Judea, for
thus it has been written through the prophet: 6And you,
Bethlehem, land of Judah, are by no means least among the

rulers of Judah; since from you shall come a ruler, who is to
shepherd my people Israel." [7]Then Herod called the magi
secretly and ascertained from them the time of the star's
appearance. [8]He sent them to Bethlehem and said, "Go and
search diligently for the child. When you have found him, bring
me word, that I too may go and do him homage." [9]After their
audience with the king they set out. And behold, the star that
they had seen at its rising preceded them, until it came and
stopped over the place where the child was. [10]They were
overjoyed at seeing the star, [11]and on entering the house they
saw the child with Mary his mother. They prostrated
themselves and did him homage. Then they opened their
treasures and offered him gifts of gold, frankincense, and
myrrh. [12]And having been warned in a dream not to return to
Herod, they departed for their country by another way.

Monday January 9, 2023

Feast of the Baptism of the Lord

First Reading – Isaiah 42:1-4, 6-7

Thus says the LORD: [1]Here is my servant whom I uphold, my
chosen one with whom I am pleased, upon whom I have put
my spirit; he shall bring forth justice to the nations, [2]not crying
out, not shouting, not making his voice heard in the street. [3]a
bruised reed he shall not break, and a smoldering wick he
shall not quench, [4]until he establishes justice on the earth; the
coastlands will wait for his teaching. [6]I, the LORD, have called
you for the victory of justice, I have grasped you by the hand; I
formed you, and set you as a covenant of the people, a light
for the nations, [7]to open the eyes of the blind, to bring out
prisoners from confinement, and from the dungeon, those who
live in darkness.

Or Isaiah 40:1-5, 9-11

[1]Comfort, give comfort to my people, says your God. [2]Speak
tenderly to Jerusalem, and proclaim to her that her service is
at an end, her guilt is expiated; indeed, she has received from
the hand of the LORD double for all her sins. [3]A voice cries
out: In the desert prepare the way of the LORD! Make straight
in the wasteland a highway for our God! [4]Every valley shall be
filled in, every mountain and hill shall be made low; the rugged
land shall be made a plain, the rough country, a broad valley.

5 Then the glory of the LORD shall be revealed, and all people
shall see it together; for the mouth of the LORD has spoken.
9 Go up on to a high mountain, Zion, herald of glad tidings; cry
out at the top of your voice, Jerusalem, herald of good news!
Fear not to cry out and say to the cities of Judah: Here is your
God! 10 Here comes with power the Lord GOD, who rules by a
strong arm; here is his reward with him, his recompense
before him. 11 Like a shepherd he feeds his flock; in his arms
he gathers the lambs, carrying them in his bosom, and leading
the ewes with care.

Responsorial Psalm – Psalms 29:1-2, 3-4, 3, 9-10.

R. (11b) The Lord will bless his people with peace.

1 Give to the LORD, you sons of God,

give to the LORD glory and praise,

2 Give to the LORD the glory due his name;

adore the LORD in holy attire.

R. The Lord will bless his people with peace.

3AC The voice of the LORD is over the waters,

the LORD, over vast waters.

4 The voice of the LORD is mighty;

the voice of the LORD is majestic.

R. The Lord will bless his people with peace.

3B The God of glory thunders,

9C and in his temple all say, “Glory!”

10 The LORD is enthroned above the flood;

the LORD is enthroned as king forever.

R. The Lord will bless his people with peace.

Or Psalms 104:1B-2, 3-4, 24-25, 27-28, 29-30

R. (1) O bless the Lord, my soul.

1B O LORD, my God, you are great indeed!

you are clothed with majesty and glory,

2 robed in light as with a cloak.

You have spread out the heavens like a tent-cloth;

R. O bless the Lord, my soul.

3 You have constructed your palace upon the waters.

You make the clouds your chariot;

you travel on the wings of the wind.

4 You make the winds your messengers,

and flaming fire your ministers.

R. O bless the Lord, my soul.

24 How manifold are your works, O LORD!

In wisdom you have wrought them all–

the earth is full of your creatures;

25 the sea also, great and wide,

in which are schools without number

of living things both small and great.

R. O bless the Lord, my soul.

27 They look to you to give them food in due time.

28 When you give it to them, they gather it;

when you open your hand, they are filled with good things.

R. O bless the Lord, my soul.

29 If you take away their breath, they perish and return to the dust.

30 When you send forth your spirit, they are created,

and you renew the face of the earth.

R. O bless the Lord, my soul.

Second Reading – Acts 10:34-38

34Peter proceeded to speak to those gathered in the house of
Cornelius, saying: "In truth, I see that God shows no partiality.
35Rather, in every nation whoever fears him and acts uprightly
is acceptable to him. 36You know the word that he sent to the
Israelites as he proclaimed peace through Jesus Christ, who is
Lord of all, 37what has happened all over Judea, beginning in

Galilee after the baptism that John preached, 38how God anointed Jesus of Nazareth with the Holy Spirit and power. He went about doing good and healing all those oppressed by the devil, for God was with him."

Or Titus 2:11-14; 3:4-7

Beloved: 11The grace of God has appeared, saving all 12and training us to reject godless ways and worldly desires and to live temperately, justly, and devoutly in this age,13as we await the blessed hope, the appearance of the glory of our great God and savior Jesus Christ, 14who gave himself for us to deliver us from all lawlessness and to cleanse for himself a people as his own, eager to do what is good. 4When the kindness and generous love of God our savior appeared, 5not because of any righteous deeds we had done but because of his mercy, He saved us through the bath of rebirth and renewal by the Holy Spirit, 6whom he richly poured out on us through Jesus Christ our savior, 7so that we might be justified by his grace and become heirs in hope of eternal life.

Alleluia – cf. Mark 9:7

R. Alleluia, alleluia.

7The heavens were opened and the voice of the Father thundered: This is my beloved Son, listen to him.

R. Alleluia, alleluia.

Or cf. Luke 3:16

R. Alleluia, alleluia.

16 John said: One mightier than I is coming; he will baptize you with the Holy Spirit and with fire.

R. Alleluia, alleluia.

Gospel – Luke 3:15-16, 21-22

15The people were filled with expectation, and all were asking in their hearts whether John might be the Christ. 16John answered them all, saying, "I am baptizing you with water, but one mightier than I is coming. I am not worthy to loosen the thongs of his sandals. He will baptize you with the Holy Spirit and fire." 21After all the people had been baptized and Jesus also had been baptized and was praying, heaven was opened

[22]and the Holy Spirit descended upon him in bodily form like a dove. And a voice came from heaven, “You are my beloved Son; with you I am well pleased.”

or Matthew 3: 13-17

[13]Then cometh Jesus from Galilee to the Jordan, unto John, to be baptized by him. [14]But John stayed him, saying: I ought to be baptized by thee, and comest thou to me? [15]And Jesus answering, said to him: Suffer it to be so now. For so it becometh us to fulfill all justice. Then he suffered him. [16]And Jesus being baptized, forthwith came out of the water: and lo, the heavens were opened to him: and he saw the Spirit of God descending as a dove, and coming upon him. [17]And behold a voice from heaven, saying: This is my beloved Son, in whom I am well pleased.

Tuesday January 10, 2023

Tuesday of the First Week in Ordinary Time

First Reading – Hebrews 2:5-12

[5]It was not to angels that God subjected the world to come, of which we are speaking. [6]Instead, someone has testified somewhere: What is man that you are mindful of him, or the son of man that you care for him? [7]You made him for a little while lower than the angels; you crowned him with glory and honor, [8]subjecting all things under his feet. In “subjecting” all things to him, he left nothing not “subject to him.” Yet at present we do not see “all things subject to him,” [9]but we do see Jesus “crowned with glory and honor” because he suffered death, he who “for a little while” was made “lower than the angels,” that by the grace of God he might taste death for everyone. [10]For it was fitting that he, for whom and through whom all things exist, in bringing many children to glory, should make the leader to their salvation perfect through suffering. [11]He who consecrates and those who are being consecrated all have one origin. Therefore, he is not ashamed to call them “brothers” [12]saying: I will proclaim your name to my brethren, in the midst of the assembly I will praise you.

Responsorial Psalm – Psalms 8:2AB AND 5, 6-7, 8-9

R. (see 7) You have given your Son rule over the works of your hands.

2AB O LORD, our Lord,

how glorious is your name over all the earth!

5 What is man that you should be mindful of him,

or the son of man that you should care for him?

R. You have given your Son rule over the works of your hands.

6 You have made him little less than the angels,

and crowned him with glory and honor.

7 You have given him rule over the works of your hands,

putting all things under his feet.

R. You have given your Son rule over the works of your hands.

8 All sheep and oxen,

yes, and the beasts of the field,

9 The birds of the air, the fishes of the sea,

and whatever swims the paths of the seas.

R. You have given your Son rule over the works of your hands.

Alleluia – 1 Thessalonians 2:13

R. Alleluia, alleluia.

13 Receive the word of God, not as the word of men, but as it truly is, the word of God.

R. Alleluia, alleluia.

Gospel – Mark 1:21-28

21 Jesus came to Capernaum with his followers, and on the Sabbath he entered the synagogue and taught.
22 The people were astonished at his teaching, for he taught them as one

having authority and not as the scribes. [23]In their synagogue
was a man with an unclean spirit; [24]he cried out, "What have
you to do with us, Jesus of Nazareth? Have you come to
destroy us? I know who you are–the Holy One of God!"
[25]Jesus rebuked him and said, "Quiet! Come out of him!" [26]The
unclean spirit convulsed him and with a loud cry came out of
him. [27]All were amazed and asked one another, "What is this?
A new teaching with authority. He commands even the
unclean spirits and they obey him. [28]His fame spread
everywhere throughout the whole region of Galilee.

Wednesday January 11, 2023

Wednesday of First Week in Ordinary Time

First Reading – Hebrews 2:14-18

[14]Since the children share in blood and Flesh, Jesus likewise
shared in them, that through death he might destroy the one
who has the power of death, that is, the Devil, [15]and free those
who through fear of death had been subject to slavery all their
life. [16]Surely he did not help angels but rather the descendants
of Abraham; [17]therefore, he had to become like his brothers
and sisters in every way, that he might be a merciful and
faithful high priest before God to expiate the sins of the
people. [18]Because he himself was tested through what he
suffered, he is able to help those who are being tested.

Responsorial Psalm – Psalms 105:1-2, 3-4, 6-7, 8-9

R. (8a) The Lord remembers his covenant for ever. or: **R. Alleluia.**

[1] Give thanks to the LORD, invoke his name;

make known among the nations his deeds.

[2] Sing to him, sing his praise,

proclaim all his wondrous deeds.

R. The Lord remembers his covenant for ever. or: **R. Alleluia.**

[3] Glory in his holy name;

rejoice, O hearts that seek the LORD!

[4] Look to the LORD in his strength;

seek to serve him constantly.

R. The Lord remembers his covenant for ever. or: **R. Alleluia.**

6 You descendants of Abraham, his servants,

sons of Jacob, his chosen ones!

7 He, the LORD, is our God;

throughout the earth his judgments prevail.

R. The Lord remembers his covenant for ever. or: **R. Alleluia.**

8 He remembers forever his covenant

which he made binding for a thousand generations

9 Which he entered into with Abraham

and by his oath to Isaac.

R. The Lord remembers his covenant for ever. or: **R. Alleluia.**

Alleluia – John 10:27

R. Alleluia, alleluia.

27 My sheep hear my voice, says the Lord. I know them, and they follow me.

R. Alleluia, alleluia.

Gospel – Mark 1:29-39

29On leaving the synagogue Jesus entered the house of
Simon and Andrew with James and John. 30Simon's mother-
in-law lay sick with a fever. They immediately told him about
her. 31He approached, grasped her hand, and helped her up.
Then the fever left her and she waited on them. 32When it was
evening, after sunset, they brought to him all who were ill or
possessed by demons. 33The whole town was gathered at the
door. 34He cured many who were sick with various diseases,
and he drove out many demons, not permitting them to speak
because they knew him. 35Rising very early before dawn, he
left and went off to a deserted place, where he prayed.
36Simon and those who were with him pursued him 37and on
finding him said, "Everyone is looking for you." 38He told them,

"Let us go on to the nearby villages that I may preach there also. For this purpose have I come." [39]So he went into their synagogues, preaching and driving out demons throughout the whole of Galilee.

Thursday January 12, 2023

Thursday of the First Week in Ordinary Time

First Reading – Hebrews 3:7-14

[7]The Holy Spirit says: Oh, that today you would hear his voice,
[8]"Harden not your hearts as at the rebellion in the day of
testing in the desert, [9]where your ancestors tested and tried
me and saw my works [10]for forty years. Because of this I was
provoked with that generation and I said, 'They have always
been of erring heart, and they do not know my ways.' [11]As I
swore in my wrath, 'They shall not enter into my rest.'" [12]Take
care, brothers and sisters, that none of you may have an evil
and unfaithful heart, so as to forsake the living God.
[13]Encourage yourselves daily while it is still "today," so that
none of you may grow hardened by the deceit of sin. [14]We
have become partners of Christ if only we hold the beginning
of the reality firm until the end.

Responsorial Psalm – Psalms 95:6-7C, 8-9, 10-11

R. (8) If today you hear his voice, harden not your hearts.

[6] Come, let us bow down in worship;

let us kneel before the LORD who made us.

[7ABC] For he is our God,

and we are the people he shepherds, the flock he guides.

R. If today you hear his voice, harden not your hearts.

[8] Oh, that today you would hear his voice:

"Harden not your hearts as at Meribah,

as in the day of Massah in the desert,

[9] Where your fathers tempted me;

they tested me though they had seen my works."

R. If today you hear his voice, harden not your hearts.

10 Forty years I was wearied of that generation;

I said: “This people’s heart goes astray,

they do not know my ways.”

11 Therefore I swore in my anger:

“They shall never enter my rest.”

R. If today you hear his voice, harden not your hearts.

Alleluia – Matthew 4:23

R. Alleluia, alleluia.

23 Jesus preached the Gospel of the Kingdom and cured every disease among the people.

R. Alleluia, alleluia.

Gospel – Mark 1:40-45

40 A leper came to him and kneeling down begged him and
said, “If you wish, you can make me clean.” 41 Moved with pity,
he stretched out his hand, touched the leper, and said to him,
“I do will it. Be made clean.” 42 The leprosy left him
immediately, and he was made clean. 43 Then, warning him
sternly, he dismissed him at once. 44 Then he said to him, “See
that you tell no one anything, but go, show yourself to the
priest and offer for your cleansing what Moses prescribed; that
will be proof for them.” 45 The man went away and began to
publicize the whole matter. He spread the report abroad so
that it was impossible for Jesus to enter a town openly. He
remained outside in deserted places, and people kept coming
to him from everywhere.

Friday January 13, 2023

Friday of the First Week in Ordinary Time

First Reading – Hebrews 4:1-5, 11

1 Let us be on our guard while the promise of entering into his
rest remains, that none of you seem to have failed. 2 For in fact
we have received the Good News just as our ancestors did.
But the word that they heard did not profit them, for they were
not united in faith with those who listened. 3 For we who
believed enter into that rest, just as he has said: As I swore in

my wrath, "They shall not enter into my rest," and yet his works were accomplished at the foundation of the world. [4]For he has spoken somewhere about the seventh day in this manner, And God rested on the seventh day from all his works; [5]and again, in the previously mentioned place, They shall not enter into my rest. [11]Therefore, let us strive to enter into that rest, so that no one may fall after the same example of disobedience.

Responsorial Psalm – Psalms 78:3 AND 4BC,6C-7, 8

R. (see 7b) **Do not forget the works of the Lord!**

3 What we have heard and know,

and what our fathers have declared to us,

4BC we will declare to the generation to come

The glorious deeds of the LORD and his strength.

R. Do not forget the works of the Lord!

6C That they too may rise and declare to their sons

7 that they should put their hope in God,

And not forget the deeds of God

but keep his commands.

R. Do not forget the works of the Lord!

8 And not be like their fathers,

a generation wayward and rebellious,

A generation that kept not its heart steadfast

nor its spirit faithful toward God.

R. Do not forget the works of the Lord!

Alleluia – Luke 7:16

R. Alleluia, alleluia.

16A great prophet has arisen in our midst and God has visited his people.

R. Alleluia, alleluia.

Gospel – Mark 2:1-12

1When Jesus returned to Capernaum after some days, it became known that he was at home. 2Many gathered together so that there was no longer room for them, not even around the door, and he preached the word to them. 3They came bringing to him a paralytic carried by four men. 4Unable to get near Jesus because of the crowd, they opened up the roof above him. After they had broken through, they let down the mat on which the paralytic was lying. 5When Jesus saw their faith, he said to him, “Child, your sins are forgiven.” 6Now some of the scribes were sitting there asking themselves, 7“Why does this man speak that way? He is blaspheming. Who but God alone can forgive sins?” 8Jesus immediately knew in his mind what they were thinking to themselves, so he said, “Why are you thinking such things in your hearts? 9Which is easier, to say to the paralytic, ‘Your sins are forgiven,’ or to say, ‘Rise, pick up your mat and walk’? 10But that you may know that the Son of Man has authority to forgive sins on earth” 11he said to the paralytic, “I say to you, rise, pick up your mat, and go home.” 12He rose, picked up his mat at once, and went away in the sight of everyone. They were all astounded and glorified God, saying, “We have never seen anything like this.”

Saturday January 14, 2023

Saturday of the First Week in Ordinary Time

First Reading – Hebrews 4:12-16

12The word of God is living and effective, sharper than any two-edged sword, penetrating even between soul and spirit, joints and marrow, and able to discern reflections and thoughts of the heart. 13No creature is concealed from him, but everything is naked and exposed to the eyes of him to whom we must render an account. 14Since we have a great high priest who has passed through the heavens, Jesus, the Son of God, let us hold fast to our confession. 15For we do not have a high priest who is unable to sympathize with our weaknesses, but one who has similarly been tested in every way, yet without sin. 16So let us confidently approach the throne of grace to receive mercy and to find grace for timely help.

Responsorial Psalm – Psalms 19:8, 9, 10, 15

R. (see John 6:63c) **Your words, Lord, are Spirit and life.**

8 The law of the LORD is perfect,

refreshing the soul;

The decree of the LORD is trustworthy,

giving wisdom to the simple.

R. Your words, Lord, are Spirit and life.

9 The precepts of the LORD are right,

rejoicing the heart;

The command of the LORD is clear,

enlightening the eye.

R. Your words, Lord, are Spirit and life.

10 The fear of the LORD is pure,

enduring forever;

The ordinances of the LORD are true,

all of them just.

R. Your words, Lord, are Spirit and life.

15 Let the words of my mouth and the thought of my heart

find favor before you,

O LORD, my rock and my redeemer.

R. Your words, Lord, are Spirit and life.

Alleluia – Luke 4:18

R. Alleluia, alleluia.

18The Lord sent me to bring glad tidings to the poor and to proclaim liberty to captives.

R. Alleluia, alleluia.

Gospel – Mark 2:13-17

13Jesus went out along the sea. All the crowd came to him and
he taught them. 14As he passed by, he saw Levi, son of
Alphaeus, sitting at the customs post. Jesus said to him,

"Follow me." And he got up and followed Jesus. [15]While he was at table in his house, many tax collectors and sinners sat with Jesus and his disciples; for there were many who followed him. [16]Some scribes who were Pharisees saw that Jesus was eating with sinners and tax collectors and said to his disciples, "Why does he eat with tax collectors and sinners?" [17]Jesus heard this and said to them, "Those who are well do not need a physician, but the sick do. I did not come to call the righteous but sinners."

Sunday January 15, 2023

Second Sunday in Ordinary Time Year A

First Reading – Isaiah 49:3, 5-6

[3]The LORD said to me: You are my servant, Israel, through whom I show my glory. [5]Now the LORD has spoken who formed me as his servant from the womb, that Jacob may be brought back to him and Israel gathered to him; and I am made glorious in the sight of the LORD, and my God is now my strength! [6]It is too little, the LORD says, for you to be my servant, to raise up the tribes of Jacob, and restore the survivors of Israel; I will make you a light to the nations, that my salvation may reach to the ends of the earth.

Responsorial Psalm – Psalms 40:2, 4, 7-8, 8-9, 10

R. (8a and 9a) **Here am I, Lord; I come to do your will.**

2 I have waited, waited for the LORD,

and he stooped toward me and heard my cry.

4 And he put a new song into my mouth,

a hymn to our God.

R. Here am I, Lord; I come to do your will.

7 Sacrifice or offering you wished not,

but ears open to obedience you gave me.

Holocausts or sin-offerings you sought not;

8A then said I, "Behold I come."

R. Here am I, Lord; I come to do your will.

8B "In the written scroll it is prescribed for me,

[9] to do your will, O my God, is my delight,

and your law is within my heart!"

R. Here am I, Lord; I come to do your will.

[10] I announced your justice in the vast assembly;

I did not restrain my lips, as you, O LORD, know.

R. Here am I, Lord; I come to do your will.

Second Reading – 1 Corinthians 1:1-3

[1]Paul, called to be an apostle of Christ Jesus by the will of
God, and Sosthenes our brother, [2]to the church of God that is
in Corinth, to you who have been sanctified in Christ Jesus,
called to be holy, with all those everywhere who call upon the
name of our Lord Jesus Christ, their Lord and ours. [3]Grace to
you and peace from God our Father and the Lord Jesus
Christ.

Alleluia – John 1:14A, 12A

R. Alleluia, alleluia.

[14A]The Word of God became flesh and dwelt among us.[12A]To
those who accepted him, he gave power to become children of
God.

R. Alleluia, alleluia.

Gospel – John 1:29-34

[29]John the Baptist saw Jesus coming toward him and said,
"Behold, the Lamb of God, who takes away the sins of the
world. [30]He is the one of whom I said, 'A man is coming after
me who ranks ahead of me because he existed before me.' [31]I
did not know him, but the reason why I came baptizing with
water was that he might be made known to Israel." [32]John
testified further, saying, "I saw the Spirit come down like a
dove from heaven and remain upon him. [33]I did not know him,
but the one who sent me to baptize with water told me, 'On
whomever you see the Spirit come down and remain, he is the
one who will baptize with the Holy Spirit.' 34Now I have seen
and testified that he is the Son of God."

Monday January 16, 2023

Monday of Second Week in Ordinary Time

First Reading – Hebrews 5:1-10

Brothers and sisters: [1]Every high priest is taken from among
men and made their representative before God, to offer gifts
and sacrifices for sins. [2]He is able to deal patiently with the
ignorant and erring, for he himself is beset by weakness [3]and
so, for this reason, must make sin offerings for himself as well
as for the people. [4]No one takes this honor upon himself but
only when called by God, just as Aaron was. [5]In the same
way, it was not Christ who glorified himself in becoming high
priest, but rather the one who said to him: You are my Son:
this day I have begotten you; [6]just as he says in another place,
You are a priest forever according to the order of Melchizedek.
[7]In the days when he was in the Flesh, he offered prayers and
supplications with loud cries and tears to the one who was
able to save him from death, and he was heard because of his
reverence. [8]Son though he was, he learned obedience from
what he suffered; [9]and when he was made perfect, he became
the source of eternal salvation for all who obey him.

Responsorial Psalm – Psalms 110:1, 2, 3, 4

R. (4b) You are a priest for ever, in the line of Melchizedek.

1 The LORD said to my Lord: "Sit at my right hand

till I make your enemies your footstool."

R. You are a priest for ever, in the line of Melchizedek.

2 The scepter of your power the LORD will stretch forth from Zion:

"Rule in the midst of your enemies."

R. You are a priest for ever, in the line of Melchizedek.

3 "Yours is princely power in the day of your birth, in holy splendor;

before the daystar, like the dew, I have begotten you."

R. You are a priest for ever, in the line of Melchizedek.

4 The LORD has sworn, and he will not repent:

"You are a priest forever, according to the order of Melchizedek."

R. You are a priest for ever, in the line of Melchizedek.

Alleluia – Hebrews 4:12

R. Alleluia, alleluia.

12 The word of God is living and effective, able to discern reflections and thoughts of the heart.

R. Alleluia, alleluia.

Gospel – Mark 2:18-22

18 The disciples of John and of the Pharisees were accustomed
to fast. People came to Jesus and objected, "Why do the
disciples of John and the disciples of the Pharisees fast, but
your disciples do not fast?" 19 Jesus answered them, "Can the
wedding guests fast while the bridegroom is with them? As
long as they have the bridegroom with them they cannot fast.
20 But the days will come when the bridegroom is taken away
from them, and then they will fast on that day. 21 No one sews
a piece of unshrunken cloth on an old cloak. If he does, its
fullness pulls away, the new from the old, and the tear gets
worse. 22 Likewise, no one pours new wine into old wineskins.
Otherwise, the wine will burst the skins, and both the wine and
the skins are ruined. Rather, new wine is poured into fresh
wineskins."

Tuesday January 17, 2023

Memorial of Saint Anthony, Abbot

First Reading – Hebrews 6:10-20

Brothers and sisters: 10 God is not unjust so as to overlook
your work and the love you have demonstrated for his name
by having served and continuing to serve the holy ones. 11 We
earnestly desire each of you to demonstrate the same
eagerness for the fulfillment of hope until the end, 12 so that
you may not become sluggish, but imitators of those who,
through faith and patience, are inheriting the promises.
13 When God made the promise to Abraham, since he had no
one greater by whom to swear, he swore by himself, 14 and
said, I will indeed bless you and multiply you. 15 And so, after

patient waiting, Abraham obtained the promise. [16]Now, men swear by someone greater than themselves; for them an oath serves as a guarantee and puts an end to all argument. [17]So when God wanted to give the heirs of his promise an even clearer demonstration of the immutability of his purpose, he intervened with an oath, [18]so that by two immutable things, in which it was impossible for God to lie, we who have taken refuge might be strongly encouraged to hold fast to the hope that lies before us. [19]This we have as an anchor of the soul, sure and firm, which reaches into the interior behind the veil, [20]where Jesus has entered on our behalf as forerunner, becoming high priest forever according to the order of Melchizedek.

Responsorial Psalm – Psalms 111:1-2, 4-5, 9 AND 10C

R. (5) The Lord will remember his covenant for ever. or: **R. Alleluia.**

1 I will give thanks to the LORD with all my heart

in the company and assembly of the just.

2 Great are the works of the LORD,

exquisite in all their delights.

R. The Lord will remember his covenant for ever. or: **R. Alleluia.**

4 He has won renown for his wondrous deeds;

gracious and merciful is the LORD.

5 He has given food to those who fear him;

he will forever be mindful of his covenant.

R. The Lord will remember his covenant for ever. or: **R. Alleluia.**

9 He has sent deliverance to his people;

he has ratified his covenant forever;

holy and awesome is his name.

10C His praise endures forever.

R. The Lord will remember his covenant for ever. or: **R. Alleluia.**

Alleluia – Ephesians 1:17-18

R. Alleluia, alleluia.

17 May the Father of our Lord Jesus Christ enlighten the eyes
of our hearts,18 that we may know what is the hope that
belongs to our call.

R. Alleluia, alleluia.

Gospel – Mark 2:23-28

23As Jesus was passing through a field of grain on the
Sabbath, his disciples began to make a path while picking the
heads of grain. 24At this the Pharisees said to him, “Look, why
are they doing what is unlawful on the Sabbath?” 25He said to
them, “Have you never read what David did when he was in
need and he and his companions were hungry? 26How he
went into the house of God when Abiathar was high priest and
ate the bread of offering that only the priests could lawfully eat,
and shared it with his companions?” 27Then he said to them,
“The Sabbath was made for man, not man for the Sabbath.
28That is why the Son of Man is lord even of the Sabbath.”

Wednesday January 18, 2023

Wednesday of Second Week in Ordinary Time

First Reading – Hebrews 7:1-3, 15-17

1Melchizedek, king of Salem and priest of God Most High, met
Abraham as he returned from his defeat of the kings and
blessed him. 2And Abraham apportioned to him a tenth of
everything. His name first means righteous king, and he was
also “king of Salem,” that is, king of peace. 3Without father,
mother, or ancestry, without beginning of days or end of life,
thus made to resemble the Son of God, he remains a priest
forever. 15It is even more obvious if another priest is raised up
after the likeness of Melchizedek,16who has become so, not by
a law expressed in a commandment concerning physical
descent but by the power of a life that cannot be destroyed.
17For it is testified: You are a priest forever according to the
order of Melchizedek.

Responsorial Psalm – Psalms 110:1, 2, 3, 4

R. (4b) You are a priest for ever, in the line of Melchizedek.

1 The LORD said to my Lord: "Sit at my right hand

till I make your enemies your footstool."

R. You are a priest for ever, in the line of Melchizedek.

2 The scepter of your power the LORD will stretch forth from Zion:

"Rule in the midst of your enemies."

R. You are a priest for ever, in the line of Melchizedek.

3 "Yours is princely power in the day of your birth, in holy splendor;

before the daystar, like the dew, I have begotten you."

R. You are a priest for ever, in the line of Melchizedek.

4 The LORD has sworn, and he will not repent:

"You are a priest forever, according to the order of Melchizedek."

R. You are a priest for ever, in the line of Melchizedek.

Alleluia – Matthew 4:23

R. Alleluia, alleluia.

23 Jesus preached the Gospel of the Kingdom and cured every disease among the people.

R. Alleluia, alleluia.

Gospel – Mark 3:1-6

1 Jesus entered the synagogue. There was a man there who
had a withered hand. 2 They watched Jesus closely to see if he
would cure him on the Sabbath so that they might accuse him.
3 He said to the man with the withered hand, "Come up here
before us." 4 Then he said to the Pharisees, "Is it lawful to do
good on the Sabbath rather than to do evil, to save life rather
than to destroy it?" But they remained silent. 5 Looking around
at them with anger and grieved at their hardness of heart,
Jesus said to the man, "Stretch out your hand." He stretched it
out and his hand was restored. 6 The Pharisees went out and

immediately took counsel with the Herodians against him to put him to death.

Thursday January 19, 2023

Thursday of Second Week in Ordinary Time

First Reading – Hebrews 7:25-8:6

[25]Jesus is always able to save those who approach God
through him, since he lives forever to make intercession for
them. [26]It was fitting that we should have such a high priest:
holy, innocent, undefiled, separated from sinners, higher than
the heavens. [27]He has no need, as did the high priests, to offer
sacrifice day after day, first for his own sins and then for those
of the people; he did that once for all when he offered himself.
[28]For the law appoints men subject to weakness to be high
priests, but the word of the oath, which was taken after the
law, appoints a son, who has been made perfect forever. [1]The
main point of what has been said is this: we have such a high
priest, who has taken his seat at the right hand of the throne of
the Majesty in heaven, [2]a minister of the sanctuary and of the
true tabernacle that the Lord, not man, set up. [3]Now every
high priest is appointed to offer gifts and sacrifices; thus the
necessity for this one also to have something to offer. [4]If then
he were on earth, he would not be a priest, since there are
those who offer gifts according to the law. [5]They worship in a
copy and shadow of the heavenly sanctuary, as Moses was
warned when he was about to erect the tabernacle. For God
says, "See that you make everything according to the pattern
shown you on the mountain." [6]Now he has obtained so much
more excellent a ministry as he is mediator of a better
covenant, enacted on better promises.

Responsorial Psalm – Psalms 40:7-8A, 8B-9, 10, 17

R. (8a and 9a) **Here am I, Lord; I come to do your will.**

[7] Sacrifice or oblation you wished not,

but ears open to obedience you gave me.

[8A] Burnt offerings or sin-offerings you sought not;

then said I, "Behold I come."

R. Here am I, Lord; I come to do your will.

[8B] "In the written scroll it is prescribed for me,

[9] To do your will, O my God, is my delight,

and your law is within my heart!"

R. Here am I, Lord; I come to do your will.

[10] I announced your justice in the vast assembly;

I did not restrain my lips, as you, O LORD, know.

R. Here am I, Lord; I come to do your will.

[17] May all who seek you

exult and be glad in you,

And may those who love your salvation

say ever, "The LORD be glorified."

R. Here am I, Lord; I come to do your will.

Alleluia – 2 Timothy 1:10

R. Alleluia, alleluia.

[10]Our Savior Jesus Christ has destroyed death and brought life to light through the Gospel.

R. Alleluia, alleluia.

Gospel – Mark 3:7-12

[7]Jesus withdrew toward the sea with his disciples. A large
number of people followed from Galilee and from Judea.
[8]Hearing what he was doing, a large number of people came
to him also from Jerusalem, from Idumea, from beyond the
Jordan, and from the neighborhood of Tyre and Sidon. [9]He
told his disciples to have a boat ready for him because of the
crowd, so that they would not crush him. [10]He had cured many
and, as a result, those who had diseases were pressing upon
him to touch him. [11]And whenever unclean spirits saw him
they would fall down before him and shout, "You are the Son
of God." [12]He warned them sternly not to make him known.

Friday January 20, 2023

Friday of the Second Week in Ordinary Time

First Reading – Hebrews 8:6-13

Brothers and sisters: 6Now our high priest has obtained so
much more excellent a ministry as he is mediator of a better
covenant, enacted on better promises. 7For if that first
covenant had been faultless, no place would have been
sought for a second one. 8But he finds fault with them and
says: Behold, the days are coming, says the Lord, when I will
conclude a new covenant with the house of Israel and the
house of Judah. 9It will not be like the covenant I made with
their fathers the day I took them by the hand to lead them forth
from the land of Egypt; for they did not stand by my covenant
and I ignored them, says the Lord. 10But this is the covenant I
will establish with the house of Israel after those days, says
the Lord: I will put my laws in their minds and I will write them
upon their hearts. I will be their God, and they shall be my
people. 11And they shall not teach, each one his fellow citizen
and kin, saying, "Know the Lord," for all shall know me, from
least to greatest. 12For I will forgive their evildoing and
remember their sins no more. 13When he speaks of a "new"
covenant, he declares the first one obsolete. And what has
become obsolete and has grown old is close to disappearing.

Responsorial Psalm – Psalms 85:8 AND 10, 11-12, 13-14

R. (11a) Kindness and truth shall meet.

8 Show us, O LORD, your mercy,

and grant us your salvation.

10 Near indeed is his salvation to those who fear him,

glory dwelling in our land.

R. Kindness and truth shall meet.

11 Kindness and truth shall meet;

justice and peace shall kiss.

12 Truth shall spring out of the earth,

and justice shall look down from heaven.

R. Kindness and truth shall meet.

13 The LORD himself will give his benefits;

our land shall yield its increase.

14 Justice shall walk before him,

and salvation, along the way of his steps.

R. Kindness and truth shall meet.

Alleluia

R. Alleluia, alleluia.

God was reconciling the world to himself in Christ, and entrusting to us the message of reconciliation.

R. Alleluia, alleluia.

Gospel – Mark 3:13-19

13 Jesus went up the mountain and summoned those whom he
wanted and they came to him. 14 He appointed Twelve, whom
he also named Apostles, that they might be with him and he
might send them forth to preach 15 and to have authority to
drive out demons: 16 He appointed the Twelve: Simon, whom
he named Peter; 17 James, son of Zebedee, and John the
brother of James, whom he named Boanerges, that is, sons of
thunder; 18 Andrew, Philip, Bartholomew, Matthew, Thomas,
James the son of Alphaeus; Thaddeus, Simon the Cananean,
19 and Judas Iscariot who betrayed him.

Saturday January 21, 2023

Memorial of Saint Agnes, Virgin and Martyr

First Reading – Hebrews 9:2-3, 11-14

2 A tabernacle was constructed, the outer one, in which were
the lampstand, the table, and the bread of offering; this is
called the Holy Place. 3 Behind the second veil was the
tabernacle called the Holy of Holies. 11 But when Christ came
as high priest of the good things that have come to be,
passing through the greater and more perfect tabernacle not
made by hands, that is, not belonging to this creation, 12 he
entered once for all into the sanctuary, not with the blood of
goats and calves but with his own Blood, thus obtaining

eternal redemption.[13]For if the blood of goats and bulls and the sprinkling of a heifer's ashes can sanctify those who are defiled so that their flesh is cleansed,[14]how much more will the Blood of Christ, who through the eternal spirit offered himself unblemished to God, cleanse our consciences from dead works to worship the living God.

Responsorial Psalm – Psalms 47:2-3, 6-7, 8-9

R. (6) God mounts his throne to shouts of joy: a blare of trumpets for the Lord.

2 All you peoples, clap your hands,

shout to God with cries of gladness,

3 For the LORD, the Most High, the awesome,

is the great king over all the earth.

R. God mounts his throne to shouts of joy: a blare of trumpets for the Lord.

6 God mounts his throne amid shouts of joy;

the LORD, amid trumpet blasts.

7 Sing praise to God, sing praise;

sing praise to our king, sing praise.

R. God mounts his throne to shouts of joy: a blare of trumpets for the Lord.

8 For king of all the earth is God:

sing hymns of praise.

9 God reigns over the nations,

God sits upon his holy throne.

R. God mounts his throne to shouts of joy: a blare of trumpets for the Lord.

Alleluia – Acts 16:14B

R. Alleluia, alleluia.

14B Open our hearts, O Lord, to listen to the words of your Son.

R. Alleluia, alleluia

Gospel – Mark 3:20-21

[20]Jesus came with his disciples into the house. Again the crowd gathered,

making it impossible for them even to eat. [21]When his relatives heard of this they set out to seize him, for they said, "He is out of his mind."

Sunday January 22, 2023

Third Sunday in Ordinary Time, Year A

First Reading – Isaiah 8:23-9:3

[23] First the Lord degraded the land of Zebulun and the land of
Naphtali; but in the end he has glorified the seaward road, the
land west of the Jordan, the District of the Gentiles. [1]Anguish
has taken wing, dispelled is darkness: for there is no gloom
where but now there was distress. The people who walked in
darkness have seen a great light; upon those who dwelt in the
land of gloom a light has shone. [2]You have brought them
abundant joy and great rejoicing, as they rejoice before you as
at the harvest, as people make merry when dividing spoils.
[3]For the yoke that burdened them, the pole on their shoulder,
and the rod of their taskmaster you have smashed, as on the
day of Midian.

Responsorial Psalm – Psalms 27:1, 4, 13-14

R. (1a) The Lord is my light and my salvation.

[1] The LORD is my light and my salvation;

whom should I fear?

The LORD is my life's refuge;

of whom should I be afraid?

R. The Lord is my light and my salvation.

[4] One thing I ask of the LORD;

this I seek:

To dwell in the house of the LORD

all the days of my life,

That I may gaze on the loveliness of the LORD

and contemplate his temple.

R. The Lord is my light and my salvation.

13 I believe that I shall see the bounty of the LORD

in the land of the living.

14 Wait for the LORD with courage;

be stouthearted, and wait for the LORD.

R. The Lord is my light and my salvation.

Second Reading – 1 Corinthians 1:10-13, 17

10I urge you, brothers and sisters, in the name of our Lord
Jesus Christ, that all of you agree in what you say, and that
there be no divisions among you, but that you be united in the
same mind and in the same purpose.11For it has been
reported to me about you, my brothers and sisters, by Chloe's
people, that there are rivalries among you. 12I mean that each
of you is saying, "I belong to Paul," or "I belong to Apollos," or
"I belong to Cephas," or "I belong to Christ." 13Is Christ divided
Was Paul crucified for you? Or were you baptized in the name
of Paul? 17For Christ did not send me to baptize but to preach
the gospel, and not with the wisdom of human eloquence, so
that the cross of Christ might not be emptied of its meaning.

Alleluia – Matthew 4:23

R. Alleluia, alleluia.

23Jesus proclaimed the Gospel of the kingdom and cured every disease among the people.

R. Alleluia, alleluia.

Gospel – Matthew 4:12-23

12When Jesus heard that John had been arrested, he withdrew
to Galilee.13 He left Nazareth and went to live in Capernaum
by the sea, in the region of Zebulun and Naphtali,14that what
had been said through Isaiah the prophet might be
fulfilled:15Land of Zebulun and land of Naphtali, the way to the
sea, beyond the Jordan, Galilee of the Gentiles,16the people
who sit in darkness have seen a great light, on those dwelling
in a land overshadowed by death light has arisen.17From that
time on, Jesus began to preach and say, "Repent, for the

kingdom of heaven is at hand." 18As he was walking by the
Sea of Galilee, he saw two brothers, Simon who is called
Peter, and his brother Andrew, casting a net into the sea; they
were fishermen.19He said to them, "Come after me, and I will
make you fishers of men." 20At once they left their nets and
followed him. 21He walked along from there and saw two other
brothers, James, the son of Zebedee, and his brother John.
They were in a boat, with their father Zebedee, mending their
nets. He called them,22and immediately they left their boat and
their father and followed him. 23He went around all of Galilee,
teaching in their synagogues, proclaiming the gospel of the
kingdom, and curing every disease and illness among the
people.

OR Matthew 4:12-17

12When Jesus heard that John had been arrested, he withdrew
to Galilee.13He left Nazareth and went to live in Capernaum by
the sea, in the region of Zebulun and Naphtali,14that what had
been said through Isaiah the prophet might be fulfilled:15Land
of Zebulun and land of Naphtali, the way to the sea, beyond
the Jordan, Galilee of the Gentiles,16the people who sit in
darkness have seen a great light, on those dwelling in a land
overshadowed by death light has arisen.17From that time on,
Jesus began to preach and say, "Repent, for the kingdom of
heaven is at hand."

Monday January 23, 2023

Monday of the Third Week in Ordinary Time

First Reading – Hebrews 9:15, 24-28

15Christ is mediator of a new covenant: since a death has
taken place for deliverance from transgressions under the first
covenant, those who are called may receive the promised
eternal inheritance. 24For Christ did not enter into a sanctuary
made by hands, a copy of the true one, but heaven itself, that
he might now appear before God on our behalf. 25Not that he
might offer himself repeatedly, as the high priest enters each
year into the sanctuary with blood that is not his own; 26if that
were so, he would have had to suffer repeatedly from the
foundation of the world. But now once for all he has appeared
at the end of the ages to take away sin by his sacrifice. 27Just
as it is appointed that human beings die once, and after this

the judgment, [28]so also Christ, offered once to take away the sins of many, will appear a second time, not to take away sin but to bring salvation to those who eagerly await him.

Responsorial Psalm – Psalms 98:1, 2-3AB, 3CD-4, 5-6

R. (1a) **Sing to the Lord a new song, for he has done marvelous deeds.**

1 Sing to the LORD a new song,

for he has done wondrous deeds;

His right hand has won victory for him,

his holy arm.

R. Sing to the Lord a new song, for he has done marvelous deeds.

2 The LORD has made his salvation known:

in the sight of the nations he has revealed his justice.

3AB He has remembered his kindness and his faithfulness

toward the house of Israel.

R. Sing to the Lord a new song, for he has done marvelous deeds.

3CD All the ends of the earth have seen

the salvation by our God.

4 Sing joyfully to the LORD, all you lands;

break into song; sing praise.

R. Sing to the Lord a new song, for he has done marvelous deeds.

5 Sing praise to the LORD with the harp,

with the harp and melodious song.

6 With trumpets and the sound of the horn

sing joyfully before the King, the LORD.

R. Sing to the Lord a new song, for he has done marvelous deeds.

Alleluia – 2 Timothy 1:10

R. Alleluia, alleluia.

[10]Our Savior Jesus Christ has destroyed death and brought
life to light through the Gospel.

R. Alleluia, alleluia.

Gospel – Mark 3:22-30

[22]The scribes who had come from Jerusalem said of Jesus,
“He is possessed by Beelzebul,” and “By the prince of demons
he drives out demons.” [23]Summoning them, he began to
speak to them in parables, “How can Satan drive out Satan?
[24]If a kingdom is divided against itself, that kingdom cannot
stand. [25]And if a house is divided against itself, that house will
not be able to stand. [26]And if Satan has risen up against
himself and is divided, he cannot stand; that is the end of him.
[27]But no one can enter a strong man’s house to plunder his
property unless he first ties up the strong man. Then he can
plunder his house. [28]Amen, I say to you, all sins and all
blasphemies that people utter will be forgiven them. [29]But
whoever blasphemes against the Holy Spirit will never have
forgiveness, but is guilty of an everlasting sin.” [30]For they had
said, “He has an unclean spirit.”

Tuesday January 24, 2023

Memorial of Saint Francis de Sales, Bishop and Doctor of the Church

First Reading – Hebrews 10:1-10

Brothers and sisters: [1]Since the law has only a shadow of the
good things to come, and not the very image of them, it can
never make perfect those who come to worship by the same
sacrifices that they offer continually each year. [2]Otherwise,
would not the sacrifices have ceased to be offered, since the
worshipers, once cleansed, would no longer have had any
consciousness of sins? [3]But in those sacrifices there is only a
yearly remembrance of sins, [4]for it is impossible that the blood
of bulls and goats take away sins. [5]For this reason, when he
came into the world, he said: Sacrifice and offering you did not
desire, but a body you prepared for me; [6]in burnt offerings and
sin offerings you took no delight. [7]Then I said, As is written of

me in the scroll, Behold, I come to do your will, O God. [8]First
he says, Sacrifices and offerings, burnt offerings and sin
offerings, you neither desired nor delighted in. These are
offered according to the law. [9]Then he says, Behold, I come to
do your will. He takes away the first to establish the second.
[10]By this "will," we have been consecrated through the offering
of the Body of Jesus Christ once for all.

Responsorial Psalm – Psalms 40:2 AND 4AB, 7-8A, 10, 11

R. (8a and 9a) **Here am I Lord; I come to do your will.**

2 I have waited, waited for the LORD,

and he stooped toward me.

4AB And he put a new song into my mouth,

a hymn to our God.

R. Here am I Lord; I come to do your will.

7 Sacrifice or oblation you wished not,

but ears open to obedience you gave me.

Burnt offerings or sin-offerings you sought not;

8A then said I, "Behold I come."

R. Here am I Lord; I come to do your will.

10 I announced your justice in the vast assembly;

I did not restrain my lips, as you, O LORD, know.

R. Here am I Lord; I come to do your will.

11 Your justice I kept not hid within my heart;

your faithfulness and your salvation I have spoken of;

I have made no secret of your kindness and your truth

in the vast assembly.

R. Here am I Lord; I come to do your will.

Alleluia – Matthew 11:25

R. Alleluia, alleluia.

25 Blessed are you, Father, Lord of heaven and earth; you have
revealed to little ones the mysteries of the Kingdom.

R. Alleluia, alleluia.

Gospel – Mark 3:31-35

31 The mother of Jesus and his brothers arrived at the house.
Standing outside, they sent word to Jesus and called him. 32 A
crowd seated around him told him, “Your mother and your
brothers and your sisters are outside asking for you.” 33 But he
said to them in reply, “Who are my mother and my brothers?”
34 And looking around at those seated in the circle he said,
“Here are my mother and my brothers. 35 For whoever does the
will of God is my brother and sister and mother.”

Wednesday January 25, 2023

Feast of Conversion of Saint Paul, Apostle

First Reading – Acts 22:3-16

3 Paul addressed the people in these words: “I am a Jew, born
in Tarsus in Cilicia, but brought up in this city. At the feet of
Gamaliel I was educated strictly in our ancestral law and was
zealous for God, just as all of you are today. 4 I persecuted this
Way to death, binding both men and women and delivering
them to prison. 5 Even the high priest and the whole council of
elders can testify on my behalf. For from them I even received
letters to the brothers and set out for Damascus to bring back
to Jerusalem in chains for punishment those there as well.
6 “On that journey as I drew near to Damascus, about noon a
great light from the sky suddenly shone around me. 7 I fell to
the ground and heard a voice saying to me, ‘Saul, Saul, why
are you persecuting me?’ 8 I replied, ‘Who are you, sir?’ And he
said to me, ‘I am Jesus the Nazorean whom you are
persecuting.’ 9 My companions saw the light but did not hear
the voice of the one who spoke to me. 10 I asked, ‘What shall I
do, sir?’ The Lord answered me, ‘Get up and go into
Damascus, and there you will be told about everything
appointed for you to do.’ 11 Since I could see nothing because
of the brightness of that light, I was led by hand by my
companions and entered Damascus. 12 “A certain Ananias, a
devout observer of the law, and highly spoken of by all the
Jews who lived there, 13 came to me and stood there and said,
‘Saul, my brother, regain your sight.’ And at that very moment I

regained my sight and saw him.14 Then he said, 'The God of
our ancestors designated you to know his will, to see the
Righteous One, and to hear the sound of his voice;15 for you
will be his witness before all to what you have seen and heard.
16Now, why delay? Get up and have yourself baptized and
your sins washed away, calling upon his name.'"

Or Acts 9:1-22

1Saul, still breathing murderous threats against the disciples of
the Lord, went to the high priest 2and asked him for letters to
the synagogues in Damascus, that, if he should find any men
or women who belonged to the Way, he might bring them back
to Jerusalem in chains.3On his journey, as he was nearing
Damascus, a light from the sky suddenly flashed around him.
4He fell to the ground and heard a voice saying to him, "Saul,
Saul, why are you persecuting me?" 5He said, "Who are you,
sir?" The reply came, "I am Jesus, whom you are persecuting.
6 Now get up and go into the city and you will be told what you
must do." 7The men who were traveling with him stood
speechless, for they heard the voice but could see no one.
8Saul got up from the ground, but when he opened his eyes he
could see nothing; so they led him by the hand and brought
him to Damascus. 9For three days he was unable to see, and
he neither ate nor drank. 10There was a disciple in Damascus
named Ananias, and the Lord said to him in a vision, Ananias."
He answered, "Here I am, Lord." 11The Lord said to him, "Get
up and go to the street called Straight and ask at the house of
Judas for a man from Tarsus named Saul. He is there praying,
12and in a vision he has seen a man named Ananias come in
and lay his hands on him, that he may regain his sight." 13But
Ananias replied, "Lord, I have heard from many sources about
this man, what evil things he has done to your holy ones in
Jerusalem. 14 And here he has authority from the chief priests
to imprison all who call upon your name." 15But the Lord said
to him, "Go, for this man is a chosen instrument of mine to
carry my name before Gentiles, kings, and children of Israel,
16and I will show him what he will have to suffer for my name."
17So Ananias went and entered the house; laying his hands on
him, he said, "Saul, my brother, the Lord has sent me, Jesus
who appeared to you on the way by which you came, that you
may regain your sight and be filled with the Holy Spirit."
18Immediately things like scales fell from his eyes and he
regained his sight. He got up and was baptized, 19and when

he had eaten, he recovered his strength. He stayed some days with the disciples in Damascus, [20]and he began at once to proclaim Jesus in the synagogues, that he is the Son of God. [21]All who heard him were astounded and said, "Is not this the man who in Jerusalem ravaged those who call upon this name, and came here expressly to take them back in chains to the chief priests?" [22]But Saul grew all the stronger and confounded the Jews who lived in Damascus, proving that this is the Christ.

Responsorial Psalm – Psalms 117:1BC, 2

R. (Mark 16:15) Go out to all the world and tell the Good News. Or R. Alleluia, alleluia.

1BC Praise the LORD, all you nations;

glorify him, all you peoples!

R. Go out to all the world, and tell the Good News. Or R. Alleluia, alleluia.

2 For steadfast is his kindness toward us,

and the fidelity of the LORD endures forever.

R. Go out to all the world, and tell the Good News. Or R. Alleluia, alleluia.

Alleluia – cf. John 15:16

R. Alleluia, alleluia.

16 I chose you from the world, To go and bear fruit that will last, says the Lord.

R. Alleluia, alleluia.

Gospel – Mark 16:15-18

[15]Jesus appeared to the Eleven and said to them: "Go into the whole world and proclaim the Gospel to every creature.[16] Whoever believes and is baptized will be saved; whoever does not believe will be condemned.[17] These signs will accompany those who believe: in my name they will drive out demons, they will speak new languages.[18] They will pick up serpents with their hands, and if they drink any deadly thing, it will not harm them. They will lay hands on the sick, and they will recover."

Thursday January 26, 2023

Memorial of Saints Timothy and Titus - Bps

First Reading – 2 Timothy 1:1-8

[1]Paul, an Apostle of Christ Jesus by the will of God for the
promise of life in Christ Jesus, [2]to Timothy, my dear child:
grace, mercy, and peace from God the Father and Christ
Jesus our Lord. [3]I am grateful to God, whom I worship with a
clear conscience as my ancestors did, as I remember you
constantly in my prayers, night and day. [4]I yearn to see you
again, recalling your tears, so that I may be filled with joy, [5]as I
recall your sincere faith that first lived in your grandmother
Lois and in your mother Eunice and that I am confident lives
also in you. [6]For this reason, I remind you to stir into flame the
gift of God that you have through the imposition of my hands.
[7]For God did not give us a spirit of cowardice but rather of
power and love and self-control. [8]So do not be ashamed of
your testimony to our Lord, nor of me, a prisoner for his sake;
but bear your share of hardship for the Gospel with the
strength that comes from God.

Or Titus 1:1-5

[1]Paul, a slave of God and Apostle of Jesus Christ for the sake
of the faith of God's chosen ones and the recognition of
religious truth, [2]in the hope of eternal life that God, who does
not lie, promised before time began, [3]who indeed at the proper
time revealed his word in the proclamation with which I was
entrusted by the command of God our savior, [4]to Titus, my
true child in our common faith: grace and peace from God the
Father and Christ Jesus our savior. [5]For this reason I left you
in Crete so that you might set right what remains to be done
and appoint presbyters in every town, as I directed you.

Responsorial Psalm – Psalms 96:1-2A, 2B-3, 7-8A, 10

R. (3) Proclaim God's marvelous deeds to all the nations.

[1] Sing to the LORD a new song;

sing to the LORD, all you lands.

[2A] Sing to the LORD; bless his name.

R. Proclaim God's marvelous deeds to all the nations.

[2B] Announce his salvation, day after day.

[3] Tell his glory among the nations;

among all peoples, his wondrous deeds.

R. Proclaim God's marvelous deeds to all the nations.

[7] Give to the LORD, you families of nations,

give to the LORD glory and praise;

[8A] give to the LORD the glory due his name!

R. Proclaim God's marvelous deeds to all the nations.

[10] Say among the nations: The LORD is king.

He has made the world firm, not to be moved;

he governs the peoples with equity.

R. Proclaim God's marvelous deeds to all the nations.

Alleluia

R. Alleluia, alleluia.

The seed is the word of God, Christ is the sower; all who come to him will live for ever.

R. Alleluia, alleluia.

Gospel – Mark 4:1-20

[1]On another occasion, Jesus began to teach by the sea. A
very large crowd gathered around him so that he got into a
boat on the sea and sat down. And the whole crowd was
beside the sea on land. [2]And he taught them at length in
parables, and in the course of his instruction he said to them,
[3]"Hear this! A sower went out to sow. [4]And as he sowed, some
seed fell on the path, and the birds came and ate it up. [5]Other
seed fell on rocky ground where it had little soil. It sprang up at
once because the soil was not deep. [6]And when the sun rose,
it was scorched and it withered for lack of roots. [7]Some seed
fell among thorns, and the thorns grew up and choked it and it
produced no grain. [8]And some seed fell on rich soil and
produced fruit. It came up and grew and yielded thirty, sixty,
and a hundredfold." [9]He added, "Whoever has ears to hear
ought to hear." [10]And when he was alone, those present along

with the Twelve questioned him about the parables. [11]He
answered them, "The mystery of the Kingdom of God has
been granted to you. But to those outside everything comes in
parables, [12]so that they may look and see but not perceive,
and hear and listen but not understand, in order that they may
not be converted and be forgiven." [13]Jesus said to them, "Do
you not understand this parable? Then how will you
understand any of the parables? [14]The sower sows the word.
[15]These are the ones on the path where the word is sown. As
soon as they hear, Satan comes at once and takes away the
word sown in them. [16]And these are the ones sown on rocky
ground who, when they hear the word, receive it at once with
joy. [17]But they have no roots; they last only for a time. Then
when tribulation or persecution comes because of the word,
they quickly fall away. [18]Those sown among thorns are
another sort. They are the people who hear the word, [19]but
worldly anxiety, the lure of riches, and the craving for other
things intrude and choke the word, and it bears no fruit. [20]But
those sown on rich soil are the ones who hear the word and
accept it and bear fruit thirty and sixty and a hundredfold."

Friday January 27, 2023

Friday of the Third Week in Ordinary Time

First Reading – Hebrews 10:32-39

[32]Remember the days past when, after you had been
enlightened, you endured a great contest of suffering. [33]At
times you were publicly exposed to abuse and affliction; at
other times you associated yourselves with those so treated.
[34]You even joined in the sufferings of those in prison and
joyfully accepted the confiscation of your property, knowing
that you had a better and lasting possession. [35]Therefore, do
not throw away your confidence; it will have great
recompense. [36]You need endurance to do the will of God and
receive what he has promised. [37]For, after just a brief moment,
he who is to come shall come; he shall not delay. [38]But my just
one shall live by faith, and if he draws back I take no pleasure
in him. [39]We are not among those who draw back and perish,
but among those who have faith and will possess life.

Responsorial Psalm – Psalms 37:3-4, 5-6, 23-24, 39-40

R. (39a) The salvation of the just comes from the Lord.

3 Trust in the LORD and do good,

that you may dwell in the land and be fed in security.

4 Take delight in the LORD,

and he will grant you your heart's requests.

R. The salvation of the just comes from the Lord.

5 Commit to the LORD your way;

trust in him, and he will act.

6 He will make justice dawn for you like the light;

bright as the noonday shall be your vindication.

R. The salvation of the just comes from the Lord.

23 By the LORD are the steps of a man made firm,

and he approves his way.

24 Though he fall, he does not lie prostrate,

for the hand of the LORD sustains him.

R. The salvation of the just comes from the Lord.

39 The salvation of the just is from the LORD;

he is their refuge in time of distress.

40 And the LORD helps them and delivers them;

he delivers them from the wicked and saves them,

because they take refuge in him.

R. The salvation of the just comes from the Lord.

Alleluia – Matthew 11:25

R. Alleluia, alleluia.

25Blessed are you, Father, Lord of heaven and earth; you have revealed to little ones the mysteries of the Kingdom.

R. Alleluia, alleluia.

Gospel – Mark 4:26-34

[26]Jesus said to the crowds: "This is how it is with the Kingdom
of God; it is as if a man were to scatter seed on the land [27]and
would sleep and rise night and day and the seed would sprout
and grow, he knows not how. [28]Of its own accord the land
yields fruit, first the blade, then the ear, then the full grain in
the ear. [29]And when the grain is ripe, he wields the sickle at
once, for the harvest has come." [30]He said, "To what shall we
compare the Kingdom of God, or what parable can we use for
it? [31]It is like a mustard seed that, when it is sown in the
ground, is the smallest of all the seeds on the earth. [32]But
once it is sown, it springs up and becomes the largest of
plants and puts forth large branches, so that the birds of the
sky can dwell in its shade." [33]With many such parables he
spoke the word to them as they were able to understand it.
[34]Without parables he did not speak to them, but to his own
disciples he explained everything in private.

Saturday January 28, 2023

Memorial of Saint Thomas Aquinas, Priest & Doctor

First Reading – Hebrews 11:1-2, 8-19

Brothers and sisters: [1]Faith is the realization of what is hoped
for and evidence of things not seen. [2]Because of it the
ancients were well attested. [8]By faith Abraham obeyed when
he was called to go out to a place that he was to receive as an
inheritance; he went out, not knowing where he was to go. [9]By
faith he sojourned in the promised land as in a foreign country,
dwelling in tents with Isaac and Jacob, heirs of the same
promise; [10]for he was looking forward to the city with
foundations, whose architect and maker is God. [11]By faith he
received power to generate, even though he was past the
normal age and Sarah herself was sterile for he thought that
the one who had made the promise was trustworthy. [12]So it
was that there came forth from one man, himself as good as
dead, descendants as numerous as the stars in the sky and as
countless as the sands on the seashore. [13]All these died in
faith. They did not receive what had been promised but saw it
and greeted it from afar and acknowledged themselves to be
strangers and aliens on earth,[14]for those who speak thus show
that they are seeking a homeland. [15]If they had been thinking
of the land from which they had come, they would have had

opportunity to return. 16 But now they desire a better homeland,
a heavenly one. Therefore, God is not ashamed to be called
their God, for he has prepared a city for them. 17 By faith
Abraham, when put to the test, offered up Isaac, and he who
had received the promises was ready to offer his only son, 18 of
whom it was said, Through Isaac descendants shall bear your
name. 19 He reasoned that God was able to raise even from
the dead, and he received Isaac back as a symbol.

Responsorial Psalm – Luke 1:69-70, 71-72, 73-75

R. (see 68) **Blessed be the Lord the God of Israel; he has come to his people.**

69 He has raised up for us a mighty savior,

born of the house of his servant David.

R. Blessed be the Lord the God of Israel; he has come to his people.

70 Through his holy prophets he promised of old.

71 that he would save us from our sins

from the hands of all who hate us.

72 He promised to show mercy to our fathers

and to remember his holy covenant.

R. Blessed be the Lord the God of Israel; he has come to his people.

73 This was the oath he swore to our father Abraham:

74 to set us free from the bonds of our enemies,

free to worship him without fear,

75 holy and righteous in his sight

all the days of our life.

R. Blessed be the Lord the God of Israel; he has come to his people.

Alleluia – John 3:16

R. Alleluia, alleluia.

16 God so loved the world that he gave his only-begotten Son, so that everyone who believes in him might have eternal life.

R. Alleluia, alleluia.

Gospel – Mark 4:35-41

[35]On that day, as evening drew on, Jesus said to his disciples: "Let us cross to the other side." [36]Leaving the crowd, they took Jesus with them in the boat just as he was. And other boats were with him. [37]A violent squall came up and waves were breaking over the boat, so that it was already filling up. [38]Jesus was in the stern, asleep on a cushion. They woke him and said to him, "Teacher, do you not care that we are perishing?" [39]He woke up, rebuked the wind, and said to the sea, "Quiet! Be still!" The wind ceased and there was great calm. [40]Then he asked them, "Why are you terrified? Do you not yet have faith?" [41]They were filled with great awe and said to one another, "Who then is this whom even wind and sea obey?"

Sunday January 29, 2023

Fourth Sunday in Ordinary Time, Year A

First Reading – Zephaniah 2:3; 3:12-13

[3]Seek the LORD, all you humble of the earth, who have observed his law; seek justice, seek humility; perhaps you may be sheltered on the day of the LORD's anger. [12]But I will leave as a remnant in your midst a people humble and lowly, who shall take refuge in the name of the LORD: [13]the remnant of Israel. They shall do no wrong and speak no lies; nor shall there be found in their mouths a deceitful tongue; they shall pasture and couch their flocks with none to disturb them.

Responsorial Psalm – Psalms 146:6-7, 8-9, 9-10

R. (Mt 5:3) **Blessed are the poor in spirit; the kingdom of heaven is theirs!** or: **R. Alleluia.**

[6C] The LORD keeps faith forever,

[7] secures justice for the oppressed,

gives food to the hungry.

The LORD sets captives free.

R. Blessed are the poor in spirit; the kingdom of heaven is theirs! or: **R. Alleluia.**

[8] The LORD gives sight to the blind;

the LORD raises up those who were bowed down.

The LORD loves the just;

9A the LORD protects strangers.

R. Blessed are the poor in spirit; the kingdom of heaven is theirs! or: **R. Alleluia.**

9B The fatherless and the widow the LORD sustains,

but the way of the wicked he thwarts.

10 The LORD shall reign forever;

your God, O Zion, through all generations. Alleluia.

R. Blessed are the poor in spirit; the kingdom of heaven is theirs! or: **R. Alleluia.**

Second Reading – 1 Corinthians 1:26-31

26 Consider your own calling, brothers and sisters. Not many of
you were wise by human standards, not many were powerful,
not many were of noble birth. 27 Rather, God chose the foolish
of the world to shame the wise, and God chose the weak of
the world to shame the strong, 28 and God chose the lowly and
despised of the world, those who count for nothing, to reduce
to nothing those who are something, 29 so that no human being
might boast before God. 30 It is due to him that you are in Christ
Jesus, who became for us wisdom from God, as well as
righteousness, sanctification, and redemption, 31 so that, as it is
written, "Whoever boasts, should boast in the Lord."

Alleluia – Matthew 5:12A

R. Alleluia, alleluia.

12A Rejoice and be glad; your reward will be great in heaven.

R. Alleluia, alleluia.

Gospel – Matthew 5:1-12A

1 When Jesus saw the crowds, he went up the mountain, and
after he had sat down, his disciples came to him. 2 He began to
teach them, saying: 3 "Blessed are the poor in spirit, for theirs
is the kingdom of heaven. 4 Blessed are they who mourn, for
they will be comforted. 5 Blessed are the meek, for they will
inherit the land. 6 Blessed are they who hunger and thirst for

righteousness, for they will be satisfied. [7]Blessed are the
merciful, for they will be shown mercy. [8]Blessed are the clean
of heart, for they will see God. [9]Blessed are the peacemakers,
for they will be called children of God. [10]Blessed are they who
are persecuted for the sake of righteousness, for theirs is the
kingdom of heaven. [11]Blessed are you when they insult you
and persecute you and utter every kind of evil against you
falsely because of me. [12A]Rejoice and be glad, for your reward
will be great in heaven."

Monday January 30, 2023

Monday of the Third Week in Ordinary Time

First Reading – Hebrews 11:32-40

Brothers and sisters: [32]What more shall I say? I have not time
to tell of Gideon, Barak, Samson, Jephthah, of David and
Samuel and the prophets, [33]who by faith conquered kingdoms,
did what was righteous, obtained the promises; they closed
the mouths of lions, [34]put out raging fires, escaped the
devouring sword; out of weakness they were made powerful,
became strong in battle, and turned back foreign invaders.
[35]Women received back their dead through resurrection. Some
were tortured and would not accept deliverance, in order to
obtain a better resurrection. [36]Others endured mockery,
scourging, even chains and imprisonment. [37]They were
stoned, sawed in two, put to death at sword's point; they went
about in skins of sheep or goats, needy, afflicted, tormented.
[38]The world was not worthy of them. They wandered about in
deserts and on mountains, in caves and in crevices in the
earth. [39]Yet all these, though approved because of their faith,
did not receive what had been promised. [40]God had foreseen
something better for us, so that without us they should not be
made perfect.

Responsorial Psalm – Psalms 31:20, 21, 22, 23, 24

R. (25) Let your hearts take comfort, all who hope in the Lord.

[20] How great is the goodness, O LORD,

which you have in store for those who fear you,

And which, toward those who take refuge in you,

you show in the sight of the children of men.

R. Let your hearts take comfort, all who hope in the Lord.

21 You hide them in the shelter of your presence

from the plottings of men;

You screen them within your abode

from the strife of tongues.

R. Let your hearts take comfort, all who hope in the Lord.

22 Blessed be the LORD whose wondrous mercy

he has shown me in a fortified city.

R. Let your hearts take comfort, all who hope in the Lord.

23 Once I said in my anguish,

"I am cut off from your sight";

Yet you heard the sound of my pleading

when I cried out to you.

R. Let your hearts take comfort, all who hope in the Lord.

24 Love the LORD, all you his faithful ones!

The LORD keeps those who are constant,

but more than requites those who act proudly.

R. Let your hearts take comfort, all who hope in the Lord.

Alleluia – Luke 7:16

R. Alleluia, alleluia.

16 A great prophet has arisen in our midst and God has visited his people.

R. Alleluia, alleluia.

Gospel – Mark 5:1-20

1 Jesus and his disciples came to the other side of the sea, to
the territory of the Gerasenes. 2 When he got out of the boat, at
once a man from the tombs who had an unclean spirit met
him. 3 The man had been dwelling among the tombs, and no
one could restrain him any longer, even with a chain. 4 In fact,
he had frequently been bound with shackles and chains, but

the chains had been pulled apart by him and the shackles
smashed, and no one was strong enough to subdue him.
[5]Night and day among the tombs and on the hillsides he was
always crying out and bruising himself with stones. [6]Catching
sight of Jesus from a distance, he ran up and prostrated
himself before him, [7]crying out in a loud voice, “What have you
to do with me, Jesus, Son of the Most High God? I adjure you
by God, do not torment me!” [8](He had been saying to him,
“Unclean spirit, come out of the man!”) [9]He asked him, “What
is your name?” He replied, “Legion is my name. There are
many of us.” [10]And he pleaded earnestly with him not to drive
them away from that territory. [11]Now a large herd of swine was
feeding there on the hillside. [12]And they pleaded with him,
“Send us into the swine. Let us enter them.” [13]And he let them,
and the unclean spirits came out and entered the swine. The
herd of about two thousand rushed down a steep bank into the
sea, where they were drowned. [14]The swineherds ran away
and reported the incident in the town and throughout the
countryside. And people came out to see what had happened.
[15]As they approached Jesus, they caught sight of the man who
had been possessed by Legion, sitting there clothed and in his
right mind. And they were seized with fear. [16]Those who
witnessed the incident explained to them what had happened
to the possessed man and to the swine. [17]Then they began to
beg him to leave their district. [18]As he was getting into the
boat, the man who had been possessed pleaded to remain
with him. [19]But Jesus would not permit him but told him
instead, “Go home to your family and announce to them all
that the Lord in his pity has done for you.” [20]Then the man
went off and began to proclaim in the Decapolis what Jesus
had done for him; and all were amazed.

Tuesday January 31, 2023

Memorial of Saint John Bosco, Priest

First Reading – Hebrews 12:1-4

Brothers and sisters: [1]Since we are surrounded by so great a
cloud of witnesses, let us rid ourselves of every burden and
sin that clings to us and persevere in running the race that lies
before us [2]while keeping our eyes fixed on Jesus, the leader
and perfecter of faith. For the sake of the joy that lay before
him Jesus endured the cross, despising its shame, and has

taken his seat at the right of the throne of God. [3]Consider how he endured such opposition from sinners, in order that you may not grow weary and lose heart. [4]In your struggle against sin you have not yet resisted to the point of shedding blood.

Responsorial Psalm – Psalms 22:26B-27, 28 AND 30, 31-32

R. (see 27b) **They will praise you, Lord, who long for you.**

26B I will fulfill my vows before those who fear him.

27 The lowly shall eat their fill;

they who seek the LORD shall praise him:

"May your hearts be ever merry!"

R. They will praise you, Lord, who long for you.

28 All the ends of the earth

shall remember and turn to the LORD;

All the families of the nations

shall bow down before him.

30 To him alone shall bow down

all who sleep in the earth;

Before him shall bend

all who go down into the dust.

R. They will praise you, Lord, who long for you.

31 And to him my soul shall live;

my descendants shall serve him.

32 Let the coming generation be told of the LORD

that they may proclaim to a people yet to be born

the justice he has shown.

R. They will praise you, Lord, who long for you.

Alleluia – Matthew 8:17

R. Alleluia, alleluia.

17 Christ took away our infirmities and bore our diseases.

R. Alleluia, alleluia.

Gospel – Mark 5:21-43

[21]When Jesus had crossed again in the boat to the other side,
a large crowd gathered around him, and he stayed close to
the sea. [22]One of the synagogue officials, named Jairus, came
forward. Seeing him he fell at his feet [23]and pleaded earnestly
with him, saying, "My daughter is at the point of death. Please,
come lay your hands on her that she may get well and live."
[24]He went off with him and a large crowd followed him. [25]There
was a woman afflicted with hemorrhages for twelve years.
[26]She had suffered greatly at the hands of many doctors and
had spent all that she had. Yet she was not helped but only
grew worse. [27]She had heard about Jesus and came up
behind him in the crowd and touched his cloak. [28]She said, "If I
but touch his clothes, I shall be cured." [29]Immediately her flow
of blood dried up. She felt in her body that she was healed of
her affliction. [30]Jesus, aware at once that power had gone out
from him, turned around in the crowd and asked, "Who has
touched my clothes?" [31]But his disciples said to him, "You see
how the crowd is pressing upon you, and yet you ask, Who
touched me?" [32]And he looked around to see who had done it.
[33]The woman, realizing what had happened to her,
approached in fear and trembling. She fell down before Jesus
and told him the whole truth. [34]He said to her, "Daughter, your
faith has saved you. Go in peace and be cured of your
affliction." [35]While he was still speaking, people from the
synagogue official's house arrived and said, "Your daughter
has died; why trouble the teacher any longer?" [36]Disregarding
the message that was reported, Jesus said to the synagogue
official, "Do not be afraid; just have faith." [37]He did not allow
anyone to accompany him inside except Peter, James and
John, the brother of James. [38]When they arrived at the house
of the synagogue official, he caught sight of a commotion,
people weeping and wailing loudly. [39]So he went in and said to
them, "Why this commotion and weeping? The child is not
dead but asleep." [40]And they ridiculed him. Then he put them
all out. He took along the child's father and mother and those
who were with him and entered the room where the child was.
[41]He took the child by the hand and said to her, "Talitha
koum," which means, "Little girl, I say to you, arise!" [42]The girl,
a child of twelve, arose immediately and walked around. At
that they were utterly astounded. [43]He gave strict orders that

no one should know this and said that she should be given something to eat.

FEBRUARY 2023

Wednesday February 1, 2023

Wednesday of Fourth Week in Ordinary Time

First Reading – Hebrew 12:4-7, 11-15

Brothers and sisters: [4]In your struggle against sin you have not yet resisted to the point of shedding blood. [5]You have also forgotten the exhortation addressed to you as children: My son, do not disdain the discipline of the Lord or lose heart when reproved by him; [6]for whom the Lord loves, he disciplines; he scourges every son he acknowledges. [7]Endure your trials as "discipline"; God treats you as his sons. For what Ason" is there whom his father does not discipline? [11]At the time, all discipline seems a cause not for joy but for pain, yet later it brings the peaceful fruit of righteousness to those who are trained by it. [12]So strengthen your drooping hands and your weak knees. [13]Make straight paths for your feet, that what is lame may not be dislocated but healed. [14]Strive for peace with everyone, and for that holiness without which no one will see the Lord. [15]See to it that no one be deprived of the grace of God, that no bitter root spring up and cause trouble, through which many may become defiled.

Responsorial Psalm – Psalms 103:1-2, 13-14, 17-18A

R. (see 17) **The Lord's kindness is everlasting to those who fear him.**

[1] Bless the LORD, O my soul;

and all my being, bless his holy name.

[2] Bless the LORD, O my soul,

and forget not all his benefits.

R. The Lord's kindness is everlasting to those who fear him.

[13] As a father has compassion on his children,

so the LORD has compassion on those who fear him,

14 For he knows how we are formed;

he remembers that we are dust.

R. The Lord's kindness is everlasting to those who fear him.

17 But the kindness of the LORD is from eternity

to eternity toward those who fear him,

18A And his justice toward children's children

among those who keep his covenant.

R. The Lord's kindness is everlasting to those who fear him.

Alleluia – John 10:27

R. Alleluia, alleluia.

27My sheep hear my voice, says the Lord; I know them, and they follow me.

R. Alleluia, alleluia.

Gospel – Mark 6:1-6

1Jesus departed from there and came to his native place,
accompanied by his disciples. 2When the Sabbath came he
began to teach in the synagogue, and many who heard him
were astonished. They said, "Where did this man get all this?
What kind of wisdom has been given him? What mighty deeds
are wrought by his hands! 3Is he not the carpenter, the son of
Mary, and the brother of James and Joseph and Judas and
Simon? And are not his sisters here with us?" And they took
offense at him. 4Jesus said to them, "A prophet is not without
honor except in his native place and among his own kin and in
his own house." 5So he was not able to perform any mighty
deed there, apart from curing a few sick people by laying his
hands on them. 6He was amazed at their lack of faith.

Thursday February 2, 2023

Feast of the Presentation of the Lord

First Reading – Malachi 3:1-4

1 Thus says the Lord God: Lo, I am sending my messenger to
prepare the way before me; And suddenly there will come to
the temple the LORD whom you seek, And the messenger of
the covenant whom you desire. Yes, he is coming, says the
LORD of hosts. 2 But who will endure the day of his coming?
And who can stand when he appears? For he is like the
refiner's fire, or like the fuller's lye. 3 He will sit refining and
purifying silver, and he will purify the sons of Levi, Refining
them like gold or like silver that they may offer due sacrifice to
the LORD. 4 Then the sacrifice of Judah and Jerusalem will
please the LORD, as in the days of old, as in years gone by.

Responsorial Psalm – Psalms 24:7, 8, 9, 10

R. (8) Who is this king of glory? It is the Lord!

7 Lift up, O gates, your lintels;

reach up, you ancient portals,

that the king of glory may come in!

R. Who is this king of glory? It is the Lord!

8 Who is this king of glory?

The LORD, strong and mighty,

the LORD, mighty in battle.

R. Who is this king of glory? It is the Lord!

9 Lift up, O gates, your lintels;

reach up, you ancient portals,

that the king of glory may come in!

R. Who is this king of glory? It is the Lord!

10 Who is this king of glory?

The LORD of hosts; he is the king of glory.

R. Who is this king of glory? It is the Lord!

Second Reading – Hebrews 2:14-18

[14]Since the children share in blood and flesh, Jesus likewise shared in them, that through death he might destroy the one who has the power of death, that is, the Devil, [15]and free those who through fear of death had been subject to slavery all their life. [16]Surely he did not help angels but rather the descendants of Abraham; [17]therefore, he had to become like his brothers and sisters in every way, that he might be a merciful and faithful high priest before God to expiate the sins of the people. [18]Because he himself was tested through what he suffered, he is able to help those who are being tested.

Alleluia – Luke 2:32

R. Alleluia, alleluia.

[32]A light of revelation to the Gentiles, and glory for your people Israel.

R. Alleluia, alleluia.

Gospel – Luke 2:22-40

[22]When the days were completed for their purification according to the law of Moses, Mary and Joseph took Jesus up to Jerusalem to present him to the Lord, [23] just as it is written in the law of the Lord, Every male that opens the womb shall be consecrated to the Lord, [24]and to offer the sacrifice of a pair of turtledoves or two young pigeons, in accordance with the dictate in the law of the Lord. [25]Now there was a man in Jerusalem whose name was Simeon. This man was righteous and devout, awaiting the consolation of Israel, and the Holy Spirit was upon him. [26]It had been revealed to him by the Holy Spirit that he should not see death before he had seen the Christ of the Lord. [27]He came in the Spirit into the temple; and when the parents brought in the child Jesus to perform the custom of the law in regard to him, [28] he took him into his arms and blessed God, saying: [29]"Now, Master, you may let your servant go in peace, according to your word, [30]for my eyes have seen your salvation,[31] which you prepared in the sight of all the peoples: [32]a light for revelation to the Gentiles, and glory for your people Israel." [33]The child's father and mother were amazed at what was said about him; [34]and Simeon blessed them and said to Mary his mother, "Behold, this child is destined for the fall and rise of many in Israel, and to be a

sign that will be contradicted [35](and you yourself a sword will pierce) so that the thoughts of many hearts may be revealed." [36]There was also a prophetess, Anna, the daughter of Phanuel, of the tribe of Asher. She was advanced in years, having lived seven years with her husband after her marriage, [37]and then as a widow until she was eighty-four. She never left the temple, but worshiped night and day with fasting and prayer. [38]And coming forward at that very time, she gave thanks to God and spoke about the child to all who were awaiting the redemption of Jerusalem. [39]When they had fulfilled all the prescriptions of the law of the Lord, they returned to Galilee, to their own town of Nazareth. [40]The child grew and became strong, filled with wisdom; and the favor of God was upon him.

Or Luke 2:22-32

[22]When the days were completed for their purification according to the law of Moses, Mary and Joseph took Jesus up to Jerusalem to present him to the Lord, [23] just as it is written in the law of the Lord, Every male that opens the womb shall be consecrated to the Lord, [24]and to offer the sacrifice of a pair of turtledoves or two young pigeons, in accordance with the dictate in the law of the Lord. [25]Now there was a man in Jerusalem whose name was Simeon. This man was righteous and devout, awaiting the consolation of Israel, and the Holy Spirit was upon him. [26]It had been revealed to him by the Holy Spirit that he should not see death before he had seen the Christ of the Lord. [27]He came in the Spirit into the temple; and when the parents brought in the child Jesus to perform the custom of the law in regard to him, [28]he took him into his arms and blessed God, saying: [29]"Now, Master, you may let your servant go in peace, according to your word, [30]for my eyes have seen your salvation, [31]which you prepared in the sight of all the peoples: [32]a light for revelation to the Gentiles, and glory for your people Israel."

Friday February 3, 2023

Friday of the Fourth Week in Ordinary Time

First Reading – Hebrews 13:1-8

[1]Let brotherly love continue. [2]Do not neglect hospitality, for through it some have unknowingly entertained angels. [3]Be

mindful of prisoners as if sharing their imprisonment, and of
the ill-treated as of yourselves, for you also are in the body.
4 Let marriage be honored among all and the marriage bed be
kept undefiled, for God will judge the immoral and adulterers.
5 Let your life be free from love of money but be content with
what you have, for he has said, I will never forsake you or
abandon you. 6 Thus we may say with confidence: The Lord is
my helper, and I will not be afraid. What can anyone do to me?
7 Remember your leaders who spoke the word of God to you.
Consider the outcome of their way of life and imitate their faith.
8 Jesus Christ is the same yesterday, today, and forever.

Responsorial Psalm – Psalms 27:1, 3, 5, 8B-9ABC

R. (1a) **The Lord is my light and my salvation.**

1 The LORD is my light and my salvation;

whom should I fear?

The LORD is my life's refuge;

of whom should I be afraid?

R. The Lord is my light and my salvation.

3 Though an army encamp against me,

my heart will not fear;

Though war be waged upon me,

even then will I trust.

R. The Lord is my light and my salvation.

5 For he will hide me in his abode

in the day of trouble;

He will conceal me in the shelter of his tent,

he will set me high upon a rock.

R. The Lord is my light and my salvation.

8B Your presence, O LORD, I seek.

9ABC Hide not your face from me;

do not in anger repel your servant.

You are my helper: cast me not off.

R. The Lord is my light and my salvation.

Alleluia – Luke 8:15

R. Alleluia, alleluia.

15 Blessed are they who have kept the word with a generous
heart, and yield a harvest through perseverance.

R. Alleluia, alleluia.

Gospel – Mark 6:14-29

14King Herod heard about Jesus, for his fame had become
widespread, and people were saying, "John the Baptist has
been raised from the dead; That is why mighty powers are at
work in him." 15Others were saying, "He is Elijah"; still others,
"He is a prophet like any of the prophets." 16But when Herod
learned of it, he said, "It is John whom I beheaded. He has
been raised up." 17Herod was the one who had John arrested
and bound in prison on account of Herodias, the wife of his
brother Philip, whom he had married. 18John had said to
Herod, "It is not lawful for you to have your brother's wife."
19Herodias harbored a grudge against him and wanted to kill
him but was unable to do so. 20Herod feared John, knowing
him to be a righteous and holy man, and kept him in custody.
When he heard him speak he was very much perplexed, yet
he liked to listen to him. 21Herodias had an opportunity one
day when Herod, on his birthday, gave a banquet for his
courtiers, his military officers, and the leading men of Galilee.
22His own daughter came in and performed a dance that
delighted Herod and his guests. The king said to the girl, "Ask
of me whatever you wish and I will grant it to you." 23He even
swore many things to her, "I will grant you whatever you ask of
me, even to half of my kingdom." 24She went out and said to
her mother, "What shall I ask for?" Her mother replied, "The
head of John the Baptist." 25The girl hurried back to the king's
presence and made her request, "I want you to give me at
once on a platter the head of John the Baptist." 26The king was
deeply distressed, but because of his oaths and the guests he
did not wish to break his word to her. 27So he promptly
dispatched an executioner with orders to bring back his head.
He went off and beheaded him in the prison. 28He brought in
the head on a platter and gave it to the girl. The girl in turn
gave it to her mother. 29When his disciples heard about it, they
came and took his body and laid it in a tomb.

Saturday February 4, 2023

Saturday of Fourth Week in Ordinary Time

First Reading – Hebrews 13:15-17, 20-21

Brothers and sisters: [15]Through Jesus, let us continually offer
God a sacrifice of praise, that is, the fruit of lips that confess
his name. [16]Do not neglect to do good and to share what you
have; God is pleased by sacrifices of that kind. [17]Obey your
leaders and defer to them, for they keep watch over you and will have to give an account, that they may fulfill their task with joy and not with sorrow, for that would be of no advantage to
you. [20]May the God of peace, who brought up from the dead
the great shepherd of the sheep by the Blood of the eternal
covenant, [21]furnish you with all that is good, that you may do
his will. May he carry out in you what is pleasing to him through Jesus Christ, to whom be glory forever and ever. Amen.

Responsorial Psalm – Psalms 23:1-3A, 3B-4, 5, 6

R. (1) The Lord is my shepherd; there is nothing I shall want.

1 The LORD is my shepherd; I shall not want.

In verdant pastures he gives me repose.

Beside restful waters he leads me;

3A he refreshes my soul.

R. The Lord is my shepherd; there is nothing I shall want.

3B He guides me in right paths

for his name's sake.

4 Even though I walk in the dark valley

I fear no evil; for you are at my side

With your rod and your staff

that give me courage.

R. The Lord is my shepherd; there is nothing I shall want.

5 You spread the table before me

in the sight of my foes;

You anoint my head with oil;

my cup overflows.

R. The Lord is my shepherd; there is nothing I shall want.

6 Only goodness and kindness follow me

all the days of my life;

And I shall dwell in the house of the LORD

for years to come.

R. The Lord is my shepherd; there is nothing I shall want.

Alleluia – John 10:27

R. Alleluia, alleluia.

27 My sheep hear my voice, says the Lord; I know them, and they follow me.

R. Alleluia, alleluia.

Gospel – Mark 6:30-34

30The Apostles gathered together with Jesus and reported all
they had done and taught. 31He said to them, "Come away by
yourselves to a deserted place and rest a while." People were
coming and going in great numbers, and they had no
opportunity even to eat. 32So they went off in the boat by
themselves to a deserted place. 33People saw them leaving
and many came to know about it. They hastened there on foot
from all the towns and arrived at the place before them.
34When Jesus disembarked and saw the vast crowd, his heart
was moved with pity for them, for they were like sheep without
a shepherd; and he began to teach them many things.

Sunday February 5, 2023

Fifth Sunday in Ordinary Time, Year A

First Reading – Isaiah 58:7-10

7Thus says the LORD: Share your bread with the hungry,
shelter the oppressed and the homeless; clothe the naked
when you see them, and do not turn your back on your own.
8Then your light shall break forth like the dawn, and your
wound shall quickly be healed; your vindication shall go before

you, and the glory of the LORD shall be your rear guard.
[9]Then you shall call, and the LORD will answer, you shall cry
for help, and he will say: Here I am! If you remove from your
midst oppression, false accusation and malicious speech; [10]if
you bestow your bread on the hungry and satisfy the afflicted;
then light shall rise for you in the darkness, and the gloom
shall become for you like midday.

Responsorial Psalm – Psalms 112:4-5, 6-7, 8-9

R. (4a) The just man is a light in darkness to the upright. or: **Alleluia.**

4 Light shines through the darkness for the upright;

he is gracious and merciful and just.

5 Well for the man who is gracious and lends,

who conducts his affairs with justice.

R. The just man is a light in darkness to the upright. or: **Alleluia.**

6 He shall never be moved;

the just one shall be in everlasting remembrance.

7 An evil report he shall not fear;

his heart is firm, trusting in the LORD.

R. The just man is a light in darkness to the upright. or: **Alleluia.**

8 His heart is steadfast; he shall not fear.

Lavishly he gives to the poor;

9 His justice shall endure forever;

his horn shall be exalted in glory.

R. The just man is a light in darkness to the upright. or: **Alleluia**

Second Reading – 1 Corinthians 2:1-5

[1]When I came to you, brothers and sisters, proclaiming the
mystery of God, I did not come with sublimity of words or of
wisdom. [2]For I resolved to know nothing while I was with you
except Jesus Christ, and him crucified. [3]I came to you in

weakness and fear and much trembling, 4and my message
and my proclamation were not with persuasive words of
wisdom, but with a demonstration of Spirit and power, 5so that
your faith might rest not on human wisdom but on the power of
God.

Alleluia – John 8:12

R. Alleluia, alleluia.

12 I am the light of the world, says the Lord; whoever follows me will have the light of life.

R. Alleluia, alleluia.

Gospel – Matthew 5:13-16

13Jesus said to his disciples: “You are the salt of the earth. But
if salt loses its taste, with what can it be seasoned? It is no
longer good for anything but to be thrown out and trampled
underfoot. 14You are the light of the world. A city set on a
mountain cannot be hidden. 15Nor do they light a lamp and
then put it under a bushel basket; it is set on a lampstand,
where it gives light to all in the house. 16Just so, your light
must shine before others, that they may see your good deeds
and glorify your heavenly Father.”

Monday February 6, 2023

Memorial of Saints Paul Miki and his Companions

First Reading – Genesis 1:1-19

1In the beginning, when God created the heavens and the
earth, 2the earth was a formless wasteland, and darkness
covered the abyss, while a mighty wind swept over the waters.
3Then God said, “Let there be light,” and there was light. 4God
saw how good the light was. God then separated the light from
the darkness. 5God called the light “day,” and the darkness he
called “night.” Thus evening came, and morning followed–the
first day. 6Then God said, “Let there be a dome in the middle
of the waters, to separate one body of water from the other.”
And so it happened: 7God made the dome, and it separated
the water above the dome from the water below it. 8God called
the dome “the sky.” Evening came, and morning followed, the
second day. 9Then God said, “Let the water under the sky be
gathered into a single basin, so that the dry land may appear.”

And so it happened: the water under the sky was gathered
into its basin, and the dry land appeared. 10God called the dry
land "the earth," and the basin of the water he called "the sea."
God saw how good it was. 11Then God said, "Let the earth
bring forth vegetation: every kind of plant that bears seed and
every kind of fruit tree on earth that bears fruit with its seed in
it." And so it happened: 12the earth brought forth every kind of
plant that bears seed and every kind of fruit tree on earth that
bears fruit with its seed in it. God saw how good it was.
13Evening came, and morning followed–the third day. 14Then
God said: "Let there be lights in the dome of the sky, to
separate day from night. Let them mark the fixed times, the
days and the years, 15and serve as luminaries in the dome of
the sky, to shed light upon the earth." And so it happened:
16God made the two great lights, the greater one to govern the
day, and the lesser one to govern the night; and he made the
stars. 17God set them in the dome of the sky, to shed light
upon the earth, 18to govern the day and the night, and to
separate the light from the darkness. God saw how good it
was. 19Evening came, and morning followed–the fourth day.

Responsorial Psalm – Psalms 104:1-2A, 5-6, 10 AND 12, 24 AND 35C

R. (31b) May the Lord be glad in his works.

1 Bless the LORD, O my soul!

O LORD, my God, you are great indeed!

You are clothed with majesty and glory,

2A robed in light as with a cloak.

R. May the Lord be glad in his works.

5 You fixed the earth upon its foundation,

not to be moved forever;

6 With the ocean, as with a garment, you covered it;

above the mountains the waters stood.

R. May the Lord be glad in his works.

10 You send forth springs into the watercourses

that wind among the mountains.

12 Beside them the birds of heaven dwell;

from among the branches they send forth their song.

R. May the Lord be glad in his works.

24 How manifold are your works, O LORD!

In wisdom you have wrought them all—

the earth is full of your creatures;

35C Bless the LORD, O my soul! Alleluia.

R. May the Lord be glad in his works.

Alleluia – Matthew 4:23

R. Alleluia, alleluia.

23 Jesus preached the Gospel of the Kingdom and cured every disease among the people.

R. Alleluia, alleluia.

Gospel – Mark 6:53-56

53After making the crossing to the other side of the sea, Jesus
and his disciples came to land at Gennesaret and tied up
there. 54As they were leaving the boat, people immediately
recognized him. 55They scurried about the surrounding country
and began to bring in the sick on mats to wherever they heard
he was. 56Whatever villages or towns or countryside he
entered, they laid the sick in the marketplaces and begged him
that they might touch only the tassel on his cloak; and as
many as touched it were healed.

Tuesday February 7, 2023

Tuesday of the Fifth Week in Ordinary Time

First Reading – Genesis 1:20-2:4A

20God said, "Let the water teem with an abundance of living
creatures, and on the earth let birds fly beneath the dome of
the sky." and so it happened: 21God created the great sea
monsters and all kinds of swimming creatures with which the
water teems, and all kinds of winged birds. God saw how good
it was, 22and God blessed them, saying, "Be fertile, multiply,
and fill the water of the seas; and let the birds multiply on the

earth." 23Evening came, and morning followed, the fifth day.
24Then God said, "Let the earth bring forth all kinds of living
creatures: cattle, creeping things, and wild animals of all
kinds." and so it happened: 25God made all kinds of wild
animals, all kinds of cattle, and all kinds of creeping things of
the earth. God saw how good it was. 26Then God said: "Let us
make man in our image, after our likeness. Let them have
dominion over the fish of the sea, the birds of the air, and the
cattle, and over all the wild animals and all the creatures that
crawl on the ground." 27God created man in his image; in the
divine image he created him; male and female he created
them. 28God blessed them, saying: "Be fertile and multiply; fill
the earth and subdue it. Have dominion over the fish of the
sea, the birds of the air, and all the living things that move on
the earth." 29God also said: "See, I give you every seed-
bearing plant all over the earth and every tree that has seed-
bearing fruit on it to be your food; 30and to all the animals of
the land, all the birds of the air, and all the living creatures that
crawl on the ground, I give all the green plants for food." And
so it happened. 31God looked at everything he had made, and
he found it very good. Evening came, and morning followed,
the sixth day. 1Thus the heavens and the earth and all their
array were completed. 2Since on the seventh day God was
finished with the work he had been doing, he rested on the
seventh day from all the work he had undertaken. 3So God
blessed the seventh day and made it holy, because on it he
rested from all the work he had done in creation. 4ASuch is the
story of the heavens and the earth at their creation.

Responsorial Psalm – Psalms 8:4-5, 6-7, 8-9

R. (2ab) O Lord, our God, how wonderful your name in all the earth!

4 When I behold your heavens, the work of your fingers,

the moon and the stars which you set in place

5 What is man that you should be mindful of him,

or the son of man that you should care for him?

R. O Lord, our God, how wonderful your name in all the earth!

6 You have made him little less than the angels,

and crowned him with glory and honor.

7 You have given him rule over the works of your hands,

putting all things under his feet.

R. O Lord, our God, how wonderful your name in all the earth!

8 All sheep and oxen,

yes, and the beasts of the field,

9 The birds of the air, the fishes of the sea,

and whatever swims the paths of the seas.

R. O Lord, our God, how wonderful your name in all the earth!

Alleluia – Psalms 119:36, 29B

R. Alleluia, alleluia.

36 Incline my heart, O God, to your decrees; 29B1 And favor me
with your law.

R. Alleluia, alleluia.

Gospel – Mark 7:1-13

1When the Pharisees with some scribes who had come from
Jerusalem gathered around Jesus, 2they observed that some
of his disciples ate their meals with unclean, that is,
unwashed, hands. 3(For the Pharisees and, in fact, all Jews,
do not eat without carefully washing their hands, keeping the
tradition of the elders. 4And on coming from the marketplace
they do not eat without purifying themselves. And there are
many other things that they have traditionally observed, the
purification of cups and jugs and kettles and beds.) 5So the
Pharisees and scribes questioned him, "Why do your disciples
not follow the tradition of the elders but instead eat a meal with
unclean hands?" 6He responded, "Well did Isaiah prophesy
about you hypocrites, as it is written: This people honors me
with their lips, but their hearts are far from me; 7in vain do they
worship me, teaching as doctrines human precepts. 8You
disregard God's commandment but cling to human tradition."
9He went on to say, "How well you have set aside the
commandment of God in order to uphold your tradition! 10For
Moses said, Honor your father and your mother, and Whoever

curses father or mother shall die. 11Yet you say, 'If someone
says to father or mother, "Any support you might have had
from me is qorban"' (meaning, dedicated to God), 12you allow
him to do nothing more for his father or mother. 13You nullify
the word of God in favor of your tradition that you have
handed on. And you do many such things."

Wednesday February 8, 2023

Wednesday of Fifth Week in Ordinary Time

First Reading – Genesis 2:4B-9, 15-17

4BAt the time when the LORD God made the earth and the
heavens, 5while as yet there was no field shrub on earth and
no grass of the field had sprouted, for the LORD God had sent
no rain upon the earth and there was no man to till the soil,
6but a stream was welling up out of the earth and was
watering all the surface of the ground, 7the LORD God formed
man out of the clay of the ground and blew into his nostrils the
breath of life, and so man became a living being. 8Then the
LORD God planted a garden in Eden, in the east, and he
placed there the man whom he had formed. 9Out of the
ground the LORD God made various trees grow that were
delightful to look at and good for food, with the tree of life in
the middle of the garden and the tree of the knowledge of
good and evil. 15The LORD God then took the man and settled
him in the garden of Eden, to cultivate and care for it. 16The
LORD God gave man this order: "You are free to eat from any
of the trees of the garden 17except the tree of knowledge of
good and evil. From that tree you shall not eat; the moment
you eat from it you are surely doomed to die."

Responsorial Psalm – Psalms 104:1-2A, 27-28, 29BC-30

R. (1a) O bless the Lord, my soul!

1 Bless the LORD, O my soul!

O LORD, my God, you are great indeed!

You are clothed with majesty and glory,

2A robed in light as with a cloak.

R. O bless the Lord, my soul!

27 All creatures look to you

to give them food in due time.

28 When you give it to them, they gather it;

when you open your hand, they are filled with good things.

R. O bless the Lord, my soul!

29BC If you take away their breath, they perish

and return to their dust.

30 When you send forth your spirit, they are created,

and you renew the face of the earth.

R. O bless the Lord, my soul!

Alleluia – John 17:17B, 17A

R. Alleluia, alleluia.

17B Your word, O Lord, is truth: 17A consecrate us in the truth.

R. Alleluia, alleluia.

Gospel – Mark 7:14-23

14Jesus summoned the crowd again and said to them, "Hear
me, all of you, and understand. 15Nothing that enters one from
outside can defile that person; but the things that come out
from within are what defile." 17When he got home away from
the crowd his disciples questioned him about the parable. 18He
said to them, "Are even you likewise without understanding?
Do you not realize that everything that goes into a person from
outside cannot defile, 19since it enters not the heart but the
stomach and passes out into the latrine?" (Thus he declared
all foods clean.) 20"But what comes out of the man, that is what
defiles him. 21From within the man, from his heart, come evil
thoughts, unchastity, theft, murder, 22adultery, greed, malice,
deceit, licentiousness, envy, blasphemy, arrogance, folly. 23All
these evils come from within and they defile."

Thursday February 9, 2023

Thursday of the Fifth Week in Ordinary Time

First Reading – Genesis 2:18-25

18The LORD God said: “It is not good for the man to be alone.
I will make a suitable partner for him.” 19So the LORD God
formed out of the ground various wild animals and various
birds of the air, and he brought them to the man to see what
he would call them; whatever the man called each of them
would be its name. 20The man gave names to all the cattle, all
the birds of the air, and all the wild animals; but none proved
to be the suitable partner for the man. 21So the LORD God
cast a deep sleep on the man, and while he was asleep, he
took out one of his ribs and closed up its place with flesh.
22The LORD God then built up into a woman the rib that he
had taken from the man. When he brought her to the man,
23the man said: “This one, at last, is bone of my bones and
flesh of my flesh; this one shall be called ‘woman,’ for out of
‘her man’ this one has been taken.” 24That is why a man
leaves his father and mother and clings to his wife, and the
two of them become one flesh. 25The man and his wife were
both naked, yet they felt no shame.

Responsorial Psalm – Psalms 128:1-2, 3, 4-5

R. (see 1a) **Blessed are those who fear the Lord.**

1 Blessed are you who fear the LORD,

who walk in his ways!

2 For you shall eat the fruit of your handiwork;

blessed shall you be, and favored.

R. Blessed are those who fear the Lord.

3 Your wife shall be like a fruitful vine

in the recesses of your home;

Your children like olive plants

around your table.

R. Blessed are those who fear the Lord.

4 Behold, thus is the man blessed

who fears the LORD.

5 The LORD bless you from Zion:

may you see the prosperity of Jerusalem

all the days of your life.

R. Blessed are those who fear the Lord.

Alleluia – James 1:21BC

R. Alleluia, alleluia.

21BC Humbly welcome the word that has been planted in you and is able to save your souls.

R. Alleluia, alleluia.

Gospel – Mark 7:24-30

24 Jesus went to the district of Tyre. He entered a house and
wanted no one to know about it, but he could not escape
notice. 25 Soon a woman whose daughter had an unclean spirit
heard about him. She came and fell at his feet. 26 The woman
was a Greek, a Syrophoenician by birth, and she begged him
to drive the demon out of her daughter. 27 He said to her, "Let
the children be fed first. For it is not right to take the food of
the children and throw it to the dogs." 28 She replied and said to
him, "Lord, even the dogs under the table eat the children's
scraps." 29 Then he said to her, "For saying this, you may go.
The demon has gone out of your daughter." 30 When the
woman went home, she found the child lying in bed and the
demon gone.

Friday February 10, 2023

Memorial of Saint Scholastica, Virgin

First Reading – Genesis 3:1-8

1 Now the serpent was the most cunning of all the animals that
the LORD God had made. The serpent asked the woman, "Did
God really tell you not to eat from any of the trees in the
garden?" 2 The woman answered the serpent: "We may eat of
the fruit of the trees in the garden; 3 it is only about the fruit of
the tree in the middle of the garden that God said, 'You shall
not eat it or even touch it, lest you die.'" 4 But the serpent said
to the woman: "You certainly will not die! 5 No, God knows well

that the moment you eat of it your eyes will be opened and
you will be like gods who know what is good and what is evil."
6The woman saw that the tree was good for food, pleasing to
the eyes, and desirable for gaining wisdom. So she took some
of its fruit and ate it; and she also gave some to her husband,
who was with her, and he ate it. 7Then the eyes of both of
them were opened, and they realized that they were naked; so
they sewed fig leaves together and made loincloths for
themselves. 8When they heard the sound of the LORD God
moving about in the garden at the breezy time of the day, the
man and his wife hid themselves from the LORD God among
the trees of the garden.

Responsorial Psalm – Psalms 32:1-2, 5, 6, 7

R. (1a) Blessed are those whose sins are forgiven.

1 Blessed is he whose fault is taken away,

whose sin is covered.

2 Blessed the man to whom the LORD imputes not guilt,

in whose spirit there is no guile.

R. Blessed are those whose sins are forgiven.

5 Then I acknowledged my sin to you,

my guilt I covered not.

I said, "I confess my faults to the LORD,"

and you took away the guilt of my sin.

R. Blessed are those whose sins are forgiven.

6 For this shall every faithful man pray to you

in time of stress.

Though deep waters overflow,

they shall not reach him.

R. Blessed are those whose sins are forgiven.

7 You are my shelter; from distress you will preserve me;

with glad cries of freedom you will ring me round.

R. Blessed are those whose sins are forgiven.

Alleluia – Acts 16:14B

R. Alleluia, alleluia.

14B Open our hearts, O Lord, to listen to the words of your Son.

R. Alleluia, alleluia.

Gospel – Mark 7:31-37

31Jesus left the district of Tyre and went by way of Sidon to the Sea of Galilee, into the district of the Decapolis. 32And people brought to him a deaf man who had a speech impediment and begged him to lay his hand on him. 33He took him off by himself away from the crowd. He put his finger into the man's ears and, spitting, touched his tongue; 34then he looked up to heaven and groaned, and said to him, "Ephphatha!" (that is, "Be opened!") 35And immediately the man's ears were opened, his speech impediment was removed, and he spoke plainly. 36He ordered them not to tell anyone. But the more he ordered them not to, the more they proclaimed it. 37They were exceedingly astonished and they said, "He has done all things well. He makes the deaf hear and the mute speak."

Saturday February 11, 2023

Saturday of the Fifth Week in Ordinary Time

First Reading – Genesis 3:9-24

9The LORD God called to Adam and asked him, "Where are you?" 10He answered, "I heard you in the garden; but I was afraid, because I was naked, so I hid myself." 11Then he asked, "Who told you that you were naked? You have eaten, then, from the tree of which I had forbidden you to eat!" 12The man replied, "The woman whom you put here with me she gave me fruit from the tree, and so I ate it." 13The LORD God then asked the woman, "Why did you do such a thing?" The woman answered, "The serpent tricked me into it, so I ate it." 14Then the LORD God said to the serpent: "Because you have done this, you shall be banned from all the animals and from all the wild creatures; On your belly shall you crawl, and dirt shall you eat all the days of your life. 15I will put enmity between you and the woman, and between your offspring and hers; He will strike at your head, while you strike at his heel." 16To the woman he said: "I will intensify the pangs of your

childbearing; in pain shall you bring forth children. Yet your
urge shall be for your husband, and he shall be your master."
17 To the man he said: "Because you listened to your wife and
ate from the tree of which I had forbidden you to eat, "Cursed
be the ground because of you! In toil shall you eat its yield all
the days of your life. 18 Thorns and thistles shall it bring forth to
you, as you eat of the plants of the field. 19 By the sweat of your
face shall you get bread to eat, Until you return to the ground,
from which you were taken; For you are dirt, and to dirt you
shall return." 20 The man called his wife Eve, because she
became the mother of all the living. 21 For the man and his wife
the LORD God made leather garments, with which he clothed
them. 22 Then the LORD God said: "See! The man has become
like one of us, knowing what is good and what is evil!
Therefore, he must not be allowed to put out his hand to take
fruit from the tree of life also, and thus eat of it and live
forever." 23 The LORD God therefore banished him from the
garden of Eden, to till the ground from which he had been
taken. 24 When he expelled the man, he settled him east of the
garden of Eden; and he stationed the cherubim and the fiery
revolving sword, to guard the way to the tree of life.

Responsorial Psalm – Psalms 90:2, 3-4ABC, 5-6, 12-13

R. (1) In every age, O Lord, you have been our refuge.

2 Before the mountains were begotten

and the earth and the world were brought forth,

from everlasting to everlasting you are God.

R. In every age, O Lord, you have been our refuge.

3 You turn man back to dust,

saying, "Return, O children of men."

4ABC For a thousand years in your sight

are as yesterday, now that it is past,

or as a watch of the night.

R. In every age, O Lord, you have been our refuge.

5 You make an end of them in their sleep;

the next morning they are like the changing grass,

6 Which at dawn springs up anew,

but by evening wilts and fades.

R. In every age, O Lord, you have been our refuge.

12 Teach us to number our days aright,

that we may gain wisdom of heart.

13 Return, O LORD! How long?

Have pity on your servants!

R. In every age, O Lord, you have been our refuge.

Alleluia – Matthew 4:4B

R. Alleluia, alleluia.

4B One does not live on bread alone, but on every word that comes forth from the mouth of God.

R. Alleluia, alleluia.

Gospel – Mark 8:1-10

1 In those days when there again was a great crowd without
anything to eat, Jesus summoned the disciples and said, 2 "My
heart is moved with pity for the crowd, because they have
been with me now for three days and have nothing to eat. 3 If I
send them away hungry to their homes, they will collapse on
the way, and some of them have come a great distance." 4 His
disciples answered him, "Where can anyone get enough bread
to satisfy them here in this deserted place?" 5 Still he asked
them, "How many loaves do you have?" They replied, "Seven."
6 He ordered the crowd to sit down on the ground. Then, taking
the seven loaves he gave thanks, broke them, and gave them
to his disciples to distribute, and they distributed them to the
crowd. 7 They also had a few fish. He said the blessing over
them and ordered them distributed also. 8 They ate and were
satisfied. They picked up the fragments left over–seven
baskets. 9 There were about four thousand people. He
dismissed the crowd 10 and got into the boat with his disciples
and came to the region of Dalmanutha.

Sunday February 12, 2023

Sixth Sunday in Ordinary Time, Year A

First Reading – Sirach 15:15-20

15 If you choose you can keep the commandments, they will
save you; if you trust in God, you too shall live; 16 he has set
before you fire and water to whichever you choose, stretch
forth your hand. 17 Before man are life and death, good and
evil, whichever he chooses shall be given him. 18 Immense is
the wisdom of the Lord; he is mighty in power, and all-seeing.
19 The eyes of God are on those who fear him; he understands
man's every deed. 20 No one does he command to act unjustly,
to none does he give license to sin.

Responsorial Psalm – Psalms 119:1-2, 4-5, 17-18, 33-34

R. (1b) Blessed are they who follow the law of the Lord!

1 Blessed are they whose way is blameless,

who walk in the law of the LORD.

2 Blessed are they who observe his decrees,

who seek him with all their heart.

R. Blessed are they who follow the law of the Lord!

4 You have commanded that your precepts

be diligently kept.

5 Oh, that I might be firm in the ways

of keeping your statutes!

R. Blessed are they who follow the law of the Lord!

17 Be good to your servant, that I may live

and keep your words.

18 Open my eyes, that I may consider

the wonders of your law.

R. Blessed are they who follow the law of the Lord!

33 Instruct me, O LORD, in the way of your statutes,

that I may exactly observe them.

34 Give me discernment, that I may observe your law

and keep it with all my heart.

R. Blessed are they who follow the law of the Lord!

Second Reading – 1 Corinthians 2:6-10

Brothers and sisters: [6]We speak a wisdom to those who are
mature, not a wisdom of this age, nor of the rulers of this age
who are passing away. [7]Rather, we speak God's wisdom,
mysterious, hidden, which God predetermined before the ages
for our glory, [8]and which none of the rulers of this age knew;
for, if they had known it, they would not have crucified the Lord
of glory. [9]But as it is written: "What eye has not seen, and ear
has not heard, and what has not entered the human heart,
what God has prepared for those who love him" [10]this God has
revealed to us through the Spirit. For the Spirit scrutinizes
everything, even the depths of God.

Alleluia – Matthew 11:25

R. Alleluia, alleluia.

25 Blessed are you, Father, Lord of heaven and earth; you
have revealed to little ones the mysteries of the kingdom.

R. Alleluia, alleluia.

Gospel – Matthew 5:17-37

Jesus said to his disciples: [17] "Do not think that I have come to
abolish the law or the prophets. I have come not to abolish but
to fulfill. [18]Amen, I say to you, until heaven and earth pass
away, not the smallest letter or the smallest part of a letter will
pass from the law, until all things have taken place.
[19]Therefore, whoever breaks one of the least of these
commandments and teaches others to do so will be called
least in the kingdom of heaven. But whoever obeys and
teaches these commandments will be called greatest in the
kingdom of heaven. [20]I tell you, unless your righteousness
surpasses that of the scribes and Pharisees, you will not enter
the kingdom of heaven. [21]"You have heard that it was said to
your ancestors, You shall not kill; and whoever kills will be
liable to judgment. [22]But I say to you, whoever is angry with his
brother will be liable to judgment; and whoever says to his

brother, 'Raqa,' will be answerable to the Sanhedrin; and whoever says, 'You fool,' will be liable to fiery Gehenna. 23Therefore, if you bring your gift to the altar, and there recall that your brother has anything against you, 24leave your gift there at the altar, go first and be reconciled with your brother, and then come and offer your gift. 25Settle with your opponent quickly while on the way to court. Otherwise your opponent will hand you over to the judge, and the judge will hand you over to the guard, and you will be thrown into prison. 26Amen, I say to you, you will not be released until you have paid the last penny. 27"You have heard that it was said, You shall not commit adultery. 28But I say to you, everyone who looks at a woman with lust has already committed adultery with her in his heart. 29If your right eye causes you to sin, tear it out and throw it away. It is better for you to lose one of your members than to have your whole body thrown into Gehenna. 30And if your right hand causes you to sin, cut it off and throw it away. It is better for you to lose one of your members than to have your whole body go into Gehenna. 31"It was also said, Whoever divorces his wife must give her a bill of divorce. 32But I say to you, whoever divorces his wife (unless the marriage is unlawful) causes her to commit adultery, and whoever marries a divorced woman commits adultery. 33"Again you have heard that it was said to your ancestors, Do not take a false oath, but make good to the Lord all that you vow. 34But I say to you, do not swear at all; not by heaven, for it is God's throne; 35nor by the earth, for it is his footstool; nor by Jerusalem, for it is the city of the great King. 36Do not swear by your head, for you cannot make a single hair white or black. 37Let your 'Yes' mean 'Yes,' and your 'No' mean 'No.' Anything more is from the evil one."

OR Matthew 5:20-22A, 27-28, 33-34A, 37

20Jesus said to his disciples: "I tell you, unless your righteousness surpasses that of the scribes and Pharisees, you will not enter the kingdom of heaven. 21"You have heard that it was said to your ancestors, You shall not kill; and whoever kills will be liable to judgment. 22ABut I say to you, whoever is angry with brother will be liable to judgment. 27"You have heard that it was said, You shall not commit adultery. 28But I say to you, everyone who looks at a woman with lust has already committed adultery with her in his heart. 33"Again you have heard that it was said to your ancestors, Do not take a false oath, but make good to the Lord all that you vow. [34A]But I say to you, do not swear at all. [37]Let your 'Yes' mean 'Yes', and your 'No' mean 'No.' Anything more is from the evil one.

Monday February 13, 2023

Monday of the Sixth Week in Ordinary Time

First Reading – Genesis 4:1-15, 25

[1]The man had relations with his wife Eve, and she conceived and bore Cain, saying, "I have produced a man with the help of the LORD." [2]Next she bore his brother Abel. Abel became a keeper of flocks, and Cain a tiller of the soil. [3]In the course of time Cain brought an offering to the LORD from the fruit of the soil, [4]while Abel, for his part, brought one of the best firstlings of his flock. The LORD looked with favor on Abel and his offering, [5]but on Cain and his offering he did not. Cain greatly resented this and was crestfallen. [6]So the LORD said to Cain: "Why are you so resentful and crestfallen. [7]If you do well, you can hold up your head; but if not, sin is a demon lurking at the door: his urge is toward you, yet you can be his master." [8]Cain said to his brother Abel, "Let us go out in the field." When they were in the field, Cain attacked his brother Abel and killed him. [9]Then the LORD asked Cain, "Where is your brother Abel?" He answered, "I do not know. Am I my brother's keeper?" [10]The LORD then said: "What have you done! Listen: your brother's blood cries out to me from the soil! [11]Therefore you shall be banned from the soil that opened its mouth to receive your brother's blood from your hand. [12]If you till the soil, it shall no longer give you its produce. You shall become a restless wanderer on the earth." [13]Cain said to the LORD: "My punishment is too great to bear. [14]Since you have now banished me from the soil, and I must avoid your presence and become a restless wanderer on the earth, anyone may kill me at sight." [15]"Not so!" the LORD said to him. "If anyone kills Cain, Cain shall be avenged sevenfold." So the LORD put a mark on Cain, lest anyone should kill him at sight. [25]Adam again had relations with his wife, and she gave birth to a son whom she called Seth. "God has granted me more offspring in place of Abel," she said, "because Cain slew him."

Responsorial Psalm – Psalms 50:1 AND 8, 16BC-17, 20-21

R. (14a) Offer to God a sacrifice of praise.

1 God the LORD has spoken and summoned the earth,

from the rising of the sun to its setting.

8 "Not for your sacrifices do I rebuke you,

for your burnt offerings are before me always."

R. Offer to God a sacrifice of praise.

16BC "Why do you recite my statutes,

and profess my covenant with your mouth

17 Though you hate discipline

and cast my words behind you?"

R. Offer to God a sacrifice of praise.

20 "You sit speaking against your brother;

against your mother's son you spread rumors.

21 When you do these things, shall I be deaf to it?

Or do you think that I am like yourself?

I will correct you by drawing them up before your eyes."

R. Offer to God a sacrifice of praise.

Alleluia – John 14:6

R. Alleluia, alleluia.

6I am the way and the truth and the life, says the Lord; no one comes to the Father except through me.

R. Alleluia, alleluia.

Gospel – Mark 8:11-13

11The Pharisees came forward and began to argue with Jesus,
seeking from him a sign from heaven to test him. 12He sighed
from the depth of his spirit and said, "Why does this generation
seek a sign? Amen, I say to you, no sign will be given to this
generation." 13Then he left them, got into the boat again, and
went off to the other shore.

Tuesday February 14, 2023

Memorial of Saints Cyril, Monk & Methodius, Bishop

First Reading – Genesis 6:5-8; 7:1-5, 10

5When the LORD saw how great was man's wickedness on
earth, and how no desire that his heart conceived was ever
anything but evil, 6he regretted that he had made man on the
earth, and his heart was grieved. 7So the LORD said: "I will
wipe out from the earth the men whom I have created, and not
only the men, but also the beasts and the creeping things and
the birds of the air, for I am sorry that I made them." 8But Noah
found favor with the LORD. 1Then the LORD said to Noah:
"Go into the ark, you and all your household, for you alone in
this age have I found to be truly just. 2Of every clean animal,
take with you seven pairs, a male and its mate; and of the
unclean animals, one pair, a male and its mate; 3likewise, of
every clean bird of the air, seven pairs, a male and a female,
and of all the unclean birds, one pair, a male and a female.
Thus you will keep their issue alive over all the earth. 4Seven
days from now I will bring rain down on the earth for forty days
and forty nights, and so I will wipe out from the surface of the
earth every moving creature that I have made." 5Noah did just
as the LORD had commanded him. 10As soon as the seven
days were over, the waters of the flood came upon the earth.

Responsorial Psalm – Psalms 29:1A AND 2, 3AC-4, 3B AND 9C-10

R. (11b) The Lord will bless his people with peace.

1A Give to the LORD, you sons of God,

give to the LORD glory and praise,

2 Give to the LORD the glory due his name;

adore the LORD in holy attire.

R. The Lord will bless his people with peace.

3AC The voice of the LORD is over the waters,

the LORD, over vast waters.

4 The voice of the LORD is mighty;

the voice of the LORD is majestic.

R. The Lord will bless his people with peace.

3B The God of glory thunders,

9C and in his temple all say, "Glory!"

10 The LORD is enthroned above the flood;

the LORD is enthroned as king forever.

R. The Lord will bless his people with peace.

Alleluia – John 14:23

R. Alleluia, alleluia.

23Whoever loves me will keep my word, says the Lord; and my Father will love him and we will come to him.

R. Alleluia, alleluia.

Gospel – Mark 8:14-21

14The disciples had forgotten to bring bread, and they had only
one loaf with them in the boat. 15Jesus enjoined them, "Watch
out, guard against the leaven of the Pharisees and the leaven
of Herod." 16They concluded among themselves that it was
because they had no bread. 17When he became aware of this
he said to them, "Why do you conclude that it is because you
have no bread? Do you not yet understand or comprehend?
Are your hearts hardened? 18Do you have eyes and not see,
ears and not hear? And do you not remember, 19when I broke
the five loaves for the five thousand, how many wicker baskets
full of fragments you picked up?" They answered him,
"Twelve." 20"When I broke the seven loaves for the four
thousand, how many full baskets of fragments did you pick
up?" They answered him, "Seven." 21He said to them, "Do you
still not understand?"

Wednesday February 15, 2023

Wednesday of Sixth Week in Ordinary Time

First Reading – Genesis 8:6-13, 20-22

6At the end of forty days Noah opened the hatch he had made
in the ark, 7and he sent out a raven, to see if the waters had
lessened on the earth. It flew back and forth until the waters
dried off from the earth. 8Then he sent out a dove, to see if the

waters had lessened on the earth. 9But the dove could find no
place to alight and perch, and it returned to him in the ark, for
there was water all over the earth. Putting out his hand, he
caught the dove and drew it back to him inside the ark. 10He
waited seven days more and again sent the dove out from the
ark. 11In the evening the dove came back to him, and there in
its bill was a plucked-off olive leaf! So Noah knew that the
waters had lessened on the earth. 12He waited still another
seven days and then released the dove once more; and this
time it did not come back. 13In the six hundred and first year of
Noah's life, in the first month, on the first day of the month, the
water began to dry up on the earth. Noah then removed the
covering of the ark and saw that the surface of the ground was
drying up. 20Noah built an altar to the LORD, and choosing
from every clean animal and every clean bird, he offered burnt
offerings on the altar. 21When the LORD smelled the sweet
odor, he said to himself: "Never again will I doom the earth
because of man since the desires of man's heart are evil from
the start; nor will I ever again strike down all living beings, as I
have done. 22As long as the earth lasts, seedtime and harvest,
cold and heat, Summer and winter, and day and night shall
not cease."

Responsorial Psalm – Psalms 116:12-13, 14-15, 18-19

R. (17a) **To you, Lord, I will offer a sacrifice of praise.** or: **R. Alleluia.**

12 How shall I make a return to the LORD

for all the good he has done for me?

13 The cup of salvation I will take up,

and I will call upon the name of the LORD.

R. To you, Lord, I will offer a sacrifice of praise. or: **R. Alleluia.**

14 My vows to the LORD I will pay

in the presence of all his people.

15 Precious in the eyes of the LORD

is the death of his faithful ones.

R. To you, Lord, I will offer a sacrifice of praise. or: **R. Alleluia.**

[18] My vows to the LORD I will pay

in the presence of all his people,

[19] In the courts of the house of the LORD,

in your midst, O Jerusalem.

R. To you, Lord, I will offer a sacrifice of praise. or: **R. Alleluia.**

Alleluia – Ephesians 1:17-18

R. Alleluia, alleluia.

[17]May the Father of our Lord Jesus Christ enlighten the eyes
of our hearts,[18]that we may know what is the hope that
belongs to his call.

R. Alleluia, alleluia.

Gospel – Mark 8:22-26

[22]When Jesus and his disciples arrived at Bethsaida, people
brought to him a blind man and begged Jesus to touch him.
[23]He took the blind man by the hand and led him outside the
village. Putting spittle on his eyes he laid his hands on the
man and asked, "Do you see anything?" [24]Looking up the man
replied, "I see people looking like trees and walking." [25]Then
he laid hands on the man's eyes a second time and he saw
clearly; his sight was restored and he could see everything
distinctly. [26]Then he sent him home and said, "Do not even go
into the village.

Thursday February 16, 2023

Thursday of the Sixth Week in Ordinary Time

First Reading – Genesis 9:1-13

[1]God blessed Noah and his sons and said to them: "Be fertile
and multiply and fill the earth. [2]Dread fear of you shall come
upon all the animals of the earth and all the birds of the air,
upon all the creatures that move about on the ground and all
the fishes of the sea; into your power they are delivered.
[3]Every creature that is alive shall be yours to eat; I give them

all to you as I did the green plants. [4]Only flesh with its lifeblood
still in it you shall not eat. [5]For your own lifeblood, too, I will
demand an accounting: from every animal I will demand it, and
from one man in regard to his fellow man I will demand an
accounting for human life. [6]If anyone sheds the blood of man,
by man shall his blood be shed; For in the image of God has
man been made. [7]Be fertile, then, and multiply; abound on
earth and subdue it." [8]God said to Noah and to his sons with
him: [9]"See, I am now establishing my covenant with you and
your descendants after you [10]and with every living creature
that was with you: all the birds, and the various tame and wild
animals that were with you and came out of the ark. [11]I will
establish my covenant with you, that never again shall all
bodily creatures be destroyed by the waters of a flood; there
shall not be another flood to devastate the earth." [12]God
added: "This is the sign that I am giving for all ages to come,
of the covenant between me and you and every living creature
with you: [13]I set my bow in the clouds to serve as a sign of the
covenant between me and the earth."

Responsorial Psalm – Psalms 102:16-18, 19-21, 29 AND 22-23

R. (20b) From heaven the Lord looks down on the earth.

[16] The nations shall revere your name, O LORD,

and all the kings of the earth your glory,

[17] When the LORD has rebuilt Zion

and appeared in his glory;

[18] When he has regarded the prayer of the destitute,

and not despised their prayer.

R. From heaven the Lord looks down on the earth.

[18] Let this be written for the generation to come,

and let his future creatures praise the LORD:

[20] "The LORD looked down from his holy height,

from heaven he beheld the earth,

[21] To hear the groaning of the prisoners,

to release those doomed to die."

R. From heaven the Lord looks down on the earth.

[29] The children of your servants shall abide,

and their posterity shall continue in your presence,

[22] That the name of the LORD may be declared in Zion,

and his praise, in Jerusalem,

[23] When the peoples gather together,

and the kingdoms, to serve the LORD.

R. From heaven the Lord looks down on the earth.

Alleluia – John 6:63C, 68C

R. Alleluia, alleluia.

[63C]Your words, Lord, are Spirit and life; [68C]you have the words of everlasting life.

R. Alleluia, alleluia.

Gospel – Mark 8:27-33

[27]Jesus and his disciples set out for the villages of Caesarea
Philippi. Along the way he asked his disciples, "Who do people
say that I am?" [28]They said in reply, "John the Baptist, others
Elijah, still others one of the prophets." [29]And he asked them,
"But who do you say that I am?" Peter said to him in reply,
"You are the Christ." [30]Then he warned them not to tell anyone
about him. [31]He began to teach them that the Son of Man
must suffer greatly and be rejected by the elders, the chief
priests, and the scribes, and be killed, and rise after three
days. [32]He spoke this openly. Then Peter took him aside and
began to rebuke him. [33]At this he turned around and, looking
at his disciples, rebuked Peter and said, "Get behind me,
Satan. You are thinking not as God does, but as human
beings do."

Friday February 17, 2023

Friday of the Sixth Week in Ordinary Time

First Reading – Genesis 11:1-9

[1]The whole world spoke the same language, using the same
words. [2]While the people were migrating in the east, they

came upon a valley in the land of Shinar and settled there.
[3]They said to one another, “Come, let us mold bricks and
harden them with fire.” They used bricks for stone, and
bitumen for mortar. [4]Then they said, “Come, let us build
ourselves a city and a tower with its top in the sky, and so
make a name for ourselves; otherwise we shall be scattered
all over the earth.” [5]The LORD came down to see the city and
the tower that they had built. [6]Then the LORD said: “If now,
while they are one people, all speaking the same language,
they have started to do this, nothing will later stop them from
doing whatever they presume to do. [7]Let us then go down and
there confuse their language, so that one will not understand
what another says.” [8]Thus the LORD scattered them from
there all over the earth, and they stopped building the city.
[9]That is why it was called Babel, because there the LORD
confused the speech of all the world. It was from that place
that he scattered them all over the earth.

Responsorial Psalm – Psalms 33:10-11, 12-13, 14-15

R. (12) Blessed the people the Lord has chosen to be his own.

10 The LORD brings to nought the plans of nations;

he foils the designs of peoples.

11 But the plan of the LORD stands forever;

the design of his heart, through all generations.

R. Blessed the people the Lord has chosen to be his own.

12 Blessed the nation whose God is the LORD,

the people he has chosen for his own inheritance.

13 From heaven the LORD looks down;

he sees all mankind.

R. Blessed the people the Lord has chosen to be his own.

14 From his fixed throne he beholds

all who dwell on the earth,

15 He who fashioned the heart of each,

he who knows all their works.

R. Blessed the people the Lord has chosen to be his own.

Alleluia – John 15:15B

R. Alleluia, alleluia.

15BI call you my friends, says the Lord, for I have made known to you all that the Father has told me.

R. Alleluia, alleluia.

Gospel – Mark 8:34-9:1

34Jesus summoned the crowd with his disciples and said to
them, "Whoever wishes to come after me must deny himself,
take up his cross, and follow me. 35For whoever wishes to
save his life will lose it, but whoever loses his life for my sake
and that of the Gospel will save it. 36What profit is there for one
to gain the whole world and forfeit his life? 37What could one
give in exchange for his life? 38Whoever is ashamed of me and
of my words in this faithless and sinful generation, the Son of
Man will be ashamed of when he comes in his Father's glory
with the holy angels." 1He also said to them, "Amen, I say to
you, there are some standing here who will not taste death
until they see that the Kingdom of God has come in power."

Saturday February 18, 2023

Saturday of the Sixth Week in Ordinary Time

First Reading – Hebrews 11:1-7

Brothers and sisters: 1Faith is the realization of what is hoped
for and evidence of things not seen. 2Because of it the
ancients were well attested. 3By faith we understand that the
universe was ordered by the word of God, so that what is
visible came into being through the invisible. 4By faith Abel
offered to God a sacrifice greater than Cain's. Through this, he
was attested to be righteous, God bearing witness to his gifts,
and through this, though dead, he still speaks. 5By faith Enoch
was taken up so that he should not see death, and he was
found no more because God had taken him. Before he was
taken up, he was attested to have pleased God. 6But without
faith it is impossible to please him, for anyone who
approaches God must believe that he exists and that he

rewards those who seek him. [7]By faith Noah, warned about what was not yet seen, with reverence built an ark for the salvation of his household. Through this, he condemned the world and inherited the righteousness that comes through faith.

Responsorial Psalm – Psalms 145:2-3, 4-5, 10-11

R. (see 1) I will praise your name for ever, Lord.

2 Every day will I bless you,

and I will praise your name forever and ever.

3 Great is the LORD and highly to be praised;

his greatness is unsearchable.

R. I will praise your name for ever, Lord.

4 Generation after generation praises your works

and proclaims your might.

5 They speak of the splendor of your glorious majesty

and tell of your wondrous works.

R. I will praise your name for ever, Lord.

10 Let all your works give you thanks, O LORD,

and let your faithful ones bless you.

11 Let them discourse of the glory of your Kingdom

and speak of your might.

R. I will praise your name for ever, Lord.

Alleluia – Mark 9:6

R. Alleluia, alleluia.

[6]The heavens were opened and the voice of the Father thundered: This is my beloved Son. Listen to him.

R. Alleluia, alleluia.

Gospel – Mark 9:2-13

[2]Jesus took Peter, James, and John and led them up a high mountain apart by themselves. And he was transfigured before them, [3]and his clothes became dazzling white, such as

no fuller on earth could bleach them. [4]Then Elijah appeared to
them along with Moses, and they were conversing with Jesus.
[5]Then Peter said to Jesus in reply, “Rabbi, it is good that we
are here! Let us make three tents: one for you, one for Moses,
and one for Elijah.” [6]He hardly knew what to say, they were so
terrified. [7]Then a cloud came, casting a shadow over them;
then from the cloud came a voice, “This is my beloved Son.
Listen to him.” [8]Suddenly, looking around, the disciples no
longer saw anyone but Jesus alone with them. [9]As they were
coming down from the mountain, he charged them not to
relate what they had seen to anyone, except when the Son of
Man had risen from the dead. [10]So they kept the matter to
themselves, questioning what rising from the dead meant.
[11]Then they asked him, “Why do the scribes say that Elijah
must come first?” [12]He told them, “Elijah will indeed come first
and restore all things, yet how is it written regarding the Son of
Man that he must suffer greatly and be treated with contempt?
[13]But I tell you that Elijah has come and they did to him
whatever they pleased, as it is written of him.”

Sunday February 19, 2023

Seventh Sunday in Ordinary Time, Year A

First Reading – Leviticus 19:1-2, 17-18

[1]The LORD said to Moses, [2]“Speak to the whole Israelite
community and tell them: Be holy, for I, the LORD, your God,
am holy. [17]“You shall not bear hatred for your brother or sister
in your heart. Though you may have to reprove your fellow
citizen, do not incur sin because of him. [18]Take no revenge
and cherish no grudge against any of your people. You shall
love your neighbor as yourself. I am the LORD.”

Responsorial Psalm – Psalms 103:1-2, 3-4, 8, 10, 12-13

R. (8a) **The Lord is kind and merciful.**

[1] Bless the LORD, O my soul;

and all my being, bless his holy name.

[2] Bless the LORD, O my soul,

and forget not all his benefits.

R. The Lord is kind and merciful.

[3] He pardons all your iniquities,

heals all your ills.

[4] He redeems your life from destruction,

crowns you with kindness and compassion.

R. The Lord is kind and merciful.

[8] Merciful and gracious is the LORD,

slow to anger and abounding in kindness.

[10] Not according to our sins does he deal with us,

nor does he requite us according to our crimes.

R. The Lord is kind and merciful.

[12] As far as the east is from the west,

so far has he put our transgressions from us.

[13] As a father has compassion on his children,

so the LORD has compassion on those who fear him.

R. The Lord is kind and merciful.

Second Reading – 1 Corinthians 3:16-23

Brothers and sisters: [16]Do you not know that you are the
temple of God, and that the Spirit of God dwells in you? [17]If
anyone destroys God's temple, God will destroy that person;
for the temple of God, which you are, is holy. [18]Let no one
deceive himself. If anyone among you considers himself wise
in this age, let him become a fool, so as to become wise. [19]For
the wisdom of this world is foolishness in the eyes of God, for
it is written: God catches the wise in their own ruses, [20]and
again: The Lord knows the thoughts of the wise, that they are
vain. [21]So let no one boast about human beings, for everything
belongs to you, [22] Paul or Apollos or Cephas, or the world or
life or death, or the present or the future: all belong to you,
[23]and you to Christ, and Christ to God.

Alleluia – 1 John 2:5

R. Alleluia, alleluia.

[5] Whoever keeps the word of Christ, the love of God is truly perfected in him.

R. Alleluia, alleluia.

Gospel – Matthew 5:38-48

Jesus said to his disciples: [38] "You have heard that it was said, An eye for an eye and a tooth for a tooth. [39]But I say to you, offer no resistance to one who is evil. When someone strikes you on your right cheek, turn the other one as well. [40]If anyone wants to go to law with you over your tunic, hand over your cloak as well. [41]Should anyone press you into service for one mile, go for two miles. [42]Give to the one who asks of you, and do not turn your back on one who wants to borrow. [43]"You have heard that it was said, You shall love your neighbor and hate your enemy. [44]But I say to you, love your enemies and pray for those who persecute you, [45]that you may be children of your heavenly Father, for he makes his sun rise on the bad and the good, and causes rain to fall on the just and the unjust. [46]For if you love those who love you, what recompense will you have? Do not the tax collectors do the same? [47]And if you greet your brothers only, what is unusual about that? Do not the pagans do the same? [48]So be perfect, just as your heavenly Father is perfect."

Monday February 20, 2023

Monday of Seventh Week in Ordinary Time

First Reading – Sirach 1:1-10

[1]All wisdom comes from the LORD and with him it remains forever, and is before all time. [2]The sand of the seashore, the drops of rain, the days of eternity: who can number these? [3]Heaven's height, earth's breadth, the depths of the abyss: who can explore these? [4]Before all things else wisdom was created; and prudent understanding, from eternity. [5]The word of God on high is the fountain of wisdom and her ways are everlasting. [6]To whom has wisdom's root been revealed? Who knows her subtleties? [7]To whom has the discipline of wisdom been revealed? And who has understood the multiplicity of her

ways? [8]There is but one, Most High all-powerful creator-king and truly awe-inspiring one, seated upon his throne and he is the God of dominion. [9]It is the LORD; he created her through the Holy Spirit, has seen her and taken note of her. He has poured her forth upon all his works, [10]upon every living thing according to his bounty; he has lavished her upon his friends.

Responsorial Psalm – Psalms 93:1AB, 1CD-2, 5

R.(1a) The Lord is king; he is robed in majesty.

1AB The LORD is king, in splendor robed;

robed is the LORD and girt about with strength.

R. The Lord is king; he is robed in majesty.

1CD And he has made the world firm,

not to be moved.

2 Your throne stands firm from of old;

from everlasting you are, O LORD.

R. The Lord is king; he is robed in majesty.

5 Your decrees are worthy of trust indeed:

holiness befits your house,

O LORD, for length of days.

R. The Lord is king; he is robed in majesty.

Alleluia – 2 Timothy 1:10

R. Alleluia, alleluia.

[10]Our Savior Jesus Christ has destroyed death and brought life to light through the Gospel.

R. Alleluia, alleluia.

Gospel – Mark 9:14-29

[14]As Jesus came down from the mountain with Peter, James, John and approached the other disciples, they saw a large crowd around them and scribes arguing with them. [15]Immediately on seeing him, the whole crowd was utterly amazed. They ran up to him and greeted him. [16]He asked them, "What are you arguing about with them?" [17]Someone

from the crowd answered him, “Teacher, I have brought to you
my son possessed by a mute spirit. [18]Wherever it seizes him,
it throws him down; he foams at the mouth, grinds his teeth,
and becomes rigid. I asked your disciples to drive it out, but
they were unable to do so.” [19]He said to them in reply, “O
faithless generation, how long will I be with you? How long will
I endure you? Bring him to me.” [20]They brought the boy to him.
And when he saw him, the spirit immediately threw the boy
into convulsions. As he fell to the ground, he began to roll
around and foam at the mouth. [21]Then he questioned his
father, “How long has this been happening to him?” He
replied, “Since childhood. [22]It has often thrown him into fire
and into water to kill him. But if you can do anything, have
compassion on us and help us.” [23]Jesus said to him, “‘If you
can!’ Everything is possible to one who has faith.” [24]Then the
boy’s father cried out, “I do believe, help my unbelief!” [25]Jesus,
on seeing a crowd rapidly gathering, rebuked the unclean
spirit and said to it, “Mute and deaf spirit, I command you:
come out of him and never enter him again!” [26]Shouting and
throwing the boy into convulsions, it came out. He became like
a corpse, which caused many to say, “He is dead!” [27]But
Jesus took him by the hand, raised him, and he stood up.
[28]When he entered the house, his disciples asked him in
private, “Why could we not drive the spirit out?” [29]He said to
them, “This kind can only come out through prayer.”

Tuesday February 21, 2023

Tuesday of Seventh Week in Ordinary Time

First Reading – Sirach 2:1-11

[1]My son, when you come to serve the LORD, stand in justice
and fear, prepare yourself for trials. [2]Be sincere of heart and
steadfast, incline your ear and receive the word of
understanding, undisturbed in time of adversity. [3]Wait on God,
with patience, cling to him, forsake him not; thus will you be
wise in all your ways. [4]Accept whatever befalls you, when
sorrowful, be steadfast, and in crushing misfortune be patient;
[5]For in fire gold and silver are tested, and worthy people in the
crucible of humiliation. [6]Trust God and God will help you; trust
in him, and he will direct your way; keep his fear and grow old
therein. [7]You who fear the LORD, wait for his mercy, turn not
away lest you fall. [8]You who fear the LORD, trust him, and

your reward will not be lost. [9]You who fear the LORD, hope for
good things, for lasting joy and mercy. You who fear the
LORD, love him, and your hearts will be enlightened. [10]Study
the generations long past and understand; has anyone hoped
in the LORD and been disappointed? Has anyone persevered
in his commandments and been forsaken? has anyone called
upon him and been rebuffed? [11]Compassionate and merciful is
the LORD; he forgives sins, he saves in time of trouble and he
is a protector to all who seek him in truth.

Responsorial Psalm – Psalms 37:3-4, 18-19, 27-28, 39-40

R. (see 5) **Commit your life to the Lord, and he will help you.**

3 Trust in the LORD and do good,

that you may dwell in the land and be fed in security.

4 Take delight in the LORD,

and he will grant you your heart's requests.

R. Commit your life to the Lord, and he will help you.

18 The LORD watches over the lives of the wholehearted;

their inheritance lasts forever.

19 They are not put to shame in an evil time;

in days of famine they have plenty.

R. Commit your life to the Lord, and he will help you.

27 Turn from evil and do good,

that you may abide forever;

28 For the LORD loves what is right,

and forsakes not his faithful ones.

R. Commit your life to the Lord, and he will help you.

39 The salvation of the just is from the LORD;

he is their refuge in time of distress.

40 And the LORD helps them and delivers them;

he delivers them from the wicked and saves them,

because they take refuge in him.

R. Commit your life to the Lord, and he will help you.

Alleluia – Galatians 6:14

R. Alleluia, alleluia.

14May I never boast except in the Cross of our Lord Jesus
Christ, through which the world has been crucified to me and I
to the world.

R. Alleluia, alleluia.

Gospel – Mark 9:30-37

30Jesus and his disciples left from there and began a journey
through Galilee, but he did not wish anyone to know about it.
31He was teaching his disciples and telling them, "The Son of
Man is to be handed over to men and they will kill him, and
three days after his death the Son of Man will rise." 32But they
did not understand the saying, and they were afraid to
question him. 33They came to Capernaum and, once inside the
house, he began to ask them, "What were you arguing about
on the way?" 34But they remained silent. For they had been
discussing among themselves on the way who was the
greatest. 35Then he sat down, called the Twelve, and said to
them, "If anyone wishes to be first, he shall be the last of all
and the servant of all." 36Taking a child, he placed it in their
midst, and putting his arms around it, he said to them,
37"Whoever receives one child such as this in my name,
receives me; and whoever receives me, receives not me but
the One who sent me."

Wednesday February 22, 2023

Ash Wednesday

First Reading – Joel 2:12-18

12Even now, says the LORD, return to me with your whole
heart, with fasting, and weeping, and mourning; 13Rend your
hearts, not your garments, and return to the LORD, your God.
For gracious and merciful is he, slow to anger, rich in
kindness, and relenting in punishment. 14Perhaps he will again
relent and leave behind him a blessing, Offerings and libations
for the LORD, your God. 15Blow the trumpet in Zion! proclaim
a fast, call an assembly; 16Gather the people, notify the
congregation; Assemble the elders, gather the children and

the infants at the breast; Let the bridegroom quit his room and
the bride her chamber. 17 Between the porch and the altar let
the priests, the ministers of the LORD, weep, And say, "Spare,
O LORD, your people, and make not your heritage a reproach,
with the nations ruling over them! Why should they say among
the peoples, 'Where is their God?'" 18 Then the LORD was
stirred to concern for his land and took pity on his people.

Responsorial Psalm – Psalms 51:3-4, 5-6AB, 12-13,14 AND 17

R. (see 3a) **Be merciful, O Lord, for we have sinned.**

3 Have mercy on me, O God, in your goodness;

in the greatness of your compassion wipe out my offense.

4 Thoroughly wash me from my guilt

and of my sin cleanse me.

R. Be merciful, O Lord, for we have sinned.

5 For I acknowledge my offense,

and my sin is before me always:

6AB "Against you only have I sinned,

and done what is evil in your sight."

R. Be merciful, O Lord, for we have sinned.

12 A clean heart create for me, O God,

and a steadfast spirit renew within me.

13 Cast me not out from your presence,

and your Holy Spirit take not from me.

R. Be merciful, O Lord, for we have sinned.

14 Give me back the joy of your salvation,

and a willing spirit sustain in me.

17 O Lord, open my lips,

and my mouth shall proclaim your praise.

R. Be merciful, O Lord, for we have sinned.

Second Reading – 2 Corinthians 5:20-6:2

[20]Brothers and sisters: We are ambassadors for Christ, as if God were appealing through us. We implore you on behalf of Christ, be reconciled to God. [21]For our sake he made him to be sin who did not know sin, so that we might become the righteousness of God in him. [1]Working together, then, we appeal to you not to receive the grace of God in vain. [2]For he says: In an acceptable time I heard you, and on the day of salvation I helped you. Behold, now is a very acceptable time; behold, now is the day of salvation.

Verse Before The Gospel – Psalms 95:8

[8]If today you hear his voice, harden not your hearts.

Gospel – Matthew 6:1-6, 16-18

Jesus said to his disciples: [1]"Take care not to perform righteous deeds in order that people may see them; otherwise, you will have no recompense from your heavenly Father. [2]When you give alms, do not blow a trumpet before you, as the hypocrites do in the synagogues and in the streets to win the praise of others. Amen, I say to you, they have received their reward. [3]But when you give alms, do not let your left hand know what your right is doing, [4]so that your almsgiving may be secret. And your Father who sees in secret will repay you. [5]"When you pray, do not be like the hypocrites, who love to stand and pray in the synagogues and on street corners so that others may see them. Amen, I say to you, they have received their reward. [6]But when you pray, go to your inner room, close the door, and pray to your Father in secret. And your Father who sees in secret will repay you. [16]"When you fast, do not look gloomy like the hypocrites. They neglect their appearance, so that they may appear to others to be fasting. Amen, I say to you, they have received their reward. [17]But when you fast, anoint your head and wash your face, [18] so that you may not appear to be fasting, except to your Father who is hidden. And your Father who sees what is hidden will repay you."

Thursday February 23, 2023

Thursday after Ash Wednesday

First Reading – Deuteronomy 30:15-20

[15]Moses said to the people: “Today I have set before you life
and prosperity, death and doom. [16]If you obey the
commandments of the LORD, your God, which I enjoin on you
today, loving him, and walking in his ways, and keeping his
commandments, statutes and decrees, you will live and grow
numerous, and the LORD, your God, will bless you in the land
you are entering to occupy. [17]If, however, you turn away your
hearts and will not listen, but are led astray and adore and
serve other gods, [18]I tell you now that you will certainly perish;
you will not have a long life on the land that you are crossing
the Jordan to enter and occupy. [19]I call heaven and earth
today to witness against you: I have set before you life and
death, the blessing and the curse. Choose life, then, that you
and your descendants may live, [20]by loving the LORD, your
God, heeding his voice, and holding fast to him. For that will
mean life for you, a long life for you to live on the land that the
LORD swore he would give to your fathers Abraham, Isaac
and Jacob.”

Responsorial Psalm – Psalms 1:1-2, 3, 4 AND 6

R. (40:5a) Blessed are they who hope in the Lord.

[1] Blessed the man who follows not

the counsel of the wicked

Nor walks in the way of sinners,

nor sits in the company of the insolent,

[2] But delights in the law of the LORD

and meditates on his law day and night.

R. Blessed are they who hope in the Lord.

[3] He is like a tree

planted near running water,

That yields its fruit in due season,

and whose leaves never fade.

Whatever he does, prospers.

R. Blessed are they who hope in the Lord.

[4] Not so the wicked, not so;

they are like chaff which the wind drives away.

[6] For the LORD watches over the way of the just,

but the way of the wicked vanishes.

R. Blessed are they who hope in the Lord.

Verse Before The Gospel – Matthew 4:17

[17] Repent, says the Lord; the Kingdom of heaven is at hand.

Gospel – Luke 9:22-25

[22]Jesus said to his disciples: “The Son of Man must suffer
greatly and be rejected by the elders, the chief priests, and the
scribes, and be killed and on the third day be raised.” [23]Then
he said to all, “If anyone wishes to come after me, he must
deny himself and take up his cross daily and follow me. [24]For
whoever wishes to save his life will lose it, but whoever loses
his life for my sake will save it. [25]What profit is there for one to
gain the whole world yet lose or forfeit himself?”

Friday February 24, 2023

Friday after Ash Wednesday

First Reading – Isaiah 58:1-9A

[1]Thus says the Lord GOD: Cry out full-throated and
unsparingly, lift up your voice like a trumpet blast; Tell my
people their wickedness, and the house of Jacob their sins.
[2]They seek me day after day, and desire to know my ways,
Like a nation that has done what is just and not abandoned
the law of their God; They ask me to declare what is due them,
pleased to gain access to God. [3]“Why do we fast, and you do
not see it? afflict ourselves, and you take no note of it?” Lo, on
your fast day you carry out your own pursuits, and drive all
your laborers. [4]Yes, your fast ends in quarreling and fighting,
striking with wicked claw. Would that today you might fast so
as to make your voice heard on high! [5]Is this the manner of
fasting I wish, of keeping a day of penance: That a man bow
his head like a reed and lie in sackcloth and ashes? Do you

call this a fast, a day acceptable to the LORD? 6This, rather, is
the fasting that I wish: releasing those bound unjustly, untying
the thongs of the yoke; Setting free the oppressed, breaking
every yoke; 7Sharing your bread with the hungry, sheltering
the oppressed and the homeless; Clothing the naked when
you see them, and not turning your back on your own. 8Then
your light shall break forth like the dawn, and your wound shall
quickly be healed; Your vindication shall go before you, and
the glory of the LORD shall be your rear guard. 9AThen you
shall call, and the LORD will answer, you shall cry for help,
and he will say: Here I am!

Responsorial Psalm – Psalms 51:3-4, 5-6AB, 18-19

R. (19b) A heart contrite and humbled, O God, you will not spurn.

3 Have mercy on me, O God, in your goodness;

in the greatness of your compassion wipe out my offense.

4 Thoroughly wash me from my guilt

and of my sin cleanse me.

R. A heart contrite and humbled, O God, you will not spurn.

5 For I acknowledge my offense,

and my sin is before me always:

6AB "Against you only have I sinned,

and done what is evil in your sight."

R. A heart contrite and humbled, O God, you will not spurn.

18 For you are not pleased with sacrifices;

should I offer a burnt offering, you would not accept it.

19 My sacrifice, O God, is a contrite spirit;

a heart contrite and humbled, O God, you will not spurn.

R. A heart contrite and humbled, O God, you will not spurn.

Verse Before The Gospel – Amos 5:14

14 Seek good and not evil so that you may live, and the Lord will be with you.

Gospel – Matthew 9:14-15

14 The disciples of John approached Jesus and said, "Why do we and the Pharisees fast much, but your disciples do not fast?" 15 Jesus answered them, "Can the wedding guests mourn as long as the bridegroom is with them? The days will come when the bridegroom is taken away from them, and then they will fast."

Saturday February 25, 2023

Saturday after Ash Wednesday

First Reading – Isaiah 58:9B-14

9B Thus says the LORD: If you remove from your midst oppression, false accusation and malicious speech; 10 If you bestow your bread on the hungry and satisfy the afflicted; Then light shall rise for you in the darkness, and the gloom shall become for you like midday; 11 Then the LORD will guide you always and give you plenty even on the parched land. He will renew your strength, and you shall be like a watered garden, like a spring whose water never fails. 12 The ancient ruins shall be rebuilt for your sake, and the foundations from ages past you shall raise up; "Repairer of the breach," they shall call you, "Restorer of ruined homesteads." 13 If you hold back your foot on the Sabbath from following your own pursuits on my holy day; If you call the Sabbath a delight, and the LORD's holy day honorable; If you honor it by not following your ways, seeking your own interests, or speaking with malice. 14 Then you shall delight in the LORD, and I will make you ride on the heights of the earth; I will nourish you with the heritage of Jacob, your father, for the mouth of the LORD has spoken.

Responsorial Psalm – Psalms 86:1-2, 3-4, 5-6

R. (11ab) Teach me your way, O Lord, that I may walk in your truth.

1 Incline your ear, O LORD; answer me,

for I am afflicted and poor.

2 Keep my life, for I am devoted to you;

save your servant who trusts in you.

You are my God.

R. Teach me your way, O Lord, that I may walk in your truth.

3 Have mercy on me, O Lord,

for to you I call all the day.

4 Gladden the soul of your servant,

for to you, O Lord, I lift up my soul.

R. Teach me your way, O Lord, that I may walk in your truth.

5 For you, O Lord, are good and forgiving,

abounding in kindness to all who call upon you.

6 Hearken, O LORD, to my prayer

and attend to the sound of my pleading.

R. Teach me your way, O Lord, that I may walk in your truth.

Verse Before The Gospel – Ezekiel 33:11

11I take no pleasure in the death of the wicked man, says the Lord, but rather in his conversion, that he may live.

Gospel – Luke 5:27-32

27Jesus saw a tax collector named Levi sitting at the customs
post. He said to him, "Follow me." 28And leaving everything
behind, he got up and followed him. 29Then Levi gave a great
banquet for him in his house, and a large crowd of tax
collectors and others were at table with them. 30The Pharisees
and their scribes complained to his disciples, saying, "Why do
you eat and drink with tax collectors and sinners?" 31Jesus
said to them in reply, "Those who are healthy do not need a
physician, but the sick do. 32I have not come to call the
righteous to repentance but sinners."

Sunday February 26, 2023

First Sunday of Lent, Year A

First Reading – Genesis 2:7-9; 3:1-7

[7]The LORD God formed man out of the clay of the ground and
blew into his nostrils the breath of life, and so man became a
living being. [8]Then the LORD God planted a garden in Eden,
in the east, and placed there the man whom he had formed.
[9]Out of the ground the LORD God made various trees grow
that were delightful to look at and good for food, with the tree
of life in the middle of the garden and the tree of the
knowledge of good and evil. [1]Now the serpent was the most
cunning of all the animals that the LORD God had made. The
serpent asked the woman, “Did God really tell you not to eat
from any of the trees in the garden?” [2]The woman answered
the serpent: “We may eat of the fruit of the trees in the garden;
[3]it is only about the fruit of the tree in the middle of the garden
that God said, ‘You shall not eat it or even touch it, lest you
die.'” [4]But the serpent said to the woman: “You certainly will
not die! No, [5]God knows well that the moment you eat of it
your eyes will be opened and you will be like gods who know
what is good and what is evil.” [6]The woman saw that the tree
was good for food, pleasing to the eyes, and desirable for
gaining wisdom. So she took some of its fruit and ate it; and
she also gave some to her husband, who was with her, and he
ate it. [7]Then the eyes of both of them were opened, and they
realized that they were naked; so they sewed fig leaves
together and made loincloths for themselves.

Responsorial Psalm – Psalms 51:3-4, 5-6, 12-13, 17

R. [(cf. 3a)] **Be merciful, O Lord, for we have sinned.**

[3] Have mercy on me, O God, in your goodness;

in the greatness of your compassion wipe out my offense.

[4] Thoroughly wash me from my guilt

and of my sin cleanse me.

R. Be merciful, O Lord, for we have sinned.

[5] For I acknowledge my offense,

and my sin is before me always:

[6] "Against you only have I sinned,

and done what is evil in your sight."

R. Be merciful, O Lord, for we have sinned.

[12] A clean heart create for me, O God,

and a steadfast spirit renew within me.

[13] Cast me not out from your presence,

and your Holy Spirit take not from me.

R. Be merciful, O Lord, for we have sinned.

[17] Give me back the joy of your salvation,

and a willing spirit sustain in me.

O Lord, open my lips,

and my mouth shall proclaim your praise.

R. Be merciful, O Lord, for we have sinned.

Second Reading – Romans 5:12-19

Brothers and sisters: [12]Through one man sin entered the
world, and through sin, death, and thus death came to all men,
inasmuch as all sinned [13]for up to the time of the law, sin was
in the world, though sin is not accounted when there is no law.
[14]But death reigned from Adam to Moses, even over those
who did not sin after the pattern of the trespass of Adam, who
is the type of the one who was to come. [15]But the gift is not
like the transgression. For if by the transgression of the one,
the many died, how much more did the grace of God and the
gracious gift of the one man Jesus Christ overflow for the
many. [16]And the gift is not like the result of the one who
sinned. For after one sin there was the judgment that brought
condemnation; but the gift, after many transgressions, brought
acquittal. [17]For if, by the transgression of the one, death came
to reign through that one, how much more will those who
receive the abundance of grace and of the gift of justification
come to reign in life through the one Jesus Christ. [18]In
conclusion, just as through one transgression condemnation
came upon all, so, through one righteous act, acquittal and life
came to all. [19]For just as through the disobedience of the one
man the many were made sinners, so, through the obedience
of the one, the many will be made righteous.

Or Romans 5:12, 17-19

Brothers and sisters: [12]Through one man sin entered the world, and through sin, death, and thus death came to all men, inasmuch as all sinned. [17]For if, by the transgression of the one, death came to reign through that one, how much more will those who receive the abundance of grace and of the gift of justification come to reign in life through the one Jesus Christ. [18]In conclusion, just as through one transgression condemnation came upon all, so, through one righteous act, acquittal and life came to all. [19]For just as through the disobedience of the one man the many were made sinners, so, through the obedience of the one, the many will be made righteous.

Verse Before The Gospel – Matthew 4:4B

[4B]One does not live on bread alone, but on every word that comes forth from the mouth of God.

Gospel – Matthew 4:1-11

[1]At that time Jesus was led by the Spirit into the desert to be tempted by the devil. [2]He fasted for forty days and forty nights, and afterwards he was hungry. [3]The tempter approached and said to him, "If you are the Son of God, command that these stones become loaves of bread." [4]He said in reply, "It is written:

One does not live on bread alone,

but on every word that comes forth

from the mouth of God."

[5]Then the devil took him to the holy city, and made him stand on the parapet of the temple, [6]and said to him, "If you are the Son of God, throw yourself down. For it is written:

He will command his angels concerning you

and with their hands they will support you,

lest you dash your foot against a stone."

[7]Jesus answered him, "Again it is written, You shall not put the Lord, your God, to the test." [8]Then the devil took him up to a very high mountain, and showed him all the kingdoms of the world in their magnificence, [9]and he said to him, "All these I

shall give to you, if you will prostrate yourself and worship me.”
[10]At this, Jesus said to him, “Get away, Satan! It is written: The
Lord, your God, shall you worship and him alone shall you
serve.” [11]Then the devil left him and, behold, angels came and
ministered to him.

Monday February 27, 2023

Monday of the First Week of Lent

First Reading – Leviticus 19:1-2, 11-18

[1]The LORD said to Moses, [2]“Speak to the whole assembly of
the children of Israel and tell them: Be holy, for I, the LORD,
your God, am holy. [11]“You shall not steal. You shall not lie or
speak falsely to one another. [12]You shall not swear falsely by
my name, thus profaning the name of your God. I am the
LORD. [13]“You shall not defraud or rob your neighbor. You
shall not withhold overnight the wages of your day laborer.
[14]You shall not curse the deaf, or put a stumbling block in front
of the blind, but you shall fear your God. I am the LORD.
[15]“You shall not act dishonestly in rendering judgment. Show
neither partiality to the weak nor deference to the mighty, but
judge your fellow men justly. [16]You shall not go about
spreading slander among your kin; nor shall you stand by idly
when your neighbor’s life is at stake. I am the LORD. [17]“You
shall not bear hatred for your brother in your heart. Though
you may have to reprove him, do not incur sin because of him.
[18]Take no revenge and cherish no grudge against your fellow
countrymen. You shall love your neighbor as yourself. I am the
LORD.”

Responsorial Psalm – Psalms 19:8, 9, 10, 15

R. (John 6:63b) **Your words, Lord, are Spirit and life.**

[8] The law of the LORD is perfect,

refreshing the soul.

The decree of the LORD is trustworthy,

giving wisdom to the simple.

R. Your words, Lord, are Spirit and life.

[9] The precepts of the LORD are right,

rejoicing the heart.

The command of the LORD is clear,

enlightening the eye.

R. Your words, Lord, are Spirit and life.

[10] The fear of the LORD is pure,

enduring forever;

The ordinances of the LORD are true,

all of them just.

R. Your words, Lord, are Spirit and life.

[15] Let the words of my mouth and the thought of my heart

find favor before you,

O LORD, my rock and my redeemer.

R. Your words, Lord, are Spirit and life.

Verse Before The Gospel – 2 Corinthians 6:2B

[2B] Behold, now is a very acceptable time; behold, now is the day of salvation.

Gospel – Matthew 25:31-46

Jesus said to his disciples: [31]"When the Son of Man comes in
his glory, and all the angels with him, he will sit upon his
glorious throne, [32]and all the nations will be assembled before
him. And he will separate them one from another, as a
shepherd separates the sheep from the goats. [33]He will place
the sheep on his right and the goats on his left. [34]Then the
king will say to those on his right, 'Come, you who are blessed
by my Father. Inherit the kingdom prepared for you from the
foundation of the world. [35]For I was hungry and you gave me
food, I was thirsty and you gave me drink, a stranger and you
welcomed me, [36]naked and you clothed me, ill and you cared
for me, in prison and you visited me.' [37]Then the righteous will
answer him and say, 'Lord, when did we see you hungry and
feed you, or thirsty and give you drink? [38]When did we see you
a stranger and welcome you, or naked and clothe you?
[39]When did we see you ill or in prison, and visit you?' [40]And
the king will say to them in reply, 'Amen, I say to you,
whatever you did for one of these least brothers of mine, you
did for me.' [41]Then he will say to those on his left, 'Depart from

me, you accursed, into the eternal fire prepared for the Devil and his angels. [42]For I was hungry and you gave me no food, I was thirsty and you gave me no drink, [43]a stranger and you gave me no welcome, naked and you gave me no clothing, ill and in prison, and you did not care for me.' [44]Then they will answer and say, 'Lord, when did we see you hungry or thirsty or a stranger or naked or ill or in prison, and not minister to your needs?' [45]He will answer them, 'Amen, I say to you, what you did not do for one of these least ones, you did not do for me.' [46]And these will go off to eternal punishment, but the righteous to eternal life."

Tuesday February 28, 2023

Tuesday of the First Week of Lent

First Reading – Isaiah 55:10-11

[10]Thus says the LORD: Just as from the heavens the rain and snow come down And do not return there till they have watered the earth, making it fertile and fruitful, giving seed to the one who sows and bread to the one who eats, [11]So shall my word be that goes forth from my mouth; It shall not return to me void, but shall do my will, achieving the end for which I sent it.

Responsorial Psalm – Psalms 34:4-5, 6-7, 16-17, 18-19

R. (18b) From all their distress God rescues the just.

4 Glorify the LORD with me,

let us together extol his name.

5 I sought the LORD, and he answered me

and delivered me from all my fears.

R. From all their distress God rescues the just.

6 Look to him that you may be radiant with joy,

and your faces may not blush with shame.

7 When the poor one called out, the LORD heard,

and from all his distress he saved him.

R. From all their distress God rescues the just.

16 The LORD has eyes for the just,

and ears for their cry.

17 The LORD confronts the evildoers,

to destroy remembrance of them from the earth.

R. From all their distress God rescues the just.

18 When the just cry out, the LORD hears them,

and from all their distress he rescues them.

19 The LORD is close to the brokenhearted;

and those who are crushed in spirit he saves.

R. From all their distress God rescues the just.

Verse Before The Gospel – Matthew 4:4B

4BOne does not live on bread alone, but on every word that comes forth from the mouth of God.

Gospel – Matthew 6:7-15

Jesus said to his disciples: 7“In praying, do not babble like the
pagans, who think that they will be heard because of their
many words. 8Do not be like them. Your Father knows what
you need before you ask him. 9“This is how you are to pray:
Our Father who art in heaven, hallowed be thy name, 10thy
Kingdom come, thy will be done, on earth as it is in heaven.
11Give us this day our daily bread; 12and forgive us our
trespasses, as we forgive those who trespass against us;
13and lead us not into temptation, but deliver us from evil. 14“If
you forgive men their transgressions, your heavenly Father will
forgive you. 15But if you do not forgive men, neither will your
Father forgive your transgressions.”

MARCH 2023

Wednesday March 1, 2023

Wednesday of the First Week of Lent

First Reading – Jonah 3:1-10

1The word of the LORD came to Jonah a second time: 2“Set
out for the great city of Nineveh, and announce to it the

message that I will tell you.” 3 So Jonah made ready and went
to Nineveh, according to the LORD’s bidding. Now Nineveh
was an enormously large city; it took three days to go through
it. 4 Jonah began his journey through the city, and had gone
but a single day’s walk announcing, “Forty days more and
Nineveh shall be destroyed,” 5 when the people of Nineveh
believed God; they proclaimed a fast and all of them, great
and small, put on sackcloth. 6 When the news reached the king
of Nineveh, he rose from his throne, laid aside his robe,
covered himself with sackcloth, and sat in the ashes. 7 Then he
had this proclaimed throughout Nineveh, by decree of the king
and his nobles: “Neither man nor beast, neither cattle nor
sheep, shall taste anything; they shall not eat, nor shall they
drink water. 8 Man and beast shall be covered with sackcloth
and call loudly to God; every man shall turn from his evil way
and from the violence he has in hand. 9 Who knows, God may
relent and forgive, and withhold his blazing wrath, so that we
shall not perish.” 10 When God saw by their actions how they
turned from their evil way, he repented of the evil that he had
threatened to do to them; he did not carry it out.

Responsorial Psalm – Psalms 51:3-4, 12-13, 18-19

R. (19b) A heart contrite and humbled, O God, you will not spurn.

3 Have mercy on me, O God, in your goodness;

in the greatness of your compassion wipe out my offense.

4 Thoroughly wash me from my guilt

and of my sin cleanse me.

R. A heart contrite and humbled, O God, you will not spurn.

12 A clean heart create for me, O God,

and a steadfast spirit renew within me.

13 Cast me not out from your presence,

and your Holy Spirit take not from me.

R. A heart contrite and humbled, O God, you will not spurn.

18 For you are not pleased with sacrifices;

should I offer a burnt offering, you would not accept it.

19 My sacrifice, O God, is a contrite spirit;

a heart contrite and humbled, O God, you will not spurn.

R. A heart contrite and humbled, O God, you will not spurn.

Verse Before The Gospel – Joel 2:12-13

12 Even now, says the LORD, 13return to me with your whole
heart for I am gracious and merciful.

Gospel – Luke 11:29-32

29 While still more people gathered in the crowd, Jesus said to
them, "This generation is an evil generation; it seeks a sign,
but no sign will be given it, except the sign of Jonah. 30Just as
Jonah became a sign to the Ninevites, so will the Son of Man
be to this generation. 31At the judgment the queen of the south
will rise with the men of this generation and she will condemn
them, because she came from the ends of the earth to hear
the wisdom of Solomon, and there is something greater than
Solomon here. 32At the judgment the men of Nineveh will arise
with this generation and condemn it, because at the preaching
of Jonah they repented, and there is something greater than
Jonah here."

Thursday March 2, 2023

Thursday of the First Week of Lent

First Reading – Esther C:12, 14-16, 23-25

12Queen Esther, seized with mortal anguish, had recourse to
the LORD. 14She lay prostrate upon the ground, together with
her handmaids, from morning until evening, and said: "God of
Abraham, God of Isaac, and God of Jacob, blessed are you.
Help me, who am alone and have no help but you,15for I am
taking my life in my hand. 16As a child I used to hear from the
books of my forefathers that you, O LORD, always free those
who are pleasing to you. 23Now help me, who am alone and
have no one but you, O LORD, my God. "And now, come to
help me, an orphan. 24Put in my mouth persuasive words in
the presence of the lion and turn his heart to hatred for our
enemy, so that he and those who are in league with him may

perish. [25]Save us from the hand of our enemies; turn our
mourning into gladness and our sorrows into wholeness."

Responsorial Psalm – Psalms 138:1-2AB, 2CDE-3, 7C-8

R. [(3a)] Lord, on the day I called for help, you answered me.

[1] I will give thanks to you, O LORD, with all my heart,

for you have heard the words of my mouth;

in the presence of the angels I will sing your praise;

[2AB] I will worship at your holy temple

and give thanks to your name.

R. Lord, on the day I called for help, you answered me.

[2CDE] Because of your kindness and your truth;

for you have made great above all things

your name and your promise.

[3] When I called, you answered me;

you built up strength within me.

R. Lord, on the day I called for help, you answered me.

[7C] Your right hand saves me.

[8] The LORD will complete what he has done for me;

your kindness, O LORD, endures forever;

forsake not the work of your hands.

R. Lord, on the day I called for help, you answered me.

Verse Before The Gospel – Psalms 51:12A, 14A

[12A] A clean heart create for me, O God; [14A]give me back the
joy of your salvation.

Gospel – Matthew 7:7-12

[7]Jesus said to his disciples: "Ask and it will be given to you;
seek and you will find; knock and the door will be opened to
you. [8]For everyone who asks, receives; and the one who
seeks, finds; and to the one who knocks, the door will be
opened. [9]Which one of you would hand his son a stone when

he asked for a loaf of bread, [10]or a snake when he asked for a
fish? [11]If you then, who are wicked, know how to give good
gifts to your children, how much more will your heavenly
Father give good things to those who ask him. [12]"Do to others
whatever you would have them do to you. This is the law and
the prophets."

Friday March 3, 2023

Friday of the First Week of Lent

First Reading – Ezekiel 18:21-28

[21]Thus says the Lord GOD: If the wicked man turns away from
all the sins he committed, if he keeps all my statutes and does
what is right and just, he shall surely live, he shall not die.
[22]None of the crimes he committed shall be remembered
against him; he shall live because of the virtue he has
practiced. [23]Do I indeed derive any pleasure from the death of
the wicked? says the Lord GOD. Do I not rather rejoice when
he turns from his evil way that he may live? [24]And if the
virtuous man turns from the path of virtue to do evil, the same
kind of abominable things that the wicked man does, can he
do this and still live? None of his virtuous deeds shall be
remembered, because he has broken faith and committed sin;
because of this, he shall die. [25]You say, "The LORD's way is
not fair!" Hear now, house of Israel: Is it my way that is unfair,
or rather, are not your ways unfair? [26]When someone virtuous
turns away from virtue to commit iniquity, and dies, it is
because of the iniquity he committed that he must die. [27]But if
the wicked, turning from the wickedness he has committed,
does what is right and just, he shall preserve his life; [28]since
he has turned away from all the sins that he committed, he
shall surely live, he shall not die.

Responsorial Psalm – Psalms 130:1-2, 3-4, 5-7A, 7BC-8

R. (3) If you, O Lord, mark iniquities, who can stand?

1 Out of the depths I cry to you, O LORD;

LORD, hear my voice!

2 Let your ears be attentive

to my voice in supplication.

R. If you, O Lord, mark iniquities, who can stand?

3 If you, O LORD, mark iniquities,

LORD, who can stand?

4 But with you is forgiveness,

that you may be revered.

R. If you, O Lord, mark iniquities, who can stand?

5 I trust in the LORD;

my soul trusts in his word.

6 My soul waits for the LORD

more than sentinels wait for the dawn.

7A Let Israel wait for the LORD.

R. If you, O Lord, mark iniquities, who can stand?

7BC For with the LORD is kindness

and with him is plenteous redemption;

8 And he will redeem Israel

from all their iniquities.

R. If you, O Lord, mark iniquities, who can stand?

Verse Before The Gospel – Ezekiel 18:31

31Cast away from you all the crimes you have committed, says the LORD, and make for yourselves a new heart and a new spirit.

Gospel – Matthew 5:20-26

Jesus said to his disciples: 20"I tell you, unless your
righteousness surpasses that of the scribes and Pharisees,
you will not enter into the Kingdom of heaven. 21"You have
heard that it was said to your ancestors, You shall not kill; and
whoever kills will be liable to judgment. 22But I say to you,
whoever is angry with his brother will be liable to judgment,
and whoever says to his brother, Raqa, will be answerable to
the Sanhedrin, and whoever says, 'You fool,' will be liable to
fiery Gehenna. 23Therefore, if you bring your gift to the altar,
and there recall that your brother has anything against you,
24leave your gift there at the altar, go first and be reconciled

with your brother, and then come and offer your gift. [25]Settle with your opponent quickly while on the way to court. Otherwise your opponent will hand you over to the judge, and the judge will hand you over to the guard, and you will be thrown into prison. [26]Amen, I say to you, you will not be released until you have paid the last penny."

Saturday March 4, 2023

Saturday of the First Week of Lent

First Reading – Deuteronomy 26:16-19

[16]Moses spoke to the people, saying: "This day the LORD, your God, commands you to observe these statutes and decrees. Be careful, then, to observe them with all your heart and with all your soul. [17]Today you are making this agreement with the LORD: he is to be your God and you are to walk in his ways and observe his statutes, commandments and decrees, and to hearken to his voice. [18]And today the LORD is making this agreement with you: you are to be a people peculiarly his own, as he promised you; and provided you keep all his commandments, [19]he will then raise you high in praise and renown and glory above all other nations he has made, and you will be a people sacred to the LORD, your God, as he promised."

Responsorial Psalm – Psalms 119:1-2, 4-5, 7-8

R. (1b) Blessed are they who follow the law of the Lord!

1 Blessed are they whose way is blameless,

who walk in the law of the LORD.

2 Blessed are they who observe his decrees,

who seek him with all their heart.

R. Blessed are they who follow the law of the Lord!

4 You have commanded that your precepts

be diligently kept.

5 Oh, that I might be firm in the ways

of keeping your statutes!

R. Blessed are they who follow the law of the Lord!

7 I will give you thanks with an upright heart,

when I have learned your just ordinances.

8 I will keep your statutes;

do not utterly forsake me.

R. Blessed are they who follow the law of the Lord!

Verse Before The Gospel – 2 Corinthians 6:2B

6BBehold, now is a very acceptable time; behold, now is the day of salvation.

Gospel – Matthew 5:43-48

Jesus said to his disciples: 43“You have heard that it was said,
You shall love your neighbor and hate your enemy. 44But I say
to you, love your enemies, and pray for those who persecute
you, 45that you may be children of your heavenly Father, for he
makes his sun rise on the bad and the good, and causes rain
to fall on the just and the unjust. 46For if you love those who
love you, what recompense will you have? Do not the tax
collectors do the same? 47And if you greet your brothers and
sisters only, what is unusual about that? Do not the pagans do
the same? 48So be perfect, just as your heavenly Father is
perfect.”

Sunday March 5, 2023

Second Sunday of Lent, Year A

First Reading – Genesis 12:1-4A

1The LORD said to Abram: “Go forth from the land of your
kinsfolk and from your father’s house to a land that I will show
you. 2“I will make of you a great nation, and I will bless you; I
will make your name great, so that you will be a blessing. 3I
will bless those who bless you and curse those who curse you.
All the communities of the earth shall find blessing in you.”
4AAbram went as the LORD directed him.

Responsorial Psalm – Psalms 33:4-5, 18-19, 20, 22

R. (22) Lord, let your mercy be on us, as we place our trust in you.

4 Upright is the word of the LORD,

and all his works are trustworthy.

5 He loves justice and right;

of the kindness of the LORD the earth is full.

R. Lord, let your mercy be on us, as we place our trust in you.

18 See, the eyes of the LORD are upon those who fear him,

upon those who hope for his kindness,

19 To deliver them from death

and preserve them in spite of famine.

R. Lord, let your mercy be on us, as we place our trust in you.

20 Our soul waits for the LORD,

who is our help and our shield.

22 May your kindness, O LORD, be upon us

who have put our hope in you.

R. Lord, let your mercy be on us, as we place our trust in you.

Second Reading – 2 Timothy 1:8B-10

8B Beloved: Bear your share of hardship for the gospel with the
strength that comes from God. 9 He saved us and called us to
a holy life, not according to our works but according to his own
design and the grace bestowed on us in Christ Jesus before
time began, 10 but now made manifest through the appearance
of our savior Christ Jesus, who destroyed death and brought
life and immortality to light through the gospel.

Verse Before The Gospel – Matthew 17:5

17 From the shining cloud the Father's voice is heard: This is my beloved Son, hear him.

Gospel – Matthew 17:1-9

1 Jesus took Peter, James, and John his brother, and led them
up a high mountain by themselves. 2 And he was transfigured
before them; his face shone like the sun and his clothes
became white as light. 3 And behold, Moses and Elijah

appeared to them, conversing with him. [4]Then Peter said to
Jesus in reply, "Lord, it is good that we are here. If you wish, I
will make three tents here, one for you, one for Moses, and
one for Elijah." [5]While he was still speaking, behold, a bright
cloud cast a shadow over them, then from the cloud came a
voice that said, "This is my beloved Son, with whom I am well
pleased; listen to him." [6]When the disciples heard this, they fell
prostrate and were very much afraid. [7]But Jesus came and
touched them, saying, "Rise, and do not be afraid." [8]And when
the disciples raised their eyes, they saw no one else but Jesus
alone. [9]As they were coming down from the mountain, Jesus
charged them, "Do not tell the vision to anyone until the Son of
Man has been raised from the dead."

Monday March 6, 2023

Monday of the Second Week of Lent

First Reading – Daniel 9:4B-10

[4B]"Lord, great and awesome God, you who keep your merciful
covenant toward those who love you and observe your
commandments! [5]We have sinned, been wicked and done
evil; we have rebelled and departed from your commandments
and your laws. [6]We have not obeyed your servants the
prophets, who spoke in your name to our kings, our princes,
our fathers, and all the people of the land. [7]Justice, O Lord, is
on your side; we are shamefaced even to this day: we, the
men of Judah, the residents of Jerusalem, and all Israel, near
and far, in all the countries to which you have scattered them
because of their treachery toward you. [8]O LORD, we are
shamefaced, like our kings, our princes, and our fathers, for
having sinned against you. [9]But yours, O Lord, our God, are
compassion and forgiveness! Yet we rebelled against you
[10]and paid no heed to your command, O LORD, our God, to
live by the law you gave us through your servants the
prophets."

Responsorial Psalm – Psalms 79:8, 9, 11 AND 13

R. (see 103:10a) **Lord, do not deal with us according to our sins.**

[8] Remember not against us the iniquities of the past;

may your compassion quickly come to us,

for we are brought very low.

R. Lord, do not deal with us according to our sins.

9 Help us, O God our savior,

because of the glory of your name;

Deliver us and pardon our sins

for your name's sake.

R. Lord, do not deal with us according to our sins.

11 Let the prisoners' sighing come before you;

with your great power free those doomed to death.

13 Then we, your people and the sheep of your pasture,

will give thanks to you forever;

through all generations we will declare your praise.

R. Lord, do not deal with us according to our sins.

Verse Before The Gospel – SEE John 6:63C, 68C

63CYour words, Lord, are Spirit and life; 68Cyou have the words of everlasting life.

Gospel – Luke 6:36-38

36Jesus said to his disciples: "Be merciful, just as your Father is merciful. 37"Stop judging and you will not be judged. Stop condemning and you will not be condemned. Forgive and you will be forgiven. 38Give and gifts will be given to you; a good measure, packed together, shaken down, and overflowing, will be poured into your lap. For the measure with which you measure will in return be measured out to you."

Tuesday March 7, 2023

Tuesday of the Second Week of Lent

First Reading – Isaiah 1:10, 16-20

10Hear the word of the LORD, princes of Sodom! Listen to the instruction of our God, people of Gomorrah! 16Wash yourselves clean! Put away your misdeeds from before my eyes; cease doing evil; 17learn to do good. Make justice your aim: redress the wronged, hear the orphan's plea, defend the widow. [18]Come now, let us set things right, says the LORD: Though your sins be like scarlet, they may become white as snow; Though they be crimson red, they may become white as wool. [19]If you are willing, and obey, you shall eat the good things of the land; [20]But if you refuse and resist, the sword shall consume you: for the mouth of the LORD has spoken!

Responsorial Psalm – Psalms 50:8-9, 16BC-17, 21 AND 23

R. (23b) To the upright I will show the saving power of God.

8 "Not for your sacrifices do I rebuke you,

for your burnt offerings are before me always.

9 I take from your house no bullock,

no goats out of your fold."

R. To the upright I will show the saving power of God.

16BC "Why do you recite my statutes,

and profess my covenant with your mouth,

17 Though you hate discipline

and cast my words behind you?"

R. To the upright I will show the saving power of God.

21 "When you do these things, shall I be deaf to it?

Or do you think that I am like yourself?

I will correct you by drawing them up before your eyes.

23 He that offers praise as a sacrifice glorifies me;

and to him that goes the right way I will show the salvation of God."

R. To the upright I will show the saving power of God.

Verse Before the Gospel – Ezekiel 18:31

[31]Cast away from you all the crimes you have committed, says the LORD, and make for yourselves a new heart and a new spirit.

Gospel – Matthew 23:1-12

1Jesus spoke to the crowds and to his disciples, 2saying, “The
scribes and the Pharisees have taken their seat on the chair of
Moses. 3Therefore, do and observe all things whatsoever they
tell you, but do not follow their example. For they preach but
they do not practice. 4They tie up heavy burdens hard to carry
and lay them on people’s shoulders, but they will not lift a
finger to move them. 5All their works are performed to be
seen. They widen their phylacteries and lengthen their tassels.
6They love places of honor at banquets, seats of honor in
synagogues, 7greetings in marketplaces, and the salutation
‘Rabbi.’ 8As for you, do not be called ‘Rabbi.’ You have but
one teacher, and you are all brothers. 9Call no one on earth
your father; you have but one Father in heaven. 10Do not be
called ‘Master’; you have but one master, the Christ. 11The
greatest among you must be your servant. 12Whoever exalts
himself will be humbled; but whoever humbles himself will be
exalted.”

Wednesday March 8, 2023

Wednesday of the Second Week of Lent

First Reading – Jeremiah 18:18-20

18The people of Judah and the citizens of Jerusalem said,
“Come, let us contrive a plot against Jeremiah. It will not mean
the loss of instruction from the priests, nor of counsel from the
wise, nor of messages from the prophets. And so, let us
destroy him by his own tongue; let us carefully note his every
word.” 19Heed me, O LORD, and listen to what my adversaries
say. 20Must good be repaid with evil that they should dig a pit
to take my life? Remember that I stood before you to speak in
their behalf, to turn away your wrath from them.

Responsorial Psalm – Psalms 31:5-6, 14, 15-16

R. (17b) **Save me, O Lord, in your kindness.**

5You will free me from the snare they set for me,

for you are my refuge.

6Into your hands I commend my spirit;

you will redeem me, O LORD, O faithful God.

R. Save me, O Lord, in your kindness.

[14]I hear the whispers of the crowd, that frighten me from every side,

as they consult together against me, plotting to take my life.

R. Save me, O Lord, in your kindness.

[15]But my trust is in you, O LORD;

I say, "You are my God."

[16]In your hands is my destiny; rescue me

from the clutches of my enemies and my persecutors.

R. Save me, O Lord, in your kindness.

Verse Before The Gospel – John 8:12

[12]I am the light of the world, says the Lord; whoever follows me will have the light of life.

Gospel – Matthew 20:17-28

[17]As Jesus was going up to Jerusalem, he took the Twelve
disciples aside by themselves, and said to them on the way, [18]
"Behold, we are going up to Jerusalem, and the Son of Man
will be handed over to the chief priests and the scribes, and
they will condemn him to death,[19]and hand him over to the
Gentiles to be mocked and scourged and crucified, and he will
be raised on the third day." [20]Then the mother of the sons of
Zebedee approached Jesus with her sons and did him
homage, wishing to ask him for something. [21]He said to her,
"What do you wish?" She answered him, "Command that
these two sons of mine sit, one at your right and the other at
your left, in your kingdom." [22]Jesus said in reply, "You do not
know what you are asking. Can you drink the chalice that I am
going to drink?" They said to him, "We can." [23]He replied, "My
chalice you will indeed drink, but to sit at my right and at my
left, this is not mine to give but is for those for whom it has
been prepared by my Father." [24]When the ten heard this, they
became indignant at the two brothers. [25]But Jesus summoned
them and said, "You know that the rulers of the Gentiles lord it
over them, and the great ones make their authority over them
felt. [26]But it shall not be so among you. Rather, whoever
wishes to be great among you shall be your servant;
[27]whoever wishes to be first among you shall be your slave.

28 Just so, the Son of Man did not come to be served but to
serve and to give his life as a ransom for many."

Thursday March 9, 2023

Thursday of the Second Week of Lent

First Reading – Jeremiah 17:5-10

5 Thus says the LORD: Cursed is the man who trusts in human
beings, who seeks his strength in flesh, whose heart turns
away from the LORD. 6 He is like a barren bush in the desert
that enjoys no change of season, But stands in a lava waste, a
salt and empty earth. 7 Blessed is the man who trusts in the
LORD, whose hope is the LORD. 8 He is like a tree planted
beside the waters that stretches out its roots to the stream: It
fears not the heat when it comes, its leaves stay green; In the
year of drought it shows no distress, but still bears fruit. 9 More
tortuous than all else is the human heart, beyond remedy; who
can understand it? 10 I, the LORD, alone probe the mind and
test the heart, To reward everyone according to his ways,
according to the merit of his deeds.

Responsorial Psalm – Psalms 1:1-2, 3, 4 AND 6

R. (40:5a) Blessed are they who hope in the Lord.

1 Blessed the man who follows not

the counsel of the wicked

Nor walks in the way of sinners,

nor sits in the company of the insolent,

2 But delights in the law of the LORD

and meditates on his law day and night.

R. Blessed are they who hope in the Lord.

3 He is like a tree

planted near running water,

That yields its fruit in due season,

and whose leaves never fade.

Whatever he does, prospers.

R. Blessed are they who hope in the Lord.

4 Not so, the wicked, not so;

they are like chaff which the wind drives away.

6 For the LORD watches over the way of the just,

but the way of the wicked vanishes.

R. Blessed are they who hope in the Lord.

Verse Before the Gospel – cf. Luke 8:15

15Blessed are they who have kept the word with a generous heart and yield a harvest through perseverance.

Gospel – Luke 16:19-31

Jesus said to the Pharisees: 19“There was a rich man who
dressed in purple garments and fine linen and dined
sumptuously each day. 20And lying at his door was a poor man
named Lazarus, covered with sores, 21who would gladly have
eaten his fill of the scraps that fell from the rich man’s table.
Dogs even used to come and lick his sores. 22When the poor
man died, he was carried away by angels to the bosom of
Abraham. The rich man also died and was buried, 23and from
the netherworld, where he was in torment, he raised his eyes
and saw Abraham far off and Lazarus at his side. 24And he
cried out, ‘Father Abraham, have pity on me. Send Lazarus to
dip the tip of his finger in water and cool my tongue, for I am
suffering torment in these flames.’ 25Abraham replied, ‘My
child, remember that you received what was good during your
lifetime while Lazarus likewise received what was bad; but
now he is comforted here, whereas you are tormented.
26Moreover, between us and you a great chasm is established
to prevent anyone from crossing who might wish to go from
our side to yours or from your side to ours.’ 27He said, ‘Then I
beg you, father, send him to my father’s house, 28for I have
five brothers, so that he may warn them, lest they too come to
this place of torment.’ 29But Abraham replied, ‘They have
Moses and the prophets. Let them listen to them.’ 30He said,
‘Oh no, father Abraham, but if someone from the dead goes to
them, they will repent.’ 31Then Abraham said, ‘If they will not
listen to Moses and the prophets, neither will they be
persuaded if someone should rise from the dead.’”

Friday March 10, 2023

Friday of the Second Week of Lent

First Reading – Genesis 37:3-4, 12-13A, 17B-28A

3Israel loved Joseph best of all his sons, for he was the child
of his old age; and he had made him a long tunic. 4When his
brothers saw that their father loved him best of all his sons,
they hated him so much that they would not even greet him.
12One day, when his brothers had gone to pasture their
father's flocks at Shechem, 13AIsrael said to Joseph, "Your
brothers, you know, are tending our flocks at Shechem. Get
ready; I will send you to them." 17BSo Joseph went after his
brothers and caught up with them in Dothan. 18They noticed
him from a distance, and before he came up to them, they
plotted to kill him. 19They said to one another: "Here comes
that master dreamer! 20Come on, let us kill him and throw him
into one of the cisterns here; we could say that a wild beast
devoured him. We shall then see what comes of his dreams."
21When Reuben heard this, he tried to save him from their
hands, saying, "We must not take his life. 22Instead of
shedding blood," he continued, "just throw him into that cistern
there in the desert; but do not kill him outright." His purpose
was to rescue him from their hands and return him to his
father. 23So when Joseph came up to them, they stripped him
of the long tunic he had on; 24then they took him and threw
him into the cistern, which was empty and dry. 25They then sat
down to their meal. Looking up, they saw a caravan of
Ishmaelites coming from Gilead, their camels laden with gum,
balm and resin to be taken down to Egypt. 26Judah said to his
brothers: "What is to be gained by killing our brother and
concealing his blood? 27Rather, let us sell him to these
Ishmaelites, instead of doing away with him ourselves. After
all, he is our brother, our own flesh." His brothers agreed.
28BThey sold Joseph to the Ishmaelites for twenty pieces of
silver.

Responsorial Psalm – Psalms 105:16-17, 18-19, 20-21

R. (5a) **Remember the marvels the Lord has done.**

16 When the LORD called down a famine on the land

and ruined the crop that sustained them,

17 He sent a man before them,

Joseph, sold as a slave.

R. Remember the marvels the Lord has done.

18 They had weighed him down with fetters,

and he was bound with chains,

19 Till his prediction came to pass

and the word of the LORD proved him true.

R. Remember the marvels the Lord has done.

20 The king sent and released him,

the ruler of the peoples set him free.

21 He made him lord of his house

and ruler of all his possessions.

R. Remember the marvels the Lord has done.

Verse Before the Gospel – John 3:16

16 God so loved the world that he gave his only-begotten Son; so that everyone who believes in him might have eternal life.

Gospel – Matthew 21:33-43, 45-46

33Jesus said to the chief priests and the elders of the people:
"Hear another parable. There was a landowner who planted a
vineyard, put a hedge around it, dug a wine press in it, and
built a tower. Then he leased it to tenants and went on a
journey. 34When vintage time drew near, he sent his servants
to the tenants to obtain his produce. 35But the tenants seized
the servants and one they beat, another they killed, and a third
they stoned. 36Again he sent other servants, more numerous
than the first ones, but they treated them in the same way.
37Finally, he sent his son to them, thinking, 'They will respect
my son.' 38But when the tenants saw the son, they said to one
another, 'This is the heir. Come, let us kill him and acquire his
inheritance.' 39They seized him, threw him out of the vineyard,
and killed him. 40What will the owner of the vineyard do to
those tenants when he comes?" 41They answered him, "He will
put those wretched men to a wretched death and lease his

vineyard to other tenants who will give him the produce at the proper times." [42]Jesus said to them, "Did you never read in the Scriptures: The stone that the builders rejected has become the cornerstone; by the Lord has this been done, and it is wonderful in our eyes? [43]Therefore, I say to you, the Kingdom of God will be taken away from you and given to a people that will produce its fruit." [45]When the chief priests and the Pharisees heard his parables, they knew that he was speaking about them. [46]And although they were attempting to arrest him, they feared the crowds, for they regarded him as a prophet.

Saturday March 11, 2023

Saturday of the Second Week of Lent

First Reading – Micah 7:14-15, 18-20

[14]Shepherd your people with your staff, the flock of your inheritance, That dwells apart in a woodland, in the midst of Carmel. Let them feed in Bashan and Gilead, as in the days of old; [15]As in the days when you came from the land of Egypt, show us wonderful signs. [18]Who is there like you, the God who removes guilt and pardons sin for the remnant of his inheritance; Who does not persist in anger forever, but delights rather in clemency, [19]And will again have compassion on us, treading underfoot our guilt? You will cast into the depths of the sea all our sins; [20]You will show faithfulness to Jacob, and grace to Abraham, As you have sworn to our fathers from days of old.

Responsorial Psalm – Psalms 103:1-2, 3-4, 9-10, 11-12

R. (8a) **The Lord is kind and merciful.**

1 Bless the LORD, O my soul;

and all my being, bless his holy name.

2 Bless the LORD, O my soul,

and forget not all his benefits.

R. The Lord is kind and merciful.

3 He pardons all your iniquities,

he heals all your ills.

4 He redeems your life from destruction,

he crowns you with kindness and compassion.

R. The Lord is kind and merciful.

9 He will not always chide,

nor does he keep his wrath forever.

10 Not according to our sins does he deal with us,

nor does he requite us according to our crimes.

R. The Lord is kind and merciful.

11 For as the heavens are high above the earth,

so surpassing is his kindness toward those who fear him.

12 As far as the east is from the west,

so far has he put our transgressions from us.

R. The Lord is kind and merciful.

Verse Before The Gospel – Luke 15:18

18 I will get up and go to my father and shall say to him, Father, I have sinned against heaven and against you.

Gospel – Luke 15:1-3, 11-32

1Tax collectors and sinners were all drawing near to listen to
Jesus, 2but the Pharisees and scribes began to complain,
saying, "This man welcomes sinners and eats with them." 3So
to them Jesus addressed this parable. 11"A man had two sons,
12and the younger son said to his father, 'Father, give me the
share of your estate that should come to me.' So the father
divided the property between them. 13After a few days, the
younger son collected all his belongings and set off to a
distant country where he squandered his inheritance on a life
of dissipation. 14When he had freely spent everything, a
severe famine struck that country, and he found himself in dire
need. 15So he hired himself out to one of the local citizens who
sent him to his farm to tend the swine. 16And he longed to eat
his fill of the pods on which the swine fed, but nobody gave
him any. 17Coming to his senses he thought, 'How many of my
father's hired workers have more than enough food to eat, but

here am I, dying from hunger. 18I shall get up and go to my
father and I shall say to him, “Father, I have sinned against
heaven and against you. 19I no longer deserve to be called
your son; treat me as you would treat one of your hired
workers.”‘ 20So he got up and went back to his father. While he
was still a long way off, his father caught sight of him, and was
filled with compassion. He ran to his son, embraced him and
kissed him. 21His son said to him, ‘Father, I have sinned
against heaven and against you; I no longer deserve to be
called your son.’ 22But his father ordered his servants,
‘Quickly, bring the finest robe and put it on him; put a ring on
his finger and sandals on his feet. 23Take the fattened calf and
slaughter it. Then let us celebrate with a feast, 24because this
son of mine was dead, and has come to life again; he was
lost, and has been found.’ Then the celebration began. 25Now
the older son had been out in the field and, on his way back,
as he neared the house, he heard the sound of music and
dancing. 26He called one of the servants and asked what this
might mean. 27The servant said to him, ‘Your brother has
returned and your father has slaughtered the fattened calf
because he has him back safe and sound.’ 28He became
angry, and when he refused to enter the house, his father
came out and pleaded with him. 29He said to his father in
reply, ‘Look, all these years I served you and not once did I
disobey your orders; yet you never gave me even a young
goat to feast on with my friends. 30But when your son returns
who swallowed up your property with prostitutes, for him you
slaughter the fattened calf.’ 31He said to him, ‘My son, you are
here with me always; everything I have is yours. 32But now we
must celebrate and rejoice, because your brother was dead
and has come to life again; he was lost and has been found.’”

Sunday March 12, 2023

Third Sunday of Lent, Year A

First Reading – Exodus 17:3-7

3In those days, in their thirst for water, the people grumbled
against Moses, saying, “Why did you ever make us leave
Egypt? Was it just to have us die here of thirst with our
children and our livestock?” 4So Moses cried out to the LORD,
“What shall I do with this people? a little more and they will
stone me!” 5The LORD answered Moses, “Go over there in

front of the people, along with some of the elders of Israel, holding in your hand, as you go, the staff with which you struck the river. [6]I will be standing there in front of you on the rock in Horeb. Strike the rock, and the water will flow from it for the people to drink." This Moses did, in the presence of the elders of Israel. [7]The place was called Massah and Meribah, because the Israelites quarreled there and tested the LORD, saying, "Is the LORD in our midst or not?"

Responsorial Psalm – Psalms 95:1-2, 6-7, 8-9

R. (8) If today you hear his voice, harden not your hearts.

1 Come, let us sing joyfully to the LORD;

let us acclaim the Rock of our salvation.

2 Let us come into his presence with thanksgiving;

let us joyfully sing psalms to him.

R. If today you hear his voice, harden not your hearts.

6 Come, let us bow down in worship;

let us kneel before the LORD who made us.

7 For he is our God,

and we are the people he shepherds, the flock he guides.

R. If today you hear his voice, harden not your hearts.

8 Oh, that today you would hear his voice:

"Harden not your hearts as at Meribah,

as in the day of Massah in the desert,

9 Where your fathers tempted me;

they tested me though they had seen my works."

R. If today you hear his voice, harden not your hearts.

Second Reading – Romans 5:1-2, 5-8

[1]Brothers and sisters: Since we have been justified by faith, we have peace with God through our Lord Jesus Christ, [2]through whom we have gained access by faith to this grace in which we stand, and we boast in hope of the glory of God. [5]And hope does not disappoint, because the love of God has been poured out into our hearts through the Holy Spirit who

has been given to us. [6]For Christ, while we were still helpless, died at the appointed time for the ungodly. [7]Indeed, only with difficulty does one die for a just person, though perhaps for a good person one might even find courage to die. [8]But God proves his love for us in that while we were still sinners Christ died for us.

Verse Before The Gospel – John 4:42, 15

[42] Lord, you are truly the Savior of the world; [15]give me living water, that I may never thirst again.

Gospel – John 4:5-42

[5]Jesus came to a town of Samaria called Sychar, near the plot of land that Jacob had given to his son Joseph. [6]Jacob's well was there. Jesus, tired from his journey, sat down there at the well. It was about noon. [7]A woman of Samaria came to draw water. Jesus said to her, "Give me a drink." [8]His disciples had gone into the town to buy food. [9]The Samaritan woman said to him, "How can you, a Jew, ask me, a Samaritan woman, for a drink?" (For Jews use nothing in common with Samaritans.) [10]Jesus answered and said to her, "If you knew the gift of God and who is saying to you, 'Give me a drink, 'you would have asked him and he would have given you living water." [11]The woman said to him, "Sir, you do not even have a bucket and the cistern is deep; where then can you get this living water? [12]Are you greater than our father Jacob, who gave us this cistern and drank from it himself with his children and his flocks?" [13]Jesus answered and said to her, "Everyone who drinks this water will be thirsty again; [14]but whoever drinks the water I shall give will never thirst; the water I shall give will become in him a spring of water welling up to eternal life." [15]The woman said to him, "Sir, give me this water, so that I may not be thirsty or have to keep coming here to draw water." [16]Jesus said to her, "Go call your husband and come back." The woman answered and said to him, "I do not have a husband." [17]Jesus answered her, "You are right in saying, 'I do not have a husband.' [18]For you have had five husbands, and the one you have now is not your husband. What you have said is true." [19]The woman said to him, "Sir, I can see that you are a prophet. [20]Our ancestors worshiped on this mountain; but you people say that the place to worship is in Jerusalem." [21]Jesus said to her, "Believe me, woman, the hour is coming when you will worship the Father neither on this mountain nor

in Jerusalem. [22]You people worship what you do not understand; we worship what we understand, because salvation is from the Jews. [23]But the hour is coming, and is now here, when true worshipers will worship the Father in Spirit and truth; and indeed the Father seeks such people to worship him. [24]God is Spirit, and those who worship him must worship in Spirit and truth." [25]The woman said to him, "I know that the Messiah is coming, the one called the Christ; when he comes, he will tell us everything." [26]Jesus said to her, "I am he, the one speaking with you." [27]At that moment his disciples returned, and were amazed that he was talking with a woman, but still no one said, "What are you looking for?" or "Why are you talking with her?" [28]The woman left her water jar and went into the town and said to the people, [29]"Come see a man who told me everything I have done. Could he possibly be the Christ?" [30]They went out of the town and came to him. [31]Meanwhile, the disciples urged him, "Rabbi, eat." [32]But he said to them, "I have food to eat of which you do not know." [33]So the disciples said to one another, "Could someone have brought him something to eat?" [34]Jesus said to them, "My food is to do the will of the one who sent me and to finish his work. [35]Do you not say, 'In four months the harvest will be here'? I tell you, look up and see the fields ripe for the harvest. [36]The reaper is already receiving payment and gathering crops for eternal life, so that the sower and reaper can rejoice together. [37]For here the saying is verified that 'One sows and another reaps.' [38]I sent you to reap what you have not worked for; others have done the work, and you are sharing the fruits of their work." [39]Many of the Samaritans of that town began to believe in him because of the word of the woman who testified, "He told me everything I have done." [40]When the Samaritans came to him, they invited him to stay with them; and he stayed there two days. [41]Many more began to believe in him because of his word, [42]and they said to the woman, "We no longer believe because of your word; for we have heard for ourselves, and we know that this is truly the savior of the world."

Monday March 13, 2023

Monday of the Third Week of Lent

First Reading – 2 Kings 5:1-15AB

[1]Naaman, the army commander of the king of Aram, was
highly esteemed and respected by his master, for through him
the LORD had brought victory to Aram. But valiant as he was,
the man was a leper. [2]Now the Arameans had captured in a
raid on the land of Israel a little girl, who became the servant
of Naaman's wife. "If only my master would present himself to
the prophet in Samaria," [3]she said to her mistress, "he would
cure him of his leprosy." [4]Naaman went and told his lord just
what the slave girl from the land of Israel had said. [5]"Go," said
the king of Aram. "I will send along a letter to the king of
Israel." So Naaman set out, taking along ten silver talents, six
thousand gold pieces, and ten festal garments. [6]To the king of
Israel he brought the letter, which read: "With this letter I am
sending my servant Naaman to you, that you may cure him of
his leprosy." [7]When he read the letter, the king of Israel tore
his garments and exclaimed: "Am I a god with power over life
and death, that this man should send someone to me to be
cured of leprosy? Take note! You can see he is only looking
for a quarrel with me!" [8]When Elisha, the man of God, heard
that the king of Israel had torn his garments, he sent word to
the king: "Why have you torn your garments? Let him come to
me and find out that there is a prophet in Israel." [9]Naaman
came with his horses and chariots and stopped at the door of
Elisha's house. [10]The prophet sent him the message: "Go and
wash seven times in the Jordan, and your flesh will heal, and
you will be clean." [11]But Naaman went away angry, saying, "I
thought that he would surely come out and stand there to
invoke the LORD his God, and would move his hand over the
spot, and thus cure the leprosy. [12]Are not the rivers of
Damascus, the Abana and the Pharpar, better than all the
waters of Israel? Could I not wash in them and be cleansed?"
With this, he turned about in anger and left. [13]But his servants
came up and reasoned with him. "My father," they said, "if the
prophet had told you to do something extraordinary, would you
not have done it? All the more now, since he said to you,
'Wash and be clean,' should you do as he said." [14]So Naaman
went down and plunged into the Jordan seven times at the
word of the man of God. His flesh became again like the flesh

of a little child, and he was clean. 15He returned with his whole retinue to the man of God. On his arrival he stood before him and said, "Now I know that there is no God in all the earth, except in Israel."

Responsorial Psalm – Psalms 42:2, 3; 43:3, 4

R. (see 42:3) **Athirst is my soul for the living God. When shall I go and behold the face of God?**

2 As the hind longs for the running waters,

so my soul longs for you, O God.

R. Athirst is my soul for the living God. When shall I go and behold the face of God?

3 Athirst is my soul for God, the living God.

When shall I go and behold the face of God?

R. Athirst is my soul for the living God. When shall I go and behold the face of God?

3 Send forth your light and your fidelity;

they shall lead me on

And bring me to your holy mountain,

to your dwelling-place.

R. Athirst is my soul for the living God. When shall I go and behold the face of God?

4 Then will I go in to the altar of God,

the God of my gladness and joy;

Then will I give you thanks upon the harp,

O God, my God!

R. Athirst is my soul for the living God. When shall I go and behold the face of God?

Verse Before the Gospel – cf. Psalms 130:5, 7

5I hope in the LORD, I trust in his word; 7with him there is kindness and plenteous redemption.

Gospel – Luke 4:24-30

[24]Jesus said to the people in the synagogue at Nazareth: "Amen, I say to you, no prophet is accepted in his own native place. [25]Indeed, I tell you, there were many widows in Israel in the days of Elijah when the sky was closed for three and a half years and a severe famine spread over the entire land. [26]It was to none of these that Elijah was sent, but only to a widow in Zarephath in the land of Sidon. [27]Again, there were many lepers in Israel during the time of Elisha the prophet; yet not one of them was cleansed, but only Naaman the Syrian." [28]When the people in the synagogue heard this, they were all filled with fury. [29]They rose up, drove him out of the town, and led him to the brow of the hill on which their town had been built, to hurl him down headlong. [30]But he passed through the midst of them and went away.

Tuesday March 14, 2023

Tuesday of the Third Week of Lent

First Reading – Daniel 3:25, 34-43

[25]Azariah stood up in the fire and prayed aloud: [34]"For your name's sake, O Lord, do not deliver us up forever, or make void your covenant. [35]Do not take away your mercy from us, for the sake of Abraham, your beloved, Isaac your servant, and Israel your holy one, [36]To whom you promised to multiply their offspring like the stars of heaven, or the sand on the shore of the sea. [37]For we are reduced, O Lord, beyond any other nation, brought low everywhere in the world this day because of our sins. [38]We have in our day no prince, prophet, or leader, no burnt offering, sacrifice, oblation, or incense, no place to offer first fruits, to find favour with you. [39]But with a contrite heart and humble spirit let us be received; As though it were burnt offerings of rams and bullocks or thousands of fat lambs, [40]So let our sacrifice be in your presence today as we follow you unreservedly; for those who trust in you cannot be put to shame. [41]And now we follow you with our whole heart, we fear you and we pray to you. Do not let us be put to shame, [42]but deal with us in your kindness and great mercy. [43]Deliver us by your wonders, and bring glory to your name, O Lord."

Responsorial Psalm – Psalms 25:4-5AB, 6 AND 7BC, 8-9

R. [(6a)] **Remember your mercies, O Lord.**

[4] Your ways, O LORD, make known to me;

teach me your paths,

[5AB] Guide me in your truth and teach me,

for you are God my savior.

R. Remember your mercies, O Lord.

[6] Remember that your compassion, O LORD,

and your kindness are from of old.

[7BC] In your kindness remember me,

because of your goodness, O LORD.

R. Remember your mercies, O Lord.

[8] Good and upright is the LORD;

thus he shows sinners the way.

[9] He guides the humble to justice,

he teaches the humble his way.

R. Remember your mercies, O Lord.

Verse Before the Gospel – Joel 2:12-13

[12]Even now, says the LORD, return to me with your whole
heart; [13]for I am gracious and merciful.

Gospel – Matthew 18:21-35

[21]Peter approached Jesus and asked him, "Lord, if my brother
sins against me, how often must I forgive him? As many as
seven times?" [22]Jesus answered, "I say to you, not seven
times but seventy-seven times. [23]That is why the Kingdom of
heaven may be likened to a king who decided to settle
accounts with his servants. [24]When he began the accounting,
a debtor was brought before him who owed him a huge
amount. [25]Since he had no way of paying it back, his master
ordered him to be sold, along with his wife, his children, and all
his property, in payment of the debt. [26]At that, the servant fell

down, did him homage, and said, 'Be patient with me, and I
will pay you back in full.' [27]Moved with compassion the master
of that servant let him go and forgave him the loan. [28]When
that servant had left, he found one of his fellow servants who
owed him a much smaller amount. He seized him and started
to choke him, demanding, 'Pay back what you owe.' [29]Falling
to his knees, his fellow servant begged him, 'Be patient with
me, and I will pay you back.' [30]But he refused. Instead, he had
him put in prison until he paid back the debt. [31]Now when his
fellow servants saw what had happened, they were deeply
disturbed, and went to their master and reported the whole
affair. [32]His master summoned him and said to him, 'You
wicked servant! I forgave you your entire debt because you
begged me to. [33]Should you not have had pity on your fellow
servant, as I had pity on you?' [34]Then in anger, his master
handed him over to the torturers until he should pay back the
whole debt. [35]So will my heavenly Father do to you, unless
each of you forgives your brother from your heart."

Wednesday March 15, 2023

Wednesday of the Third Week of Lent

First Reading – Deuteronomy 4:1, 5-9

[1]Moses spoke to the people and said: "Now, Israel, hear the
statutes and decrees which I am teaching you to observe, that
you may live, and may enter in and take possession of the
land which the LORD, the God of your fathers, is giving you.
[5]Therefore, I teach you the statutes and decrees as the LORD,
my God, has commanded me, that you may observe them in
the land you are entering to occupy. [6]Observe them carefully,
for thus will you give evidence of your wisdom and intelligence
to the nations, who will hear of all these statutes and say, 'This
great nation is truly a wise and intelligent people.' [7]For what
great nation is there that has gods so close to it as the LORD,
our God, is to us whenever we call upon him? [8]Or what great
nation has statutes and decrees that are as just as this whole
law which I am setting before you today? [9]"However, take care
and be earnestly on your guard not to forget the things which
your own eyes have seen, nor let them slip from your memory
as long as you live, but teach them to your children and to
your children's children."

Responsorial Psalm – Psalms 147:12-13, 15-16, 19-20

R. (12a) Praise the Lord, Jerusalem.

12Glorify the LORD, O Jerusalem;

praise your God, O Zion.

13For he has strengthened the bars of your gates;

he has blessed your children within you.

R. Praise the Lord, Jerusalem.

15He sends forth his command to the earth;

swiftly runs his word!

16He spreads snow like wool;

frost he strews like ashes.

R. Praise the Lord, Jerusalem.

19He has proclaimed his word to Jacob,

his statutes and his ordinances to Israel.

20He has not done thus for any other nation;

his ordinances he has not made known to them.

R. Praise the Lord, Jerusalem.

Verse Before The Gospel – John 6:63C, 68C

63CYour words, Lord, are Spirit and life; 68Cyou have the words of everlasting life.

Gospel – Matthew 5:17-19

Jesus said to his disciples: 17"Do not think that I have come to abolish the law or the prophets. I have come not to abolish but to fulfill. 18Amen, I say to you, until heaven and earth pass away, not the smallest letter or the smallest part of a letter will pass from the law, until all things have taken place.
19Therefore, whoever breaks one of the least of these commandments and teaches others to do so will be called least in the Kingdom of heaven. But whoever obeys and teaches these commandments will be called greatest in the Kingdom of heaven."

Thursday March 16, 2023

Thursday of the Third Week of Lent

First Reading – Jeremiah 7:23-28

Thus says the LORD: [23]This is what I commanded my people:
Listen to my voice; then I will be your God and you shall be my
people. Walk in all the ways that I command you, so that you
may prosper. [24]But they obeyed not, nor did they pay heed.
They walked in the hardness of their evil hearts and turned
their backs, not their faces, to me. [25]From the day that your
fathers left the land of Egypt even to this day, I have sent you
untiringly all my servants the prophets. [26]Yet they have not
obeyed me nor paid heed; they have stiffened their necks and
done worse than their fathers. [27]When you speak all these
words to them, they will not listen to you either; when you call
to them, they will not answer you. [28]Say to them: This is the
nation that does not listen to the voice of the LORD, its God,
or take correction. Faithfulness has disappeared; the word
itself is banished from their speech.

Responsorial Psalm – Psalms 95:1-2, 6-7, 8-9

R. (8) If today you hear his voice, harden not your hearts.

[1] Come, let us sing joyfully to the LORD;

let us acclaim the Rock of our salvation.

[2] Let us come into his presence with thanksgiving;

let us joyfully sing psalms to him.

R. If today you hear his voice, harden not your hearts.

[6] Come, let us bow down in worship;

let us kneel before the LORD who made us.

[7ABC] For he is our God,

and we are the people he shepherds, the flock he guides.

R. If today you hear his voice, harden not your hearts.

[7D] Oh, that today you would hear his voice:

[8] “Harden not your hearts as at Meribah,

as in the day of Massah in the desert,

9 Where your fathers tempted me;

they tested me though they had seen my works."

R. If today you hear his voice, harden not your hearts.

Verse Before the Gospel – Joel 2:12-13

12Even now, says the LORD, return to me with your whole
heart,13for I am gracious and merciful.

Gospel – Luke 11:14-23

14Jesus was driving out a demon that was mute, and when the
demon had gone out, the mute man spoke and the crowds
were amazed. 15Some of them said, "By the power of
Beelzebul, the prince of demons, he drives out demons."
16Others, to test him, asked him for a sign from heaven. 17But
he knew their thoughts and said to them, "Every kingdom
divided against itself will be laid waste and house will fall
against house. 18And if Satan is divided against himself, how
will his kingdom stand? For you say that it is by Beelzebul that
I drive out demons. 19If I, then, drive out demons by Beelzebul,
by whom do your own people drive them out? Therefore they
will be your judges. 20But if it is by the finger of God that I drive
out demons, then the Kingdom of God has come upon you.
21When a strong man fully armed guards his palace, his
possessions are safe. 22But when one stronger than he
attacks and overcomes him, he takes away the armour on
which he relied and distributes the spoils. 23Whoever is not
with me is against me, and whoever does not gather with me
scatters."

Friday March 17, 2023

Friday of the Third Week of Lent

First Reading – Hosea 14:2-10

2Thus says the LORD: Return, O Israel, to the LORD, your
God; you have collapsed through your guilt. 3Take with you
words, and return to the LORD; Say to him, "Forgive all
iniquity, and receive what is good, that we may render as
offerings the bullocks from our stalls. 4Assyria will not save us,
nor shall we have horses to mount; We shall say no more,
'Our god,' to the work of our hands; for in you the orphan finds
compassion." 5I will heal their defection, says the LORD, I will

love them freely; for my wrath is turned away from them. 6I will
be like the dew for Israel: he shall blossom like the lily; He
shall strike root like the Lebanon cedar, 7and put forth his
shoots. His splendor shall be like the olive tree and his
fragrance like the Lebanon cedar. 8Again they shall dwell in
his shade and raise grain; They shall blossom like the vine,
and his fame shall be like the wine of Lebanon. 9Ephraim!
What more has he to do with idols? I have humbled him, but I
will prosper him. "I am like a verdant cypress tree" Because of
me you bear fruit! 10Let him who is wise understand these
things; let him who is prudent know them. Straight are the
paths of the LORD, in them the just walk, but sinners stumble
in them.

Responsorial Psalm – Psalms 81:6C-8A, 8BC-9, 10-11AB, 14 AND 17

R. (see 11 and 9a) **I am the Lord your God: hear my voice.**

7 An unfamiliar speech I hear:

"I relieved his shoulder of the burden;

his hands were freed from the basket.

8A In distress you called, and I rescued you."

R. I am the Lord your God: hear my voice.

8BC "Unseen, I answered you in thunder;

I tested you at the waters of Meribah.

9 Hear, my people, and I will admonish you;

O Israel, will you not hear me?"

R. I am the Lord your God: hear my voice.

10 "There shall be no strange god among you

nor shall you worship any alien god.

11AB I, the LORD, am your God

who led you forth from the land of Egypt."

R. I am the Lord your God: hear my voice.

14 "If only my people would hear me,

and Israel walk in my ways,

[17] I would feed them with the best of wheat,

and with honey from the rock I would fill them."

R. I am the Lord your God: hear my voice.

Verse Before The Gospel – Matthew 4:17

[17] Repent, says the Lord; the Kingdom of heaven is at hand.

Gospel – Mark 12:28-34

[28]One of the scribes came to Jesus and asked him, "Which is
the first of all the commandments?" [29]Jesus replied, "The first
is this: Hear, O Israel! The Lord our God is Lord alone! [30]You
shall love the Lord your God with all your heart, with all your
soul, with all your mind, and with all your strength. [31]The
second is this: You shall love your neighbor as yourself. There
is no other commandment greater than these." [32]The scribe
said to him, "Well said, teacher. You are right in saying, He is
One and there is no other than he. [33]And to love him with all
your heart, with all your understanding, with all your strength,
and to love your neighbor as yourself is worth more than all
burnt offerings and sacrifices." [34]And when Jesus saw that he
answered with understanding, he said to him, "You are not far
from the Kingdom of God." And no one dared to ask him any
more questions.

Saturday March 18, 2023

Saturday of the Third Week of Lent

First Reading – Hosea 6:1-6

[1]"Come, let us return to the LORD, it is he who has rent, but
he will heal us; he has struck us, but he will bind our wounds.
[2]He will revive us after two days; on the third day he will raise
us up, to live in his presence. [3]Let us know, let us strive to
know the LORD; as certain as the dawn is his coming, and his
judgment shines forth like the light of day! He will come to us
like the rain, like spring rain that waters the earth." [4]What can I
do with you, Ephraim? What can I do with you, Judah? Your
piety is like a morning cloud, like the dew that early passes
away. [5]For this reason I smote them through the prophets, I
slew them by the words of my mouth; [6]For it is love that I
desire, not sacrifice, and knowledge of God rather than burnt
offerings.

Responsorial Psalm – Psalms 51:3-4, 18-19, 20-21AB

R. (see Hosea 6:6) **It is mercy I desire, and not sacrifice.**

3 Have mercy on me, O God, in your goodness;

in the greatness of your compassion wipe out my offense.

4 Thoroughly wash me from my guilt

and of my sin cleanse me.

R. It is mercy I desire, and not sacrifice.

18 For you are not pleased with sacrifices;

should I offer a burnt offering, you would not accept it.

19 My sacrifice, O God, is a contrite spirit;

a heart contrite and humbled, O God, you will not spurn.

R. It is mercy I desire, and not sacrifice.

20 Be bountiful, O LORD, to Zion in your kindness

by rebuilding the walls of Jerusalem;

21AB Then shall you be pleased with due sacrifices,

burnt offerings and holocausts.

R. It is mercy I desire, and not sacrifice.

Verse Before the Gospel – Psalms 95:8

8 If today you hear his voice, harden not your hearts.

Gospel – Luke 18:9-14

9Jesus addressed this parable to those who were convinced of
their own righteousness and despised everyone else. 10"Two
people went up to the temple area to pray; one was a
Pharisee and the other was a tax collector. 11The Pharisee
took up his position and spoke this prayer to himself, 'O God, I
thank you that I am not like the rest of humanity – greedy,
dishonest, adulterous – or even like this tax collector. 12I fast
twice a week, and I pay tithes on my whole income.' 13But the
tax collector stood off at a distance and would not even raise
his eyes to heaven but beat his breast and prayed, 'O God, be
merciful to me a sinner.' 14I tell you, the latter went home

justified, not the former; for everyone who exalts himself will be humbled, and the one who humbles himself will be exalted."

Sunday March 19, 2023

Fourth Sunday of Lent, Year A

First Reading – 1 Samuel 16:1B, 6-7, 10-13A

1B The LORD said to Samuel: "Fill your horn with oil, and be on
your way. I am sending you to Jesse of Bethlehem, for I have
chosen my king from among his sons." 6 As Jesse and his sons
came to the sacrifice, Samuel looked at Eliab and thought,
"Surely the LORD's anointed is here before him." 7 But the
LORD said to Samuel: "Do not judge from his appearance or
from his lofty stature, because I have rejected him. Not as man
sees does God see, because man sees the appearance but
the LORD looks into the heart." 10 In the same way Jesse
presented seven sons before Samuel, but Samuel said to
Jesse, "The LORD has not chosen any one of these." 11 Then
Samuel asked Jesse, "Are these all the sons you have?"
Jesse replied, "There is still the youngest, who is tending the
sheep." Samuel said to Jesse, "Send for him; we will not begin
the sacrificial banquet until he arrives here." 12 Jesse sent and
had the young man brought to them. He was ruddy, a youth
handsome to behold and making a splendid appearance. The
LORD said, "There – anoint him, for this is the one!" 13 Then
Samuel, with the horn of oil in hand, anointed David in the
presence of his brothers; and from that day on, the spirit of the
LORD rushed upon David.

Responsorial Psalm – Psalms 23:1-3A, 3B-4, 5, 6.

R. (1) The Lord is my shepherd; there is nothing I shall want.

1 The LORD is my shepherd; I shall not want.

2 In verdant pastures he gives me repose;

beside restful waters he leads me;

3A he refreshes my soul.

R. The Lord is my shepherd; there is nothing I shall want.

3B He guides me in right paths

for his name's sake.

4 Even though I walk in the dark valley

I fear no evil; for you are at my side

With your rod and your staff

that give me courage.

R. The Lord is my shepherd; there is nothing I shall want.

5 You spread the table before me

in the sight of my foes;

you anoint my head with oil;

my cup overflows.

R. The Lord is my shepherd; there is nothing I shall want.

6 Only goodness and kindness follow me

all the days of my life;

and I shall dwell in the house of the LORD

for years to come.

R. The Lord is my shepherd; there is nothing I shall want.

Second Reading – Ephesians 5:8-14

Brothers and sisters: 8You were once darkness, but now you
are light in the Lord. Live as children of light, 9for light
produces every kind of goodness and righteousness and truth.
10Try to learn what is pleasing to the Lord. 11Take no part in
the fruitless works of darkness; rather expose them, 12for it is
shameful even to mention the things done by them in secret;
13but everything exposed by the light becomes visible, 14for
everything that becomes visible is light. Therefore, it says:
"Awake, O sleeper, and arise from the dead, and Christ will
give you light."

Verse Before The Gospel – John 8:12

12 I am the light of the world, says the Lord; whoever follows me will have the light of life.

Gospel – John 9:1-41

1As Jesus passed by he saw a man blind from birth. 2His
disciples asked him, "Rabbi, who sinned, this man or his
parents, that he was born blind?" 3Jesus answered, "Neither
he nor his parents sinned; it is so that the works of God might
be made visible through him. 4We have to do the works of the
one who sent me while it is day. Night is coming when no one
can work. 5While I am in the world, I am the light of the world."
6When he had said this, he spat on the ground and made clay
with the saliva, and smeared the clay on his eyes, 7and said to
him, "Go wash in the Pool of Siloam" – which means Sent -.
So he went and washed, and came back able to see. 8His
neighbors and those who had seen him earlier as a beggar
said, "Isn't this the one who used to sit and beg?" 9Some said,
"It is," but others said, "No, he just looks like him." He said, "I
am." 10So they said to him, "How were your eyes opened?"
11He replied, "The man called Jesus made clay and anointed
my eyes and told me, 'Go to Siloam and wash.' So I went
there and washed and was able to see." 12And they said to
him, "Where is he?" He said, "I don't know." 13They brought
the one who was once blind to the Pharisees. 14Now Jesus
had made clay and opened his eyes on a Sabbath. 15So then
the Pharisees also asked him how he was able to see. He said
to them, "He put clay on my eyes, and I washed, and now I
can see." 16So some of the Pharisees said, "This man is not
from God, because he does not keep the Sabbath." But others
said, "How can a sinful man do such signs?" And there was a
division among them. 17So they said to the blind man again,
"What do you have to say about him, since he opened your
eyes?" He said, "He is a prophet." 18Now the Jews did not
believe that he had been blind and gained his sight until they
summoned the parents of the one who had gained his sight.
19They asked them, "Is this your son, who you say was born
blind? How does he now see?" 20His parents answered and
said, "We know that this is our son and that he was born blind.
21We do not know how he sees now, nor do we know who
opened his eyes. Ask him, he is of age; he can speak for
himself." 22His parents said this because they were afraid of
the Jews, for the Jews had already agreed that if anyone
acknowledged him as the Christ, he would be expelled from
the synagogue. 23For this reason his parents said, "He is of
age; question him." 24So a second time they called the man

who had been blind and said to him, "Give God the praise! We
know that this man is a sinner." 25He replied, "If he is a sinner,
I do not know. One thing I do know is that I was blind and now
I see." 26So they said to him, "What did he do to you? How did
he open your eyes?" 27He answered them, "I told you already
and you did not listen. Why do you want to hear it again? Do
you want to become his disciples, too?" 28They ridiculed him
and said, "You are that man's disciple; we are disciples of
Moses! 29We know that God spoke to Moses, but we do not
know where this one is from." 30The man answered and said to
them, "This is what is so amazing, that you do not know where
he is from, yet he opened my eyes. 31We know that God does
not listen to sinners, but if one is devout and does his will, he
listens to him. 32It is unheard of that anyone ever opened the
eyes of a person born blind. 33If this man were not from God,
he would not be able to do anything." 34They answered and
said to him, "You were born totally in sin, and are you trying to
teach us?" Then they threw him out. 35When Jesus heard that
they had thrown him out, he found him and said, "Do you
believe in the Son of Man?" 36He answered and said, "Who is
he, sir, that I may believe in him?" 37Jesus said to him, "You
have seen him, the one speaking with you is he." 38He said, "I
do believe, Lord," and he worshiped him. 39Then Jesus said, "I
came into this world for judgment, so that those who do not
see might see, and those who do see might become blind."
40Some of the Pharisees who were with him heard this and
said to him, "Surely we are not also blind, are we?" 41Jesus
said to them, "If you were blind, you would have no sin; but
now you are saying, 'We see,' so your sin remains.

Monday March 20, 2023

Solemnity of Saint Joseph, Husband of Virgin Mary

First Reading – 2 Samuel 7:4-5A, 12-14A, 16

4The LORD spoke to Nathan and said: 5A"Go, tell my servant
David, 12'When your time comes and you rest with your
ancestors, I will raise up your heir after you, sprung from your
loins, and I will make his kingdom firm. 13It is he who shall
build a house for my name. And I will make his royal throne
firm forever. 14AI will be a father to him, and he shall be a son
to me. 16Your house and your kingdom shall endure forever
before me; your throne shall stand firm forever.'"

Responsorial Psalm – Psalms 89:2-3, 4-5, 27 and 29

R. (37) The son of David will live for ever.

2 The promises of the LORD I will sing forever;

through all generations my mouth shall proclaim your faithfulness,

3 For you have said, “My kindness is established forever”;

in heaven you have confirmed your faithfulness.

R. The son of David will live for ever.

4 “I have made a covenant with my chosen one,

I have sworn to David my servant:

5 Forever will I confirm your posterity

and establish your throne for all generations.”

R. The son of David will live for ever.

27 “He shall say of me, ‘You are my father,

my God, the Rock, my savior.’

29 Forever I will maintain my kindness toward him,

and my covenant with him stands firm.”

R. The son of David will live for ever.

Second Reading – Romans 4:13, 16-18, 22

Brothers and sisters: 13It was not through the law that the
promise was made to Abraham and his descendants that he
would inherit the world, but through the righteousness that
comes from faith. 16For this reason, it depends on faith, so that
it may be a gift, and the promise may be guaranteed to all his
descendants, not to those who only adhere to the law but to
those who follow the faith of Abraham, who is the father of all
of us, 17as it is written, I have made you father of many
nations. He is our father in the sight of God, in whom he
believed, who gives life to the dead and calls into being what
does not exist. 18He believed, hoping against hope, that he
would become the father of many nations, according to what

was said, Thus shall your descendants be. 22That is why it was
credited to him as righteousness.

Verse Before the Gospel – Psalms 84:5

5Blessed are those who dwell in your house, O Lord; they
never cease to praise you.

Gospel – Matthew 1:16, 18-21, 24A

16Jacob was the father of Joseph, the husband of Mary. Of her
was born Jesus who is called the Christ. 18Now this is how the
birth of Jesus Christ came about. When his mother Mary was
betrothed to Joseph, but before they lived together, she was
found with child through the Holy Spirit. 19Joseph her husband,
since he was a righteous man, yet unwilling to expose her to
shame, decided to divorce her quietly. 20Such was his
intention when, behold, the angel of the Lord appeared to him
in a dream and said, "Joseph, son of David, do not be afraid to
take Mary your wife into your home. For it is through the Holy
Spirit that this child has been conceived in her. 21She will bear
a son and you are to name him Jesus, because he will save
his people from their sins." 24When Joseph awoke, he did as
the angel of the Lord had commanded him and took his wife
into his home.

Or Luke 2:41-51A

41Each year Jesus' parents went to Jerusalem for the feast of
Passover, 42and when he was twelve years old, they went up
according to festival custom. 43After they had completed its
days, as they were returning, the boy Jesus remained behind
in Jerusalem, but his parents did not know it. 44Thinking that
he was in the caravan, they journeyed for a day and looked for
him among their relatives and acquaintances, 45but not finding
him, they returned to Jerusalem to look for him. 46After three
days they found him in the temple, sitting in the midst of the
teachers, listening to them and asking them questions, 47and
all who heard him were astounded at his understanding and
his answers. 48When his parents saw him, they were
astonished, and his mother said to him, "Son, why have you
done this to us? Your father and I have been looking for you
with great anxiety." 49And he said to them, "Why were you
looking for me? Did you not know that I must be in my Father's
house?" 50But they did not understand what he said to them.

[51A]He went down with them and came to Nazareth, and was obedient to them.

Tuesday March 21, 2023

Tuesday of the Fourth Week of Lent

First Reading – Ezekiel 47:1-9, 12

[1]The angel brought me, Ezekiel, back to the entrance of the
temple of the LORD, and I saw water flowing out from beneath
the threshold of the temple toward the east, for the façade of
the temple was toward the east; the water flowed down from
the right side of the temple, south of the altar. [2]He led me
outside by the north gate, and around to the outer gate facing
the east, where I saw water trickling from the right side. [3]Then
when he had walked off to the east with a measuring cord in
his hand, he measured off a thousand cubits and had me
wade through the water, which was ankle-deep. [4]He
measured off another thousand and once more had me wade
through the water, which was now knee-deep. Again he
measured off a thousand and had me wade; the water was up
to my waist. [5]Once more he measured off a thousand, but
there was now a river through which I could not wade; for the
water had risen so high it had become a river that could not be
crossed except by swimming. [6]He asked me, "Have you seen
this, son of man?" Then he brought me to the bank of the river,
where he had me sit. [7]Along the bank of the river I saw very
many trees on both sides. [8]He said to me, "This water flows
into the eastern district down upon the Arabah, and empties
into the sea, the salt waters, which it makes fresh. [9]Wherever
the river flows, every sort of living creature that can multiply
shall live, and there shall be abundant fish, for wherever this
water comes the sea shall be made fresh. [12]Along both banks
of the river, fruit trees of every kind shall grow; their leaves
shall not fade, nor their fruit fail. Every month they shall bear
fresh fruit, for they shall be watered by the flow from the
sanctuary. Their fruit shall serve for food, and their leaves for
medicine."

Responsorial Psalm – Psalms 46:2-3, 5-6, 8-9

R. (8) The Lord of hosts is with us; our stronghold is the God of Jacob.

[2] God is our refuge and our strength,

an ever-present help in distress.

3 Therefore we fear not, though the earth be shaken

and mountains plunge into the depths of the sea.

R. The Lord of hosts is with us; our stronghold is the God of Jacob.

5 There is a stream whose runlets gladden the city of God,

the holy dwelling of the Most High.

6 God is in its midst; it shall not be disturbed;

God will help it at the break of dawn.

R. The Lord of hosts is with us; our stronghold is the God of Jacob.

8 The LORD of hosts is with us;

our stronghold is the God of Jacob.

9 Come! behold the deeds of the LORD,

the astounding things he has wrought on earth.

R. The Lord of hosts is with us; our stronghold is the God of Jacob.

Verse Before the Gospel – Psalms 51:12A, 14A

12A A clean heart create for me, O God; 14A give me back the joy of your salvation.

Gospel – John 5:1-16

1 There was a feast of the Jews, and Jesus went up to
Jerusalem. 2 Now there is in Jerusalem at the Sheep Gate a
pool called in Hebrew Bethesda, with five porticoes. 3 In these
lay a large number of ill, blind, lame, and crippled. 5 One man
was there who had been ill for thirty-eight years. 6 When Jesus
saw him lying there and knew that he had been ill for a long
time, he said to him, "Do you want to be well?" 7 The sick man
answered him, "Sir, I have no one to put me into the pool
when the water is stirred up; while I am on my way, someone
else gets down there before me." 8 Jesus said to him, "Rise,
take up your mat, and walk." 9 Immediately the man became
well, took up his mat, and walked. Now that day was a
Sabbath. 10 So the Jews said to the man who was cured, "It is

the Sabbath, and it is not lawful for you to carry your mat." [11]He answered them, "The man who made me well told me, 'Take up your mat and walk.'" [12]They asked him, "Who is the man who told you, 'Take it up and walk'?" [13]The man who was healed did not know who it was, for Jesus had slipped away, since there was a crowd there. [14]After this Jesus found him in the temple area and said to him, "Look, you are well; do not sin anymore, so that nothing worse may happen to you." [15]The man went and told the Jews that Jesus was the one who had made him well. [16]Therefore, the Jews began to persecute Jesus because he did this on a Sabbath.

Wednesday March 22, 2023

Wednesday of the Fourth Week of Lent

First Reading – Isaiah 49:8-15

[8]Thus says the LORD: In a time of favor I answer you, on the day of salvation I help you; and I have kept you and given you as a covenant to the people, To restore the land and allot the desolate heritages, [9]Saying to the prisoners: Come out! To those in darkness: Show yourselves! Along the ways they shall find pasture, on every bare height shall their pastures be. [10]They shall not hunger or thirst, nor shall the scorching wind or the sun strike them; For he who pities them leads them and guides them beside springs of water. [11]I will cut a road through all my mountains, and make my highways level. [12]See, some shall come from afar, others from the north and the west, and some from the land of Syene. [13]Sing out, O heavens, and rejoice, O earth, break forth into song, you mountains. For the LORD comforts his people and shows mercy to his afflicted. [14]But Zion said, "The LORD has forsaken me; my Lord has forgotten me." [15]Can a mother forget her infant, be without tenderness for the child of her womb? Even should she forget, I will never forget you.

Responsorial Psalm – Psalms 145:8-9, 13CD-14, 17-18

R. (8a) The Lord is gracious and merciful.

[8] The LORD is gracious and merciful,

slow to anger and of great kindness.

[9] The LORD is good to all

and compassionate toward all his works.

R. The Lord is gracious and merciful.

[13CD] The LORD is faithful in all his words

and holy in all his works.

[14] The LORD lifts up all who are falling

and raises up all who are bowed down.

R. The Lord is gracious and merciful.

[17] The LORD is just in all his ways

and holy in all his works.

[18] The LORD is near to all who call upon him,

to all who call upon him in truth.

R. The Lord is gracious and merciful.

Verse Before the Gospel – John 11:25A, 26

[25A]I am the resurrection and the life, says the Lord; [26]whoever believes in me will never die.

Gospel – John 5:17-30

[17]Jesus answered the Jews: "My Father is at work until now,
so I am at work." [18]For this reason they tried all the more to kill
him, because he not only broke the Sabbath but he also called
God his own father, making himself equal to God. [19]Jesus
answered and said to them, "Amen, amen, I say to you, the
Son cannot do anything on his own, but only what he sees the
Father doing; for what he does, the Son will do also. [20]For the
Father loves the Son and shows him everything that he
himself does, and he will show him greater works than these,
so that you may be amazed. [21]For just as the Father raises the
dead and gives life, so also does the Son give life to
whomever he wishes. [22]Nor does the Father judge anyone, but
he has given all judgment to the Son, [23]so that all may honor
the Son just as they honor the Father. Whoever does not
honor the Son does not honor the Father who sent him.
[24]Amen, amen, I say to you, whoever hears my word and
believes in the one who sent me has eternal life and will not
come to condemnation, but has passed from death to life.

[25]Amen, amen, I say to you, the hour is coming and is now here when the dead will hear the voice of the Son of God, and those who hear will live. [26]For just as the Father has life in himself, so also he gave to the Son the possession of life in himself. [27]And he gave him power to exercise judgment, because he is the Son of Man. [28]Do not be amazed at this, because the hour is coming in which all who are in the tombs will hear his voice [29]and will come out, those who have done good deeds to the resurrection of life, but those who have done wicked deeds to the resurrection of condemnation. [30]"I cannot do anything on my own; I judge as I hear, and my judgment is just, because I do not seek my own will but the will of the one who sent me."

Thursday March 23, 2023

Thursday of the Fourth Week of Lent

First Reading – Exodus 32:7-14

[7]The LORD said to Moses, "Go down at once to your people whom you brought out of the land of Egypt, for they have become depraved. [8]They have soon turned aside from the way I pointed out to them, making for themselves a molten calf and worshiping it, sacrificing to it and crying out, 'This is your God, O Israel, who brought you out of the land of Egypt!' [9]The LORD said to Moses, "I see how stiff-necked this people is. [10]Let me alone, then, that my wrath may blaze up against them to consume them. Then I will make of you a great nation." [11]But Moses implored the LORD, his God, saying, "Why, O LORD, should your wrath blaze up against your own people, whom you brought out of the land of Egypt with such great power and with so strong a hand? [12]Why should the Egyptians say, 'With evil intent he brought them out, that he might kill them in the mountains and exterminate them from the face of the earth'? Let your blazing wrath die down; relent in punishing your people. [13]Remember your servants Abraham, Isaac and Israel, and how you swore to them by your own self, saying, 'I will make your descendants as numerous as the stars in the sky; and all this land that I promised, I will give your descendants as their perpetual heritage.'" [14]So the LORD relented in the punishment he had threatened to inflict on his people.

Responsorial Psalm – Psalms 106:19-20, 21-22, 23

R. (4a) Remember us, O Lord, as you favor your people.

19 Our fathers made a calf in Horeb

and adored a molten image;

20 They exchanged their glory

for the image of a grass-eating bullock.

R. Remember us, O Lord, as you favor your people.

21 They forgot the God who had saved them,

who had done great deeds in Egypt,

22 Wondrous deeds in the land of Ham,

terrible things at the Red Sea.

R. Remember us, O Lord, as you favor your people.

23 Then he spoke of exterminating them,

but Moses, his chosen one,

Withstood him in the breach

to turn back his destructive wrath.

R. Remember us, O Lord, as you favor your people.

Verse Before the Gospel – John 3:16

16God so loved the world that he gave his only-begotten Son, so that everyone who believes in him might have eternal life.

Gospel – John 5:31-47

31Jesus said to the Jews: "If I testify on my own behalf, my
testimony is not true. 32But there is another who testifies on my
behalf, and I know that the testimony he gives on my behalf is
true. 33You sent emissaries to John, and he testified to the
truth. 34I do not accept human testimony, but I say this so that
you may be saved. 35He was a burning and shining lamp, and
for a while you were content to rejoice in his light. 36But I have
testimony greater than John's. The works that the Father gave
me to accomplish, these works that I perform testify on my
behalf that the Father has sent me. 37Moreover, the Father
who sent me has testified on my behalf. But you have never

heard his voice nor seen his form, 38and you do not have his
word remaining in you, because you do not believe in the one
whom he has sent. 39You search the Scriptures, because you
think you have eternal life through them; even they testify on
my behalf. 40But you do not want to come to me to have life.
41"I do not accept human praise; 42moreover, I know that you
do not have the love of God in you. 43I came in the name of my
Father, but you do not accept me; yet if another comes in his
own name, you will accept him. 44How can you believe, when
you accept praise from one another and do not seek the
praise that comes from the only God? 45Do not think that I will
accuse you before the Father: the one who will accuse you is
Moses, in whom you have placed your hope. 46For if you had
believed Moses, you would have believed me, because he
wrote about me. 47But if you do not believe his writings, how
will you believe my words?"

Friday March 24, 2023

Friday of the Fourth Week of Lent

First Reading – Wisdom 2:1A, 12-22

1AThe wicked said among themselves, thinking not aright:
12"Let us beset the just one, because he is obnoxious to us; he
sets himself against our doings, Reproaches us for
transgressions of the law and charges us with violations of our
training. 13He professes to have knowledge of God and styles
himself a child of the LORD. 14To us he is the censure of our
thoughts; merely to see him is a hardship for us, 15Because his
life is not like that of others, and different are his ways. 16He
judges us debased; he holds aloof from our paths as from
things impure. He calls blest the destiny of the just and boasts
that God is his Father. 17Let us see whether his words be true;
let us find out what will happen to him. 18For if the just one be
the son of God, he will defend him and deliver him from the
hand of his foes. 19With revilement and torture let us put him to
the test that we may have proof of his gentleness and try his
patience. 20Let us condemn him to a shameful death; for
according to his own words, God will take care of him."
21These were their thoughts, but they erred; for their
wickedness blinded them, 22and they knew not the hidden
counsels of God; neither did they count on a recompense of
holiness nor discern the innocent souls' reward.

Responsorial Psalm – Psalms 34:17-18, 19-20, 21 AND 23

R. (19a) The Lord is close to the brokenhearted.

17 The LORD confronts the evildoers,

to destroy remembrance of them from the earth.

18 When the just cry out, the LORD hears them,

and from all their distress he rescues them.

R. The Lord is close to the brokenhearted.

19 The LORD is close to the brokenhearted;

and those who are crushed in spirit he saves.

20 Many are the troubles of the just man,

but out of them all the LORD delivers him.

R. The Lord is close to the brokenhearted.

21 He watches over all his bones;

not one of them shall be broken.

23 The LORD redeems the lives of his servants;

no one incurs guilt who takes refuge in him.

R. The Lord is close to the brokenhearted.

Verse Before the Gospel – Matthew 4:4B

4B One does not live on bread alone, but on every word that comes forth from the mouth of God.

Gospel – John 7:1-2, 10, 25-30

1 Jesus moved about within Galilee; he did not wish to travel in
Judea, because the Jews were trying to kill him. 2 But the
Jewish feast of Tabernacles was near. 10 But when his brothers
had gone up to the feast, he himself also went up, not openly
but as it were in secret. 25 Some of the inhabitants of
Jerusalem said, “Is he not the one they are trying to kill? 26 And
look, he is speaking openly and they say nothing to him. Could
the authorities have realized that he is the Christ? 27 But we
know where he is from. When the Christ comes, no one will
know where he is from.” 28 So Jesus cried out in the temple

area as he was teaching and said, “You know me and also
know where I am from. Yet I did not come on my own, but the
one who sent me, whom you do not know, is true. [29]I know
him, because I am from him, and he sent me.” [30]So they tried
to arrest him, but no one laid a hand upon him, because his
hour had not yet come.

Saturday March 25, 2023

Solemnity of the Annunciation of the Lord

First Reading – Isaiah 7:10-14; 8:10

[10]The LORD spoke to Ahaz, saying: [11]Ask for a sign from the
LORD, your God; let it be deep as the netherworld, or high as
the sky! [12]But Ahaz answered, “I will not ask! I will not tempt
the LORD!” [13]Then Isaiah said: Listen, O house of David! Is it
not enough for you to weary people, must you also weary my
God? [14]Therefore the Lord himself will give you this sign: the
virgin shall be with child, and bear a son, and shall name him
Emmanuel, which means “God is with us!”

Responsorial Psalm – Psalms 40:7-8A, 8B-9, 10, 11

R. (8a and 9a) **Here I am, Lord; I come to do your will.**

[7] Sacrifice or oblation you wished not,

but ears open to obedience you gave me.

[8A] Holocausts or sin-offerings you sought not;

then said I, “Behold I come.”

R. Here I am, Lord; I come to do your will.

[8B] “In the written scroll it is prescribed for me,

[9] To do your will, O my God, is my delight,

and your law is within my heart!”

R. Here I am, Lord; I come to do your will.

[10] I announced your justice in the vast assembly;

I did not restrain my lips, as you, O LORD, know.

R. Here I am, Lord; I come to do your will.

[11] Your justice I kept not hid within my heart;

your faithfulness and your salvation I have spoken of;

I have made no secret of your kindness and your truth

in the vast assembly.

R. Here I am, Lord; I come to do your will.

Second Reading – Hebrews 10:4-10

Brothers and sisters: 4It is impossible that the blood of bulls and goats take away sins. 5For this reason, when Christ came into the world, he said: “Sacrifice and offering you did not desire, but a body you prepared for me; 6in holocausts and sin offerings you took no delight. 7Then I said, ‘As is written of me in the scroll, behold, I come to do your will, O God.’” 8First, he says, “Sacrifices and offerings, holocausts and sin offerings, you neither desired nor delighted in.” These are offered according to the law. 9Then he says, “Behold, I come to do your will.” He takes away the first to establish the second. 10By this “will,” we have been consecrated through the offering of the Body of Jesus Christ once for all.

Verse Before The Gospel – John 1:14AB

14ABThe Word of God became flesh and made his dwelling among us; and we saw his glory.

Gospel – Luke 1:26-38

26The angel Gabriel was sent from God to a town of Galilee called Nazareth, 27to a virgin betrothed to a man named Joseph, of the house of David, and the virgin’s name was Mary. 28And coming to her, he said, “Hail, full of grace! The Lord is with you.” 29But she was greatly troubled at what was said and pondered what sort of greeting this might be. 30Then the angel said to her, “Do not be afraid, Mary, for you have found favor with God. 31Behold, you will conceive in your womb and bear a son, and you shall name him Jesus. 32He will be great and will be called Son of the Most High, and the Lord God will give him the throne of David his father, 33and he will rule over the house of Jacob forever, and of his Kingdom there will be no end.” 34But Mary said to the angel, “How can this be, since I have no relations with a man?” 35And the angel said to her in reply, “The Holy Spirit will come upon you, and the power of the Most High will overshadow you. Therefore the child to be born will be called holy, the Son of God. 36And behold, Elizabeth, your relative, has also conceived a son in her old age, and this is the sixth month for her who was called barren; [37]for nothing will be impossible for God." [38]Mary said, "Behold, I am the handmaid of the Lord. May it be done to me according to your word." Then the angel departed from her.

Sunday March 26, 2023

Fifth Sunday of Lent, Year A

First Reading – Ezekiel 37:12-14

[12]Thus says the Lord GOD: O my people, I will open your graves and have you rise from them, and bring you back to the land of Israel. [13]Then you shall know that I am the LORD, when I open your graves and have you rise from them, O my people! [14]I will put my spirit in you that you may live, and I will settle you upon your land; thus you shall know that I am the LORD. I have promised, and I will do it, says the LORD.

Responsorial Psalm – Psalms 130:1-2, 3-4, 5-6, 7-8

R. (7) With the Lord there is mercy and fullness of redemption.

1 Out of the depths I cry to you, O LORD;

LORD, hear my voice!

2 Let your ears be attentive

to my voice in supplication.

R. With the Lord there is mercy and fullness of redemption.

3 If you, O LORD, mark iniquities,

LORD, who can stand?

4 But with you is forgiveness,

that you may be revered.

R. With the Lord there is mercy and fullness of redemption.

5 I trust in the LORD;

my soul trusts in his word.

6 More than sentinels wait for the dawn,

let Israel wait for the LORD.

R. With the Lord there is mercy and fullness of redemption.

7 For with the LORD is kindness

and with him is plenteous redemption;

8 And he will redeem Israel

from all their iniquities.

R. With the Lord there is mercy and fullness of redemption.

Second Reading – Romans 8:8-11

Brothers and sisters: 8 Those who are in the flesh cannot
please God. 9 But you are not in the flesh; on the contrary, you
are in the spirit, if only the Spirit of God dwells in you.
Whoever does not have the Spirit of Christ does not belong to
him. 10 But if Christ is in you, although the body is dead
because of sin, the spirit is alive because of righteousness. 11 If
the Spirit of the one who raised Jesus from the dead dwells in
you, the one who raised Christ from the dead will give life to
your mortal bodies also, through his Spirit dwelling in you.

Verse Before The Gospel – John 11:25A, 26

25A I am the resurrection and the life, says the Lord; 26 whoever
believes in me, even if he dies, will never die.

Gospel – John 11:1-45

1 Now a man was ill, Lazarus from Bethany, the village of Mary
and her sister Martha. 2 Mary was the one who had anointed
the Lord with perfumed oil and dried his feet with her hair; it
was her brother Lazarus who was ill. 3 So the sisters sent word
to him saying, “Master, the one you love is ill.” 4 When Jesus
heard this he said, “This illness is not to end in death, but is for
the glory of God, that the Son of God may be glorified through
it.” 5 Now Jesus loved Martha and her sister and Lazarus. 6 So
when he heard that he was ill, he remained for two days in the
place where he was. 7 Then after this he said to his disciples,
“Let us go back to Judea.” 8 The disciples said to him, “Rabbi,
the Jews were just trying to stone you, and you want to go
back there?” 9 Jesus answered, “Are there not twelve hours in

a day? If one walks during the day, he does not stumble,
because he sees the light of this world. 10But if one walks at
night, he stumbles, because the light is not in him." 11He said
this, and then told them, "Our friend Lazarus is asleep, but I
am going to awaken him." 12So the disciples said to him,
"Master, if he is asleep, he will be saved." 13But Jesus was
talking about his death, while they thought that he meant
ordinary sleep. 14So then Jesus said to them clearly, "Lazarus
has died. 15And I am glad for you that I was not there, that you
may believe. Let us go to him." 16So Thomas, called Didymus,
said to his fellow disciples, "Let us also go to die with him."
17When Jesus arrived, he found that Lazarus had already
been in the tomb for four days. 18Now Bethany was near
Jerusalem, only about two miles away. 19And many of the
Jews had come to Martha and Mary to comfort them about
their brother. 20When Martha heard that Jesus was coming,
she went to meet him; but Mary sat at home. 21Martha said to
Jesus, "Lord, if you had been here, my brother would not have
died. 22But even now I know that whatever you ask of God,
God will give you." 23Jesus said to her, "Your brother will rise."
24Martha said to him, "I know he will rise, in the resurrection on
the last day." 25Jesus told her, "I am the resurrection and the
life; whoever believes in me, even if he dies, will live, 26and
everyone who lives and believes in me will never die. Do you
believe this?" 27She said to him, "Yes, Lord. I have come to
believe that you are the Christ, the Son of God, the one who is
coming into the world." 28When she had said this, she went
and called her sister Mary secretly, saying, "The teacher is
here and is asking for you." 29As soon as she heard this, she
rose quickly and went to him. 30For Jesus had not yet come
into the village, but was still where Martha had met him. 31So
when the Jews who were with her in the house comforting her
saw Mary get up quickly and go out, they followed her,
presuming that she was going to the tomb to weep there.
32When Mary came to where Jesus was and saw him, she fell
at his feet and said to him, "Lord, if you had been here, my
brother would not have died." 33When Jesus saw her weeping
and the Jews who had come with her weeping, he became
perturbed and deeply troubled, 34and said, "Where have you
laid him?" They said to him, "Sir, come and see." 35And Jesus
wept. 36So the Jews said, "See how he loved him." 37But some
of them said, "Could not the one who opened the eyes of the
blind man have done something so that this man would not

have died?” 38So Jesus, perturbed again, came to the tomb. It was a cave, and a stone lay across it. 39Jesus said, “Take away the stone.” Martha, the dead man’s sister, said to him, “Lord, by now there will be a stench; he has been dead for four days.” 40Jesus said to her, “Did I not tell you that if you believe you will see the glory of God?” 41So they took away the stone. And Jesus raised his eyes and said, “Father, I thank you for hearing me. 42I know that you always hear me; but because of the crowd here I have said this, that they may believe that you sent me.” 43And when he had said this, He cried out in a loud voice, “Lazarus, come out!” 44The dead man came out, tied hand and foot with burial bands, and his face was wrapped in a cloth. So Jesus said to them, “Untie him and let him go.” 45Now many of the Jews who had come to Mary and seen what he had done began to believe in him.

Monday March 27, 2023

Monday of the Fifth Week of Lent

First Reading – Daniel 13:1-9, 15-17, 19-30, 33-62

1In Babylon there lived a man named Joakim, 2who married a very beautiful and God-fearing woman, Susanna, the daughter of Hilkiah; 3her pious parents had trained their daughter according to the law of Moses. 4Joakim was very rich; he had a garden near his house, and the Jews had recourse to him often because he was the most respected of them all. 5That year, two elders of the people were appointed judges, of whom the Lord said, “Wickedness has come out of Babylon: from the elders who were to govern the people as judges.” 6These men, to whom all brought their cases, frequented the house of Joakim. 7When the people left at noon, Susanna used to enter her husband’s garden for a walk. 8When the old men saw her enter every day for her walk, they began to lust for her. 9They suppressed their consciences; they would not allow their eyes to look to heaven, and did not keep in mind just judgments. 15One day, while they were waiting for the right moment, she entered the garden as usual, with two maids only. She decided to bathe, for the weather was warm. 16Nobody else was there except the two elders, who had hidden themselves and were watching her. 17“Bring me oil and soap,” she said to the maids, “and shut the garden doors while I bathe.” 19As soon as the maids had left, the two old men got

up and hurried to her. 20“Look,” they said, “the garden doors
are shut, and no one can see us; give in to our desire, and lie
with us. 21If you refuse, we will testify against you that you
dismissed your maids because a young man was here with
you.” 22“I am completely trapped,” Susanna groaned. “If I yield,
it will be my death; if I refuse, I cannot escape your power.
23Yet it is better for me to fall into your power without guilt than
to sin before the Lord.” 24Then Susanna shrieked, and the old
men also shouted at her, 25as one of them ran to open the
garden doors. 26When the people in the house heard the cries
from the garden, they rushed in by the side gate to see what
had happened to her. 27At the accusations by the old men, the
servants felt very much ashamed, for never had any such
thing been said about Susanna. 28When the people came to
her husband Joakim the next day, the two wicked elders also
came, fully determined to put Susanna to death. 29Before all
the people they ordered: “Send for Susanna, the daughter of
Hilkiah, the wife of Joakim.” When she was sent for, 30she
came with her parents, children and all her relatives. 33All her
relatives and the onlookers were weeping. 34In the midst of the
people the two elders rose up and laid their hands on her
head. 35Through tears she looked up to heaven, for she
trusted in the Lord wholeheartedly. 36The elders made this
accusation: “As we were walking in the garden alone, this
woman entered with two girls and shut the doors of the
garden, dismissing the girls. 37A young man, who was hidden
there, came and lay with her. 38When we, in a corner of the
garden, saw this crime, we ran toward them. 39We saw them
lying together, but the man we could not hold, because he was
stronger than we; he opened the doors and ran off. 40Then we
seized her and asked who the young man was, 41but she
refused to tell us. We testify to this.” The assembly believed
them, since they were elders and judges of the people, and
they condemned her to death. 42But Susanna cried aloud: “O
eternal God, you know what is hidden and are aware of all
things before they come to be: 43you know that they have
testified falsely against me. Here I am about to die, though I
have done none of the things with which these wicked men
have charged me.” 44The Lord heard her prayer. 45As she was
being led to execution, God stirred up the holy spirit of a
young boy named Daniel, 46and he cried aloud: “I will have no
part in the death of this woman.” 47All the people turned and
asked him, “What is this you are saying?” 48He stood in their

midst and continued, "Are you such fools, O children of Israel!
To condemn a woman of Israel without examination and
without clear evidence? 49 Return to court, for they have
testified falsely against her." 50Then all the people returned in
haste. To Daniel the elders said, "Come, sit with us and inform
us, since God has given you the prestige of old age." 51But he
replied, "Separate these two far from each other that I may
examine them." 52After they were separated one from the
other, he called one of them and said: "How you have grown
evil with age! Now have your past sins come to term:
53passing unjust sentences, condemning the innocent, and
freeing the guilty, although the Lord says, 'The innocent and
the just you shall not put to death.' 54Now, then, if you were a
witness, tell me under what tree you saw them together."
55"Under a mastic tree," he answered. Daniel replied, "Your
fine lie has cost you your head, for the angel of God shall
receive the sentence from him and split you in two." 56Putting
him to one side, he ordered the other one to be brought.
Daniel said to him, "Offspring of Canaan, not of Judah, beauty
has seduced you, lust has subverted your conscience. 57This
is how you acted with the daughters of Israel, and in their fear
they yielded to you; but a daughter of Judah did not tolerate
your wickedness. 58Now, then, tell me under what tree you
surprised them together." 59"Under an oak," he said. Daniel
replied, "Your fine lie has cost you also your head, for the
angel of God waits with a sword to cut you in two so as to
make an end of you both." 60The whole assembly cried aloud,
blessing God who saves those who hope in him. 61They rose
up against the two elders, for by their own words Daniel had
convicted them of perjury. 62According to the law of Moses,
they inflicted on them the penalty they had plotted to impose
on their neighbor: they put them to death. Thus was innocent
blood spared that day.

Responsorial Psalm – Psalms 23:1-3A, 3B-4, 5, 6

R. (4ab) Even though I walk in the dark valley I fear no evil; for you are at my side.

1The LORD is my shepherd; I shall not want.

2In verdant pastures he gives me repose;

Beside restful waters he leads me;

3A he refreshes my soul.

R. Even though I walk in the dark valley I fear no evil; for you are at my side.

3BC He guides me in right paths

for his name's sake.

4 Even though I walk in the dark valley

I fear no evil; for you are at my side

With your rod and your staff

that give me courage.

R. Even though I walk in the dark valley I fear no evil; for you are at my side.

5 You spread the table before me

in the sight of my foes;

You anoint my head with oil;

my cup overflows.

R. Even though I walk in the dark valley I fear no evil; for you are at my side.

6 Only goodness and kindness follow me

all the days of my life;

And I shall dwell in the house of the LORD

for years to come.

R. Even though I walk in the dark valley I fear no evil; for you are at my side.

Verse Before the Gospel – Ezekiel 33:11

11 I take no pleasure in the death of the wicked man, says the Lord, but rather in his conversion, that he may live.

Gospel – John 8:1-11

1 Jesus went to the Mount of Olives. 2 But early in the morning
he arrived again in the temple area, and all the people started
coming to him, and he sat down and taught them. 3 Then the
scribes and the Pharisees brought a woman who had been
caught in adultery and made her stand in the middle. 4 They
said to him, "Teacher, this woman was caught in the very act

of committing adultery. [5]Now in the law, Moses commanded
us to stone such women. So what do you say?” [6]They said
this to test him, so that they could have some charge to bring
against him. Jesus bent down and began to write on the
ground with his finger. [7]But when they continued asking him,
he straightened up and said to them, “Let the one among you
who is without sin be the first to throw a stone at her.” [8]Again
he bent down and wrote on the ground. [9]And in response, they
went away one by one, beginning with the elders. So he was
left alone with the woman before him. [10]Then Jesus
straightened up and said to her, “Woman, where are they?
Has no one condemned you?” [11]She replied, “No one, sir.”
Then Jesus said, “Neither do I condemn you. Go, and from
now on do not sin anymore.”

Tuesday March 28, 2023

Tuesday of the Fifth Week of Lent

First Reading – Numbers 21:4-9

[4]From Mount Hor the children of Israel set out on the Red Sea
road, to bypass the land of Edom. But with their patience worn
out by the journey, [5]the people complained against God and
Moses, “Why have you brought us up from Egypt to die in this
desert, where there is no food or water? We are disgusted
with this wretched food!” [6]In punishment the LORD sent
among the people saraph serpents, which bit the people so
that many of them died. [7]Then the people came to Moses and
said, “We have sinned in complaining against the LORD and
you. Pray the LORD to take the serpents away from us.” So
Moses prayed for the people, [8]and the LORD said to Moses,
“Make a saraph and mount it on a pole, and whoever looks at
it after being bitten will live.” [9]Moses accordingly made a
bronze serpent and mounted it on a pole, and whenever
anyone who had been bitten by a serpent looked at the bronze
serpent, he lived.

Responsorial Psalm – Psalms 102:2-3, 16-18, 19-21

R. (2) O Lord, hear my prayer, and let my cry come to you.

[2]O LORD, hear my prayer,

and let my cry come to you.

[3]Hide not your face from me

in the day of my distress.

Incline your ear to me;

in the day when I call, answer me speedily.

R. O Lord, hear my prayer, and let my cry come to you.

16The nations shall revere your name, O LORD,

and all the kings of the earth your glory,

17When the LORD has rebuilt Zion

and appeared in his glory;

18When he has regarded the prayer of the destitute,

and not despised their prayer.

R. O Lord, hear my prayer, and let my cry come to you.

19 Let this be written for the generation to come,

and let his future creatures praise the LORD:

20"The LORD looked down from his holy height,

from heaven he beheld the earth,

21To hear the groaning of the prisoners,

to release those doomed to die."

R. O Lord, hear my prayer, and let my cry come to you.

Verse Before the Gospel

The seed is the word of God, Christ is the sower; all who come to him will live forever.

Gospel – John 8:21-30

21Jesus said to the Pharisees: "I am going away and you will
look for me, but you will die in your sin. Where I am going you
cannot come." 22So the Jews said, "He is not going to kill
himself, is he, because he said, 'Where I am going you cannot
come'?" 23He said to them, "You belong to what is below, I
belong to what is above. You belong to this world, but I do not
belong to this world. 24That is why I told you that you will die in
your sins. For if you do not believe that I AM, you will die in
your sins." 25So they said to him, "Who are you?" Jesus said to
them, "What I told you from the beginning. 26I have much to

say about you in condemnation. But the one who sent me is
true, and what I heard from him I tell the world." [27]They did not
realize that he was speaking to them of the Father. [28]So Jesus
said to them, "When you lift up the Son of Man, then you will
realize that I AM, and that I do nothing on my own, but I say
only what the Father taught me. [29]The one who sent me is with
me. He has not left me alone, because I always do what is
pleasing to him." [30]Because he spoke this way, many came to
believe in him.

Wednesday March 29, 2023

Wednesday of the Fifth Week of Lent

First Reading – Daniel 3:14-20, 91-92, 95

[14]King Nebuchadnezzar said: "Is it true, Shadrach, Meshach,
and Abednego, that you will not serve my god, or worship the
golden statue that I set up? [15]Be ready now to fall down and
worship the statue I had made, whenever you hear the sound
of the trumpet, flute, lyre, harp, psaltery, bagpipe, and all the
other musical instruments; otherwise, you shall be instantly
cast into the white-hot furnace; and who is the God who can
deliver you out of my hands?" [16]Shadrach, Meshach, and
Abednego answered King Nebuchadnezzar, "There is no need
for us to defend ourselves before you in this matter. [17]If our
God, whom we serve, can save us from the white-hot furnace
and from your hands, O king, may he save us! [18]But even if he
will not, know, O king, that we will not serve your god or
worship the golden statue that you set up." [19]King
Nebuchadnezzar's face became livid with utter rage against
Shadrach, Meshach, and Abednego. He ordered the furnace
to be heated seven times more than usual [20]and had some of
the strongest men in his army bind Shadrach, Meshach, and
Abednego and cast them into the white-hot furnace.
[91]Nebuchadnezzar rose in haste and asked his nobles, "Did
we not cast three men bound into the fire?" "Assuredly, O
king," they answered. [92]"But," he replied, "I see four men
unfettered and unhurt, walking in the fire, and the fourth looks
like a son of God." [95]Nebuchadnezzar exclaimed, "Blessed be
the God of Shadrach, Meshach, and Abednego, who sent his
angel to deliver the servants who trusted in him; they
disobeyed the royal command and yielded their bodies rather
than serve or worship any god except their own God."

Responsorial Psalm – Daniel 3:52, 53, 54, 55, 56

R. (52b) Glory and praise for ever!

52 "Blessed are you, O Lord, the God of our fathers,
praiseworthy and exalted above all forever;
And blessed is your holy and glorious name,
praiseworthy and exalted above all for all ages."

R. Glory and praise for ever!

53 "Blessed are you in the temple of your holy glory,
praiseworthy and exalted above all forever.

R. Glory and praise for ever!

54 "Blessed are you on the throne of your Kingdom,
praiseworthy and exalted above all forever."

R. Glory and praise for ever!

55 "Blessed are you who look into the depths
from your throne upon the cherubim;
praiseworthy and exalted above all forever."

R. Glory and praise for ever!

56 "Blessed are you in the firmament of heaven,
praiseworthy and glorious forever."

R. Glory and praise for ever!

Verse Before the Gospel – Luke 8:15

15 Blessed are they who have kept the word with a generous heart and yield a harvest through perseverance.

Gospel – John 8:31-42

31 "If you remain in my word, you will truly be my disciples,
32 and you will know the truth, and the truth will set you free."
33 They answered him, "We are descendants of Abraham and
have never been enslaved to anyone. How can you say, 'You
will become free'?" 34 Jesus answered them, "Amen, amen, I
say to you, everyone who commits sin is a slave of sin. 35 A
slave does not remain in a household forever, but a son

always remains. [36]So if the Son frees you, then you will truly be free. [37]I know that you are descendants of Abraham. But you are trying to kill me, because my word has no room among you. [38]I tell you what I have seen in the Father's presence; then do what you have heard from the Father." [39]They answered and said to him, "Our father is Abraham." Jesus said to them, "If you were Abraham's children, you would be doing the works of Abraham. [40]But now you are trying to kill me, a man who has told you the truth that I heard from God; Abraham did not do this. [41]You are doing the works of your father!" So they said to him, "We were not born of fornication. We have one Father, God." [42] Jesus said to them, "If God were your Father, you would love me, for I came from God and am here; I did not come on my own, but he sent me."

Thursday March 30, 2023

Thursday of the Fifth Week of Lent

First Reading – Genesis 17:3-9

[3]When Abram prostrated himself, God spoke to him: [4]"My covenant with you is this: you are to become the father of a host of nations. [5]No longer shall you be called Abram; your name shall be Abraham, for I am making you the father of a host of nations. [6]I will render you exceedingly fertile; I will make nations of you; kings shall stem from you. [7]I will maintain my covenant with you and your descendants after you throughout the ages as an everlasting pact, to be your God and the God of your descendants after you. [8]I will give to you and to your descendants after you the land in which you are now staying, the whole land of Canaan, as a permanent possession; and I will be their God." [9]God also said to Abraham: "On your part, you and your descendants after you must keep my covenant throughout the ages."

Responsorial Psalm – Psalms 105:4-5, 6-7, 8-9

R. (8a) The Lord remembers his covenant for ever.

[4]Look to the LORD in his strength;

seek to serve him constantly.

[5]Recall the wondrous deeds that he has wrought,

his portents, and the judgments he has uttered.

R. The Lord remembers his covenant for ever.

[6]You descendants of Abraham, his servants,

sons of Jacob, his chosen ones!

[7]He, the LORD, is our God;

throughout the earth his judgments prevail.

R. The Lord remembers his covenant for ever.

[8]He remembers forever his covenant

which he made binding for a thousand generations –

[9]Which he entered into with Abraham

and by his oath to Isaac.

R. The Lord remembers his covenant for ever.

Verse Before the Gospel – Psalms 95:8

[8]If today you hear his voice, harden not your hearts.

Gospel – John 8:51-59

[51]Jesus said to the Jews: "Amen, amen, I say to you, whoever
keeps my word will never see death." [52]So the Jews said to
him, "Now we are sure that you are possessed. Abraham died,
as did the prophets, yet you say, 'Whoever keeps my word will
never taste death.' [53]Are you greater than our father Abraham,
who died? Or the prophets, who died? Who do you make
yourself out to be?" [54]Jesus answered, "If I glorify myself, my
glory is worth nothing; but it is my Father who glorifies me, of
whom you say, 'He is our God.' [55]You do not know him, but I
know him. And if I should say that I do not know him, I would
be like you a liar. But I do know him and I keep his word.
[56]Abraham your father rejoiced to see my day; he saw it and
was glad." [57]So the Jews said to him, "You are not yet fifty
years old and you have seen Abraham?" [58]Jesus said to them,
"Amen, amen, I say to you, before Abraham came to be, I
AM." [59] So they picked up stones to throw at him; but Jesus
hid and went out of the temple area.

Friday March 31, 2023

Friday of the Fifth Week of Lent

First Reading – Jeremiah 20:10-13

10I hear the whisperings of many: "Terror on every side! Denounce! let us denounce him!" All those who were my friends are on the watch for any misstep of mine. "Perhaps he will be trapped; then we can prevail, and take our vengeance on him." 11But the LORD is with me, like a mighty champion: my persecutors will stumble, they will not triumph. In their failure they will be put to utter shame, to lasting, unforgettable confusion. 12O LORD of hosts, you who test the just, who probe mind and heart, Let me witness the vengeance you take on them, for to you I have entrusted my cause. 13 Sing to the LORD, praise the LORD, For he has rescued the life of the poor from the power of the wicked!

Responsorial Psalm – Psalms 18:2-3A, 3BC-4, 5-6, 7

R. (see 7) **In my distress I called upon the Lord, and he heard my voice.**

2I love you, O LORD, my strength,

3AO LORD, my rock, my fortress, my deliverer.

R. In my distress I called upon the Lord, and he heard my voice.

3BCMy God, my rock of refuge,

my shield, the horn of my salvation, my stronghold!

4Praised be the LORD, I exclaim,

and I am safe from my enemies.

R. In my distress I called upon the Lord, and he heard my voice.

5The breakers of death surged round about me,

the destroying floods overwhelmed me;

6The cords of the nether world enmeshed me,

the snares of death overtook me.

R. In my distress I called upon the Lord, and he heard my voice.

[7]In my distress I called upon the LORD

and cried out to my God;

From his temple he heard my voice,

and my cry to him reached his ears.

R. In my distress I called upon the Lord, and he heard my voice.

Verse Before the Gospel – John 6:63C, 68C

[63C]Your words, Lord, are Spirit and life; [68C]you have the words
of everlasting life.

Gospel – John 10:31-42

[31]The Jews picked up rocks to stone Jesus. [32]Jesus answered
them, "I have shown you many good works from my Father.
For which of these are you trying to stone me?" [33]The Jews
answered him, "We are not stoning you for a good work but for
blasphemy. You, a man, are making yourself God." [34]Jesus
answered them, "Is it not written in your law, 'I said, 'You are
gods"'? [35]If it calls them gods to whom the word of God came,
and Scripture cannot be set aside, [36]can you say that the one
whom the Father has consecrated and sent into the world
blasphemes because I said, 'I am the Son of God'? [37]If I do
not perform my Father's works, do not believe me; [38]but if I
perform them, even if you do not believe me, believe the
works, so that you may realize and understand that the Father
is in me and I am in the Father." [39]Then they tried again to
arrest him; but he escaped from their power. [40]He went back
across the Jordan to the place where John first baptized, and
there he remained. [41]Many came to him and said, "John
performed no sign, but everything John said about this man
was true." [42]And many there began to believe in him.

APRIL 2023

Saturday April 1, 2023

Saturday of the Fifth Week of Lent

First Reading – Ezekiel 37:21-28

[21]Thus says the Lord GOD: I will take the children of Israel from among the nations to which they have come, and gather them from all sides to bring them back to their land. [22]I will make them one nation upon the land, in the mountains of Israel, and there shall be one prince for them all. Never again shall they be two nations, and never again shall they be divided into two kingdoms. [23]No longer shall they defile themselves with their idols, their abominations, and all their transgressions. I will deliver them from all their sins of apostasy, and cleanse them so that they may be my people and I may be their God. [24]My servant David shall be prince over them, and there shall be one shepherd for them all; they shall live by my statutes and carefully observe my decrees. [25]They shall live on the land that I gave to my servant Jacob, the land where their fathers lived; they shall live on it forever, they, and their children, and their children's children, with my servant David their prince forever. [26]I will make with them a covenant of peace; it shall be an everlasting covenant with them, and I will multiply them, and put my sanctuary among them forever. [27]My dwelling shall be with them; I will be their God, and they shall be my people. [28]Thus the nations shall know that it is I, the LORD, who make Israel holy, when my sanctuary shall be set up among them forever.

Responsorial Psalm – Jeremiah 31:10, 11-12ABCD, 13

R. (see 10d) **The Lord will guard us, as a shepherd guards his flock.**

[10]Hear the word of the LORD, O nations,

proclaim it on distant isles, and say:

He who scattered Israel, now gathers them together,

he guards them as a shepherd his flock.

R. The Lord will guard us, as a shepherd guards his flock.

11The LORD shall ransom Jacob,

he shall redeem him from the hand of his conqueror.

12Shouting, they shall mount the heights of Zion,

they shall come streaming to the LORD's blessings:

The grain, the wine, and the oil,

the sheep and the oxen.

R. The Lord will guard us, as a shepherd guards his flock.

13Then the virgins shall make merry and dance,

and young men and old as well.

I will turn their mourning into joy,

I will console and gladden them after their sorrows.

R. The Lord will guard us, as a shepherd guards his flock.

Verse Before the Gospel – Ezekiel 18:31

31Cast away from you all the crimes you have committed, says the LORD, and make for yourselves a new heart and a new spirit.

Gospel – John 11:45-56

45Many of the Jews who had come to Mary and seen what Jesus had done began to believe in him. 46But some of them went to the Pharisees and told them what Jesus had done. 47So the chief priests and the Pharisees convened the Sanhedrin and said, "What are we going to do? This man is performing many signs. 48If we leave him alone, all will believe in him, and the Romans will come and take away both our land and our nation." 49But one of them, Caiaphas, who was high priest that year, said to them, "You know nothing, 50nor do you consider that it is better for you that one man should die instead of the people, so that the whole nation may not perish." 51He did not say this on his own, but since he was high priest for that year, he prophesied that Jesus was going to die for the nation, 52and not only for the nation, but also to gather into one the dispersed children of God. 53So from that day on they planned to kill him. 54So Jesus no longer walked about in public among the Jews, but he left for the region near the desert, to a town called Ephraim, and there he remained with his disciples. [55]Now the Passover of the Jews was near, and many went up from the country to Jerusalem before Passover to purify themselves. [56] They looked for Jesus and said to one another as they were in the temple area, “What do you think? That he will not come to the feast?”

Sunday April 2, 2023

Palm Sunday, Year A

At The Procession with Palms – Gospel – Matthew 21: 1-11

[1]And when they drew nigh to Jerusalem, and were come to Bethphage, unto mount Olivet, then Jesus sent two disciples, [2]Saying to them: Go ye into the village that is over against you, and immediately you shall find an ass tied, and a colt with her: loose them and bring them to me. [3]And if any man shall say anything to you, say ye, that the Lord hath need of them: and forthwith he will let them go. [4]Now all this was done that it might be fulfilled which was spoken by the prophet, saying: [5] Tell ye the daughter of Sion: Behold thy king cometh to thee, meek, and sitting upon an ass, and a colt the foal of her that is used to the yoke. [6]And the disciples going, did as Jesus commanded them. [7]And they brought the ass and the colt, and laid their garments upon them, and made him sit thereon. [8]And a very great multitude spread their garments in the way: and others cut boughs from the trees, and strewed them in the way: [9]And the multitudes that went before and that followed, cried, saying: Hosanna to the son of David: Blessed is he that cometh in the name of the Lord: Hosanna in the highest. [10]And when he was come into Jerusalem, the whole city was moved, saying: Who is this? [11]And the people said: This is Jesus the prophet, from Nazareth of Galilee.

At The Mass – First Reading - Isaiah 50:4-7

[4]The Lord GOD has given me a well-trained tongue, that I might know how to speak to the weary a word that will rouse them. Morning after morning he opens my ear that I may hear; [5]and I have not rebelled, have not turned back. [6]I gave my back to those who beat me, my cheeks to those who plucked my beard; my face I did not shield from buffets and spitting. [7]The Lord GOD is my help, therefore I am not disgraced; I

have set my face like flint, knowing that I shall not be put to shame.

Responsorial Psalm – Psalms 22:8-9, 17-18, 19-20, 23-24

R. (2a) My God, my God, why have you abandoned me?

8All who see me scoff at me;

they mock me with parted lips, they wag their heads:

9 "He relied on the LORD; let him deliver him,

let him rescue him, if he loves him."

R. My God, my God, why have you abandoned me?

17Indeed, many dogs surround me,

a pack of evildoers closes in upon me;

18They have pierced my hands and my feet;

I can count all my bones.

R. My God, my God, why have you abandoned me?

19They divide my garments among them,

and for my vesture they cast lots.

20But you, O LORD, be not far from me;

O my help, hasten to aid me.

R. My God, my God, why have you abandoned me?

23I will proclaim your name to my brethren;

in the midst of the assembly I will praise you:

24"You who fear the LORD, praise him;

all you descendants of Jacob, give glory to him;

revere him, all you descendants of Israel!"

R. My God, my God, why have you abandoned me?

Second Reading – Philippians 2:6-11

6Christ Jesus, though he was in the form of God, did not
regard equality with God something to be grasped. 7Rather, he
emptied himself, taking the form of a slave, coming in human

likeness; and found human in appearance, [8]he humbled
himself, becoming obedient to the point of death, even death
on a cross. [9]Because of this, God greatly exalted him and
bestowed on him the name which is above every name, [10]that
at the name of Jesus every knee should bend, of those in
heaven and on earth and under the earth, [11]and every tongue
confess that Jesus Christ is Lord, to the glory of God the
Father.

Verse Before the Gospel – Philippians 2:8-9

[8]Christ became obedient to the point of death, even death on
a cross. [9]Because of this, God greatly exalted him and
bestowed on him the name which is above every name.

Gospel – Matthew 26: 14 – 27: 66 or Matthew 27: 11-54

[14]Then went one of the twelve, who was called Judas Iscariot,
to the chief priests, [15]And said to them: What will you give me,
and I will deliver him unto you? But they appointed him thirty
pieces of silver. [16]And from thenceforth he sought opportunity
to betray him. [17]And on the first day of the Azymes, the
disciples came to Jesus, saying: Where wilt thou that we
prepare for thee to eat the pasch? [18]But Jesus said: Go ye into
the city to a certain man, and say to him: the master saith, My
time is near at hand, with thee I make the pasch with my
disciples. [19]And the disciples did as Jesus appointed to them,
and they prepared the pasch. [20]But when it was evening, he
sat down with his twelve disciples. [21]And whilst they were
eating, he said: Amen I say to you, that one of you is about to
betray me. [22]And they being very much troubled, began
everyone to say: Is it I, Lord? [23]But he answering, said: He that
dippeth his hand with me in the dish, he shall betray me. [24]The
Son of man indeed goeth, as it is written of him: but woe to
that man by whom the Son of man shall be betrayed: it were
better for him, if that man had not been born. [25]And Judas that
betrayed him, answering, said: Is it I, Rabbi? He saith to him:
Thou hast said it. [26]And whilst they were at supper, Jesus took
bread, and blessed, and broke: and gave to his disciples, and
said: Take ye, and eat. This is my body. [27]And taking the
chalice, he gave thanks, and gave to them, saying: Drink ye all
of this. [28]For this is my blood of the new testament, which shall
be shed for many unto remission of sins. [29]And I say to you, I

will not drink from henceforth of this fruit of the vine, until that
day when I shall drink it with you new in the kingdom of my
Father. 30And a hymn being said, they went out unto mount
Olivet. 31Then Jesus said to them: All you shall be scandalized
in me this night. For it is written: I will strike the shepherd, and
the sheep of the flock shall be dispersed. 32But after I shall be
risen again, I will go before you into Galilee. 33And Peter
answering, said to him: Although all shall be scandalized in
thee, I will never be scandalized. 34Jesus said to him: Amen I
say to thee, that in this night before the cock crow, thou wilt
deny me thrice. 35Peter saith to him: Yea, though I should die
with thee, I will not deny thee. And in like manner said all the
disciples. 36Then Jesus came with them into a country place
which is called Gethsemani; and he said to his disciples: Sit
you here, till I go yonder and pray. 37And taking with him Peter
and the two sons of Zebedee, he began to grow sorrowful and
to be sad. 38Then he saith to them: My soul is sorrowful even
unto death: stay you here, and watch with me. 39And going a
little further, he fell upon his face, praying, and saying: My
Father, if it be possible, let this chalice pass from me.
Nevertheless not as I will, but as thou wilt. 40And he cometh to
his disciples, and findeth them asleep, and he saith to Peter:
What? Could you not watch one hour with me? 41Watch ye,
and pray that ye enter not into temptation. The spirit indeed is
willing, but the flesh weak. 42Again the second time, he went
and prayed, saying: My Father, if this chalice may not pass
away, but I must drink it, thy will be done. 43And he cometh
again and findeth them sleeping: for their eyes were heavy.
44And leaving them, he went again: and he prayed the third
time, saying the selfsame word. 45Then he cometh to his
disciples, and saith to them: Sleep ye now and take your rest;
behold the hour is at hand, and the Son of man shall be
betrayed into the hands of sinners. 46Rise, let us go: behold he
is at hand that will betray me. 47As he yet spoke, behold
Judas, one of the twelve, came, and with him a great multitude
with swords and clubs, sent from the chief priests and the
ancients of the people. 48And he that betrayed him, gave them
a sign, saying: Whomsoever I shall kiss, that is he, hold him
fast. 49And forthwith coming to Jesus, he said: Hail, Rabbi.
And he kissed him. 50And Jesus said to him: Friend, where to
art thou come? Then they came up, and laid hands on Jesus,
and held him. 51And behold one of them that were with Jesus,
stretching forth his hand, drew out his sword: and striking the

servant of the high priest, cut off his ear. [52]Then Jesus saith to
him: Put up again thy sword into its place: for all that take the
sword shall perish with the sword. [53]Thinkest thou that I cannot
ask my Father, and he will give me presently more than twelve
legions of angels? [54]How then shall the scriptures be fulfilled,
that so it must be done? [55]In that same hour Jesus said to the
multitudes: You are come out as it were to a robber with
swords and clubs to apprehend me. I sat daily with you,
teaching in the temple, and you laid not hands on me. [56]Now
all this was done, that the scriptures of the prophets might be
fulfilled. Then the disciples all leaving him, fled. [57]But they
holding Jesus led him to Caiphas the high priest, where the
scribes and the ancients were assembled. [58]And Peter
followed him afar off, even to the court of the high priest. And
going in, he sat with the servants, that he might see the end.
[59]And the chief priests and the whole council sought false
witness against Jesus, that they might put him to death: [60]And
they found not, whereas many false witnesses had come in.
And last of all there came two false witnesses: [61]And they
said: This man said, I am able to destroy the temple of God,
and after three days to rebuild it. [62]And the high priest rising
up, said to him: Answerest thou nothing to the things which
these witness against thee? [63]But Jesus held his peace. And
the high priest said to him: I adjure thee by the living God, that
thou tell us if thou be the Christ the Son of God. [64]Jesus saith
to him: Thou hast said it. Nevertheless I say to you, hereafter
you shall see the Son of man sitting on the right hand of the
power of God, and coming in the clouds of heaven. [65]Then the
high priests rent his garments, saying: He hath blasphemed;
what further need have we of witnesses? Behold, now you
have heard the blasphemy: [66]What think you? But they
answering, said: He is guilty of death. [67]Then did they spit in
his face, and buffeted him: and others struck his face with the
palms of their hands, [68]Saying: Prophesy unto us, O Christ,
who is he that struck thee? [69]But Peter sat without in the court:
and there came to him a servant maid, saying: Thou also wast
with Jesus the Galilean. [70]But he denied before them all,
saying: I know not what thou sayest. [71]And as he went out of
the gate, another maid saw him, and she saith to them that
were there: This man also was with Jesus of Nazareth. [72]And
again he denied with an oath, I know not the man. [73]And after
a little while they came that stood by, and said to Peter: Surely
thou also art one of them; for even thy speech doth discover

thee. [74]Then he began to curse and to swear that he knew not
the man. And immediately the cock crew. [75]And Peter
remembered the word of Jesus which he had said: Before the
cock crow, thou wilt deny me thrice. And going forth, he wept
bitterly. [27:1]And when morning was come, all the chief priests
and ancients of the people took counsel against Jesus, that
they might put him to death. [2]And they brought him bound,
and delivered him to Pontius Pilate the governor. [3]Then Judas,
who betrayed him, seeing that he was condemned, repenting
himself, brought back the thirty pieces of silver to the chief
priests and ancients, [4]Saying: I have sinned in betraying
innocent blood. But they said: What is that to us? look thou to
it. [5]And casting down the pieces of silver in the temple, he
departed: and went and hanged himself with an halter. [6]But
the chief priests having taken the pieces of silver, said: It is not
lawful to put them into the *corbona*, because it is the price of
blood. [7]And after they had consulted together, they bought
with them the potter's field, to be a burying place for strangers.
[8]For this cause the field was called Haceldama, that is, The
field of blood, even to this day. [9]Then was fulfilled that which
was spoken by Jeremias the prophet, saying: And they took
the thirty pieces of silver, the price of him that was prized,
whom they prized of the children of Israel. [10]And they gave
them unto the potter's field, as the Lord appointed to me.
[11]And Jesus stood before the governor, and the governor
asked him, saying: Art thou the king of the Jews? Jesus saith
to him: Thou sayest it. [12]And when he was accused by the
chief priests and ancients, he answered nothing. [13]Then Pilate
saith to him: Dost not thou hear how great testimonies they
allege against thee? [14]And he answered him to never a word;
so that the governor wondered exceedingly. [15]Now upon the
solemn day the governor was accustomed to release to the
people one prisoner, whom they would. [16]And he had then a
notorious prisoner, that was called Barabbas. [17]They therefore
being gathered together, Pilate said: Whom will you that I
release to you, Barabbas, or Jesus that is called Christ? [18]For
he knew that for envy they had delivered him. [19]And as he was
sitting in the place of judgment, his wife sent to him, saying:
Have thou nothing to do with that just man; for I have suffered
many things this day in a dream because of him. [20]But the
chief priests and ancients persuaded the people, that they
should ask Barabbas, and make Jesus away. [21]And the
governor answering, said to them: Whether will you of the two

to be released unto you? But they said, Barabbas. 22Pilate
saith to them: What shall I do then with Jesus that is called
Christ? They say all: Let him be crucified. 23The governor said
to them: Why, what evil hath he done? But they cried out the
more, saying: Let him be crucified. 24And Pilate seeing that he
prevailed nothing, but that rather a tumult was made; taking
water washed his hands before the people, saying: I am
innocent of the blood of this just man; look you to it. 25And the
whole people answering, said: His blood be upon us and our
children. 26Then he released to them Barabbas, and having
scourged Jesus, delivered him unto them to be crucified.
27Then the soldiers of the governor taking Jesus into the hall,
gathered together unto him the whole band; 28And stripping
him, they put a scarlet cloak about him. 29And platting a crown
of thorns, they put it upon his head, and a reed in his right
hand. And bowing the knee before him, they mocked him,
saying: Hail, king of the Jews. 30And spitting upon him, they
took the reed, and struck his head. 31And after they had
mocked him, they took off the cloak from him, and put on him
his own garments, and led him away to crucify him. 32And
going out, they found a man of Cyrene, named Simon: him
they forced to take up his cross. 33And they came to the place
that is called Golgotha, which is the place of Calvary. 34And
they gave him wine to drink mingled with gall. And when he
had tasted, he would not drink. 35And after they had crucified
him, they divided his garments, casting lots; that it might be
fulfilled which was spoken by the prophet, saying: They
divided my garments among them; and upon my vesture they
cast lots. 36And they sat and watched him. 37And they put over
his head his cause written: **THIS IS JESUS THE KING OF
THE JEWS.** 38Then were crucified with him two thieves: one
on the right hand, and one on the left. 39And they that passed
by, blasphemed him, wagging their heads, 40And saying: Vah,
thou that destroyest the temple of God, and in three days dost
rebuild it: save thy own self: if thou be the Son of God, come
down from the cross. 41In like manner also the chief priests,
with the scribes and ancients, mocking, said: 42He saved
others; himself he cannot save. If he be the king of Israel, let
him now come down from the cross, and we will believe him.
43He trusted in God; let him now deliver him if he will have him;
for he said: I am the Son of God. 44And the selfsame thing the
thieves also, that were crucified with him, reproached him with.
45Now from the sixth hour there was darkness over the whole

earth, until the ninth hour. [46]And about the ninth hour Jesus
cried with a loud voice, saying: *Eli, Eli, lamma sabacthani*?
that is, My God, my God, why hast thou forsaken me? [47]And
some that stood there and heard, said: This man calleth Elias.
[48]And immediately one of them running took a sponge, and
filled it with vinegar; and put it on a reed, and gave him to
drink. [49]And the others said: Let be, let us see whether Elias
will come to deliver him. [50]And Jesus again crying with a loud
voice, yielded up the ghost. [51]And behold the veil of the temple
was rent in two from the top even to the bottom, and the earth
quaked, and the rocks were rent. [52]And the graves were
opened: and many bodies of the saints that had slept arose,
[53]And coming out of the tombs after his resurrection, came into
the holy city, and appeared to many. [54]Now the centurion and
they that were with him watching Jesus, having seen the
earthquake, and the things that were done, were sore afraid,
saying: Indeed this was the Son of God. [55]And there were
there many women afar off, who had followed Jesus from
Galilee, ministering unto him: [56]Among whom was Mary
Magdalen, and Mary the mother of James and Joseph, and
the mother of the sons of Zebedee. [57]And when it was
evening, there came a certain rich man of Arimathea, named
Joseph, who also himself was a disciple of Jesus. [58]He went to
Pilate, and asked the body of Jesus. Then Pilate commanded
that the body should be delivered. [59]And Joseph taking the
body, wrapped it up in a clean linen cloth. [60]And laid it in his
own new monument, which he had hewed out in a rock. And
he rolled a great stone to the door of the monument, and went
his way. [61]And there was there Mary Magdalen, and the other
Mary sitting over against the sepulchre. [62]And the next day,
which followed the day of preparation, the chief priests and the
Pharisees came together to Pilate, [63]Saying: Sir, we have
remembered, that that seducer said, while he was yet alive:
After three days I will rise again. [64]Command therefore the
sepulchre to be guarded until the third day: lest perhaps his
disciples come and steal him away, and say to the people: He
is risen from the dead; and the last error shall be worse than
the first. [65]Pilate saith to them: You have a guard; go, guard it
as you know. [66]And they departing, made the sepulchre sure,
sealing the stone, and setting guards.

Or

[11]And Jesus stood before the governor, and the governor
asked him, saying: Art thou the king of the Jews? Jesus saith
to him: Thou sayest it. [12]And when he was accused by the
chief priests and ancients, he answered nothing. [13]Then Pilate
saith to him: Dost not thou hear how great testimonies they
allege against thee? [14]And he answered him to never a word;
so that the governor wondered exceedingly. [15]Now upon the
solemn day the governor was accustomed to release to the
people one prisoner, whom they would. [16]And he had then a
notorious prisoner, that was called Barabbas. [17]They therefore
being gathered together, Pilate said: Whom will you that I
release to you, Barabbas, or Jesus that is called Christ? [18]For
he knew that for envy they had delivered him. [19]And as he was
sitting in the place of judgment, his wife sent to him, saying:
Have thou nothing to do with that just man; for I have suffered
many things this day in a dream because of him. [20]But the
chief priests and ancients persuaded the people, that they
should ask Barabbas, and make Jesus away. [21]And the
governor answering, said to them: Whether will you of the two
to be released unto you? But they said, Barabbas. [22]Pilate
saith to them: What shall I do then with Jesus that is called
Christ? They say all: Let him be crucified. [23]The governor said
to them: Why, what evil hath he done? But they cried out the
more, saying: Let him be crucified. [24]And Pilate seeing that he
prevailed nothing, but that rather a tumult was made; taking
water washed his hands before the people, saying: I am
innocent of the blood of this just man; look you to it. [25]And the
whole people answering, said: His blood be upon us and our
children. [26]Then he released to them Barabbas, and having
scourged Jesus, delivered him unto them to be crucified.
[27]Then the soldiers of the governor taking Jesus into the hall,
gathered together unto him the whole band; [28]And stripping
him, they put a scarlet cloak about him. [29]And platting a crown
of thorns, they put it upon his head, and a reed in his right
hand. And bowing the knee before him, they mocked him,
saying: Hail, king of the Jews. [30]And spitting upon him, they
took the reed, and struck his head. [31]And after they had
mocked him, they took off the cloak from him, and put on him
his own garments, and led him away to crucify him. [32]And
going out, they found a man of Cyrene, named Simon: him
they forced to take up his cross. [33]And they came to the place
that is called Golgotha, which is the place of Calvary. [34]And
they gave him wine to drink mingled with gall. And when he

had tasted, he would not drink. [35]And after they had crucified
him, they divided his garments, casting lots; that it might be
fulfilled which was spoken by the prophet, saying: They
divided my garments among them; and upon my vesture they
cast lots. [36]And they sat and watched him. [37]And they put over
his head his cause written: **THIS IS JESUS THE KING OF
THE JEWS.** [38]Then were crucified with him two thieves: one
on the right hand, and one on the left. [39]And they that passed
by, blasphemed him, wagging their heads, [40]And saying: Vah,
thou that destroyest the temple of God, and in three days dost
rebuild it: save thy own self: if thou be the Son of God, come
down from the cross. [41]In like manner also the chief priests,
with the scribes and ancients, mocking, said: [42]He saved
others; himself he cannot save. If he be the king of Israel, let
him now come down from the cross, and we will believe him.
[43]He trusted in God; let him now deliver him if he will have him;
for he said: I am the Son of God. [44]And the selfsame thing the
thieves also, that were crucified with him, reproached him with.
[45]Now from the sixth hour there was darkness over the whole
earth, until the ninth hour. [46]And about the ninth hour Jesus
cried with a loud voice, saying: Eli, Eli, lamma sabacthani?
that is, My God, my God, why hast thou forsaken me? [47]And
some that stood there and heard, said: This man calleth Elias.
[48]And immediately one of them running took a sponge, and
filled it with vinegar; and put it on a reed, and gave him to
drink. [49]And the others said: Let be, let us see whether Elias
will come to deliver him. [50]And Jesus again crying with a loud
voice, yielded up the ghost. [51]And behold the veil of the temple
was rent in two from the top even to the bottom, and the earth
quaked, and the rocks were rent. [52]And the graves were
opened: and many bodies of the saints that had slept arose,
[53]And coming out of the tombs after his resurrection, came into
the holy city, and appeared to many. [54]Now the centurion and
they that were with him watching Jesus, having seen the
earthquake, and the things that were done, were sore afraid,
saying: Indeed this was the Son of God.

Monday April 3, 2023

Monday of Holy Week

First Reading – Isaiah 42:1-7

1Here is my servant whom I uphold, my chosen one with
whom I am pleased, Upon whom I have put my Spirit; he shall
bring forth justice to the nations, 2Not crying out, not shouting,
not making his voice heard in the street. 3A bruised reed he
shall not break, and a smoldering wick he shall not quench,
4Until he establishes justice on the earth; the coastlands will
wait for his teaching. 5Thus says God, the LORD, who created
the heavens and stretched them out, who spreads out the
earth with its crops, Who gives breath to its people and spirit
to those who walk on it: 6I, the LORD, have called you for the
victory of justice, I have grasped you by the hand; I formed
you, and set you as a covenant of the people, a light for the
nations, 7To open the eyes of the blind, to bring out prisoners
from confinement, and from the dungeon, those who live in
darkness.

Responsorial Psalm – Psalms 27:1, 2, 3, 13-14

R. (1a) The Lord is my light and my salvation.

1 The LORD is my light and my salvation;

whom should I fear?

The LORD is my life's refuge;

of whom should I be afraid?

R. The Lord is my light and my salvation.

2 When evildoers come at me

to devour my flesh,

My foes and my enemies

themselves stumble and fall.

R. The Lord is my light and my salvation.

3 Though an army encamp against me,

my heart will not fear;

Though war be waged upon me,

even then will I trust.

R. The Lord is my light and my salvation.

13 I believe that I shall see the bounty of the LORD

in the land of the living.

14 Wait for the LORD with courage;

be stouthearted, and wait for the LORD.

R. The Lord is my light and my salvation.

Verse Before the Gospel

Hail to you, our King; you alone are compassionate with our faults.

Gospel – John 12:1-11

1Six days before Passover Jesus came to Bethany, where
Lazarus was, whom Jesus had raised from the dead. 2They
gave a dinner for him there, and Martha served, while Lazarus
was one of those reclining at table with him. 3Mary took a liter
of costly perfumed oil made from genuine aromatic nard and
anointed the feet of Jesus and dried them with her hair; the
house was filled with the fragrance of the oil. 4Then Judas the
Iscariot, one of his disciples, and the one who would betray
him, said, 5"Why was this oil not sold for three hundred days'
wages and given to the poor?" 6He said this not because he
cared about the poor but because he was a thief and held the
money bag and used to steal the contributions. 7So Jesus
said, "Leave her alone. Let her keep this for the day of my
burial. 8You always have the poor with you, but you do not
always have me." 9The large crowd of the Jews found out that
he was there and came, not only because of him, but also to
see Lazarus, whom he had raised from the dead. 10And the
chief priests plotted to kill Lazarus too, 11because many of the
Jews were turning away and believing in Jesus because of
him.

Tuesday April 4, 2023

Tuesday of Holy Week

First Reading – Isaiah 49:1-6

1 Hear me, O islands, listen, O distant peoples. The LORD
called me from birth, from my mother's womb he gave me my
name. 2 He made of me a sharp-edged sword and concealed
me in the shadow of his arm. He made me a polished arrow, in
his quiver he hid me. 3 You are my servant, he said to me,
Israel, through whom I show my glory. 4 Though I thought I had
toiled in vain, and for nothing, uselessly, spent my strength,
Yet my reward is with the LORD, my recompense is with my
God. 5 For now the LORD has spoken who formed me as his
servant from the womb, That Jacob may be brought back to
him and Israel gathered to him; And I am made glorious in the
sight of the LORD, and my God is now my strength! 6 It is too
little, he says, for you to be my servant, to raise up the tribes
of Jacob, and restore the survivors of Israel; I will make you a
light to the nations, that my salvation may reach to the ends of
the earth.

Responsorial Psalm – Psalms 71:1-2, 3-4A,5AB-6AB,15and 17

R. (see 15ab) **I will sing of your salvation.**

1 In you, O LORD, I take refuge;

let me never be put to shame.

2 In your justice rescue me, and deliver me;

incline your ear to me, and save me.

R. I will sing of your salvation.

3 Be my rock of refuge,

a stronghold to give me safety,

for you are my rock and my fortress.

4A O my God, rescue me from the hand of the wicked.

R. I will sing of your salvation.

5AB For you are my hope, O Lord;

my trust, O God, from my youth.

[6AB] On you I depend from birth;

from my mother's womb you are my strength.

R. I will sing of your salvation.

[15] My mouth shall declare your justice,

day by day your salvation.

[17] O God, you have taught me from my youth,

and till the present I proclaim your wondrous deeds.

R. I will sing of your salvation.

Verse Before the Gospel

Hail to you, our King, obedient to the Father; you were led to your crucifixion like a gentle lamb to the slaughter.

Gospel – John 13:21-33, 36-38

[21]Reclining at table with his disciples, Jesus was deeply
troubled and testified, "Amen, amen, I say to you, one of you
will betray me." [22]The disciples looked at one another, at a
loss as to whom he meant. [23]One of his disciples, the one
whom Jesus loved, was reclining at Jesus' side. [24]So Simon
Peter nodded to him to find out whom he meant. [25]He leaned
back against Jesus' chest and said to him, "Master, who is it?"
[26]Jesus answered, "It is the one to whom I hand the morsel
after I have dipped it." So he dipped the morsel and took it and
handed it to Judas, son of Simon the Iscariot. [27]After Judas
took the morsel, Satan entered him. So Jesus said to him,
"What you are going to do, do quickly." [28]Now none of those
reclining at table realized why he said this to him. [29]Some
thought that since Judas kept the money bag, Jesus had told
him, "Buy what we need for the feast," or to give something to
the poor. [30]So Judas took the morsel and left at once. And it
was night. [31]When he had left, Jesus said, "Now is the Son of
Man glorified, and God is glorified in him. [32]If God is glorified in
him, God will also glorify him in himself, and he will glorify him
at once. [33]My children, I will be with you only a little while
longer. You will look for me, and as I told the Jews, 'Where I
go you cannot come,' so now I say it to you." [36]Simon Peter
said to him, "Master, where are you going?" Jesus answered
him, "Where I am going, you cannot follow me now, though

you will follow later." [37]Peter said to him, "Master, why can I
not follow you now? I will lay down my life for you." [38]Jesus
answered, "Will you lay down your life for me? Amen, amen, I
say to you, the cock will not crow before you deny me three
times."

Wednesday April 5, 2023

Wednesday of Holy Week

First Reading – Isaiah 50:4-9A

[4]The Lord GOD has given me a well-trained tongue, That I
might know how to speak to the weary a word that will rouse
them. Morning after morning he opens my ear that I may hear;
[5]And I have not rebelled, have not turned back. [6]I gave my
back to those who beat me, my cheeks to those who plucked
my beard; My face I did not shield from buffets and spitting.
[7]The Lord GOD is my help, therefore I am not disgraced; I
have set my face like flint, knowing that I shall not be put to
shame. [8]He is near who upholds my right; if anyone wishes to
oppose me, let us appear together. Who disputes my right?
Let him confront me. [9]See, the Lord GOD is my help; who will
prove me wrong?

Responsorial Psalm – Psalms 69:8-10, 21-22, 31 and 33-34

R. (14c) Lord, in your great love, answer me.

[8] For your sake I bear insult,

and shame covers my face.

[9] I have become an outcast to my brothers,

a stranger to my mother's sons,

[10] because zeal for your house consumes me,

and the insults of those who blaspheme you fall upon me.

R. Lord, in your great love, answer me.

[21] Insult has broken my heart, and I am weak,

I looked for sympathy, but there was none;

for consolers, not one could I find.

22 Rather they put gall in my food,

and in my thirst they gave me vinegar to drink.

R. Lord, in your great love, answer me.

31 I will praise the name of God in song,

and I will glorify him with thanksgiving:

33 “See, you lowly ones, and be glad;

you who seek God, may your hearts revive!

34 For the LORD hears the poor,

and his own who are in bonds he spurns not.”

R. Lord, in your great love, answer me.

Verse Before the Gospel

Hail to you, our King; you alone are compassionate with our errors.

Or

Hail to you, our King, obedient to the Father; you were led to your crucifixion like a gentle lamb to the slaughter.

Gospel – Matthew 26:14-25

14One of the Twelve, who was called Judas Iscariot, went to
the chief priests 15and said, “What are you willing to give me if
I hand him over to you?” They paid him thirty pieces of silver,
16and from that time on he looked for an opportunity to hand
him over. 17On the first day of the Feast of Unleavened Bread,
the disciples approached Jesus and said, “Where do you want
us to prepare for you to eat the Passover?” 18He said, “Go into
the city to a certain man and tell him, ‘The teacher says, “My
appointed time draws near; in your house I shall celebrate the
Passover with my disciples.”’” 19The disciples then did as
Jesus had ordered, and prepared the Passover. 20When it was
evening, he reclined at table with the Twelve. 21And while they
were eating, he said, “Amen, I say to you, one of you will
betray me.” 22Deeply distressed at this, they began to say to
him one after another, “Surely it is not I, Lord?” 23He said in
reply, “He who has dipped his hand into the dish with me is the
one who will betray me. 24The Son of Man indeed goes, as it is
written of him, but woe to that man by whom the Son of Man is

betrayed. It would be better for that man if he had never been born." [25]Then Judas, his betrayer, said in reply, "Surely it is not I, Rabbi?" He answered, "You have said so."

Thursday April 6, 2023

Holy Thursday of the Lord's Supper

First Reading – Exodus 12:1-8, 11-14

[1]The LORD said to Moses and Aaron in the land of Egypt,
[2]"This month shall stand at the head of your calendar; you
shall reckon it the first month of the year. [3]Tell the whole
community of Israel: On the tenth of this month every one of
your families must procure for itself a lamb, one apiece for
each household. [4]If a family is too small for a whole lamb, it
shall join the nearest household in procuring one and shall
share in the lamb in proportion to the number of persons who
partake of it. [5]The lamb must be a year-old male and without
blemish. You may take it from either the sheep or the goats.
[6]You shall keep it until the fourteenth day of this month, and
then, with the whole assembly of Israel present, it shall be
slaughtered during the evening twilight. [7]They shall take some
of its blood and apply it to the two doorposts and the lintel of
every house in which they partake of the lamb. [8]That same
night they shall eat its roasted flesh with unleavened bread
and bitter herbs. [11]"This is how you are to eat it: with your loins
girt, sandals on your feet and your staff in hand, you shall eat
like those who are in flight. It is the Passover of the LORD.
[12]For on this same night I will go through Egypt, striking down
every firstborn of the land, both man and beast, and executing
judgment on all the gods of Egypt-I, the LORD! [13]But the blood
will mark the houses where you are. Seeing the blood, I will
pass over you; thus, when I strike the land of Egypt, no
destructive blow will come upon you. [14]"This day shall be a
memorial feast for you, which all your generations shall
celebrate with pilgrimage to the LORD, as a perpetual
institution."

Responsorial Psalm – Psalms 116:12-13, 15-16BC, 17-18

R. (cf. 1 Cor 10:16) **Our blessing-cup is a communion with the Blood of Christ.**

12 How shall I make a return to the LORD

for all the good he has done for me?

13 The cup of salvation I will take up,

and I will call upon the name of the LORD.

R. Our blessing-cup is a communion with the Blood of Christ.

15 Precious in the eyes of the LORD

is the death of his faithful ones.

16BC I am your servant, the son of your handmaid;

you have loosed my bonds.

R. Our blessing-cup is a communion with the Blood of Christ.

17 To you will I offer sacrifice of thanksgiving,

and I will call upon the name of the LORD.

18 My vows to the LORD I will pay

in the presence of all his people.

R. Our blessing-cup is a communion with the Blood of Christ.

Second Reading – 1 Corinthians 11:23-26

Brothers and sisters: 23I received from the Lord what I also
handed on to you, that the Lord Jesus, on the night he was
handed over, took bread, 24and, after he had given thanks,
broke it and said, "This is my body that is for you. Do this in
remembrance of me." 25In the same way also the cup, after
supper, saying, "This cup is the new covenant in my blood. Do
this, as often as you drink it, in remembrance of me." 26For as
often as you eat this bread and drink the cup, you proclaim the
death of the Lord until he comes.

Verse Before The Gospel – John 13:34

34 I give you a new commandment, says the Lord: love one another as I have loved you.

Gospel – John 13:1-15

[1]Before the feast of Passover, Jesus knew that his hour had come to pass from this world to the Father. He loved his own in the world and he loved them to the end. [2]The devil had already induced Judas, son of Simon the Iscariot, to hand him over. So, during supper, [3]fully aware that the Father had put everything into his power and that he had come from God and was returning to God, [4]he rose from supper and took off his outer garments. He took a towel and tied it around his waist. [5]Then he poured water into a basin and began to wash the disciples' feet and dry them with the towel around his waist. [6]He came to Simon Peter, who said to him, “Master, are you going to wash my feet?” [7]Jesus answered and said to him, “What I am doing, you do not understand now, but you will understand later.” [8]Peter said to him, “You will never wash my feet.” Jesus answered him, “Unless I wash you, you will have no inheritance with me.” [9]Simon Peter said to him, “Master, then not only my feet, but my hands and head as well.” [10]Jesus said to him, “Whoever has bathed has no need except to have his feet washed, for he is clean all over; so you are clean, but not all.” [11]For he knew who would betray him; for this reason, he said, “Not all of you are clean.” [12]So when he had washed their feet and put his garments back on and reclined at table again, he said to them, “Do you realize what I have done for you? [13]You call me ‘teacher’ and ‘master,’ and rightly so, for indeed I am. [14]If I, therefore, the master and teacher, have washed your feet, you ought to wash one another's feet. [15]I have given you a model to follow, so that as I have done for you, you should also do.”

Friday April 7, 2023

Good Friday of the Lord's Passion

First Reading – Isaiah 52:13-53:12

[13]See, my servant shall prosper, he shall be raised high and greatly exalted. [14]Even as many were amazed at him so marred was his look beyond human semblance and his appearance beyond that of the sons of man [15]so shall he startle many nations, because of him kings shall stand speechless; for those who have not been told shall see, those who have not heard shall ponder it.[1]Who would believe what we have heard? To whom has the arm of the LORD been

revealed? 2He grew up like a sapling before him, like a shoot from the parched earth; there was in him no stately bearing to make us look at him, nor appearance that would attract us to him. 3He was spurned and avoided by people, a man of suffering, accustomed to infirmity, one of those from whom people hide their faces, spurned, and we held him in no esteem. 4Yet it was our infirmities that he bore, our sufferings that he endured, while we thought of him as stricken, as one smitten by God and afflicted. 5But he was pierced for our offenses, crushed for our sins; upon him was the chastisement that makes us whole, by his stripes we were healed. 6We had all gone astray like sheep, each following his own way; but the LORD laid upon him the guilt of us all. 7Though he was harshly treated, he submitted and opened not his mouth; like a lamb led to the slaughter or a sheep before the shearers, he was silent and opened not his mouth. 8Oppressed and condemned, he was taken away, and who would have thought any more of his destiny? When he was cut off from the land of the living, and smitten for the sin of his people, 9a grave was assigned him among the wicked and a burial place with evildoers, though he had done no wrong nor spoken any falsehood. 10But the LORD was pleased to crush him in infirmity. If he gives his life as an offering for sin, he shall see his descendants in a long life, and the will of the LORD shall be accomplished through him. 11Because of his affliction he shall see the light in fullness of days; through his suffering, my servant shall justify many, and their guilt he shall bear. 12 Therefore I will give him his portion among the great, and he shall divide the spoils with the mighty, because he surrendered himself to death and was counted among the wicked; and he shall take away the sins of many, and win pardon for their offenses.

Responsorial Psalm – Psalms 31:2, 6, 12-13, 15-16, 17, 25

R. (Luke 23:46) **Father, into your hands I commend my spirit.**

2 In you, O LORD, I take refuge;

let me never be put to shame.

In your justice rescue me.

6Into your hands I commend my spirit;

you will redeem me, O LORD, O faithful God.

R. Father, into your hands I commend my spirit.

[12]For all my foes I am an object of reproach,

a laughingstock to my neighbors, and a dread to my friends;

they who see me abroad flee from me.

[13]I am forgotten like the unremembered dead;

I am like a dish that is broken.

R. Father, into your hands I commend my spirit.

[15]But my trust is in you, O LORD;

I say, "You are my God.

[16]In your hands is my destiny; rescue me

from the clutches of my enemies and my persecutors."

R. Father, into your hands I commend my spirit.

[17]Let your face shine upon your servant;

save me in your kindness.

[25]Take courage and be stouthearted,

all you who hope in the LORD.

R. Father, into your hands I commend my spirit.

Second Reading – Hebrews 4:14-16; 5:7-9

[14]Brothers and sisters: Since we have a great high priest who
has passed through the heavens, Jesus, the Son of God, let
us hold fast to our confession. [15]For we do not have a high
priest who is unable to sympathize with our weaknesses, but
one who has similarly been tested in every way, yet without
sin. [16]So let us confidently approach the throne of grace to
receive mercy and to find grace for timely help. [7]In the days
when Christ was in the flesh, he offered prayers and
supplications with loud cries and tears to the one who was
able to save him from death, and he was heard because of his
reverence. [8]Son though he was, he learned obedience from
what he suffered; [9]and when he was made perfect, he became
the source of eternal salvation for all who obey him.

Verse Before The Gospel – Philippians 2:8-9

[8]Christ became obedient to the point of death, even death on
a cross. [9]Because of this, God greatly exalted him and
bestowed on him the name which is above every other name.

Gospel – John 18:1-19:42

[1]Jesus went out with his disciples across the Kidron valley to
where there was a garden, into which he and his disciples
entered. [2]Judas his betrayer also knew the place, because
Jesus had often met there with his disciples. [3]So Judas got a
band of soldiers and guards from the chief priests and the
Pharisees and went there with lanterns, torches, and
weapons. [4]Jesus, knowing everything that was going to
happen to him, went out and said to them, "Whom are you
looking for?" [5]They answered him, "Jesus the Nazorean." He
said to them, "**I AM**." Judas his betrayer was also with them. [6]
When he said to them, "I AM," they turned away and fell to the
ground. [7]So he again asked them, "Whom are you looking
for?" They said, "Jesus the Nazorean." [8]Jesus answered, "I
told you that I AM. So if you are looking for me, let these men
go." [9]This was to fulfill what he had said, "I have not lost any of
those you gave me." [10]Then Simon Peter, who had a sword,
drew it, struck the high priest's slave, and cut off his right ear.
The slave's name was Malchus. [11]Jesus said to Peter, "Put
your sword into its scabbard. Shall I not drink the cup that the
Father gave me?" [12]So the band of soldiers, the tribune, and
the Jewish guards seized Jesus, bound him, [13]and brought
him to Annas first. He was the father-in-law of Caiaphas, who
was high priest that year. [14]It was Caiaphas who had
counseled the Jews that it was better that one man should die
rather than the people. [15]Simon Peter and another disciple
followed Jesus. Now the other disciple was known to the high
priest, and he entered the courtyard of the high priest with
Jesus. [16]But Peter stood at the gate outside. So the other
disciple, the acquaintance of the high priest, went out and
spoke to the gatekeeper and brought Peter in. [17]Then the maid
who was the gatekeeper said to Peter, "You are not one of this
man's disciples, are you?" He said, "I am not." [18]Now the
slaves and the guards were standing around a charcoal fire
that they had made, because it was cold, and were warming
themselves. Peter was also standing there keeping warm.
[19]The high priest questioned Jesus about his disciples and

about his doctrine. 20Jesus answered him, “I have spoken
publicly to the world. I have always taught in a synagogue or in
the temple area where all the Jews gather, and in secret I
have said nothing. 21Why ask me? Ask those who heard me
what I said to them. They know what I said.” 22When he had
said this, one of the temple guards standing there struck Jesus
and said, “Is this the way you answer the high priest?” 23 Jesus
answered him, “If I have spoken wrongly, testify to the wrong;
but if I have spoken rightly, why do you strike me?” 24Then
Annas sent him bound to Caiaphas the high priest. 25Now
Simon Peter was standing there keeping warm. And they said
to him, “You are not one of his disciples, are you?” He denied
it and said, “I am not.” 26One of the slaves of the high priest, a
relative of the one whose ear Peter had cut off, said, “Didn’t I
see you in the garden with him?” 27Again Peter denied it. And
immediately the cock crowed. 28Then they brought Jesus from
Caiaphas to the praetorium. It was morning. And they
themselves did not enter the praetorium, in order not to be
defiled so that they could eat the Passover. 29So Pilate came
out to them and said, “What charge do you bring against this
man?” 30They answered and said to him, “If he were not a
criminal, we would not have handed him over to you.” 31At this,
Pilate said to them, “Take him yourselves, and judge him
according to your law.” The Jews answered him, “We do not
have the right to execute anyone, “ 32 in order that the word of
Jesus might be fulfilled that he said indicating the kind of
death he would die. 33So Pilate went back into the praetorium
and summoned Jesus and said to him, “Are you the King of
the Jews?” 34Jesus answered, “Do you say this on your own or
have others told you about me?” 35Pilate answered, “I am not
a Jew, am I? Your own nation and the chief priests handed
you over to me. What have you done?” 36Jesus answered, “My
kingdom does not belong to this world. If my kingdom did
belong to this world, my attendants would be fighting to keep
me from being handed over to the Jews. But as it is, my
kingdom is not here.” 37So Pilate said to him, “Then you are a
king?” Jesus answered, “You say I am a king. For this I was
born and for this I came into the world, to testify to the truth.
Everyone who belongs to the truth listens to my voice.” 38Pilate
said to him, “What is truth?” When he had said this, he again
went out to the Jews and said to them, “I find no guilt in him.
39But you have a custom that I release one prisoner to you at
Passover. Do you want me to release to you the King of the

Jews?” [40]They cried out again, “Not this one but Barabbas!”
Now Barabbas was a revolutionary. [1]Then Pilate took Jesus
and had him scourged. [2]And the soldiers wove a crown out of
thorns and placed it on his head, and clothed him in a purple
cloak, [3]and they came to him and said, “Hail, King of the
Jews!” And they struck him repeatedly. [4]Once more Pilate
went out and said to them, “Look, I am bringing him out to you,
so that you may know that I find no guilt in him.” [5] So Jesus
came out, wearing the crown of thorns and the purple cloak.
And he said to them, “Behold, the man!” [6]When the chief
priests and the guards saw him they cried out, “Crucify him,
crucify him!” Pilate said to them, “Take him yourselves and
crucify him. I find no guilt in him.” [7]The Jews answered, “We
have a law, and according to that law he ought to die, because
he made himself the Son of God.” [8]Now when Pilate heard this
statement, he became even more afraid, [9]and went back into
the praetorium and said to Jesus, “Where are you from?”
Jesus did not answer him. [10]So Pilate said to him, “Do you not
speak to me? Do you not know that I have power to release
you and I have power to crucify you?” [11]Jesus answered him,
“You would have no power over me if it had not been given to
you from above. For this reason the one who handed me over
to you has the greater sin.” [12]Consequently, Pilate tried to
release him; but the Jews cried out, “If you release him, you
are not a Friend of Caesar. Everyone who makes himself a
king opposes Caesar.” [13]When Pilate heard these words he
brought Jesus out and seated him on the judge’s bench in the
place called Stone Pavement, in Hebrew, Gabbatha. [14]It was
preparation day for Passover, and it was about noon. And he
said to the Jews, “Behold, your king!” [15]They cried out, “Take
him away, take him away! Crucify him!” Pilate said to them,
“Shall I crucify your king?” The chief priests answered, “We
have no king but Caesar.” [16] Then he handed him over to them
to be crucified. So they took Jesus, [17]and, carrying the cross
himself, he went out to what is called the Place of the Skull, in
Hebrew, Golgotha. [18] There they crucified him, and with him
two others, one on either side, with Jesus in the middle.
[19]Pilate also had an inscription written and put on the cross. It
read, “Jesus the Nazorean, the King of the Jews.” [20]Now many
of the Jews read this inscription, because the place where
Jesus was crucified was near the city; and it was written in
Hebrew, Latin, and Greek. [21]So the chief priests of the Jews
said to Pilate, “Do not write ‘The King of the Jews,’ but that he

said, 'I am the King of the Jews'." [22]Pilate answered, "What I
have written, I have written." [23]When the soldiers had crucified
Jesus, they took his clothes and divided them into four shares,
a share for each soldier. They also took his tunic, but the tunic
was seamless, woven in one piece from the top down. [24]So
they said to one another, "Let's not tear it, but cast lots for it to
see whose it will be, " in order that the passage of Scripture
might be fulfilled that says: They divided my garments among
them, and for my vesture they cast lots. This is what the
soldiers did. [25]Standing by the cross of Jesus were his mother
and his mother's sister, Mary the wife of Clopas, and Mary of
Magdala. [26]When Jesus saw his mother and the disciple there
whom he loved he said to his mother, "Woman, behold, your
son." [27]Then he said to the disciple, "Behold, your mother."
And from that hour the disciple took her into his home. [28]After
this, aware that everything was now finished, in order that the
Scripture might be fulfilled, Jesus said, "I thirst." [29]There was a
vessel filled with common wine. So they put a sponge soaked
in wine on a sprig of hyssop and put it up to his mouth. [30]When
Jesus had taken the wine, he said, "It is finished." And bowing
his head, he handed over the spirit.

During Good Friday Readings all kneel and pause for a short time.

[31]Now since it was preparation day, in order that the bodies
might not remain on the cross on the Sabbath, for the Sabbath
day of that week was a solemn one, the Jews asked Pilate
that their legs be broken and that they be taken down. [32]So the
soldiers came and broke the legs of the first and then of the
other one who was crucified with Jesus. [33]But when they came
to Jesus and saw that he was already dead, they did not break
his legs, [34]but one soldier thrust his lance into his side, and
immediately blood and water flowed out. [35]An eyewitness has
testified, and his testimony is true; he knows that he is
speaking the truth, so that you also may come to believe. [36]For
this happened so that the Scripture passage might be fulfilled:
Not a bone of it will be broken. [37]And again another passage
says: They will look upon him whom they have pierced. [38]After
this, Joseph of Arimathea, secretly a disciple of Jesus for fear
of the Jews, asked Pilate if he could remove the body of
Jesus. And Pilate permitted it. So he came and took his body.
[39]Nicodemus, the one who had first come to him at night, also
came bringing a mixture of myrrh and aloes weighing about

one hundred pounds. [40]They took the body of Jesus and
bound it with burial cloths along with the spices, according to
the Jewish burial custom. [41]Now in the place where he had
been crucified there was a garden, and in the garden a new
tomb, in which no one had yet been buried. [42]So they laid
Jesus there because of the Jewish preparation day; for the
tomb was close by.

Saturday April 8, 2023

Holy Saturday Night of Easter – Easter Vigil

First Reading – Genesis 1:1-2:2

[1]In the beginning, when God created the heavens and the
earth, [2]the earth was a formless wasteland, and darkness
covered the abyss, while a mighty wind swept over the waters.
[3]Then God said, "Let there be light," and there was light. [4]God
saw how good the light was. God then separated the light from
the darkness. [5]God called the light "day," and the darkness he
called "night." Thus evening came, and morning followed – the
first day. [6]Then God said, "Let there be a dome in the middle
of the waters, to separate one body of water from the other."
And so it happened: [7]God made the dome, and it separated
the water above the dome from the water below it. [8]God called
the dome "the sky." Evening came, and morning followed – the
second day. [9]Then God said, "Let the water under the sky be
gathered into a single basin, so that the dry land may appear."
And so it happened: the water under the sky was gathered
into its basin, and the dry land appeared. [10]God called the dry
land "the earth, " and the basin of the water he called "the
sea." God saw how good it was. [11]Then God said, "Let the
earth bring forth vegetation: every kind of plant that bears
seed and every kind of fruit tree on earth that bears fruit with
its seed in it." And so it happened: [12] the earth brought forth
every kind of plant that bears seed and every kind of fruit tree
on earth that bears fruit with its seed in it. God saw how good
it was. [13]Evening came, and morning followed – the third day.
[14]Then God said: "Let there be lights in the dome of the sky, to
separate day from night. Let them mark the fixed times, the
days and the years, [15]and serve as luminaries in the dome of
the sky, to shed light upon the earth." And so it happened:
[16]God made the two great lights, the greater one to govern the
day, and the lesser one to govern the night; and he made the

stars. 17God set them in the dome of the sky, to shed light
upon the earth, 18to govern the day and the night, and to
separate the light from the darkness. God saw how good it
was. 19Evening came, and morning followed – the fourth day.
20Then God said, “Let the water teem with an abundance of
living creatures, and on the earth let birds fly beneath the
dome of the sky.” And so it happened: 21God created the great
sea monsters and all kinds of swimming creatures with which
the water teems, and all kinds of winged birds. God saw how
good it was, 22and God blessed them, saying, “Be fertile,
multiply, and fill the water of the seas; and let the birds multiply
on the earth.” 23Evening came, and morning followed – the fifth
day. 24Then God said, “Let the earth bring forth all kinds of
living creatures: cattle, creeping things, and wild animals of all
kinds.” And so it happened: 25God made all kinds of wild
animals, all kinds of cattle, and all kinds of creeping things of
the earth. God saw how good it was. 26Then God said: “Let us
make man in our image, after our likeness. Let them have
dominion over the fish of the sea, the birds of the air, and the
cattle, and over all the wild animals and all the creatures that
crawl on the ground.” 27God created man in his image; in the
image of God he created him; male and female he created
them. 28God blessed them, saying: “Be fertile and multiply; fill
the earth and subdue it. Have dominion over the fish of the
sea, the birds of the air, and all the living things that move on
the earth.” 29God also said: “See, I give you every seed-
bearing plant all over the earth and every tree that has seed-
bearing fruit on it to be your food; 30and to all the animals of
the land, all the birds of the air, and all the living creatures that
crawl on the ground, I give all the green plants for food.” And
so it happened. 31God looked at everything he had made, and
he found it very good. Evening came, and morning followed –
the sixth day. 1 Thus the heavens and the earth and all their
array were completed. 2Since on the seventh day God was
finished with the work he had been doing, he rested on the
seventh day from all the work he had undertaken.

Or Genesis 1:1, 26-31A

1In the beginning, when God created the heavens and the
earth, 26God said: “Let us make man in our image, after our
likeness. Let them have dominion over the fish of the sea, the
birds of the air, and the cattle, and over all the wild animals
and all the creatures that crawl on the ground.” 27God created

man in his image; in the image of God he created him; male
and female he created them. [28]God blessed them, saying: "Be
fertile and multiply; fill the earth and subdue it. Have dominion
over the fish of the sea, the birds of the air, and all the living
things that move on the earth." [29] God also said: "See, I give
you every seed-bearing plant all over the earth and every tree
that has seed-bearing fruit on it to be your food; [30]and to all the
animals of the land, all the birds of the air, and all the living
creatures that crawl on the ground, I give all the green plants
for food." And so it happened. [31A]God looked at everything he
had made, and found it very good.

Responsorial Psalm – Psalms 104:1-2, 5-6, 10,12,13-14, 24, 35

R. (30) Lord, send out your Spirit, and renew the face of the earth.

[1]Bless the LORD, O my soul!

O LORD, my God, you are great indeed!

[2]You are clothed with majesty and glory,

robed in light as with a cloak.

R. Lord, send out your Spirit, and renew the face of the earth.

[5]You fixed the earth upon its foundation,

not to be moved forever;

[6]with the ocean, as with a garment, you covered it;

above the mountains the waters stood.

R. Lord, send out your Spirit, and renew the face of the earth.

[10]You send forth springs into the watercourses

that wind among the mountains.

[12]Beside them the birds of heaven dwell;

from among the branches they send forth their song.

R. Lord, send out your Spirit, and renew the face of the earth.

[13]You water the mountains from your palace;

the earth is replete with the fruit of your works.

14 You raise grass for the cattle,

and vegetation for man's use,

Producing bread from the earth.

R. Lord, send out your Spirit, and renew the face of the earth.

24 How manifold are your works, O LORD!

In wisdom you have wrought them all –

the earth is full of your creatures.

35 Bless the LORD, O my soul! Alleluia.

R. Lord, send out your Spirit, and renew the face of the earth.

Or Psalms 33:4-5, 6-7, 12-13, 20 and 22

R. (5b) **The earth is full of the goodness of the Lord.**

4 Upright is the word of the LORD,

and all his works are trustworthy.

5 He loves justice and right;

of the kindness of the LORD the earth is full.

R. The earth is full of the goodness of the Lord.

6 By the word of the LORD the heavens were made;

by the breath of his mouth all their host.

7 He gathers the waters of the sea as in a flask;

in cellars he confines the deep.

R. The earth is full of the goodness of the Lord.

12 Blessed the nation whose God is the LORD,

the people he has chosen for his own inheritance.

13 From heaven the LORD looks down;

he sees all mankind.

R. The earth is full of the goodness of the Lord.

[20]Our soul waits for the LORD,

who is our help and our shield.

[22]May your kindness, O LORD, be upon us

who have put our hope in you.

R. The earth is full of the goodness of the Lord.

Second Reading – Genesis 22:1-18

[1]God put Abraham to the test. He called to him, "Abraham!"
"Here I am, " he replied. [2]Then God said: "Take your son
Isaac, your only one, whom you love, and go to the land of
Moriah. There you shall offer him up as a holocaust on a
height that I will point out to you." [3]Early the next morning
Abraham saddled his donkey, took with him his son Isaac and
two of his servants as well, and with the wood that he had cut
for the holocaust, set out for the place of which God had told
him. [4]On the third day Abraham got sight of the place from
afar. [5]Then he said to his servants: "Both of you stay here with
the donkey, while the boy and I go on over yonder. We will
worship and then come back to you." [6]Thereupon Abraham
took the wood for the holocaust and laid it on his son Isaac's
shoulders, while he himself carried the fire and the knife. As
the two walked on together, [7]Isaac spoke to his father
Abraham: "Father!" Isaac said. "Yes, son," he replied. Isaac
continued, "Here are the fire and the wood, but where is the
sheep for the holocaust?" [8]"Son," Abraham answered, "God
himself will provide the sheep for the holocaust." Then the two
continued going forward. [9]When they came to the place of
which God had told him, Abraham built an altar there and
arranged the wood on it. Next he tied up his son Isaac, and
put him on top of the wood on the altar. [10] Then he reached
out and took the knife to slaughter his son. [11]But the LORD's
messenger called to him from heaven, "Abraham, Abraham!"
"Here I am!" he answered. [12]"Do not lay your hand on the boy,"
said the messenger. "Do not do the least thing to him. I know
now how devoted you are to God, since you did not withhold
from me your own beloved son." [13]As Abraham looked about,
he spied a ram caught by its horns in the thicket. So he went
and took the ram and offered it up as a holocaust in place of
his son. [14]Abraham named the site Yahweh-yireh; hence
people now say, "On the mountain the LORD will see." [15]Again
the LORD's messenger called to Abraham from heaven [16]and

said: “I swear by myself, declares the LORD, that because you
acted as you did in not withholding from me your beloved son,
17I will bless you abundantly and make your descendants as
countless as the stars of the sky and the sands of the
seashore; 18your descendants shall take possession of the
gates of their enemies, and in your descendants all the
nations of the earth shall find blessings all this because you
obeyed my command.”

Or Genesis 22:1-2, 9A, 10-13, 15-18

1God put Abraham to the test. He called to him, “Abraham!”
“Here I am, ” he replied. 2Then God said: “Take your son
Isaac, your only one, whom you love, and go to the land of
Moriah. There you shall offer him up as a holocaust on a
height that I will point out to you.” 9AWhen they came to the
place of which God had told him, Abraham built an altar there
and arranged the wood on it. 10Then he reached out and took
the knife to slaughter his son. 11But the LORD’s messenger
called to him from heaven, “Abraham, Abraham!” “Here I am,”
he answered. 12“Do not lay your hand on the boy, ” said the
messenger. “Do not do the least thing to him. I know now how
devoted you are to God, since you did not withhold from me
your own beloved son.” 13As Abraham looked about, he spied
a ram caught by its horns in the thicket. So he went and took
the ram and offered it up as a holocaust in place of his son.
15Again the LORD’s messenger called to Abraham from
heaven 16and said: “I swear by myself, declares the LORD,
that because you acted as you did in not withholding from me
your beloved son, 17I will bless you abundantly and make your
descendants as countless as the stars of the sky and the
sands of the seashore; 18your descendants shall take
possession of the gates of their enemies, and in your
descendants all the nations of the earth shall find blessing, all
this because you obeyed my command.”

Responsorial Psalm – Psalms 16:5, 8, 9-10, 11

R. (1) You are my inheritance, O Lord.

5O LORD, my allotted portion and my cup,

you it is who hold fast my lot.

8I set the LORD ever before me;

with him at my right hand I shall not be disturbed.

R. You are my inheritance, O Lord.

9 Therefore my heart is glad and my soul rejoices,

my body, too, abides in confidence;

10 because you will not abandon my soul to the netherworld,

nor will you suffer your faithful one to undergo corruption.

R. You are my inheritance, O Lord.

11 You will show me the path to life,

fullness of joys in your presence,

the delights at your right hand forever.

R. You are my inheritance, O Lord.

Third Reading – Exodus 14:15-15:1

15 The LORD said to Moses, "Why are you crying out to me?
Tell the Israelites to go forward. 16 And you, lift up your staff
and, with hand outstretched over the sea, split the sea in two,
that the Israelites may pass through it on dry land. 17 But I will
make the Egyptians so obstinate that they will go in after them.
Then I will receive glory through Pharaoh and all his army, his
chariots and charioteers. 18 The Egyptians shall know that I am
the LORD, when I receive glory through Pharaoh and his
chariots and charioteers." 19 The angel of God, who had been
leading Israel's camp, now moved and went around behind
them. The column of cloud also, leaving the front, took up its
place behind them, 20 so that it came between the camp of the
Egyptians and that of Israel. But the cloud now became dark,
and thus the night passed without the rival camps coming any
closer together all night long. 21 Then Moses stretched out his
hand over the sea, and the LORD swept the sea with a strong
east wind throughout the night and so turned it into dry land.
22 When the water was thus divided, the Israelites marched into
the midst of the sea on dry land, with the water like a wall to
their right and to their left. 23 The Egyptians followed in pursuit;
all Pharaoh's horses and chariots and charioteers went after
them right into the midst of the sea. 24 In the night watch just
before dawn the LORD cast through the column of the fiery
cloud upon the Egyptian force a glance that threw it into a
panic; 25 and he so clogged their chariot wheels that they could
hardly drive. With that the Egyptians sounded the retreat

before Israel, because the LORD was fighting for them against the Egyptians. [26]Then the LORD told Moses, stretch out your hand over the sea, that the water may flow back upon the Egyptians, upon their chariots and their charioteers." [27]So Moses stretched out his hand over the sea, and at dawn the sea flowed back to its normal depth. The Egyptians were fleeing head on toward the sea, when the LORD hurled them into its midst. [28]As the water flowed back, it covered the chariots and the charioteers of Pharaoh's whole army which had followed the Israelites into the sea. Not a single one of them escaped. [29]But the Israelites had marched on dry land through the midst of the sea, with the water like a wall to their right and to their left. [30]Thus the LORD saved Israel on that day from the power of the Egyptians. When Israel saw the Egyptians lying dead on the seashore [31]and beheld the great power that the LORD had shown against the Egyptians, they feared the LORD and believed in him and in his servant Moses. [1]Then Moses and the Israelites sang this song to the LORD: I will sing to the LORD, for he is gloriously triumphant; horse and chariot he has cast into the sea.

Responsorial Psalm – Exodus 15:1-2, 3-4, 5-6, 17-18

R. (1b) Let us sing to the Lord; he has covered himself in glory.

[1] I will sing to the LORD, for he is gloriously triumphant;

horse and chariot he has cast into the sea.

[2]My strength and my courage is the LORD,

and he has been my savior.

He is my God, I praise him;

the God of my father, I extol him.

R. Let us sing to the Lord; he has covered himself in glory.

[3]The LORD is a warrior,

LORD is his name!

[4]Pharaoh's chariots and army he hurled into the sea;

the elite of his officers were submerged in the Red Sea.

R. Let us sing to the Lord; he has covered himself in glory.

5The flood waters covered them,

they sank into the depths like a stone.

6Your right hand, O LORD, magnificent in power,

your right hand, O LORD, has shattered the enemy.

R. Let us sing to the Lord; he has covered himself in glory.

17You brought in the people you redeemed

and planted them on the mountain of your inheritance

the place where you made your seat, O LORD,

the sanctuary, LORD, which your hands established.

18The LORD shall reign forever and ever.

R. Let us sing to the Lord; he has covered himself in glory.

Fourth Reading – Isaiah 54:5-14

5The One who has become your husband is your Maker; his
name is the LORD of hosts; your redeemer is the Holy One of
Israel, called God of all the earth. 6The LORD calls you back,
like a wife forsaken and grieved in spirit, a wife married in
youth and then cast off, says your God. 7 For a brief moment I
abandoned you, but with great tenderness I will take you back.
8In an outburst of wrath, for a moment I hid my face from you;
but with enduring love I take pity on you, says the LORD, your
redeemer. 9This is for me like the days of Noah, when I swore
that the waters of Noah should never again deluge the earth;
so I have sworn not to be angry with you, or to rebuke you.
10Though the mountains leave their place and the hills be
shaken, my love shall never leave you nor my covenant of
peace be shaken, says the LORD, who has mercy on you. 11O
afflicted one, storm-battered and unconsoled, I lay your
pavements in carnelians, and your foundations in sapphires;
12I will make your battlements of rubies, your gates of
carbuncles, and all your walls of precious stones. 13All your
children shall be taught by the LORD, and great shall be the
peace of your children. 14In justice shall you be established, far

from the fear of oppression, where destruction cannot come near you.

Responsorial Psalm – Psalms 30:2, 4, 5-6, 11-12, 13

R. (2a) I will praise you, Lord, for you have rescued me.

2I will extol you, O LORD, for you drew me clear

and did not let my enemies rejoice over me.

4O LORD, you brought me up from the netherworld;

you preserved me from among those going down into the pit.

R. I will praise you, Lord, for you have rescued me.

5Sing praise to the LORD, you his faithful ones,

and give thanks to his holy name.

6For his anger lasts but a moment;

a lifetime, his good will.

At nightfall, weeping enters in,

but with the dawn, rejoicing.

R. I will praise you, Lord, for you have rescued me.

11Hear, O LORD, and have pity on me;

O LORD, be my helper.

12You changed my mourning into dancing;

13O LORD, my God, forever will I give you thanks.

R. I will praise you, Lord, for you have rescued me.

Fifth Reading – Isaiah 55:1-11

1Thus says the LORD: All you who are thirsty, come to the
water! You who have no money, come, receive grain and eat;
come, without paying and without cost, drink wine and milk!
2Why spend your money for what is not bread, your wages for
what fails to satisfy? Heed me, and you shall eat well, you
shall delight in rich fare. 3Come to me heedfully, listen, that
you may have life. I will renew with you the everlasting
covenant, the benefits assured to David. 4As I made him a
witness to the peoples, a leader and commander of nations,

5 so shall you summon a nation you knew not, and nations that
knew you not shall run to you, because of the LORD, your
God, the Holy One of Israel, who has glorified you. 6 Seek the
LORD while he may be found, call him while he is near. 7 Let
the scoundrel forsake his way, and the wicked man his
thoughts; let him turn to the LORD for mercy; to our God, who
is generous in forgiving. 8 For my thoughts are not your
thoughts, nor are your ways my ways, says the LORD. 9 As
high as the heavens are above the earth, so high are my ways
above your ways and my thoughts above your thoughts. 10 For
just as from the heavens the rain and snow come down and
do not return there till they have watered the earth, making it
fertile and fruitful, giving seed to the one who sows and bread
to the one who eats, 11 so shall my word be that goes forth
from my mouth; my word shall not return to me void, but shall
do my will, achieving the end for which I sent it.

Responsorial Psalm – Isaiah 12:2-3, 4, 5-6

R. (3) You will draw water joyfully from the springs of salvation.

2 God indeed is my savior;

I am confident and unafraid.

My strength and my courage is the LORD,

and he has been my savior.

3 With joy you will draw water

at the fountain of salvation.

R. You will draw water joyfully from the springs of salvation.

4 Give thanks to the LORD, acclaim his name;

among the nations make known his deeds,

proclaim how exalted is his name.

R. You will draw water joyfully from the springs of salvation.

5 Sing praise to the LORD for his glorious achievement;

let this be known throughout all the earth.

6 Shout with exultation, O city of Zion,

for great in your midst

is the Holy One of Israel!

R. You will draw water joyfully from the springs of salvation.

Sixth Reading – Baruch 3:9-15, 32C4:4

[9]Hear, O Israel, the commandments of life: listen, and know prudence! [10]How is it, Israel, that you are in the land of your foes, grown old in a foreign land, [11]defiled with the dead, accounted with those destined for the netherworld? [12]You have forsaken the fountain of wisdom! [13]Had you walked in the way of God, you would have dwelt in enduring peace. [14]Learn where prudence is, where strength, where understanding; that you may know also where are length of days, and life, where light of the eyes, and peace. [15]Who has found the place of wisdom, who has entered into her treasuries? [32]The One who knows all things knows her; he has probed her by his knowledge The One who established the earth for all time, and filled it with four-footed beasts; [33] he who dismisses the light, and it departs, calls it, and it obeys him trembling; [34]before whom the stars at their posts shine and rejoice; [35]when he calls them, they answer, "Here we are!" shining with joy for their Maker. [36]Such is our God; no other is to be compared to him: [37]he has traced out the whole way of understanding, and has given her to Jacob, his servant, to Israel, his beloved son. [38]Since then she has appeared on earth, and moved among people. [1] She is the book of the precepts of God, the law that endures forever; all who cling to her will live, but those will die who forsake her. [2]Turn, O Jacob, and receive her: walk by her light toward splendor. [3]Give not your glory to another, your privileges to an alien race. [4]Blessed are we, O Israel; for what pleases God is known to us!

Responsorial Psalm – Psalms 19:8, 9, 10, 11

R. (John 6:68c) **Lord, you have the words of everlasting life.**

[8]The law of the LORD is perfect,

refreshing the soul;

the decree of the LORD is trustworthy,

giving wisdom to the simple.

R. Lord, you have the words of everlasting life.

9The precepts of the LORD are right,

rejoicing the heart;

the command of the LORD is clear,

enlightening the eye.

R. Lord, you have the words of everlasting life.

10The fear of the LORD is pure,

enduring forever;

the ordinances of the LORD are true,

all of them just.

R. Lord, you have the words of everlasting life.

11They are more precious than gold,

than a heap of purest gold;

sweeter also than syrup

or honey from the comb.

R. Lord, you have the words of everlasting life.

Seventh Reading – Ezekiel 36:16-17A, 18-28

16The word of the LORD came to me, saying: 17Son of man,
when the house of Israel lived in their land, they defiled it by
their conduct and deeds. 18Therefore I poured out my fury
upon them because of the blood that they poured out on the
ground, and because they defiled it with idols. 19I scattered
them among the nations, dispersing them over foreign lands;
according to their conduct and deeds I judged them. 20 But
when they came among the nations wherever they came, they
served to profane my holy name, because it was said of them:
"These are the people of the LORD, yet they had to leave their
land." 21So I have relented because of my holy name which
the house of Israel profaned among the nations where they
came. 22Therefore say to the house of Israel: Thus says the
Lord GOD: Not for your sakes do I act, house of Israel, but for
the sake of my holy name, which you profaned among the
nations to which you came. 23I will prove the holiness of my
great name, profaned among the nations, in whose midst you

have profaned it. Thus the nations shall know that I am the LORD, says the Lord GOD, when in their sight I prove my
holiness through you. [24] For I will take you away from among the nations, gather you from all the foreign lands, and bring
you back to your own land. [25]I will sprinkle clean water upon you to cleanse you from all your impurities, and from all your
idols I will cleanse you. [26]I will give you a new heart and place a new spirit within you, taking from your bodies your stony
hearts and giving you natural hearts. [27]I will put my spirit within you and make you live by my statutes, careful to observe my
decrees. [28]You shall live in the land I gave your fathers; you shall be my people, and I will be your God.

Responsorial Psalm – Psalms 42:3, 5; 43:3, 4

When baptism is celebrated on Easter Vigil

R. (42:2) **Like a deer that longs for running streams, my soul longs for you, my God.**

[3]Athirst is my soul for God, the living God.

When shall I go and behold the face of God?

R. Like a deer that longs for running streams, my soul longs for you, my God.

[5] I went with the throng

and led them in procession to the house of God,

Amid loud cries of joy and thanksgiving,

with the multitude keeping festival.

R. Like a deer that longs for running streams, my soul longs for you, my God.

[3] Send forth your light and your fidelity;

they shall lead me on

And bring me to your holy mountain,

to your dwelling-place.

R. Like a deer that longs for running streams, my soul longs for you, my God.

[4]Then will I go in to the altar of God,

the God of my gladness and joy;

then will I give you thanks upon the harp,

O God, my God!

R. Like a deer that longs for running streams, my soul longs for you, my God.

Or Isaiah 12:2-3, 4BCD, 5-6

When baptism is not celebrated During Easter Vigil

R. (3) You will draw water joyfully from the springs of salvation.

2God indeed is my savior;

I am confident and unafraid.

My strength and my courage is the LORD,

and he has been my savior.

3With joy you will draw water

at the fountain of salvation.

R. You will draw water joyfully from the springs of salvation.

4BCDGive thanks to the LORD, acclaim his name;

among the nations make known his deeds,

proclaim how exalted is his name.

R. You will draw water joyfully from the springs of salvation.

5Sing praise to the LORD for his glorious achievement;

let this be known throughout all the earth.

6Shout with exultation, O city of Zion,

for great in your midst

is the Holy One of Israel!

R. You will draw water joyfully from the springs of salvation.

Or Psalms 51:12-13, 14-15, 18-19

When baptism is not celebrated During Easter Vigil

R. (12a) **Create a clean heart in me, O God.**

12 A clean heart create for me, O God,

and a steadfast spirit renew within me.

13 Cast me not out from your presence,

and your Holy Spirit take not from me.

R. Create a clean heart in me, O God.

14 Give me back the joy of your salvation,

and a willing spirit sustain in me.

15 I will teach transgressors your ways,

and sinners shall return to you.

R. Create a clean heart in me, O God.

18 For you are not pleased with sacrifices;

should I offer a holocaust, you would not accept it.

19 My sacrifice, O God, is a contrite spirit;

a heart contrite and humbled, O God, you will not spurn.

R. Create a clean heart in me, O God.

Epistle – Romans 6:3-11

Brothers and sisters:

3 Are you unaware that we who were baptized into Christ Jesus
were baptized into his death? 4 We were indeed buried with
him through baptism into death, so that, just as Christ was
raised from the dead by the glory of the Father, we too might
live in newness of life. 5 For if we have grown into union with
him through a death like his, we shall also be united with him
in the resurrection. 6 We know that our old self was crucified
with him, so that our sinful body might be done away with, that
we might no longer be in slavery to sin. 7 For a dead person
has been absolved from sin. 8 If, then, we have died with
Christ, we believe that we shall also live with him. 9 We know
that Christ, raised from the dead, dies no more; death no
longer has power over him. 10 As to his death, he died to sin

once and for all; as to his life, he lives for God.
[11]Consequently, you too must think of yourselves as being
dead to sin and living for God in Christ Jesus.

Responsorial Psalm – Psalms 118:1-2, 16-17, 22-23

R. Alleluia, alleluia, alleluia.

[1]Give thanks to the LORD, for he is good,

for his mercy endures forever.

[2]Let the house of Israel say,

"His mercy endures forever."

R. Alleluia, alleluia, alleluia.

[16]The right hand of the LORD has struck with power;

the right hand of the LORD is exalted.

[17]I shall not die, but live,

and declare the works of the LORD.

R. Alleluia, alleluia, alleluia.

[22]The stone the builders rejected

has become the cornerstone.

[23]By the LORD has this been done;

it is wonderful in our eyes.

R. Alleluia, alleluia, alleluia.

Gospel – Matthew 28: 1-10

[1]And in the end of the Sabbath, when it began to dawn
towards the first day of the week, came Mary Magdalen and
the other Mary, to see the sepulchre. [2]And behold there was a
great earthquake. For an angel of the Lord descended from
heaven, and coming, rolled back the stone, and sat upon it.
[3]And his countenance was as lightning, and his raiment as
snow. [4]And for fear of him, the guards were struck with terror,
and became as dead men. [5]And the angel answering, said to
the women: Fear not you; for I know that you seek Jesus who
was crucified. [6]He is not here, for he is risen, as he said.
Come, and see the place where the Lord was laid. [7]And going
quickly, tell ye his disciples that he is risen: and behold he will

go before you into Galilee; there you shall see him. Lo, I have
foretold it to you. [8]And they went out quickly from the
sepulchre with fear and great joy, running to tell his disciples.
[9]And behold Jesus met them, saying: All hail. But they came
up and took hold of his feet, and adored him. [10]Then Jesus
said to them: Fear not. Go, tell my brethren that they go into
Galilee, there they shall see me.

Sunday April 9, 2023

Easter Sunday 2023

First Reading – Acts 10:34A, 37-43

[34A]Peter proceeded to speak and said: [37] "You know what has
happened all over Judea, beginning in Galilee after the
baptism that John preached, [38]how God anointed Jesus of
Nazareth with the Holy Spirit and power. He went about doing
good and healing all those oppressed by the devil, for God
was with him. [39]We are witnesses of all that he did both in the
country of the Jews and in Jerusalem. They put him to death
by hanging him on a tree. [40]This man God raised on the third
day and granted that he be visible, [41]not to all the people, but
to us, the witnesses chosen by God in advance, who ate and
drank with him after he rose from the dead. [42] He
commissioned us to preach to the people and testify that he is
the one appointed by God as judge of the living and the dead.
[43]To him all the prophets bear witness, that everyone who
believes in him will receive forgiveness of sins through his
name."

Responsorial Psalm – Psalms 118:1-2, 16-17, 22-23.

R. [(24)] **This is the day the Lord has made; let us rejoice and be glad.** or: **R. Alleluia.**

[1]Give thanks to the LORD, for he is good,

for his mercy endures forever.

[2]Let the house of Israel say,

"His mercy endures forever."

R. This is the day the Lord has made; let us rejoice and be glad. or: **R. Alleluia.**

[16] "The right hand of the LORD has struck with power;

the right hand of the LORD is exalted.

[17] I shall not die, but live,

and declare the works of the LORD."

R. This is the day the Lord has made; let us rejoice and be glad. or: **R. Alleluia.**

[22]The stone which the builders rejected

has become the cornerstone.

[23]By the LORD has this been done;

it is wonderful in our eyes.

R. This is the day the Lord has made; let us rejoice and be glad. or: **R. Alleluia.**

Second Reading – Colossians 3:1-4

Brothers and sisters: [1]If then you were raised with Christ, seek
what is above, where Christ is seated at the right hand of God.
[2]Think of what is above, not of what is on earth. [3]For you have
died, and your life is hidden with Christ in God. [4]When Christ
your life appears, then you too will appear with him in glory.

Or 1 Corinthians 5:6B-8

Brothers and sisters: [6B]Do you not know that a little yeast
leavens all the dough? [7]Clear out the old yeast, so that you
may become a fresh batch of dough, inasmuch as you are
unleavened. For our paschal lamb, Christ, has been sacrificed.
[8]Therefore, let us celebrate the feast, not with the old yeast,
the yeast of malice and wickedness, but with the unleavened
bread of sincerity and truth.

Sequence - *Victimae Paschali Laudes*

Christians, to the Paschal Victim

Offer your thankful praises!

A Lamb the sheep redeems;

Christ, who only is sinless,

Reconciles sinners to the Father.

Death and life have contended in that combat stupendous:

The Prince of life, who died, reigns immortal.

Speak, Mary, declaring

What you saw, wayfaring.

“The tomb of Christ, who is living,

The glory of Jesus’ resurrection;

bright angels attesting,

The shroud and napkin resting.

Yes, Christ my hope is arisen;

to Galilee he goes before you.”

Christ indeed from death is risen, our new life obtaining.

Have mercy, victor King, ever reigning!

Amen. Alleluia.

Alleluia – cf. 1 Corinthians 5:7B-8A

R. Alleluia, alleluia.

[7B]Christ, our paschal lamb, has been sacrificed; [8A]let us then
feast with joy in the Lord.

R. Alleluia, alleluia.

Gospel – John 20:1-9

[1]On the first day of the week, Mary of Magdala came to the
tomb early in the morning, while it was still dark, and saw the
stone removed from the tomb. [2]So she ran and went to Simon
Peter and to the other disciple whom Jesus loved, and told
them, “They have taken the Lord from the tomb, and we don’t
know where they put him.” [3]So Peter and the other disciple
went out and came to the tomb. [4]They both ran, but the other
disciple ran faster than Peter and arrived at the tomb first; [5]he
bent down and saw the burial cloths there, but did not go in. [6]
When Simon Peter arrived after him, he went into the tomb
and saw the burial cloths there, [7]and the cloth that had
covered his head, not with the burial cloths but rolled up in a
separate place. [8]Then the other disciple also went in, the one
who had arrived at the tomb first, and he saw and believed.

9For they did not yet understand the Scripture that he had to
rise from the dead.

OR Gospel – Matthew 28:1-10

1After the Sabbath, as the first day of the week was dawning,
Mary Magdalene and the other Mary came to see the tomb.
2And behold, there was a great earthquake; for an angel of the
Lord descended from heaven, approached, rolled back the
stone, and sat upon it. 3His appearance was like lightning and
his clothing was white as snow. 4The guards were shaken with
fear of him and became like dead men. 5Then the angel said
to the women in reply, "Do not be afraid! I know that you are
seeking Jesus the crucified. 6He is not here, for he has been
raised just as he said. Come and see the place where he lay.
7Then go quickly and tell his disciples, 'He has been raised
from the dead, and he is going before you to Galilee; there
you will see him.' Behold, I have told you." 8Then they went
away quickly from the tomb, fearful yet overjoyed, and ran to
announce this to his disciples. 9And behold, Jesus met them
on their way and greeted them. They approached, embraced
his feet, and did him homage. 10Then Jesus said to them, "Do
not be afraid. Go tell my brothers to go to Galilee, and there
they will see me."

Or Gospel – Mark 16:1-7

1When the Sabbath was over, Mary Magdalene, Mary, the
mother of James, and Salome bought spices so that they
might go and anoint him. 2Very early when the sun had risen,
on the first day of the week, they came to the tomb. 3They
were saying to one another, "Who will roll back the stone for
us from the entrance to the tomb?" 4When they looked up,
they saw that the stone had been rolled back; it was very
large. 5On entering the tomb they saw a young man sitting on
the right side, clothed in a white robe, and they were utterly
amazed. 6He said to them, "Do not be amazed! You seek
Jesus of Nazareth, the crucified. He has been raised; he is not
here. Behold the place where they laid him. 7But go and tell
his disciples and Peter, 'He is going before you to Galilee;
there you will see him, as he told you.'"

Or Gospel Luke – 24:13-35

At an afternoon or evening Mass.

[13]That very day, the first day of the week, two of Jesus' disciples were going to a village seven miles from Jerusalem called Emmaus, [14]and they were conversing about all the things that had occurred. [15]And it happened that while they were conversing and debating, Jesus himself drew near and walked with them, [16] but their eyes were prevented from recognizing him. [17] He asked them, "What are you discussing as you walk along?" They stopped, looking downcast. [18]One of them, named Cleopas, said to him in reply, "Are you the only visitor to Jerusalem who does not know of the things that have taken place there in these days?" [19]And he replied to them, "What sort of things?" They said to him, "The things that happened to Jesus the Nazarene, who was a prophet mighty in deed and word before God and all the people, [20]how our chief priests and rulers both handed him over to a sentence of death and crucified him. [21]But we were hoping that he would be the one to redeem Israel; and besides all this, it is now the third day since this took place. [22]Some women from our group, however, have astounded us: they were at the tomb early in the morning [23]and did not find his body; they came back and reported that they had indeed seen a vision of angels who announced that he was alive. [24]Then some of those with us went to the tomb and found things just as the women had described, but him they did not see." [25]And he said to them, "Oh, how foolish you are! How slow of heart to believe all that the prophets spoke! [26]Was it not necessary that the Christ should suffer these things and enter into his glory?" [27]Then beginning with Moses and all the prophets, he interpreted to them what referred to him in all the Scriptures. [28]As they approached the village to which they were going, he gave the impression that he was going on farther. [29]But they urged him, "Stay with us, for it is nearly evening and the day is almost over." So he went in to stay with them. [30]And it happened that, while he was with them at table, he took bread, said the blessing, broke it, and gave it to them. [31]With that their eyes were opened and they recognized him, but he vanished from their sight. [32]Then they said to each other, "Were not our hearts burning within us while he spoke to us on the way and opened the Scriptures to us?" [33]So they set out at once and returned to Jerusalem where they found gathered together the

eleven and those with them [34]who were saying, "The Lord has truly been raised and has appeared to Simon!" [35]Then the two recounted what had taken place on the way and how he was made known to them in the breaking of bread.

Monday April 10, 2023

Monday in the Octave of Easter

First Reading – Acts 2:14, 22-33

[14]On the day of Pentecost, Peter stood up with the Eleven, raised his voice, and proclaimed: "You who are Jews, indeed all of you staying in Jerusalem. Let this be known to you, and listen to my words. [22]"You who are children of Israel, hear these words. Jesus the Nazorean was a man commended to you by God with mighty deeds, wonders, and signs, which God worked through him in your midst, as you yourselves know. [23]This man, delivered up by the set plan and foreknowledge of God, you killed, using lawless men to crucify him. [24]But God raised him up, releasing him from the throes of death, because it was impossible for him to be held by it. [25]For David says of him: I saw the Lord ever before me, with him at my right hand I shall not be disturbed. [26] Therefore my heart has been glad and my tongue has exulted; my flesh, too, will dwell in hope, [27]because you will not abandon my soul to the nether world, nor will you suffer your holy one to see corruption. [28]You have made known to me the paths of life; you will fill me with joy in your presence. [29]My brothers, one can confidently say to you about the patriarch David that he died and was buried, and his tomb is in our midst to this day. [30]But since he was a prophet and knew that God had sworn an oath to him that he would set one of his descendants upon his throne, [31]he foresaw and spoke of the resurrection of the Christ, that neither was he abandoned to the netherworld nor did his flesh see corruption.[32]God raised this Jesus; of this we are all witnesses. [33]Exalted at the right hand of God, he poured forth the promise of the Holy Spirit that he received from the Father, as you both see and hear."

Responsorial Psalm – Psalms 16:1-2A AND 5, 7-8, 9-10, 11

R. (1) **Keep me safe, O God; you are my hope.** or: **R. Alleluia.**

1Keep me, O God, for in you I take refuge;

2AI say to the LORD, "My Lord are you."

5 O LORD, my allotted portion and my cup,

you it is who hold fast my lot.

R. Keep me safe, O God; you are my hope. or: **R. Alleluia.**

7I bless the LORD who counsels me;

even in the night my heart exhorts me.

8I set the LORD ever before me;

with him at my right hand I shall not be disturbed.

R. Keep me safe, O God; you are my hope. or: **R. Alleluia.**

9Therefore my heart is glad and my soul rejoices,

my body, too, abides in confidence;

10Because you will not abandon my soul to the nether world,

nor will you suffer your faithful one to undergo corruption.

R. Keep me safe, O God; you are my hope. or: **R. Alleluia.**

11You will show me the path to life,

fullness of joys in your presence,

the delights at your right hand forever.

R. Keep me safe, O God; you are my hope. or: **R. Alleluia.**

Alleluia – Psalms 118:24

R. Alleluia, alleluia.

24This is the day the LORD has made; let us be glad and rejoice in it.

R. Alleluia, alleluia.

Gospel – Matthew 28:8-15

[8]Mary Magdalene and the other Mary went away quickly from
the tomb, fearful yet overjoyed, and ran to announce the news
to his disciples. [9]And behold, Jesus met them on their way and
greeted them. They approached, embraced his feet, and did
him homage. [10]Then Jesus said to them, "Do not be afraid. Go
tell my brothers to go to Galilee, and there they will see me."
[11]While they were going, some of the guard went into the city
and told the chief priests all that had happened. [12]The chief
priests assembled with the elders and took counsel; then they
gave a large sum of money to the soldiers, [13]telling them, "You
are to say, 'His disciples came by night and stole him while we
were asleep.' [14]And if this gets to the ears of the governor, we
will satisfy him and keep you out of trouble." [15]The soldiers
took the money and did as they were instructed. And this story
has circulated among the Jews to the present day.

Tuesday April 11, 2023

Tuesday in the Octave of Easter

First Reading – Acts 2:36-41

[36]On the day of Pentecost, Peter said to the Jewish people,
"Let the whole house of Israel know for certain that God has
made him both Lord and Christ, this Jesus whom you
crucified." [37]Now when they heard this, they were cut to the
heart, and they asked Peter and the other Apostles, "What are
we to do, my brothers?" [38]Peter said to them, "Repent and be
baptized, every one of you, in the name of Jesus Christ, for
the forgiveness of your sins; and you will receive the gift of the
Holy Spirit. [39]For the promise is made to you and to your
children and to all those far off, whomever the Lord our God
will call." [40]He testified with many other arguments, and was
exhorting them, "Save yourselves from this corrupt
generation." [41]Those who accepted his message were
baptized, and about three thousand persons were added that
day.

Responsorial Psalm – Psalms 33:4-5, 18-19, 20 AND 22

R. (5b) The earth is full of the goodness of the Lord. or: **R. Alleluia.**

4 Upright is the word of the LORD,

and all his works are trustworthy.

5 He loves justice and right;

of the kindness of the LORD the earth is full.

R. The earth is full of the goodness of the Lord. or: **R. Alleluia.**

18 See, the eyes of the LORD are upon those who fear him,

upon those who hope for his kindness,

19 To deliver them from death

and preserve them in spite of famine.

R. The earth is full of the goodness of the Lord. or: **R. Alleluia.**

20 Our soul waits for the LORD,

who is our help and our shield.

22 May your kindness, O LORD, be upon us

who have put our hope in you.

R. The earth is full of the goodness of the Lord. or: **R. Alleluia.**

Alleluia – Psalms 118:24

R. Alleluia, alleluia.

24 This is the day the LORD has made; let us be glad and rejoice in it.

R. Alleluia, alleluia.

Gospel – John 20:11-18

11Mary Magdalene stayed outside the tomb weeping. And as
she wept, she bent over into the tomb
12and saw two angels in
white sitting there, one at the head and one at the feet where

the Body of Jesus had been. [13]And they said to her, “Woman,
why are you weeping?” She said to them, “They have taken
my Lord, and I don’t know where they laid him.” [14]When she
had said this, she turned around and saw Jesus there, but did
not know it was Jesus. [15]Jesus said to her, “Woman, why are
you weeping? Whom are you looking for?” She thought it was
the gardener and said to him, “Sir, if you carried him away, tell
me where you laid him, and I will take him.” [16]Jesus said to
her, “Mary!” She turned and said to him in Hebrew,
“Rabbouni,” which means Teacher. [17]Jesus said to her, “Stop
holding on to me, for I have not yet ascended to the Father.
But go to my brothers and tell them, ‘I am going to my Father
and your Father, to my God and your God.’” [18]Mary went and
announced to the disciples, “I have seen the Lord,” and then
reported what he had told her.

Wednesday April 12, 2023

Wednesday in the Octave of Easter

First Reading – Acts 3:1-10

[1]Peter and John were going up to the temple area for the three
o’clock hour of prayer. [2]And a man crippled from birth was
carried and placed at the gate of the temple called “the
Beautiful Gate” every day to beg for alms from the people who
entered the temple. [3]When he saw Peter and John about to go
into the temple, he asked for alms. [4]But Peter looked intently
at him, as did John, and said, “Look at us.” [5]He paid attention
to them, expecting to receive something from them. [6]Peter
said, “I have neither silver nor gold, but what I do have I give
you: in the name of Jesus Christ the Nazorean, rise and walk.”
[7]Then Peter took him by the right hand and raised him up, and
immediately his feet and ankles grew strong. [8]He leaped up,
stood, and walked around, and went into the temple with
them, walking and jumping and praising God. [9]When all the
people saw him walking and praising God, [10]they recognized
him as the one who used to sit begging at the Beautiful Gate
of the temple, and they were filled with amazement and
astonishment at what had happened to him.

Responsorial Psalm – Psalms 105:1-2, 3-4, 6-7, 8-9

R. [3b] **Rejoice, O hearts that seek the Lord.** or: **R. Alleluia.**

[1] Give thanks to the LORD, invoke his name;

make known among the nations his deeds.

2 Sing to him, sing his praise,

proclaim all his wondrous deeds.

R. Rejoice, O hearts that seek the Lord. or: **R. Alleluia.**

3 Glory in his holy name;

rejoice, O hearts that seek the LORD!

4 Look to the LORD in his strength;

seek to serve him constantly.

R. Rejoice, O hearts that seek the Lord. or: **R. Alleluia.**

6 You descendants of Abraham, his servants,

sons of Jacob, his chosen ones!

7 He, the LORD, is our God;

throughout the earth his judgments prevail.

R. Rejoice, O hearts that seek the Lord. or: **R. Alleluia.**

8 He remembers forever his covenant

which he made binding for a thousand generations

9 Which he entered into with Abraham

and by his oath to Isaac.

R. Rejoice, O hearts that seek the Lord. or: **R. Alleluia.**

Alleluia – Psalms 118:24

R. Alleluia, alleluia.

24 This is the day the LORD has made; let us be glad and rejoice in it.

R. Alleluia, alleluia.

Gospel – Luke 24:13-35

13That very day, the first day of the week, two of Jesus'
disciples were going to a village seven miles from Jerusalem
called Emmaus, 14and they were conversing about all the
things that had occurred. 15And it happened that while they
were conversing and debating, Jesus himself drew near and
walked with them, 16but their eyes were prevented from

recognizing him. [17]He asked them, “What are you discussing as you walk along?” They stopped, looking downcast. [18]One of them, named Cleopas, said to him in reply, “Are you the only visitor to Jerusalem who does not know of the things that have taken place there in these days?” [19]And he replied to them, “What sort of things?” They said to him, “The things that happened to Jesus the Nazarene, who was a prophet mighty in deed and word before God and all the people, [20]how our chief priests and rulers both handed him over to a sentence of death and crucified him. [21]But we were hoping that he would be the one to redeem Israel; and besides all this, it is now the third day since this took place. [22]Some women from our group, however, have astounded us: they were at the tomb early in the morning [23]and did not find his Body; they came back and reported that they had indeed seen a vision of angels who announced that he was alive. [24]Then some of those with us went to the tomb and found things just as the women had described, but him they did not see.” [25]And he said to them, “Oh, how foolish you are! How slow of heart to believe all that the prophets spoke! [26]Was it not necessary that the Christ should suffer these things and enter into his glory?” [27]Then beginning with Moses and all the prophets, he interpreted to them what referred to him in all the Scriptures. [28]As they approached the village to which they were going, he gave the impression that he was going on farther. [29]But they urged him, “Stay with us, for it is nearly evening and the day is almost over.” So he went in to stay with them. [30]And it happened that, while he was with them at table, he took bread, said the blessing, broke it, and gave it to them. [31]With that their eyes were opened and they recognized him, but he vanished from their sight. [32]Then they said to each other, “Were not our hearts burning within us while he spoke to us on the way and opened the Scriptures to us?” [33]So they set out at once and returned to Jerusalem where they found gathered together the Eleven and those with them [34]who were saying, “The Lord has truly been raised and has appeared to Simon!” [35]Then the two recounted what had taken place on the way and how he was made known to them in the breaking of the bread.

Thursday April 13, 2023

Thursday in the Octave of Easter

First Reading – Acts 3:11-26

11 As the crippled man who had been cured clung to Peter and
John, all the people hurried in amazement toward them in the
portico called "Solomon's Portico." 12 When Peter saw this, he
addressed the people, "You children of Israel, why are you
amazed at this, and why do you look so intently at us as if we
had made him walk by our own power or piety? 13 The God of
Abraham, the God of Isaac, and the God of Jacob, the God of
our fathers, has glorified his servant Jesus whom you handed
over and denied in Pilate's presence, when he had decided to
release him. 14 You denied the Holy and Righteous One and
asked that a murderer be released to you. 15 The author of life
you put to death, but God raised him from the dead; of this we
are witnesses. 16 And by faith in his name, this man, whom you
see and know, his name has made strong, and the faith that
comes through it has given him this perfect health, in the
presence of all of you. 17 Now I know, brothers and sisters, that
you acted out of ignorance, just as your leaders did; 18 but God
has thus brought to fulfillment what he had announced
beforehand through the mouth of all the prophets, that his
Christ would suffer. 19 Repent, therefore, and be converted,
that your sins may be wiped away, 20 and that the Lord may
grant you times of refreshment and send you the Christ
already appointed for you, Jesus, 21 whom heaven must
receive until the times of universal restoration of which God
spoke through the mouth of his holy prophets from of old.
22 For Moses said: A prophet like me will the Lord, your God,
raise up for you from among your own kin; to him you shall
listen in all that he may say to you. 23 Everyone who does not
listen to that prophet will be cut off from the people.
24 "Moreover, all the prophets who spoke, from Samuel and
those afterwards, also announced these days. 25 You are the
children of the prophets and of the covenant that God made
with your ancestors when he said to Abraham, In your
offspring all the families of the earth shall be blessed. 26 For
you first, God raised up his servant and sent him to bless you
by turning each of you from your evil ways."

Responsorial Psalm – Psalms 8:2AB and 5, 6-7, 8-9

R. [(2ab)] **O Lord, our God, how wonderful your name in all the earth!** or: **R. Alleluia.**

[2AB] O LORD, our Lord,

how glorious is your name over all the earth!

[5] What is man that you should be mindful of him,

or the son of man that you should care for him?

R. O Lord, our God, how wonderful your name in all the earth! or: **R. Alleluia.**

[6] You have made him little less than the angels,

and crowned him with glory and honor.

[7] You have given him rule over the works of your hands,

putting all things under his feet.

R. O Lord, our God, how wonderful your name in all the earth! or: **R. Alleluia.**

[8] All sheep and oxen,

yes, and the beasts of the field,

[9] The birds of the air, the fishes of the sea,

and whatever swims the paths of the seas.

R. O Lord, our God, how wonderful your name in all the earth! or: **R. Alleluia.**

Alleluia – Psalms 118:24

R. Alleluia, alleluia.

[24] This is the day the LORD has made; let us be glad and rejoice in it.

R. Alleluia, alleluia.

Gospel – Luke 24:35-48

[35]The disciples of Jesus recounted what had taken place along the way, and how they had come to recognize him in the
breaking of bread. [36]While they were still speaking about this,
he stood in their midst and said to them, “Peace be with you.”

37But they were startled and terrified and thought that they
were seeing a ghost. 38Then he said to them, “Why are you
troubled? And why do questions arise in your hearts? 39Look
at my hands and my feet, that it is I myself. Touch me and
see, because a ghost does not have flesh and bones as you
can see I have.” 40And as he said this, he showed them his
hands and his feet. 41While they were still incredulous for joy
and were amazed, he asked them, “Have you anything here to
eat?” 42They gave him a piece of baked fish; 43he took it and
ate it in front of them. 44He said to them, “These are my words
that I spoke to you while I was still with you, that everything
written about me in the law of Moses and in the prophets and
psalms must be fulfilled.” 45Then he opened their minds to
understand the Scriptures. 46And he said to them, “Thus it is
written that the Christ would suffer and rise from the dead on
the third day 47and that repentance, for the forgiveness of sins,
would be preached in his name to all the nations, beginning
from Jerusalem. 48You are witnesses of these things.”

Friday April 14, 2023

Friday in the Octave of Easter

First Reading – Acts 4:1-12

1After the crippled man had been cured, while Peter and John
were still speaking to the people, the priests, the captain of the
temple guard, and the Sadducees confronted them, 2disturbed
that they were teaching the people and proclaiming in Jesus
the resurrection of the dead. 3They laid hands on Peter and
John and put them in custody until the next day, since it was
already evening. 4But many of those who heard the word
came to believe and the number of men grew to about five
thousand. 5On the next day, their leaders, elders, and scribes
were assembled in Jerusalem, 6with Annas the high priest,
Caiaphas, John, Alexander, and all who were of the high-
priestly class. 7They brought them into their presence and
questioned them, “By what power or by what name have you
done this?” 8Then Peter, filled with the Holy Spirit, answered
them, “Leaders of the people and elders: 9If we are being
examined today about a good deed done to a cripple, namely,
by what means he was saved, 10then all of you and all the
people of Israel should know that it was in the name of Jesus
Christ the Nazorean whom you crucified, whom God raised

from the dead; in his name this man stands before you healed.
11 He is the stone rejected by you, the builders, which has
become the cornerstone. 12 There is no salvation through
anyone else, nor is there any other name under heaven given
to the human race by which we are to be saved."

Responsorial Psalm – Psalms 118:1-2 and 4, 22-24, 25-27A

R. (22) The stone rejected by the builders has become the cornerstone. or: **R. Alleluia.**

1 Give thanks to the LORD, for he is good,

for his mercy endures forever.

2 Let the house of Israel say,

"His mercy endures forever."

4 Let those who fear the LORD say,

"His mercy endures forever."

R. The stone rejected by the builders has become the cornerstone. or: **R. Alleluia.**

22 The stone which the builders rejected

has become the cornerstone.

23 By the LORD has this been done;

it is wonderful in our eyes.

24 This is the day the LORD has made;

let us be glad and rejoice in it.

R. The stone rejected by the builders has become the cornerstone. or: **R. Alleluia.**

25 O LORD, grant salvation!

O LORD, grant prosperity!

26 Blessed is he who comes in the name of the LORD;

we bless you from the house of the LORD.

27A The LORD is God, and he has given us light.

R. The stone rejected by the builders has become the cornerstone. or: **R. Alleluia.**

Alleluia – Psalms 118:24

R. Alleluia, alleluia.

[24] This is the day the LORD has made; let us be glad and rejoice in it.

R. Alleluia, alleluia.

Gospel – John 21:1-14

[1]Jesus revealed himself again to his disciples at the Sea of
Tiberias. He revealed himself in this way. [2]Together were
Simon Peter, Thomas called Didymus, Nathanael from Cana
in Galilee, Zebedee's sons, and two others of his disciples.
[3]Simon Peter said to them, "I am going fishing." They said to
him, "We also will come with you." So they went out and got
into the boat, but that night they caught nothing. [4]When it was
already dawn, Jesus was standing on the shore; but the
disciples did not realize that it was Jesus. [5]Jesus said to them,
"Children, have you caught anything to eat?" They answered
him, "No." [6]So he said to them, "Cast the net over the right
side of the boat and you will find something." So they cast it,
and were not able to pull it in because of the number of fish.
[7]So the disciple whom Jesus loved said to Peter, "It is the
Lord." When Simon Peter heard that it was the Lord, he tucked
in his garment, for he was lightly clad, and jumped into the
sea. [8]The other disciples came in the boat, for they were not
far from shore, only about a hundred yards, dragging the net
with the fish. [9]When they climbed out on shore, they saw a
charcoal fire with fish on it and bread. [10]Jesus said to them,
"Bring some of the fish you just caught." [11]So Simon Peter
went over and dragged the net ashore full of one hundred fifty-
three large fish. Even though there were so many, the net was
not torn. [12]Jesus said to them, "Come, have breakfast." And
none of the disciples dared to ask him, "Who are you?"
because they realized it was the Lord.[13]Jesus came over and
took the bread and gave it to them, and in like manner the fish.
[14]This was now the third time Jesus was revealed to his
disciples after being raised from the dead.

Saturday April 15, 2023

Saturday in the Octave of Easter

First Reading – Acts 4:13-21

[13]Observing the boldness of Peter and John and perceiving
them to be uneducated, ordinary men, the leaders, elders, and
scribes were amazed, and they recognized them as the
companions of Jesus. [14]Then when they saw the man who
had been cured standing there with them, they could say
nothing in reply. [15]So they ordered them to leave the
Sanhedrin, and conferred with one another, saying, [16]"What
are we to do with these men? Everyone living in Jerusalem
knows that a remarkable sign was done through them, and we
cannot deny it. [17]But so that it may not be spread any further
among the people, let us give them a stern warning never
again to speak to anyone in this name." [18]So they called them
back and ordered them not to speak or teach at all in the
name of Jesus. [19]Peter and John, however, said to them in
reply, "Whether it is right in the sight of God for us to obey you
rather than God, you be the judges. [20]It is impossible for us not
to speak about what we have seen and heard." [21]After
threatening them further, they released them, finding no way
to punish them, on account of the people who were all praising
God for what had happened.

Responsorial Psalm – Psalms 118:1 and 14-15AB,16-18,19-21

R. [(21a)] **I will give thanks to you, for you have answered me.**
or: **R. Alleluia.**

[1] Give thanks to the LORD, for he is good,

for his mercy endures forever.

[14] My strength and my courage is the LORD,

and he has been my savior.

[15AB] The joyful shout of victory

in the tents of the just.

R. I will give thanks to you, for you have answered me. or:
R. Alleluia.

16 "The right hand of the LORD is exalted;

the right hand of the LORD has struck with power."

17 I shall not die, but live,

and declare the works of the LORD.

18 Though the LORD has indeed chastised me,

yet he has not delivered me to death.

R. I will give thanks to you, for you have answered me. or:
R. Alleluia.

19 Open to me the gates of justice;

I will enter them and give thanks to the LORD.

20 This is the gate of the LORD;

the just shall enter it.

21 I will give thanks to you, for you have answered me

and have been my savior.

R. I will give thanks to you, for you have answered me. or:
R. Alleluia.

Alleluia – Psalms 118:24

R. Alleluia, alleluia.

24 This is the day the LORD has made; let us be glad and rejoice in it.

R. Alleluia, alleluia.

Gospel – Mark 16:9-15

9When Jesus had risen, early on the first day of the week, he
appeared first to Mary Magdalene, out of whom he had driven
seven demons. 10She went and told his companions who were
mourning and weeping. 11When they heard that he was alive
and had been seen by her, they did not believe. 12After this he
appeared in another form to two of them walking along on their
way to the country. 13They returned and told the others; but
they did not believe them either. 14But later, as the Eleven
were at table, he appeared to them and rebuked them for their
unbelief and hardness of heart because they had not believed
those who saw him after he had been raised. 15He said to

them, "Go into the whole world and proclaim the Gospel to every creature."

Sunday April 16, 2023

Second Sunday of Easter - Divine Mercy Sunday

First Reading – Acts 2:42-47

42They devoted themselves to the teaching of the apostles and
to the communal life, to the breaking of bread and to the
prayers. 43Awe came upon everyone, and many wonders and
signs were done through the apostles. 44All who believed were
together and had all things in common; 45they would sell their
property and possessions and divide them among all
according to each one's need. 46Every day they devoted
themselves to meeting together in the temple area and to
breaking bread in their homes. They ate their meals with
exultation and sincerity of heart, 47praising God and enjoying
favor with all the people. And every day the Lord added to
their number those who were being saved.

Responsorial Psalm – Psalms 118:2-4, 13-15, 22-24

R. (1) Give thanks to the LORD, for he is good, his love is everlasting. or: **R. Alleluia.**

2 Let the house of Israel say,

"His mercy endures forever."

3 Let the house of Aaron say,

"His mercy endures forever."

4 Let those who fear the LORD say,

"His mercy endures forever."

R. Give thanks to the LORD, for he is good, his love is everlasting. or: **R. Alleluia.**

13 I was hard pressed and was falling,

but the LORD helped me.

14 My strength and my courage is the LORD,

and he has been my savior.

15 The joyful shout of victory

in the tents of the just:

R. Give thanks to the LORD, for he is good, his love is everlasting. or: **R. Alleluia.**

22 The stone which the builders rejected

has become the cornerstone.

23 By the LORD has this been done;

it is wonderful in our eyes.

24 This is the day the LORD has made;

let us be glad and rejoice in it.

R. Give thanks to the LORD, for he is good, his love is everlasting. or: **R. Alleluia.**

Second Reading – 1 Peter 1:3-9

3Blessed be the God and Father of our Lord Jesus Christ, who
in his great mercy gave us a new birth to a living hope through
the resurrection of Jesus Christ from the dead, 4to an
inheritance that is imperishable, undefiled, and unfading, kept
in heaven for you 5who by the power of God are safeguarded
through faith, to a salvation that is ready to be revealed in the
final time. 6In this you rejoice, although now for a little while
you may have to suffer through various trials, 7so that the
genuineness of your faith, more precious than gold that is
perishable even though tested by fire, may prove to be for
praise, glory, and honor at the revelation of Jesus Christ.
8Although you have not seen him you love him; even though
you do not see him now yet believe in him, you rejoice with an
indescribable and glorious joy, 9as you attain the goal of your
faith, the salvation of your souls.

Alleluia – John 20:29

R. Alleluia, alleluia.

29You believe in me, Thomas, because you have seen me, says the Lord; Blessed are those who have not seen me, but still believe!

R. Alleluia, alleluia.

Gospel – John 20:19-31

[19]On the evening of that first day of the week, when the doors
were locked, where the disciples were, for fear of the Jews,
Jesus came and stood in their midst and said to them, "Peace
be with you." [20]When he had said this, he showed them his
hands and his side. The disciples rejoiced when they saw the
Lord. [21]Jesus said to them again, "Peace be with you. As the
Father has sent me, so I send you." [22]And when he had said
this, he breathed on them and said to them, "Receive the Holy
Spirit. [23]Whose sins you forgive are forgiven them, and whose
sins you retain are retained." [24]Thomas, called Didymus, one
of the Twelve, was not with them when Jesus came. [25]So the
other disciples said to him, "We have seen the Lord." But he
said to them, "Unless I see the mark of the nails in his hands
and put my finger into the nailmarks and put my hand into his
side, I will not believe." [26]Now a week later his disciples were
again inside and Thomas was with them. Jesus came,
although the doors were locked, and stood in their midst and
said, "Peace be with you." [27]Then he said to Thomas, "Put
your finger here and see my hands, and bring your hand and
put it into my side, and do not be unbelieving, but believe."
[28]Thomas answered and said to him, "My Lord and my God!"
[29]Jesus said to him, "Have you come to believe because you
have seen me? Blessed are those who have not seen and
have believed." [30]Now Jesus did many other signs in the
presence of his disciples that are not written in this book. [31]But
these are written that you may come to believe that Jesus is
the Christ, the Son of God, and that through this belief you
may have life in his name.

Monday April 17, 2023

Monday of the Second Week of Easter

First Reading – Acts 4:23-31

[23]After their release Peter and John went back to their own
people and reported what the chief priests and elders had told
them. [24]And when they heard it, they raised their voices to
God with one accord and said, "Sovereign Lord, maker of
heaven and earth and the sea and all that is in them, [25]you
said by the Holy Spirit through the mouth of our father David,
your servant: Why did the Gentiles rage and the peoples
entertain folly? [26]The kings of the earth took their stand and

the princes gathered together against the Lord and against his
anointed. [27]Indeed they gathered in this city against your holy
servant Jesus whom you anointed, Herod and Pontius Pilate,
together with the Gentiles and the peoples of Israel, [28]to do
what your hand and your will had long ago planned to take
place. [29]And now, Lord, take note of their threats, and enable
your servants to speak your word with all boldness, [30]as you
stretch forth your hand to heal, and signs and wonders are
done through the name of your holy servant Jesus." [31]As they
prayed, the place where they were gathered shook, and they
were all filled with the Holy Spirit and continued to speak the
word of God with boldness.

Responsorial Psalm – Psalms 2:1-3, 4-7A, 7B-9

R. (see 11d) **Blessed are all who take refuge in the Lord.** or: **R. Alleluia.**

1 Why do the nations rage

and the peoples utter folly?

2 The kings of the earth rise up,

and the princes conspire together

against the LORD and against his anointed:

3 "Let us break their fetters

and cast their bonds from us!"

R. Blessed are all who take refuge in the Lord. or: **R. Alleluia.**

4 He who is throned in heaven laughs;

the LORD derides them.

5 Then in anger he speaks to them;

he terrifies them in his wrath:

6 "I myself have set up my king

on Zion, my holy mountain."

7A I will proclaim the decree of the LORD.

R. Blessed are all who take refuge in the Lord. or: **R. Alleluia.**

7B The LORD said to me, "You are my Son;

this day I have begotten you.

8 Ask of me and I will give you

the nations for an inheritance

and the ends of the earth for your possession.

9 You shall rule them with an iron rod;

you shall shatter them like an earthen dish."

R. Blessed are all who take refuge in the Lord. or: **R. Alleluia.**

Alleluia – Colossians 3:1

R. Alleluia, alleluia.

1 If then you were raised with Christ, seek what is above, where Christ is seated at the right hand of God.

R. Alleluia, alleluia.

Gospel – John 3:1-8

1 There was a Pharisee named Nicodemus, a ruler of the Jews.
2 He came to Jesus at night and said to him, "Rabbi, we know
that you are a teacher who has come from God, for no one
can do these signs that you are doing unless God is with him."
3 Jesus answered and said to him, "Amen, amen, I say to you,
unless one is born from above, he cannot see the Kingdom of
God." 4 Nicodemus said to him, "How can a man once grown
old be born again? Surely he cannot reenter his mother's
womb and be born again, can he?" 5 Jesus answered, "Amen,
amen, I say to you, unless one is born of water and Spirit he
cannot enter the Kingdom of God. 6 What is born of flesh is
flesh and what is born of spirit is spirit. 7 Do not be amazed that
I told you, 'You must be born from above.' 8 The wind blows
where it wills, and you can hear the sound it makes, but you
do not know where it comes from or where it goes; so it is with
everyone who is born of the Spirit."

Tuesday April 18, 2023

Tuesday of the Second Week of Easter

First Reading – Acts 4:32-37

[32]The community of believers was of one heart and mind, and
no one claimed that any of his possessions was his own, but
they had everything in common. [33]With great power the
Apostles bore witness to the resurrection of the Lord Jesus,
and great favour was accorded them all. [34]There was no
needy person among them, for those who owned property or
houses would sell them, bring the proceeds of the sale, [35]and
put them at the feet of the Apostles, and they were distributed
to each according to need. [36]Thus Joseph, also named by the
Apostles Barnabas (which is translated "son of
encouragement"), a Levite, a Cypriot by birth, [37]sold a piece of
property that he owned, then brought the money and put it at
the feet of the Apostles.

Responsorial Psalm – Psalms 93:1AB, 1CD-2, 5

R. [(1a)] **The Lord is king; he is robed in majesty.** or: **R. Alleluia.**

[1AB] The LORD is king, in splendor robed;

robed is the LORD and girt about with strength.

R. The Lord is king; he is robed in majesty. or: **R. Alleluia.**

[1CD] And he has made the world firm,

not to be moved.

[2] Your throne stands firm from of old;

from everlasting you are, O LORD.

R. The Lord is king; he is robed in majesty. or: **R. Alleluia.**

[5] Your decrees are worthy of trust indeed:

holiness befits your house,

O LORD, for length of days.

R. The Lord is king; he is robed in majesty. or: **R. Alleluia.**

Alleluia – John 3:14-15

R. Alleluia, alleluia.

[14] The Son of Man must be lifted up, [15] so that everyone who
believes in him may have eternal life.

R. Alleluia, alleluia.

Gospel – John 3:7B-15

[7B]Jesus said to Nicodemus: "'You must be born from above.'
[8]The wind blows where it wills, and you can hear the sound it
makes, but you do not know where it comes from or where it
goes; so it is with everyone who is born of the Spirit."
[9]Nicodemus answered and said to him, 'How can this
happen?" [10]Jesus answered and said to him, "You are the
teacher of Israel and you do not understand this? [11]Amen,
amen, I say to you, we speak of what we know and we testify
to what we have seen, but you people do not accept our
testimony. [12]If I tell you about earthly things and you do not
believe, how will you believe if I tell you about heavenly
things? [13]No one has gone up to heaven except the one who
has come down from heaven, the Son of Man. [14]And just as
Moses lifted up the serpent in the desert, so must the Son of
Man be lifted up, so that everyone who believes in him may
have eternal life."

Wednesday April 19, 2023

Wednesday of the Second Week of Easter

First Reading – Acts 5:17-26

[17]The high priest rose up and all his companions, that is, the
party of the Sadducees, and, filled with jealousy, [18]laid hands
upon the Apostles and put them in the public jail. [19]But during
the night, the angel of the Lord opened the doors of the prison,
led them out, and said, [20]"Go and take your place in the
temple area, and tell the people everything about this life."
[21]When they heard this, they went to the temple early in the
morning and taught. When the high priest and his companions
arrived, they convened the Sanhedrin, the full senate of the
children of Israel, and sent to the jail to have them brought in.
[22]But the court officers who went did not find them in the
prison, so they came back and reported, [23]"We found the jail

securely locked and the guards stationed outside the doors, but when we opened them, we found no one inside."
24When
the captain of the temple guard and the chief priests heard this report, they were at a loss about them, as to what this would come to.
25Then someone came in and reported to them, "The men whom you put in prison are in the temple area and are teaching the people."
26Then the captain and the court officers went and brought them, but without force, because they were afraid of being stoned by the people.

Responsorial Psalm – Psalms 34:2-3, 4-5, 6-7, 8-9

R. (7a) **The Lord hears the cry of the poor.** or: **R. Alleluia.**

2 I will bless the LORD at all times;

his praise shall be ever in my mouth.

3 Let my soul glory in the LORD;

the lowly will hear me and be glad.

R. The Lord hears the cry of the poor. or: **R. Alleluia.**

4 Glorify the LORD with me,

let us together extol his name.

5 I sought the LORD, and he answered me

and delivered me from all my fears.

R. The Lord hears the cry of the poor. or: **R. Alleluia.**

6 Look to him that you may be radiant with joy,

and your faces may not blush with shame.

7 When the poor one called out, the LORD heard,

and from all his distress he saved him.

R. The Lord hears the cry of the poor. or: **R. Alleluia.**

8 The angel of the LORD encamps

around those who fear him, and delivers them.

9 Taste and see how good the LORD is;

blessed the man who takes refuge in him.

R. The Lord hears the cry of the poor. or: **R. Alleluia.**

Alleluia – John 3:16

R. Alleluia, alleluia.

[16] God so love the world that he gave his only-begotten Son, so that everyone who believes in him might have eternal life.

R. Alleluia, alleluia.

Gospel – John 3:16-21

[16]God so loved the world that he gave his only-begotten Son, so that everyone who believes in him might not perish but might have eternal life. [17]For God did not send his Son into the world to condemn the world, but that the world might be saved through him.[18]Whoever believes in him will not be condemned, but whoever does not believe has already been condemned, because he has not believed in the name of the only-begotten Son of God.[19]And this is the verdict, that the light came into the world, but people preferred darkness to light, because their works were evil.[20]For everyone who does wicked things hates the light and does not come toward the light, so that his works might not be exposed. [21]But whoever lives the truth comes to the light, so that his works may be clearly seen as done in God.

Thursday April 20, 2023

Thursday of the Second Week of Easter

First Reading – Acts 5:27-33

[27]When the court officers had brought the Apostles in and made them stand before the Sanhedrin, the high priest questioned them, [28]"We gave you strict orders did we not, to stop teaching in that name. Yet you have filled Jerusalem with your teaching and want to bring this man's blood upon us." [29]But Peter and the Apostles said in reply, "We must obey God rather than men. [30]The God of our ancestors raised Jesus, though you had him killed by hanging him on a tree. [31]God exalted him at his right hand as leader and savior to grant Israel repentance and forgiveness of sins. [32]We are witnesses of these things, as is the Holy Spirit whom God has given to those who obey him." [33]When they heard this, they became infuriated and wanted to put them to death.

Responsorial Psalm – Psalms 34:2 and 9, 17-18, 19-20

R. (7a) **The Lord hears the cry of the poor.** or: **R. Alleluia.**

2 I will bless the LORD at all times;

his praise shall be ever in my mouth.

9 Taste and see how good the LORD is;

blessed the man who takes refuge in him.

R. The Lord hears the cry of the poor. or: **R. Alleluia.**

17 The LORD confronts the evildoers,

to destroy remembrance of them from the earth.

18 When the just cry out, the LORD hears them,

and from all their distress he rescues them.

R. The Lord hears the cry of the poor. or: **R. Alleluia.**

19 The LORD is close to the brokenhearted;

and those who are crushed in spirit he saves.

20 Many are the troubles of the just man,

but out of them all the LORD delivers him.

R. The Lord hears the cry of the poor. or: **R. Alleluia.**

Alleluia – John 20:29

R. Alleluia, alleluia.

29 You believe in me, Thomas, because you have seen me, says the Lord; blessed are those who have not seen, but still believe!

R. Alleluia, alleluia.

Gospel – John 3:31-36

31The one who comes from above is above all. The one who is
of the earth is earthly and speaks of earthly things. But the
one who comes from heaven is above all. 32He testifies to
what he has seen and heard, but no one accepts his
testimony. 33Whoever does accept his testimony certifies that
God is trustworthy. 34For the one whom God sent speaks the

words of God. He does not ration his gift of the Spirit. [35]The Father loves the Son and has given everything over to him. [36]Whoever believes in the Son has eternal life, but whoever disobeys the Son will not see life, but the wrath of God remains upon him.

Friday April 21, 2023

Friday of the Second Week of Easter

First Reading – Acts 5:34-42

[34]A Pharisee in the Sanhedrin named Gamaliel, a teacher of the law, respected by all the people, stood up, ordered the Apostles to be put outside for a short time, [35]and said to the Sanhedrin, “Fellow children of Israel, be careful what you are about to do to these men. [36]Some time ago, Theudas appeared, claiming to be someone important, and about four hundred men joined him, but he was killed, and all those who were loyal to him were disbanded and came to nothing. [37]After him came Judas the Galilean at the time of the census. He also drew people after him, but he too perished and all who were loyal to him were scattered. [38]So now I tell you, have nothing to do with these men, and let them go. For if this endeavor or this activity is of human origin, it will destroy itself. [39]But if it comes from God, you will not be able to destroy them; you may even find yourselves fighting against God.” They were persuaded by him. [40]After recalling the Apostles, they had them flogged, ordered them to stop speaking in the name of Jesus, and dismissed them. [41]So they left the presence of the Sanhedrin, rejoicing that they had been found worthy to suffer dishonor for the sake of the name. [42]And all day long, both at the temple and in their homes, they did not stop teaching and proclaiming the Christ, Jesus.

Responsorial Psalm – Psalms 27:1, 4, 13-14

R. (see 4abc) **One thing I seek: to dwell in the house of the Lord.** or: **R. Alleluia.**

[1] The LORD is my light and my salvation;

whom should I fear?

The LORD is my life’s refuge;

of whom should I be afraid?

R. One thing I seek: to dwell in the house of the Lord. or: **R. Alleluia.**

4 One thing I ask of the LORD

this I seek:

To dwell in the house of the LORD

all the days of my life,

That I may gaze on the loveliness of the LORD

and contemplate his temple.

R. One thing I seek: to dwell in the house of the Lord. or: **R. Alleluia.**

13 I believe that I shall see the bounty of the LORD

in the land of the living.

14 Wait for the LORD with courage;

be stouthearted, and wait for the LORD.

R. One thing I seek: to dwell in the house of the Lord. or: **R. Alleluia.**

Alleluia – Matthew 4:4B

R. Alleluia, alleluia.

4B One does not live on bread alone, but on every word that comes forth from the mouth of God.

R. Alleluia, alleluia.

Gospel – John 6:1-15

1Jesus went across the Sea of Galilee. 2A large crowd
followed him, because they saw the signs he was performing
on the sick. 3Jesus went up on the mountain, and there he sat
down with his disciples. 4The Jewish feast of Passover was
near. 5When Jesus raised his eyes and saw that a large crowd
was coming to him, he said to Philip, "Where can we buy
enough food for them to eat?" 6He said this to test him,
because he himself knew what he was going to do. Philip
answered him, 7"Two hundred days' wages worth of food
would not be enough for each of them to have a little." 8One of
his disciples, Andrew, the brother of Simon Peter, said to him,
9"There is a boy here who has five barley loaves and two fish;

but what good are these for so many?" [10]Jesus said, "Have the
people recline." Now there was a great deal of grass in that
place. So the men reclined, about five thousand in number.
[11]Then Jesus took the loaves, gave thanks, and distributed
them to those who were reclining, and also as much of the fish
as they wanted. [12]When they had had their fill, he said to his
disciples, "Gather the fragments left over, so that nothing will
be wasted." [13]So they collected them, and filled twelve wicker
baskets with fragments from the five barley loaves that had
been more than they could eat. [14]When the people saw the
sign he had done, they said, "This is truly the Prophet, the one
who is to come into the world." [15]Since Jesus knew that they
were going to come and carry him off to make him king, he
withdrew again to the mountain alone.

Saturday April 22, 2023

Saturday of the Second Week of Easter

First Reading – Acts 6:1-7

[1]As the number of disciples continued to grow, the Hellenists
complained against the Hebrews because their widows were
being neglected in the daily distribution. [2]So the Twelve called
together the community of the disciples and said, "It is not right
for us to neglect the word of God to serve at table.[3]Brothers,
select from among you seven reputable men, filled with the
Spirit and wisdom, whom we shall appoint to this
task,[4]whereas we shall devote ourselves to prayer and to the
ministry of the word." [5]The proposal was acceptable to the
whole community, so they chose Stephen, a man filled with
faith and the Holy Spirit, also Philip, Prochorus, Nicanor,
Timon, Parmenas, and Nicholas of Antioch, a convert to
Judaism. [6]They presented these men to the Apostles who
prayed and laid hands on them. [7]The word of God continued
to spread, and the number of the disciples in Jerusalem
increased greatly; even a large group of priests were
becoming obedient to the faith.

Responsorial Psalm – Psalms 33:1-2, 4-5, 18-19

R. (22) **Lord, let your mercy be on us, as we place our trust in you.** or: **R. Alleluia.**

[1] Exult, you just, in the LORD;

praise from the upright is fitting.

2 Give thanks to the LORD on the harp;

with the ten-stringed lyre chant his praises.

R. Lord, let your mercy be on us, as we place our trust in you. or: **R. Alleluia.**

4 Upright is the word of the LORD,

and all his works are trustworthy.

5 He loves justice and right;

of the kindness of the LORD the earth is full.

R. Lord, let your mercy be on us, as we place our trust in you. or: **R. Alleluia.**

18 See, the eyes of the LORD are upon those who fear him,

upon those who hope for his kindness,

19 To deliver them from death

and preserve them in spite of famine.

R. Lord, let your mercy be on us, as we place our trust in you. or: **R. Alleluia.**

Alleluia

R. Alleluia, alleluia.

Christ is risen, who made all things; he has shown mercy on all people.

R. Alleluia, alleluia.

Gospel – John 6:16-21

16When it was evening, the disciples of Jesus went down to
the sea, 17embarked in a boat, and went across the sea to
Capernaum. It had already grown dark, and Jesus had not yet
come to them.18The sea was stirred up because a strong wind
was blowing.19When they had rowed about three or four miles,
they saw Jesus walking on the sea and coming near the boat,
and they began to be afraid.20But he said to them, "It is I. Do
not be afraid." 21They wanted to take him into the boat, but the
boat immediately arrived at the shore to which they were
heading.

Sunday April 23, 2023

Third Sunday of Easter, Year A

First Reading – Acts 2:14, 22-33

14 Then Peter stood up with the Eleven, raised his voice, and
proclaimed: “You who are Jews, indeed all of you staying in
Jerusalem. Let this be known to you, and listen to my
words. 22 You who are Israelites, hear these words. Jesus the
Nazarene was a man commended to you by God with mighty
deeds, wonders, and signs, which God worked through him in
your midst, as you yourselves know. 23 This man, delivered up
by the set plan and foreknowledge of God, you killed, using
lawless men to crucify him. 24 But God raised him up, releasing
him from the throes of death, because it was impossible for
him to be held by it. 25 For David says of him: I saw the Lord
ever before me, with him at my right hand I shall not be
disturbed. 26 Therefore my heart has been glad and my tongue
has exulted; my flesh, too, will dwell in hope, 27 because you
will not abandon my soul to the netherworld, nor will you suffer
your holy one to see corruption. 28 You have made known to
me the paths of life; you will fill me with joy in your presence.
29 “My brothers, one can confidently say to you about the
patriarch David that he died and was buried, and his tomb is in
our midst to this day. 30 But since he was a prophet and knew
that God had sworn an oath to him that he would set one of
his descendants upon his throne, 31 he foresaw and spoke of
the resurrection of the Christ, that neither was he abandoned
to the netherworld nor did his flesh see corruption. 32 God
raised this Jesus; of this we are all witnesses. 33 Exalted at the
right hand of God, he received the promise of the Holy Spirit
from the Father and poured him forth, as you see and hear.”

Responsorial Psalm – Psalms 16:1-2, 5, 7-8, 9-10, 11

R. (11a) **Lord, you will show us the path of life.** or: **R. Alleluia.**

1 Keep me, O God, for in you I take refuge;

2 I say to the LORD, “My Lord are you.”

5 O LORD, my allotted portion and my cup,

you it is who hold fast my lot.

R. Lord, you will show us the path of life. or: **R. Alleluia.**

[7] I bless the LORD who counsels me;

even in the night my heart exhorts me.

[8] I set the LORD ever before me;

with him at my right hand I shall not be disturbed.

R. Lord, you will show us the path of life. or: **R. Alleluia.**

[9] Therefore my heart is glad and my soul rejoices,

my body, too, abides in confidence;

[10] because you will not abandon my soul to the netherworld,

nor will you suffer your faithful one to undergo corruption.

R. Lord, you will show us the path of life. or: **R. Alleluia.**

[11] You will show me the path to life,

abounding joy in your presence,

the delights at your right hand forever.

R. Lord, you will show us the path of life. or: **R. Alleluia.**

Second Reading – 1 Peter 1:17-21

[17]Beloved: If you invoke as Father him who judges impartially
according to each one's works, conduct yourselves with
reverence during the time of your sojourning,[18]realizing that
you were ransomed from your futile conduct, handed on by
your ancestors, not with perishable things like silver or gold
[19]but with the precious blood of Christ as of a spotless
unblemished lamb. [20]He was known before the foundation of
the world but revealed in the final time for you, [21]who through
him believe in God who raised him from the dead and gave
him glory, so that your faith and hope are in God.

Alleluia – Luke 24:32

R. Alleluia, alleluia.

[32] Lord Jesus, open the Scriptures to us; make our hearts burn while you speak to us.

R. Alleluia, alleluia.

Gospel – Luke 24:13-35

[13]That very day, the first day of the week, two of Jesus'
disciples were going to a village seven miles from Jerusalem
called Emmaus, [14]and they were conversing about all the
things that had occurred. [15]And it happened that while they
were conversing and debating, Jesus himself drew near and
walked with them,[16]but their eyes were prevented from
recognizing him. [17]He asked them, "What are you discussing
as you walk along?" They stopped, looking downcast. [18]One of
them, named Cleopas, said to him in reply, "Are you the only
visitor to Jerusalem who does not know of the things that have
taken place there in these days?" [19]And he replied to them,
"What sort of things?" They said to him, "The things that
happened to Jesus the Nazarene, who was a prophet mighty
in deed and word before God and all the people, [20]how our
chief priests and rulers both handed him over to a sentence of
death and crucified him. [21]But we were hoping that he would
be the one to redeem Israel; and besides all this, it is now the
third day since this took place. [22]Some women from our group,
however, have astounded us: they were at the tomb early in
the morning [23]and did not find his body; they came back and
reported that they had indeed seen a vision of angels who
announced that he was alive. [24]Then some of those with us
went to the tomb and found things just as the women had
described, but him they did not see." [25]And he said to them,
"Oh, how foolish you are! How slow of heart to believe all that
the prophets spoke! [27]Was it not necessary that the Christ
should suffer these things and enter into his glory?" Then
beginning with Moses and all the prophets, he interpreted to
them what referred to him in all the Scriptures. [28]As they
approached the village to which they were going, he gave the
impression that he was going on farther. [29]But they urged him,
"Stay with us, for it is nearly evening and the day is almost
over." So he went in to stay with them. [30]And it happened that,
while he was with them at table, he took bread, said the
blessing, broke it, and gave it to them. [31]With that their eyes
were opened and they recognized him, but he vanished from
their sight. [32]Then they said to each other, "Were not our
hearts burning within us while he spoke to us on the way and
opened the Scriptures to us?" [33]So they set out at once and
returned to Jerusalem where they found gathered together the
eleven and those with them [34]who were saying, "The Lord has

truly been raised and has appeared to Simon!" 35Then the two
recounted what had taken place on the way and how he was
made known to them in the breaking of bread.

Monday April 24, 2023

Monday of the Third Week of Easter

First Reading – Acts 6:8-15

8Stephen, filled with grace and power, was working great
wonders and signs among the people. 9Certain members of
the so-called Synagogue of Freedmen, Cyreneans, and
Alexandrians, and people from Cilicia and Asia, came forward
and debated with Stephen,10but they could not withstand the
wisdom and the Spirit with which he spoke.11Then they
instigated some men to say, "We have heard him speaking
blasphemous words against Moses and God." 12They stirred
up the people, the elders, and the scribes, accosted him,
seized him, and brought him before the Sanhedrin.13They
presented false witnesses who testified, "This man never
stops saying things against this holy place and the law.14For
we have heard him claim that this Jesus the Nazorean will
destroy this place and change the customs that Moses
handed down to us." 15All those who sat in the Sanhedrin
looked intently at him and saw that his face was like the face
of an angel.

Responsorial Psalm – Psalms 119:23-24, 26-27, 29-30

R. (1ab) **Blessed are they who follow the law of the Lord!** or: **R. Alleluia.**

23 Though princes meet and talk against me,

your servant meditates on your statutes.

24 Yes, your decrees are my delight;

they are my counselors.

R. Blessed are they who follow the law of the Lord! or: **R. Alleluia.**

26 I declared my ways, and you answered me;

teach me your statutes.

27 Make me understand the way of your precepts,

and I will meditate on your wondrous deeds.

R. Blessed are they who follow the law of the Lord! or: **R. Alleluia.**

29 Remove from me the way of falsehood,

and favor me with your law.

30 The way of truth I have chosen;

I have set your ordinances before me.

R. Blessed are they who follow the law of the Lord! or: **R. Alleluia.**

Alleluia – Matthew 4:4B

R. Alleluia, alleluia.

4B One does not live on bread alone but on every word that comes forth from the mouth of God.

R. Alleluia, alleluia.

Gospel – John 6:22-29

[After Jesus had fed the five thousand men, his disciples saw
him walking on the sea.] 22 The next day, the crowd that
remained across the sea saw that there had been only one
boat there, and that Jesus had not gone along with his
disciples in the boat, but only his disciples had left. 23 Other
boats came from Tiberias near the place where they had
eaten the bread when the Lord gave thanks. 24 When the
crowd saw that neither Jesus nor his disciples were there, they
themselves got into boats and came to Capernaum looking for
Jesus. 25 And when they found him across the sea they said to
him, "Rabbi, when did you get here?" 26 Jesus answered them
and said, "Amen, amen, I say to you, you are looking for me
not because you saw signs but because you ate the loaves
and were filled. 27 Do not work for food that perishes but for the
food that endures for eternal life, which the Son of Man will
give you. For on him the Father, God, has set his seal." 28 So
they said to him, "What can we do to accomplish the works of
God?" 29 Jesus answered and said to them, "This is the work of
God, that you believe in the one he sent."

Tuesday April 25, 2023

Feast of Saint Mark the Evangelist

First Reading – 1 Peter 5:5B-14

[5B]Beloved: Clothe yourselves with humility in your dealings
with one another, for God opposes the proud but bestows
favor on the humble. [6]So humble yourselves under the mighty
hand of God, that he may exalt you in due time.[7]Cast all your
worries upon him because he cares for you. [8]Be sober and
vigilant. Your opponent the Devil is prowling around like a
roaring lion looking for someone to devour. [9]Resist him,
steadfast in faith, knowing that your brothers and sisters
throughout the world undergo the same sufferings. [10]The God
of all grace who called you to his eternal glory through Christ
Jesus will himself restore, confirm, strengthen, and establish
you after you have suffered a little.[11]To him be dominion
forever. Amen. [12]I write you this briefly through Silvanus,
whom I consider a faithful brother, exhorting you and testifying
that this is the true grace of God. Remain firm in it. [13]The
chosen one at Babylon sends you greeting, as does Mark, my
son. [14]Greet one another with a loving kiss. Peace to all of you
who are in Christ.

Responsorial Psalm – Psalms 89:2-3, 6-7, 16-17

R. [(2)] **For ever I will sing the goodness of the Lord.** or: **R. Alleluia.**

[2] The favors of the LORD I will sing forever;

through all generations my mouth shall proclaim your faithfulness.

[3] For you have said, “My kindness is established forever”;

in heaven you have confirmed your faithfulness.

R. For ever I will sing the goodness of the Lord. or: **R. Alleluia.**

[6] The heavens proclaim your wonders, O LORD,

and your faithfulness, in the assembly of the holy ones.

[7] For who in the skies can rank with the LORD?

Who is like the LORD among the sons of God?

R. For ever I will sing the goodness of the Lord. or: **R. Alleluia.**

16 Blessed the people who know the joyful shout;

in the light of your countenance, O LORD, they walk.

17 At your name they rejoice all the day,

and through your justice they are exalted.

R. For ever I will sing the goodness of the Lord. or: **R. Alleluia.**

Alleluia – 1 Corinthians 1:23A-24B

R. Alleluia, alleluia.

23A We proclaim Christ crucified; 24B he is the power of God
and the wisdom of God.

R. Alleluia, alleluia.

Gospel – Mark 16:15-20

15Jesus appeared to the Eleven and said to them: “Go into the
whole world and proclaim the Gospel to every creature.
16Whoever believes and is baptized will be saved; whoever
does not believe will be condemned. 17These signs will
accompany those who believe: in my name they will drive out
demons, they will speak new languages.18They will pick up
serpents with their hands, and if they drink any deadly thing, it
will not harm them. They will lay hands on the sick, and they
will recover.” 19Then the Lord Jesus, after he spoke to them,
was taken up into heaven and took his seat at the right hand
of God. 20But they went forth and preached everywhere, while
the Lord worked with them and confirmed the word through
accompanying signs.

Wednesday April 26, 2023

Wednesday of the Third Week of Easter

First Reading – Acts 8:1B-8

1BThere broke out a severe persecution of the Church in
Jerusalem, and all were scattered throughout the countryside
of Judea and Samaria, except the Apostles. 2Devout men
buried Stephen and made a loud lament over him.3Saul,

meanwhile, was trying to destroy the Church; entering house after house and dragging out men and women, he handed them over for imprisonment.
4Now those who had been scattered went about preaching the word.
5Thus Philip went down to the city of Samaria and proclaimed the Christ to them.
6With one accord, the crowds paid attention to what was said by Philip when they heard it and saw the signs he was doing.
7For unclean spirits, crying out in a loud voice, came out of many possessed people, and many paralyzed and crippled people were cured.
8There was great joy in that city.

Responsorial Psalm – Psalms 66:1-3A, 4-5, 6-7A

R. (1) Let all the earth cry out to God with joy. or: **R. Alleluia.**

2 Shout joyfully to God, all the earth,

sing praise to the glory of his name;

proclaim his glorious praise.

3A Say to God, "How tremendous are your deeds!"

R. Let all the earth cry out to God with joy. or: **R. Alleluia.**

4 "Let all on earth worship and sing praise to you,

sing praise to your name!"

5 Come and see the works of God,

his tremendous deeds among the children of Adam.

R. Let all the earth cry out to God with joy. or: **R. Alleluia.**

6 He has changed the sea into dry land;

through the river they passed on foot;

therefore let us rejoice in him.

7A He rules by his might forever.

R. Let all the earth cry out to God with joy. or: **R. Alleluia.**

Alleluia – cf. John 6:40

R. Alleluia, alleluia.

40 Everyone who believes in the Son has eternal life, and I shall raise him on the last day, says the Lord.

R. Alleluia, alleluia.

Gospel – John 6:35-40

[35]Jesus said to the crowds, "I am the bread of life; whoever
comes to me will never hunger, and whoever believes in me
will never thirst. [36]But I told you that although you have seen
me, you do not believe. [37]Everything that the Father gives me
will come to me, and I will not reject anyone who comes to
me,[38]because I came down from heaven not to do my own will
but the will of the one who sent me.[39]And this is the will of the
one who sent me, that I should not lose anything of what he
gave me, but that I should raise it on the last day. [40]For this is
the will of my Father, that everyone who sees the Son and
believes in him may have eternal life, and I shall raise him on
the last day."

Thursday April 27, 2023

Thursday of the Third Week of Easter

First Reading – Acts 8:26-40

[26]The angel of the Lord spoke to Philip, "Get up and head
south on the road that goes down from Jerusalem to Gaza, the
desert route." [27]So he got up and set out. Now there was an
Ethiopian eunuch, a court official of the Candace, that is, the
queen of the Ethiopians, in charge of her entire treasury, who
had come to Jerusalem to worship, [28]and was returning home.
Seated in his chariot, he was reading the prophet Isaiah.[29]The
Spirit said to Philip, "Go and join up with that chariot."[30]Philip
ran up and heard him reading Isaiah the prophet and said, "Do
you understand what you are reading?" [31]He replied, "How can
I, unless someone instructs me?" So he invited Philip to get in
and sit with him. [32]This was the Scripture passage he was
reading: Like a sheep he was led to the slaughter, and as a
lamb before its shearer is silent, so he opened not his mouth.
[33]In his humiliation justice was denied him. Who will tell of his
posterity? For his life is taken from the earth. [34]Then the
eunuch said to Philip in reply, "I beg you, about whom is the
prophet saying this? About himself, or about someone else?"
[35]Then Philip opened his mouth and, beginning with this
Scripture passage, he proclaimed Jesus to him. [36]As they
traveled along the road they came to some water, and the
eunuch said, "Look, there is water. What is to prevent my

being baptized?” [38]Then he ordered the chariot to stop, and
Philip and the eunuch both went down into the water, and he
baptized him. [39]When they came out of the water, the Spirit of
the Lord snatched Philip away, and the eunuch saw him no
more, but continued on his way rejoicing. [40]Philip came to
Azotus, and went about proclaiming the good news to all the
towns until he reached Caesarea.

Responsorial Psalm – Psalms 66:8-9, 16-17, 20

R. [(1)] **Let all the earth cry out to God with joy.** or: **R. Alleluia.**

[8] Bless our God, you peoples,

loudly sound his praise;

[9] He has given life to our souls,

and has not let our feet slip.

R. Let all the earth cry out to God with joy. or: **R. Alleluia.**

[16] Hear now, all you who fear God, while I declare

what he has done for me.

[17] When I appealed to him in words,

praise was on the tip of my tongue.

R. Let all the earth cry out to God with joy. or: **R. Alleluia.**

[20] Blessed be God who refused me not

my prayer or his kindness!

R. Let all the earth cry out to God with joy. or: **R. Alleluia.**

Alleluia – John 6:51

R. Alleluia, alleluia.

[51]I am the living bread that came down from heaven, says the Lord; whoever eats this bread will live forever.

R. Alleluia, alleluia.

Gospel – John 6:44-51

[44]Jesus said to the crowds: “No one can come to me unless
the Father who sent me draw him, and I will raise him on the
last day. [45]It is written in the prophets: They shall all be taught

by God. Everyone who listens to my Father and learns from
him comes to me. [46]Not that anyone has seen the Father
except the one who is from God; he has seen the Father.
[47]Amen, amen, I say to you, whoever believes has eternal life.
[48]I am the bread of life. [49]Your ancestors ate the manna in the
desert, but they died; [50]this is the bread that comes down from
heaven so that one may eat it and not die. [51]I am the living
bread that came down from heaven; whoever eats this bread
will live forever; and the bread that I will give is my Flesh for
the life of the world."

Friday April 28, 2023

Friday of the Third Week of Easter

First Reading – Acts 9:1-20

[1]Saul, still breathing murderous threats against the disciples of
the Lord, went to the high priest [2]and asked him for letters to
the synagogues in Damascus, that, if he should find any men
or women who belonged to the Way, he might bring them back
to Jerusalem in chains.[3]On his journey, as he was nearing
Damascus, a light from the sky suddenly flashed around him.
[4]He fell to the ground and heard a voice saying to him, "Saul,
Saul, why are you persecuting me?" [5]He said, "Who are you,
sir?" The reply came, "I am Jesus, whom you are persecuting.
[6]Now get up and go into the city and you will be told what you
must do." [7]The men who were traveling with him stood
speechless, for they heard the voice but could see no one.
[8]Saul got up from the ground, but when he opened his eyes he
could see nothing; so they led him by the hand and brought
him to Damascus. [9]For three days he was unable to see, and
he neither ate nor drank. [10]There was a disciple in Damascus
named Ananias, and the Lord said to him in a vision,
"Ananias." He answered, "Here I am, Lord." [11]The Lord said to
him, "Get up and go to the street called Straight and ask at the
house of Judas for a man from Tarsus named Saul. He is
there praying, [12]and in a vision he has seen a man named
Ananias come in and lay his hands on him, that he may regain
his sight." [13]But Ananias replied, "Lord, I have heard from
many sources about this man, what evil things he has done to
your holy ones in Jerusalem. [14]And here he has authority from
the chief priests to imprison all who call upon your name."
[15]But the Lord said to him, "Go, for this man is a chosen

instrument of mine to carry my name before Gentiles, kings,
and children of Israel,16and I will show him what he will have to
suffer for my name.” 17So Ananias went and entered the
house; laying his hands on him, he said, “Saul, my brother, the
Lord has sent me, Jesus who appeared to you on the way by
which you came, that you may regain your sight and be filled
with the Holy Spirit.” 18Immediately things like scales fell from
his eyes and he regained his sight. He got up and was
baptized, 19and when he had eaten, he recovered his strength.
He stayed some days with the disciples in Damascus, 20and
he began at once to proclaim Jesus in the synagogues, that
he is the Son of God.

Responsorial Psalm – Psalms 117:1BC, 2

R. (Mark 16:15) **Go out to all the world and tell the Good News.**
or: **R. Alleluia.**

1BC Praise the LORD, all you nations;

glorify him, all you peoples!

R. Go out to all the world and tell the Good News. or: **R. Alleluia.**

2 For steadfast is his kindness toward us,

and the fidelity of the LORD endures forever.

R. Go out to all the world and tell the Good News. or: **R. Alleluia.**

Alleluia – John 6:56

R. Alleluia, alleluia.

56 Whoever eats my Flesh and drinks my Blood, remains in me and I in him, says the Lord.

R. Alleluia, alleluia.

Gospel – John 6:52-59

52The Jews quarreled among themselves, saying, “How can
this man give us his Flesh to eat?” 53Jesus said to them,
“Amen, amen, I say to you, unless you eat the Flesh of the
Son of Man and drink his Blood, you do not have life within
you. 54Whoever eats my Flesh and drinks my Blood has
eternal life, and I will raise him on the last day. 55For my Flesh

is true food, and my Blood is true drink.[56]Whoever eats my Flesh and drinks my Blood remains in me and I in him. [57]Just as the living Father sent me and I have life because of the Father, so also the one who feeds on me will have life because of me.[58]This is the bread that came down from heaven. Unlike your ancestors who ate and still died, whoever eats this bread will live forever." [59]These things he said while teaching in the synagogue in Capernaum.

Saturday April 29, 2023

Memorial of Saint Catherine of Siena – Virgin & Doctor

First Reading – Acts 9:31-42

[31]The Church throughout all Judea, Galilee, and Samaria was at peace. She was being built up and walked in the fear of the Lord, and with the consolation of the Holy Spirit she grew in numbers. [32]As Peter was passing through every region, he went down to the holy ones living in Lydda. [33]There he found a man named Aeneas, who had been confined to bed for eight years, for he was paralyzed.[34]Peter said to him, "Aeneas, Jesus Christ heals you. Get up and make your bed." He got up at once. [35]And all the inhabitants of Lydda and Sharon saw him, and they turned to the Lord. [36]Now in Joppa there was a disciple named Tabitha (which translated is Dorcas). She was completely occupied with good deeds and almsgiving. [37]Now during those days she fell sick and died, so after washing her, they laid her out in a room upstairs. [38]Since Lydda was near Joppa, the disciples, hearing that Peter was there, sent two men to him with the request, "Please come to us without delay." [39]So Peter got up and went with them. When he arrived, they took him to the room upstairs where all the widows came to him weeping and showing him the tunics and cloaks that Dorcas had made while she was with them. [40]Peter sent them all out and knelt down and prayed. Then he turned to her body and said, "Tabitha, rise up." She opened her eyes, saw Peter, and sat up. [41]He gave her his hand and raised her up, and when he had called the holy ones and the widows, he presented her alive.[42]This became known all over Joppa, and many came to believe in the Lord.

Responsorial Psalm – Psalms 116:12-13, 14-15, 16-17

R. [(12)] **How shall I make a return to the Lord for all the good he has done for me?** or: **R. Alleluia.**

12 How shall I make a return to the LORD

for all the good he has done for me?

13 The cup of salvation I will take up,

and I will call upon the name of the LORD

R. How shall I make a return to the Lord for all the good he has done for me? or: **R. Alleluia.**

14 My vows to the LORD I will pay

in the presence of all his people.

15 Precious in the eyes of the LORD

is the death of his faithful ones.

R. How shall I make a return to the Lord for all the good he has done for me? or: **R. Alleluia.**

16 O LORD, I am your servant;

I am your servant, the son of your handmaid;

you have loosed my bonds.

17 To you will I offer sacrifice of thanksgiving,

and I will call upon the name of the LORD.

R. How shall I make a return to the Lord for all the good he has done for me? or: **R. Alleluia.**

Alleluia – cf. John 6:63C, 68C

R. Alleluia, alleluia.

63C Your words, Lord, are Spirit and life; 68C you have the words of everlasting life.

R. Alleluia, alleluia.

Gospel – John 6:60-69

60 Many of the disciples of Jesus who were listening said, "This
saying is hard; who can accept it?" 61 Since Jesus knew that

his disciples were murmuring about this, he said to them,
"Does this shock you? 62What if you were to see the Son of
Man ascending to where he was before? 63It is the Spirit that
gives life, while the flesh is of no avail. The words I have
spoken to you are Spirit and life. 64But there are some of you
who do not believe." Jesus knew from the beginning the ones
who would not believe and the one who would betray him.
65And he said, "For this reason I have told you that no one can
come to me unless it is granted him by my Father." 66As a
result of this, many of his disciples returned to their former way
of life and no longer walked with him. 67Jesus then said to the
Twelve, "Do you also want to leave?" 68Simon Peter answered
him, "Master, to whom shall we go? You have the words of
eternal life. 69We have come to believe and are convinced that
you are the Holy One of God."

Sunday April 30, 2023

Fourth Sunday of Easter, Year A

First Reading – Acts 2:14A, 36-41

14AThen Peter stood up with the Eleven, raised his voice, and
proclaimed: 36"Let the whole house of Israel know for certain
that God has made both Lord and Christ, this Jesus whom you
crucified." 37Now when they heard this, they were cut to the
heart, and they asked Peter and the other apostles, "What are
we to do, my brothers?" 38Peter said to them, "Repent and be
baptized, every one of you, in the name of Jesus Christ for the
forgiveness of your sins; and you will receive the gift of the
Holy Spirit. 39For the promise is made to you and to your
children and to all those far off, whomever the Lord our God
will call." 40He testified with many other arguments, and was
exhorting them, "Save yourselves from this corrupt
generation." 41Those who accepted his message were
baptized, and about three thousand persons were added that
day.

Responsorial Psalm – Psalms 23: 1-3a, 3b, 4, 5, 6

R. (1) The Lord is my shepherd; there is nothing I shall want. or: **R. Alleluia.**

1 The LORD is my shepherd; I shall not want.

2 In verdant pastures he gives me repose;

beside restful waters he leads me;

3A he refreshes my soul.

R. The Lord is my shepherd; there is nothing I shall want.
or: **R. Alleluia.**

3BC He guides me in right paths

for his name's sake.

4 Even though I walk in the dark valley

I fear no evil; for you are at my side.

With your rod and your staff

that give me courage.

R. The Lord is my shepherd; there is nothing I shall want.
or: **R. Alleluia.**

5 You spread the table before me

in the sight of my foes;

you anoint my head with oil;

my cup overflows.

R. The Lord is my shepherd; there is nothing I shall want.
or: **R. Alleluia.**

6 Only goodness and kindness follow me

all the days of my life;

and I shall dwell in the house of the LORD

for years to come.

R. The Lord is my shepherd; there is nothing I shall want.
or: **R. Alleluia.**

Second Reading – 1 Peter 2:20B-25

20BBeloved: If you are patient when you suffer for doing what is
good, this is a grace before God. 21For to this you have been
called, because Christ also suffered for you, leaving you an
example that you should follow in his footsteps. 22He
committed no sin, and no deceit was found in his mouth.
23When he was insulted, he returned no insult; when he
suffered, he did not threaten; instead, he handed himself over

to the one who judges justly. [24]He himself bore our sins in his
body upon the cross, so that, free from sin, we might live for
righteousness. By his wounds you have been healed. [25]For
you had gone astray like sheep, but you have now returned to
the shepherd and guardian of your souls.

Alleluia – John 10:14

R. Alleluia, alleluia.

[14] I am the good shepherd, says the Lord; I know my sheep, and mine know me.

R. Alleluia, alleluia.

Gospel – John 10:1-10

[1]Jesus said: "Amen, amen, I say to you, whoever does not
enter a sheepfold through the gate but climbs over elsewhere
is a thief and a robber. [2]But whoever enters through the gate
is the shepherd of the sheep. [3]The gatekeeper opens it for
him, and the sheep hear his voice, as the shepherd calls his
own sheep by name and leads them out. [4]When he has driven
out all his own, he walks ahead of them, and the sheep follow
him, because they recognize his voice. [5]But they will not follow
a stranger; they will run away from him, because they do not
recognize the voice of strangers." [6]Although Jesus used this
figure of speech, the Pharisees did not realize what he was
trying to tell them. [7]So Jesus said again, "Amen, amen, I say
to you, I am the gate for the sheep. [8]All who came before me
are thieves and robbers, but the sheep did not listen to them.
[9]I am the gate. Whoever enters through me will be saved, and
will come in and go out and find pasture. [10]A thief comes only
to steal and slaughter and destroy; I came so that they might
have life and have it more abundantly."

MAY 2023

Monday May 1, 2023

Monday of the Fourth Week of Easter

First Reading – Acts 11:1-18

[1]The Apostles and the brothers who were in Judea heard that
the Gentiles too had accepted the word of God. [2]So when
Peter went up to Jerusalem the circumcised believers

confronted him, 3saying, 'You entered the house of
uncircumcised people and ate with them." 4Peter began and
explained it to them step by step, saying, 5"I was at prayer in
the city of Joppa when in a trance I had a vision, something
resembling a large sheet coming down, lowered from the sky
by its four corners, and it came to me. 6Looking intently into it,
I observed and saw the four-legged animals of the earth, the
wild beasts, the reptiles, and the birds of the sky. 7I also heard
a voice say to me, 'Get up, Peter. Slaughter and eat.' 8But I
said, 'Certainly not, sir, because nothing profane or unclean
has ever entered my mouth.' 9But a second time a voice from
heaven answered, 'What God has made clean, you are not to
call profane.' 10This happened three times, and then
everything was drawn up again into the sky. 11Just then three
men appeared at the house where we were, who had been
sent to me from Caesarea. 12The Spirit told me to accompany
them without discriminating. These six brothers also went with
me, and we entered the man's house. 13He related to us how
he had seen the angel standing in his house, saying, 'Send
someone to Joppa and summon Simon, who is called Peter, 14
who will speak words to you by which you and all your
household will be saved.' 15As I began to speak, the Holy Spirit
fell upon them as it had upon us at the beginning,16and I
remembered the word of the Lord, how he had said, 'John
baptized with water but you will be baptized with the Holy
Spirit.' 17If then God gave them the same gift he gave to us
when we came to believe in the Lord Jesus Christ, who was I
to be able to hinder God?" 18When they heard this, they
stopped objecting and glorified God, saying, "God has then
granted life-giving repentance to the Gentiles too."

Responsorial Psalm – Psalms 42:2-3; 43:3, 4

R. (see 3a) **Athirst is my soul for the living God.** or: **R. Alleluia.**

2 As the hind longs for the running waters,

so my soul longs for you, O God.

3 Athirst is my soul for God, the living God.

When shall I go and behold the face of God?

R. Athirst is my soul for the living God. or: **R. Alleluia.**

3 Send forth your light and your fidelity;

they shall lead me on

And bring me to your holy mountain,

to your dwelling-place.

R. Athirst is my soul for the living God. or: **R. Alleluia.**

4 Then will I go in to the altar of God,

the God of my gladness and joy;

Then will I give you thanks upon the harp,

O God, my God!

R. Athirst is my soul for the living God. or: **R. Alleluia.**

Alleluia – John 10:14

R. Alleluia, alleluia.

14 I am the good shepherd, says the Lord; I know my sheep, and mine know me.

R. Alleluia, alleluia.

Gospel – John 10:1-10

1Jesus said: "Amen, amen, I say to you, whoever does not enter a sheepfold through the gate but climbs over elsewhere
is a thief and a robber. 2But whoever enters through the gate
is the shepherd of the sheep. 3The gatekeeper opens it for
him, and the sheep hear his voice, as the shepherd calls his
own sheep by name and leads them out. 4When he has driven
out all his own, he walks ahead of them, and the sheep follow
him, because they recognize his voice. 5But they will not follow
a stranger; they will run away from him, because they do not
recognize the voice of strangers." 6Although Jesus used this
figure of speech, the Pharisees did not realize what he was
trying to tell them. 7So Jesus said again, "Amen, amen, I say
to you, I am the gate for the sheep. 8All who came before me
are thieves and robbers, but the sheep did not listen to them.
9I am the gate. Whoever enters through me will be saved, and
will come in and go out and find pasture. 10A thief comes only
to steal and slaughter and destroy; I came so that they might have life and have it more abundantly."

Tuesday May 2, 2023

Memorial of Athanasius – Bishop & Bishop

First Reading – Acts 11:19-26

19 Those who had been scattered by the persecution that arose
because of Stephen went as far as Phoenicia, Cyprus, and
Antioch, preaching the word to no one but Jews. 20 There were
some Cypriots and Cyrenians among them, however, who
came to Antioch and began to speak to the Greeks as well,
proclaiming the Lord Jesus. 21 The hand of the Lord was with
them and a great number who believed turned to the Lord.
22 The news about them reached the ears of the Church in
Jerusalem, and they sent Barnabas to go to Antioch. 24 When
he arrived and saw the grace of God, he rejoiced and
encouraged them all to remain faithful to the Lord in firmness
of heart, for he was a good man, filled with the Holy Spirit and
faith. And a large number of people was added to the Lord.
25 Then he went to Tarsus to look for Saul, 26 and when he had
found him he brought him to Antioch. For a whole year they
met with the Church and taught a large number of people, and
it was in Antioch that the disciples were first called Christians.

Responsorial Psalm – Psalms 87:1B-3, 4-5, 6-7

R. (117:1a) **All you nations, praise the Lord.** or: **R. Alleluia.**

1B His foundation upon the holy mountains

the LORD loves:

2 The gates of Zion,

more than any dwelling of Jacob.

3 Glorious things are said of you,

O city of God!

R. All you nations, praise the Lord. or: **R. Alleluia.**

4 I tell of Egypt and Babylon

among those who know the LORD;

Of Philistia, Tyre, Ethiopia:

"This man was born there."

5 And of Zion they shall say:

"One and all were born in her;

And he who has established her

is the Most High LORD."

R. All you nations, praise the Lord. or: **R. Alleluia.**

6 They shall note, when the peoples are enrolled:

"This man was born there."

7 And all shall sing, in their festive dance:

"My home is within you."

R. All you nations, praise the Lord. or: **R. Alleluia.**

Alleluia – John 10:27

R. Alleluia, alleluia.

27 My sheep hear my voice, says the Lord; I know them, and they follow me.

R. Alleluia, alleluia.

Gospel – John 10:22-30

22The feast of the Dedication was taking place in Jerusalem. It
was winter. 23And Jesus walked about in the temple area on
the Portico of Solomon. 24So the Jews gathered around him
and said to him, "How long are you going to keep us in
suspense? If you are the Christ, tell us plainly." 25Jesus
answered them, "I told you and you do not believe. The works
I do in my Father's name testify to me. 26But you do not
believe, because you are not among my sheep. 27My sheep
hear my voice; I know them, and they follow me. 28I give them
eternal life, and they shall never perish. No one can take them
out of my hand. 29My Father, who has given them to me, is
greater than all, and no one can take them out of the Father's
hand. 30The Father and I are one."

Wednesday May 3, 2023

Feast of Saints Philip and James, Apostles

First Reading – 1 Corinthians 15:1-8

1I am reminding you, brothers and sisters, of the Gospel I preached to you, which you indeed received and in which you

also stand. 2Through it you are also being saved, if you hold
fast to the word I preached to you, unless you believed in vain.
3For I handed on to you as of first importance what I also
received: that Christ died for our sins in accordance with the
Scriptures; 4that he was buried; that he was raised on the third
day in accordance with the Scriptures; 5that he appeared to
Cephas, then to the Twelve. 6After that, he appeared to more
than five hundred brothers and sisters at once, most of whom
are still living, though some have fallen asleep. 7After that he
appeared to James, then to all the Apostles. 8Last of all, as to
one born abnormally, he appeared to me.

Responsorial Psalm – Psalms 19:2-3, 4-5

R. (5) **Their message goes out through all the earth.** or: **R. Alleluia.**

2 The heavens declare the glory of God;

and the firmament proclaims his handiwork.

3 Day pours out the word to day;

and night to night imparts knowledge.

R. Their message goes out through all the earth. or: **R. Alleluia.**

4 Not a word nor a discourse

whose voice is not heard;

5 Through all the earth their voice resounds,

and to the ends of the world, their message.

R. Their message goes out through all the earth. or: **R. Alleluia.**

Alleluia – John 14:6B, 9C

R. Alleluia, alleluia.

6B I am the way, the truth, and the life, says the Lord; 9C Philip, whoever has seen me has seen the Father.

R. Alleluia, alleluia.

Gospel – John 14:6-14

[6]Jesus said to Thomas, "I am the way and the truth and the
life. No one comes to the Father except through me. [7]If you
know me, then you will also know my Father. From now on
you do know him and have seen him." [8]Philip said to him,
"Master, show us the Father, and that will be enough for us."
[9]Jesus said to him, "Have I been with you for so long a time
and you still do not know me, Philip? Whoever has seen me
has seen the Father. How can you say, 'Show us the Father'?
[10]Do you not believe that I am in the Father and the Father is
in me? The words that I speak to you I do not speak on my
own. The Father who dwells in me is doing his works.
[11]Believe me that I am in the Father and the Father is in me, or
else, believe because of the works themselves.[12]Amen, amen,
I say to you, whoever believes in me will do the works that I
do, and will do greater ones than these, because I am going to
the Father. [13]And whatever you ask in my name, I will do, so
that the Father may be glorified in the Son. [14]If you ask
anything of me in my name, I will do it."

Thursday May 4, 2023

Thursday of the Fourth Week of Easter

First Reading – Acts 13:13-25

[13]From Paphos, Paul and his companions set sail and arrived
at Perga in Pamphylia. But John left them and returned to
Jerusalem. [14]They continued on from Perga and reached
Antioch in Pisidia. On the Sabbath they entered into the
synagogue and took their seats. [15]After the reading of the law
and the prophets, the synagogue officials sent word to them,
"My brothers, if one of you has a word of exhortation for the
people, please speak." [16]So Paul got up, motioned with his
hand, and said, "Fellow children of Israel and you others who
are God-fearing, listen. [17]The God of this people Israel chose
our ancestors and exalted the people during their sojourn in
the land of Egypt. With uplifted arm he led them out, [18]and for
about forty years he put up with them in the desert. [19]When he
had destroyed seven nations in the land of Canaan, he gave
them their land as an inheritance [20]at the end of about four
hundred and fifty years. After these things he provided judges
up to Samuel the prophet. [21]Then they asked for a king. God
gave them Saul, son of Kish, a man from the tribe of

Benjamin, for forty years. 22 Then he removed him and raised
up David as their king; of him he testified, I have found David,
son of Jesse, a man after my own heart; he will carry out my
every wish. 23 From this man's descendants God, according to
his promise, has brought to Israel a savior, Jesus. 24 John
heralded his coming by proclaiming a baptism of repentance
to all the people of Israel; 25 and as John was completing his
course, he would say, 'What do you suppose that I am? I am
not he. Behold, one is coming after me; I am not worthy to
unfasten the sandals of his feet.'"

Responsorial Psalm – Psalms 89:2-3, 21-22, 25 AND 27

R. (2) **For ever I will sing the goodness of the Lord.** or: **R. Alleluia.**

2 The favors of the LORD I will sing forever;

through all generations my mouth shall proclaim your faithfulness.

3 For you have said, "My kindness is established forever";

in heaven you have confirmed your faithfulness.

R. For ever I will sing the goodness of the Lord. or: **R. Alleluia.**

21 "I have found David, my servant;

with my holy oil I have anointed him,

22 That my hand may be always with him,

and that my arm may make him strong."

R. For ever I will sing the goodness of the Lord. or: **R. Alleluia.**

25 "My faithfulness and my mercy shall be with him,

and through my name shall his horn be exalted.

27 He shall say of me, 'You are my father,

my God, the Rock, my savior.'"

R. For ever I will sing the goodness of the Lord. or: **R. Alleluia.**

Alleluia – cf. Revelation 1:5AB

R. Alleluia, alleluia.

[5AB] Jesus Christ, you are the faithful witness, the firstborn of
the dead, you have loved us and freed us from our sins by
your Blood.

R. Alleluia, alleluia.

Gospel – John 13:16-20

[16]When Jesus had washed the disciples' feet, he said to them:
"Amen, amen, I say to you, no slave is greater than his master
nor any messenger greater than the one who sent him. [17]If you
understand this, blessed are you if you do it. [18]I am not
speaking of all of you. I know those whom I have chosen. But
so that the Scripture might be fulfilled, The one who ate my
food has raised his heel against me. [19]From now on I am
telling you before it happens, so that when it happens you may
believe that **I AM**. [20]Amen, amen, I say to you, whoever
receives the one I send receives me, and whoever receives
me receives the one who sent me."

Friday May 5, 2023

Friday of the Fourth Week of Easter

First Reading – Acts 13:26-33

[26]When Paul came to Antioch in Pisidia, he said in the
synagogue: "My brothers, children of the family of Abraham,
and those others among you who are God-fearing, to us this
word of salvation has been sent. [27]The inhabitants of
Jerusalem and their leaders failed to recognize him, and by
condemning him they fulfilled the oracles of the prophets that
are read Sabbath after Sabbath. [28]For even though they found
no grounds for a death sentence, they asked Pilate to have
him put to death, [29]and when they had accomplished all that
was written about him, they took him down from the tree and
placed him in a tomb.[30]But God raised him from the dead,
[31]and for many days he appeared to those who had come up
with him from Galilee to Jerusalem. These are now his
witnesses before the people. [32]We ourselves are proclaiming
this good news to you that what God promised our fathers [33]he
has brought to fulfillment for us, their children, by raising up

Jesus, as it is written in the second psalm, You are my Son; this day I have begotten you."

Responsorial Psalm – Psalms 2:6-7, 8-9, 10-11AB

R. (7bc) **You are my Son; this day I have begotten you.** or: **R. Alleluia.**

6 "I myself have set up my king

on Zion, my holy mountain."

7 I will proclaim the decree of the LORD:

The LORD said to me, "You are my Son;

this day I have begotten you."

R. You are my Son; this day I have begotten you. or: **R. Alleluia.**

8 "Ask of me and I will give you

the nations for an inheritance

and the ends of the earth for your possession.

9 You shall rule them with an iron rod;

you shall shatter them like an earthen dish."

R. You are my Son; this day I have begotten you. or: **R. Alleluia.**

10 And now, O kings, give heed;

take warning, you rulers of the earth.

11AB Serve the LORD with fear, and rejoice before him;

with trembling rejoice.

R. You are my Son; this day I have begotten you. or: **R. Alleluia.**

Alleluia – John 14:6

R. Alleluia, alleluia.

6 I am the way and the truth and the life, says the Lord; No one comes to the Father except through me.

R. Alleluia, alleluia.

Gospel – John 14:1-6

[1]Jesus said to his disciples: “Do not let your hearts be
troubled. You have faith in God; have faith also in me. [2]In my
Father’s house there are many dwelling places. If there were
not, would I have told you that I am going to prepare a place
for you? [3]And if I go and prepare a place for you, I will come
back again and take you to myself, so that where I am you
also may be. [4]Where I am going you know the way.” [5]Thomas
said to him, “Master, we do not know where you are going;
how can we know the way?” [6]Jesus said to him, “I am the way
and the truth and the life. No one comes to the Father except
through me.”

Saturday May 6, 2023

Saturday of the Fourth Week of Easter

First Reading – Acts 13:44-52

[44]On the following Sabbath almost the whole city gathered to
hear the word of the Lord. [45]When the Jews saw the crowds,
they were filled with jealousy and with violent abuse
contradicted what Paul said. [46]Both Paul and Barnabas spoke
out boldly and said, “It was necessary that the word of God be
spoken to you first, but since you reject it and condemn
yourselves as unworthy of eternal life, we now turn to the
Gentiles. [47]For so the Lord has commanded us, I have made
you a light to the Gentiles, that you may be an instrument of
salvation to the ends of the earth.” [48]The Gentiles were
delighted when they heard this and glorified the word of the
Lord. All who were destined for eternal life came to believe,
[49]and the word of the Lord continued to spread through the
whole region. [50]The Jews, however, incited the women of
prominence who were worshipers and the leading men of the
city, stirred up a persecution against Paul and Barnabas, and
expelled them from their territory. [51]So they shook the dust
from their feet in protest against them and went to Iconium.
[52]The disciples were filled with joy and the Holy Spirit.

Responsorial Psalm – Psalms 98:1, 2-3AB, 3CD-4

R. (3cd) **All the ends of the earth have seen the saving power of God.** or: **R. Alleluia.**

[1] Sing to the LORD a new song,

for he has done wondrous deeds;

His right hand has won victory for him,

his holy arm.

R. All the ends of the earth have seen the saving power of God. or: **R. Alleluia.**

[2] The LORD has made his salvation known:

in the sight of the nations he has revealed his justice.

[3AB] He has remembered his kindness and his faithfulness

toward the house of Israel.

R. All the ends of the earth have seen the saving power of God. or: **R. Alleluia.**

[3CD] All the ends of the earth have seen

the salvation by our God.

[4] Sing joyfully to the LORD, all you lands;

break into song; sing praise.

R. All the ends of the earth have seen the saving power of God. or: **R. Alleluia.**

Alleluia – John 8:31B-32

R. Alleluia, alleluia.

[31B] If you remain in my word, you will truly be my disciples, [32]
and you will know the truth, says the Lord.

R. Alleluia, alleluia.

Gospel – John 14:7-14

[7]Jesus said to his disciples: "If you know me, then you will also
know my Father. From now on you do know him and have
seen him." [8]Philip said to Jesus, "Master, show us the Father,
and that will be enough for us." [9]Jesus said to him, "Have I
been with you for so long a time and you still do not know me,
Philip? Whoever has seen me has seen the Father. How can
you say, 'Show us the Father'? [10]Do you not believe that I am
in the Father and the Father is in me? The words that I speak
to you I do not speak on my own. The Father who dwells in me
is doing his works. [11]Believe me that I am in the Father and

the Father is in me, or else, believe because of the works
themselves. [12]Amen, amen, I say to you, whoever believes in
me will do the works that I do, and will do greater ones than
these, because I am going to the Father. [13]And whatever you
ask in my name, I will do, so that the Father may be glorified in
the Son. [14]If you ask anything of me in my name, I will do it."

Sunday May 7, 2023

Fifth Sunday of Easter, Year A

First Reading – Acts 6:1-7

[1]As the number of disciples continued to grow, the Hellenists
complained against the Hebrews because their widows were
being neglected in the daily distribution. [2]So the Twelve called
together the community of the disciples and said, "It is not right
for us to neglect the word of God to serve at table.[3]Brothers,
select from among you seven reputable men, filled with the
Spirit and wisdom, whom we shall appoint to this task,
[4]whereas we shall devote ourselves to prayer and to the
ministry of the word." [5]The proposal was acceptable to the
whole community, so they chose Stephen, a man filled with
faith and the Holy Spirit, also Philip, Prochorus, Nicanor,
Timon, Parmenas, and Nicholas of Antioch, a convert to
Judaism. [6]They presented these men to the apostles who
prayed and laid hands on them. [7]The word of God continued
to spread, and the number of the disciples in Jerusalem
increased greatly; even a large group of priests were
becoming obedient to the faith.

Responsorial Psalm – Psalms 33:1-2, 4-5, 18-19

R. (22) Lord, let your mercy be on us, as we place our trust in you. or: **R. Alleluia.**

[1] Exult, you just, in the LORD;

praise from the upright is fitting.

[2] Give thanks to the LORD on the harp;

with the ten-stringed lyre chant his praises.

R. Lord, let your mercy be on us, as we place our trust in you. or: **R. Alleluia.**

[4] Upright is the word of the LORD,

and all his works are trustworthy.

5 He loves justice and right;

of the kindness of the LORD the earth is full.

R. Lord, let your mercy be on us, as we place our trust in you. or: **R. Alleluia.**

18 See, the eyes of the LORD are upon those who fear him,

upon those who hope for his kindness,

19 To deliver them from death

and preserve them in spite of famine.

R. Lord, let your mercy be on us, as we place our trust in you. or: **R. Alleluia.**

Second Reading – 1 Peter 2:4-9

4Beloved: Come to him, a living stone, rejected by human
beings but chosen and precious in the sight of God, 5and, like
living stones, let yourselves be built into a spiritual house to be
a holy priesthood to offer spiritual sacrifices acceptable to God
through Jesus Christ. 6For it says in Scripture: Behold, I am
laying a stone in Zion, a cornerstone, chosen and precious,
and whoever believes in it shall not be put to shame.
7Therefore, its value is for you who have faith, but for those
without faith: The stone that the builders rejected has become
the cornerstone, and A stone that will make people stumble,
8and a rock that will make them fall. They stumble by
disobeying the word, as is their destiny. 9You are "a chosen
race, a royal priesthood, a holy nation, a people of his own, so
that you may announce the praises" of him who called you out
of darkness into his wonderful light.

Alleluia – John 14:6

R. Alleluia, alleluia.

6 I am the way, the truth and the life, says the Lord; no one comes to the Father, except through me.

R. Alleluia, alleluia.

Gospel – John 14:1-12

[1]Jesus said to his disciples: “Do not let your hearts be
troubled. You have faith in God; have faith also in me. [2]In my
Father’s house there are many dwelling places. If there were
not, would I have told you that I am going to prepare a place
for you? [3]And if I go and prepare a place for you, I will come
back again and take you to myself, so that where I am you
also may be. [4]Where I am going you know the way.” [5]Thomas
said to him, “Master, we do not know where you are going;
how can we know the way?” [6]Jesus said to him, I am the way
and the truth and the life. No one comes to the Father except
through me. [7]If you know me, then you will also know my
Father. From now on you do know him and have seen him.”
[8]Philip said to him, “Master, show us the Father, and that will
be enough for us.” [9]Jesus said to him, “Have I been with you
for so long a time and you still do not know me, Philip?
Whoever has seen me has seen the Father. How can you say,
‘Show us the Father’? [10]Do you not believe that I am in the
Father and the Father is in me? The words that I speak to you
I do not speak on my own. The Father who dwells in me is
doing his works. [11]Believe me that I am in the Father and the
Father is in me, or else, believe because of the works
themselves. [12]Amen, amen, I say to you, whoever believes in
me will do the works that I do, and will do greater ones than
these, because I am going to the Father.”

Monday May 8, 2023

Monday of the Fifth Week of Easter

First Reading – Acts 14:5-18

[5]There was an attempt in Iconium by both the Gentiles and the
Jews, together with their leaders, to attack and stone Paul and
Barnabas. [6]They realized it, and fled to the Lycaonian cities of
Lystra and Derbe and to the surrounding countryside,[7]where
they continued to proclaim the Good News. [8]At Lystra there
was a crippled man, lame from birth, who had never walked.
[9]He listened to Paul speaking, who looked intently at him, saw
that he had the faith to be healed, [10]and called out in a loud
voice, “Stand up straight on your feet.” He jumped up and
began to walk about. [11]When the crowds saw what Paul had
done, they cried out in Lycaonian, “The gods have come down
to us in human form.” [12]They called Barnabas “Zeus” and Paul

"Hermes," because he was the chief speaker. [13]And the priest of Zeus, whose temple was at the entrance to the city, brought oxen and garlands to the gates, for he together with the people intended to offer sacrifice. [14]The Apostles Barnabas and Paul tore their garments when they heard this and rushed out into the crowd, shouting, [15]"Men, why are you doing this? We are of the same nature as you, human beings. We proclaim to you good news that you should turn from these idols to the living God, who made heaven and earth and sea and all that is in them. [16]In past generations he allowed all Gentiles to go their own ways; [17]yet, in bestowing his goodness, he did not leave himself without witness, for he gave you rains from heaven and fruitful seasons, and filled you with nourishment and gladness for your hearts."[18]Even with these words, they scarcely restrained the crowds from offering sacrifice to them.

Responsorial Psalm – Psalms 115:1-2, 3-4, 15-16

R. (1ab) **Not to us, O Lord, but to your name give the glory.** or: **R. Alleluia.**

1 Not to us, O LORD, not to us

but to your name give glory

because of your mercy, because of your truth.

2 Why should the pagans say,

"Where is their God?"

R. Not to us, O Lord, but to your name give the glory. or: **R. Alleluia.**

3 Our God is in heaven;

whatever he wills, he does.

4 Their idols are silver and gold,

the handiwork of men.

R. Not to us, O Lord, but to your name give the glory. or: **R. Alleluia.**

15 May you be blessed by the LORD,

who made heaven and earth.

16 Heaven is the heaven of the LORD,

but the earth he has given to the children of men.

R. Not to us, O Lord, but to your name give the glory. or:
R. Alleluia.

Alleluia – John 14:26

R. Alleluia, alleluia.

26 The Holy Spirit will teach you everything and remind you of all I told you.

R. Alleluia, alleluia.

Gospel – John 14:21-26

21 Jesus said to his disciples: "Whoever has my commandments and observes them is the one who loves me. Whoever loves me will be loved by my Father, and I will love him and reveal myself to him." 22 Judas, not the Iscariot, said to him, "Master, then what happened that you will reveal yourself to us and not to the world?" 23 Jesus answered and said to him, "Whoever loves me will keep my word, and my Father will love him, and we will come to him and make our dwelling with him. 24 Whoever does not love me does not keep my words; yet the word you hear is not mine but that of the Father who sent me. 25 "I have told you this while I am with you. 26 The Advocate, the Holy Spirit whom the Father will send in my name, he will teach you everything and remind you of all that I told you."

Tuesday May 9, 2023

Tuesday of the Fifth Week of Easter

First Reading – Acts 14:19-28

19 In those days, some Jews from Antioch and Iconium arrived and won over the crowds. They stoned Paul and dragged him out of the city, supposing that he was dead. 20 But when the disciples gathered around him, he got up and entered the city. On the following day he left with Barnabas for Derbe. 21 After they had proclaimed the good news to that city and made a considerable number of disciples, they returned to Lystra and to Iconium and to Antioch. 22 They strengthened the spirits of the disciples and exhorted them to persevere in the faith, saying, "It is necessary for us to undergo many hardships to enter the Kingdom of God." 23 They appointed presbyters for

them in each Church and, with prayer and fasting, commended them to the Lord in whom they had put their faith.
24Then they traveled through Pisidia and reached Pamphylia.
25After proclaiming the word at Perga they went down to
Attalia. 26From there they sailed to Antioch, where they had been commended to the grace of God for the work they had
now accomplished. 27And when they arrived, they called the Church together and reported what God had done with them and how he had opened the door of faith to the Gentiles.
28Then they spent no little time with the disciples.

Responsorial Psalm – Psalms 145:10-11, 12-13AB, 21

R. (see 12) **Your friends make known, O Lord, the glorious splendor of your kingdom.** or: **R. Alleluia.**

10 Let all your works give you thanks, O LORD,

and let your faithful ones bless you.

11 Let them discourse of the glory of your kingdom

and speak of your might.

R. Your friends make known, O Lord, the glorious splendor of your kingdom. or: **R. Alleluia.**

12 Making known to men your might

and the glorious splendor of your kingdom.

13AB Your kingdom is a kingdom for all ages,

and your dominion endures through all generations.

R. Your friends make known, O Lord, the glorious splendor of your kingdom. or: **R. Alleluia.**

21 May my mouth speak the praise of the LORD,

and may all flesh bless his holy name forever and ever.

R. Your friends make known, O Lord, the glorious splendor of your kingdom. or: **R. Alleluia.**

Alleluia – cf. Luke 24:46, 26

R. Alleluia, alleluia.

[46] Christ had to suffer and to rise from the dead, [26] and so enter into his glory.

R. Alleluia, alleluia.

Gospel – John 14:27-31A

[27]Jesus said to his disciples: "Peace I leave with you; my peace I give to you. Not as the world gives do I give it to you. Do not let your hearts be troubled or afraid. [28]You heard me tell you, 'I am going away and I will come back to you.' If you loved me, you would rejoice that I am going to the Father; for the Father is greater than I. [29]And now I have told you this before it happens, so that when it happens you may believe. [30]I will no longer speak much with you, for the ruler of the world is coming. He has no power over me, [31A]but the world must know that I love the Father and that I do just as the Father has commanded me."

Wednesday May 10, 2023

Wednesday of the Fifth Week of Easter

First Reading – Acts 15:1-6

[1]Some who had come down from Judea were instructing the brothers, "Unless you are circumcised according to the Mosaic practice, you cannot be saved." [2]Because there arose no little dissension and debate by Paul and Barnabas with them, it was decided that Paul, Barnabas, and some of the others should go up to Jerusalem to the Apostles and presbyters about this question. [3]They were sent on their journey by the Church, and passed through Phoenicia and Samaria telling of the conversion of the Gentiles, and brought great joy to all the brethren. [4]When they arrived in Jerusalem, they were welcomed by the Church, as well as by the Apostles and the presbyters, and they reported what God had done with them. [5]But some from the party of the Pharisees who had become believers stood up and said, "It is necessary to circumcise them and direct them to observe the Mosaic law." [6]The Apostles and the presbyters met together to see about this matter.

Responsorial Psalm – Psalms 122:1-2, 3-4AB, 4CD-5

R. (see 1) **Let us go rejoicing to the house of the Lord.** or: **R. Alleluia**.

1 I rejoiced because they said to me,

“We will go up to the house of the LORD.”

2 And now we have set foot

within your gates, O Jerusalem.

R. Let us go rejoicing to the house of the Lord. or: **R. Alleluia.**

3 Jerusalem, built as a city

with compact unity.

4AB To it the tribes go up,

the tribes of the LORD.

R. Let us go rejoicing to the house of the Lord. or: **R. Alleluia.**

4CD According to the decree for Israel,

to give thanks to the name of the LORD.

5 In it are set up judgment seats,

seats for the house of David.

R. Let us go rejoicing to the house of the Lord. or: **R. Alleluia.**

Alleluia – John 15:4A, 5B

R. Alleluia, alleluia.

4A Remain in me, as I remain in you, says the Lord; 5B whoever remains in me will bear much fruit.

R. Alleluia, alleluia.

Gospel – John 15:1-8

1Jesus said to his disciples: “I am the true vine, and my Father is the vine grower.
2He takes away every branch in me that does not bear fruit, and everyone that does he prunes so that

it bears more fruit. [3]You are already pruned because of the word that I spoke to you. [4]Remain in me, as I remain in you. Just as a branch cannot bear fruit on its own unless it remains on the vine, so neither can you unless you remain in me. [5]I am the vine, you are the branches. Whoever remains in me and I in him will bear much fruit, because without me you can do nothing. [6]Anyone who does not remain in me will be thrown out like a branch and wither; people will gather them and throw them into a fire and they will be burned. [7]If you remain in me and my words remain in you, ask for whatever you want and it will be done for you. [8]By this is my Father glorified, that you bear much fruit and become my disciples."

Thursday May 11, 2023

Thursday of the Fifth Week of Easter

First Reading – Acts 15:7-21

[7]After much debate had taken place, Peter got up and said to the Apostles and the presbyters, "My brothers, you are well aware that from early days God made his choice among you that through my mouth the Gentiles would hear the word of the Gospel and believe. [8]And God, who knows the heart, bore witness by granting them the Holy Spirit just as he did us. [9]He made no distinction between us and them, for by faith he purified their hearts. [10]Why, then, are you now putting God to the test by placing on the shoulders of the disciples a yoke that neither our ancestors nor we have been able to bear? [11]On the contrary, we believe that we are saved through the grace of the Lord Jesus, in the same way as they." [12]The whole assembly fell silent, and they listened while Paul and Barnabas described the signs and wonders God had worked among the Gentiles through them. [13]After they had fallen silent, James responded, "My brothers, listen to me. [14]Symeon has described how God first concerned himself with acquiring from among the Gentiles a people for his name. [15]The words of the prophets agree with this, as is written: [16]After this I shall return and rebuild the fallen hut of David; from its ruins I shall rebuild it and raise it up again, [17]so that the rest of humanity may seek out the Lord, even all the Gentiles on whom my name is invoked. Thus says the Lord who accomplishes these things, [18]known from of old. [19]It is my judgment, therefore, that we ought to stop troubling the Gentiles who turn to God, [20]but

tell them by letter to avoid pollution from idols, unlawful marriage, the meat of strangled animals, and blood. [21]For Moses, for generations now, has had those who proclaim him in every town, as he has been read in the synagogues every Sabbath."

Responsorial Psalm – Psalms 96:1-2A, 2B-3, 10

R. (3) Proclaim God's marvelous deeds to all the nations. or: **R. Alleluia.**

1 Sing to the LORD a new song;

sing to the LORD, all you lands.

2A Sing to the LORD; bless his name.

R. Proclaim God's marvelous deeds to all the nations. or: **R. Alleluia.**

2B Announce his salvation, day after day.

3 Tell his glory among the nations;

among all peoples, his wondrous deeds.

R. Proclaim God's marvelous deeds to all the nations. or: **R. Alleluia.**

10 Say among the nations: The LORD is king.

He has made the world firm, not to be moved;

he governs the peoples with equity.

R. Proclaim God's marvelous deeds to all the nations. or: **R. Alleluia.**

Alleluia – John 10:27

R. Alleluia, alleluia.

27 My sheep hear my voice, says the Lord; I know them, and they follow me.

R. Alleluia, alleluia.

Gospel – John 15:9-11

9Jesus said to his disciples: "As the Father loves me, so I also love you. Remain in my love. 10If you keep my commandments, you will remain in my love, just as I have kept

my Father's commandments and remain in his love. 11"I have
told you this so that my joy might be in you and your joy might
be complete."

Friday May 12, 2023

Friday of the Fifth Week of Easter

First Reading – Acts 15:22-31

22The Apostles and presbyters, in agreement with the whole
Church, decided to choose representatives and to send them
to Antioch with Paul and Barnabas. The ones chosen were
Judas, who was called Barsabbas, and Silas, leaders among
the brothers. 23This is the letter delivered by them: "The
Apostles and the presbyters, your brothers, to the brothers in
Antioch, Syria, and Cilicia of Gentile origin: greetings. 24Since
we have heard that some of our number who went out without
any mandate from us have upset you with their teachings and
disturbed your peace of mind, 25we have with one accord
decided to choose representatives and to send them to you
along with our beloved Barnabas and Paul, 26who have
dedicated their lives to the name of our Lord Jesus Christ.
27So we are sending Judas and Silas who will also convey this
same message by word of mouth: 28'It is the decision of the
Holy Spirit and of us not to place on you any burden beyond
these necessities, 29namely, to abstain from meat sacrificed to
idols, from blood, from meats of strangled animals, and from
unlawful marriage. If you keep free of these, you will be doing
what is right. Farewell.'" 30And so they were sent on their
journey. Upon their arrival in Antioch they called the assembly
together and delivered the letter. 31When the people read it,
they were delighted with the exhortation.

Responsorial Psalm – Psalms 57:8-9, 10-12

R. (10a) I will give you thanks among the peoples, O Lord.
or: **R. Alleluia.**

8 My heart is steadfast, O God; my heart is steadfast;

I will sing and chant praise.

9 Awake, O my soul; awake, lyre and harp!

I will wake the dawn.

R. I will give you thanks among the peoples, O Lord. or: **R. Alleluia.**

10 I will give thanks to you among the peoples, O LORD,

I will chant your praise among the nations.

11 For your mercy towers to the heavens,

and your faithfulness to the skies.

12 Be exalted above the heavens, O God;

above all the earth be your glory!

R. I will give you thanks among the peoples, O Lord. or: **R. Alleluia.**

Alleluia – John 15:15B

R. Alleluia, alleluia.

15B I call you my friends, says the Lord, For I have made known to you all that the Father has told me.

R. Alleluia, alleluia.

Gospel – John 15:12-17

12 Jesus said to his disciples: "This is my commandment: love
one another as I love you. 13 No one has greater love than this,
to lay down one's life for one's friends. 14 You are my friends if
you do what I command you. 15 I no longer call you slaves,
because a slave does not know what his master is doing. I
have called you friends, because I have told you everything I
have heard from my Father. 16 It was not you who chose me,
but I who chose you and appointed you to go and bear fruit
that will remain, so that whatever you ask the Father in my
name he may give you. 17 This I command you: love one
another."

Saturday May 13, 2023

Saturday of the Fifth Week of Easter

First Reading – Acts 16:1-10

1 Paul reached also Derbe and Lystra where there was a
disciple named Timothy, the son of a Jewish woman who was
a believer, but his father was a Greek. 2 The brothers in Lystra

and Iconium spoke highly of him, [3]and Paul wanted him to come along with him. On account of the Jews of that region, Paul had him circumcised, for they all knew that his father was a Greek. [4]As they traveled from city to city, they handed on to the people for observance the decisions reached by the Apostles and presbyters in Jerusalem. [5]Day after day the churches grew stronger in faith and increased in number. [6]They travelled through the Phrygian and Galatian territory because they had been prevented by the Holy Spirit from preaching the message in the province of Asia. [7]When they came to Mysia, they tried to go on into Bithynia, but the Spirit of Jesus did not allow them, [8]so they crossed through Mysia and came down to Troas. [9]During the night Paul had a vision. A Macedonian stood before him and implored him with these words, "Come over to Macedonia and help us." [10]When he had seen the vision, we sought passage to Macedonia at once, concluding that God had called us to proclaim the Good News to them.

Responsorial Psalm – Psalms 100:1B-2, 3, 5

R. (2a) Let all the earth cry out to God with joy. or: **R. Alleluia.**

[1B] Sing joyfully to the LORD, all you lands;

[2] serve the LORD with gladness;

come before him with joyful song.

R. Let all the earth cry out to God with joy. or: **R. Alleluia.**

[3] Know that the LORD is God;

he made us, his we are;

his people, the flock he tends.

R. Let all the earth cry out to God with joy. or: **R. Alleluia.**

[5] The LORD is good:

his kindness endures forever,

and his faithfulness, to all generations.

R. Let all the earth cry out to God with joy. or: **R. Alleluia.**

Alleluia – Colossians 3:1

R. Alleluia, alleluia.

[1] If then you were raised with Christ, seek what is above,
where Christ is seated at the right hand of God.

R. Alleluia, alleluia.

Gospel – John 15:18-21

[18]Jesus said to his disciples: "If the world hates you, realize
that it hated me first. [19]If you belonged to the world, the world
would love its own; but because you do not belong to the
world, and I have chosen you out of the world, the world hates
you. [20]Remember the word I spoke to you, 'No slave is greater
than his master.' If they persecuted me, they will also
persecute you. If they kept my word, they will also keep yours.
[21]And they will do all these things to you on account of my
name, because they do not know the one who sent me."

Sunday May 14, 2023

Sixth Sunday of Easter, Year A

First Reading – Acts 8:5-8, 14-17

[5]Philip went down to the city of Samaria and proclaimed the
Christ to them. [6]With one accord, the crowds paid attention to
what was said by Philip when they heard it and saw the signs
he was doing. [7]For unclean spirits, crying out in a loud voice,
came out of many possessed people, and many paralyzed or
crippled people were cured. [8]There was great joy in that city.
[14]Now when the apostles in Jerusalem heard that Samaria had
accepted the word of God, they sent them Peter and
John,[15]who went down and prayed for them, that they might
receive the Holy Spirit,[16]for it had not yet fallen upon any of
them; they had only been baptized in the name of the Lord
Jesus.[17]Then they laid hands on them and they received the
Holy Spirit.

Responsorial Psalm – Psalms 66:1-3, 4-5, 6-7, 16, 20

R. (1) **Let all the earth cry out to God with joy.** or: **R. Alleluia.**

[2] Shout joyfully to God, all the earth,

sing praise to the glory of his name;

proclaim his glorious praise.

3 Say to God, “How tremendous are your deeds!”

R. Let all the earth cry out to God with joy. or: **R. Alleluia.**

4 “Let all on earth worship and sing praise to you,

sing praise to your name!”

5 Come and see the works of God,

his tremendous deeds among the children of Adam.

R. Let all the earth cry out to God with joy. or: **R. Alleluia.**

6 He has changed the sea into dry land;

through the river they passed on foot;

therefore let us rejoice in him.

7 He rules by his might forever.

R. Let all the earth cry out to God with joy. or: **R. Alleluia.**

16 Hear now, all you who fear God, while I declare

what he has done for me.

20 Blessed be God who refused me not

my prayer or his kindness!

R. Let all the earth cry out to God with joy. or: **R. Alleluia.**

Second Reading – 1 Peter 3:15-18

15Beloved: Sanctify Christ as Lord in your hearts. Always be
ready to give an explanation to anyone who asks you for a
reason for your hope,16but do it with gentleness and
reverence, keeping your conscience clear, so that, when you
are maligned, those who defame your good conduct in Christ
may themselves be put to shame. 17For it is better to suffer for
doing good, if that be the will of God, than for doing evil. 18For
Christ also suffered for sins once, the righteous for the sake of
the unrighteous, that he might lead you to God. Put to death in
the flesh, he was brought to life in the Spirit.

Alleluia – John 14:23

R. Alleluia, alleluia.

[23] Whoever loves me will keep my word, says the Lord, and my Father will love him and we will come to him.

R. Alleluia, alleluia.

Gospel – John 14:15-21

[15]Jesus said to his disciples: "If you love me, you will keep my commandments. [16]And I will ask the Father, and he will give you another Advocate to be with you always,[17]the Spirit of truth, whom the world cannot accept, because it neither sees nor knows him. But you know him, because he remains with you, and will be in you. [18]I will not leave you orphans; I will come to you. [19]In a little while the world will no longer see me, but you will see me, because I live and you will live. [20]On that day you will realize that I am in my Father and you are in me and I in you. [21]Whoever has my commandments and observes them is the one who loves me. And whoever loves me will be loved by my Father, and I will love him and reveal myself to him."

Monday May 15, 2023

Monday of the Sixth Week of Easter

First Reading – Acts 16:11-15

[11]We set sail from Troas, making a straight run for Samothrace, and on the next day to Neapolis,[12]and from there to Philippi, a leading city in that district of Macedonia and a Roman colony. We spent some time in that city. [13]On the Sabbath we went outside the city gate along the river where we thought there would be a place of prayer. We sat and spoke with the women who had gathered there.[14]One of them, a woman named Lydia, a dealer in purple cloth, from the city of Thyatira, a worshiper of God, listened, and the Lord opened her heart to pay attention to what Paul was saying.[15]After she and her household had been baptized, she offered us an invitation, "If you consider me a believer in the Lord, come and stay at my home," and she prevailed on us.

Responsorial Psalm – Psalms 149:1B-2, 3-4, 5-6A AND 9B

R. (see 4a) **The Lord takes delight in his people.** or: **R. Alleluia.**

1B Sing to the LORD a new song

of praise in the assembly of the faithful.

2 Let Israel be glad in their maker,

let the children of Zion rejoice in their king.

R. The Lord takes delight in his people. or: **R. Alleluia.**

3 Let them praise his name in the festive dance,

let them sing praise to him with timbrel and harp.

4 For the LORD loves his people,

and he adorns the lowly with victory.

R. The Lord takes delight in his people. or: **R. Alleluia.**

5 Let the faithful exult in glory;

let them sing for joy upon their couches.

6A Let the high praises of God be in their throats.

9B This is the glory of all his faithful. Alleluia.

R. The Lord takes delight in his people. or: **R. Alleluia.**

Alleluia – John 15:26B, 27A

R. Alleluia, alleluia.

26B The Spirit of truth will testify to me, says the Lord, 27A and you also will testify.

R. Alleluia, alleluia.

Gospel – John 15:26-16:4A

26Jesus said to his disciples: "When the Advocate comes
whom I will send you from the Father, the Spirit of truth who
proceeds from the Father, he will testify to me. 27And you also
testify, because you have been with me from the beginning. 1"I
have told you this so that you may not fall away. 2They will
expel you from the synagogues; in fact, the hour is coming

when everyone who kills you will think he is offering worship to
God. 3They will do this because they have not known either
the Father or me. 4AI have told you this so that when their hour
comes you may remember that I told you.

Tuesday May 16, 2023

Tuesday of the Sixth Week of Easter

First Reading – Acts 16:22-34

22The crowd in Philippi joined in the attack on Paul and Silas,
and the magistrates had them stripped and ordered them to
be beaten with rods. 23After inflicting many blows on them,
they threw them into prison and instructed the jailer to guard
them securely. 24When he received these instructions, he put
them in the innermost cell and secured their feet to a stake.
25About midnight, while Paul and Silas were praying and
singing hymns to God as the prisoners listened, 26 there was
suddenly such a severe earthquake that the foundations of the
jail shook; all the doors flew open, and the chains of all were
pulled loose. 27When the jailer woke up and saw the prison
doors wide open, he drew his sword and was about to kill
himself, thinking that the prisoners had escaped. 28But Paul
shouted out in a loud voice, "Do no harm to yourself; we are all
here." 29He asked for a light and rushed in and, trembling with
fear, he fell down before Paul and Silas. 30Then he brought
them out and said, "Sirs, what must I do to be saved?" 31And
they said, "Believe in the Lord Jesus and you and your
household will be saved." 32So they spoke the word of the Lord
to him and to everyone in his house. 33He took them in at that
hour of the night and bathed their wounds; then he and all his
family were baptized at once. 34He brought them up into his
house and provided a meal and with his household rejoiced at
having come to faith in God.

Responsorial Psalm – Psalms 138:1-2AB, 2CDE-3, 7C-8

R. (7c) **Your right hand saves me, O Lord.** or: **R. Alleluia.**

1 I will give thanks to you, O LORD, with all my heart,

for you have heard the words of my mouth;

in the presence of the angels I will sing your praise;

[2AB] I will worship at your holy temple,

and give thanks to your name.

R. Your right hand saves me, O Lord. or: **R. Alleluia.**

[2CDE] Because of your kindness and your truth,

you have made great above all things

your name and your promise.

[3] When I called, you answered me;

you built up strength within me.

R. Your right hand saves me, O Lord. or: **R. Alleluia.**

[7C] Your right hand saves me.

[8] The LORD will complete what he has done for me;

your kindness, O LORD, endures forever;

forsake not the work of your hands.

R. Your right hand saves me, O Lord. or: **R. Alleluia.**

Alleluia – cf. John 16:7, 13

R. Alleluia, alleluia.

[7] I will send to you the Spirit of truth, says the Lord; [13] he will guide you to all truth.

R. Alleluia, alleluia.

Gospel – John 16:5-11

[5]Jesus said to his disciples: "Now I am going to the one who sent me, and not one of you asks me, 'Where are you going?'
[6]But because I told you this, grief has filled your hearts. [7]But I tell you the truth, it is better for you that I go. For if I do not go, the Advocate will not come to you. But if I go, I will send him to
you. [8]And when he comes he will convict the world in regard to
sin and righteousness and condemnation: [9]sin, because they
do not believe in me; [10]righteousness, because I am going to
the Father and you will no longer see me; [11]condemnation,
because the ruler of this world has been condemned."

Wednesday May 17, 2023

Wednesday of the Sixth Week of Easter

First Reading – Acts 17:15, 22-18:1

[15]After Paul's escorts had taken him to Athens, they came
away with instructions for Silas and Timothy to join him as
soon as possible. [22]Then Paul stood up at the Areopagus and
said: "You Athenians, I see that in every respect you are very
religious. [23]For as I walked around looking carefully at your
shrines, I even discovered an altar inscribed, 'To an Unknown
God.' What therefore you unknowingly worship, I proclaim to
you. [24]The God who made the world and all that is in it, the
Lord of heaven and earth, does not dwell in sanctuaries made
by human hands, [25]nor is he served by human hands because
he needs anything. Rather it is he who gives to everyone life
and breath and everything. [26]He made from one the whole
human race to dwell on the entire surface of the earth, and he
fixed the ordered seasons and the boundaries of their regions,
[27]so that people might seek God, even perhaps grope for him
and find him, though indeed he is not far from any one of us.
[28]For 'In him, we live and move and have our being,' as even
some of your poets have said, 'For we too are his offspring.'
[29]Since therefore we are the offspring of God, we ought not to
think that the divinity is like an image fashioned from gold,
silver, or stone by human art and imagination.[30]God has
overlooked the times of ignorance, but now he demands that
all people everywhere repent [31]because he has established a
day on which he will 'judge the world with justice' through a
man, he has appointed, and he has provided confirmation for
all by raising him from the dead." [32]When they heard about
resurrection of the dead, some began to scoff, but others said,
"We should like to hear you on this some other time." [33]And so
Paul left them. [34]But some did join him and became believers.
Among them were Dionysius, a member of the Court of the
Areopagus, a woman named Damaris, and others with them.
[1]After this he left Athens and went to Corinth.

Responsorial Psalm – Psalms 148:1-2, 11-12, 13, 14

R. Heaven and earth are full of your glory. or: **R. Alleluia.**

[1] Praise the LORD from the heavens;

praise him in the heights.

2 Praise him, all you his angels;

praise him, all you his hosts.

R. Heaven and earth are full of your glory. or: **R. Alleluia.**

11 Let the kings of the earth and all peoples,

the princes and all the judges of the earth,

12 Young men too, and maidens,

old men and boys.

R. Heaven and earth are full of your glory. or: **R. Alleluia.**

13 Praise the name of the LORD,

for his name alone is exalted;

His majesty is above earth and heaven.

R. Heaven and earth are full of your glory. or: **R. Alleluia.**

14 He has lifted up the horn of his people;

Be this his praise from all his faithful ones,

from the children of Israel, the people close to him.

Alleluia.

R. Heaven and earth are full of your glory. or: **R. Alleluia.**

Alleluia – John 14:16

R. Alleluia, alleluia.

16 I will ask the Father and he will give you another Advocate to be with you always.

R. Alleluia, alleluia.

Gospel – John 16:12-15

Jesus said to his disciples:
12"I have much more to tell you, but you cannot bear it now.
13But when he comes, the Spirit of truth, he will guide you to all truth. He will not speak on his own, but he will speak what he hears and will declare to you the things that are coming.
14He will glorify me because he will take from what is mine and declare it to you.
15Everything that

the Father has is mine; for this reason, I told you that he will take from what is mine and declare it to you."

Thursday May 18, 2023

Thursday of the Sixth Week of Easter

First Reading – Acts 18:1-8

[1]Paul left Athens and went to Corinth. [2]There he met a Jew
named Aquila, a native of Pontus, who had recently come
from Italy with his wife Priscilla because Claudius had ordered
all the Jews to leave Rome. He went to visit them [3]and,
because he practised the same trade, stayed with them and
worked, for they were tentmakers by trade. [4]Every Sabbath,
he entered into discussions in the synagogue, attempting to
convince both Jews and Greeks.[5]When Silas and Timothy
came down from Macedonia, Paul began to occupy himself
totally with preaching the word, testifying to the Jews that the
Christ was Jesus.[6]When they opposed him and reviled him, he
shook out his garments and said to them, "Your blood be on
your heads! I am clear of responsibility. From now on I will go
to the Gentiles." [7]So he left there and went to a house
belonging to a man named Titus Justus, a worshiper of God;
his house was next to a synagogue. [8]Crispus, the synagogue
official, came to believe in the Lord along with his entire
household, and many of the Corinthians who heard believed
and were baptized.

Responsorial Psalm – Psalms 98:1, 2-3AB, 3CD-4

R.(see 2b) **The Lord has revealed to the nations his saving power.** or: **R. Alleluia.**

[1] Sing to the LORD a new song,

for he has done wondrous deeds;

His right hand has won victory for him,

his holy arm.

R. The Lord has revealed to the nations his saving power. or: **R. Alleluia.**

[2] The LORD has made his salvation known:

in the sight of the nations, he has revealed his justice.

3AB He has remembered his kindness and his faithfulness

toward the house of Israel.

R. The Lord has revealed to the nations his saving power.
or: **R. Alleluia.**

3CD All the ends of the earth have seen

the salvation by our God.

4 Sing joyfully to the LORD, all you lands;

break into song; sing praise.

R. The Lord has revealed to the nations his saving power.
or: **R. Alleluia.**

Alleluia – John 14:18

R. Alleluia, alleluia.

15 I will not leave you orphans, says the Lord; I will come back to you, and your hearts will rejoice.

R. Alleluia, alleluia.

Gospel – John 16:16-20

16 Jesus said to his disciples: "A little while and you will no
longer see me, and again a little while later and you will see
me." 17 So some of his disciples said to one another, "What
does this mean that he is saying to us, 'A little while and you
will not see me, and again a little while and you will see me,'
and 'Because I am going to the Father'?" 18 So they said,
"What is this 'little while' of which he speaks? We do not know
what he means." 19 Jesus knew that they wanted to ask him, so
he said to them, "Are you discussing with one another what I
said, 'A little while and you will not see me, and again a little
while and you will see me'? 20 Amen, amen, I say to you, you
will weep and mourn, while the world rejoices; you will grieve,
but your grief will become joy."

Friday May 19, 2023

Friday of the Sixth Week of Easter

First Reading – Acts 18:9-18

[9]One night while Paul was in Corinth, the Lord said to him in a vision, "Do not be afraid. Go on speaking, and do not be silent, [10]for I am with you. No one will attack and harm you, for I have many people in this city." [11]He settled there for a year and a half and taught the word of God among them. [12]But when Gallio was proconsul of Achaia, the Jews rose up together against Paul and brought him to the tribunal,[13]saying, "This man is inducing people to worship God contrary to the law." [14]When Paul was about to reply, Gallio spoke to the Jews, "If it were a matter of some crime or malicious fraud, I should with reason hear the complaint of you Jews; [15]but since it is a question of arguments over doctrine and titles and your own law, see to it yourselves. I do not wish to be a judge of such matters." [16]And he drove them away from the tribunal. [17]They all seized Sosthenes, the synagogue official, and beat him in full view of the tribunal. But none of this was of concern to Gallio. [18]Paul remained for quite some time, and after saying farewell to the brothers he sailed for Syria, together with Priscilla and Aquila. At Cenchreae he had shaved his head because he had taken a vow.

Responsorial Psalm – Psalms 47:2-3, 4-5, 6-7

R. [(8a)] God is king of all the earth. or: **R. Alleluia.**

[2] All you peoples, clap your hands,

shout to God with cries of gladness,

[3] For the LORD, the Most High, the awesome,

is the great king over all the earth.

R. God is king of all the earth. or: **R. Alleluia.**

[4] He brings people under us;

nations under our feet.

[5] He chooses for us our inheritance,

the glory of Jacob, whom he loves.

R. God is king of all the earth. or: **R. Alleluia.**

[6] God mounts his throne amid shouts of joy;

the LORD, amid trumpet blasts.

[7] Sing praise to God, sing praise;

sing praise to our king, sing praise.

R. God is king of all the earth. or: **R. Alleluia.**

Alleluia – cf. Luke 24:46, 26

R. Alleluia, alleluia.

[46] Christ had to suffer and to rise from the dead, [26] and so enter into his glory.

R. Alleluia, alleluia.

Gospel – John 16:20-23

[20]Jesus said to his disciples: "Amen, amen, I say to you, you
will weep and mourn, while the world rejoices; you will grieve,
but your grief will become joy. [21]When a woman is in labor,
she is in anguish because her hour has arrived; but when she
has given birth to a child, she no longer remembers the pain
because of her joy that a child has been born into the world.
[22]So you also are now in anguish. But I will see you again, and
your hearts will rejoice, and no one will take your joy away
from you. [23]On that day you will not question me about
anything. Amen, amen, I say to you, whatever you ask the
Father in my name he will give you."

Saturday May 20, 2023

Saturday of the Sixth Week of Easter

First Reading – Acts 18:23-28

[23]After staying in Antioch some time, Paul left and travelled in
orderly sequence through the Galatian country and Phrygia,
bringing strength to all the disciples. [24]A Jew named Apollos, a
native of Alexandria, an eloquent speaker arrived in Ephesus.
He was an authority on the Scriptures. [25]He had been
instructed in the Way of the Lord and, with ardent spirit, spoke
and taught accurately about Jesus, although he knew only the
baptism of John. [26]He began to speak boldly in the
synagogue; but when Priscilla and Aquila heard him, they took
him aside and explained to him the Way of God more

accurately. [27]And when he wanted to cross to Achaia, the brothers encouraged him and wrote to the disciples there to welcome him. After his arrival, he gave great assistance to those who had come to believe through grace. [28]He vigorously refuted the Jews in public, establishing from the Scriptures that the Christ is Jesus.

Responsorial Psalm – Psalms 47:2-3, 8-9, 10

R.[(8a)] **God is king of all the earth.** or: **R. Alleluia.**

2 All you peoples, clap your hands;

shout to God with cries of gladness.

3 For the LORD, the Most High, the awesome,

is the great king over all the earth.

R. God is king of all the earth. or: **R. Alleluia.**

8 For king of all the earth is God;

sing hymns of praise.

9 God reigns over the nations,

God sits upon his holy throne.

R. God is king of all the earth. or: **R. Alleluia.**

10 The princes of the peoples are gathered together

with the people of the God of Abraham.

For God's are the guardians of the earth;

he is supreme.

R. God is king of all the earth. or: **R. Alleluia.**

Alleluia – John 16:28

R. Alleluia, alleluia.

[28]I came from the Father and have come into the world; now I am leaving the world and going back to the Father.

R. Alleluia, alleluia.

Gospel – John 16:23B-28

Jesus said to his disciples: [23B]"Amen, amen, I say to you, whatever you ask the Father in my name he will give you.

[24]Until now you have not asked anything in my name; ask and
you will receive, so that your joy may be complete. [25]"I have
told you this in figures of speech. The hour is coming when I
will no longer speak to you in figures but I will tell you clearly
about the Father. [26]On that day you will ask in my name, and I
do not tell you that I will ask the Father for you. [27]For the
Father himself loves you because you have loved me and
have come to believe that I came from God. [28]I came from the
Father and have come into the world. Now I am leaving the
world and going back to the Father."

Sunday May 21, 2023

Solemnity of Ascension of the Lord

First Reading – Acts 1:1-11

[1]In the first book, Theophilus, I dealt with all that Jesus did and
taught [2]until the day he was taken up, after giving instructions
through the Holy Spirit to the apostles whom he had chosen.
[3]He presented himself alive to them by many proofs after he
had suffered, appearing to them during forty days and
speaking about the kingdom of God. [4]While meeting with
them, he enjoined them not to depart from Jerusalem, but to
wait for "the promise of the Father about which you have
heard me speak; [5]for John baptized with water, but in a few
days you will be baptized with the Holy Spirit." [6]When they had
gathered together they asked him, "Lord, are you at this time
going to restore the kingdom to Israel?" [7]He answered them,
"It is not for you to know the times or seasons that the Father
has established by his own authority. [8]But you will receive
power when the Holy Spirit comes upon you, and you will be
my witnesses in Jerusalem, throughout Judea and Samaria,
and to the ends of the earth." [9]When he had said this, as they
were looking on, he was lifted up, and a cloud took him from
their sight. [10]While they were looking intently at the sky as he
was going, suddenly two men dressed in white garments
stood beside them. [11]They said, "Men of Galilee, why are you
standing there looking at the sky? This Jesus who has been
taken up from you into heaven will return in the same way as
you have seen him going into heaven."

Responsorial Psalm – Psalms 47:2-3, 6-7, 8-9

R. (6) God mounts his throne to shouts of joy: a blare of trumpets for the Lord. or: **R. Alleluia.**

2 All you peoples, clap your hands,

shout to God with cries of gladness,

3 For the LORD, the Most High, the awesome,

is the great king over all the earth.

R. God mounts his throne to shouts of joy: a blare of trumpets for the Lord. or: **R. Alleluia.**

6 God mounts his throne amid shouts of joy;

the LORD, amid trumpet blasts.

7 Sing praise to God, sing praise;

sing praise to our king, sing praise.

R. God mounts his throne to shouts of joy: a blare of trumpets for the Lord. or: **R. Alleluia.**

8 For king of all the earth is God;

sing hymns of praise.

9 God reigns over the nations,

God sits upon his holy throne.

R. God mounts his throne to shouts of joy: a blare of trumpets for the Lord. or: **R. Alleluia.**

Second Reading – Ephesians 1:17-23

Brothers and sisters: 17May the God of our Lord Jesus Christ,
the Father of glory, give you a Spirit of wisdom and revelation
resulting in knowledge of him. 18May the eyes of your hearts
be enlightened, that you may know what is the hope that
belongs to his call, what are the riches of glory in his
inheritance among the holy ones,19and what is the surpassing
greatness of his power for us who believe, in accord with the
exercise of his great might: 20which he worked in Christ,
raising him from the dead and seating him at his right hand in
the heavens,21far above every principality, authority, power,
and dominion, and every name that is named not only in this
age but also in the one to come. 22And he put all things

beneath his feet and gave him as head over all things to the church, which is his body, the fullness of the one who fills all things in every way.

Or Hebrews 9:24-28; 10:19-23

[24]Christ did not enter into a sanctuary made by hands, a copy of the true one, but heaven itself, that he might now appear before God on our behalf. [25]Not that he might offer himself repeatedly, as the high priest enters each year into the sanctuary with blood that is not his own; [26]if that were so, he would have had to suffer repeatedly from the foundation of the world. But now once for all he has appeared at the end of the ages to take away sin by his sacrifice. [27]Just as it is appointed that men and women die once, and after this the judgment, [28]so also Christ, offered once to take away the sins of many, will appear a second time, not to take away sin but to bring salvation to those who eagerly await him. [19]Therefore, brothers and sisters, since through the blood of Jesus we have confidence of entrance into the sanctuary [20]by the new and living way he opened for us through the veil, that is, his flesh, [21]and since we have a great priest over the house of God, [22]"let us approach with a sincere heart and in absolute trust, with our hearts sprinkled clean from an evil conscience and our bodies washed in pure water. [23]Let us hold unwaveringly to our confession that gives us hope, for he who made the promise is trustworthy.

OR Ephesians 4:1-13

[1]Brothers and sisters, I, a prisoner for the Lord, urge you to live in a manner worthy of the call you have received, [2]with all humility and gentleness, with patience, bearing with one another through love, [3]striving to preserve the unity of the spirit through the bond of peace: [4]one body and one Spirit, as you were also called to the one hope of your call; [5]one Lord, one faith, one baptism; [6]one God and Father of all, who is over all and through all and in all. [7]But grace was given to each of us according to the measure of Christ's gift. [8]Therefore, it says: He ascended on high and took prisoners captive; he gave gifts to men. [9]What does "he ascended" mean except that he also descended into the lower regions of the earth? [10]The one who descended is also the one who ascended far above all the heavens, that he might fill all things. [11]And he gave some as apostles, others as prophets, others as

evangelists, others as pastors and teachers,12to equip the holy
ones for the work of ministry, for building up the body of Christ,
13until we all attain to the unity of faith and knowledge of the
Son of God, to mature to manhood, to the extent of the full
stature of Christ.

OR Ephesians 4:1-7, 11-13

1Brothers and sisters, I, a prisoner for the Lord, urge you to
live in a manner worthy of the calling you have received, 2with
all humility and gentleness, with patience, bearing with one
another through love, 3striving to preserve the unity of the
Spirit through the bond of peace: 4one body and one Spirit, as
you were also called to the one hope of your calling; 5one
Lord, one faith, one baptism; 6one God and Father of all, who
is over all and through all and in all. 7But grace was given to
each of us according to the measure of Christ's gift. 11And he
gave some as apostles, others as prophets, others as
evangelists, others as pastors and teachers, 12to equip the
holy ones for the work of ministry, for building up the body of
Christ, 13until we all attain to the unity of faith and knowledge
of the Son of God, to mature to manhood, to the extent of the
full stature of Christ.

Alleluia – Matthew 28:19A, 20B

R. Alleluia, alleluia.

19A Go and teach all nations, says the Lord; 20B I am with you
always, until the end of the world.

R. Alleluia, alleluia.

Gospel – Luke 24:46-53

46Jesus said to his disciples: "Thus it is written that the Christ
would suffer and rise from the dead on the third day 47and that
repentance, for the forgiveness of sins, would be preached in
his name to all the nations, beginning from Jerusalem. 48You
are witnesses of these things.49And behold I am sending the
promise of my Father upon you; but stay in the city until you
are clothed with power from on high." 50Then he led them out
as far as Bethany, raised his hands, and blessed them. 51As
he blessed them he parted from them and was taken up to
heaven. 52They did him homage and then returned to

Jerusalem with great joy, [53]and they were continually in the temple praising God.

Monday May 22, 2023

Monday of the Seventh Week of Easter

First Reading – Acts 19:1-8

[1]While Apollos was in Corinth, Paul travelled through the interior of the country and down to Ephesus where he found some disciples. [2]He said to them, "Did you receive the Holy Spirit when you became believers?" They answered him, "We have never even heard that there is a Holy Spirit." [3]He said, "How were you baptized?" They replied, "With the baptism of John." [4]Paul then said, "John baptized with a baptism of repentance, telling the people to believe in the one who was to come after him, that is, in Jesus." [5]When they heard this, they were baptized in the name of the Lord Jesus. [6]And when Paul laid his hands on them, the Holy Spirit came upon them, and they spoke in tongues and prophesied. [7]Altogether there were about twelve men. [8]He entered the synagogue, and for three months debated boldly with persuasive arguments about the Kingdom of God.

Responsorial Psalm – Psalms 68:2-3AB, 4-5ACD, 6-7AB

R.[(33a)] **Sing to God, O kingdoms of the earth.** or: **R. Alleluia.**

[2] God arises; his enemies are scattered,

and those who hate him flee before him.

[3AB] As smoke is driven away, so are they driven;

as wax melts before the fire.

R. Sing to God, O kingdoms of the earth. or: **R. Alleluia.**

[4] But the just rejoice and exult before God;

they are glad and rejoice.

[5ACD] Sing to God, chant praise to his name;

whose name is the LORD.

R. Sing to God, O kingdoms of the earth. or: **R. Alleluia.**

[6] The father of orphans and the defender of widows

is God in his holy dwelling.

[7AB] God gives a home to the forsaken;

he leads forth prisoners to prosperity.

R. Sing to God, O kingdoms of the earth. or: **R. Alleluia.**

Alleluia – Colossians 3:1

R. Alleluia, alleluia.

[1] If then you were raised with Christ, seek what is above, where Christ is seated at the right hand of God.

R. Alleluia, alleluia.

Gospel – John 16:29-33

[29]The disciples said to Jesus, "Now you are talking plainly, and
not in any figure of speech.[30]Now we realize that you know
everything and that you do not need to have anyone question
you. Because of this, we believe that you came from God."
[31]Jesus answered them, "Do you believe now? [32]Behold, the
hour is coming and has arrived when each of you will be
scattered to his own home and you will leave me alone. But I
am not alone, because the Father is with me. [33]I have told you
this so that you might have peace in me. In the world, you will
have trouble, but take courage, I have conquered the world.

Tuesday May 23, 2023

Tuesday of the Seventh Week of Easter

First Reading – Acts 20:17-27

[17]From Miletus Paul had the presbyters of the Church at
Ephesus summoned.[18]When they came to him, he addressed
them, "You know how I lived among you the whole time from
the day I first came to the province of Asia. [19]I served the Lord
with all humility and with the tears and trials that came to me
because of the plots of the Jews, [20]and I did not at all shrink
from telling you what was for your benefit, or from teaching
you in public or in your homes. [21]I earnestly bore witness for
both Jews and Greeks to repentance before God and to faith
in our Lord Jesus. [22]But now, compelled by the Spirit, I am
going to Jerusalem. What will happen to me there I do not

know, 23except that in one city after another the Holy Spirit has
been warning me that imprisonment and hardships await me.
24Yet I consider life of no importance to me, if only I may finish
my course and the ministry that I received from the Lord
Jesus, to bear witness to the Gospel of God's grace. 25"But
now I know that none of you to whom I preached the kingdom
during my travels will ever see my face again. 26And so I
solemnly declare to you this day that I am not responsible for
the blood of any of you, 27for I did not shrink from proclaiming
to you the entire plan of God."

Responsorial Psalm – Psalms 68:10-11, 20-21

R. (33a) **Sing to God, O kingdoms of the earth.** or: **R. Alleluia.**

10 A bountiful rain you showered down, O God, upon your inheritance;

you restored the land when it languished;

11 Your flock settled in it;

in your goodness, O God, you provided it for the needy.

R. Sing to God, O kingdoms of the earth. or: **R. Alleluia.**

20 Blessed day by day be the Lord,

who bears our burdens; God, who is our salvation.

21 God is a saving God for us;

the LORD, my Lord, controls the passageways of death.

R. Sing to God, O kingdoms of the earth. or: **R. Alleluia.**

Alleluia – John 14:16

R. Alleluia, alleluia.

16 I will ask the father and he will give you another Advocate to be with you always.

R. Alleluia, alleluia.

Gospel – John 17:1-11A

1Jesus raised his eyes to heaven and said, "Father, the hour
has come. Give glory to your son, so that your son may glorify
you, 2just as you gave him authority over all people, so that

your son may give eternal life to all you gave him. [3]Now, this is eternal life, that they should know you, the only true God, and the one whom you sent, Jesus Christ. [4]I glorified you on earth by accomplishing the work that you gave me to do. [5]Now glorify me, Father, with you, with the glory that I had with you before the world began. [6]"I revealed your name to those whom you gave me out of the world. They belonged to you, and you gave them to me, and they have kept your word. [7]Now they know that everything you gave me is from you, [8]because the words you gave to me I have given to them, and they accepted them and truly understood that I came from you, and they have believed that you sent me. [9]I pray for them. I do not pray for the world but for the ones you have given me, because they are yours, and everything of mine is yours [10]and everything of yours is mine, and I have been glorified in them. [11A]And now I will no longer be in the world, but they are in the world, while I am coming to you."

Wednesday May 24, 2023

Wednesday of the Seventh Week of Easter

First Reading – Acts 20:28-38

[28]At Miletus, Paul spoke to the presbyters of the Church of Ephesus: "Keep watch over yourselves and over the whole flock of which the Holy Spirit has appointed you overseers, in which you tend the Church of God that he acquired with his own Blood. [29]I know that after my departure savage wolves will come among you, and they will not spare the flock. [30]And from your own group, men will come forward perverting the truth to draw the disciples away after them. [31]So be vigilant and remember that for three years, night and day, I unceasingly admonished each of you with tears. [32]And now I commend you to God and to that gracious word of his that can build you up and give you the inheritance among all who are consecrated. [33]I have never wanted anyone's silver or gold or clothing. [34]You know well that these very hands have served my needs and my companions. [35]In every way I have shown you that by hard work of that sort we must help the weak, and keep in mind the words of the Lord Jesus who himself said, 'It is more blessed to give than to receive.'" [36]When he had finished speaking he knelt down and prayed with them all. [37]They were all weeping loudly as they threw their arms around Paul and

kissed him, [38]for they were deeply distressed that he had said that they would never see his face again. Then they escorted him to the ship.

Responsorial Psalm – Psalms 68:29-30, 33-35A, 35BC-36AB

R.[(33a)] **Sing to God, O kingdoms of the earth.** or: **R. Alleluia.**

29 Show forth, O God, your power,

the power, O God, with which you took our part;

30 For your temple in Jerusalem

let the kings bring you gifts.

R. Sing to God, O Kingdoms of the earth. or: **R. Alleluia.**

33 You kingdoms of the earth, sing to God,

chant praise to the Lord

34 who rides on the heights of the ancient heavens.

Behold, his voice resounds, the voice of power:

35A "Confess the power of God!"

R. Sing to God, O kingdoms of the earth. or: **R. Alleluia.**

35BC Over Israel is his majesty;

his power is in the skies.

36AB Awesome in his sanctuary is God, the God of Israel;

he gives power and strength to his people.

R. Sing to God, O kingdoms of the earth. or: **R. Alleluia.**

Alleluia – cf. John 17:17B, 17A

R. Alleluia, alleluia.

Your word, O Lord, is truth; consecrate us in the truth.

R. Alleluia, alleluia.

Gospel – John 17:11B-19

Lifting up his eyes to heaven, Jesus prayed, saying: [11B] "Holy Father, keep them in your name that you have given me, so that they may be one just as we are one. [12]When I was with

them I protected them in your name that you gave me, and I
guarded them, and none of them was lost except the son of
destruction, in order that the Scripture might be fulfilled.[13]But
now I am coming to you. I speak this in the world so that they
may share my joy completely. [14]I gave them your word, and
the world hated them because they do not belong to the world
any more than I belong to the world. [15]I do not ask that you
take them out of the world but that you keep them from the
Evil One. [16]They do not belong to the world any more than I
belong to the world. [17]Consecrate them in the truth. Your word
is truth. [18]As you sent me into the world, so I sent them into
the world. [19]And I consecrate myself for them, so that they
also may be consecrated in truth."

Thursday May 25, 2023

Thursday of the Seventh Week of Easter

First Reading – Acts 22:30; 23:6-11

[30]Wishing to determine the truth about why Paul was being
accused by the Jews, the commander freed him and ordered
the chief priests and the whole Sanhedrin to convene. Then
he brought Paul down and made him stand before them. [6]Paul
was aware that some were Sadducees and some Pharisees,
so he called out before the Sanhedrin, "My brothers, I am a
Pharisee, the son of Pharisees; I am on trial for hope in the
resurrection of the dead." [7]When he said this, a dispute broke
out between the Pharisees and Sadducees, and the group
became divided. [8]For the Sadducees say that there is no
resurrection or angels or spirits, while the Pharisees
acknowledge all three. [9]A great uproar occurred, and some
scribes belonging to the Pharisee party stood up and sharply
argued, "We find nothing wrong with this man. Suppose a
spirit or an angel has spoken to him?" [10]The dispute was so
serious that the commander, afraid that Paul would be torn to
pieces by them, ordered his troops to go down and rescue
Paul from their midst and take him into the compound. [11]The
following night the Lord stood by him and said, "Take courage.
For just as you have borne witness to my cause in Jerusalem,
so you must also bear witness in Rome."

Responsorial Psalm – Psalms 16:1-2A AND 5, 7-8, 9-10, 11

R. (1) **Keep me safe, O God; you are my hope.** or: **R. Alleluia**.

1 Keep me, O God, for in you I take refuge;

2A I say to the LORD, "My Lord are you."

5 O LORD, my allotted portion and my cup,

it is you who hold fast my lot.

R. Keep me safe, O God; you are my hope. or: **R. Alleluia.**

7 I bless the LORD who counsels me;

even in the night, my heart exhorts me.

8 I set the LORD ever before me;

with him, at my right hand, I shall not be disturbed.

R. Keep me safe, O God; you are my hope. or: **R. Alleluia.**

9 Therefore my heart is glad and my soul rejoices,

my body, too, abides in confidence;

10 Because you will not abandon my soul to the nether world,

nor will you suffer your faithful one to undergo corruption.

R. Keep me safe, O God; you are my hope. or: **R. Alleluia.**

11 You will show me the path to life,

fullness of joys in your presence,

the delights at your right hand forever.

R. Keep me safe, O God; you are my hope. or: **R. Alleluia.**

Alleluia – John 17:21

R. Alleluia, alleluia.

21 May they all be one as you, Father, are in me and I in you, that the world may believe that you sent me, says the Lord.

R. Alleluia, alleluia.

Gospel – John 17:20-26

Lifting up his eyes to heaven, Jesus prayed saying: [20]"I pray not only for these but also for those who will believe in me through their word, [21]so that they may all be one, as you, Father, are in me and I in you, that they also may be in us, that the world may believe that you sent me. [22]And I have given them the glory you gave me, so that they may be one, as we are one, [23]I in them and you in me, that they may be brought to perfection as one, that the world may know that you sent me, and that you loved them even as you loved me. [24]Father, they are your gift to me. I wish that where I am they also may be with me, that they may see my glory that you gave me because you loved me before the foundation of the world. [25]Righteous Father, the world also does not know you, but I know you, and they know that you sent me. [26]I made known to them your name and I will make it known, that the love with which you loved me may be in them and I in them."

Friday May 26, 2023

Memorial of Saint Philip Neri - Priest

First Reading – Acts 25:13B-21

[13B]King Agrippa and Bernice arrived in Caesarea on a visit to Festus. [14]Since they spent several days there, Festus referred Paul's case to the king, saying, "There is a man here left in custody by Felix. [15]When I was in Jerusalem the chief priests and the elders of the Jews brought charges against him and demanded his condemnation. [16]I answered them that it was not Roman practice to hand over an accused person before he has faced his accusers and had the opportunity to defend himself against their charge.[17]So when they came together here, I made no delay; the next day I took my seat on the tribunal and ordered the man to be brought in. [18]His accusers stood around him, but did not charge him with any of the crimes I suspected.[19]Instead, they had some issues with him about their own religion and about a certain Jesus who had died but who Paul claimed was alive. [20]Since I was at a loss on how to investigate this controversy, I asked if he were willing to go to Jerusalem and there stand trial on these charges. [21]And when Paul appealed that he be held in custody for the Emperor's decision, I ordered him held until I could send him to Caesar."

Responsorial Psalm – Psalms 103:1-2, 11-12, 19-20AB

R. (19a) **The Lord has established his throne in heaven.** or: **R. Alleluia.**

1 Bless the LORD, O my soul;

and all my being, bless his holy name.

2 Bless the LORD, O my soul,

and forget not all his benefits.

R. The Lord has established his throne in heaven. or: **R. Alleluia.**

11 For as the heavens are high above the earth,

so surpassing is his kindness toward those who fear him.

12 As far as the east is from the west,

so far has he put our transgressions from us.

R. The Lord has established his throne in heaven. or: **R. Alleluia.**

19 The LORD has established his throne in heaven,

and his kingdom rules over all.

20AB Bless the LORD, all you his angels,

you mighty in strength, who do his bidding.

R. The Lord has established his throne in heaven. or: **R. Alleluia.**

Alleluia – John 14:26

R. Alleluia, alleluia.

26 The Holy Spirit will teach you everything and remind you of all I told you.

R. Alleluia, alleluia.

Gospel – John 21:15-19

15After Jesus had revealed himself to his disciples and eaten breakfast with them, he said to Simon Peter, “Simon, son of John, do you love me more than these?” Simon Peter

answered him, “Yes, Lord, you know that I love you.” Jesus
said to him, “Feed my lambs.” 16He then said to Simon Peter a
second time, “Simon, son of John, do you love me?” Simon
Peter answered him, “Yes, Lord, you know that I love you.” He
said to him, “Tend my sheep.” 17He said to him the third time,
“Simon, son of John, do you love me?” Peter was distressed
that he had said to him a third time, “Do you love me?” and he
said to him, “Lord, you know everything; you know that I love
you.” Jesus said to him, “Feed my sheep. 18Amen, amen, I say
to you, when you were younger, you used to dress yourself
and go where you wanted; but when you grow old, you will
stretch out your hands, and someone else will dress you and
lead you where you do not want to go.” 19He said this
signifying by what kind of death he would glorify God. And
when he had said this, he said to him, “Follow me.”

Saturday May 27, 2023

Saturday of the Seventh Week of Easter

First Reading – Acts 28:16-20, 30-31

16When he entered Rome, Paul was allowed to live by himself,
with the soldier who was guarding him. 17Three days later he
called together the leaders of the Jews. When they had
gathered he said to them, “My brothers, although I had done
nothing against our people or our ancestral customs, I was
handed over to the Romans as a prisoner from Jerusalem.
18After trying my case the Romans wanted to release me,
because they found nothing against me deserving the death
penalty. 19But when the Jews objected, I was obliged to appeal
to Caesar, even though I had no accusation to make against
my own nation. 20This is the reason, then, I have requested to
see you and to speak with you, for it is on account of the hope
of Israel that I wear these chains.” 30He remained for two full
years in his lodgings. He received all who came to him, 31and
with complete assurance and without hindrance he proclaimed
the Kingdom of God and taught about the Lord Jesus Christ.

Responsorial Psalm – Psalms 11:4, 5 AND 7

R. (see 7b) **The just will gaze on your face, O Lord.** or: **R. Alleluia.**

4 The LORD is in his holy temple;

the LORD's throne is in heaven.

His eyes behold,

his searching glance is on mankind.

R. The just will gaze on your face, O Lord. or: **R. Alleluia.**

5 The LORD searches the just and the wicked;

the lover of violence he hates.

7 For the LORD is just, he loves just deeds;

the upright shall see his face.

R. The just will gaze on your face, O Lord. or: **R. Alleluia.**

Alleluia – John 16:7, 13

R. Alleluia, alleluia.

7 I will send to you the Spirit of truth, says the Lord; 13 he will guide you to all truth.

R. Alleluia, alleluia.

Gospel – John 21:20-25

20Peter turned and saw the disciple following whom Jesus
loved, the one who had also reclined upon his chest during the
supper and had said, "Master, who is the one who will betray
you?" 21When Peter saw him, he said to Jesus, "Lord, what
about him?" 22Jesus said to him, "What if I want him to remain
until I come? What concern is it of yours? You follow me." 23So
the word spread among the brothers that that disciple would
not die. But Jesus had not told him that he would not die, just
"What if I want him to remain until I come? What concern is it
of yours?" 24It is this disciple who testifies to these things and
has written them, and we know that his testimony is true.
25There are also many other things that Jesus did, but if these
were to be described individually, I do not think the whole
world would contain the books that would be written.

Saturday May 27, 2023

Pentecost Vigil

First Reading – Genesis 11:1-9

[1]The whole world spoke the same language, using the same
words. [2]While the people were migrating in the east, they
came upon a valley in the land of Shinar and settled there.
[3]They said to one another, “Come, let us mold bricks and
harden them with fire.” They used bricks for stone, and
bitumen for mortar. [4]Then they said, “Come, let us build
ourselves a city and a tower with its top in the sky, and so
make a name for ourselves; otherwise we shall be scattered
all over the earth.” [5]The LORD came down to see the city and
the tower that the people had built. [6]Then the LORD said: “If
now, while they are one people, all speaking the same
language, they have started to do this, nothing will later stop
them from doing whatever they presume to do. [7]Let us then go
down there and confuse their language, so that one will not
understand what another says.” [8]Thus the LORD scattered
them from there all over the earth, and they stopped building
the city. [9]That is why it was called Babel, because there the
LORD confused the speech of all the world. It was from that
place that he scattered them all over the earth.

OR Exodus 19:3-8A, 16-20B

[3]Moses went up the mountain to God. Then the LORD called
to him and said, “Thus shall you say to the house of Jacob; tell
the Israelites: [4]You have seen for yourselves how I treated the
Egyptians and how I bore you up on eagle wings and brought
you here to myself. [5]Therefore, if you hearken to my voice and
keep my covenant, you shall be my special possession, dearer
to me than all other people, though all the earth is mine. [6]You
shall be to me a kingdom of priests, a holy nation. That is what
you must tell the Israelites.” [7]So Moses went and summoned
the elders of the people. When he set before them all that the
LORD had ordered him to tell them, [8A]the people all answered
together, “Everything the LORD has said, we will do.” [16]On the
morning of the third day there were peals of thunder and
lightning, and a heavy cloud over the mountain, and a very
loud trumpet blast, so that all the people in the camp trembled.
[17]But Moses led the people out of the camp to meet God, and
they stationed themselves at the foot of the mountain. [18]Mount

Sinai was all wrapped in smoke, for the LORD came down
upon it in fire. The smoke rose from it as though from a
furnace, and the whole mountain trembled violently. [19]The
trumpet blast grew louder and louder, while Moses was
speaking, and God answering him with thunder. [20]When the
LORD came down to the top of Mount Sinai, he summoned
Moses to the top of the mountain.

OR Ezekiel 37:1-14

[1]The hand of the LORD came upon me, and he led me out in
the spirit of the LORD and set me in the center of the plain,
which was now filled with bones. [2]He made me walk among
the bones in every direction so that I saw how many they were
on the surface of the plain. How dry they were! [3]He asked me:
Son of man, can these bones come to life? I answered, “Lord
GOD, you alone know that.” [4]Then he said to me: Prophesy
over these bones, and say to them: Dry bones, hear the word
of the LORD! [5]Thus says the Lord GOD to these bones: See! I
will bring spirit into you, that you may come to life. [6]I will put
sinews upon you, make flesh grow over you, cover you with
skin, and put spirit in you so that you may come to life and
know that I am the LORD. [7]I, Ezekiel, prophesied as I had
been told, and even as I was prophesying I heard a noise; it
was a rattling as the bones came together, bone joining bone.
[8]I saw the sinews and the flesh come upon them, and the skin
cover them, but there was no spirit in them. [9]Then the LORD
said to me: Prophesy to the spirit, prophesy, son of man, and
say to the spirit: Thus says the Lord GOD: From the four winds
come, O spirit, and breathe into these slain that they may
come to life. [10]I prophesied as he told me, and the spirit came
into them; they came alive and stood upright, a vast
army.[11]Then he said to me: Son of man, these bones are the
whole house of Israel. They have been saying, “Our bones are
dried up, our hope is lost, and we are cut off.” [12]Therefore,
prophesy and say to them: Thus says the Lord GOD: O my
people, I will open your graves and have you rise from them,
and bring you back to the land of Israel. [13]Then you shall know
that I am the LORD, when I open your graves and have you
rise from them, O my people! [14]I will put my spirit in you that
you may live, and I will settle you upon your land; thus you
shall know that I am the LORD. I have promised, and I will do
it, says the LORD.

OR Joel 3:1-5

1 Thus says the LORD: I will pour out my spirit upon all flesh.
Your sons and daughters shall prophesy, your old men shall
dream dreams, your young men shall see visions; 2 even upon
the servants and the handmaids, in those days, I will pour out
my spirit. 3 And I will work wonders in the heavens and on the
earth, blood, fire, and columns of smoke; 4 the sun will be
turned to darkness, and the moon to blood, at the coming of
the day of the LORD, the great and terrible day. 5 Then
everyone shall be rescued who calls on the name of the
LORD; for on Mount Zion there shall be a remnant, as the
LORD has said, and in Jerusalem survivors whom the LORD
shall call.

Responsorial Psalm – Psalms 104:1-2,24 AND 35,27-28, 29-30

R. (cf. 30) **Lord, send out your Spirit, and renew the face of the earth.** or: **R. Alleluia.**

1 Bless the LORD, O my soul!

O LORD, my God, you are great indeed!

2 You are clothed with majesty and glory,

robed in light as with a cloak.

R. Lord, send out your Spirit, and renew the face of the earth. or: **R. Alleluia.**

24 How manifold are your works, O LORD!

In wisdom you have wrought them all

the earth is full of your creatures;

35C bless the LORD, O my soul! Alleluia.

R. Lord, send out your Spirit, and renew the face of the earth. or: **R. Alleluia.**

27 Creatures all look to you

to give them food in due time.

28 When you give it to them, they gather it;

when you open your hand, they are filled with good things.

R. Lord, send out your Spirit, and renew the face of the earth. or: **R. Alleluia.**

29 If you take away their breath, they perish

and return to their dust.

30 When you send forth your spirit, they are created,

and you renew the face of the earth.

R. Lord, send out your Spirit, and renew the face of the earth. or: **R. Alleluia.**

Second Reading – Romans 8:22-27

Brothers and sisters: 22We know that all creation is groaning in
labor pains even until now; 23and not only that, but we
ourselves, who have the first fruits of the Spirit, we also groan
within ourselves as we wait for adoption, the redemption of our
bodies. 24For in hope we were saved. Now hope that sees is
not hope. For who hopes for what one sees? 25But if we hope
for what we do not see, we wait with endurance. 26In the same
way, the Spirit too comes to the aid of our weakness; for we
do not know how to pray as we ought, but the Spirit himself
intercedes with inexpressible groanings. 27And the one who
searches hearts knows what is the intention of the Spirit,
because he intercedes for the holy ones according to God's
will.

Alleluia

R. Alleluia, alleluia.

Come, Holy Spirit, fill the hearts of your faithful and kindle in them the fire of your love.

R. Alleluia, alleluia.

Gospel – John 7:37-39

37Jesus stood up and exclaimed, "Let anyone who thirsts
come to me and drink. 38As Scripture says: Rivers of living
water will flow from within him who believes in me." 39He said
this in reference to the Spirit that those who came to believe in
him were to receive. There was, of course, no Spirit yet,
because Jesus had not yet been glorified.

Sunday May 28, 2023

Pentecost Sunday

First Reading – Acts 2:1-11

[1]When the time for Pentecost was fulfilled, they were all in one
place together. [2]And suddenly there came from the sky a
noise like a strong driving wind, and it filled the entire house in
which they were. [3]Then there appeared to them tongues as of
fire, which parted and came to rest on each one of them. [4]And
they were all filled with the Holy Spirit and began to speak in
different tongues, as the Spirit enabled them to proclaim. [5]Now
there were devout Jews from every nation under heaven
staying in Jerusalem.[6]At this sound, they gathered in a large
crowd, but they were confused because each one heard them
speaking in his own language. [7]They were astounded, and in
amazement, they asked, "Are not all these people who are
speaking Galileans? [8]Then how does each of us hear them in
his native language? [9]We are Parthians, Medes, and Elamites,
inhabitants of Mesopotamia, Judea and Cappadocia, Pontus
and Asia, [10]Phrygia and Pamphylia, Egypt and the districts of
Libya near Cyrene, as well as travellers from Rome, [11]both
Jews and converts to Judaism, Cretans and Arabs, yet we
hear them speaking in our own tongues of the mighty acts of
God."

Responsorial Psalm – Psalms 104:1, 24, 29-30, 31, 34

R. (cf. 30) **Lord, send out your Spirit and renew the face of the earth.** or: **R. Alleluia.**

[1] Bless the LORD, O my soul!

O LORD, my God, you are great indeed!

[24] How manifold are your works, O LORD!

the earth is full of your creatures;

R. Lord, send out your Spirit, and renew the face of the earth. or: **R. Alleluia.**

[31] May the glory of the LORD endure forever;

may the LORD be glad in his works!

[34] Pleasing to him be my theme;

I will be glad in the LORD.

R. Lord, send out your Spirit, and renew the face of the earth. or: **R. Alleluia.**

[29] If you take away their breath, they perish

and return to their dust.

[30] When you send forth your spirit, they are created,

and you renew the face of the earth.

R. Lord, send out your Spirit, and renew the face of the earth. or: **R. Alleluia.**

Second Reading – 1 Corinthians 12:3B-7, 12-13

Brothers and sisters: [3B]No one can say, “Jesus is Lord,” except by the Holy Spirit. [4]There are different kinds of spiritual gifts but the same Spirit; [5]there are different forms of service but the same Lord; [6]there are different workings but the same God who produces all of them in everyone. [7]To each individual, the manifestation of the Spirit is given for some benefit. [12]As a body is one though it has many parts, and all the parts of the body, though many, are one body, so also Christ. [13]For in one Spirit we were all baptized into one body, whether Jews or Greeks, slaves or free persons, and we were all given to drink of one Spirit.

Or: Romans 8:8-17

Brothers and sisters: [8]Those who are in the flesh cannot please God. [9]But you are not in the flesh; on the contrary, you are in the spirit, if only the Spirit of God dwells in you. Whoever does not have the Spirit of Christ does not belong to him.[10]But if Christ is in you, although the body is dead because of sin, the spirit is alive because of righteousness. [11]If the Spirit of the one who raised Jesus from the dead dwells in you, the one who raised Christ from the dead will give life to your mortal bodies also, through his Spirit that dwells in you.[12]Consequently, brothers and sisters, we are not debtors to the flesh, to live according to the flesh.[13]For if you live according to the flesh, you will die, but if by the Spirit you put to death the deeds of the body, you will live.[14]For those who are led by the Spirit of God are sons of God.[15]For you did not receive a spirit of slavery to fall back into fear, but you received a Spirit of adoption, through whom we cry, "Abba, Father!" [16]The Spirit himself bears witness with our spirit that we are children of God,[17]and if children, then heirs, heirs of God and joint heirs with Christ, if only we suffer with him so that we may also be glorified with him.

OR Galatians 5:16-25

[16]Brothers and sisters, live by the Spirit and you will certainly not gratify the desire of the flesh.[17]For the flesh has desires against the Spirit, and the Spirit against the flesh; these are opposed to each other, so that you may not do what you want.[18]But if you are guided by the Spirit, you are not under the law.[19]Now the works of the flesh are obvious: immorality, impurity, lust, [20]idolatry, sorcery, hatreds, rivalry, jealousy, outbursts of fury, acts of selfishness, dissensions, factions,[21]occasions of envy, drinking bouts, orgies, and the like. I warn you, as I warned you before, that those who do such things will not inherit the kingdom of God. [22]In contrast, the fruit of the Spirit is love, joy, peace, patience, kindness, generosity, faithfulness,[23]gentleness, self-control. Against such there is no law. [24]Now those who belong to Christ Jesus have crucified their flesh with its passions and desires.[25]If we live in the Spirit, let us also follow the Spirit.

Sequence -*Veni, Sancte Spiritus*

Come, Holy Spirit, come!

And from your celestial home

Shed a ray of light divine!

Come, Father of the poor!

Come, source of all our store!

Come, within our bosoms shine.

You, of comforters the best;

You, the soul's most welcome guest;

Sweet refreshment here below;

In our labour, rest most sweet;

Grateful coolness in the heat;

Solace in the midst of woe.
O most blessed Light divine,
Shine within these hearts of yours,
And our inmost being fill!
Where you are not, we have naught,
Nothing good in deed or thought,
Nothing free from taint of ill.
Heal our wounds, our strength renew;
On our dryness pour your dew;
Wash the stains of guilt away:
Bend the stubborn heart and will;
Melt the frozen, warm the chill;
Guide the steps that go astray.
On the faithful, who adore
And confess you, evermore
In your sevenfold gift descend;
Give them virtue's sure reward;
Give them your salvation, Lord;
Give them joys that never end. Amen. **Alleluia.**

Alleluia

R. Alleluia, alleluia.

Come, Holy Spirit, fill the hearts of your faithful and kindle in them the fire of your love.

R. Alleluia, alleluia.

Gospel – John 20:19-23

19On the evening of that first day of the week, when the doors were locked, where the disciples were, for fear of the Jews, Jesus came and stood in their midst and said to them, "Peace be with you."
20When he had said this, he showed them his hands and his side. The disciples rejoiced when they saw the Lord.
21Jesus said to them again, "Peace be with you. As the

Father has sent me, so I send you." 22And when he had said this, he breathed on them and said to them, "Receive the Holy Spirit. 23Whose sins you forgive are forgiven them, and whose sins you retain are retained."

Or: John 14:15-16, 23B-26

Jesus said to his disciples: 15"If you love me, you will keep my commandments.16And I will ask the Father, and he will give you another Advocate to be with you always. 23B "Whoever loves me will keep my word, and my Father will love him, and we will come to him and make our dwelling with him. 24Those who do not love me do not keep my words; yet the word you hear is not mine but that of the Father who sent me. 25"I have told you this while I am with you. 26The Advocate, the Holy Spirit whom the Father will send in my name, will teach you everything and remind you of all that I told you."

Or: John 15:26-27; 16:12-15

Jesus said to his disciples: 26"When the Advocate comes whom I will send you from the Father, the Spirit of truth that proceeds from the Father, he will testify to me. 27And you also testify, because you have been with me from the beginning.12"I have much more to tell you, but you cannot bear it now. 13But when he comes, the Spirit of truth, he will guide you to all truth. He will not speak on his own, but he will speak what he hears, and will declare to you the things that are coming.14He will glorify me, because he will take from what is mine and declare it to you.15Everything that the Father has is mine; for this reason, I told you that he will take from what is mine and declare it to you."

Monday May 29, 2023

Monday of the Eighth Week in Ordinary Time

First Reading – Sirach 17:20-24

24To the penitent, God provides a way back, he encourages those who are losing hope and has chosen for them the lot of truth.25Return to him and give up sin, pray to the LORD and make your offences few.26Turn again to the Most High and away from your sin, hate intensely what he loathes, and know the justice and judgments of God, Stand firm in the way set before you, in prayer to the Most High God.27Who in the nether world can glorify the Most High in place of the living who offer their praise? Dwell no longer in the error of the ungodly, but offer your praise before death.[28]No more can the dead give praise than those who have never lived; You who are alive and well shall praise and glorify God in his mercies.[29]How great the mercy of the LORD, his forgiveness of those who return to him!

Responsorial Psalm – Psalms 32:1-2, 5, 6, 7

R. (11a) **Let the just exult and rejoice in the Lord.**

1 Blessed is he whose fault is taken away,

whose sin is covered.

2 Blessed the man to whom the LORD imputes not guilt,

in whose spirit there is no guile.

R. Let the just exult and rejoice in the Lord.

5 Then I acknowledged my sin to you,

my guilt I covered not.

I said, "I confess my faults to the LORD,"

and you took away the guilt of my sin.

R. Let the just exult and rejoice in the Lord.

6 For this shall every faithful man pray to you

in time of stress.

Though deep waters overflow,

they shall not reach him.

R. Let the just exult and rejoice in the Lord

7 You are my shelter; from distress you will preserve me;

with glad cries of freedom you will ring me round.

R. Let the just exult and rejoice in the Lord.

Alleluia – 2 Corinthians 8:9

R. Alleluia, alleluia.

9 Jesus Christ became poor although he was rich, so that by his poverty you might become rich.

R. Alleluia, alleluia.

Gospel – Mark 10:17-27

[17]As Jesus was setting out on a journey, a man ran up, knelt
down before him, and asked him, “Good teacher, what must I
do to inherit eternal life?” [18]Jesus answered him, “Why do you
call me good? No one is good but God alone.[19]You know the
commandments: You shall not kill; you shall not commit
adultery; you shall not steal; you shall not bear false witness;
you shall not defraud; honor your father and your mother.”
[20]He replied and said to him, “Teacher, all of these I have
observed from my youth.” [21]Jesus, looking at him, loved him
and said to him, “You are lacking in one thing. Go, sell what
you have, and give to the poor and you will have treasure in
heaven; then come, follow me.” [22]At that statement, his face
fell, and he went away sad, for he had many possessions.
[23]Jesus looked around and said to his disciples, “How hard it is
for those who have wealth to enter the Kingdom of God!”
[24]The disciples were amazed at his words. So Jesus again
said to them in reply, “Children, how hard it is to enter the
Kingdom of God! [25]It is easier for a camel to pass through the
eye of a needle, than for one who is rich to enter the Kingdom
of God.” [26]They were exceedingly astonished and said among
themselves, “Then who can be saved?” [27]Jesus looked at
them and said, “For men it is impossible, but not for God. All
things are possible for God.”

Tuesday May 30, 2023

Tuesday of the Eighth Week in Ordinary Time

First Reading – Sirach 35:1-15

[1]To keep the law is a great oblation,[2]and he who observes the
commandments sacrifices a peace offering. [3]In works of
charity one offers fine flour,[4]and when he gives alms he
presents his sacrifice of praise. [5]To refrain from evil pleases
the LORD, and to avoid injustice is an atonement. [6]Appear not
before the LORD empty-handed, [7]for all that you offer is in
fulfilment of the precepts. [8]The just one’s offering enriches the
altar and rises as a sweet odour before the Most High.[9]The
just one’s sacrifice is most pleasing, nor will it ever be
forgotten.[10]In a generous spirit pay homage to the LORD, be
not sparing of freewill gifts.[11]With each contribution show a

cheerful countenance, and pay your tithes in a spirit of
joy.[12]Give to the Most High as he has given to you,
generously, according to your means.[13]For the LORD is one
who always repays, and he will give back to you
sevenfold.[14]But offer no bribes, these he does not accept!
[15]Trust not in sacrifice of the fruits of extortion. For he is a God
of justice, who knows no favourites.

Responsorial Psalm – Psalms 50:5-6, 7-8, 14 And 23

R. (23b) To the upright I will show the saving power of God.

5 “Gather my faithful ones before me,

those who have made a covenant with me by sacrifice.”

6 And the heavens proclaim his justice;

for God himself is the judge.

R. To the upright I will show the saving power of God.

7 “Hear, my people, and I will speak;

Israel, I will testify against you;

God, your God, am I.

8 Not for your sacrifices do I rebuke you,

for your burnt offerings are before me always.”

R. To the upright I will show the saving power of God.

14 “Offer to God praise as your sacrifice

and fulfil your vows to the Most High.

23 He that offers praise as a sacrifice glorifies me;

and to him, that goes the right way I will show the salvation of God.”

R. To the upright I will show the saving power of God.

Alleluia – Matthew 11:25

R. Alleluia, alleluia.

25 Blessed are you, Father, Lord of heaven and earth; you have revealed to little ones the mysteries of the Kingdom.

R. Alleluia, alleluia.

Gospel – Mark 10:28-31

[28]Peter began to say to Jesus, 'We have given up everything
and followed you." [29]Jesus said, "Amen, I say to you, there is
no one who has given up house or brothers or sisters or
mother or father or children or lands for my sake and for the
sake of the Gospel [30]who will not receive a hundred times
more now in this present age: houses and brothers and sisters
and mothers and children and lands, with persecutions, and
eternal life in the age to come.[31]But many that are first will be
last, and the last will be first."

Wednesday May 31, 2023

Feast of the Visitation of the Blessed Virgin Mary

First Reading – Zephaniah 3:14-18A

[14]Shout for joy, O daughter Zion! Sing joyfully, O Israel! Be
glad and exult with all your heart, O daughter Jerusalem!
[15]The LORD has removed the judgment against you, he has
turned away your enemies; The King of Israel, the LORD, is in
your midst, you have no further misfortune to fear. [16]On that
day, it shall be said to Jerusalem: Fear not, O Zion, be not
discouraged! [17]The LORD, your God, is in your midst, a mighty
saviour; He will rejoice over you with gladness, and renew you
in his love, He will sing joyfully because of you, [18A] as one
sings at festivals.

Or Romans 12:9-16

[9]Brothers and sisters: Let love be sincere; hate what is evil,
hold on to what is good; [10]love one another with mutual
affection; anticipate one another in showing honor. [11]Do not
grow slack in zeal, be fervent in spirit, serve the Lord.[12]Rejoice
in hope, endure in affliction, persevere in prayer.[13]Contribute
to the needs of the holy ones, exercise hospitality.[14]Bless
those who persecute you, bless and do not curse
them.[15]Rejoice with those who rejoice, weep with those who
weep.[16]Have the same regard for one another; do not be
haughty but associate with the lowly; do not be wise in your
own estimation.

Responsorial Psalm – Isaiah 12:2-3, 4BCD, 5-6

R.(6) Among you is the great and Holy One of Israel.

2 God indeed is my savior;
I am confident and unafraid.
My strength and my courage is the LORD,
and he has been my savior.
3 With joy you will draw water
at the fountain of salvation.

R. Among you is the great and Holy One of Israel.

4BCD Give thanks to the LORD, acclaim his name;
among the nations make known his deeds,
proclaim how exalted is his name.

R. Among you is the great and Holy One of Israel.

5 Sing praise to the LORD for his glorious achievement;
let this be known throughout all the earth.
6 Shout with exultation, O city of Zion,
for great in your midst
is the Holy One of Israel!

R. Among you is the great and Holy One of Israel.

Alleluia – cf. Luke 1:45

R. Alleluia, alleluia.

45 Blessed are you, O Virgin Mary, who believed that what was spoken to you by the Lord would be fulfilled.

R. Alleluia, alleluia.

Gospel – Luke 1:39-56

39 Mary set out and travelled to the hill country in haste to a
town of Judah, 40 where she entered the house of Zechariah
and greeted Elizabeth. 41 When Elizabeth heard Mary's
greeting, the infant leaped in her womb, and Elizabeth, filled
with the Holy Spirit, 42 cried out in a loud voice and said, "Most

blessed are you among women, and blessed is the fruit of your womb.[43]And how does this happen to me, that the mother of my Lord should come to me? [44]For at the moment the sound of your greeting reached my ears, the infant in my womb leaped for joy. [45]Blessed are you who believed that what was spoken to you by the Lord would be fulfilled." [46]*And Mary said:"My soul proclaims the greatness of the Lord;* [47]*my spirit rejoices in God my Savior,* [48]*for he has looked with favour on his lowly servant. From this day all generations will call me blessed:* [49]*the Almighty has done great things for me, and holy is his Name.* [50]*He has mercy on those who fear him in every generation.* [51]*He has shown the strength of his arm, he has scattered the proud in their conceit.* [52]*He has cast down the mighty from their thrones and has lifted up the lowly.* [53]*He has filled the hungry with good things, and the rich he has sent away empty.* [54]*He has come to the help of his servant Israel for he has remembered his promise of mercy,*[55]*the promise he made to our fathers, to Abraham and his children forever."* [56]Mary remained with her about three months and then returned to her home.

JUNE 2023

Thursday June 1, 2023

Thursday of Eighth Week in Ordinary Time

First Reading – Sirach 42:15-25

[15]Now will I recall God's works; what I have seen, I will describe. At God's word were his works brought into being; they do his will as he has ordained for them.[16]As the rising sun is clear to all, so the glory of the LORD fills all his works; [17]Yet even God's holy ones must fail in recounting the wonders of the LORD, Though God has given these, his hosts, the strength to stand firm before his glory.[18]He plumbs the depths and penetrates the heart; their innermost being he understands. The Most High possesses all knowledge, and sees from of old the things that are to come: [19]He makes known the past and the future, and reveals the deepest secrets. [20]No understanding does he lack; no single thing escapes him. [21]Perennial is his almighty wisdom; he is from all eternity one and the same, With nothing added, nothing taken away; no need of a counselor for him! [22]How beautiful are all

his works! even to the spark and fleeting vision! [23]The universe lives and abides forever; to meet each need, each creature is preserved. [24]All of them differ, one from another, yet none of them has he made in vain, [25]For each in turn, as it comes, is good; can one ever see enough of their splendor?

Responsorial Psalm – Psalms 33:2-3, 4-5, 6-7, 8-9

R. (6a) By the word of the Lord the heavens were made.

2 Give thanks to the LORD on the harp;

with the ten-stringed lyre chant his praises.

3 Sing to him a new song;

pluck the strings skillfully, with shouts of gladness.

R. By the word of the Lord the heavens were made.

4 For upright is the word of the LORD

and all his works are trustworthy.

5 He loves justice and right;

of the kindness of the LORD the earth is full.

R. By the word of the Lord the heavens were made.

6 By the word of the LORD the heavens were made;

by the breath of his mouth all their host.

7 He gathers the waters of the sea as in a flask;

in cellars he confines the deep.

R. By the word of the Lord the heavens were made.

8 Let all the earth fear the LORD;

let all who dwell in the world revere him.

9 For he spoke, and it was made;

he commanded, and it stood forth.

R. By the word of the Lord the heavens were made.

Alleluia – John 8:12

R. Alleluia, alleluia.

[12] I am the light of the world, says the Lord; whoever follows me will have the light of life.

R. Alleluia, alleluia.

Gospel – Mark 10:46-52

[46]As Jesus was leaving Jericho with his disciples and a sizable crowd, Bartimaeus, a blind man, the son of Timaeus, sat by the roadside begging. [47]On hearing that it was Jesus of Nazareth, he began to cry out and say, "Jesus, son of David, have pity on me." [48]And many rebuked him, telling him to be silent. But he kept calling out all the more, "Son of David, have pity on me." [49]Jesus stopped and said, "Call him." So they called the blind man, saying to him, "Take courage; get up, Jesus is calling you." [50]He threw aside his cloak, sprang up, and came to Jesus. [51]Jesus said to him in reply, "What do you want me to do for you?" The blind man replied to him, "Master, I want to see." [52]Jesus told him, 'Go your way; your faith has saved you." Immediately he received his sight and followed him on the way.

Friday June 2, 2023

Friday of the Eighth Week in Ordinary Time

First Reading – Sirach 44:1, 9-13

[1]Now will I praise those godly men, our ancestors, each in his own time. [9]But of others there is no memory, for when they ceased, they ceased. And they are as though they had not lived, they and their children after them. [10]Yet these also were godly men whose virtues have not been forgotten; [11]Their wealth remains in their families, their heritage with their descendants; [12]Through God's covenant with them their family endures, their posterity, for their sake. [13]And for all time their progeny will endure, their glory will never be blotted out.

Responsorial Psalm – Psalms 149:1B-2, 3-4, 5-6A AND 9B

R. (see 4a) **The Lord takes delight in his people.** or: **R. Alleluia.**

[1B] Sing to the LORD a new song

of praise in the assembly of the faithful.

[2] Let Israel be glad in their maker,

let the children of Zion rejoice in their king.

R. The Lord takes delight in his people. or: **R. Alleluia.**

[3] Let them praise his name in the festive dance,

let them sing praise to him with timbrel and harp.

[4] For the LORD loves his people,

and he adorns the lowly with victory.

R. The Lord takes delight in his people. or: **R. Alleluia.**

[5] Let the faithful exult in glory;

let them sing for joy upon their couches;

[6A] Let the high praises of God be in their throats.

[9B] This is the glory of all his faithful. Alleluia.

R. The Lord takes delight in his people. or: **R. Alleluia.**

Alleluia – John 15:16

R. Alleluia, alleluia.

[16] I chose you from the world, to go and bear fruit that will last, says the Lord.

R. Alleluia, alleluia.

Gospel – Mark 11:11-26

[11]Jesus entered Jerusalem and went into the temple area. He
looked around at everything and, since it was already late,
went out to Bethany with the Twelve.
[12]The next day as they
were leaving Bethany he was hungry.
[13]Seeing from a
distance a fig tree in leaf, he went over to see if he could find
anything on it. When he reached it he found nothing but
leaves; it was not the time for figs.
[14]And he said to it in reply,
"May no one ever eat of your fruit again!" And his disciples
heard it.
[15]They came to Jerusalem, and on entering the
temple area he began to drive out those selling and buying
there. He overturned the tables of the money changers and
the seats of those who were selling doves.
[16]He did not permit

anyone to carry anything through the temple area. [17]Then he
taught them saying, “Is it not written: My house shall be called
a house of prayer for all peoples? But you have made it a den
of thieves.” [18]The chief priests and the scribes came to hear of
it and were seeking a way to put him to death, yet they feared
him because the whole crowd was astonished at his teaching.
[19]When evening came, they went out of the city. [20]Early in the
morning, as they were walking along, they saw the fig tree
withered to its roots. [21]Peter remembered and said to him,
“Rabbi, look! The fig tree that you cursed has withered.”
[22]Jesus said to them in reply, “Have faith in God. [23]Amen, I say
to you, whoever says to this mountain, ‘Be lifted up and thrown
into the sea,’ and does not doubt in his heart but believes that
what he says will happen, it shall be done for him. [24]Therefore
I tell you, all that you ask for in prayer, believe that you will
receive it and it shall be yours. [25]When you stand to pray,
forgive anyone against whom you have a grievance, so that
your heavenly Father may in turn forgive you your
transgressions.”

Saturday June 3, 2023

Memorial of Saints Charles Lwanga and Companions

First Reading – Sirach 51:12CD-20

[12CD]I thank the LORD and I praise him; I bless the name of the
LORD. [13]When I was young and innocent, I sought wisdom
openly in my prayer [14] I prayed for her before the temple, and I
will seek her until the end, [15]and she flourished as a grape
soon ripe. My heart delighted in her, My feet kept to the level
path because from earliest youth I was familiar with her. [16]In
the short time I paid heed, I met with great instruction.[17]Since
in this way I have profited, I will give my teacher grateful
praise.[18]I became resolutely devoted to her the good I
persistently strove for.[19]My soul was tormented in seeking her,
My hand opened her gate and I came to know her secrets.[20]I
directed my soul to her, and in cleanness I attained to her.

Responsorial Psalm – Psalms 19:8, 9, 10, 11

R. [(9ab)] The precepts of the Lord give joy to the heart.

[8] The law of the LORD is perfect,

refreshing the soul.

The decree of the LORD is trustworthy,

giving wisdom to the simple.

R. The precepts of the Lord give joy to the heart.

9 The precepts of the LORD are right,

rejoicing the heart.

The command of the LORD is clear,

enlightening the eye.

R. The precepts of the Lord give joy to the heart.

10 The fear of the LORD is pure,

enduring forever;

The ordinances of the LORD are true,

all of them just.

R. The precepts of the Lord give joy to the heart.

11 They are more precious than gold,

than a heap of purest gold;

Sweeter also than syrup

or honey from the comb.

R. The precepts of the Lord give joy to the heart.

Alleluia – Colossians 3:16A, 17C

R. Alleluia, alleluia.

16A Let the word of Christ dwell in you richly; 17C giving thanks to God the Father through him.

R. Alleluia, alleluia.

Gospel – Mark 11:27-33

27Jesus and his disciples returned once more to Jerusalem. As he was walking in the temple area, the chief priests, the scribes, and the elders approached him 28and said to him, "By what authority are you doing these things? Or who gave you this authority to do them?" 29Jesus said to them, "I shall ask you one question. Answer me, and I will tell you by what authority I do these things. 30Was John's baptism of heavenly or of human origin? Answer me." 31 They discussed this among themselves and said, "If we say, 'Of heavenly origin,' he will say, 'Then why did you not believe him?' 32 But shall we say, 'Of human origin'?" they feared the crowd, for they all thought John really was a prophet. 33 So they said to Jesus in reply, "We do not know." Then Jesus said to them, "Neither shall I tell you by what authority I do these things."

Sunday June 4, 2023

Solemnity of the Most Holy Trinity, Year A

First Reading – Exodus 34:4B-6, 8-9

4B Early in the morning Moses went up Mount Sinai as the LORD had commanded him, taking along the two stone tablets. 5 Having come down in a cloud, the LORD stood with Moses there and proclaimed his name, "LORD." 6 Thus the LORD passed before him and cried out, "The LORD, the LORD, a merciful and gracious God, slow to anger and rich in kindness and fidelity." 8 Moses at once bowed down to the ground in worship. 9 Then he said, "If I find favor with you, O Lord, do come along in our company. This is indeed a stiff-necked people; yet pardon our wickedness and sins, and receive us as your own."

Responsorial Psalm – Daniel 3:52, 53, 54, 55, 56

R. (52b) Glory and praise for ever!

52 Blessed are you, O Lord, the God of our fathers,

praiseworthy and exalted above all forever;

And blessed is your holy and glorious name,

praiseworthy and exalted above all for all ages.

R. Glory and praise for ever!

53 Blessed are you in the temple of your holy glory,

praiseworthy and glorious above all forever.

R. Glory and praise for ever!

54 Blessed are you on the throne of your kingdom,

praiseworthy and exalted above all forever.

R. Glory and praise for ever!

[55] Blessed are you who look into the depths

from your throne upon the cherubim,

praiseworthy and exalted above all forever.

R. Glory and praise for ever!

Second Reading – 2 Corinthians 13:11-13

[11]Brothers and sisters, rejoice. Mend your ways, encourage
one another, agree with one another, live in peace, and the
God of love and peace will be with you. [12]Greet one another
with a holy kiss. All the holy ones greet you. [13]The grace of the
Lord Jesus Christ and the love of God and the fellowship of
the Holy Spirit be with all of you.

Alleluia – Revelation 1:8

R. Alleluia, alleluia.

[8]Glory to the Father, the Son, and the Holy Spirit; to God who is, who was, and who is to come.

R. Alleluia, alleluia.

Gospel – John 3:16-18

[16]God so loved the world that he gave his only Son, so that
everyone who believes in him might not perish but might have
eternal life. [17]For God did not send his Son into the world to
condemn the world, but that the world might be saved through
him. [18]Whoever believes in him will not be condemned, but
whoever does not believe has already been condemned,
because he has not believed in the name of the only Son of
God.

Monday June 5, 2023

Memorial of Saint Boniface – Bishop & Doctor

First Reading – Tobit 1:3; 2:1A-8

[3]I, Tobit, have walked all the days of my life on the paths of
truth and righteousness. I performed many charitable works
for my kinsmen and my people who had been deported with
me to Nineveh, in Assyria. [1A]On our festival of Pentecost, the
feast of Weeks, a fine dinner was prepared for me, and I
reclined to eat. [2]The table was set for me, and when many

different dishes were placed before me, I said to my son
Tobiah: "My son, go out and try to find a poor man from
among our kinsmen exiled here in Nineveh. If he is a sincere
worshiper of God, bring him back with you, so that he can
share this meal with me. Indeed, son, I shall wait for you to
come back." [3]Tobiah went out to look for some poor kinsman
of ours. When he returned he exclaimed, "Father!" I said to
him, "What is it, son?" He answered, "Father, one of our
people has been murdered! His body lies in the market place
where he was just strangled!" [4]I sprang to my feet, leaving the
dinner untouched; and I carried the dead man from the street
and put him in one of the rooms, so that I might bury him after
sunset. [5]Returning to my own quarters, I washed myself and
ate my food in sorrow. [6]I was reminded of the oracle
pronounced by the prophet Amos against Bethel: "All your
festivals shall be turned into mourning, and all your songs into
lamentation." [7]And I wept. Then at sunset I went out, dug a
grave, and buried him. [8]The neighbors mocked me, saying to
one another: "He is still not afraid! Once before he was hunted
down for execution because of this very thing; yet now that he
has scarcely escaped, here he is again burying the dead!"

Responsorial Psalm – Psalms 112:1B-2, 3B-4, 5-6

R. [(1b)] **Blessed the man who fears the Lord.** or: **R. Alleluia.**

[1B] Blessed the man who fears the LORD,

who greatly delights in his commands.

[2] His posterity shall be mighty upon the earth;

the upright generation shall be blessed.

R. Blessed the man who fears the Lord. or: **R. Alleluia.**

[3B] His generosity shall endure forever.

[4] Light shines through the darkness for the upright;

he is gracious and merciful and just.

R. Blessed the man who fears the Lord. or: **R. Alleluia.**

[5] Well for the man who is gracious and lends,

who conducts his affairs with justice;

[6] He shall never be moved;

the just man shall be in everlasting remembrance.

R. Blessed the man who fears the Lord. or: **R. Alleluia.**

Alleluia – Revelation 1:5AB

R. Alleluia, alleluia.

[5AB]Jesus Christ, you are the faithful witness, the firstborn of the dead; you have loved us and freed us from our sins by your Blood.

R. Alleluia, alleluia.

Gospel – Mark 12:1-12

[1]Jesus began to speak to the chief priests, the scribes, and the elders in parables. “A man planted a vineyard, put a hedge around it, dug a wine press, and built a tower. Then he leased it to tenant farmers and left on a journey. [2]At the proper time he sent a servant to the tenants to obtain from them some of the produce of the vineyard. [3]But they seized him, beat him, and sent him away empty-handed. [4]Again he sent them another servant. And that one they beat over the head and treated shamefully. [5]He sent yet another whom they killed. So, too, many others; some they beat, others they killed. [6]He had one other to send, a beloved son. He sent him to them last of all, thinking, ‘They will respect my son.’ [7]But those tenants said to one another, ‘This is the heir. Come, let us kill him, and the inheritance will be ours.’ [8]So they seized him and killed him, and threw him out of the vineyard. [9]What then will the owner of the vineyard do? He will come, put the tenants to death, and give the vineyard to others. [10]Have you not read this Scripture passage: The stone that the builders rejected has become the cornerstone; [11]by the Lord has this been done, and it is wonderful in our eyes?” [12]They were seeking to arrest him, but they feared the crowd, for they realized that he had addressed the parable to them. So they left him and went away.

Tuesday June 6, 2023

Tuesday of the Ninth Week in Ordinary Time

First Reading – Tobit 2:9-14

9On the night of Pentecost, after I had buried the dead, I,
Tobit, went into my courtyard to sleep next to the courtyard
wall. My face was uncovered because of the heat. 10I did not
know there were birds perched on the wall above me, till their
warm droppings settled in my eyes, causing cataracts. I went
to see some doctors for a cure but the more they anointed my
eyes with various salves, the worse the cataracts became,
until I could see no more. For four years I was deprived of
eyesight, and all my kinsmen were grieved at my condition.
Ahiqar, however, took care of me for two years, until he left for
Elymais. 11At that time, my wife Anna worked for hire at
weaving cloth, the kind of work women do. 12When she sent
back the goods to their owners, they would pay her. Late in
winter on the seventh of Dystrus, she finished the cloth and
sent it back to the owners. They paid her the full salary and
also gave her a young goat for the table. 13On entering my
house the goat began to bleat. I called to my wife and said:
"Where did this goat come from? Perhaps it was stolen! Give it
back to its owners; we have no right to eat stolen food!" 14She
said to me, "It was given to me as a bonus over and above my
wages." Yet I would not believe her, and told her to give it
back to its owners. I became very angry with her over this. So
she retorted: "Where are your charitable deeds now? Where
are your virtuous acts? See! Your true character is finally
showing itself!"

Responsorial Psalm – Psalms 112:1-2, 7-8, 9

R. (see 7c) **The heart of the just one is firm, trusting in the Lord.** or: **R. Alleluia.**

1 Blessed the man who fears the LORD,

who greatly delights in his commands.

2 His posterity shall be mighty upon the earth;

the upright generation shall be blessed.

R. The heart of the just one is firm, trusting in the Lord. or: **R. Alleluia.**

[7] An evil report he shall not fear;

his heart is firm, trusting in the LORD.

[8] His heart is steadfast; he shall not fear

till he looks down upon his foes.

R. The heart of the just one is firm, trusting in the Lord. or: **R. Alleluia.**

[9] Lavishly he gives to the poor;

his generosity shall endure forever;

his horn shall be exalted in glory.

R. The heart of the just one is firm, trusting in the Lord. or: **R. Alleluia.**

Alleluia – Ephesians 1:17-18

R. Alleluia, alleluia.

[17]May the Father of our Lord Jesus Christ enlighten the eyes
of our hearts,[18]that we may know what is the hope that
belongs to his call.

R. Alleluia, alleluia.

Gospel – Mark 12:13-17

[13]Some Pharisees and Herodians were sent to Jesus to
ensnare him in his speech. [14]They came and said to him,
"Teacher, we know that you are a truthful man and that you
are not concerned with anyone's opinion. You do not regard a
person's status but teach the way of God in accordance with
the truth. Is it lawful to pay the census tax to Caesar or not?
Should we pay or should we not pay?" [15]Knowing their
hypocrisy he said to them, "Why are you testing me? Bring me
a denarius to look at." [16]They brought one to him and he said
to them, "Whose image and inscription is this?" They replied to
him, "Caesar's." [17]So Jesus said to them, "Repay to Caesar
what belongs to Caesar and to God what belongs to God."
They were utterly amazed at him.

Wednesday June 7, 2023

Wednesday of Ninth Week in Ordinary Time

First Reading – Tobit 3:1-11A, 16-17A

[1]Grief-stricken in spirit, I, Tobit, groaned and wept aloud. Then
with sobs I began to pray: [2]"You are righteous, O Lord, and all
your deeds are just; All your ways are mercy and truth; you
are the judge of the world. [3]And now, O Lord, may you be
mindful of me, and look with favor upon me. Punish me not for
my sins, nor for my inadvertent offenses, nor for those of my
ancestors. "We sinned against you,[4]and disobeyed your
commandments. So you handed us over to plundering, exile,
and death, till you made us the talk and reproach of all the
nations among whom you had dispersed us. [5]"Yes, your
judgments are many and true in dealing with me as my sins
and those of my ancestors deserve. For we have not kept your
commandments, nor have we trodden the paths of truth before
you. [6]"So now, deal with me as you please, and command my
life breath to be taken from me, that I may go from the face of
the earth into dust. It is better for me to die than to live,
because I have heard insulting calumnies, and I am
overwhelmed with grief. "Lord, command me to be delivered
from such anguish; let me go to the everlasting abode; Lord,
refuse me not. For it is better for me to die than to endure so
much misery in life, and to hear these insults!" [7]On the same
day, at Ecbatana in Media, it so happened that Raguel's
daughter Sarah also had to listen to abuse, from one of her
father's maids. [8]For she had been married to seven husbands,
but the wicked demon Asmodeus killed them off before they
could have intercourse with her, as it is prescribed for wives.
So the maid said to her: "You are the one who strangles your
husbands! Look at you! You have already been married seven
times, but you have had no joy with any one of your husbands.
[9]Why do you beat us? Is it on account of your seven
husbands, Because they are dead? May we never see a son
or daughter of yours!" [10]The girl was deeply saddened that
day, and she went into an upper chamber of her house, where
she planned to hang herself. But she reconsidered, saying to
herself: "No! People would level this insult against my father:
'You had only one beloved daughter, but she hanged herself
because of ill fortune!' And thus would I cause my father in his
old age to go down to the nether world laden with sorrow. It is

far better for me not to hang myself, but to beg the Lord to have me die, so that I need no longer live to hear such insults." [11A]At that time, then, she spread out her hands, and facing the window, poured out her prayer: "Blessed are you, O Lord, merciful God, and blessed is your holy and honorable name. Blessed are you in all your works for ever!" [16]At that very time, the prayer of these two suppliants was heard in the glorious presence of Almighty God. [17A]So Raphael was sent to heal them both: to remove the cataracts from Tobit's eyes, so that he might again see God's sunlight; and to marry Raguel's daughter Sarah to Tobit's son Tobiah, and then drive the wicked demon Asmodeus from her.

Responsorial Psalm – Psalms 25:2-3, 4-5AB, 6 AND 7BC, 8-9

R. (1) To you, O Lord, I lift my soul.

2 In you I trust; let me not be put to shame,

let not my enemies exult over me.

3 No one who waits for you shall be put to shame;

those shall be put to shame who heedlessly break faith.

R. To you, O Lord, I lift my soul.

4 Your ways, O LORD, make known to me;

teach me your paths,

5AB Guide me in your truth and teach me,

for you are God my savior.

R. To you, O Lord, I lift my soul.

6 Remember that your compassion, O LORD,

and your kindness are from of old.

7BC In your kindness remember me,

because of your goodness, O LORD.

R. To you, O Lord, I lift my soul.

8 Good and upright is the LORD;

thus he shows sinners the way.

9 He guides the humble to justice,

he teaches the humble his way.

R. To you, O Lord, I lift my soul.

Alleluia – John 11:25A, 26

R. Alleluia, alleluia.

[25A] I am the resurrection and the life, says the Lord; [26] whoever believes in me will never die.

R. Alleluia, alleluia.

Gospel – Mark 12:18-27

[18]Some Sadducees, who say there is no resurrection, came to Jesus and put this question to him, [19]saying, "Teacher, Moses wrote for us, If someone's brother dies, leaving a wife but no child, his brother must take the wife and raise up descendants for his brother. [20]Now there were seven brothers. The first married a woman and died, leaving no descendants. [21]So the second brother married her and died, leaving no descendants, and the third likewise. [22]And the seven left no descendants. Last of all the woman also died. [23]At the resurrection when they arise whose wife will she be? For all seven had been married to her." [24]Jesus said to them, "Are you not misled because you do not know the Scriptures or the power of God? [25]When they rise from the dead, they neither marry nor are given in marriage, but they are like the angels in heaven. [26]As for the dead being raised, have you not read in the Book of Moses, in the passage about the bush, how God told him, I am the God of Abraham, the God of Isaac, and the God of Jacob? [27]He is not God of the dead but of the living. You are greatly misled."

Thursday June 8, 2023

Thursday of the Ninth Week in Ordinary Time

First Reading – Tobit 6:10-11; 7:1 BCDE, 9-17; 8:4-9A

[10]When the angel Raphael and Tobiah had entered Media and were getting close to Ecbatana, [11]Raphael said to the boy, "Tobiah, my brother!" He replied: "Here I am!" He said: "Tonight we must stay with Raguel, who is a relative of yours. He has a daughter named Sarah." [1]So he brought him to the

house of Raguel, whom they found seated by his courtyard
gate. They greeted him first. He said to them, "Greetings to
you too, brothers! Good health to you, and welcome!" And he
brought them into his home. [9]Raguel slaughtered a ram from
the flock and gave them a cordial reception. When they had
bathed and reclined to eat, Tobiah said to Raphael, "Brother
Azariah, ask Raguel to let me marry my kinswoman Sarah."
[10]Raguel overheard the words; so he said to the boy: "Eat and
drink and be merry tonight, for no man is more entitled to
marry my daughter Sarah than you, brother. Besides, not even
I have the right to give her to anyone but you, because you
are my closest relative. But I will explain the situation to you
very frankly. [11]I have given her in marriage to seven men, all of
whom were kinsmen of ours, and all died on the very night
they approached her. But now, son, eat and drink. I am sure
the Lord will look after you both." Tobiah answered, "I will eat
or drink nothing until you set aside what belongs to me."
Raguel said to him: "I will do it. She is yours according to the
decree of the Book of Moses. Your marriage to her has been
decided in heaven! Take your kinswoman; from now on you
are her love, and she is your beloved. She is yours today and
ever after. And tonight, son, may the Lord of heaven prosper
you both. May he grant you mercy and peace." [12]Then Raguel
called his daughter Sarah, and she came to him. He took her
by the hand and gave her to Tobiah with the words: "Take her
according to the law. According to the decree written in the
Book of Moses she is your wife. Take her and bring her back
safely to your father. And may the God of heaven grant both of
you peace and prosperity." [13]Raguel then called Sarah's
mother and told her to bring a scroll, so that he might draw up
a marriage contract stating that he gave Sarah to Tobiah as
his wife according to the decree of the Mosaic law. Her mother
brought the scroll, and Raguel drew up the contract, to which
they affixed their seals. [14]Afterward they began to eat and
drink. [15]Later Raguel called his wife Edna and said, "My love,
prepare the other bedroom and bring the girl there." [16]She
went and made the bed in the room, as she was told, and
brought the girl there. After she had cried over her, she wiped
away the tears and said: [17]"Be brave, my daughter. May the
Lord grant you joy in place of your grief. Courage, my
daughter." Then she left. [4]When the girl's parents left the
bedroom and closed the door behind them, Tobiah arose from
bed and said to his wife, "My love, get up. Let us pray and beg

our Lord to have mercy on us and to grant us deliverance.”
5She got up, and they started to pray and beg that deliverance
might be theirs. And they began to say: “Blessed are you, O
God of our fathers, praised be your name forever and ever.
Let the heavens and all your creation praise you forever. 6You
made Adam and you gave him his wife Eve to be his help and
support; and from these two the human race descended. You
said, ‘It is not good for the man to be alone; let us make him a
partner like himself.’ Now, Lord, you know that I take this wife
of mine 7not because of lust, but for a noble purpose. Call
down your mercy on me and on her, and allow us to live
together to a happy old age.” 8They said together, “Amen,
amen,” 9Aand went to bed for the night.

Responsorial Psalm – Psalms 128:1-2, 3, 4-5

R. (see 1a) **Blessed are those who fear the Lord.**

1 Blessed are you who fear the LORD,

who walk in his ways!

2 For you shall eat the fruit of your handiwork;

Blessed shall you be, and favored.

R. Blessed are those who fear the Lord.

3 Your wife shall be like a fruitful vine

in the recesses of your home;

Your children like olive plants

around your table.

R. Blessed are those who fear the Lord.

4 Behold, thus is the man blessed

who fears the LORD.

5 The LORD bless you from Zion:

may you see the prosperity of Jerusalem

all the days of your life.

R. Blessed are those who fear the Lord.

Alleluia – 2 Timothy 1:10

R. Alleluia, alleluia.

10 Our Savior Jesus Christ has destroyed death and brought
life to light through the Gospel.

R. Alleluia, alleluia.

Gospel – Mark 12:28-34

28One of the scribes came to Jesus and asked him, "Which is
the first of all the commandments?" 29Jesus replied, "The first
is this: Hear, O Israel! The Lord our God is Lord alone! 30You
shall love the Lord your God with all your heart, with all your
soul, with all your mind, and with all your strength. 31The
second is this: You shall love your neighbor as yourself. There
is no other commandment greater than these." 32The scribe
said to him, "Well said, teacher. You are right in saying, He is
One and there is no other than he. 33And to love him with all
your heart, with all your understanding, with all your strength,
and to love your neighbor as yourself is worth more than all
burnt offerings and sacrifices." 34And when Jesus saw that he
answered with understanding, he said to him, "You are not far
from the Kingdom of God." And no one dared to ask him any
more questions.

Friday June 9, 2023

Friday of the Ninth Week in Ordinary Time

First Reading – Tobit 11:5-17

5Anna sat watching the road by which her son was to come.
6When she saw him coming, she exclaimed to his father,
"Tobit, your son is coming, and the man who traveled with
him!" 7Raphael said to Tobiah before he reached his father: "I
am certain that his eyes will be opened. 8Smear the fish gall
on them. This medicine will make the cataracts shrink and
peel off from his eyes; then your father will again be able to
see the light of day." 9Then Anna ran up to her son, threw her
arms around him, and said to him, "Now that I have seen you
again, son, I am ready to die!" And she sobbed aloud. 10Tobit
got up and stumbled out through the courtyard gate. Tobiah
went up to him 11with the fish gall in his hand, and holding him
firmly, blew into his eyes. "Courage, father," he said. Next he

smeared the medicine on his eyes, and it made them smart. Then, beginning at the corners of Tobit's eyes, 13Tobiah used both hands to peel off the cataracts. When Tobit saw his son, he threw his arms around him and wept. 14He exclaimed, "I can see you, son, the light of my eyes!" Then he said: "Blessed be God, and praised be his great name, and blessed be all his holy angels. May his holy name be praised throughout all the ages, 15Because it was he who scourged me, and it is he who has had mercy on me. Behold, I now see my son Tobiah!" Then Tobit went back in, rejoicing and praising God with full voice for everything that had happened. Tobiah told his father that the Lord God had granted him a successful journey; that he had brought back the money; and that he had married Raguel's daughter Sarah, who would arrive shortly, for she was approaching the gate of Nineveh. 16Tobit and Anna rejoiced and went out to the gate of Nineveh to meet their daughter-in-law. When the people of Nineveh saw Tobit walking along briskly, with no one leading him by the hand, they were amazed. 17Before them all Tobit proclaimed how God had mercifully restored sight to his eyes. When Tobit reached Sarah, the wife of his son Tobiah, he greeted her: "Welcome, my daughter! Blessed be your God for bringing you to us, daughter! Blessed is your father, and blessed is my son Tobiah, and blessed are you, daughter! Welcome to your home with blessing and joy. Come in, daughter!" That day there was joy for all the Jews who lived in Nineveh.

Responsorial Psalm – Psalms 146:1B-2, 6C-7, 8-9A, 9BC-10

R. (1b) **Praise the Lord, my soul!** or: **R. Alleluia.**

2 Praise the LORD, O my soul;

I will praise the LORD all my life;

I will sing praise to my God while I live.

R. Praise the Lord, my soul! or: **R. Alleluia.**

6C The LORD keeps faith forever,

7 secures justice for the oppressed,

gives food to the hungry.

The LORD sets captives free.

R. Praise the Lord, my soul! or: **R. Alleluia.**

8 The LORD gives sight to the blind.

The LORD raises up those who are bowed down;

the LORD loves the just.

9A The LORD protects strangers.

R. Praise the Lord, my soul! or: **R. Alleluia.**

9BC The fatherless and the widow he sustains,

but the way of the wicked he thwarts

10 The LORD shall reign forever,

your God, O Zion, through all generations! Alleluia.

R. Praise the Lord, my soul! or: **R. Alleluia.**

Alleluia – John 14:23

R. Alleluia, alleluia.

23 Whoever loves me will keep my word, and my Father will love him and we will come to him.

R. Alleluia, alleluia.

Gospel – Mark 12:35-37

35As Jesus was teaching in the temple area he said, "How do
the scribes claim that the Christ is the son of David? 36David
himself, inspired by the Holy Spirit, said: The Lord said to my
lord, 'Sit at my right hand until I place your enemies under your
feet.' 37David himself calls him 'lord'; so how is he his son?"
The great crowd heard this with delight.

Saturday June 10, 2023

Saturday of the Ninth Week in Ordinary Time

First Reading – Tobit 12:1, 5-15, 20

1Tobit called his son Tobiah and said to him, "Son, see to it
that you give what is due to the man who made the journey
with you; give him a bonus too." 5So he called Raphael and
said, "Take as your wages half of all that you have brought
back, and go in peace." 6Raphael called the two men aside
privately and said to them: "Thank God! Give him the praise

and the glory. Before all the living, acknowledge the many
good things he has done for you, by blessing and extolling his
name in song. Honor and proclaim God's deeds, and do not
be slack in praising him. [7]A king's secret it is prudent to keep,
but the works of God are to be declared and made known.
Praise them with due honor. Do good, and evil will not find its
way to you. [8]Prayer and fasting are good, but better than
either is alms-giving accompanied by righteousness. A little
with righteousness is better than abundance with wickedness.
It is better to give alms than to store up gold; [9]for alms-giving
saves one from death and expiates every sin. Those who
regularly give alms shall enjoy a full life; [10]but those habitually
guilty of sin are their own worst enemies. [11]"I will now tell you
the whole truth; I will conceal nothing at all from you. I have
already said to you, 'A king's secret it is prudent to keep, but
the works of God are to be made known with due honor.' [12]I
can now tell you that when you, Tobit, and Sarah prayed, it
was I who presented and read the record of your prayer before
the Glory of the Lord; and I did the same thing when you used
to bury the dead. [13]When you did not hesitate to get up and
leave your dinner in order to go and bury the dead, [14]I was
sent to put you to the test. At the same time, however, God
commissioned me to heal you and your daughter-in-law
Sarah. [15]I am Raphael, one of the seven angels who enter and
serve before the Glory of the Lord." [20]"So now get up from the
ground and praise God. Behold, I am about to ascend to him
who sent me; write down all these things that have happened
to you."

Responsorial Psalm – Tobit 13:2, 6EFGH, 7, 8

R. (1b) Blessed be God, who lives for ever.

[2] He scourges and then has mercy;

he casts down to the depths of the nether world,

and he brings up from the great abyss.

No one can escape his hand.

R. Blessed be God, who lives for ever.

[6EFGH] So now consider what he has done for you,

and praise him with full voice.

Bless the Lord of righteousness,

and exalt the King of ages.

R. Blessed be God, who lives for ever.

7 In the land of my exile I praise him

and show his power and majesty to a sinful nation.

R. Blessed be God, who lives for ever.

8 Bless the Lord, all you his chosen ones,

and may all of you praise his majesty.

Celebrate days of gladness, and give him praise.

R. Blessed be God, who lives for ever.

Alleluia – Matthew 5:3

R. Alleluia, alleluia.

3Blessed are the poor in spirit; for theirs is the Kingdom of heaven.

R. Alleluia, alleluia.

Gospel – Mark 12:38-44

38In the course of his teaching Jesus said, "Beware of the
scribes, who like to go around in long robes and accept
greetings in the marketplaces, 39seats of honor in synagogues,
and places of honor at banquets. 40They devour the houses of
widows and, as a pretext, recite lengthy prayers. They will
receive a very severe condemnation." 41He sat down opposite
the treasury and observed how the crowd put money into the
treasury. Many rich people put in large sums. 42A poor widow
also came and put in two small coins worth a few cents.
43Calling his disciples to himself, he said to them, "Amen, I say
to you, this poor widow put in more than all the other
contributors to the treasury. 44For they have all contributed
from their surplus wealth, but she, from her poverty, has
contributed all she had, her whole livelihood."

Sunday June 11, 2023

Solemnity of Body & Blood of Christ – Corpus Christi

First Reading – Deuteronomy 8:2-3, 14B-16A

[2]Moses said to the people: “Remember how for forty years
now the LORD, your God, has directed all your journeying in
the desert, so as to test you by affliction and find out whether
or not it was your intention to keep his commandments. [3]He,
therefore, let you be afflicted with hunger, and then fed you
with manna, a food unknown to you and your fathers, in order
to show you that not by bread alone does one live, but by
every word that comes forth from the mouth of the LORD.
[14B]“Do not forget the LORD, your God, who brought you out of
the land of Egypt, that place of slavery; [15]who guided you
through the vast and terrible desert with its saraph serpents
and scorpions, its parched and waterless ground; who brought
forth water for you from the flinty rock [16A]and fed you in the
desert with manna, a food unknown to your fathers.”

Responsorial Psalm – Psalms 147:12-13, 14-15, 19-20

R. [(12)] **Praise the Lord, Jerusalem.** or: **R. Alleluia.**

[12] Glorify the LORD, O Jerusalem;

praise your God, O Zion.

[13] For he has strengthened the bars of your gates;

he has blessed your children within you.

R. Praise the Lord, Jerusalem. or: **R. Alleluia.**

[14] He has granted peace in your borders;

with the best of wheat he fills you.

[15] He sends forth his command to the earth;

swiftly runs his word!

R. Praise the Lord, Jerusalem. or: **R. Alleluia.**

[19] He has proclaimed his word to Jacob,

his statutes and his ordinances to Israel.

[20] He has not done thus for any other nation;

his ordinances he has not made known to them. Alleluia.

R. Praise the Lord, Jerusalem. or: **R. Alleluia.**

Second Reading – 1 Corinthians 10:16-17

16Brothers and sisters: The cup of blessing that we bless, is it not a participation in the blood of Christ? The bread that we break, is it not a participation in the body of Christ? 17Because the loaf of bread is one, we, though many, are one body, for we all partake of the one loaf.

Sequence – *Lauda Sion*

Laud, O Zion, your salvation,

Laud with hymns of exultation,

Christ, your king and shepherd true:

Bring him all the praise you know,

He is more than you bestow.

Never can you reach his due.

Special theme for glad thanksgiving

Is the quick'ning and the living

Bread today before you set:

From his hands of old partaken,

As we know, by faith unshaken,

Where the Twelve at supper met.

Full and clear ring out your chanting,

Joy nor sweetest grace be wanting,

From your heart let praises burst:

For today the feast is holden,

When the institution olden
Of that supper was rehearsed.

Here the new law's new oblation,
By the new king's revelation,
Ends the form of ancient rite:

Now the new the old effaces,
Truth away the shadow chases,
Light dispels the gloom of night.

What he did at supper seated,
Christ ordained to be repeated,
His memorial ne'er to cease:

And his rule for guidance taking,
Bread and wine we hallow, making
Thus our sacrifice of peace.

This the truth each Christian learns,
Bread into his flesh he turns,
To his precious blood the wine:

Sight has fail'd, nor thought conceives,
But a dauntless faith believes,
Resting on a pow'r divine.

Here beneath these signs are hidden
Priceless things to sense forbidden;

Signs, not things are all we see:

Blood is poured and flesh is broken,
Yet in either wondrous token
Christ entire we know to be.

Whoso of this food partakes,
Does not rend the Lord nor breaks;
Christ is whole to all that taste:

Thousands are, as one, receivers,
One, as thousands of believers,
Eats of him who cannot waste.

Bad and good the feast are sharing,
Of what divers dooms preparing,
Endless death, or endless life.

Life to these, to those damnation,
See how like participation
Is with unlike issues rife.

When the sacrament is broken,
Doubt not, but believe 'tis spoken,
That each sever'd outward token
doth the very whole contain.

Nought the precious gift divides,
Breaking but the sign betides

Jesus still the same abides,
still unbroken does remain.

The shorter form of the sequence begins here
Lo! the angel's food is given
To the pilgrim who has striven;
see the children's bread from heaven,
which on dogs may not be spent.

Truth the ancient types fulfilling,
Isaac bound, a victim willing,
Paschal lamb, its lifeblood spilling,
manna to the fathers sent.

Very bread, good shepherd, tend us,
Jesus, of your love befriend us,
You refresh us, you defend us,
Your eternal goodness send us
In the land of life to see.

You who all things can and know,
Who on earth such food bestow,
Grant us with your saints, though lowest,
Where the heav'nly feast you show,
Fellow heirs and guests to be. Amen. **Alleluia.**

Alleluia – John 6:51

R. Alleluia, alleluia.

51 I am the living bread that came down from heaven, says the Lord; whoever eats this bread will live forever.

R. Alleluia, alleluia.

Gospel – John 6:51-58

[51]Jesus said to the Jewish crowds: “I am the living bread that
came down from heaven; whoever eats this bread will live
forever; and the bread that I will give is my flesh for the life of
the world.” [52]The Jews quarreled among themselves, saying,
“How can this man give us his flesh to eat?” [53]Jesus said to
them, “Amen, amen, I say to you, unless you eat the flesh of
the Son of Man and drink his blood, you do not have life within
you. [54]Whoever eats my flesh and drinks my blood has eternal
life, and I will raise him on the last day. [55]For my flesh is true
food, and my blood is true drink. [56]Whoever eats my flesh and
drinks my blood remains in me and I in him. [57]Just as the living
Father sent me and I have life because of the Father, so also
the one who feeds on me will have life because of me. [58]This
is the bread that came down from heaven. Unlike your
ancestors who ate and still died, whoever eats this bread will
live forever.”

Monday June 12, 2023

Monday of the Tenth Week in Ordinary Time

First Reading – 2 Corinthians 1:1-7

[1]Paul, an Apostle of Christ Jesus by the will of God, and
Timothy our brother, to the Church of God that is at Corinth,
with all the holy ones throughout Achaia: [2]grace to you and
peace from God our Father and the Lord Jesus Christ.
[3]Blessed be the God and Father of our Lord Jesus Christ, the
Father of compassion and the God of all encouragement,
[4]who encourages us in our every affliction, so that we may be
able to encourage those who are in any affliction with the
encouragement with which we ourselves are encouraged by
God. [5]For as Christ’s sufferings overflow to us, so through
Christ does our encouragement also overflow. [6]If we are
afflicted, it is for your encouragement and salvation; if we are
encouraged, it is for your encouragement, which enables you
to endure the same sufferings that we suffer. [7]Our hope for
you is firm, for we know that as you share in the sufferings,
you also share in the encouragement.

Responsorial Psalm – Psalms 34:2-3, 4-5, 6-7, 8-9

R. (9a) Taste and see the goodness of the Lord.

2 I will bless the LORD at all times;

his praise shall be ever in my mouth.

3 Let my soul glory in the LORD;

the lowly will hear me and be glad.

R. Taste and see the goodness of the Lord.

4 Glorify the LORD with me,

let us together extol his name.

5 I sought the LORD, and he answered me

and delivered me from all my fears.

R. Taste and see the goodness of the Lord.

6 Look to him that you may be radiant with joy,

and your faces may not blush with shame.

7 When the poor one called out, the LORD heard,

and from all his distress he saved him.

R. Taste and see the goodness of the Lord.

8 The angel of the LORD encamps

around those who fear him, and delivers them.

9 Taste and see how good the LORD is;

blessed the man who takes refuge in him.

R. Taste and see the goodness of the Lord.

Alleluia – Matthew 5:12A

R. Alleluia, alleluia.

12A Rejoice and be glad; for your reward will be great in heaven.

R. Alleluia, alleluia.

Gospel – Matthew 5:1-12

1When Jesus saw the crowds, he went up the mountain, and
after he had sat down, his disciples came to him. 2He began to
teach them, saying: 3"Blessed are the poor in spirit, for theirs
is the Kingdom of heaven. 4Blessed are they who mourn, for
they will be comforted. 5Blessed are the meek, for they will
inherit the land. 6Blessed are they who hunger and thirst for
righteousness, for they will be satisfied. 7Blessed are the
merciful, for they will be shown mercy. 8Blessed are the clean
of heart, for they will see God. 9Blessed are the peacemakers,
for they will be called children of God. 10Blessed are they who
are persecuted for the sake of righteousness, for theirs is the
Kingdom of heaven. 11Blessed are you when they insult you
and persecute you and utter every kind of evil against you
falsely because of me. 12Rejoice and be glad, for your reward
will be great in heaven. Thus they persecuted the prophets
who were before you."

Tuesday June 13, 2023

Memorial of Saint Anthony of Padua - Priest & Doctor

First Reading – 2 Corinthians 1:18-22

Brothers and sisters: 18As God is faithful, our word to you is
not "yes" and "no." 19 For the Son of God, Jesus Christ, who
was proclaimed to you by us, Silvanus and Timothy and me,
was not "yes" and "no," but "yes" has been in him. 20For
however many are the promises of God, their Yes is in him;
therefore, the Amen from us also goes through him to God for
glory. 21But the one who gives us security with you in Christ
and who anointed us is God; 22he has also put his seal upon
us and given the Spirit in our hearts as a first installment.

Responsorial Psalm – Psalms 119:129, 130, 131, 132, 133, 135

R. (135a) Lord, let your face shine on me.

129 Wonderful are your decrees;

therefore I observe them.

R. Lord, let your face shine on me.

130 The revelation of your words sheds light,

gives understanding to the simple.

R. Lord, let your face shine on me.

131 I gasp with open mouth

in my yearning for your commands.

R. Lord, let your face shine on me.

132 Turn to me in pity

as you turn to those who love your name.

R. Lord, let your face shine on me.

133 Steady my footsteps according to your promise,

and let no iniquity rule over me.

R. Lord, let your face shine on me.

135 Let your countenance shine upon your servant,

and teach me your statutes.

R. Lord, let your face shine on me.

Alleluia – Matthew 5:16

R. Alleluia, alleluia.

16 Let your light shine before others that they may see your good deeds and glorify your heavenly Father.

R. Alleluia, alleluia.

Gospel – Matthew 5:13-16

Jesus said to his disciples: 13"You are the salt of the earth. But
if salt loses its taste, with what can it be seasoned? It is no
longer good for anything but to be thrown out and trampled
underfoot. 14You are the light of the world. A city set on a
mountain cannot be hidden.15Nor do they light a lamp and
then put it under a bushel basket; it is set on a lampstand,
where it gives light to all in the house.16Just so, your light must
shine before others, that they may see your good deeds and
glorify your heavenly Father."

Wednesday June 14, 2023

Wednesday of Tenth Week in Ordinary Time

First Reading – 2 Corinthians 3:4-11

4 Brothers and sisters: Such confidence we have through
Christ toward God. 5 Not that of ourselves we are qualified to
take credit for anything as coming from us; rather, our
qualification comes from God, 6 who has indeed qualified us as
ministers of a new covenant, not of letter but of spirit; for the
letter brings death, but the Spirit gives life. 7 Now if the ministry
of death, carved in letters on stone, was so glorious that the
children of Israel could not look intently at the face of Moses
because of its glory that was going to fade, 8 how much more
will the ministry of the Spirit be glorious? 9 For if the ministry of
condemnation was glorious, the ministry of righteousness will
abound much more in glory. 10 Indeed, what was endowed with
glory has come to have no glory in this respect because of the
glory that surpasses it. 11 For if what was going to fade was
glorious, how much more will what endures be glorious.

Responsorial Psalm – Psalms 99:5, 6, 7, 8, 9

R. (see 9c) **Holy is the Lord our God.**

5 Extol the LORD, our God,

and worship at his footstool;

holy is he!

R. Holy is the Lord our God.

6 Moses and Aaron were among his priests,

and Samuel, among those who called upon his name;

they called upon the LORD, and he answered them.

R. Holy is the Lord our God.

7 From the pillar of cloud he spoke to them;

they heard his decrees and the law he gave them.

R. Holy is the Lord our God.

8 O LORD, our God, you answered them;

a forgiving God you were to them,

though requiting their misdeeds.

R. Holy is the Lord our God.

9 Extol the LORD, our God,

and worship at his holy mountain;

for holy is the LORD, our God.

R. Holy is the Lord our God.

Alleluia – Psalms 25:4B, 5A

R. Alleluia, alleluia.

4BTeach me your paths, my God, 5A and guide me in your truth.

R. Alleluia, alleluia.

Gospel – Matthew 5:17-19

17Jesus said to his disciples: "Do not think that I have come to abolish the law or the prophets. I have come not to abolish but to fulfill. 18Amen, I say to you, until heaven and earth pass away, not the smallest letter or the smallest part of a letter will pass from the law, until all things have taken place. 19Therefore, whoever breaks one of the least of these commandments and teaches others to do so will be called least in the Kingdom of heaven. But whoever obeys and teaches these commandments will be called greatest in the Kingdom of heaven."

Thursday June 15, 2023

Thursday of Tenth Week in Ordinary Time

First Reading – 2 Corinthians 3:15-4:1, 3-6

Brothers and sisters: 15To this day, whenever Moses is read, a veil lies over the hearts of the children of Israel, 16but whenever a person turns to the Lord the veil is removed. 17Now the Lord is the Spirit and where the Spirit of the Lord is, there is freedom. 18All of us, gazing with unveiled face on the glory of the Lord, are being transformed into the same image from glory to glory, as from the Lord who is the Spirit. 1Therefore, since we have this ministry through the mercy shown us, we are not discouraged. 3And even though our

Gospel is veiled, it is veiled for those who are perishing, [4]in
whose case the god of this age has blinded the minds of the
unbelievers, so that they may not see the light of the Gospel of
the glory of Christ, who is the image of God. [5]For we do not
preach ourselves but Jesus Christ as Lord, and ourselves as
your slaves for the sake of Jesus. [6]For God who said, Let light
shine out of darkness, has shone in our hearts to bring to light
the knowledge of the glory of God on the face of Jesus Christ.

Responsorial Psalm – Psalms 85:9AB and 10, 11-12, 13-14

R. (see 10b) **The glory of the Lord will dwell in our land.**

9AB I will hear what God proclaims;

the LORD–for he proclaims peace to his people.

10 Near indeed is his salvation to those who fear him,

glory dwelling in our land.

R. The glory of the Lord will dwell in our land.

11 Kindness and truth shall meet;

justice and peace shall kiss.

12 Truth shall spring out of the earth,

and justice shall look down from heaven.

R. The glory of the Lord will dwell in our land.

13 The LORD himself will give his benefits;

our land shall yield its increase.

14 Justice shall walk before him,

and salvation, along the way of his steps.

R. The glory of the Lord will dwell in our land.

Alleluia – John 13:34

R. Alleluia, alleluia.

34 I give you a new commandment: love one another as I have loved you.

R. Alleluia, alleluia.

Gospel – Matthew 5:20-26

20Jesus said to his disciples: “I tell you, unless your
righteousness surpasses that of the scribes and Pharisees,
you will not enter into the Kingdom of heaven. 21“You have
heard that it was said to your ancestors, You shall not kill; and
whoever kills will be liable to judgment. 22But I say to you,
whoever is angry with his brother will be liable to judgment,
and whoever says to his brother, Raqa, will be answerable to
the Sanhedrin, and whoever says, ‘You fool,’ will be liable to
fiery Gehenna. 23Therefore, if you bring your gift to the altar,
and there recall that your brother has anything against you,
24leave your gift there at the altar, go first and be reconciled
with your brother, and then come and offer your gift. 25Settle
with your opponent quickly while on the way to court with him.
Otherwise your opponent will hand you over to the judge, and
the judge will hand you over to the guard, and you will be
thrown into prison. 26Amen, I say to you, you will not be
released until you have paid the last penny.”

Friday June 16, 2023

Solemnity of Most Sacred Heart of Jesus

First Reading - Deuteronomy 7: 6-11

6Because thou art a holy people to the Lord thy God. The Lord
thy God hath chosen thee, to be his peculiar people of all
peoples that are upon the earth. 7Not because you surpass all
nations in number, is the Lord joined unto you, and hath
chosen you, for you are the fewest of any people: 8But
because the Lord hath loved you, and hath kept his oath,
which he swore to your fathers: and hath brought you out with
a strong hand, and redeemed you from the house of bondage,
out of the hand of Pharao the king of Egypt. 9And thou shalt
know that the Lord thy God, he is a strong and faithful God,
keeping his covenant and mercy to them that love him, and to
them that keep his commandments, unto a thousand
generations: 10And repaying forthwith them that hate him, so
as to destroy them, without further delay immediately
rendering to them what they deserve. 11Keep therefore the
precepts and ceremonies and judgments, which I command
thee this day to do.

Responsorial Psalm - Psalms 103: 1-2, 3-4, 6-7, 8, 10

R. (17) The Lord's kindness is everlasting to those who fear him.

1Bless the Lord, O my soul: and let all that is within me bless his holy name.

2 Bless the Lord, O my soul, and never forget all he hath done for thee.

R. The Lord's kindness is everlasting to those who fear him.

3 Who forgiveth all thy iniquities: who healeth all thy diseases.

4 Who redeemeth thy life from destruction: who crowneth thee with mercy and compassion.

R. The Lord's kindness is everlasting to those who fear him.

6 The Lord doth mercies, and judgment for all that suffer wrong.

7 He hath made his ways known to Moses: his wills to the children of Israel.

R. The Lord's kindness is everlasting to those who fear him.

8 The Lord is compassionate and merciful: longsuffering and plenteous in mercy.

10 He hath not dealt with us according to our sins: nor rewarded us according to our iniquities.

R. The Lord's kindness is everlasting to those who fear him.

Second Reading - 1 John 4: 7-16

7Dearly beloved, let us love one another, for charity is of God.
And every one that loveth, is born of God, and knoweth God.
8He that loveth not, knoweth not God: for God is charity. 9By
this hath the charity of God appeared towards us, because
God hath sent his only begotten Son into the world, that we
may live by him. 10In this is charity: not as though we had
loved God, but because he hath first loved us, and sent his

Son to be a propitiation for our sins. [11]My dearest, if God hath so loved us; we also ought to love one another. [12]No man hath seen God at any time. If we love one another, God abideth in us, and his charity is perfected in us. [13]In this we know that we abide in him, and he in us: because he hath given us of his spirit. [14]And we have seen, and do testify, that the Father hath sent his Son to be the Saviour of the world. [15]Whosoever shall confess that Jesus is the Son of God, God abideth in him, and he in God. [16]And we have known, and have believed the charity, which God hath to us. God is charity: and he that abideth in charity, abideth in God, and God in him.

Alleluia - Matthew 11: 29a

R. Alleluia, alleluia.

[29a]Take my yoke upon you, says the Lord; and learn from me, for I am meek and humble of heart.

R. Alleluia, alleluia.

Gospel - Matthew 11: 25-30

[25]At that time Jesus answered and said: I confess to thee, O Father, Lord of heaven and earth, because thou hast hid these things from the wise and prudent, and hast revealed them to the little ones. [26]Yea, Father; for so hath it seemed good in thy sight. [27]All things are delivered to me by my Father. And no one knoweth the Son, but the Father: neither doth any one know the Father, but the Son, and he to whom it shall please the Son to reveal him. [28]Come to me, all you that labour, and are burdened, and I will refresh you. [29]Take up my yoke upon you, and learn of me, because I am meek, and humble of heart: and you shall find rest to your souls. [30]For my yoke is sweet and my burden light.

Saturday June 17, 2023

Memorial of the Immaculate Heart of Mary

First Reading – 2 Corinthians 5:14-21

Brothers and sisters: [14]The love of Christ impels us, once we have come to the conviction that one died for all; therefore, all have died. [15]He indeed died for all, so that those who live might no longer live for themselves but for him who for their sake died and was raised. [16]Consequently, from now on we

regard no one according to the flesh; even if we once knew
Christ according to the flesh, yet now we know him so no
longer. [17]So whoever is in Christ is a new creation: the old
things have passed away; behold, new things have come.
[18]And all this is from God, who has reconciled us to himself
through Christ and given us the ministry of reconciliation,
[19]namely, God was reconciling the world to himself in Christ,
not counting their trespasses against them and entrusting to
us the message of reconciliation. [20]So we are ambassadors
for Christ as if God were appealing through us. We implore
you on behalf of Christ, be reconciled to God. [21]For our sake
he made him to be sin who did not know sin, so that we might
become the righteousness of God in him.

Responsorial Psalm – Psalms 103:1-2, 3-4, 9-10, 11-12

R. (8a) The Lord is kind and merciful.

1 Bless the LORD, O my soul;

and all my being, bless his holy name.

2 Bless the LORD, O my soul,

and forget not all his benefits.

R. The Lord is kind and merciful.

3 He pardons all your iniquities,

he heals all your ills.

4 He redeems your life from destruction,

he crowns you with kindness and compassion.

R. The Lord is kind and merciful.

9 He will not always chide,

nor does he keep his wrath forever.

10 Not according to our sins does he deal with us,

nor does he requite us according to our crimes.

R. The Lord is kind and merciful.

11 For as the heavens are high above the earth,

so surpassing is his kindness toward those who fear him.

12 As far as the east is from the west,

so far has he put our transgressions from us.

R. The Lord is kind and merciful.

Alleluia – Psalms 119:36A, 29B

R. Alleluia, alleluia.

36A Incline my heart, O God, to your decrees; 29B and favour
me with your law.

R. Alleluia, alleluia.

Gospel – Matthew 5:33-37

Jesus said to his disciples: 33“You have heard that it was said
to your ancestors, Do not take a false oath, but make good to
the Lord all that you vow. 34But I say to you, do not swear at
all; not by heaven, for it is God’s throne; 35nor by the earth, for
it is his footstool; nor by Jerusalem, for it is the city of the great
King. 36Do not swear by your head, for you cannot make a
single hair white or black. 37Let your ‘Yes’ mean ‘Yes,’ and
your ‘No’ mean ‘No.’ Anything more is from the Evil One.”

Sunday June 18, 2023

Eleventh Sunday in Ordinary Time, Year A

First Reading – Exodus 19:2-6a

2After they made the journey from Rephidim and entered the
wilderness of Sinai, they then pitched camp in the wilderness.
While Israel was encamped there in front of the mountain,
3Moses went up to the mountain of God. Then the Lord called
to him from the mountain, saying: This is what you will say to
the house of Jacob; tell the Israelites: 4You have seen how I
treated the Egyptians and how I bore you up on eagles’ wings
and brought you to myself. 5Now, if you obey me completely
and keep my covenant, you will be my treasured possession
among all peoples, though all the earth is mine. 6AYou will be
to me a kingdom of priests, a holy nation.

Responsorial Psalm – Psalms 100:1-2, 3, 5

R. We are His people, the sheep of His flock.

1 Shout joyfully to the Lord, all you lands;

2 serve the Lord with gladness;

come before him with joyful song.

R. We are His people, the sheep of His flock.

3 Know that the Lord is God,

he made us, we belong to him,

we are his people, the flock he shepherds.

R. We are His people, the sheep of His flock.

5 Good indeed is the Lord,

His mercy endures forever,

his faithfulness lasts through every generation.

R. We are His people, the sheep of His flock.

Second Reading – Romans 5:6-11

Brothers and sisters: 6For Christ, while we were still helpless,
yet died at the appointed time for the ungodly. 7Indeed, only
with difficulty does one die for a just person, though perhaps
for a good person one might even find courage to die. 8But
God proves his love for us in that while we were still sinners
Christ died for us. 9How much more then, since we are now
justified by his blood, will we be saved through him from the
wrath. 10Indeed, if, while we were enemies, we were
reconciled to God through the death of his Son, how much
more, once reconciled, will we be saved by his life. 11Not only
that, but we also boast of God through our Lord Jesus Christ,
through whom we have now received reconciliation.

Alleluia – Mark 1:15

R. Alleluia, alleluia.

15 The Kingdom of God is at Hand; repent and believe in the Gospel.

R. Alleluia, alleluia.

Gospel – Matthew 9:36-10:8

36At the sight of the crowds, his heart was moved with pity for
them because they were troubled and abandoned, like sheep
without a shepherd. 37Then he said to his disciples, "The

harvest is abundant but the laborers are few; [38]so ask the
master of the harvest to send out laborers for his harvest."
[1]Then he summoned his twelve disciples and gave them
authority over unclean spirits to drive them out and to cure
every disease and every illness. [2]The names of the twelve
apostles are these: first, Simon called Peter, and his brother
Andrew; James, the son of Zebedee, and his brother John;
[3]Philip and Bartholomew, Thomas and Matthew the tax
collector; James, the son of Alphaeus, and Thaddeus; [4]Simon
the Cananean, and Judas Iscariot who betrayed him. [5]Jesus
sent out these twelve after instructing them thus, "Do not go
into pagan territory or enter a Samaritan town. [6]Go rather to
the lost sheep of the house of Israel. [7]As you go, make this
proclamation: 'The kingdom of heaven is at hand.' [8]Cure the
sick, raise the dead, cleanse lepers, drive out demons.
Without cost you have received; without cost you are to give.

Monday June 19, 2023

Monday of Eleventh Week in Ordinary Time

First Reading – 2 Corinthians 6:1-10

Brothers and sisters: [1]As your fellow workers, we appeal to
you not to receive the grace of God in vain. [2]For he says: In an
acceptable time, I heard you, and on the day of salvation, I
helped you. Behold, now is a very acceptable time; behold,
now is the day of salvation. [3]We cause no one to stumble in
anything, in order that no fault may be found with our ministry;
[4]on the contrary, in everything we commend ourselves as
ministers of God, through much endurance, in afflictions,
hardships, constraints, [5]beatings, imprisonments, riots,
labours, vigils, fasts; [6]by purity, knowledge, patience,
kindness, in the Holy Spirit, in unfeigned love, [7]in truthful
speech, in the power of God; with weapons of righteousness
at the right and at the left; [8]through glory and dishonour, insult
and praise. We are treated as deceivers and yet are truthful;
[9]as unrecognized and yet acknowledged; as dying and behold
we live; as chastised and yet not put to death; [10]as sorrowful
yet always rejoicing; as poor yet enriching many; as having
nothing and yet possessing all things.

Responsorial Psalm – Psalms 98:1, 2B-3AB, 3CD-4

R. (2a) The Lord has made known his salvation.

[1] Sing to the LORD a new song,

for he has done wondrous deeds;

His right hand has won victory for him, his holy arm.

R. The Lord has made known his salvation.

[2B] In the sight of the nations, he has revealed his justice.

[3AB] He has remembered his kindness and his faithfulness

toward the house of Israel.

R. The Lord has made known his salvation.

[3CD] All the ends of the earth have seen

the salvation by our God.

[4] Sing joyfully to the LORD, all you lands;

break into song; sing praise.

R. The Lord has made known his salvation.

Alleluia – Psalms 119:105

R. Alleluia, alleluia.

[105] A lamp to my feet is your word, a light to my path.

R. Alleluia, alleluia.

Gospel – Matthew 5:38-42

Jesus said to his disciples: [38]"You have heard that it was said,
An eye for an eye and a tooth for a tooth. [39]But I say to you,
offer no resistance to one who is evil. When someone strikes
you on your right cheek, turn the other one to him as well. [40]If
anyone wants to go to law with you over your tunic, hand him
your cloak as well. [41]Should anyone press you into service for
one mile, go with him for two miles. [42]Give to the one who
asks of you, and do not turn your back on one who wants to
borrow."

Tuesday June 20, 2023

Tuesday of Eleventh Week in Ordinary Time

First Reading – 2 Corinthians 8:1-9

[1]We want you to know, brothers and sisters, of the grace of
God that has been given to the churches of Macedonia, [2]for in
a severe test of affliction, the abundance of their joy and their
profound poverty overflowed in a wealth of generosity on their
part. [3]For according to their means, I can testify, and beyond
their means, spontaneously, [4]they begged us insistently for
the favour of taking part in the service to the holy ones, [5]and
this, not as we expected, but they gave themselves first to the
Lord and to us through the will of God, [6]so that we urged Titus
that, as he had already begun, he should also complete for
you this gracious act also. [7]Now as you excel in every respect,
in faith, discourse, knowledge, all earnestness, and in the love
we have for you, may you excel in this gracious act also. [8]I say
this not by way of command, but to test the genuineness of
your love by your concern for others. [9]For you know the
gracious act of our Lord Jesus Christ, that for your sake he
became poor although he was rich so that by his poverty you
might become rich.

Responsorial Psalm – Psalms 146:2, 5-6AB, 6C- 7, 8-9A

R. (1b) **Praise the Lord, my soul!** or: **R. Alleluia.**

[2] Praise the LORD, my soul!

I will praise the LORD all my life;

I will sing praise to my God while I live.

R. Praise the Lord, my soul! or: **R. Alleluia.**

[5] Blessed he whose help is the God of Jacob,

whose hope is in the LORD, his God,

[6AB] Who made heaven and earth,

the sea and all that is in them.

R. Praise the Lord, my soul! or: **R. Alleluia.**

[6C] Who keeps faith forever,

[7] secures justice for the oppressed,

gives food to the hungry.

The LORD sets captives free.

R. Praise the Lord, my soul! or: **R. Alleluia.**

[8] The LORD gives sight to the blind.

The LORD raises up those who were bowed down;

the LORD loves the just.

[9A] The LORD protects strangers.

R. Praise the Lord, my soul! or: **R. Alleluia.**

Alleluia – John 13:34

R. Alleluia, alleluia.

[34] I give you a new commandment: love one another as I have loved you.

R. Alleluia, alleluia.

Gospel – Matthew 5:43-48

Jesus said to his disciples: [43]"You have heard that it was said,
You shall love your neighbour and hate your enemy. [44]But I
say to you, love your enemies and pray for those who
persecute you, [45]that you may be children of your heavenly
Father, for he makes his sun rise on the bad and the good,
and causes rain to fall on the just and the unjust. [46]For if you
love those who love you, what recompense will you have? Do
not the tax collectors do the same? [47]And if you greet your
brothers only, what is unusual about that? Do not the pagans
do the same? [48]So be perfect, just as your heavenly Father is
perfect."

Wednesday June 21, 2023

Memorial of Saint Aloysius Gonzaga - Religious

First Reading – 2 Corinthians 9:6-11

[6]Brothers and sisters, consider this: whoever sows sparingly
will also reap sparingly, and whoever sows bountifully will also
reap bountifully. [7]Each must do as already determined, without
sadness or compulsion, for God loves a cheerful giver.

8 Moreover, God is able to make every grace abundant for you,
so that in all things, always having all you need, you may have
an abundance for every good work. 9 As it is written: He
scatters abroad, he gives to the poor; his righteousness
endures forever. 10 The one who supplies seed to the sower
and bread for food will supply and multiply your seed and
increase the harvest of your righteousness. 11 You are being
enriched in every way for all generosity, which through us
produces thanksgiving to God.

Responsorial Psalm – Psalms 112:1BC-2, 3-4, 9

R. (1b) **Blessed the man who fears the Lord.** or: **R. Alleluia.**

1BC Blessed the man who fears the LORD,

who greatly delights in his commands.

2 His posterity shall be mighty upon the earth;

the upright generation shall be blessed.

R. Blessed the man who fears the Lord. or: **R. Alleluia.**

3 Wealth and riches shall be in his house;

his generosity shall endure forever.

4 Light shines through the darkness for the upright;

he is gracious and merciful and just.

R. Blessed the man who fears the Lord. or: **R. Alleluia.**

9 Lavishly he gives to the poor;

his generosity shall endure forever;

his horn shall be exalted in glory.

R. Blessed the man who fears the Lord. or: **R. Alleluia.**

Alleluia – John 14:23

R. Alleluia, alleluia.

23 Whoever loves me will keep my word, and my Father will love him and we will come to him.

R. Alleluia, alleluia.

Gospel – Matthew 6:1-6, 16-18

Jesus said to his disciples: 1"Take care not to perform righteous deeds in order that people may see them; otherwise, you will have no recompense from your heavenly Father. 2When you give alms, do not blow a trumpet before you, as the hypocrites do in the synagogues and in the streets to win the praise of others. Amen, I say to you, they have received their reward. 3But when you give alms, do not let your left hand know what your right is doing, 4so that your almsgiving may be secret. And your Father who sees in secret will repay you. 5"When you pray, do not be like the hypocrites, who love to stand and pray in the synagogues and on street corners so that others may see them. Amen, I say to you, they have received their reward. 6But when you pray, go to your inner room, close the door, and pray to your Father in secret. And your Father who sees in secret will repay you. 16"When you fast, do not look gloomy like the hypocrites. They neglect their appearance, so that they may appear to others to be fasting. Amen, I say to you, they have received their reward. 17But when you fast, anoint your head and wash your face, 18so that you may not appear to others to be fasting, except to your Father who is hidden. And your Father who sees what is hidden will repay you."

Thursday June 22, 2023

Thursday of Eleventh Week in Ordinary Time

First Reading – 2 Corinthians 11:1-11

Brothers and sisters: 1If only you would put up with a little foolishness from me! Please put up with me. 2For I am jealous of you with the jealousy of God, since I betrothed you to one husband to present you as a chaste virgin to Christ. 3But I am afraid that, as the serpent deceived Eve by his cunning, your thoughts may be corrupted from a sincere and pure commitment to Christ. 4For if someone comes and preaches another Jesus than the one we preached, or if you receive a different spirit from the one you received or a different gospel from the one you accepted, you put up with it well enough. 5For I think that I am not in any way inferior to these "super-apostles." 6Even if I am untrained in speaking, I am not so in knowledge; in every way, we have made this plain to you in all things. 7Did I make a mistake when I humbled myself so that

you might be exalted because I preached the Gospel of God
to you without charge? [8]I plundered other churches by
accepting from them in order to minister to you. [9]And when I
was with you and in need, I did not burden anyone, for the
brothers who came from Macedonia supplied my needs. So I
refrained and will refrain from burdening you in any way. [10]By
the truth of Christ in me, this boast of mine shall not be
silenced in the regions of Achaia. [11]And why? Because I do
not love you? God knows I do!

Responsorial Psalm – Psalms 111:1B-2, 3-4, 7-8

R. (7a) **Your works, O Lord, are justice and truth.** or: **R. Alleluia.**

1B I will give thanks to the LORD with all my heart

in the company and assembly of the just.

2 Great are the works of the LORD,

exquisite in all their delights.

R. Your works, O Lord, are justice and truth. or: **R. Alleluia.**

3 Majesty and glory are his work,

and his justice endures forever.

4 He has won renown for his wondrous deeds;

gracious and merciful is the LORD.

R. Your works, O Lord, are justice and truth. or: **R. Alleluia.**

7 The works of his hands are faithful and just;

sure are all his precepts,

8 Reliable forever and ever,

wrought in truth and equity.

R. Your works, O Lord, are justice and truth. or: **R. Alleluia.**

Alleluia – Romans 8:15BC

R. Alleluia, alleluia.

[15BC]You have received a spirit of adoption as sons through which we cry: Abba! Father!

R. Alleluia, alleluia.

Gospel – Matthew 6:7-15

Jesus said to his disciples: [7]“In praying, do not babble like the pagans, who think that they will be heard because of their many words. [8]Do not be like them. Your Father knows what you need before you ask him. [9]“This is how you are to pray: ‘Our Father who art in heaven, hallowed be thy name, [10]thy Kingdom come, thy will be done, on earth as it is in heaven. [11]Give us this day our daily bread; [12]and forgive us our trespasses, as we forgive those who trespass against us; [13]and lead us not into temptation, but deliver us from evil.’ [14]“If you forgive others their transgressions, your heavenly Father will forgive you. [15]But if you do not forgive others, neither will your Father forgive your transgressions.”

Friday June 23, 2023

Friday of the Eleventh Week in Ordinary Time

First Reading – 2 Corinthians 11:18, 21-30

Brothers and sisters: [18]Since many boast according to the flesh, I too will boast. [21]To my shame I say that we were too weak! But what anyone dares to boast of (I am speaking in foolishness) I also dare. [22]Are they Hebrews? So am I. Are they children of Israel? So am I. Are they descendants of Abraham? So am I. [23]Are they ministers of Christ? (I am talking like an insane person). I am still more, with far greater labours, far more imprisonments, far worse beatings, and numerous brushes with death. [24]Five times at the hands of the Jews I received forty lashes minus one. [25]Three times I was beaten with rods, once I was stoned, three times I was shipwrecked, I passed a night and a day on the deep; [26]on frequent journeys, in dangers from rivers, dangers from robbers, dangers from my own race, dangers from Gentiles, dangers in the city, dangers in the wilderness, dangers at sea, dangers among false brothers; [27]in toil and hardship, through many sleepless nights, through hunger and thirst, through frequent fastings, through cold and exposure. [28]And apart from these things, there is the daily pressure upon me of my anxiety for all the churches. [29]Who is weak, and I am not weak? Who is led to sin, and I am not indignant? [30]If I must boast, I will boast of the things that show my weakness.

Responsorial Psalm – Psalms 34:2-3, 4-5, 6-7

R. (see 18b) From all their distress God rescues the just.

2 I will bless the LORD at all times;

his praise shall be ever in my mouth.

3 Let my soul glory in the LORD;

the lowly will hear me and be glad.

R. From all their distress God rescues the just.

4 Glorify the LORD with me,

let us together extol his name.

5 I sought the LORD, and he answered me

and delivered me from all my fears.

R. From all their distress God rescues the just.

6 Look to him that you may be radiant with joy,

and your faces may not blush with shame.

7 When the poor one called out, the LORD heard,

and from all his distress he saved him.

R. From all their distress God rescues the just.

Alleluia – Matthew 5:3

R. Alleluia, alleluia.

3Blessed are the poor in spirit; for theirs is the Kingdom of heaven.

R. Alleluia, alleluia.

Gospel – Matthew 6:19-23

Jesus said to his disciples: [19]"Do not store up for yourselves treasures on earth, where moth and decay destroy, and thieves break in and steal. [20]But store up treasures in heaven, where neither moth nor decay destroys, nor thieves break in and steal. [21]For where your treasure is, there also will your heart be. [22]"The lamp of the body is the eye. If your eye is sound, your whole body will be filled with light; [23]but if your eye is bad, your whole body will be in darkness. And if the light in you is darkness, how great will the darkness be."

Saturday June 24, 2023

Solemnity of Birth of Saint John the Baptist

First Reading – Isaiah 49:1-6

[1]Hear me, O coastlands, listen, O distant peoples. The LORD called me from birth, from my mother's womb, he gave me my name. [2]He made of me a sharp-edged sword and concealed me in the shadow of his arm. He made me a polished arrow, in his quiver, he hid me. [3]You are my servant, he said to me, Israel, through whom I show my glory. [4]Though I thought I had toiled in vain, and for nothing, uselessly, spent my strength, yet my reward is with the LORD, my recompense is with my God. [5]For now, the LORD has spoken who formed me as his servant from the womb, that Jacob may be brought back to him and Israel gathered to him; and I am made glorious in the sight of the LORD, and my God is now my strength! [6]It is too little, he says, for you to be my servant, to raise up the tribes of Jacob, and restore the survivors of Israel; I will make you a light to the nations, that my salvation may reach to the ends of the earth.

Responsorial Psalm – Psalms 139:1B-3, 13-14AB, 14C-15

R.[(14)] I praise you, for I am wonderfully made.

[1B] O LORD, you have probed me, you know me:

[2] you know when I sit and when I stand;

you understand my thoughts from afar.

[3] My journeys and my rest you scrutinize,

with all my ways you are familiar.

R. I praise you for I am wonderfully made.

13 Truly you have formed my inmost being;

you knit me in my mother's womb.

14AB I give you thanks that I am fearfully, wonderfully made;

wonderful are your works.

R. I praise you, for I am wonderfully made.

14C My soul also you knew full well;

15 nor was my frame unknown to you

When I was made in secret,

when I was fashioned in the depths of the earth.

R. I praise you, for I am wonderfully made.

Second Reading – Acts13:22-26

In those days, Paul said: 22“God raised up David as king; of
him, God testified, I have found David, son of Jesse, a man
after my own heart; he will carry out my every wish. 23From
this man's descendants God, according to his promise, has
brought to Israel a saviour, Jesus. 24John heralded his coming
by proclaiming a baptism of repentance to all the people of
Israel; 25and as John was completing his course, he would
say, 'What do you suppose that I am? I am not he. Behold,
one is coming after me; I am not worthy to unfasten the
sandals of his feet.' 26“My brothers, sons of the family of
Abraham, and those others among you who are God-fearing,
to us this word of salvation has been sent.”

Alleluia – Luke 1:76

R. Alleluia, alleluia.

76You, child, will be called prophet of the Most High, for you will go before the Lord to prepare his way.

R. Alleluia, alleluia.

Gospel – Luke 1:57-66, 80

57When the time arrived for Elizabeth to have her child she
gave birth to a son. 58Her neighbours and relatives heard that
the Lord had shown his great mercy toward her, and they
rejoiced with her. 59When they came on the eighth day to
circumcise the child, they were going to call him Zechariah

after his father, [60]but his mother said in reply, “No. He will be called John.” [61]But they answered her, “There is no one among your relatives who has this name.” [62]So they made signs, asking his father what he wished him to be called. [63]He asked for a tablet and wrote, “John is his name,” and all were amazed. [64]Immediately his mouth was opened, his tongue freed, and he spoke blessing God. [65]Then fear came upon all their neighbours, and all these matters were discussed throughout the hill country of Judea. [66]All who heard these things took them to heart, saying, “What, then, will this child be?” For surely the hand of the Lord was with him. [80]The child grew and became strong in spirit, and he was in the desert until the day of his manifestation to Israel.

Sunday June 25, 2023

Twelfth Sunday in Ordinary Time, Year A

First Reading – Jeremiah 20:10-13

[10]Jeremiah said: “I hear the whisperings of many: ‘Terror on every side! Denounce! let us denounce him!’ All those who were my friends are on the watch for any misstep of mine. ‘Perhaps he will be trapped; then we can prevail, and take our vengeance on him.’ [11]But the LORD is with me, like a mighty champion: my persecutors will stumble, they will not triumph. In their failure they will be put to utter shame, to lasting, unforgettable confusion. [12]O LORD of hosts, you who test the just, who probe mind and heart, let me witness the vengeance you take on them, for to you I have entrusted my cause. [13]Sing to the LORD, praise the LORD, for he has rescued the life of the poor from the power of the wicked!”

Responsorial Psalm – Psalms 69:8-10, 14, 17, 33-35

R. (14c) **Lord, in your great love, answer me.**

[8] For your sake I bear insult,

and shame covers my face.

[9] I have become an outcast to my brothers,

a stranger to my children,

[10] Because zeal for your house consumes me,

and the insults of those who blaspheme you fall upon me.

R. Lord, in your great love, answer me.

[14] I pray to you, O LORD,

for the time of your favor, O God!

In your great kindness answer me

with your constant help.

[17] Answer me, O LORD, for bounteous is your kindness;

in your great mercy turn toward me.

R. Lord, in your great love, answer me.

[33] "See, you lowly ones, and be glad;

you who seek God, may your hearts revive!

[34] For the LORD hears the poor,

and his own who are in bonds he spurns not.

[35] Let the heavens and the earth praise him,

the seas and whatever moves in them!"

R. Lord, in your great love, answer me.

Second Reading – Romans 5:12-15

[12]Brothers and sisters: Through one man sin entered the
world, and through sin, death, and thus death came to all men,
inasmuch as all sinned [13]for up to the time of the law, sin was
in the world, though sin is not accounted when there is no law.
[14]But death reigned from Adam to Moses, even over those
who did not sin after the pattern of the trespass of Adam, who
is the type of the one who was to come. [15]But the gift is not
like the transgression. For if by the transgression of the one
the many died, how much more did the grace of God and the
gracious gift of the one man Jesus Christ overflow for the
many.

Alleluia – John 15:26B, 27A

R. Alleluia, alleluia.

[26B] The Spirit of truth will testify to me, says the Lord; [27A] and you also will testify.

R. Alleluia, alleluia.

Gospel – Matthew 10:26-33

[26]Jesus said to the Twelve: "Fear no one. Nothing is concealed that will not be revealed, nor secret that will not be known. [27]What I say to you in the darkness, speak in the light; what you hear whispered, proclaim on the housetops. [28]And do not be afraid of those who kill the body but cannot kill the soul; rather, be afraid of the one who can destroy both soul and body in Gehenna. [29]Are not two sparrows sold for a small coin? Yet not one of them falls to the ground without your Father's knowledge. [30]Even all the hairs of your head are counted. [31]So do not be afraid; you are worth more than many sparrows. [32]Everyone who acknowledges me before others I will acknowledge before my heavenly Father. [33]But whoever denies me before others, I will deny before my heavenly Father."

Monday June 26, 2023

Monday of Twelfth Week in Ordinary Time

First Reading – Genesis 12:1-9

[1]The LORD said to Abram: "Go forth from the land of your kinsfolk and from your father's house to a land that I will show you. [2]"I will make of you a great nation, and I will bless you; I will make your name great, so that you will be a blessing. [3]I will bless those who bless you and curse those who curse you. All the communities of the earth shall find blessing in you." [4]Abram went as the LORD directed him, and Lot went with him. Abram was seventy-five years old when he left Haran. [5]Abram took his wife, Sarai, his brother's son Lot, all the possessions that they had accumulated, and the persons they had acquired in Haran, and they set out for the land of Canaan. When they came to the land of Canaan, [6]Abram passed through the land as far as the sacred place at Shechem, by the terebinth of Moreh. (The Canaanites were then in the land.) [7]The LORD appeared to Abram and said, "To your descendants I will give this land." So Abram built an altar there to the LORD who had appeared to him. [8]From there he moved on to the hill country east of Bethel, pitching his tent with Bethel to the west and Ai to the east. He built an altar

there to the LORD and invoked the LORD by name. [9]Then Abram journeyed on by stages to the Negeb.

Responsorial Psalm – Psalms 33:12-13, 18-19, 20 AND 22

R. (12) Blessed the people the Lord has chosen to be his own.

12 Blessed the nation whose God is the LORD,

the people he has chosen for his own inheritance.

13 From heaven the LORD looks down;

he sees all mankind.

R. Blessed the people the Lord has chosen to be his own.

18 See, the eyes of the LORD are upon those who fear him,

upon those who hope for his kindness,

19 To deliver them from death

and preserve them in spite of famine.

R. Blessed the people the Lord has chosen to be his own.

20 Our soul waits for the LORD,

who is our help and our shield.

22 May your kindness, O LORD, be upon us

who have put our hope in you.

R. Blessed the people the Lord has chosen to be his own.

Alleluia – Hebrews 4:12

R. Alleluia, alleluia.

12 The word of God is living and effective, able to discern reflections and thoughts of the heart.

R. Alleluia, alleluia.

Gospel – Matthew 7:1-5

Jesus said to his disciples: [1]"Stop judging, that you may not be judged. [2]For as you judge, so will you be judged, and the measure with which you measure will be measured out to you. [3]Why do you notice the splinter in your brother's eye, but do

not perceive the wooden beam in your own eye? [4]How can
you say to your brother, 'Let me remove that splinter from your
eye,' while the wooden beam is in your eye? [5]You hypocrite,
remove the wooden beam from your eye first; then you will
see clearly to remove the splinter from your brother's eye."

Tuesday June 27, 2023

Tuesday of Twelfth Week in Ordinary Time

First Reading – Genesis 13:2, 5-18

[2]Abram was very rich in livestock, silver, and gold. [5]Lot, who
went with Abram, also had flocks and herds and tents, [6]so that
the land could not support them if they stayed together; their
possessions were so great that they could not dwell together.
[7]There were quarrels between the herdsmen of Abram's
livestock and those of Lot's. (At this time the Canaanites and
the Perizzites were occupying the land.) [8]So Abram said to
Lot: "Let there be no strife between you and me, or between
your herdsmen and mine, for we are kinsmen. [9]Is not the
whole land at your disposal? Please separate from me. If you
prefer the left, I will go to the right; if you prefer the right, I will
go to the left." [10]Lot looked about and saw how well watered
the whole Jordan Plain was as far as Zoar, like the LORD's
own garden, or like Egypt. (This was before the LORD had
destroyed Sodom and Gomorrah.) [11]Lot, therefore, chose for
himself the whole Jordan Plain and set out eastward. Thus
they separated from each other; [12]Abram stayed in the land of
Canaan, while Lot settled among the cities of the Plain,
pitching his tents near Sodom. [13]Now the inhabitants of
Sodom were very wicked in the sins they committed against
the LORD. [14]After Lot had left, the LORD said to Abram: "Look
about you, and from where you are, gaze to the north and
south, east and west; [15]all the land that you see I will give to
you and your descendants forever. [16]I will make your
descendants like the dust of the earth; if anyone could count
the dust of the earth, your descendants too might be counted.
[17]Set forth and walk about in the land, through its length and
breadth, for to you I will give it." [18]Abram moved his tents and
went on to settle near the terebinth of Mamre, which is at
Hebron. There he built an altar to the LORD.

Responsorial Psalm – Psalms 15:2-3A, 3BC-4AB, 5

R. (1b) He who does justice will live in the presence of the Lord.

2 He who walks blamelessly and does justice;

who thinks the truth in his heart

3A and slanders not with his tongue.

R. He who does justice will live in the presence of the Lord.

3BC Who harms not his fellow man,

nor takes up a reproach against his neighbour;

4AB By whom the reprobate is despised,

while he honours those who fear the LORD.

R. He who does justice will live in the presence of the Lord.

5 Who lends not his money at usury

and accepts no bribe against the innocent.

He who does these things

shall never be disturbed.

R. He who does justice will live in the presence of the Lord.

Alleluia – John 8:12

R. Alleluia, alleluia.

12 I am the light of the world, says the Lord; whoever follows me will have the light of life.

R. Alleluia, alleluia.

Gospel – Matthew 7:6, 12-14

Jesus said to his disciples: 6"Do not give what is holy to dogs,
or throw your pearls before swine, lest they trample them
underfoot, and turn and tear you to pieces. 12"Do to others
whatever you would have them do to you. This is the Law and
the Prophets. 13"Enter through the narrow gate; for the gate is
wide and the road broad that leads to destruction, and those

who enter through it are many. [14]How narrow the gate and constricted the road that leads to life. And those who find it are few."

Wednesday June 28, 2023

Wednesday of Twelfth Week Ordinary Time

First Reading – Genesis 15:1-12, 17-18

[1]The word of the LORD came to Abram in a vision: "Fear not,
Abram! I am your shield; I will make your reward very great."
[2]But Abram said, "O Lord GOD, what good will your gifts be, if
I keep on being childless and have as my heir the steward of
my house, Eliezer?" [3]Abram continued, "See, you have given
me no offspring, and so one of my servants will be my heir."
[4]Then the word of the LORD came to him: "No, that one shall
not be your heir; your own issue shall be your heir." [5]He took
him outside and said: "Look up at the sky and count the stars if
you can. Just so," he added, "shall your descendants be."
[6]Abram put his faith in the LORD, who credited it to him as an
act of righteousness. [7]He then said to him, "I am the LORD
who brought you from Ur of the Chaldeans to give you this
land as a possession." [8]"O Lord GOD," he asked, "how am I to
know that I shall possess it?" [9]He answered him, "Bring me a
three-year-old heifer, a three-year-old she-goat, a three-year-
old ram, a turtledove, and a young pigeon." [10]Abram brought
him all these, split them in two, and placed each half opposite
the other; but the birds he did not cut up. [11]Birds of prey
swooped down on the carcasses, but Abram stayed with them.
[12]As the sun was about to set, a trance fell upon Abram, and a
deep, terrifying darkness enveloped him. [17]When the sun had
set and it was dark, there appeared a smoking fire pot and a
flaming torch, which passed between those pieces. [18]It was on
that occasion that the LORD made a covenant with Abram,
saying: "To your descendants, I give this land, from the Wadi
of Egypt to the Great River the Euphrates."

Responsorial Psalm – Psalms 105:1-2, 3-4, 6-7, 8-9

R. [(8a)] **The Lord remembers his covenant forever.** or: **R. Alleluia.**

[1] Give thanks to the LORD, invoke his name;

make known among the nations his deeds.

2 Sing to him, sing his praise,

proclaim all his wondrous deeds.

R. The Lord remembers his covenant forever. or: **R. Alleluia.**

3 Glory in his holy name;

rejoice, O hearts that seek the LORD!

4 Look to the LORD in his strength;

seek to serve him constantly.

R. The Lord remembers his covenant forever. or: **R. Alleluia.**

6 You descendants of Abraham, his servants,

sons of Jacob, his chosen ones!

7 He, the LORD, is our God;

throughout the earth, his judgments prevail.

R. The Lord remembers his covenant forever. or: **R. Alleluia.**

8 He remembers forever his covenant

which he made binding for a thousand generations

9 Which he entered into with Abraham

and by his oath to Isaac.

R. The Lord remembers his covenant forever. or: **R. Alleluia.**

Alleluia – John 15:4A, 5B

R. Alleluia, alleluia.

4A Remain in me, as I remain in you, says the Lord; 5B whoever remains in me will bear much fruit.

R. Alleluia, alleluia.

Gospel – Matthew 7:15-20

Jesus said to his disciples: 15“Beware of false prophets, who come to you in sheep’s clothing, but underneath are ravenous wolves. 16By their fruits, you will know them. Do people pick grapes from thorn bushes or figs from thistles? [17]Just so, every good tree bears good fruit, and a rotten tree bears bad fruit. [18]A good tree cannot bear bad fruit, nor can a rotten tree bear good fruit. [19]Every tree that does not bear good fruit will be cut down and thrown into the fire. [20]So by their fruits, you will know them."

Thursday June 29, 2023

Solemnity of Saints Peter and Paul, Apostles

First Reading – Acts 12:1-11

[1]In those days, King Herod laid hands upon some members of the Church to harm them. [2]He had James, the brother of John, killed by the sword, [3]and when he saw that this was pleasing to the Jews he proceeded to arrest Peter also. –It was the feast of Unleavened Bread. [4]He had him taken into custody and put in prison under the guard of four squads of four soldiers each. He intended to bring him before the people after Passover. [5]Peter thus was being kept in prison, but prayer by the Church was fervently being made to God on his behalf. [6]On the very night before Herod was to bring him to trial, Peter, secured by double chains, was sleeping between two soldiers, while outside the door guards kept watch on the prison. [7]Suddenly the angel of the Lord stood by him and a light shone in the cell. He tapped Peter on the side and awakened him, saying, "Get up quickly." The chains fell from his wrists. [8]The angel said to him, "Put on your belt and your sandals." He did so. Then he said to him, "Put on your cloak and follow me." [9]So he followed him out, not realizing that what was happening through the angel was real; he thought he was seeing a vision. [10]They passed the first guard, then the second, and came to the iron gate leading out to the city, which opened for them by itself. They emerged and made their way down an alley, and suddenly the angel left him. [11]Then Peter recovered his senses and said, "Now I know for certain that the Lord sent his angel and rescued me from the hand of Herod and from all that the Jewish people had been expecting."

Responsorial Psalm – Psalms 34:2-3, 4-5, 6-7, 8-9

R. (5) The angel of the Lord will rescue those who fear him.

[2] I will bless the LORD at all times;

his praise shall be ever in my mouth.

3 Let my soul glory in the LORD;

the lowly will hear me and be glad.

R. The angel of the Lord will rescue those who fear him.

4 Glorify the LORD with me,

let us together extol his name.

5 I sought the LORD, and he answered me

and delivered me from all my fears.

R. The angel of the Lord will rescue those who fear him.

6 Look to him that you may be radiant with joy,

and your faces may not blush with shame.

7 When the poor one called out, the LORD heard,

and from all his distress he saved him.

R. The angel of the Lord will rescue those who fear him.

8 The angel of the LORD encamps

around those who fear him and delivers them.

9 Taste and see how good the LORD is;

blessed the man who takes refuge in him.

R. The angel of the Lord will rescue those who fear him.

Second Reading – 2 Timothy 4:6-8, 17-18

6I, Paul, am already being poured out like a libation, and the
time of my departure is at hand. 7I have competed well; I have
finished the race; I have kept the faith. 8From now on the
crown of righteousness awaits me, which the Lord, the just
judge, will award to me on that day, and not only to me but to
all who have longed for his appearance. 17The Lord stood by
me and gave me strength so that through me the proclamation
might be completed and all the Gentiles might hear it. And I
was rescued from the lion's mouth. 18The Lord will rescue me
from every evil threat and will bring me safe to his heavenly
Kingdom. To him be glory forever and ever. Amen.

Alleluia – Matthew 16:18

R. Alleluia, alleluia.

[18]You are Peter and upon this rock, I will build my Church, and the gates of the netherworld shall not prevail against it.

R. Alleluia, alleluia.

Gospel – Matthew 16:13-19

[13]When Jesus went into the region of Caesarea Philippi he asked his disciples, “Who do people say that the Son of Man is?” [14]They replied, “Some say John the Baptist, others Elijah, still others Jeremiah or one of the prophets.” [15]He said to them, “But who do you say that I am?” [16]Simon Peter said in reply, “You are the Christ, the Son of the living God.” [17]Jesus said to him in reply, “Blessed are you, Simon son of Jonah. For flesh and blood has not revealed this to you, but my heavenly Father. [18]And so I say to you, you are Peter, and upon this rock, I will build my Church, and the gates of the netherworld shall not prevail against it. [19]I will give you the keys to the Kingdom of heaven. Whatever you bind on earth shall be bound in heaven, and whatever you loose on earth shall be loosed in heaven.”

Friday June 30, 2023

Friday of the Twelfth Week in Ordinary Time

First Reading – Genesis 17:1, 9-10, 15-22

[1]When Abram was ninety-nine years old, the LORD appeared to him and said: “I am God the Almighty. Walk in my presence and be blameless.” [9]God also said to Abraham: “On your part, you and your descendants after you must keep my covenant throughout the ages. [10]This is my covenant with you and your descendants after you that you must keep: every male among you shall be circumcised.” [15]God further said to Abraham: “As for your wife Sarai, do not call her Sarai; her name shall be Sarah. [16]I will bless her, and I will give you a son by her. Him also will I bless; he shall give rise to nations, and rulers of peoples shall issue from him.” [17]Abraham prostrated himself and laughed as he said to himself, “Can a child be born to a man who is a hundred years old? Or can Sarah give birth at ninety?” [18]Then Abraham said to God, “Let but Ishmael live on

by your favor!" [19]God replied: "Nevertheless, your wife Sarah
is to bear you a son, and you shall call him Isaac. I will
maintain my covenant with him as an everlasting pact, to be
his God and the God of his descendants after him. [20]As for
Ishmael, I am heeding you: I hereby bless him. I will make him
fertile and will multiply him exceedingly. He shall become the
father of twelve chieftains, and I will make of him a great
nation. [21]But my covenant I will maintain with Isaac, whom
Sarah shall bear to you by this time next year." [22]When he had
finished speaking with him, God departed from Abraham.

Responsorial Psalm – Psalms 128:1-2, 3, 4-5

R. (4) See how the Lord blesses those who fear him.

1 Blessed are you who fear the LORD,

who walk in his ways!

2 For you shall eat the fruit of your handiwork;

blessed shall you be, and favored.

R. See how the Lord blesses those who fear him.

3 Your wife shall be like a fruitful vine

in the recesses of your home;

Your children like olive plants

around your table.

R. See how the Lord blesses those who fear him.

4 Behold, thus is the man blessed

who fears the LORD.

5 The LORD bless you from Zion:

may you see the prosperity of Jerusalem

all the days of your life.

R. See how the Lord blesses those who fear him.

Alleluia – Matthew 8:17

R. Alleluia, alleluia.

17 Christ took away our infirmities and bore our diseases.

R. Alleluia, alleluia.

Gospel – Matthew 8:1-4

[1]When Jesus came down from the mountain, great crowds followed him. [2]And then a leper approached, did him homage, and said, “Lord, if you wish, you can make me clean.” [3]He stretched out his hand, touched him, and said, “I will do it. Be made clean.” His leprosy was cleansed immediately. [4]Then Jesus said to him, “See that you tell no one, but go show yourself to the priest, and offer the gift that Moses prescribed; that will be proof for them.”

JULY 2023

Saturday July 1, 2023

Saturday of Twelfth Week in Ordinary Time

First Reading – Genesis 18:1-15

[1]The LORD appeared to Abraham by the Terebinth of Mamre, as Abraham sat in the entrance of his tent, while the day was growing hot. [2]Looking up, he saw three men standing nearby. When he saw them, he ran from the entrance of the tent to greet them; and bowing to the ground, [3]he said: “Sir, if I may ask you this favor, please do not go on past your servant. [4]Let some water be brought, that you may bathe your feet, and then rest yourselves under the tree. [5]Now that you have come this close to your servant, let me bring you a little food, that you may refresh yourselves; and afterward you may go on your way.” The men replied, “Very well, do as you have said.” [6]Abraham hastened into the tent and told Sarah, “Quick, three measures of fine flour! Knead it and make rolls.” [7]He ran to the herd, picked out a tender, choice steer, and gave it to a servant, who quickly prepared it. [8]Then Abraham got some curds and milk, as well as the steer that had been prepared, and set these before them; and he waited on them under the tree while they ate. [9]They asked him, “Where is your wife Sarah?” He replied, “There in the tent.” [10]One of them said, “I will surely return to you about this time next year, and Sarah will then have a son.” Sarah was listening at the entrance of the tent, just behind him. [11]Now Abraham and Sarah were old, advanced in years, and Sarah had stopped having her womanly periods. [12]So Sarah laughed to herself and said, “Now that I am so withered and my husband is so old, am I still to have sexual pleasure?” [13]But the LORD said to Abraham:

“Why did Sarah laugh and say, ‘Shall I really bear a child, old as I am?’ 14Is anything too marvelous for the LORD to do? At the appointed time, about this time next year, I will return to you, and Sarah will have a son.” 15Because she was afraid, Sarah dissembled, saying, “I didn’t laugh.” But he replied, “Yes you did.”

Responsorial Psalm – Luke 1:46-47, 48-49, 50 AND 53, 54-55

R. (see 54b) **The Lord has remembered his mercy.**

46 “My soul proclaims the greatness of the Lord,

47 my spirit rejoices in God my Savior.”

R. The Lord has remembered his mercy.

48 “For he has looked with favor on his lowly servant.

From this day all generations will call me blessed:

49 the Almighty has done great things for me,

and holy is his Name.”

R. The Lord has remembered his mercy.

50 “He has mercy on those who fear him

in every generation.

53 He has filled the hungry with good things,

and the rich he has sent away empty.”

R. The Lord has remembered his mercy.

54 “He has come to the help of his servant Israel

for he has remembered his promise of mercy,

55 The promise he made to our fathers,

to Abraham and his children for ever.”

R. The Lord has remembered his mercy.

Alleluia – Matthew 8:17

R. Alleluia, alleluia.

17 Christ took away our infirmities and bore our diseases.

R. Alleluia, alleluia.

Gospel – Matthew 8:5-17

[5]When Jesus entered Capernaum, a centurion approached him and appealed to him, [6]saying, “Lord, my servant is lying at home paralyzed, suffering dreadfully.” [7]He said to him, “I will come and cure him.” [8]The centurion said in reply, “Lord, I am not worthy to have you enter under my roof; only say the word and my servant will be healed. [9]For I too am a man subject to authority, with soldiers subject to me. And I say to one, ‘Go,’ and he goes; and to another, ‘Come here,’ and he comes; and to my slave, ‘Do this,’ and he does it.” [10]When Jesus heard this, he was amazed and said to those following him, “Amen, I say to you, in no one in Israel have I found such faith. [11]I say to you, many will come from the east and the west, and will recline with Abraham, Isaac, and Jacob at the banquet in the Kingdom of heaven, [12]but the children of the Kingdom will be driven out into the outer darkness, where there will be wailing and grinding of teeth.” [13]And Jesus said to the centurion, “You may go; as you have believed, let it be done for you.” And at that very hour his servant was healed. [14]Jesus entered the house of Peter, and saw his mother-in-law lying in bed with a fever. [15]He touched her hand, the fever left her, and she rose and waited on him. [16]When it was evening, they brought him many who were possessed by demons, and he drove out the spirits by a word and cured all the sick, [17]to fulfill what had been said by Isaiah the prophet: *He took away our infirmities and bore our diseases.*

Sunday July 2, 2023

Thirteenth Sunday in Ordinary Time, Year A

First Reading – 2 Kings 4:8-11, 14-16A

[8]One day Elisha came to Shunem, where there was a woman of influence, who urged him to dine with her. Afterward, whenever he passed by, he used to stop there to dine. [9]So she said to her husband, “I know that Elisha is a holy man of God. Since he visits us often, [10]let us arrange a little room on the roof and furnish it for him with a bed, table, chair, and lamp, so that when he comes to us he can stay there.” [11]Sometime later Elisha arrived and stayed in the room overnight. [14]Later Elisha asked, “Can something be done for

her?" His servant Gehazi answered, "Yes! She has no son,
and her husband is getting on in years." 15Elisha said, "Call
her." When the woman had been called and stood at the door,
16Elisha promised, "This time next year you will be fondling a
baby son."

Responsorial Psalm – Psalms 89:2-3, 16-17, 18-19

R. (2a) For ever I will sing the goodness of the Lord.

2 The promises of the LORD I will sing forever,

through all generations my mouth shall proclaim your faithfulness.

3 For you have said, "My kindness is established forever;"

in heaven you have confirmed your faithfulness.

R. For ever I will sing the goodness of the Lord.

16 Blessed the people who know the joyful shout;

in the light of your countenance, O LORD, they walk.

17 At your name they rejoice all the day,

and through your justice they are exalted.

R. For ever I will sing the goodness of the Lord.

18 You are the splendor of their strength,

and by your favor our horn is exalted.

19 For to the LORD belongs our shield,

and the Holy One of Israel, our king.

R. For ever I will sing the goodness of the Lord.

Second Reading – Romans 6:3-4, 8-11

3Brothers and sisters: Are you unaware that we who were
baptized into Christ Jesus were baptized into his death? 4We
were indeed buried with him through baptism into death, so
that, just as Christ was raised from the dead by the glory of the
Father, we too might live in newness of life. 8If, then, we have
died with Christ, we believe that we shall also live with him.
9We know that Christ, raised from the dead, dies no more;
death no longer has power over him. 10As to his death, he died
to sin once and for all; as to his life, he lives for God.

[11]Consequently, you too must think of yourselves as dead to sin and living for God in Christ Jesus.

Alleluia – 1 Peter 2:9

R. Alleluia, alleluia.

[9] You are a chosen race, a royal priesthood, a holy nation; announce the praises of him who called you out of darkness into his wonderful light.

R. Alleluia, alleluia.

Gospel – Matthew 10:37-42

[37]Jesus said to his apostles: "Whoever loves father or mother more than me is not worthy of me, and whoever loves son or daughter more than me is not worthy of me; [38]and whoever does not take up his cross and follow after me is not worthy of me. [39]Whoever finds his life will lose it, and whoever loses his life for my sake will find it. [40]"Whoever receives you receives me, and whoever receives me receives the one who sent me. [41]Whoever receives a prophet because he is a prophet will receive a prophet's reward, and whoever receives a righteous man because he is a righteous man will receive a righteous man's reward. [42]And whoever gives only a cup of cold water to one of these little ones to drink because the little one is a disciple amen, I say to you, he will surely not lose his reward."

Monday July 3, 2023

Feast of Saint Thomas – Apostle

First Reading – Ephesians 2:19-22

Brothers and sisters: [19]You are no longer strangers and sojourners, but you are fellow citizens with the holy ones and members of the household of God, [20]built upon the foundation of the Apostles and prophets, with Christ Jesus himself as the capstone. [21]Through him, the whole structure is held together and grows into a temple sacred in the Lord; [22]in him, you also are being built together into a dwelling place of God in the Spirit.

Responsorial Psalm – Psalms 117:1BC, 2

R. (Mark 16:15) **Go out to all the world and tell the Good News.**

[1BC] Praise the LORD, all you nations;

glorify him, all you peoples!

R. Go out to all the world and tell the Good News.

[2] For steadfast is his kindness for us,

and the fidelity of the LORD endures forever.

R. Go out to all the world and tell the Good News.

Alleluia – John 20:29

R. Alleluia, alleluia.

[29] You believe in me, Thomas, because you have seen me, says the Lord; blessed are those who have not seen, but still, believe!

R. Alleluia, alleluia.

Gospel – John 20:24-29

[24]Thomas, called Didymus, one of the Twelve, was not with
them when Jesus came. [25]So the other disciples said to him,
"We have seen the Lord." But Thomas said to them, "Unless I
see the mark of the nails in his hands and put my finger into
the nail marks and put my hand into his side, I will not believe."
[26]Now a week later his disciples were again inside and
Thomas was with them. Jesus came, although the doors were
locked, and stood in their midst and said, "Peace be with you."
[27]Then he said to Thomas, "Put your finger here and see my
hands, and bring your hand and put it into my side, and do not
be unbelieving, but believe." [28]Thomas answered and said to
him, "My Lord and my God!" [29]Jesus said to him, "Have you
come to believe because you have seen me? Blessed are
those who have not seen and have believed."

Tuesday July 4, 2023

Tuesday of Thirteenth Week in Ordinary Time

First Reading – Genesis 19:15-29

[15]As dawn was breaking, the angels urged Lot on, saying, "On
your way! Take with you your wife and your two daughters
who are here, or you will be swept away in the punishment of
Sodom." [16]When he hesitated, the men, by the LORD's mercy,

seized his hand and the hands of his wife and his two
daughters and led them to safety outside the city. [17]As soon as
they had been brought outside, he was told: "Flee for your life!
Don't look back or stop anywhere on the Plain. Get off to the
hills at once, or you will be swept away." [18]"Oh, no, my lord!"
Lot replied, [19]"You have already thought enough of your
servant to do me the great kindness of intervening to save my
life. But I cannot flee to the hills to keep the disaster from
overtaking me, and so I shall die. [20]Look, this town ahead is
near enough to escape to. It's only a small place. Let me flee
there – it's a small place, is it not? – that my life may be
saved." [21]"Well, then," he replied, "I will also grant you the
favour you now ask. I will not overthrow the town you speak of.
[22]Hurry, escape there! I cannot do anything until you arrive
there." That is why the town is called Zoar. [23]The sun was just
rising over the earth as Lot arrived in Zoar; [24]at the same time,
the LORD rained down sulphurous fire upon Sodom and
Gomorrah from the LORD out of heaven. [25]He overthrew
those cities and the whole Plain, together with the inhabitants
of the cities and the produce of the soil. [26]But Lot's wife looked
back, and she was turned into a pillar of salt. [27]Early the next
morning Abraham went to the place where he had stood in the
LORD's presence. [28]As he looked down toward Sodom and
Gomorrah and the whole region of the Plain, he saw dense
smoke over the land rising like fumes from a furnace. Thus it
came to pass: [29]when God destroyed the Cities of the Plain,
he was mindful of Abraham by sending Lot away from the
upheaval by which God overthrew the cities where Lot had
been living.

Responsorial Psalm – Psalms 26:2-3, 9-10, 11-12

R. [(3a)] O Lord, your mercy is before my eyes.

[2] Search me, O LORD, and try me;

test my soul and my heart.

[3] For your mercy is before my eyes,

and I walk in your truth.

R. O Lord, your mercy is before my eyes.

[9] Gather not my soul with those of sinners,

nor with men of blood my life.

10 On their hands are crimes,

and their right hands are full of bribes.

R. O Lord, your mercy is before my eyes.

11 But I walk in integrity;

redeem me, and have mercy on me.

12 My foot stands on level ground;

in the assemblies, I will bless the LORD.

R. O Lord, your mercy is before my eyes.

Alleluia – Psalms 130:5

R. Alleluia, alleluia.

5 I trust in the LORD; my soul trusts in his word.

R. Alleluia, alleluia.

Gospel – Matthew 8:23-27

23 As Jesus got into a boat, his disciples followed him.
24 Suddenly a violent storm came upon the sea so that the boat
was being swamped by waves, but he was asleep. 25 They
came and woke him, saying, “Lord, save us! We are
perishing!” 26 He said to them, “Why are you terrified, O you of
little faith?” Then he got up, rebuked the winds and the sea,
and there was great calm. 27 The men were amazed and said,
“What sort of man is this, whom even the winds and the sea
obey?”

Wednesday July 5, 2023

Wednesday of the Thirteenth Week in Ordinary Time

First Reading – Genesis 21:5, 8-20A

5 Abraham was a hundred years old when his son Isaac was
born to him. 8 Isaac grew, and on the day of the child’s
weaning Abraham held a great feast. 9 Sarah noticed the son
whom Hagar the Egyptian had borne to Abraham playing with
her son Isaac; 10 so she demanded of Abraham: “Drive out that
slave and her son! No son of that slave is going to share the
inheritance with my son Isaac!” 11 Abraham was greatly
distressed, especially on account of his son Ishmael. 12 But
God said to Abraham: “Do not be distressed about the boy or

about your slave woman. Heed the demands of Sarah, no
matter what she is asking of you; for it is through Isaac that
descendants shall bear your name. 13As for the son of the
slave woman, I will make a great nation of him also, since he
too is your offspring." 14Early the next morning Abraham got
some bread and a skin of water and gave them to Hagar.
Then, placing the child on her back, he sent her away. As she
roamed aimlessly in the wilderness of Beer-sheba, 15the water
in the skin was used up. So she put the child down under a
shrub, 16and then went and sat down opposite him, about a
bowshot away; for she said to herself, "Let me not watch to
see the child die." As she sat opposite Ishmael, he began to
cry. 17God heard the boy's cry, and God's messenger called to
Hagar from heaven: "What is the matter, Hagar? Don't be
afraid; God has heard the boy's cry in this plight of his. 18Arise,
lift up the boy and hold him by the hand; for I will make of him
a great nation." 19Then God opened her eyes, and she saw a
well of water. She went and filled the skin with water, and then
let the boy drink. 20AGod was with the boy as he grew up.

Responsorial Psalm – Psalms 34:7-8, 10-11, 12-13

R. (7a) The Lord hears the cry of the poor.

7 When the poor one called out, the LORD heard,

and from all his distress he saved him.

8 The angel of the LORD encamps

around those who fear him, and delivers them.

R. The Lord hears the cry of the poor.

10 Fear the LORD, you his holy ones,

for nought is lacking to those who fear him.

11 The great grow poor and hungry;

but those who seek the LORD want for no good thing.

R. The Lord hears the cry of the poor.

12 Come, children, hear me;

I will teach you the fear of the LORD.

13 Which of you desires life,

and takes delight in prosperous days?

R. The Lord hears the cry of the poor.

Alleluia – James 1:18

R. Alleluia, alleluia.

18The Father willed to give us birth by the word of truth that we may be a kind of first fruits of his creatures.

R. Alleluia, alleluia.

Gospel – Matthew 8:28-34

28When Jesus came to the territory of the Gadarenes, two
demoniacs who were coming from the tombs met him. They
were so savage that no one could travel by that road. 29They
cried out, "What have you to do with us, Son of God? Have
you come here to torment us before the appointed time?"
30Some distance away a herd of many swine was feeding.
31The demons pleaded with him, "If you drive us out, send us
into the herd of swine." 32And he said to them, "Go then!" They
came out and entered the swine, and the whole herd rushed
down the steep bank into the sea where they drowned. 33The
swineherds ran away, and when they came to the town they
reported everything, including what had happened to the
demoniacs. 34Thereupon the whole town came out to meet
Jesus, and when they saw him they begged him to leave their
district.

Thursday July 6, 2023

Thursday of Thirteenth Week Ordinary Time

First Reading – Genesis 22:1B-19

1BGod put Abraham to the test. He called to him, "Abraham!"
"Here I am," he replied. 2Then God said: "Take your son Isaac,
your only one, whom you love, and go to the land of Moriah.
There you shall offer him up as a burnt offering on a height
that I will point out to you." 3Early the next morning Abraham
saddled his donkey, took with him his son Isaac, and two of
his servants as well, and with the wood that he had cut for the
burnt offering, set out for the place of which God had told him.
4On the third day, Abraham got sight of the place from afar.
5Then he said to his servants: "Both of you stay here with the
donkey, while the boy and I go on over yonder. We will
worship and then come back to you." 6Thereupon Abraham

took the wood for the burnt offering and laid it on his son
Isaac’s shoulders, while he himself carried the fire and the
knife. As the two walked on together, 7 Isaac spoke to his
father Abraham: “Father!” he said. “Yes, son,” he replied.
Isaac continued, “Here are the fire and the wood, but where is
the sheep for the burnt offering?” 8“Son,” Abraham answered,
“God himself will provide the sheep for the burnt offering.”
Then the two continued going forward. 9When they came to
the place of which God had told him, Abraham built an altar
there and arranged the wood on it. Next, he tied up his son
Isaac and put him on top of the wood on the altar. 10Then he
reached out and took the knife to slaughter his son. 11But the
LORD’s messenger called to him from heaven, “Abraham,
Abraham!” “Here I am,” he answered. 12“Do not lay your hand
on the boy,” said the messenger. “Do not do the least thing to
him. I know now how devoted you are to God since you did
not withhold from me your own beloved son.” 13As Abraham
looked about, he spied a ram caught by its horns in the thicket.
So he went and took the ram and offered it up as a burnt
offering in place of his son. 14Abraham named the site
Yahweh-yireh; hence people now say, “On the mountain, the
LORD will see.” 15Again the LORD’s messenger called to
Abraham from heaven and said: 16“I swear by myself, declares
the LORD, that because you acted as you did in not
withholding from me your beloved son, 17I will bless you
abundantly and make your descendants as countless as the
stars of the sky and the sands of the seashore; your
descendants shall take possession of the gates of their
enemies, 18and in your descendants all the nations of the earth
shall find blessing all this because you obeyed my command.”
19Abraham then returned to his servants, and they set out
together for Beer-sheba, where Abraham made his home.

Responsorial Psalm – Psalms 115:1-2, 3-4, 5-6, 8-9

R. (9) I will walk in the presence of the Lord, in the land of the living. or: **R. Alleluia.**

1 Not to us, O LORD, not to us

but to your name give glory

because of your kindness, because of your truth.

2 Why should the pagans say,

"Where is their God?"

R. I will walk in the presence of the Lord, in the land of the living. or: **R. Alleluia.**

3 Our God is in heaven;

whatever he wills, he does.

4 Their idols are silver and gold,

the handiwork of men.

R. I will walk in the presence of the Lord, in the land of the living. or: **R. Alleluia.**

5 They have mouths but speak not;

they have eyes but see not;

6 They have ears but hear not;

they have noses but smell not.

R. I will walk in the presence of the Lord, in the land of the living. or: **R. Alleluia.**

8 Their makers shall be like them,

everyone who trusts in them.

9 The house of Israel trusts in the LORD;

he is their help and their shield.

R. I will walk in the presence of the Lord, in the land of the living. or: **R. Alleluia.**

Alleluia – 2 Corinthians 5:19

R. Alleluia, alleluia.

19 God was reconciling the world to himself in Christ and entrusting to us the message of reconciliation.

R. Alleluia, alleluia.

Gospel – Matthew 9:1-8

1 After entering a boat, Jesus made the crossing and came into
his own town. 2 And there, people brought to him a paralytic
lying on a stretcher. When Jesus saw their faith, he said to the
paralytic, "Courage, child, your sins are forgiven." 3 At that,
some of the scribes said to themselves, "This man is

blaspheming.” [4]Jesus knew what they were thinking, and said,
Why do you harbour evil thoughts? [5]Which is easier, to say,
‘Your sins are forgiven,’ or to say, ‘Rise and walk’? [6]But that
you may know that the Son of Man has authority on earth to
forgive sins”– he then said to the paralytic, “Rise, pick up your
stretcher and go home.” [7]He rose and went home. [8]When the
crowds saw this they were struck with awe and glorified God
who had given such authority to men.

Friday July 7, 2023

Friday of Thirteenth Week in Ordinary Time

First Reading – Genesis 23:1-4, 19; 24:1-8, 62-67

[1]The span of Sarah’s life was one hundred and twenty-seven
years. [2]She died in Kiriatharba (that is, Hebron) in the land of
Canaan, and Abraham performed the customary mourning
rites for her. [3]Then he left the side of his dead one and
addressed the Hittites: [4]“Although I am a resident alien among
you, sell me from your holdings a piece of property for a burial
ground, that I may bury my dead wife.” [19]After the transaction,
Abraham buried his wife Sarah in the cave of the field of
Machpelah, facing Mamre (that is, Hebron) in the land of
Canaan. [1]Abraham had now reached a ripe old age, and the
LORD had blessed him in every way. [2]Abraham said to the
senior servant of his household, who had charge of all his
possessions: “Put your hand under my thigh, [3]and I will make
you swear by the LORD, the God of heaven and the God of
earth, that you will not procure a wife for my son from the
daughters of the Canaanites among whom I live, [4]but that you
will go to my own land and to my kindred to get a wife for my
son Isaac.” [5]The servant asked him: “What if the woman is
unwilling to follow me to this land? Should I then take your son
back to the land from which you migrated?” [6]“Never take my
son back there for any reason,” Abraham told him. [7]“The
LORD, the God of heaven, who took me from my father’s
house and the land of my kin, and who confirmed by oath the
promise he then made to me, ‘I will give this land to your
descendants’– he will send his messenger before you, and
you will obtain a wife for my son there. [8]If the woman is
unwilling to follow you, you will be released from this oath. But
never take my son back there!” [62]A long time later, Isaac went
to live in the region of the Negeb. [63]One day toward evening

he went out . . . in the field, and as he looked around, he
noticed that camels were approaching. [64]Rebekah, too, was
looking about, and when she saw him, she alighted from her
camel. [65]She asked the servant, "Who is the man out there,
walking through the fields toward us?" "That is my master,"
replied the servant. Then she covered herself with her veil.
[66]The servant recounted to Isaac all the things he had done.
[67]Then Isaac took Rebekah into his tent; he married her, and
thus she became his wife. In his love for her, Isaac found
solace after the death of his mother Sarah.

Responsorial Psalm – Psalms 106:1B-2, 3-4A, 4B-5

R. [(1b)] Give thanks to the Lord, for he is good.

[1B] Give thanks to the LORD, for he is good,

for his mercy endures forever.

[2] Who can tell the mighty deeds of the LORD,

or proclaim all his praises?

R. Give thanks to the Lord, for he is good.

[3] Blessed are they who observe what is right,

who do always what is just.

[4A] Remember us, O LORD, as you favour your people.

R. Give thanks to the Lord, for he is good.

[4B] Visit me with your saving help,

[5] That I may see the prosperity of your chosen ones,

rejoice in the joy of your people,

and glory with your inheritance.

R. Give thanks to the Lord, for he is good.

Alleluia – Matthew 11:28

R. Alleluia, alleluia.

[28] Come to me, all you who labour and are burdened, and I will give you rest, says the Lord.

R. Alleluia, alleluia.

Gospel – Matthew 9:9-13

9As Jesus passed by, he saw a man named Matthew sitting at
the customs post. He said to him, “Follow me.” And he got up
and followed him. 10While he was at table in his house, many
tax collectors and sinners came and sat with Jesus and his
disciples. 11The Pharisees saw this and said to his disciples,
“Why does your teacher eat with tax collectors and sinners?”
12He heard this and said, “Those who are well, do not need a
physician, but the sick do. 13Go and learn the meaning of the
words, I desire mercy, not sacrifice. I did not come to call the
righteous but sinners.”

Saturday July 8, 2023

Saturday of Thirteenth Week Ordinary Time

First Reading – Genesis 27:1-5, 15-29

1When Isaac was so old that his eyesight had failed him, he
called his older son Esau and said to him, “Son!” “Yes, father!”
he replied. 2Isaac then said, “As you can see, I am so old that I
may now die at any time. 3Take your gear, therefore–your
quiver and bow–and go out into the country to hunt some
game for me. 4With your catch prepare an appetizing dish for
me, such as I like, and bring it to me to eat, so that I may give
you my special blessing before I die.” 5Rebekah had been
listening while Isaac was speaking to his son Esau. So, when
Esau went out into the country to hunt some game for his
father, 15Rebekah [then] took the best clothes of her older son
Esau that she had in the house, and gave them to her younger
son Jacob to wear; 16and with the skins of the kids she
covered up his hands and the hairless parts of his neck.
17Then she handed her son Jacob the appetizing dish and the
bread she had prepared. 18Bringing them to his father, Jacob
said, “Father!” “Yes?” replied Isaac. “Which of my sons are
you?” 19Jacob answered his father: “I am Esau, your first-born.
I did as you told me. Please sit up and eat some of my game,
so that you may give me your special blessing.” 20But Isaac
asked, “How did you succeed so quickly, son?” He answered,
21“The LORD, your God, let things turn out well with me.” Isaac
then said to Jacob, “Come closer, son, that I may feel you, to
learn whether you really are my son Esau or not.” 22So Jacob
moved up closer to his father. When Isaac felt him, he said,
“Although the voice is Jacob’s, the hands are Esau’s.” 23(He

failed to identify him because his hands were hairy, like those of his brother Esau; so in the end, he gave him his blessing.)
24Again he asked Jacob, "Are you really my son Esau?" "Certainly," Jacob replied. 25Then Isaac said, "Serve me your game, son, that I may eat of it and then give you my blessing." Jacob served it to him, and Isaac ate; he brought him wine, and he drank. 26Finally, his father Isaac said to Jacob, "Come closer, son, and kiss me." 27As Jacob went up and kissed him, Isaac smelled the fragrance of his clothes. With that, he blessed him saying, *"Ah, the fragrance of my son is like the fragrance of a field that the LORD has blessed!* 28*"May God give to you of the dew of the heavens And of the fertility of the earth abundance of grain and wine.* 29*"Let peoples serve you, and nations pay you homage; Be master of your brothers, and may your mother's sons bow down to you. Cursed be those who curse you, and blessed be those who bless you."*

Responsorial Psalm – Psalms 135:1B-2, 3-4, 5-6

R. (3a) **Praise the Lord for the Lord is good!** or: **R. Alleluia.**

1B Praise the name of the LORD;

Praise, you servants of the LORD

2 Who stand in the house of the LORD,

in the courts of the house of our God.

R. Praise the Lord for the Lord is good! or: **R. Alleluia.**

3 Praise the LORD, for the LORD is good;

sing praise to his name, which we love;

4 For the LORD has chosen Jacob for himself,

Israel for his own possession.

R. Praise the Lord for the Lord is good! or: **R. Alleluia.**

5 For I know that the LORD is great;

our LORD is greater than all gods.

6 All that the LORD wills he does

in heaven and on earth,

in the seas and in all the deeps.

R. Praise the Lord for the Lord is good! or: **R. Alleluia.**

Alleluia – John 10:27

R. Alleluia, alleluia.

27 My sheep hear my voice, says the Lord; I know them, and they follow me.

R. Alleluia, alleluia.

Gospel – Matthew 9:14-17

14 The disciples of John approached Jesus and said, "Why do
we and the Pharisees fast much, but your disciples do not
fast?" 15 Jesus answered them, "Can the wedding guests
mourn as long as the bridegroom is with them? The days will
come when the bridegroom is taken away from them, and then
they will fast. 16 No one patches an old cloak with a piece of
unshrunken cloth, for its fullness pulls away from the cloak and
the tear gets worse. 17 People do not put new wine into old
wineskins. Otherwise the skins burst, the wine spills out, and
the skins are ruined. Rather, they pour new wine into fresh
wineskins, and both are preserved."

Sunday July 9, 2023

Fourteenth Sunday in Ordinary Time, Year A

First Reading – Zechariah 9:9-10

9 Thus says the LORD: Rejoice heartily, O daughter Zion,
shout for joy, O daughter Jerusalem! See, your king shall
come to you; a just savior is he, meek, and riding on an ass,
on a colt, the foal of an ass. 10 He shall banish the chariot from
Ephraim, and the horse from Jerusalem; the warrior's bow
shall be banished, and he shall proclaim peace to the nations.
His dominion shall be from sea to sea, and from the River to
the ends of the earth.

Responsorial Psalm – Psalms 145:1-2, 8-9, 10-11, 13-14

R. (cf. 1) **I will praise your name for ever, my king and my God.** or: **R. Alleluia.**

1 I will extol you, O my God and King,

and I will bless your name forever and ever.

2 Every day will I bless you,

and I will praise your name forever and ever.

R. I will praise your name for ever, my king and my God.
or: **R. Alleluia.**

8 The LORD is gracious and merciful,

slow to anger and of great kindness.

9 The LORD is good to all

and compassionate toward all his works.

R. I will praise your name for ever, my king and my God.
or: **R. Alleluia.**

10 Let all your works give you thanks, O LORD,

and let your faithful ones bless you.

11 Let them discourse of the glory of your kingdom

and speak of your might.

R. I will praise your name for ever, my king and my God.
or: **R. Alleluia.**

13 The LORD is faithful in all his words

and holy in all his works.

14 The LORD lifts up all who are falling

and raises up all who are bowed down.

R. I will praise your name for ever, my king and my God.
or: **R. Alleluia.**

Second Reading – Romans 8:9, 11-13

9Brothers and sisters: You are not in the flesh; on the contrary, you are in the spirit, if only the Spirit of God dwells in you. Whoever does not have the Spirit of Christ does not belong to
him. 11If the Spirit of the one who raised Jesus from the dead dwells in you, the one who raised Christ from the dead will give life to your mortal bodies also, through his Spirit that
dwells in you. 12Consequently, brothers and sisters, we are not
debtors to the flesh, to live according to the flesh. 13For if you live according to the flesh, you will die, but if by the Spirit you put to death the deeds of the body, you will live.

Alleluia – Matthew 11:25

R. Alleluia, alleluia.

25 Blessed are you, Father, Lord of heaven and earth; you have revealed to little ones the mysteries of the kingdom.

R. Alleluia, alleluia.

Gospel – Matthew 11:25-30

25At that time Jesus exclaimed: "I give praise to you, Father,
Lord of heaven and earth, for although you have hidden these
things from the wise and the learned you have revealed them
to little ones. 26Yes, Father, such has been your gracious will.
27All things have been handed over to me by my Father. No
one knows the Son except the Father, and no one knows the
Father except the Son and anyone to whom the Son wishes to
reveal him." 28"Come to me, all you who labor and are
burdened, and I will give you rest. 29Take my yoke upon you
and learn from me, for I am meek and humble of heart; and
you will find rest for yourselves. 30For my yoke is easy, and my
burden light."

Monday July 10, 2023

Monday of Fourteenth Week Ordinary Time

First Reading – Genesis 28:10-22A

10Jacob departed from Beer-sheba and proceeded toward
Haran. 11When he came upon a certain shrine, as the sun had
already set, he stopped there for the night. Taking one of the
stones at the shrine, he put it under his head and lay down to
sleep at that spot. 12Then he had a dream: a stairway rested
on the ground, with its top reaching to the heavens; and God's
messengers were going up and down on it. 13And there was
the LORD standing beside him and saying: "I, the LORD, am
the God of your forefather Abraham and the God of Isaac; the
land on which you are lying I will give to you and your
descendants. 14These shall be as plentiful as the dust of the
earth, and through them, you shall spread out east and west,
north and south. In you and your descendants, all the nations
of the earth shall find blessing. 15Know that I am with you; I will
protect you wherever you go, and bring you back to this land. I
will never leave you until I have done what I promised you."

16 When Jacob awoke from his sleep, he exclaimed, “Truly, the
LORD is in this spot, although I did not know it!” 17 In solemn
wonder, he cried out: “How awesome is this shrine! This is
nothing else but an abode of God, and that is the gateway to
heaven!” 18 Early the next morning Jacob took the stone that he
had put under his head, set it up as a memorial stone, and
poured oil on top of it. 19 He called the site Bethel, whereas the
former name of the town had been Luz. 20 Jacob then made
this vow: “If God remains with me, to protect me on this
journey I am making and to give me enough bread to eat and
clothing to wear, 21 and I come back safe to my father’s house,
the LORD shall be my God. 22 This stone that I have set up as
a memorial stone shall be God’s abode.”

Responsorial Psalm – Psalms 91:1-2, 3-4, 14-15AB

R. (see 2b) **In you, my God, I place my trust.**

1 You who dwell in the shelter of the Most High,

who abide in the shadow of the Almighty,

2 Say to the LORD, “My refuge and my fortress,

my God, in whom I trust.”

R. In you, my God, I place my trust.

3 For he will rescue you from the snare of the fowler,

from the destroying pestilence.

4 With his pinions, he will cover you,

and under his wings, you shall take refuge.

R. In you, my God, I place my trust.

14 Because he clings to me, I will deliver him;

I will set him on high because he acknowledges my name.

15AB He shall call upon me, and I will answer him;

I will be with him in distress.

R. In you, my God, I place my trust.

Alleluia – 2 Timothy 1:10

R. Alleluia, alleluia.

10 Our Savior Jesus Christ has destroyed death and brought life to light through the Gospel.

R. Alleluia, alleluia.

Gospel – Matthew 9:18-26

18 While Jesus was speaking, an official came forward, knelt
down before him, and said, "My daughter has just died. But
come, lay your hand on her, and she will live." 19 Jesus rose
and followed him, and so did his disciples. 20 A woman
suffering haemorrhages for twelve years came up behind him
and touched the tassel on his cloak. 21 She said to herself, "If
only I can touch his cloak, I shall be cured." 22 Jesus turned
around and saw her, and said, "Courage, daughter! Your faith
has saved you." And from that hour the woman was cured.
23 When Jesus arrived at the official's house and saw the flute
players and the crowd who were making a commotion, 24 he
said, "Go away! The girl is not dead but sleeping." And they
ridiculed him. 25 When the crowd was put out, he came and
took her by the hand, and the little girl arose. 26 And news of
this spread throughout all that land.

Tuesday July 11, 2023

Memorial of Saint Benedict, Abbot

First Reading – Genesis 32:23-33

23 In the course of the night, Jacob arose, took his two wives,
with the two maidservants and his eleven children, and
crossed the ford of the Jabbok. 24 After he had taken them
across the stream and had brought over all his possessions,
25 Jacob was left there alone. Then some man wrestled with
him until the break of dawn. 26 When the man saw that he
could not prevail over him, he struck Jacob's hip at its socket,
so that the hip socket was wrenched as they wrestled. 27 The
man then said, "Let me go, for it is daybreak." But Jacob said,
"I will not let you go until you bless me." 28 The man asked,
"What is your name?" He answered, "Jacob." 29 Then the man
said, "You shall no longer be spoken of as Jacob, but as
Israel, because you have contended with divine and human

beings and have prevailed." [30]Jacob then asked him, "Do tell me your name, please." He answered, "Why should you want to know my name?" With that, he bade him farewell. [31]Jacob named the place Peniel, "Because I have seen God face to face," he said, "yet my life has been spared." [32]At sunrise, as he left Penuel, Jacob limped along because of his hip. [33]That is why, to this day, the children of Israel do not eat the sciatic muscle that is on the hip socket, inasmuch as Jacob's hip socket was struck at the sciatic muscle.

Responsorial Psalm – Psalms 17:1B, 2-3, 6-7AB, 8B AND 15

R. [(15a)] **In justice, I shall behold your face, O Lord.**

[1B] Hear, O LORD, a just suit;

attend to my outcry;

hearken to my prayer from lips without deceit.

R. In justice, I shall behold your face, O Lord.

[2] From you let my judgment come;

your eyes behold what is right.

[3] Though you test my heart, searching it in the night,

though you try me with fire, you shall find no malice in me.

R. In justice, I shall behold your face, O Lord.

[6] I call upon you, for you will answer me, O God;

incline your ear to me; hear my word.

[7AB] Show your wondrous mercies,

O saviour of those who flee from their foes.

R. In justice, I shall behold your face, O Lord.

[8B] Hide me in the shadow of your wings.

[15] I in justice shall behold your face;

on waking, I shall be content in your presence.

R. In justice, I shall behold your face, O Lord.

Alleluia – John 10:14

R. Alleluia, alleluia.

[14] I am the good shepherd, says the Lord; I know my sheep, and mine know me.

R. Alleluia, alleluia.

Gospel – Matthew 9:32-38

[32]A demoniac who could not speak was brought to Jesus, [33]and when the demon was driven out the mute man spoke. The crowds were amazed and said, "Nothing like this has ever been seen in Israel." [34]But the Pharisees said, "He drives out demons by the prince of demons." [35]Jesus went around to all the towns and villages, teaching in their synagogues, proclaiming the Gospel of the Kingdom, and curing every disease and illness. [36]At the sight of the crowds, his heart was moved with pity for them because they were troubled and abandoned, like sheep without a shepherd. [37]Then he said to his disciples, "The harvest is abundant but the labourers are few; [38]so ask the master of the harvest to send out labourers for his harvest."

Wednesday July 12, 2023

Wednesday of the Fourteenth Week in Ordinary Time

First Reading – Genesis 41:55-57; 42:5-7A, 17-24A

[55]When hunger came to be felt throughout the land of Egypt and the people cried to Pharaoh for bread, Pharaoh directed all the Egyptians to go to Joseph and do whatever he told them. [56]When the famine had spread throughout the land, Joseph opened all the cities that had grain and rationed it to the Egyptians, since the famine had gripped the land of Egypt. [57]In fact, all the world came to Joseph to obtain rations of grain, for famine had gripped the whole world. [5]The sons of Israel were among those who came to procure rations. [6]It was Joseph, as governor of the country, who dispensed the rations to all the people. When Joseph's brothers came and knelt down before him with their faces to the ground, [7A]he recognized them as soon as he saw them. But Joseph concealed his own identity from them and spoke sternly to them. [17]With that, he locked them up in the guardhouse for three days. [18]On the third day Joseph said to his brothers: "Do

this, and you shall live; for I am a God-fearing man. [19]If you
have been honest, only one of your brothers need be confined
in this prison, while the rest of you may go and take home
provisions for your starving families. [20]But you must come
back to me with your youngest brother. Your words will thus
be verified, and you will not die." To this they agreed. [21]To one
another, however, they said: "Alas, we are being punished
because of our brother. We saw the anguish of his heart when
he pleaded with us, yet we paid no heed; that is why this
anguish has now come upon us." [22]Reuben broke in, "Did I not
tell you not to do wrong to the boy? But you would not listen!
Now comes the reckoning for his blood." [23]The brothers did
not know, of course, that Joseph understood what they said,
since he spoke with them through an interpreter. [24A]But turning
away from them, he wept.

Responsorial Psalm – Psalms 33:2-3, 10-11, 18-19

R. [(22)] Lord, let your mercy be on us, as we place our trust in you.

[2] Give thanks to the LORD on the harp;

with the ten-stringed lyre chant his praises.

[3] Sing to him a new song;

pluck the strings skillfully, with shouts of gladness.

R. Lord, let your mercy be on us, as we place our trust in you.

[10] The LORD brings to nought the plans of nations;

he foils the designs of peoples.

[11] But the plan of the LORD stands forever;

the design of his heart, through all generations.

R. Lord, let your mercy be on us, as we place our trust in you.

[18] But see, the eyes of the LORD are upon those who fear him,

upon those who hope for his kindness,

[19] To deliver them from death

and preserve them in spite of famine.

R. Lord, let your mercy be on us, as we place our trust in you.

Alleluia – Mark 1:15

R. Alleluia, alleluia.

15 The Kingdom of God is at hand: repent and believe in the Gospel.

R. Alleluia, alleluia.

Gospel – Matthew 10:1-7

1Jesus summoned his Twelve disciples and gave them
authority over unclean spirits to drive them out and to cure
every disease and every illness. 2The names of the Twelve
Apostles are these: first, Simon called Peter, and his brother
Andrew; James, the son of Zebedee, and his brother John;
3Philip and Bartholomew, Thomas and Matthew the tax
collector; James, the son of Alphaeus, and Thaddeus; 4Simon
the Cananean, and Judas Iscariot who betrayed Jesus. 5Jesus
sent out these Twelve after instructing them thus, "Do not go
into pagan territory or enter a Samaritan town. 6Go rather to
the lost sheep of the house of Israel. 7As you go, make this
proclamation: 'The Kingdom of heaven is at hand.'"

Thursday July 13, 2023

Thursday of Fourteenth Week Ordinary Time

First Reading – Genesis 44:18-21, 23B-29; 45:1-5

18Judah approached Joseph and said: "I beg you, my lord, let
your servant speak earnestly to my lord, and do not become
angry with your servant, for you are the equal of Pharaoh.
19My lord asked your servants, 'Have you a father, or another
brother?' 20So we said to my lord, 'We have an aged father,
and a young brother, the child of his old age. This one's full
brother is dead, and since he is the only one by that mother
who is left, his father dotes on him.' 21Then you told your
servants, 'Bring him down to me that my eyes may look on
him. 23BUnless your youngest brother comes back with you,
you shall not come into my presence again.' 24When we
returned to your servant our father, we reported to him the
words of my lord. 25"Later, our father told us to come back and
buy some food for the family. 26So we reminded him, 'We

cannot go down there; only if our youngest brother is with us
can we go, for we may not see the man if our youngest brother
is not with us.' 27Then your servant our father said to us, 'As
you know, my wife bore me two sons. 28One of them, however,
disappeared, and I had to conclude that he must have been
torn to pieces by wild beasts; I have not seen him since. 29If
you now take this one away from me, too, and some disaster
befalls him, you will send my white head down to the nether
world in grief.'" 1Joseph could no longer control himself in the
presence of all his attendants, so he cried out, "Have everyone
withdraw from me!" Thus no one else was about when he
made himself known to his brothers. 2But his sobs were so
loud that the Egyptians heard him, and so the news reached
Pharaoh's palace. 3"I am Joseph," he said to his brothers. "Is
my father still in good health?" But his brothers could give him
no answer, so dumbfounded were they at him. 4"Come closer
to me," he told his brothers. When they had done so, he said:
"I am your brother Joseph, whom you once sold into Egypt.
5But now do not be distressed, and do not reproach
yourselves for having sold me here. It was really for the sake
of saving lives that God sent me here ahead of you."

Responsorial Psalm – Psalms 105:16-17, 18-19, 20-21

R. (5a) **Remember the marvels the Lord has done.** or: **R. Alleluia.**

16 When the LORD called down a famine on the land

and ruined the crop that sustained them,

17 He sent a man before them,

Joseph, sold as a slave.

R. Remember the marvels the Lord has done. or: **R. Alleluia.**

18 They had weighed him down with fetters,

and he was bound with chains,

19 Till his prediction came to pass

and the word of the LORD proved him true.

R. Remember the marvels the Lord has done. or: **R. Alleluia.**

[20] The king sent and released him,

the ruler of the peoples set him free.

[21] He made him lord of his house

and ruler of all his possessions.

R. Remember the marvels the Lord has done. or: **R. Alleluia.**

Alleluia – Mark 1:15

R. Alleluia, alleluia.

[15] The Kingdom of God is at hand: repent and believe in the Gospel.

R. Alleluia, alleluia.

Gospel – Matthew 10:7-15

[7]Jesus said to his Apostles: "As you go, make this
proclamation: 'The Kingdom of heaven is at hand.' [8]Cure the
sick, raise the dead, cleanse the lepers, drive out demons.
Without cost you have received; without cost you are to give.
[9]Do not take gold or silver or copper for your belts; [10]no sack
for the journey, or a second tunic, or sandals, or walking stick.
The labourer deserves his keep. [11]Whatever town or village
you enter, look for a worthy person in it, and stay there until
you leave. [12]As you enter a house, wish it peace. [13]If the
house is worthy, let your peace come upon it; if not, let your
peace return to you. [14]Whoever will not receive you or listen to
your words go outside that house or town and shake the dust
from your feet. [15]Amen, I say to you, it will be more tolerable
for the land of Sodom and Gomorrah on the day of judgment
than for that town."

Friday July 14, 2023

Memorial of Saint Kateri Tekakwitha, Virgin

First Reading – Genesis 46:1-7, 28-30

[1]Israel set out with all that was his. When he arrived at Beer-
sheba, he offered sacrifices to the God of his father Isaac.
[2]There God, speaking to Israel in a vision by night, called,
"Jacob! Jacob!" He answered, "Here I am." [3]Then he said: "I
am God, the God of your father. Do not be afraid to go down

to Egypt, for there I will make you a great nation. [4]Not only will I go down to Egypt with you; I will also bring you back here, after Joseph has closed your eyes." [5]So Jacob departed from Beer-sheba, and the sons of Israel put their father and their wives and children on the wagons that Pharaoh had sent for his transport. [6]They took with them their livestock and the possessions they had acquired in the land of Canaan. Thus Jacob and all his descendants migrated to Egypt. [7]His sons and his grandsons, his daughters and his granddaughters all his descendants-he took with him to Egypt. [28]Israel had sent Judah ahead to Joseph so that he might meet him in Goshen. On his arrival in the region of Goshen, [29]Joseph hitched the horses to his chariot and rode to meet his father Israel in Goshen. As soon as Joseph saw him, he flung himself on his neck and wept a long time in his arms. [30]And Israel said to Joseph, "At last I can die, now that I have seen for myself that Joseph is still alive."

Responsorial Psalm – Psalms 37:3-4, 18-19, 27-28, 39-40

R. (39a) The salvation of the just comes from the Lord.

3 Trust in the LORD and do good,

that you may dwell in the land and be fed in security.

4 Take delight in the LORD,

and he will grant you your heart's requests.

R. The salvation of the just comes from the Lord.

18 The LORD watches over the lives of the wholehearted;

their inheritance lasts forever.

19 They are not put to shame in an evil time;

in days of famine, they have plenty.

R. The salvation of the just comes from the Lord.

27 Turn from evil and do good,

that you may abide forever;

28 For the LORD loves what is right,

and forsakes not his faithful ones.

R. The salvation of the just comes from the Lord.

39 The salvation of the just is from the LORD;

he is their refuge in time of distress.

40 And the LORD helps them and delivers them;

he delivers them from the wicked and saves them,

because they take refuge in him.

R. The salvation of the just comes from the Lord.

Alleluia – John 16:13A, 14:26D

R. Alleluia, alleluia.

13A When the Spirit of truth comes, he will guide you to all truth
26D and remind you of all I told you.

R. Alleluia, alleluia.

Gospel – Matthew 10:16-23

Jesus said to his Apostles: 16“Behold, I am sending you like
sheep in the midst of wolves; so be shrewd as serpents and
simple as doves. 17But beware of men, for they will hand you
over to courts and scourge you in their synagogues, 18and you
will be led before governors and kings for my sake as a
witness before them and the pagans. 19When they hand you
over, do not worry about how you are to speak or what you are
to say. You will be given at that moment what you are to say.
20For it will not be you who speak but the Spirit of your Father
speaking through you. 21Brother will hand over brother to
death, and the father his child; children will rise up against
parents and have them put to death. 22You will be hated by all
because of my name, but whoever endures to the end will be
saved. 23When they persecute you in one town, flee to
another. Amen, I say to you, you will not finish the towns of
Israel before the Son of Man comes.”

Saturday July 15, 2023

Memorial of Saint Bonaventure, Bishop and Doctor

First Reading – Genesis 49:29-32; 50:15-26A

29Jacob gave his sons this charge: “Since I am about to be
taken to my people, bury me with my fathers in the cave that

lies in the field of Ephron the Hittite, 30the cave in the field of
Machpelah, facing on Mamre, in the land of Canaan, the field
that Abraham bought from Ephron the Hittite for a burial
ground. 31There Abraham and his wife Sarah are buried, and
so are Isaac and his wife Rebekah, and there, too, I buried
Leah 32the field and the cave in it that had been purchased
from the Hittites." 15Now that their father was dead, Joseph's
brothers became fearful and thought, "Suppose Joseph has
been nursing a grudge against us and now plans to pay us
back in full for all the wrong we did him!" 16So they approached
Joseph and said: "Before your father died, he gave us these
instructions: 17'You shall say to Joseph, Jacob begs you to
forgive the criminal wrongdoing of your brothers, who treated
you so cruelly.' Please, therefore, forgive the crime that we,
the servants of your father's God, committed." When they
spoke these words to him, Joseph broke into tears. 18Then his
brothers proceeded to fling themselves down before him and
said, "Let us be your slaves!" 19But Joseph replied to them:
"Have no fear. Can I take the place of God? 20Even though
you meant harm to me, God meant it for good, to achieve his
present end, the survival of many people. 21Therefore have no
fear. I will provide for you and for your children." By thus
speaking kindly to them, he reassured them. 22Joseph
remained in Egypt, together with his father's family. He lived a
hundred and ten years. 23He saw Ephraim's children to the
third generation, and the children of Manasseh's son Machir
were also born on Joseph's knees. 24Joseph said to his
brothers: "I am about to die. God will surely take care of you
and lead you out of this land to the land that he promised on
oath to Abraham, Isaac and Jacob." 25Then, putting the sons
of Israel under oath, he continued, "When God thus takes care
of you, you must bring my bones up with you from this place."
26AJoseph died at the age of a hundred and ten.

Responsorial Psalm – Psalms 105:1-2, 3-4, 6-7

R. (see Psalm 69:33) **Be glad you lowly ones; may your hearts be glad!**

1 Give thanks to the LORD, invoke his name;

make known among the nations his deeds.

2 Sing to him, sing his praise,

proclaim all his wondrous deeds.

R. Be glad you lowly ones; may your hearts be glad!

3 Glory in his holy name;

rejoice, O hearts that seek the LORD!

4 Look to the LORD in his strength;

seek to serve him constantly.

R. Be glad you lowly ones; may your hearts be glad!

6 You descendants of Abraham, his servants,

sons of Jacob, his chosen ones!

7 He, the LORD, is our God;

throughout the earth his judgments prevail.

R. Be glad you lowly ones; may your hearts be glad!

Alleluia – 1 Peter 4:14

R. Alleluia, alleluia.

14 If you are insulted for the name of Christ, blessed are you, for the Spirit of God rests upon you.

R. Alleluia, alleluia.

Gospel – Matthew 10:24-33

Jesus said to his Apostles: 24"No disciple is above his teacher,
no slave above his master. 25It is enough for the disciple that
he become like his teacher, for the slave that he become like
his master. If they have called the master of the house
Beelzebul, how much more those of his household!
26"Therefore do not be afraid of them. Nothing is concealed
that will not be revealed, nor secret that will not be known.
27What I say to you in the darkness, speak in the light; what
you hear whispered, proclaim on the housetops. 28And do not
be afraid of those who kill the body but cannot kill the soul;
rather, be afraid of the one who can destroy both soul and
body in Gehenna. 29Are not two sparrows sold for a small
coin? Yet not one of them falls to the ground without your
Father's knowledge. 30Even all the hairs of your head are
counted. 31So do not be afraid; you are worth more than many
sparrows. 32Everyone who acknowledges me before others I
will acknowledge before my heavenly Father. 33But whoever

denies me before others, I will deny before my heavenly Father."

Sunday July 16, 2023

Fifteenth Sunday in Ordinary Time, Year A

First Reading – Isaiah 55:10-11

10 Thus says the LORD: Just as from the heavens the rain and
snow come down and do not return there till they have
watered the earth, making it fertile and fruitful, giving seed to
the one who sows and bread to the one who eats,
11 so shall
my word be that goes forth from my mouth; my word shall not
return to me void, but shall do my will, achieving the end for
which I sent it.

Responsorial Psalm – Psalms 65:10, 11, 12-13, 14

R. (Luke 8:8) **The seed that falls on good ground will yield a fruitful harvest.**

10 You have visited the land and watered it;

greatly have you enriched it.

God's watercourses are filled;

you have prepared the grain.

R. The seed that falls on good ground will yield a fruitful harvest.

11 Thus have you prepared the land: drenching its furrows,

breaking up its clods,

Softening it with showers, blessing its yield.

R. The seed that falls on good ground will yield a fruitful harvest.

12 You have crowned the year with your bounty,

and your paths overflow with a rich harvest;

13 The untilled meadows overflow with it,

and rejoicing clothes the hills.

R. The seed that falls on good ground will yield a fruitful harvest.

14 The fields are garmented with flocks

and the valleys blanketed with grain.

They shout and sing for joy.

R. The seed that falls on good ground will yield a fruitful harvest.

Second Reading – Romans 8:18-23

18 Brothers and sisters: I consider that the sufferings of this
present time are as nothing compared with the glory to be
revealed for us. 19 For creation awaits with eager expectation
the revelation of the children of God; 20 for creation was made
subject to futility, not of its own accord but because of the one
who subjected it, in hopen 21 that creation itself would be set
free from slavery to corruption and share in the glorious
freedom of the children of God. 22 We know that all creation is
groaning in labor pains even until now; 23 and not only that, but
we ourselves, who have the firstfruits of the Spirit, we also
groan within ourselves as we wait for adoption, the redemption
of our bodies.

Alleluia

R. Alleluia, alleluia.

The seed is the word of God, Christ is the sower. All who come to him will have life forever.

R. Alleluia, alleluia.

Gospel – Matthew 13:1-23

1 On that day, Jesus went out of the house and sat down by
the sea. 2 Such large crowds gathered around him that he got
into a boat and sat down, and the whole crowd stood along
the shore. 3 And he spoke to them at length in parables,
saying: "A sower went out to sow. 4 And as he sowed, some
seed fell on the path, and birds came and ate it up. 5 Some fell
on rocky ground, where it had little soil. It sprang up at once
because the soil was not deep, 6 and when the sun rose it was
scorched, and it withered for lack of roots. 7 Some seed fell
among thorns, and the thorns grew up and choked it. 8 But
some seed fell on rich soil, and produced fruit, a hundred or
sixty or thirtyfold. 9 Whoever has ears ought to hear." 10 The
disciples approached him and said, "Why do you speak to

them in parables?” [11]He said to them in reply, “Because
knowledge of the mysteries of the kingdom of heaven has
been granted to you, but to them it has not been granted. [12]To
anyone who has, more will be given and he will grow rich; from
anyone who has not, even what he has will be taken away.
[13]This is why I speak to them in parables, because they look
but do not see and hear but do not listen or understand.
[14]Isaiah’s prophecy is fulfilled in them, which says: You shall
indeed hear but not understand, you shall indeed look but
never see. [15]Gross is the heart of this people, they will hardly
hear with their ears, they have closed their eyes, lest they see
with their eyes and hear with their ears and understand with
their hearts and be converted, and I heal them. [16]“But blessed
are your eyes, because they see, and your ears, because they
hear. [17]Amen, I say to you, many prophets and righteous
people longed to see what you see but did not see it, and to
hear what you hear but did not hear it. [18]“Hear then the
parable of the sower. [19]The seed sown on the path is the one
who hears the word of the kingdom without understanding it,
and the evil one comes and steals away what was sown in his
heart. [20]The seed sown on rocky ground is the one who hears
the word and receives it at once with joy. [21]But he has no root
and lasts only for a time. When some tribulation or persecution
comes because of the word, he immediately falls away. [22]The
seed sown among thorns is the one who hears the word, but
then worldly anxiety and the lure of riches choke the word and
it bears no fruit. [23]But the seed sown on rich soil is the one
who hears the word and understands it, who indeed bears fruit
and yields a hundred or sixty or thirtyfold.”

Or Matthew 13:1-9

[1]On that day, Jesus went out of the house and sat down by
the sea. [2]Such large crowds gathered around him that he got
into a boat and sat down, and the whole crowd stood along
the shore. [3]And he spoke to them at length in parables,
saying: “A sower went out to sow. [4]And as he sowed, some
seed fell on the path, and birds came and ate it up. [5]Some fell
on rocky ground, where it had little soil. It sprang up at once
because the soil was not deep, [6]and when the sun rose it was
scorched, and it withered for lack of roots. [7]Some seed fell
among thorns, and the thorns grew up and choked it. [8]But
some seed fell on rich soil, and produced fruit, a hundred or
sixty or thirtyfold. [9]Whoever has ears ought to hear.”

Monday July 17, 2023

Monday of Fifteenth Week in Ordinary Time

First Reading – Exodus 1:8-14, 22

[8]A new king, who knew nothing of Joseph, came to power in Egypt. [9]He said to his subjects, “Look how numerous and powerful the people of the children of Israel are growing, more so than we ourselves! [10]Come, let us deal shrewdly with them to stop their increase; otherwise, in time of war they too may join our enemies to fight against us, and so leave our country.” [11]Accordingly, taskmasters were set over the children of Israel to oppress them with forced labour. Thus they had to build for Pharaoh the supply cities of Pithom and Raamses. [12]Yet the more they were oppressed, the more they multiplied and spread. [13]The Egyptians, then, dreaded the children of Israel and reduced them to cruel slavery, [14]making life bitter for them with hard work in mortar and brick and all kinds of field work – the whole cruel fate of slaves. [22]Pharaoh then commanded all his subjects, “Throw into the river every boy that is born to the Hebrews, but you may let all the girls live.”

Responsorial Psalm – Psalms 124:1B-3, 4-6, 7-8

R. (8a) Our help is in the name of the Lord.

[1B] Had not the LORD been with us – let Israel say,

[2] had not the LORD been with us–

When men rose up against us,

[3] then would they have swallowed us alive,

When their fury was inflamed against us.

R. Our help is in the name of the Lord.

[4] Then would the waters have overwhelmed us;

The torrent would have swept over us;

[5] over us then would have swept

the raging waters.

[6] Blessed be the LORD, who did not leave us

a prey to their teeth.

R. Our help is in the name of the Lord.

7 We were rescued like a bird

from the fowlers' snare;

Broken was the snare,

and we were freed.

8 Our help is in the name of the LORD,

who made heaven and earth.

R. Our help is in the name of the Lord.

Alleluia – Matthew 5:10

R. Alleluia, alleluia.

10 Blessed are they who are persecuted for the sake of righteousness, for theirs is the Kingdom of heaven.

R. Alleluia, alleluia.

Gospel – Matthew 10:34-11:1

34Jesus said to his Apostles: "Do not think that I have come to
bring peace upon the earth. I have come to bring not peace
but the sword. 35For I have come to set a man against his
father, a daughter against her mother, and a daughter-in-law
against her mother-in-law; 36and one's enemies will be those
of his household. 37"Whoever loves father or mother more than
me is not worthy of me, and whoever loves son or daughter
more than me is not worthy of me; 38and whoever does not
take up his cross and follow after me is not worthy of me.
39Whoever finds his life will lose it, and whoever loses his life
for my sake will find it. 40"Whoever receives you receives me,
and whoever receives me receives the one who sent me.
41Whoever receives a prophet because he is a prophet will
receive a prophet's reward, and whoever receives a righteous
man because he is righteous will receive a righteous man's
reward. 42And whoever gives only a cup of cold water to one of
these little ones to drink because he is a disciple, amen, I say
to you, he will surely not lose his reward." 1When Jesus
finished giving these commands to his Twelve disciples, he
went away from that place to teach and to preach in their
towns.

Tuesday July 18, 2023

Tuesday of Fifteenth Week in Ordinary Time

First Reading – Exodus 2:1-15A

[1]A certain man of the house of Levi married a Levite woman,
[2]who conceived and bore a son. Seeing that he was a goodly
child, she hid him for three months. [3]When she could hide him
no longer, she took a papyrus basket, daubed it with bitumen
and pitch, and putting the child in it, placed it among the reeds
on the river bank. [4]His sister stationed herself at a distance to
find out what would happen to him. [5]Pharaoh's daughter came
down to the river to bathe, while her maids walked along the
river bank. Noticing the basket among the reeds, she sent her
handmaid to fetch it. [6]On opening it, she looked, and lo, there
was a baby boy, crying! She was moved with pity for him and
said, "It is one of the Hebrews' children." [7]Then his sister
asked Pharaoh's daughter, "Shall I go and call one of the
Hebrew women to nurse the child for you?" [8]"Yes, do so," she
answered. So the maiden went and called the child's own
mother. [9]Pharaoh's daughter said to her, "Take this child and
nurse it for me, and I will repay you." The woman therefore
took the child and nursed it. [10]When the child grew, she
brought him to Pharaoh's daughter, who adopted him as her
son and called him Moses; for she said, "I drew him out of the
water." [11]On one occasion, after Moses had grown up, when
he visited his kinsmen and witnessed their forced labor, he
saw an Egyptian striking a Hebrew, one of his own kinsmen.
[12]Looking about and seeing no one, he slew the Egyptian and
hid him in the sand. [13]The next day he went out again, and
now two Hebrews were fighting! So he asked the culprit, "Why
are you striking your fellow Hebrew?" [14]But the culprit replied,
"Who has appointed you ruler and judge over us? Are you
thinking of killing me as you killed the Egyptian?" Then Moses
became afraid and thought, "The affair must certainly be
known." [15A]Pharaoh, too, heard of the affair and sought to put
Moses to death. But Moses fled from him and stayed in the
land of Midian.

Responsorial Psalm – Psalms 69:3, 14, 30-31, 33-34

R. (see 33) **Turn to the Lord in your need, and you will live.**

[3] I am sunk in the abysmal swamp

where there is no foothold;

I have reached the watery depths;

the flood overwhelms me.

R. Turn to the Lord in your need, and you will live.

[14] But I pray to you, O LORD,

for the time of your favor, O God!

In your great kindness answer me

with your constant help.

R. Turn to the Lord in your need, and you will live.

[30] But I am afflicted and in pain;

let your saving help, O God, protect me;

[31] I will praise the name of God in song,

and I will glorify him with thanksgiving.

R. Turn to the Lord in your need, and you will live.

[33] "See, you lowly ones, and be glad;

you who seek God, may your hearts revive!

[34] For the LORD hears the poor,

and his own who are in bonds he spurns not."

R. Turn to the Lord in your need, and you will live.

Alleluia – Psalms 95:8

R. Alleluia, alleluia.

[8] If today you hear his voice, harden not your hearts.

R. Alleluia, alleluia.

Gospel – Matthew 11:20-24

[20]Jesus began to reproach the towns where most of his mighty
deeds had been done, since they had not repented. [21]"Woe to
you, Chorazin! Woe to you, Bethsaida! For if the mighty deeds
done in your midst had been done in Tyre and Sidon, they
would long ago have repented in sackcloth and ashes. [22]But I

tell you, it will be more tolerable for Tyre and Sidon on the day of judgment than for you. [23]And as for you, Capernaum: Will you be exalted to heaven? You will go down to the netherworld. For if the mighty deeds done in your midst had been done in Sodom, it would have remained until this day. [24]But I tell you, it will be more tolerable for the land of Sodom on the day of judgment than for you."

Wednesday July 19, 2023

Wednesday of Fifteenth Week Ordinary Time

First Reading – Exodus 3:1-6, 9-12

[1]Moses was tending the flock of his father-in-law Jethro, the priest of Midian. Leading the flock across the desert, he came to Horeb, the mountain of God. [2]There an angel of the LORD appeared to him in fire flaming out of a bush. As he looked on, he was surprised to see that the bush, though on fire, was not consumed. [3]So Moses decided, "I must go over to look at this remarkable sight, and see why the bush is not burned." [4]When the LORD saw him coming over to look at it more closely, God called out to him from the bush, "Moses! Moses!" He answered, "Here I am." [5]God said, "Come no nearer! Remove the sandals from your feet, for the place where you stand is holy ground. [6]I am the God of your father," he continued, "the God of Abraham, the God of Isaac, the God of Jacob. [9]The cry of the children of Israel has reached me, and I have truly noted that the Egyptians are oppressing them. [10]Come, now! I will send you to Pharaoh to lead my people, the children of Israel, out of Egypt." [11]But Moses said to God, "Who am I that I should go to Pharaoh and lead the children of Israel out of Egypt?" [12]He answered, "I will be with you; and this shall be your proof that it is I who have sent you: when you bring my people out of Egypt, you will worship God on this very mountain."

Responsorial Psalm – Psalms 103:1B-2, 3-4, 6-7

R. [8a] The Lord is kind and merciful.

[1B] Bless the LORD, O my soul;

and all my being, bless his holy name.

[2] Bless the LORD, O my soul,

and forget not all his benefits.

R. The Lord is kind and merciful.

3 He pardons all your iniquities,

he heals all your ills.

4 He redeems your life from destruction,

he crowns you with kindness and compassion.

R. The Lord is kind and merciful.

6 The LORD secures justice

and the rights of all the oppressed.

7 He has made known his ways to Moses,

and his deeds to the children of Israel.

R. The Lord is kind and merciful.

Alleluia – Matthew 11:25

R. Alleluia, alleluia.

25 Blessed are you, Father, Lord of heaven and earth; you have revealed to little ones the mysteries of the Kingdom.

R. Alleluia, alleluia.

Gospel – Matthew 11:25-27

25 At that time Jesus exclaimed: "I give praise to you, Father,
Lord of heaven and earth, for although you have hidden these
things from the wise and the learned you have revealed them
to the childlike. 26 Yes, Father, such has been your gracious
will. 27 All things have been handed over to me by my Father.
No one knows the Son except the Father, and no one knows
the Father except the Son and anyone to whom the Son
wishes to reveal him."

Thursday July 20, 2023

Thursday of Fifteenth Week in Ordinary Time

First Reading – Exodus 3:13-20

13 Moses, hearing the voice of the LORD from the burning
bush, said to him, "When I go to the children of Israel and say

to them, ‘The God of your fathers has sent me to you,’ if they ask me, ‘What is his name?’ what am I to tell them?” 14God replied, “I am who am.” Then he added, “This is what you shall tell the children of Israel: **I AM** sent me to you.” 15God spoke further to Moses, “Thus shall you say to the children of Israel: The LORD, the God of your fathers, the God of Abraham, the God of Isaac, the God of Jacob, has sent me to you. “This is my name forever; this my title for all generations. 16“Go and assemble the elders of Israel, and tell them: The LORD, the God of your fathers, the God of Abraham, Isaac, and Jacob, has appeared to me and said: I am concerned about you and about the way you are being treated in Egypt; 17so I have decided to lead you up out of the misery of Egypt into the land of the Canaanites, Hittites, Amorites, Perizzites, Hivites, and Jebusites, a land flowing with milk and honey. 18“Thus they will heed your message. Then you and the elders of Israel shall go to the king of Egypt and say to him: “The LORD, the God of the Hebrews, has sent us word. Permit us, then, to go a three-days’ journey in the desert, that we may offer sacrifice to the LORD, our God. 19“Yet I know that the king of Egypt will not allow you to go unless he is forced. 20I will stretch out my hand, therefore, and smite Egypt by doing all kinds of wondrous deeds there. After that he will send you away.”

Responsorial Psalm – Psalms 105:1 AND 5, 8-9, 24-25, 26-27

R. (8a) The Lord remembers his covenant for ever. or: **R. Alleluia.**

1 Give thanks to the LORD, invoke his name;

make known among the nations his deeds.

5 Recall the wondrous deeds that he has wrought,

his portents, and the judgments he has uttered.

R. The Lord remembers his covenant for ever. or: **R. Alleluia.**

8 He remembers forever his covenant

which he made binding for a thousand generations

9 Which he entered into with Abraham

and by his oath to Isaac.

R. The Lord remembers his covenant for ever. or: **R. Alleluia.**

[24] He greatly increased his people

and made them stronger than their foes,

[25] Whose hearts he changed, so that they hated his people,

and dealt deceitfully with his servants.

R. The Lord remembers his covenant for ever. or: **R. Alleluia.**

[26] He sent Moses his servant;

Aaron, whom he had chosen.

[27] They wrought his signs among them,

and wonders in the land of Ham.

R. The Lord remembers his covenant for ever. or: **R. Alleluia.**

Alleluia – Matthew 11:28

R. Alleluia, alleluia.

[28] Come to me, all you who labor and are burdened, and I will give you rest, says the Lord.

R. Alleluia, alleluia.

Gospel – Matthew 11:28-30

Jesus said: [28]"Come to me, all you who labor and are burdened, and I will give you rest. [29]Take my yoke upon you and learn from me, for I am meek and humble of heart; and you will find rest for yourselves. [30]For my yoke is easy, and my burden light."

Friday July 21, 2023

Friday of Fifteenth Week in Ordinary Time

First Reading – Exodus 11:10-12:14

[10]Although Moses and Aaron performed various wonders in Pharaoh's presence, the LORD made Pharaoh obstinate, and he would not let the children of Israel leave his land. [1]The LORD said to Moses and Aaron in the land of Egypt, [2]"This

month shall stand at the head of your calendar; you shall
reckon it the first month of the year. [3]Tell the whole community
of Israel: On the tenth of this month every one of your families
must procure for itself a lamb, one apiece for each household.
[4]If a family is too small for a whole lamb, it shall join the
nearest household in procuring one and shall share in the
lamb in proportion to the number of persons who partake of it.
[5]The lamb must be a year-old male and without blemish. You
may take it from either the sheep or the goats. [6]You shall keep
it until the fourteenth day of this month, and then, with the
whole assembly of Israel present, it shall be slaughtered
during the evening twilight. [7]They shall take some of its blood
and apply it to the two doorposts and the lintel of every house
in which they partake of the lamb. [8]That same night they shall
eat its roasted flesh with unleavened bread and bitter herbs. [9]It
shall not be eaten raw or boiled, but roasted whole, with its
head and shanks and inner organs. [10]None of it must be kept
beyond the next morning; whatever is leftover in the morning
shall be burned up. [11]"This is how you are to eat it: with your
loins girt, sandals on your feet and your staff in hand, you shall
eat like those who are in flight. It is the Passover of the LORD.
[12]For on this same night I will go through Egypt, striking down
every first born of the land, both man and beast, and
executing judgment on all the gods of Egypt – I, the LORD!
[13]But the blood will mark the houses where you are. Seeing
the blood, I will pass over you; thus, when I strike the land of
Egypt, no destructive blow will come upon you. [14]"This day
shall be a memorial feast for you, which all your generations
shall celebrate with pilgrimage to the LORD, as a perpetual
institution."

Responsorial Psalm – Psalms 116:12-13, 15 AND 16BC, 17-18

R. (13) I will take the cup of salvation, and call on the name of the Lord.

[12] How shall I make a return to the LORD

for all the good he has done for me?

[13] The cup of salvation I will take up,

and I will call upon the name of the LORD.

R. I will take the cup of salvation, and call on the name of the Lord.

15 Precious in the eyes of the LORD

is the death of his faithful ones.

16B I am your servant, the son of your handmaid;

you have loosed my bonds.

R. I will take the cup of salvation, and call on the name of the Lord.

17 To you will I offer sacrifice of thanksgiving,

and I will call upon the name of the LORD.

18 My vows to the LORD I will pay

in the presence of all his people.

R. I will take the cup of salvation, and call on the name of the Lord.

Alleluia – John 10:27

R. Alleluia, alleluia.

27 My sheep hear my voice, says the Lord; I know them, and they follow me.

R. Alleluia, alleluia.

Gospel – Matthew 12:1-8

1 Jesus was going through a field of grain on the Sabbath. His
disciples were hungry and began to pick the heads of grain
and eat them. 2 When the Pharisees saw this, they said to him,
“See, your disciples are doing what is unlawful to do on the
Sabbath.” 3 He said to the them, “Have you not read what
David did when he and his companions were hungry, 4 how he
went into the house of God and ate the bread of offering,
which neither he nor his companions but only the priests could
lawfully eat? 5 Or have you not read in the law that on the
Sabbath the priests serving in the temple violate the Sabbath
and are innocent? 6 I say to you, something greater than the
temple is here. 7 If you knew what this meant, I desire mercy,
not sacrifice, you would not have condemned these innocent
men. 8 For the Son of Man is Lord of the Sabbath.”

Saturday July 22, 2023

Feast of Saint Mary Magdalene

First Reading – Songs of Solomon 3:1-4B

The Bride says: [1]On my bed at night I sought him whom my heart loves, I sought him but I did not find him. [2]I will rise then and go about the city; in the streets and crossings I will seek Him whom my heart loves. I sought him but I did not find him. [3]The watchmen came upon me, as they made their rounds of the city: Have you seen him whom my heart loves? [4]I had hardly left them when I found him whom my heart loves.

OR 2 Corinthians 5:14-17

Brothers and sisters: [14]The love of Christ impels us, once we have come to the conviction that one died for all; therefore, all have died. [15]He indeed died for all, so that those who live might no longer live for themselves but for him who for their sake died and was raised. [16]Consequently, from now on we regard no one according to the flesh; even if we once knew Christ according to the flesh, yet now we know him so no longer. [17]So whoever is in Christ is a new creation: the old things have passed away; behold, new things have come.

Responsorial Psalm – Psalms 63:2, 3-4, 5-6, 8-9

R. (2) My soul is thirsting for you, O Lord my God.

[2] O God, you are my God whom I seek;

for you my flesh pines and my soul thirsts

like the earth, parched, lifeless and without water.

R. My soul is thirsting for you, O Lord my God.

[3] Thus have I gazed toward you in the sanctuary

to see your power and your glory,

[4] For your kindness is a greater good than life;

my lips shall glorify you.

R. My soul is thirsting for you, O Lord my God.

[5] Thus will I bless you while I live;

lifting up my hands, I will call upon your name.

6 As with the riches of a banquet shall my soul be satisfied,

and with exultant lips my mouth shall praise you.

R. My soul is thirsting for you, O Lord my God.

8 You are my help,

and in the shadow of your wings I shout for joy.

9 My soul clings fast to you;

your right hand upholds me.

R. My soul is thirsting for you, O Lord my God.

Alleluia

R. Alleluia, alleluia.

Tell us Mary, what did you see on the way? I saw the glory of the risen Christ, I saw his empty tomb.

R. Alleluia, alleluia.

Gospel – John 20:1-2, 11-18

1On the first day of the week, Mary Magdalene came to the
tomb early in the morning, while it was still dark, and saw the
stone removed from the tomb. 2So she ran and went to Simon
Peter and to the other disciple whom Jesus loved, and told
them, "They have taken the Lord from the tomb, and we don't
know where they put him." 11Mary stayed outside the tomb
weeping. And as she wept, she bent over into the tomb 12and
saw two angels in white sitting there, one at the head and one
at the feet where the Body of Jesus had been. 13And they said
to her, "Woman, why are you weeping?" She said to them,
"They have taken my Lord, and I don't know where they laid
him." 14When she had said this, she turned around and saw
Jesus there, but did not know it was Jesus. 15Jesus said to
her, "Woman, why are you weeping? Whom are you looking
for?" She thought it was the gardener and said to him, "Sir, if
you carried him away, tell me where you laid him, and I will
take him." 16Jesus said to her, "Mary!" She turned and said to
him in Hebrew, "Rabbouni," which means Teacher. 17Jesus
said to her, "Stop holding on to me, for I have not yet
ascended to the Father. But go to my brothers and tell them, 'I
am going to my Father and your Father, to my God and your
God.'" 18Mary Magdalene went and announced to the

disciples, "I have seen the Lord," and then reported what he told her.

Sunday July 23, 2023

Sixteenth Sunday in Ordinary Time, Year A

First Reading – Wisdom 12:13, 16-19

13 There is no god besides you who have the care of all, that
you need show you have not unjustly condemned. 16 For your
might is the source of justice; your mastery over all things
makes you lenient to all. 17 For you show your might when the
perfection of your power is disbelieved; and in those who know
you, you rebuke temerity. 18 But though you are master of
might, you judge with clemency, and with much lenience you
govern us; for power, whenever you will, attends you. 19 And
you taught your people, by these deeds, that those who are
just must be kind; and you gave your children good ground for
hope that you would permit repentance for their sins.

Responsorial Psalm – Psalms 86:5-6, 9-10, 15-16

R. (5a) Lord, you are good and forgiving.

5 You, O LORD, are good and forgiving,

abounding in kindness to all who call upon you.

6 Hearken, O LORD, to my prayer

and attend to the sound of my pleading.

R. Lord, you are good and forgiving.

9 All the nations you have made shall come

and worship you, O LORD,

and glorify your name.

10 For you are great, and you do wondrous deeds;

you alone are God.

R. Lord, you are good and forgiving.

15 You, O LORD, are a God merciful and gracious,

slow to anger, abounding in kindness and fidelity.

16 Turn toward me, and have pity on me;

give your strength to your servant.

R. Lord, you are good and forgiving.

Second Reading – Romans 8:26-27

[26]Brothers and sisters: The Spirit comes to the aid of our
weakness; for we do not know how to pray as we ought, but
the Spirit himself intercedes with inexpressible groanings.
[27]And the one who searches hearts knows what is the
intention of the Spirit, because he intercedes for the holy ones
according to God's will.

Alleluia – Matthew 11:25

R. Alleluia, alleluia.

[25]Blessed are you, Father, Lord of heaven and earth; you have revealed to little ones the mysteries of the kingdom.

R. Alleluia, alleluia.

Gospel – Matthew 13:24-43

[24]Jesus proposed another parable to the crowds, saying: "The
kingdom of heaven may be likened to a man who sowed good
seed in his field. [25]While everyone was asleep his enemy
came and sowed weeds all through the wheat, and then went
off. [26]When the crop grew and bore fruit, the weeds appeared
as well. [27]The slaves of the householder came to him and
said, 'Master, did you not sow good seed in your field? Where
have the weeds come from?' [28]He answered, 'An enemy has
done this.' His slaves said to him, 'Do you want us to go and
pull them up?' [29]He replied, 'No, if you pull up the weeds you
might uproot the wheat along with them. [30]Let them grow
together until harvest; then at harvest time I will say to the
harvesters, "First collect the weeds and tie them in bundles for
burning; but gather the wheat into my barn."'" [31]He proposed
another parable to them. "The kingdom of heaven is like a
mustard seed that a person took and sowed in a field. [32]It is
the smallest of all the seeds, yet when full-grown it is the
largest of plants. It becomes a large bush, and the 'birds of the
sky come and dwell in its branches.'" [33]He spoke to them
another parable. "The kingdom of heaven is like yeast that a
woman took and mixed with three measures of wheat flour
until the whole batch was leavened." [34]All these things Jesus
spoke to the crowds in parables. He spoke to them only in

parables, [35]to fulfill what had been said through the prophet: I
will open my mouth in parables, I will announce what has lain
hidden from the foundation of the world. [36]Then, dismissing
the crowds, he went into the house. His disciples approached
him and said, “Explain to us the parable of the weeds in the
field.” [37]He said in reply, “He who sows good seed is the Son
of Man, [38]the field is the world, the good seed the children of
the kingdom. The weeds are the children of the evil one, [39]and
the enemy who sows them is the devil. The harvest is the end
of the age, and the harvesters are angels. [40]Just as weeds are
collected and burned up with fire, so will it be at the end of the
age. [41]The Son of Man will send his angels, and they will
collect out of his kingdom all who cause others to sin and all
evildoers. [42]They will throw them into the fiery furnace, where
there will be wailing and grinding of teeth. [43]Then the righteous
will shine like the sun in the kingdom of their Father. Whoever
has ears ought to hear.”

Or Matthew 13:24-30

[24]Jesus proposed another parable to the crowds, saying: “The
kingdom of heaven may be likened to a man who sowed good
seed in his field. [25]While everyone was asleep his enemy
came and sowed weeds all through the wheat, and then went
off. [26]When the crop grew and bore fruit, the weeds appeared
as well. [27]The slaves of the householder came to him and
said, ‘Master, did you not sow good seed in your field? Where
have the weeds come from?’ [28]He answered, ‘An enemy has
done this.’ His slaves said to him, ‘Do you want us to go and
pull them up?’ [29]He replied, ‘No, if you pull up the weeds you
might uproot the wheat along with them. [30]Let them grow
together until harvest; then at harvest time I will say to the
harvesters, “First collect the weeds and tie them in bundles for
burning; but gather the wheat into my barn.”’

Monday July 24, 2023

Monday of Sixteenth Week in Ordinary Time

First Reading – Exodus 14:5-18

[5]When it was reported to the king of Egypt that the people had
fled, Pharaoh and his servants changed their minds about
them. They exclaimed, “What have we done! Why, we have
released Israel from our service!” [6]So Pharaoh made his

chariots ready and mustered his soldiers 7six hundred first-class chariots and all the other chariots of Egypt, with warriors on them all. 8So obstinate had the LORD made Pharaoh that he pursued the children of Israel even while they were marching away in triumph. 9The Egyptians, then, pursued them; Pharaoh's whole army, his horses, chariots and charioteers, caught up with them as they lay encamped by the sea, at Pi-hahiroth, in front of Baal-zephon. 10Pharaoh was already near when the children of Israel looked up and saw that the Egyptians were on the march in pursuit of them. In great fright they cried out to the LORD. 11And they complained to Moses, "Were there no burial places in Egypt that you had to bring us out here to die in the desert? Why did you do this to us? Why did you bring us out of Egypt? 12Did we not tell you this in Egypt, when we said, 'Leave us alone. Let us serve the Egyptians'? Far better for us to be the slaves of the Egyptians than to die in the desert." 13But Moses answered the people, "Fear not! Stand your ground, and you will see the victory the LORD will win for you today. These Egyptians whom you see today you will never see again. 14The LORD himself will fight for you; you have only to keep still." 15Then the LORD said to Moses, "Why are you crying out to me? Tell the children of Israel to go forward. 16And you, lift up your staff and, with hand outstretched over the sea, split the sea in two, that the children of Israel may pass through it on dry land. 17But I will make the Egyptians so obstinate that they will go in after them. Then I will receive glory through Pharaoh and all his army, his chariots and charioteers. 18The Egyptians shall know that I am the LORD, when I receive glory through Pharaoh and his chariots and charioteers."

Responsorial Psalm – Exodus 15:1BC-2, 3-4, 5-6

R. (1b) Let us sing to the Lord; he has covered himself in glory.

1BC I will sing to the LORD, for he is gloriously triumphant;

horse and chariot he has cast into the sea.

2 My strength and my courage is the LORD,

and he has been my savior.

He is my God, I praise him;

the God of my father, I extol him.

R. Let us sing to the Lord; he has covered himself in glory.

3 The LORD is a warrior,

LORD is his name!

4 Pharaoh's chariots and army he hurled into the sea;

the elite of his officers were submerged in the Red Sea.

R. Let us sing to the Lord; he has covered himself in glory.

5 The flood waters covered them,

they sank into the depths like a stone.

6 Your right hand, O LORD, magnificent in power,

your right hand, O LORD, has shattered the enemy.

R. Let us sing to the Lord; he has covered himself in glory.

Alleluia – Psalms 95:8

R. Alleluia, alleluia.

8 If today you hear his voice, harden not your hearts.

R. Alleluia, alleluia.

Gospel – Matthew 12:38-42

38Some of the scribes and Pharisees said to Jesus, "Teacher,
we wish to see a sign from you." 39He said to them in reply,
"An evil and unfaithful generation seeks a sign, but no sign will
be given it except the sign of Jonah the prophet. 40Just as
Jonah was in the belly of the whale three days and three
nights, so will the Son of Man be in the heart of the earth three
days and three nights. 41At the judgment, the men of Nineveh
will arise with this generation and condemn it, because they
repented at the preaching of Jonah; and there is something
greater than Jonah here. 42At the judgment the queen of the
south will arise with this generation and condemn it, because
she came from the ends of the earth to hear the wisdom of
Solomon; and there is something greater than Solomon here."

Tuesday July 25, 2023

Feast of Saint James, Apostle

First Reading – 2 Corinthians 4:7-15

Brothers and sisters: 7We hold this treasure in earthen
vessels, that the surpassing power may be of God and not
from us. 8We are afflicted in every way, but not constrained;
perplexed, but not driven to despair; 9persecuted, but not
abandoned; struck down, but not destroyed; 10always carrying
about in the body the dying of Jesus, so that the life of Jesus
may also be manifested in our body. 11For we who live are
constantly being given up to death for the sake of Jesus, so
that the life of Jesus may be manifested in our mortal flesh.
12So death is at work in us, but life in you. 13Since, then, we
have the same spirit of faith, according to what is written, I
believed, therefore I spoke, we too believe and therefore
speak, 14knowing that the one who raised the Lord Jesus will
raise us also with Jesus and place us with you in his presence.
15Everything indeed is for you, so that the grace bestowed in
abundance on more and more people may cause the
thanksgiving to overflow for the glory of God.

Responsorial Psalm – Psalms 126:1BC-2AB, 2CD-3, 4-5, 6

R.(5) Those who sow in tears shall reap rejoicing.

1BC When the LORD brought back the captives of Zion,

we were like men dreaming.

2AB Then our mouth was filled with laughter,

and our tongue with rejoicing.

R. Those who sow in tears shall reap rejoicing.

2CD Then they said among the nations,

“The LORD has done great things for them.”

3 The LORD has done great things for us;

we are glad indeed.

R. Those who sow in tears shall reap rejoicing.

4 Restore our fortunes, O LORD,

like the torrents in the southern desert.

5 Those that sow in tears

shall reap rejoicing.

R. Those who sow in tears shall reap rejoicing.

6 Although they go forth weeping,

carrying the seed to be sown,

They shall come back rejoicing,

carrying their sheaves.

R. Those who sow in tears shall reap rejoicing.

Alleluia – cf. John 15:16

R. Alleluia, alleluia.

16 I chose you from the world, to go and bear fruit that will last, says the Lord.

R. Alleluia, alleluia.

Gospel – Matthew 20:20-28

20 The mother of the sons of Zebedee approached Jesus with
her sons and did him homage, wishing to ask him for
something. 21 He said to her, "What do you wish?" She
answered him, "Command that these two sons of mine sit, one
at your right and the other at your left, in your Kingdom."
22 Jesus said in reply, "You do not know what you are asking.
Can you drink the chalice that I am going to drink?" They said
to him, "We can." 23 He replied, "My chalice you will indeed
drink, but to sit at my right and at my left, this is not mine to
give but is for those for whom it has been prepared by my
Father." 24 When the ten heard this, they became indignant at
the two brothers. 25 But Jesus summoned them and said, "You
know that the rulers of the Gentiles lord it over them, and the
great ones make their authority over them felt. 26 But it shall not
be so among you. Rather, whoever wishes to be great among
you shall be your servant; 27 whoever wishes to be first among
you shall be your slave. 28 Just so, the Son of Man did not
come to be served but to serve and to give his life as a
ransom for many."

Wednesday July 26, 2023

Memorial of Saints Joachim and Anne

First Reading – Exodus 16:1-5, 9-15

[1]The children of Israel set out from Elim, and came into the
desert of Sin, which is between Elim and Sinai, on the fifteenth
day of the second month after their departure from the land of
Egypt. [2]Here in the desert the whole assembly of the children
of Israel grumbled against Moses and Aaron. [3]The children of
Israel said to them, “Would that we had died at the LORD’s
hand in the land of Egypt, as we sat by our fleshpots and ate
our fill of bread! But you had to lead us into this desert to make
the whole community die of famine!” [4]Then the LORD said to
Moses, “I will now rain down bread from heaven for you. Each
day the people are to go out and gather their daily portion;
thus will I test them, to see whether they follow my instructions
or not. [5]On the sixth day, however, when they prepare what
they bring in, let it be twice as much as they gather on the
other days.” [9]Then Moses said to Aaron, “Tell the whole
congregation of the children of Israel: Present yourselves
before the LORD, for he has heard your grumbling.” [10]When
Aaron announced this to the whole assembly of the children of
Israel, they turned toward the desert, and lo, the glory of the
LORD appeared in the cloud! [11]The LORD spoke to Moses
and said, [12]“I have heard the grumbling of the children of
Israel. Tell them: In the evening twilight you shall eat flesh,
and in the morning you shall have your fill of bread, so that
you may know that I, the LORD, am your God.” [13]In the
evening quail came up and covered the camp. In the morning
a dew lay all about the camp, [14]and when the dew evaporated,
there on the surface of the desert were fine flakes like
hoarfrost on the ground. [15]On seeing it, the children of Israel
asked one another, “What is this?” for they did not know what
it was. But Moses told them, “This is the bread which the
LORD has given you to eat.”

Responsorial Psalm – Psalms 78:18-19, 23-24, 25-26, 27-28

R. [(24b)] The Lord gave them bread from heaven.

[18] They tempted God in their hearts

by demanding the food they craved.

19 Yes, they spoke against God, saying,

"Can God spread a table in the desert?"

R. The Lord gave them bread from heaven.

23 Yet he commanded the skies above

and the doors of heaven he opened;

24 He rained manna upon them for food

and gave them heavenly bread.

R. The Lord gave them bread from heaven.

25 Man ate the bread of angels,

food he sent them in abundance.

26 He stirred up the east wind in the heavens,

and by his power brought on the south wind.

R. The Lord gave them bread from heaven.

27 And he rained meat upon them like dust,

and, like the sand of the sea, winged fowl,

28 Which fell in the midst of their camp

round about their tents.

R. The Lord gave them bread from heaven.

Alleluia

R. Alleluia, alleluia.

The seed is the word of God, Christ is the sower; all who come to him will live for ever.

R. Alleluia, alleluia.

Gospel – Matthew 13:1-9

1On that day, Jesus went out of the house and sat down by
the sea. 2Such large crowds gathered around him that he got
into a boat and sat down, and the whole crowd stood along
the shore. 3And he spoke to them at length in parables,
saying: "A sower went out to sow. 4And as he sowed, some
seed fell on the path, and birds came and ate it up. 5Some fell

on rocky ground, where it had little soil. It sprang up at once because the soil was not deep, [6]and when the sun rose it was scorched, and it withered for lack of roots. [7]Some seed fell among thorns, and the thorns grew up and choked it. [8]But some seed fell on rich soil, and produced fruit, a hundred or sixty or thirtyfold. [9]Whoever has ears ought to hear."

Thursday July 27, 2023

Thursday of Sixteenth Week Ordinary Time

First Reading – Exodus 19:1-2, 9-11, 16-20B

[1]In the third month after their departure from the land of Egypt, on its first day, the children of Israel came to the desert of Sinai. [2]After the journey from Rephidim to the desert of Sinai, they pitched camp. While Israel was encamped here in front of the mountain, [9]the LORD told Moses, "I am coming to you in a dense cloud, so that when the people hear me speaking with you, they may always have faith in you also." When Moses, then, had reported to the LORD the response of the people, [10]the LORD added, "Go to the people and have them sanctify themselves today and tomorrow. Make them wash their garments [11]and be ready for the third day; for on the third day the LORD will come down on Mount Sinai before the eyes of all the people." [16]On the morning of the third day there were peals of thunder and lightning, and a heavy cloud over the mountain, and a very loud trumpet blast, so that all the people in the camp trembled. [17]But Moses led the people out of the camp to meet God, and they stationed themselves at the foot of the mountain. [18]Mount Sinai was all wrapped in smoke, for the LORD came down upon it in fire. The smoke rose from it as though from a furnace, and the whole mountain trembled violently. [19]The trumpet blast grew louder and louder, while Moses was speaking and God answering him with thunder. [20AB]When the LORD came down to the top of Mount Sinai, he summoned Moses to the top of the mountain.

Responsorial Psalm – Daniel 3:52, 53, 54, 55, 56

R. (52b) Glory and praise for ever!

[52] "Blessed are you, O Lord, the God of our fathers,

praiseworthy and exalted above all forever;

And blessed is your holy and glorious name,

praiseworthy and exalted above all for all ages.”

R. Glory and praise for ever!

53 “Blessed are you in the temple of your holy glory,

praiseworthy and glorious above all forever.”

R. Glory and praise for ever!

54 “Blessed are you on the throne of your Kingdom,

praiseworthy and exalted above all forever.”

R. Glory and praise for ever!

55 “Blessed are you who look into the depths

from your throne upon the cherubim,

praiseworthy and exalted above all forever.”

R. Glory and praise for ever!

56 “Blessed are you in the firmament of heaven,

praiseworthy and glorious forever.”

R. Glory and praise for ever!

Alleluia – Matthew 11:25

R. Alleluia, alleluia.

25 Blessed are you, Father, Lord of heaven and earth; you have revealed to little ones the mysteries of the Kingdom.

R. Alleluia, alleluia.

Gospel – Matthew 13:10-17

10 The disciples approached Jesus and said, “Why do you
speak to the crowd in parables?” 11 He said to them in reply,
“Because knowledge of the mysteries of the Kingdom of
heaven has been granted to you, but to them it has not been
granted. 12 To anyone who has, more will be given and he will
grow rich; from anyone who has not, even what he has will be
taken away. 13 This is why I speak to them in parables,
because they look but do not see and hear but do not listen or
understand. 14 Isaiah’s prophecy is fulfilled in them, which says:
You shall indeed hear but not understand, you shall indeed
look but never see. 15 Gross is the heart of this people, they will
hardly hear with their ears, they have closed their eyes, lest

they see with their eyes and hear with their ears and
understand with their hearts and be converted and I heal
them. [16]"But blessed are your eyes, because they see, and
your ears, because they hear. [17]Amen, I say to you, many
prophets and righteous people longed to see what you see but
did not see it, and to hear what you hear but did not hear it."

Friday July 28, 2023

Friday of Sixteenth Week in Ordinary Time

First Reading – Exodus 20:1-17

In those days: [1]God delivered all these commandments: [2]"I,
the LORD, am your God, who brought you out of the land of
Egypt, that place of slavery. [3]You shall not have other gods
besides me. [4]You shall not carve idols for yourselves in the
shape of anything in the sky above or on the earth below or in
the waters beneath the earth; [5]you shall not bow down before
them or worship them. For I, the LORD, your God, am a
jealous God, inflicting punishment for their fathers' wickedness
on the children of those who hate me, down to the third and
fourth generation; [6]but bestowing mercy down to the
thousandth generation on the children of those who love me
and keep my commandments. [7]"You shall not take the name
of the LORD, your God, in vain. For the LORD will not leave
unpunished him who takes his name in vain. [8]"Remember to
keep holy the Sabbath day. [9]Six days you may labor and do all
your work, [10]but the seventh day is the Sabbath of the LORD,
your God. No work may be done then either by you, or your
son or daughter, or your male or female slave, or your beast,
or by the alien who lives with you. [11]In six days the LORD
made the heavens and the earth, the sea and all that is in
them; but on the seventh day he rested. That is why the LORD
has blessed the Sabbath day and made it holy. [12]"Honor your
father and your mother, that you may have a long life in the
land which the LORD, your God, is giving you. [13]"You shall not
kill. [14]"You shall not commit adultery. [15]"You shall not steal.
[16]"You shall not bear false witness against your neighbor.
[17]"You shall not covet your neighbor's house. You shall not
covet your neighbor's wife, nor his male or female slave, nor
his ox or ass, nor anything else that belongs to him."

Responsorial Psalm – Psalms 19:8, 9, 10, 11

R. (John 6:68c) **Lord, you have the words of everlasting life.**

8 he law of the LORD is perfect,

refreshing the soul;

The decree of the LORD is trustworthy,

giving wisdom to the simple.

R. Lord, you have the words of everlasting life.

9 The precepts of the LORD are right,

rejoicing the heart;

The command of the LORD is clear,

enlightening the eye.

R. Lord, you have the words of everlasting life.

10 The fear of the LORD is pure,

enduring forever;

The ordinances of the LORD are true,

all of them just.

R. Lord, you have the words of everlasting life.

11 They are more precious than gold,

than a heap of purest gold;

Sweeter also than syrup

or honey from the comb.

R. Lord, you have the words of everlasting life.

Alleluia – Luke 8:15

R. Alleluia, alleluia.

15 Blessed are they who have kept the word with a generous heart and yield a harvest through perseverance.

R. Alleluia, alleluia.

Gospel – Matthew 13:18-23

Jesus said to his disciples: 18“Hear the parable of the sower.
19The seed sown on the path is the one who hears the word of
the Kingdom without understanding it, and the Evil One comes
and steals away what was sown in his heart. 20The seed sown
on rocky ground is the one who hears the word and receives it
at once with joy. 21But he has no root and lasts only for a time.
When some tribulation or persecution comes because of the
word, he immediately falls away. 22The seed sown among
thorns is the one who hears the word, but then worldly anxiety
and the lure of riches choke the word and it bears no fruit.
23But the seed sown on rich soil is the one who hears the word
and understands it, who indeed bears fruit and yields a
hundred or sixty or thirty-fold.”

Saturday July 29, 2023

Memorial of Saints Martha

First Reading – Exodus 24:3-8

3When Moses came to the people and related all the words
and ordinances of the LORD, they all answered with one
voice, “We will do everything that the LORD has told us.”
4Moses then wrote down all the words of the LORD and, rising
early the next day, he erected at the foot of the mountain an
altar and twelve pillars for the twelve tribes of Israel. 5Then,
having sent certain young men of the children of Israel to offer
burnt offerings and sacrifice young bulls as peace offerings to
the LORD, 6Moses took half of the blood and put it in large
bowls; the other half he splashed on the altar. 7Taking the
book of the covenant, he read it aloud to the people, who
answered, “All that the LORD has said, we will heed and do.”
8Then he took the blood and sprinkled it on the people, saying,
“This is the blood of the covenant that the LORD has made
with you in accordance with all these words of his.”

Responsorial Psalm – Psalms 50:1B-2, 5-6, 14-15

R. (14a) Offer to God a sacrifice of praise.

1B God the LORD has spoken and summoned the earth,

from the rising of the sun to its setting.

2 From Zion, perfect in beauty,

God shines forth.

R. Offer to God a sacrifice of praise.

[5] "Gather my faithful ones before me,

those who have made a covenant with me by sacrifice."

[6] And the heavens proclaim his justice;

for God himself is the judge.

R. Offer to God a sacrifice of praise.

[14] "Offer to God praise as your sacrifice

and fulfill your vows to the Most High;

[15] Then call upon me in time of distress;

I will rescue you, and you shall glorify me."

R. Offer to God a sacrifice of praise.

Alleluia – James 1:21BC

R. Alleluia, alleluia.

[21BC] Humbly welcome the word that has been planted in you and is able to save your souls.

R. Alleluia, alleluia.

Gospel – Matthew 13:24-30

[24]Jesus proposed a parable to the crowds. "The Kingdom of
heaven may be likened to a man who sowed good seed in his
field. [25]While everyone was asleep his enemy came and
sowed weeds all through the wheat, and then went off. [26]When
the crop grew and bore fruit, the weeds appeared as well.
[27]The slaves of the householder came to him and said,
'Master, did you not sow good seed in your field? Where have
the weeds come from?' [28]He answered, 'An enemy has done
this.' His slaves said to him, 'Do you want us to go and pull
them up?' [29]He replied, 'No, if you pull up the weeds you might
uproot the wheat along with them. [30]Let them grow together
until harvest; then at harvest time I will say to the harvesters,
"First collect the weeds and tie them in bundles for burning;
but gather the wheat into my barn."

Sunday July 30, 2023

Seventeenth Sunday in Ordinary Time Year A

First Reading – 1 Kings 3:5, 7-12

5 The LORD appeared to Solomon in a dream at night. God
said, "Ask something of me and I will give it to you." 7 Solomon
answered: "O LORD, my God, you have made me, your
servant, king to succeed my father David; but I am a mere
youth, not knowing at all how to act. 8 I serve you in the midst
of the people whom you have chosen, a people so vast that it
cannot be numbered or counted. 9 Give your servant,
therefore, an understanding heart to judge your people and to
distinguish right from wrong. For who is able to govern this
vast people of yours?" 10 The LORD was pleased that Solomon
made this request. 11 So God said to him: "Because you have
asked for this not for a long life for yourself, nor for riches, nor
for the life of your enemies, but for understanding so that you
may know what is right 12 I do as you requested. I give you a
heart so wise and understanding that there has never been
anyone like you up to now, and after you there will come no
one to equal you."

Responsorial Psalm – Psalms 119:57, 72, 76-77, 127-128, 129-130

R. (97a) Lord, I love your commands.

57 I have said, O LORD, that my part

is to keep your words.

72 The law of your mouth is to me more precious

than thousands of gold and silver pieces.

R. Lord, I love your commands.

76 Let your kindness comfort me

according to your promise to your servants.

77 Let your compassion come to me that I may live,

for your law is my delight.

R. Lord, I love your commands.

127 For I love your command

more than gold, however fine.

128 For in all your precepts I go forward;

every false way I hate.

R. Lord, I love your commands.

129 Wonderful are your decrees;

therefore I observe them.

130 The revelation of your words sheds light,

giving understanding to the simple.

R. Lord, I love your commands.

Second Reading – Romans 8:28-30

Brothers and sisters: 28We know that all things work for good
for those who love God, who are called according to his
purpose. 29For those he foreknew he also predestined to be
conformed to the image of his Son, so that he might be the
firstborn among many brothers and sisters. 30And those he
predestined he also called; and those he called he also
justified; and those he justified he also glorified.

Alleluia – Matthew 11:25

R. Alleluia, alleluia.

25 Blessed are you, Father, Lord of heaven and earth; for you
have revealed to little ones the mysteries of the kingdom.

R. Alleluia, alleluia.

Gospel – Matthew 13:44-52

Jesus said to his disciples: 44"The kingdom of heaven is like a
treasure buried in a field, which a person finds and hides
again, and out of joy goes and sells all that he has and buys
that field. 45Again, the kingdom of heaven is like a merchant
searching for fine pearls. 46When he finds a pearl of great
price, he goes and sells all that he has and buys it. 47Again,
the kingdom of heaven is like a net thrown into the sea, which
collects fish of every kind. 48When it is full they haul it ashore
and sit down to put what is good into buckets. What is bad
they throw away. 49Thus it will be at the end of the age. The
angels will go out and separate the wicked from the righteous

[50]and throw them into the fiery furnace, where there will be wailing and grinding of teeth. [51]"Do you understand all these things?" They answered, "Yes." [52]And he replied, "Then every scribe who has been instructed in the kingdom of heaven is like the head of a household who brings from his storeroom both the new and the old."

Or Matthew 13:44-46

Jesus said to his disciples: [44]"The kingdom of heaven is like a treasure buried in a field, which a person finds and hides again, and out of joy goes and sells all that he has and buys that field. [45]Again, the kingdom of heaven is like a merchant searching for fine pearls. [46]When he finds a pearl of great price, he goes and sells all that he has and buys it.

Monday June 31, 2023

Memorial of Saint Ignatius Loyola – Priest

First Reading – Exodus 32:15-24, 30-34

[15]Moses turned and came down the mountain with the two tablets of the commandments in his hands, tablets that were written on both sides, front and back; [16]tablets that were made by God, having inscriptions on them that were engraved by God himself. [17]Now, when Joshua heard the noise of the people shouting, he said to Moses, "That sounds like a battle in the camp." [18]But Moses answered, "It does not sound like cries of victory, nor does it sound like cries of defeat; the sounds that I hear are cries of revelry." [19]As he drew near the camp, he saw the calf and the dancing. With that, Moses' wrath flared up, so that he threw the tablets down and broke them on the base of the mountain. [20]Taking the calf they had made, he fused it in the fire and then ground it down to powder, which he scattered on the water and made the children of Israel drink. [21]Moses asked Aaron, "What did this people ever do to you that you should lead them into so grave a sin?" [22]Aaron replied, "Let not my lord be angry. You know well enough how prone the people are to evil. [23]They said to me, 'Make us a god to be our leader; as for the man Moses who brought us out of the land of Egypt, we do not know what has happened to him.' [24]So I told them, 'Let anyone who has gold jewelry take it off.' They gave it to me, and I threw it into the fire, and this calf came out." [30]On the next day Moses said

to the people, “You have committed a grave sin. I will go up to the LORD, then; perhaps I may be able to make atonement for your sin.”
31So Moses went back to the LORD and said, “Ah, this people has indeed committed a grave sin in making a god of gold for themselves!
32If you would only forgive their sin! If you will not, then strike me out of the book that you have written.”
33The LORD answered, “Him only who has sinned against me will I strike out of my book.
34Now, go and lead the people to the place I have told you. My angel will go before you. When it is time for me to punish, I will punish them for their sin.”

Responsorial Psalm – Psalms 106:19-20, 21-22, 23

R. (1a) Give thanks to the Lord, for he is good.

19 Our fathers made a calf in Horeb

and adored a molten image;

20 They exchanged their glory

for the image of a grass-eating bullock.

R. Give thanks to the Lord, for he is good.

21 They forgot the God who had saved them,

who had done great deeds in Egypt,

22 Wondrous deeds in the land of Ham,

terrible things at the Red Sea.

R. Give thanks to the Lord, for he is good.

23 Then he spoke of exterminating them,

but Moses, his chosen one,

Withstood him in the breach

to turn back his destructive wrath.

R. Give thanks to the Lord, for he is good.

Alleluia – James 1:18

R. Alleluia, alleluia.

18 The Father willed to give us birth by the word of truth that we may be a kind of first-fruits of his creatures.

R. Alleluia, alleluia.

Gospel – Matthew 13:31-35

[31]Jesus proposed a parable to the crowds. "The Kingdom of heaven is like a mustard seed that a person took and sowed in a field. [32]It is the smallest of all the seeds, yet when full-grown it is the largest of plants. It becomes a large bush, and the birds of the sky come and dwell in its branches." [33]He spoke to them another parable. "The Kingdom of heaven is like yeast that a woman took and mixed with three measures of wheat flour until the whole batch was leavened." [34]All these things Jesus spoke to the crowds in parables. He spoke to them only in parables, [35]to fulfill what had been said through the prophet: I will open my mouth in parables, I will announce what has lain hidden from the foundation of the world.

AUGUST 2023

Tuesday August 1, 2023

Memorial of Saint Alphonsus Liguori, Bishop & Doctor

First Reading - Exodus 33: 7-11; 34: 5b-9, 28

[7]Moses also taking the tabernacle, pitched it without the camp afar off, and called the name thereof, The tabernacle of the covenant. And all the people that had any question, went forth to the tabernacle of the covenant, without the camp. [8]And when Moses went forth to the tabernacle, all the people rose up, and every one stood in the door of his pavilion, and they beheld the back of Moses, till he went into the tabernacle. [9]And when he was gone into the tabernacle of the covenant, the pillar of the cloud came down, and stood at the door, and he spoke with Moses. [10]And all saw that the pillar of the cloud stood at the door of the tabernacle. And they stood, and worshipped at the doors of their tents. [11]And the Lord spoke to Moses face to face, as a man is wont to speak to his friend. And when he returned into the camp, his servant Josue the son of Nun, a young man, departed not from the tabernacle. [34:5b] Moses stood with him, calling upon the name of the Lord. [6]And when he passed before him, he said: O the Lord, the Lord God, merciful and gracious, patient and of much compassion, and true, [7]Who keepest mercy unto thousands: who takest away iniquity, and wickedness, and sin, and no

man of himself is innocent before thee. Who renderest the
iniquity of the fathers to the children, and to the grandchildren,
unto the third and fourth generation. 8 And Moses making
haste, bowed down prostrate unto the earth, and adoring,
9 Said: If I have found grace in thy sight: O Lord, I beseech
thee, that thou wilt go with us, (for it is a stiffnecked people,)
and take away our iniquities and sin, and possess us. 28 And
he was there with the Lord forty days and forty nights: he
neither ate bread nor drank water, and he wrote upon the
tables the ten words of the covenant.

Responsorial Psalm - Psalms 103: 6-7, 8-9, 10-11, 12-13

R. (8a) The Lord is kind and merciful.

6 The Lord doth mercies, and judgment for all that suffer wrong.

7 He hath made his ways known to Moses: his wills to the children of Israel.

R. The Lord is kind and merciful.

8 The Lord is compassionate and merciful: longsuffering and plenteous in mercy.

9 He will not always be angry: nor will he threaten for ever.

R. The Lord is kind and merciful.

10 He hath not dealt with us according to our sins: nor rewarded us according to our iniquities.

11 For according to the height of the heaven above the earth: he hath strengthened his mercy towards them that fear him.

R. The Lord is kind and merciful.

12 As far as the east is from the west, so far hath he removed our iniquities from us.

13 As a father hath compassion on his children, so hath the Lord compassion on them that fear him:

R. The Lord is kind and merciful.

Alleluia

R. Alleluia, alleluia.

The seed is the word of God, Christ is the sower; all who come to him will live for ever.

R. Alleluia, alleluia.

Gospel - Matthew 13: 36-43

[36]Then having sent away the multitudes, he came into the
house, and his disciples came to him, saying: Expound to us
the parable of the cockle of the field. [37]Who made answer and
said to them: He that soweth the good seed, is the Son of
man. [38]And the field, is the world. And the good seed are the
children of the kingdom. And the cockle, are the children of the
wicked one. [39]And the enemy that sowed them, is the devil.
But the harvest is the end of the world. And the reapers are
the angels. [40]Even as cockle therefore is gathered up, and
burnt with fire: so shall it be at the end of the world. [41]The Son
of man shall send his angels, and they shall gather out of his
kingdom all scandals, and them that work iniquity. [42]And shall
cast them into the furnace of fire: there shall be weeping and
gnashing of teeth. [43]Then shall the just shine as the sun, in the
kingdom of their Father. He that hath ears to hear, let him
hear.

Wednesday August 2, 2023

Wednesday of Seventeenth Week in Ordinary Time

First Reading – Exodus 34:29-35

[29]As Moses came down from Mount Sinai with the two tablets
of the commandments in his hands, he did not know that the
skin of his face had become radiant while he conversed with
the LORD. [30]When Aaron, then, and the other children of
Israel saw Moses and noticed how radiant the skin of his face
had become, they were afraid to come near him. [31]Only after
Moses called to them did Aaron and all the rulers of the
community come back to him. Moses then spoke to them.
[32]Later on, all the children of Israel came up to him, and he
enjoined on them all that the LORD had told him on Mount
Sinai. [33]When he finished speaking with them, he put a veil
over his face. [34]Whenever Moses entered the presence of the
LORD to converse with him, he removed the veil until he came

out again. On coming out, he would tell the children of Israel all that had been commanded. [35]Then the children of Israel would see that the skin of Moses' face was radiant; so he would again put the veil over his face until he went in to converse with the LORD.

Responsorial Psalm – Psalms 99:5, 6, 7, 9

R. (see 9c) Holy is the Lord our God.

[5] Extol the LORD, our God,

and worship at his footstool;

holy is he!

R. Holy is the Lord our God.

[6] Moses and Aaron were among his priests,

and Samuel, among those who called upon his name;

they called upon the LORD, and he answered them.

R. Holy is the Lord our God.

[7] From the pillar of cloud he spoke to them;

they heard his decrees and the law he gave them.

R. Holy is the Lord our God.

[9] Extol the LORD, our God,

and worship at his holy mountain;

for holy is the LORD, our God.

R. Holy is the Lord our God.

Alleluia – John 15:15B

R. Alleluia, alleluia.

[15B] I call you my friends, says the Lord, for I have made known to you all that the Father has told me.

R. Alleluia, alleluia.

Gospel – Matthew 13:44-46

Jesus said to his disciples: [44]"The Kingdom of heaven is like a treasure buried in a field, which a person finds and hides again, and out of joy goes and sells all that he has and buys

that field. [45]Again, the Kingdom of heaven is like a merchant
searching for fine pearls. [46]When he finds a pearl of great
price, he goes and sells all that he has and buys it."

Thursday August 3, 2023

Thursday of Seventeenth Week in Ordinary Time

First Reading – Exodus 40:16-21, 34-38

[16]Moses did exactly as the LORD had commanded him. [17]On
the first day of the first month of the second year the Dwelling
was erected. [18]It was Moses who erected the Dwelling. He
placed its pedestals, set up its boards, put in its bars, and set
up its columns. [19]He spread the tent over the Dwelling and put
the covering on top of the tent, as the LORD had commanded
him. [20]He took the commandments and put them in the ark; he
placed poles alongside the ark and set the propitiatory upon it.
[21]He brought the ark into the Dwelling and hung the curtain
veil, thus screening off the ark of the commandments, as the
LORD had commanded him. [34]Then the cloud covered the
meeting tent, and the glory of the LORD filled the Dwelling.
[35]Moses could not enter the meeting tent, because the cloud
settled down upon it and the glory of the LORD filled the
Dwelling. [36]Whenever the cloud rose from the Dwelling, the
children of Israel would set out on their journey. [37]But if the
cloud did not lift, they would not go forward; only when it lifted
did they go forward. [38]In the daytime the cloud of the LORD
was seen over the Dwelling; whereas at night, fire was seen in
the cloud by the whole house of Israel in all the stages of their
journey.

Responsorial Psalm – Psalms 84:3, 4, 5-6A AND 8A, 11

R. (2) How lovely is your dwelling place, O Lord, mighty God!

[3] My soul yearns and pines

for the courts of the LORD.

My heart and my flesh

cry out for the living God.

R. How lovely is your dwelling place, O Lord, mighty God!

[4] Even the sparrow finds a home,

and the swallow a nest

in which she puts her young–

Your altars, O LORD of hosts,

my king and my God!

R. How lovely is your dwelling place, O Lord, mighty God!

[5] Blessed they who dwell in your house!

continually they praise you.

[36A] Blessed the men whose strength you are!

[8A] They go from strength to strength.

R. How lovely is your dwelling place, O Lord, mighty God!

[11] I had rather one day in your courts

than a thousand elsewhere;

I had rather lie at the threshold of the house of my God

than dwell in the tents of the wicked.

R. How lovely is your dwelling place, O Lord, mighty God!

Alleluia – Acts 16:14B

R. Alleluia, alleluia.

[14B] Open our hearts, O Lord, to listen to the words of your Son.

R. Alleluia, alleluia.

Gospel – Matthew 13:47-53

Jesus said to the disciples: [47]"The Kingdom of heaven is like a
net thrown into the sea, which collects fish of every kind.
[48]When it is full they haul it ashore and sit down to put what is
good into buckets. What is bad they throw away. [49]Thus it will
be at the end of the age. The angels will go out and separate
the wicked from the righteous. [50]and throw them into the fiery
furnace, where there will be wailing and grinding of teeth."
[51]"Do you understand all these things?" They answered, "Yes."
[52]And he replied, "Then every scribe who has been instructed
in the Kingdom of heaven is like the head of a household who

brings from his storeroom both the new and the old." 53When
Jesus finished these parables, he went away from there.

Friday August 4, 2023

Memorial of Saint John Vianney, Priest

First Reading – Leviticus 23:1, 4-11, 15-16, 27, 34B-37

1The LORD said to Moses, 4"These are the festivals of the
LORD which you shall celebrate at their proper time with a
sacred assembly. 5The Passover of the LORD falls on the
fourteenth day of the first month, at the evening twilight. 6The
fifteenth day of this month is the LORD's feast of Unleavened
Bread. For seven days you shall eat unleavened bread. 7On
the first of these days you shall hold a sacred assembly and
do no sort of work. 8On each of the seven days you shall offer
an oblation to the LORD. Then on the seventh day you shall
again hold a sacred assembly and do no sort of work." 9The
LORD said to Moses, 10"Speak to the children of Israel and tell
them: When you come into the land which I am giving you,
and reap your harvest, you shall bring a sheaf of the first fruits
of your harvest to the priest, 11who shall wave the sheaf before
the LORD that it may be acceptable for you. On the day after
the Sabbath the priest shall do this.15"Beginning with the day
after the Sabbath, the day on which you bring the wave-
offering sheaf, 16you shall count seven full weeks, and then on
the day after the seventh week, the fiftieth day, you shall
present the new cereal offering to the LORD. 27"The tenth of
this seventh month is the Day of Atonement, when you shall
hold a sacred assembly and mortify yourselves and offer an
oblation to the LORD. 34B"The fifteenth day of this seventh
month is the LORD's feast of Booths, which shall continue for
seven days. 35On the first day there shall be a sacred
assembly, and you shall do no sort of work. 36For seven days
you shall offer an oblation to the LORD, and on the eighth day
you shall again hold a sacred assembly and offer an oblation
to the LORD. On that solemn closing you shall do no sort of
work. 37"These, therefore, are the festivals of the LORD on
which you shall proclaim a sacred assembly, and offer as an
oblation to the LORD burnt offerings and cereal offerings,
sacrifices and libations, as prescribed for each day."

Responsorial Psalm – Psalms 81:3-4, 5-6, 10-11AB

R. (2a) Sing with joy to God our help.

3 Take up a melody, and sound the timbrel,

the pleasant harp and the lyre.

4 Blow the trumpet at the new moon,

at the full moon, on our solemn feast.

R. Sing with joy to God our help.

5 For it is a statute in Israel,

an ordinance of the God of Jacob,

6 Who made it a decree for Joseph

when he came forth from the land of Egypt.

R. Sing with joy to God our help.

10 There shall be no strange god among you

nor shall you worship any alien god.

11AB I, the LORD, am your God

who led you forth from the land of Egypt.

R. Sing with joy to God our help.

Alleluia – 1 Peter 1:25

R. Alleluia, alleluia.

25 The word of the Lord remains forever; This is the word that has been proclaimed to you.

R. Alleluia, alleluia.

Gospel – Matthew 13:54-58

54Jesus came to his native place and taught the people in their
synagogue. They were astonished and said, "Where did this
man get such wisdom and mighty deeds? 55Is he not the
carpenter's son? Is not his mother named Mary and his
brothers James, Joseph, Simon, and Judas? 56Are not his
sisters all with us? Where did this man get all this?" 57And they
took offense at him. But Jesus said to them, "A prophet is not
without honor except in his native place and in his own

house." [58]And he did not work many mighty deeds there because of their lack of faith.

Saturday August 5, 2023

Saturday of Seventeenth Week in Ordinary Time

First Reading – Leviticus 25:1, 8-17

[1]The LORD said to Moses on Mount Sinai, [8]"Seven weeks of years shall you count–seven times seven years– so that the seven cycles amount to forty-nine years. [9]Then, on the tenth day of the seventh month, let the trumpet resound; on this, the Day of Atonement, the trumpet blast shall re-echo throughout your land. [10]This fiftieth year you shall make sacred by proclaiming liberty in the land for all its inhabitants. It shall be a jubilee for you, when every one of you shall return to his own property, everyone to his own family estate. [11]In this fiftieth year, your year of jubilee, you shall not sow, nor shall you reap the after growth or pick the grapes from the untrimmed vines. [12]Since this is the jubilee, which shall be sacred for you, you may not eat of its produce, except as taken directly from the field. [13]"In this year of jubilee, then, every one of you shall return to his own property. [14]Therefore, when you sell any land to your neighbor or buy any from him, do not deal unfairly. [15]On the basis of the number of years since the last jubilee shall you purchase the land from your neighbor; and so also, on the basis of the number of years for crops, shall he sell it to you. [16]When the years are many, the price shall be so much the more; when the years are few, the price shall be so much the less. For it is really the number of crops that he sells you.[17]Do not deal unfairly, then; but stand in fear of your God. I, the LORD, am your God."

Responsorial Psalm – Psalms 67:2-3, 5, 7-8

R. (4) O God, let all the nations praise you!

[2] May God have pity on us and bless us;

may he let his face shine upon us.

[3] So may your way be known upon earth;

among all nations, your salvation.

R. O God, let all the nations praise you!

[5] May the nations be glad and exult

because you rule the peoples in equity;

the nations on the earth you guide.

R. O God, let all the nations praise you!

[7] The earth has yielded its fruits;

God, our God, has blessed us.

[8] May God bless us,

and may all the ends of the earth fear him!

R. O God, let all the nations praise you!

Alleluia – Matthew 5:10

R. Alleluia, alleluia.

[10] Blessed are they who are persecuted for the sake of righteousness for theirs is the Kingdom of heaven.

R. Alleluia, alleluia.

Gospel – Matthew 14:1-12

[1]Herod the tetrarch heard of the reputation of Jesus [2]and said
to his servants, "This man is John the Baptist. He has been
raised from the dead; that is why mighty powers are at work in
him." [3]Now Herod had arrested John, bound him, and put him
in prison on account of Herodias, the wife of his brother Philip,
[4]for John had said to him, "It is not lawful for you to have her."
[5]Although he wanted to kill him, he feared the people, for they
regarded him as a prophet. [6]But at a birthday celebration for
Herod, the daughter of Herodias performed a dance before
the guests and delighted Herod [7]so much that he swore to
give her whatever she might ask for. [8]Prompted by her
mother, she said, "Give me here on a platter the head of John
the Baptist." [9]The king was distressed, but because of his
oaths and the guests who were present, he ordered that it be
given, [10]and he had John beheaded in the prison. [11]His head
was brought in on a platter and given to the girl, who took it to
her mother. [12]His disciples came and took away the corpse
and buried him; and they went and told Jesus.

Sunday August 6, 2023

Feast of the Transfiguration of the Lord

First Reading – Daniel 7:9-10, 13-14

9 Thrones were set up and the Ancient One took his throne. His
clothing was bright as snow, and the hair on his head as white
as wool; his throne was flames of fire, with wheels of burning
fire. 10 A surging stream of fire flowed out from where he sat;
Thousands upon thousands were ministering to him, and
myriads upon myriads attended him. The court was convened
and the books were opened. 13 As the visions during the night
continued, I saw: One like a Son of man coming, on the clouds
of heaven; When he reached the Ancient One and was
presented before him, 14 The one like a Son of man received
dominion, glory, and kingship; all peoples, nations, and
languages serve him. His dominion is an everlasting dominion
that shall not be taken away, his kingship shall not be
destroyed.

Responsorial Psalm – Psalms 97:1-2, 5-6, 9

R.(1a and 9a) The Lord is king, the Most High over all the earth.

1 The LORD is king; let the earth rejoice;

let the many islands be glad.

2 Clouds and darkness are round about him,

justice and judgment are the foundation of his throne.

R. The Lord is king, the Most High over all the earth.

5 The mountains melt like wax before the LORD,

before the LORD of all the earth.

6 The heavens proclaim his justice,

and all peoples see his glory.

R. The Lord is king, the Most High over all the earth.

9 Because you, O LORD, are the Most High over all the earth,

exalted far above all gods.

R. The Lord is king, the Most High over all the earth.

Second Reading – 2 Peter 1:16-19

Beloved: [16]We did not follow cleverly devised myths when we made known to you the power and coming of our Lord Jesus Christ, but we had been eyewitnesses of his majesty. [17]For he received honor and glory from God the Father when that unique declaration came to him from the majestic glory, "This is my Son, my beloved, with whom I am well pleased." [18]We ourselves heard this voice come from heaven while we were with him on the holy mountain.[19]Moreover, we possess the prophetic message that is altogether reliable. You will do well to be attentive to it, as to a lamp shining in a dark place, until day dawns and the morning star rises in your hearts.

Alleluia – Matthew 17:5C

R. Alleluia, alleluia.

[5C] This is my beloved Son, with whom I am well-pleased; listen to him.

R. Alleluia, alleluia.

Gospel – Mark 9:2-10

[2]Jesus took Peter, James, and his brother John, and led them up a high mountain apart by themselves. And he was transfigured before them, [3]and his clothes became dazzling white, such as no fuller on earth could bleach them. [4]Then Elijah appeared to them along with Moses, and they were conversing with Jesus. [5]Then Peter said to Jesus in reply, "Rabbi, it is good that we are here! Let us make three tents: one for you, one for Moses, and one for Elijah." [6]He hardly knew what to say, they were so terrified. [7]Then a cloud came, casting a shadow over them; from the cloud came a voice, "This is my beloved Son. Listen to him." [8]Suddenly, looking around, they no longer saw anyone but Jesus alone with them. [9]As they were coming down from the mountain, he charged them not to relate what they had seen to anyone, except when the Son of Man had risen from the dead. [10]So they kept the matter to themselves, questioning what rising from the dead meant.

Monday August 7, 2023

Monday of Eighteenth Week in Ordinary Time

First Reading – Numbers 11:4B-15

The children of Israel lamented, [4B]"Would that we had meat for food! [5]We remember the fish we used to eat without cost in Egypt, and the cucumbers, the melons, the leeks, the onions, and the garlic. [6]But now we are famished; we see nothing before us but this manna." [7]Manna was like coriander seed and had the color of resin. [8]When they had gone about and gathered it up, the people would grind it between millstones or pound it in a mortar, then cook it in a pot and make it into loaves, which tasted like cakes made with oil. [9]At night, when the dew fell upon the camp, the manna also fell. [10]When Moses heard the people, family after family, crying at the entrance of their tents, so that the LORD became very angry, he was grieved. [11]"Why do you treat your servant so badly?" Moses asked the LORD. "Why are you so displeased with me that you burden me with all this people? [12]Was it I who conceived all this people? Or was it I who gave them birth, that you tell me to carry them at my bosom, like a foster father carrying an infant, to the land you have promised under oath to their fathers? [13]Where can I get meat to give to all this people? For they are crying to me, 'Give us meat for our food.' [14]I cannot carry all this people by myself, for they are too heavy for me. [15]If this is the way you will deal with me, then please do me the favor of killing me at once, so that I need no longer face this distress."

Responsorial Psalm – Psalms 81:12-13, 14-15, 16-17

R. [(2a)]Sing with joy to God our help.

[12] "My people heard not my voice,

and Israel obeyed me not;

[13] So I gave them up to the hardness of their hearts;

they walked according to their own counsels."

R. Sing with joy to God our help.

[14] "If only my people would hear me,

and Israel walk in my ways,

15 Quickly would I humble their enemies;

against their foes I would turn my hand."

R. Sing with joy to God our help.

16 "Those who hated the LORD would seek to flatter me,

but their fate would endure forever,

17 While Israel I would feed with the best of wheat,

and with honey from the rock I would fill them."

R. Sing with joy to God our help.

Alleluia – Matthew 4:4

R. Alleluia, alleluia.

4 One does not live on bread alone, but on every word that comes forth from the mouth of God.

R. Alleluia, alleluia.

Gospel – Matthew 14:13-21

13 When Jesus heard of the death of John the Baptist, he
withdrew in a boat to a deserted place by himself. The crowds
heard of this and followed him on foot from their towns.
14 When he disembarked and saw the vast crowd, his heart
was moved with pity for them, and he cured their sick. 15 When
it was evening, the disciples approached him and said, "This is
a deserted place and it is already late; dismiss the crowds so
that they can go to the villages and buy food for themselves."
16 He said to them, "There is no need for them to go away; give
them some food yourselves." 17 But they said to him, "Five
loaves and two fish are all we have here." 18 Then he said,
"Bring them here to me," 19 and he ordered the crowds to sit
down on the grass. Taking the five loaves and the two fish,
and looking up to heaven, he said the blessing, broke the
loaves, and gave them to the disciples, who in turn gave them
to the crowds. 20 They all ate and were satisfied, and they
picked up the fragments left over– twelve wicker baskets full.
21 Those who ate were about five thousand men, not counting
women and children.

Tuesday August 8, 2023

Memorial of Saint Dominic - Priest

First Reading – Numbers 12:1-13

[1]Miriam and Aaron spoke against Moses on the pretext of the
marriage he had contracted with a Cushite woman. [2]They
complained, “Is it through Moses alone that the LORD
speaks? Does he not speak through us also?” And the LORD
heard this. [3]Now, Moses himself was by far the meekest man
on the face of the earth. [4]So at once the LORD said to Moses
and Aaron and Miriam, “Come out, you three, to the meeting
tent.” And the three of them went. [5]Then the LORD came
down in the column of cloud, and standing at the entrance of
the tent, called Aaron and Miriam. When both came forward,
[6]he said, “Now listen to the words of the LORD: Should there
be a prophet among you, in visions will I reveal myself to him,
in dreams will I speak to him; [7]not so with my servant Moses!
Throughout my house he bears my trust: [8]face to face I speak
to him; plainly and not in riddles. The presence of the LORD
he beholds. Why, then, did you not fear to speak against my
servant Moses?” [9]So angry was the LORD against them that
when he departed, [10]and the cloud withdrew from the tent,
there was Miriam, a snow-white leper! When Aaron turned and
saw her a leper, [11]he said to Moses, “Ah, my lord! Please do
not charge us with the sin that we have foolishly committed!
[12]Let her not thus be like the stillborn babe that comes forth
from its mother’s womb with its flesh half consumed.” [13]Then
Moses cried to the LORD, “Please, not this! Pray, heal her!”

Responsorial Psalm – Psalms 51:3-4, 5-6AB, 6CD-7, 12-13

R. (see 3a) **Be merciful, O Lord, for we have sinned.**

[3] Have mercy on me, O God, in your goodness;

in the greatness of your compassion wipe out my offense.

[4] Thoroughly wash me from my guilt

and of my sin cleanse me.

R. Be merciful, O Lord, for we have sinned.

[5] For I acknowledge my offense;

and my sin is before me always:

6AB "Against you only have I sinned;

and done what is evil in your sight."

R. Be merciful, O Lord, for we have sinned.

6CD That you may be justified in your sentence,

vindicated when you condemn.

7 Indeed, in guilt was I born,

and in sin my mother conceived me.

R. Be merciful, O Lord, for we have sinned.

12 A clean heart create for me, O God,

and a steadfast spirit renew within me.

13 Cast me not off from your presence,

and your Holy Spirit take not from me.

R. Be merciful, O Lord, for we have sinned.

Alleluia – John 1:49B

R. Alleluia, alleluia.

49B Rabbi, you are the Son of God; you are the King of Israel.

R. Alleluia, alleluia.

Gospel – Matthew 15:1-2, 10-14

1Some Pharisees and scribes came to Jesus from Jerusalem
and said, 2"Why do your disciples break the tradition of the
elders? They do not wash their hands when they eat a meal."
10He summoned the crowd and said to them, "Hear and
understand. 11It is not what enters one's mouth that defiles the
man; but what comes out of the mouth is what defiles one."
12Then his disciples approached and said to him, "Do you
know that the Pharisees took offense when they heard what
you said?" 13He said in reply, "Every plant that my heavenly
Father has not planted will be uprooted. 14Let them alone; they
are blind guides of the blind. If a blind man leads a blind man,
both will fall into a pit."

Wednesday August 9, 2023

Wednesday of Eighteenth Week in Ordinary Time

First Reading – Numbers 13:1-2, 25-14:1, 26A-29A, 34-35

1The LORD said to Moses [in the desert of Paran,] 2"Send
men to reconnoitre the land of Canaan, which I am giving the
children of Israel. You shall send one man from each ancestral
tribe, all of them princes." 25After reconnoitring the land for
forty days they returned, 26met Moses and Aaron and the
whole congregation of the children of Israel in the desert of
Paran at Kadesh, made a report to them all, and showed the
fruit of the country to the whole congregation. 27They told
Moses: "We went into the land to which you sent us. It does
indeed flow with milk and honey, and here is its fruit.
28However, the people who are living in the land are fierce,
and the towns are fortified and very strong. Besides, we saw
descendants of the Anakim there. 29Amalekites live in the
region of the Negeb; Hittites, Jebusites, and Amorites dwell in
the highlands, and Canaanites along the seacoast and the
banks of the Jordan." 30Caleb, however, to quiet the people
toward Moses, said, "We ought to go up and seize the land,
for we can certainly do so." 31But the men who had gone up
with him said, "We cannot attack these people; they are too
strong for us." 32So they spread discouraging reports among
the children of Israel about the land they had scouted, saying,
"The land that we explored is a country that consumes its
inhabitants. 33And all the people we saw there are huge,
veritable giants (the Anakim were a race of giants); we felt like
mere grasshoppers, and so we must have seemed to them."
1At this, the whole community broke out with loud cries, and
even in the night the people wailed. 26AThe LORD said to
Moses and Aaron: 27"How long will this wicked assembly
grumble against me? I have heard the grumblings of the
children of Israel against me. 28Tell them: By my life, says the
LORD, I will do to you just what I have heard you say. 29AHere
in the desert shall your dead bodies fall. 34Forty days you
spent in scouting the land; forty years shall you suffer for your
crimes: one year for each day. Thus you will realize what it
means to oppose me.35I, the LORD, have sworn to do this to
all this wicked assembly that conspired against me: here in the
desert they shall die to the last man."

Responsorial Psalm – Psalms 106:6-7AB, 13-14, 21-22, 23

R.(4a) Remember us, O Lord, as you favor your people.

6 We have sinned, we and our fathers;

we have committed crimes; we have done wrong.

7AB Our fathers in Egypt

considered not your wonders.

R. Remember us, O Lord, as you favor your people.

13 But soon they forgot his works;

they waited not for his counsel.

14 They gave way to craving in the desert

and tempted God in the wilderness.

R. Remember us, O Lord, as you favor your people.

21 They forgot the God who had saved them,

who had done great deeds in Egypt,

22 Wondrous deeds in the land of Ham,

terrible things at the Red Sea.

R. Remember us, O Lord, as you favor your people.

23 Then he spoke of exterminating them,

but Moses, his chosen one,

Withstood him in the breach

to turn back his destructive wrath.

R. Remember us, O Lord, as you favor your people.

Alleluia – Luke 7:16

R. Alleluia, alleluia.

16 A great prophet has arisen in our midst and God has visited his people.

R. Alleluia, alleluia.

Gospel – Matthew 15:21-28

[21]At that time Jesus withdrew to the region of Tyre and Sidon. [22]And behold, a Canaanite woman of that district came and called out, “Have pity on me, Lord, Son of David! My daughter is tormented by a demon.” [23]But he did not say a word in answer to her. His disciples came and asked him, “Send her away, for she keeps calling out after us.” [24]He said in reply, “I was sent only to the lost sheep of the house of Israel.” [25]But the woman came and did him homage, saying, “Lord, help me.” [26]He said in reply, “It is not right to take the food of the children and throw it to the dogs.” [27]She said, “Please, Lord, for even the dogs eat the scraps that fall from the table of their masters.” [28]Then Jesus said to her in reply, “O woman, great is your faith! Let it be done for you as you wish.” And her daughter was healed from that hour.

Thursday August 10, 2023

Feast of Saint Lawrence, Deacon and Martyr

First Reading – 2 Corinthians 9:6-10

Brothers and sisters: [6]Whoever sows sparingly will also reap sparingly, and whoever sows bountifully will also reap bountifully. [7]Each must do as already determined, without sadness or compulsion, for God loves a cheerful giver. [8]Moreover, God is able to make every grace abundant for you, so that in all things, always having all you need, you may have an abundance for every good work. [9]As it is written: He scatters abroad, he gives to the poor; his righteousness endures forever. [10]The one who supplies seed to the sower and bread for food will supply and multiply your seed and increase the harvest of your righteousness.

Responsorial Psalm – Psalms 112:1-2, 5-6, 7-8, 9

R. (5) Blessed the man who is gracious and lends to those in need.

[1] Blessed the man who fears the LORD,

who greatly delights in his commands.

[2] His posterity shall be mighty upon the earth;

the upright generation shall be blessed.

R. Blessed the man who is gracious and lends to those in need.

[5] Well for the man who is gracious and lends,

who conducts his affairs with justice;

[6] He shall never be moved;

the just one shall be in everlasting remembrance.

R. Blessed the man who is gracious and lends to those in need.

[7] An evil report he shall not fear;

his heart is firm, trusting in the LORD.

[8] His heart is steadfast; he shall not fear

till he looks down upon his foes.

R. Blessed the man who is gracious and lends to those in need.

[9] Lavishly he gives to the poor,

his generosity shall endure forever;

his horn shall be exalted in glory.

R. Blessed the man who is gracious and lends to those in need.

Alleluia – John 8:12BC

R. Alleluia, alleluia.

[12BC]Whoever follows me will not walk in darkness but will have the light of life, says the Lord.

R. Alleluia, alleluia.

Gospel – John 12:24-26

Jesus said to his disciples: [24]"Amen, amen, I say to you, unless a grain of wheat falls to the ground and dies, it remains just a grain of wheat; but if it dies, it produces much fruit.
[25]Whoever loves his life loses it, and whoever hates his life in this world will preserve it for eternal life. [26]Whoever serves me must follow me, and where I am, there also will my servant be. The Father will honor whoever serves me."

Friday August 11, 2023

Memorial of Saint Clare - Virgin

First Reading – Deuteronomy 4:32-40

Moses said to the people: [32]"Ask now of the days of old, before your time, ever since God created man upon the earth; ask from one end of the sky to the other: Did anything so great ever happen before? Was it ever heard of? [33]Did a people ever hear the voice of God speaking from the midst of fire, as you did, and live? [34]Or did any god venture to go and take a nation for himself from the midst of another nation, by testings, by signs and wonders, by war, with his strong hand and outstretched arm, and by great terrors, all of which the LORD, your God, did for you in Egypt before your very eyes? [35]All this you were allowed to see that you might know the LORD is God and there is no other. [36]Out of the heavens he let you hear his voice to discipline you; on earth he let you see his great fire, and you heard him speaking out of the fire. [37]For love of your fathers he chose their descendants and personally led you out of Egypt by his great power, [38]driving out of your way nations greater and mightier than you, so as to bring you in and to make their land your heritage, as it is today. [39]This is why you must now know, and fix in your heart, that the LORD is God in the heavens above and on earth below, and that there is no other. [40]You must keep his statutes and commandments which I enjoin on you today, that you and your children after you may prosper, and that you may have long life on the land which the LORD, your God, is giving you forever."

Responsorial Psalm – Psalms 77:12-13, 14-15, 16 AND 21

R. (12a) I remember the deeds of the Lord.

[12] I remember the deeds of the LORD;

yes, I remember your wonders of old.

[13] And I meditate on your works;

your exploits I ponder.

R. I remember the deeds of the Lord.

14 O God, your way is holy;

what great god is there like our God?

15 You are the God who works wonders;

among the peoples you have made known your power.

R. I remember the deeds of the Lord.

16 With your strong arm you redeemed your people,

the sons of Jacob and Joseph.

21 You led your people like a flock

under the care of Moses and Aaron.

R. I remember the deeds of the Lord.

Alleluia – Matthew 5:10

R. Alleluia, alleluia.

10 Blessed are they who are persecuted for the sake of righteousness; for theirs is the Kingdom of heaven.

R. Alleluia, alleluia.

Gospel – Matthew 16:24-28

24Jesus said to his disciples, "Whoever wishes to come after
me must deny himself, take up his cross, and follow me. 25For
whoever wishes to save his life will lose it, but whoever loses
his life for my sake will find it. 26What profit would there be for
one to gain the whole world and forfeit his life? Or what can
one give in exchange for his life? 27For the Son of Man will
come with his angels in his Father's glory, and then he will
repay each according to his conduct. 28Amen, I say to you,
there are some standing here who will not taste death until
they see the Son of Man coming in his Kingdom."

Saturday August 12, 2023

Saturday of Eighteenth Week Ordinary Time

First Reading – Deuteronomy 6:4-13

Moses said to the people: 4"Hear, O Israel! The LORD is our
God, the LORD alone! 5Therefore, you shall love the LORD,
your God, with all your heart, and with all your soul, and with

all your strength. [6]Take to heart these words which I enjoin on you today. [7]Drill them into your children. Speak of them at home and abroad, whether you are busy or at rest. [8]Bind them at your wrist as a sign and let them be as a pendant on your forehead. [9]Write them on the doorposts of your houses and on your gates. [10]"When the LORD, your God, brings you into the land which he swore to your fathers: Abraham, Isaac and Jacob, that he would give you, a land with fine, large cities that you did not build, [11]with houses full of goods of all sorts that you did not garner, with cisterns that you did not dig, with vineyards and olive groves that you did not plant; and when, therefore, you eat your fill, [12]take care not to forget the LORD, who brought you out of the land of Egypt, that place of slavery. [13]The LORD, your God, shall you fear; him shall you serve, and by his name shall you swear."

Responsorial Psalm – Psalms 18:2-3A, 3BC-4, 47 AND 51

R. [(2)] I love you, Lord, my strength.

[2] I love you, O LORD, my strength,

[3A] O LORD, my rock, my fortress, my deliverer.

R. I love you, Lord, my strength.

[3BC] My God, my rock of refuge,

my shield, the horn of my salvation, my stronghold!

[4] Praised be the LORD, I exclaim!

And I am safe from my enemies.

R. I love you, Lord, my strength.

[47] The LORD live! And blessed be my Rock!

Extolled be God my savior!

[51] You who gave great victories to your king,

and showed kindness to your anointed,

to David and his posterity forever.

R. I love you, Lord, my strength.

Alleluia – 2 Timothy 1:10

R. Alleluia, alleluia.

[10] Our Savior Jesus Christ has destroyed death and brought life to light through the Gospel.

R. Alleluia, alleluia.

Gospel – Matthew 17:14-20

[14]A man came up to Jesus, knelt down before him, [15]and said, "Lord, have pity on my son, who is a lunatic and suffers severely; often he falls into fire, and often into water. [16]I brought him to your disciples, but they could not cure him." [17]Jesus said in reply, "O faithless and perverse generation, how long will I be with you? How long will I endure you? Bring the boy here to me." [18]Jesus rebuked him and the demon came out of him, and from that hour the boy was cured. [19]Then the disciples approached Jesus in private and said, "Why could we not drive it out?" [20]He said to them, "Because of your little faith. Amen, I say to you, if you have faith the size of a mustard seed, you will say to this mountain, 'Move from here to there,' and it will move. Nothing will be impossible for you."

Sunday August 13, 2023

Nineteenth Sunday in Ordinary Time, Year A

First Reading – 1 Kings 19:9A, 11-13A

[9A]At the mountain of God, Horeb, Elijah came to a cave where he took shelter.[11]Then the LORD said to him, "Go outside and stand on the mountain before the LORD; the LORD will be passing by." A strong and heavy wind was rending the mountains and crushing rocks before the LORD but the LORD was not in the wind. After the wind there was an earthquake but the LORD was not in the earthquake. [12]After the earthquake there was fire but the LORD was not in the fire. After the fire there was a tiny whispering sound. [13A]When he heard this, Elijah hid his face in his cloak and went and stood at the entrance of the cave.

Responsorial Psalm – Psalms 85:9, 10, 11-12, 13-14

R. (8) Lord, let us see your kindness, and grant us your salvation.

9 I will hear what God proclaims;

the LORD for he proclaims peace.

10 Near indeed is his salvation to those who fear him,

glory dwelling in our land.

R. Lord, let us see your kindness, and grant us your salvation.

11 Kindness and truth shall meet;

justice and peace shall kiss.

12 Truth shall spring out of the earth,

and justice shall look down from heaven.

R. Lord, let us see your kindness, and grant us your salvation.

13 The LORD himself will give his benefits;

our land shall yield its increase.

14 Justice shall walk before him,

and prepare the way of his steps.

R. Lord, let us see your kindness, and grant us your salvation.

Second Reading – Romans 9:1-5

Brothers and sisters: 1I speak the truth in Christ, I do not lie;
my conscience joins with the Holy Spirit in bearing me witness
2that I have great sorrow and constant anguish in my heart.
3For I could wish that I myself were accursed and cut off from
Christ for the sake of my own people, my kindred according to
the flesh.4They are Israelites; theirs the adoption, the glory,
the covenants, the giving of the law, the worship, and the
promises; 5theirs the patriarchs, and from them, according to
the flesh, is the Christ, who is over all, God blessed forever.
Amen.

Alleluia – Psalms 130:5

R. Alleluia, alleluia.

[5] I wait for the Lord; my soul waits for his word.

R. Alleluia, alleluia.

Gospel – Matthew 14:22-33

[22]After he had fed the people, Jesus made the disciples get into a boat and precede him to the other side, while he dismissed the crowds. [23]After doing so, he went up on the mountain by himself to pray. When it was evening he was there alone. [24]Meanwhile the boat, already a few miles offshore, was being tossed about by the waves, for the wind was against it. [25]During the fourth watch of the night, he came toward them walking on the sea. [26]When the disciples saw him walking on the sea they were terrified. "It is a ghost," they said, and they cried out in fear. [27]At once Jesus spoke to them, "Take courage, it is I; do not be afraid." [28]Peter said to him in reply, "Lord, if it is you, command me to come to you on the water." [29]He said, "Come." Peter got out of the boat and began to walk on the water toward Jesus. [30]But when he saw how strong the wind was he became frightened; and, beginning to sink, he cried out, "Lord, save me!" [31]Immediately Jesus stretched out his hand and caught Peter, and said to him, "O you of little faith, why did you doubt?" [32]After they got into the boat, the wind died down [33]Those who were in the boat did him homage, saying, "Truly, you are the Son of God."

Monday August 14, 2023

Memorial of Saint Maximilian Kolbe – Priest & Martyr

First Reading – Deuteronomy 10:12-22

Moses said to the people: [12]"And now, Israel, what does the LORD, your God, ask of you but to fear the LORD, your God, and follow his ways exactly, to love and serve the LORD, your God, with all your heart and all your soul,[13]to keep the commandments and statutes of the LORD which I enjoin on you today for your own good? [14]Think! The heavens, even the highest heavens, belong to the LORD, your God, as well as the earth and everything on it. [15]Yet in his love for your fathers the LORD was so attached to them as to choose you, their descendants, in preference to all other peoples, as indeed he

has now done. 16 Circumcise your hearts, therefore, and be no
longer stiff-necked. 17 For the LORD, your God, is the God of
gods, the LORD of lords, the great God, mighty and awesome,
who has no favourites, accepts no bribes; 18 who executes
justice for the orphan and the widow, and befriends the alien,
feeding and clothing him. 19 So you too must befriend the alien,
for you were once aliens yourselves in the land of Egypt. 20 The
LORD, your God, shall you fear, and him shall you serve; hold
fast to him and swear by his name. 21 He is your glory, he, your
God, who has done for you those great and terrible things
which your own eyes have seen. 22 Your ancestors went down
to Egypt seventy strong, and now the LORD, your God, has
made you as numerous as the stars of the sky."

Responsorial Psalm – Psalms 147:12-13, 14-15, 19-20

R. (12a) **Praise the Lord, Jerusalem.**

12 Glorify the LORD, O Jerusalem;

praise your God, O Zion.

13 For he has strengthened the bars of your gates;

he has blessed your children within you.

R. Praise the Lord, Jerusalem.

14 He has granted peace in your borders;

with the best of wheat he fills you.

15 He sends forth his command to the earth;

swiftly runs his word!

R. Praise the Lord, Jerusalem.

19 He has proclaimed his word to Jacob,

his statutes and his ordinances to Israel.

20 He has not done thus for any other nation;

his ordinances he has not made known to them. Alleluia.

R. Praise the Lord, Jerusalem.

Alleluia – 2 Thessalonians 2:14

R. Alleluia, alleluia.

14 God has called you through the Gospel To possess the glory of our Lord Jesus Christ.

R. Alleluia, alleluia.

Gospel – Matthew 17:22-27

22As Jesus and his disciples were gathering in Galilee, Jesus
said to them, "The Son of Man is to be handed over to men,
23and they will kill him, and he will be raised on the third day."
And they were overwhelmed with grief. 24When they came to
Capernaum, the collectors of the temple tax approached Peter
and said, "Does not your teacher pay the temple tax?" 25"Yes,"
he said. When he came into the house, before he had time to
speak, Jesus asked him, "What is your opinion, Simon? From
whom do the kings of the earth take tolls or census tax? From
their subjects or from foreigners?" 26When he said, "From
foreigners," Jesus said to him, "Then the subjects are exempt.
27But that we may not offend them, go to the sea, drop in a
hook, and take the first fish that comes up. Open its mouth
and you will find a coin worth twice the temple tax. Give that to
them for me and for you."

Monday August 14, 2023

Assumption of the Blessed Virgin Mary – Vigil Mass

First Reading – 1 Chronicles 15:3-4, 15-16; 16:1-2

3David assembled all Israel in Jerusalem to bring the ark of the
LORD to the place which he had prepared for it. 4David also
called together the sons of Aaron and the Levites. 15The
Levites bore the ark of God on their shoulders with poles, as
Moses had ordained according to the word of the
LORD.16David commanded the chiefs of the Levites to appoint
their kinsmen as chanters, to play on musical instruments,
harps, lyres, and cymbals, to make a loud sound of
rejoicing.1They brought in the ark of God and set it within the
tent which David had pitched for it. Then they offered up burnt
offerings and peace offerings to God. 2When David had
finished offering up the burnt offerings and peace offerings, he
blessed the people in the name of the LORD.

Responsorial Psalm – Psalms 132:6-7, 9-10, 13-14

R.(8) Lord, go up to the place of your rest, you and the ark of your holiness.

6 Behold, we heard of it in Ephrathah;

we found it in the fields of Jaar.

7 Let us enter his dwelling,

let us worship at his footstool.

R. Lord, go up to the place of your rest, you and the ark of your holiness.

9 May your priests be clothed with justice;

let your faithful ones shout merrily for joy.

10 For the sake of David your servant,

reject not the plea of your anointed.

R. Lord, go up to the place of your rest, you and the ark of your holiness.

13 For the LORD has chosen Zion;

he prefers her for his dwelling.

14 "Zion is my resting place forever;

in her will I dwell, for I prefer her."

R. Lord, go up to the place of your rest, you and the ark of your holiness.

Second Reading – 1 Corinthians 15:54B-57

Brothers and sisters: 54B When that which is mortal clothes
itself with immortality, then the word that is written shall come
about: 55 Death is swallowed up in victory. Where, O death, is
your victory? Where, O death, is your sting? 56 The sting of
death is sin, and the power of sin is the law. 57 But thanks be to
God who gives us the victory through our Lord Jesus Christ.

Alleluia – Luke 11:28

R. Alleluia, alleluia.

28 Blessed are they who hear the word of God and observe it.

R. Alleluia, alleluia.

Gospel – Luke 11:27-28

[27]While Jesus was speaking, a woman from the crowd called
out and said to him, “Blessed is the womb that carried you and
the breasts at which you nursed.” [28]He replied, “Rather,
blessed are those who hear the word of God and observe it.”

Tuesday August 15, 2023

Solemnity of the Assumption of the Blessed Virgin Mary (Mass during the Day)

First Reading – Revelation 11:19A; 12:1-6A, 10AB

[19A]God’s temple in heaven was opened, and the ark of his
covenant could be seen in the temple. [1]A great sign appeared
in the sky, a woman clothed with the sun, with the moon under
her feet, and on her head a crown of twelve stars. [2]She was
with child and wailed aloud in pain as she labored to give
birth.[3]Then another sign appeared in the sky; it was a huge
red dragon, with seven heads and ten horns, and on its heads
were seven diadems.[4]Its tail swept away a third of the stars in
the sky and hurled them down to the earth. Then the dragon
stood before the woman about to give birth, to devour her
child when she gave birth.[5]She gave birth to a son, a male
child, destined to rule all the nations with an iron rod. Her child
was caught up to God and his throne.[6A]The woman herself
fled into the desert where she had a place prepared by
God.[10AB]Then I heard a loud voice in heaven say: “Now have
salvation and power come, and the Kingdom of our God and
the authority of his Anointed One.”

Responsorial Psalm – Psalms 45:10, 11, 12, 16

R. (10bc) The queen stands at your right hand, arrayed in gold.

[10] The queen takes her place at your right hand in gold of Ophir.

R. The queen stands at your right hand, arrayed in gold.

[11] Hear, O daughter, and see; turn your ear,

forget your people and your father’s house.

R. The queen stands at your right hand, arrayed in gold.

12 So shall the king desire your beauty;

for he is your lord.

R. The queen stands at your right hand, arrayed in gold.

16 They are borne in with gladness and joy;

they enter the palace of the king.

R. The queen stands at your right hand, arrayed in gold.

Second Reading – 1 Corinthians 15:20-27

Brothers and sisters: 20 Christ has been raised from the dead,
the first fruits of those who have fallen asleep. 21 For since
death came through man, the resurrection of the dead came
also through man. 22 For just as in Adam all die, so too in Christ
shall all be brought to life, 23 but each one in proper order:
Christ the first fruits; then, at his coming, those who belong to
Christ; 24 then comes the end, when he hands over the
Kingdom to his God and Father, when he has destroyed every
sovereignty and every authority and power. 25 For he must reign
until he has put all his enemies under his feet. 26 The last
enemy to be destroyed is death, 27 for "he subjected everything
under his feet."

Alleluia

R. Alleluia, alleluia.

Mary is taken up to heaven; a chorus of angels exults.

R. Alleluia, alleluia.

Gospel – Luke 1:39-56

39 Mary set out and traveled to the hill country in haste to a
town of Judah, 40 where she entered the house of Zechariah
and greeted Elizabeth. 41 When Elizabeth heard Mary's
greeting, the infant leaped in her womb, and Elizabeth, filled
with the Holy Spirit, 42 cried out in a loud voice and said,
"Blessed are you among women, and blessed is the fruit of
your womb. 43 And how does this happen to me that the mother
of my Lord should come to me? 44 For at the moment the
sound of your greeting reached my ears, the infant in my
womb leaped for joy. 45 Blessed are you who believed that

what was spoken to you by the Lord would be fulfilled." 46And
Mary said: *"My soul proclaims the greatness of the Lord;* *47 my
spirit rejoices in God my Savior 48for he has looked with favor
on his lowly servant. From this day all generations will call me
blessed: 49the Almighty has done great things for me and holy
is his Name. 50He has mercy on those who fear him in every
generation. 51He has shown the strength of his arm, and has
scattered the proud in their conceit. 52He has cast down the
mighty from their thrones, and has lifted up the lowly. 53He has
filled the hungry with good things, and the rich he has sent
away empty. 54He has come to the help of his servant Israel
for he has remembered his promise of mercy,* 55the promise
he made to our fathers, to Abraham and his children forever."
56Mary remained with her about three months and then
returned to her home.

Wednesday August 16, 2023

Wednesday of Nineteenth Week in Ordinary Time

First Reading – Deuteronomy 34:1-12

1Moses went up from the plains of Moab to Mount Nebo, the
headland of Pisgah which faces Jericho, and the LORD
showed him all the land – Gilead, and as far as Dan, 2all
Naphtali, the land of Ephraim and Manasseh, all the land of
Judah as far as the Western Sea, 3the Negeb, the circuit of the
Jordan with the lowlands at Jericho, city of palms, and as far
as Zoar.4The LORD then said to him, "This is the land which I
swore to Abraham, Isaac, and Jacob that I would give to their
descendants. I have let you feast your eyes upon it, but you
shall not cross over." 5So there, in the land of Moab, Moses,
the servant of the LORD, died as the LORD had said; 6and he
was buried in the ravine opposite Beth-peor in the land of
Moab, but to this day no one knows the place of his burial.
7Moses was one hundred and twenty years old when he died,
yet his eyes were undimmed and his vigor unabated. 8For
thirty days the children of Israel wept for Moses in the plains of
Moab, till they had completed the period of grief and mourning
for Moses. 9Now Joshua, son of Nun, was filled with the spirit
of wisdom, since Moses had laid his hands upon him; and so
the children of Israel gave him their obedience, thus carrying
out the LORD's command to Moses. 10Since then no prophet
has arisen in Israel like Moses, whom the LORD knew face to

face. [11]He had no equal in all the signs and wonders the LORD sent him to perform in the land of Egypt against Pharaoh and all his servants and against all his land, [12]and for the might and the terrifying power that Moses exhibited in the sight of all Israel.

Responsorial Psalm – Psalms 66:1-3A, 5 AND 8, 16-17

R. (see 20a and 10b) **Blessed be God who filled my soul with fire!**

2 Shout joyfully to God, all the earth;

sing praise to the glory of his name;

proclaim his glorious praise.

3A Say to God: “How tremendous are your deeds!”

R. Blessed be God who filled my soul with fire!

5 Come and see the works of God,

his tremendous deeds among the children of Adam.

8 Bless our God, you peoples;

loudly sound his praise.

R. Blessed be God who filled my soul with fire!

16 Hear now, all you who fear God, while I declare

what he has done for me.

17 When I appealed to him in words,

praise was on the tip of my tongue.

R. Blessed be God who filled my soul with fire!

Alleluia – 2 Corinthians 5:19

R. Alleluia, alleluia.

19 God was reconciling the world to himself in Christ, and entrusting to us the message of reconciliation.

R. Alleluia, alleluia.

Gospel – Matthew 18:15-20

Jesus said to his disciples: 15“If your brother sins against you,
go and tell him his fault between you and him alone. If he
listens to you, you have won over your brother. 16If he does
not listen, take one or two others along with you, so that every
fact may be established on the testimony of two or three
witnesses. 17If he refuses to listen to them, tell the Church. If
he refuses to listen even to the Church, then treat him as you
would a Gentile or a tax collector. 18Amen, I say to you,
whatever you bind on earth shall be bound in heaven, and
whatever you loose on earth shall be loosed in heaven.
19Again, amen, I say to you, if two of you agree on earth about
anything for which they are to pray, it shall be granted to them
by my heavenly Father. 20For where two or three are gathered
together in my name, there am I in the midst of them.”

Thursday August 17, 2023

Thursday of Nineteenth Week Ordinary Time

First Reading – Joshua 3:7-10A, 11, 13-17

7The LORD said to Joshua, “Today I will begin to exalt you in
the sight of all Israel, that they may know I am with you, as I
was with Moses. 8Now command the priests carrying the ark
of the covenant to come to a halt in the Jordan when you
reach the edge of the waters.” 9So Joshua said to the children
of Israel, “Come here and listen to the words of the LORD,
your God. 10AThis is how you will know that there is a living
God in your midst, who at your approach will dispossess the
Canaanites. 11The ark of the covenant of the LORD of the
whole earth will precede you into the Jordan. 13When the soles
of the feet of the priests carrying the ark of the LORD, the Lord
of the whole earth, touch the water of the Jordan, it will cease
to flow; for the water flowing down from upstream will halt in a
solid bank.” 14The people struck their tents to cross the
Jordan, with the priests carrying the ark of the covenant ahead
of them. 15No sooner had these priestly bearers of the ark
waded into the waters at the edge of the Jordan, which
overflows all its banks during the entire season of the harvest,
16than the waters flowing from upstream halted, backing up in
a solid mass for a very great distance indeed, from Adam, a
city in the direction of Zarethan; while those flowing
downstream toward the Salt Sea of the Arabah disappeared

entirely. Thus the people crossed over opposite Jericho.
[17]While all Israel crossed over on dry ground, the priests
carrying the ark of the covenant of the LORD remained
motionless on dry ground in the bed of the Jordan until the
whole nation had completed the passage.

Responsorial Psalm – Psalms 114:1-2, 3-4, 5-6

R. Alleluia!

1 When Israel came forth from Egypt,

the house of Jacob from a people of alien tongue,

2 Judah became his sanctuary,

Israel his domain.

R. Alleluia!

3 The sea beheld and fled;

Jordan turned back.

4 The mountains skipped like rams,

the hills like the lambs of the flock.

R. Alleluia!

5 Why is it, O sea, that you flee?

O Jordan, that you turn back?

6 You mountains, that you skip like rams?

You hills, like the lambs of the flock?

R. Alleluia!

Alleluia – Psalms 119:135

R. Alleluia, alleluia.

135 Let your countenance shine upon your servant and teach me your statutes.

R. Alleluia, alleluia.

Gospel – Matthew 18:21-19:1

[21]Peter approached Jesus and asked him, "Lord, if my brother
sins against me, how often must I forgive him? As many as
seven times?" [22]Jesus answered, "I say to you, not seven

times but seventy-seven times. [23]That is why the Kingdom of heaven may be likened to a king who decided to settle accounts with his servants. [24]When he began the accounting, a debtor was brought before him who owed him a huge amount. [25]Since he had no way of paying it back, his master ordered him to be sold, along with his wife, his children, and all his property, in payment of the debt. [26]At that, the servant fell down, did him homage, and said, ‘Be patient with me, and I will pay you back in full.’ [27]Moved with compassion the master of that servant let him go and forgave him the loan. [28]When that servant had left, he found one of his fellow servants who owed him a much smaller amount. He seized him and started to choke him, demanding, ‘Pay back what you owe.’ [29]Falling to his knees, his fellow servant begged him, ‘Be patient with me, and I will pay you back.’ [30]But he refused. Instead, he had the fellow servant put in prison until he paid back the debt. [31]Now when his fellow servants saw what had happened, they were deeply disturbed, and went to their master and reported the whole affair. [32]His master summoned him and said to him, ‘You wicked servant! I forgave you your entire debt because you begged me to. [33]Should you not have had pity on your fellow servant, as I had pity on you?’ [34]Then in anger his master handed him over to the torturers until he should pay back the whole debt. [35]So will my heavenly Father do to you, unless each of you forgives his brother from his heart.” [1]When Jesus finished these words, he left Galilee and went to the district of Judea across the Jordan.

Friday August 18, 2023

Friday of Nineteenth Week in Ordinary Time

First Reading – Joshua 24:1-13

[1]Joshua gathered together all the tribes of Israel at Shechem, summoning their elders, their leaders, their judges and their officers. When they stood in ranks before God, [2]Joshua addressed all the people: “Thus says the LORD, the God of Israel: In times past your fathers, down to Terah, father of Abraham and Nahor, dwelt beyond the River and served other gods. [3]But I brought your father Abraham from the region beyond the River and led him through the entire land of Canaan. I made his descendants numerous, and gave him Isaac. [4]To Isaac I gave Jacob and Esau. To Esau I assigned

the mountain region of Seir in which to settle, while Jacob and
his children went down to Egypt. 5“Then I sent Moses and
Aaron, and smote Egypt with the prodigies which I wrought in
her midst. 6Afterward I led you out of Egypt, and when you
reached the sea, the Egyptians pursued your fathers to the
Red Sea with chariots and horsemen. 7Because they cried out
to the LORD, he put darkness between your people and the
Egyptians, upon whom he brought the sea so that it engulfed
them. After you witnessed what I did to Egypt, and dwelt a
long time in the desert, 8I brought you into the land of the
Amorites who lived east of the Jordan. They fought against
you, but I delivered them into your power. You took
possession of their land, and I destroyed them, the two kings
of the Amorites, before you. 9Then Balak, son of Zippor, king
of Moab, prepared to war against Israel. He summoned
Balaam, son of Beor, to curse you; 10but I would not listen to
Balaam. On the contrary, he had to bless you, and I saved you
from him. 11Once you crossed the Jordan and came to
Jericho, the men of Jericho fought against you, but I delivered
them also into your power. 12And I sent the hornets ahead of
you that drove them (the Amorites, Perizzites, Canaanites,
Hittites, Girgashites, Hivites and Jebusites) out of your way; it
was not your sword or your bow. 13“I gave you a land that you
had not tilled and cities that you had not built, to dwell in; you
have eaten of vineyards and olive groves which you did not
plant.”

Responsorial Psalm – Psalms 136:1-3, 16-18, 21-22 AND 24

R. His mercy endures forever.

1 Give thanks to the LORD, for he is good,

for his mercy endures forever;

2 Give thanks to the God of gods,

for his mercy endures forever;

3 Give thanks to the LORD of lords,

for his mercy endures forever.

R. His mercy endures forever.

16 Who led his people through the wilderness,

for his mercy endures forever;

17 Who smote great kings,

for his mercy endures forever;

18 And slew powerful kings,

for his mercy endures forever.

R. His mercy endures forever.

21 And made their land a heritage,

for his mercy endures forever;

22 The heritage of Israel his servant,

for his mercy endures forever;

24 And freed us from our foes,

for his mercy endures forever.

R. His mercy endures forever.

Alleluia – 1 Thessalonians 2:13

R. Alleluia, alleluia.

13 Receive the word of god, not as the word of men, but, as it truly is, the word of God.

R. Alleluia, alleluia.

Gospel – Matthew 19:3-12

3Some Pharisees approached Jesus, and tested him, saying, "Is it lawful for a man to divorce his wife for any cause whatever?" 4He said in reply, "Have you not read that from the beginning the Creator made them male and female and said, 5For this reason a man shall leave his father and mother and be joined to his wife, and the two shall become one flesh? 6So they are no longer two, but one flesh. Therefore, what God has joined together, man must not separate." 7They said to him, "Then why did Moses command that the man give the woman a bill of divorce and dismiss her? 8He said to them, "Because of the hardness of your hearts Moses allowed you to divorce your wives, but from the beginning it was not so. 9I say to you, whoever divorces his wife (unless the marriage is unlawful) and marries another commits adultery." 10His disciples said to him, "If that is the case of a man with his wife, it is better not to marry." [11]He answered, "Not all can accept this word, but only those to whom that is granted. [12]Some are incapable of marriage because they were born so; some, because they were made so by others; some, because they have renounced marriage for the sake of the Kingdom of heaven. Whoever can accept this ought to accept it."

Saturday August 19, 2023

Saturday of Nineteenth Week Ordinary Time

First Reading – Joshua 24:14-29

Joshua gathered together all the tribes of Israel at Shechem, and addressed them, saying: [14]"Fear the LORD and serve him completely and sincerely. Cast out the gods your fathers served beyond the River and in Egypt, and serve the LORD. [15]If it does not please you to serve the LORD, decide today whom you will serve, the gods your fathers served beyond the River or the gods of the Amorites in whose country you are dwelling. As for me and my household, we will serve the LORD." [16]But the people answered, "Far be it from us to forsake the LORD for the service of other gods. [17]For it was the LORD, our God, who brought us and our fathers up out of the land of Egypt, out of a state of slavery. He performed those great miracles before our very eyes and protected us along our entire journey and among all the peoples through whom we passed. [18]At our approach the LORD drove out all the peoples, including the Amorites who dwelt in the land. Therefore we also will serve the LORD, for he is our God." [19]Joshua in turn said to the people, "You may not be able to serve the LORD, for he is a holy God; he is a jealous God who will not forgive your transgressions or your sins. [20]If, after the good he has done for you, you forsake the LORD and serve strange gods, he will do evil to you and destroy you." [21]But the people answered Joshua, "We will still serve the LORD." [22]Joshua therefore said to the people, "You are your own witnesses that you have chosen to serve the LORD." They replied, "We are, indeed!" Joshua continued: [23]"Now, therefore, put away the strange gods that are among you and turn your hearts to the LORD, the God of Israel." [24]Then the people promised Joshua, "We will serve the LORD, our God, and obey his voice." [25]So Joshua made a covenant with the people that day and made statutes and ordinances for them at

Shechem, 26which he recorded in the book of the law of God.
Then he took a large stone and set it up there under the oak
that was in the sanctuary of the LORD. 27And Joshua said to
all the people, "This stone shall be our witness, for it has heard
all the words which the LORD spoke to us. It shall be a
witness against you, should you wish to deny your God."
28Then Joshua dismissed the people, each to his own
heritage. 29After these events, Joshua, son of Nun, servant of
the LORD, died at the age of a hundred and ten.

Responsorial Psalm – Psalms 16:1-2A AND 5, 7-8, 11

R.(see 5a) You are my inheritance, O Lord.

1 Keep me, O God, for in you I take refuge;

2A I say to the LORD, "My Lord are you."

5 O LORD, my allotted portion and my cup,

you it is who hold fast my lot.

R. You are my inheritance, O Lord.

7 I bless the LORD who counsels me;

even in the night my heart exhorts me.

8 I set the LORD ever before me;

with him at my right hand I shall not be disturbed.

R. You are my inheritance, O Lord.

11 You will show me the path to life,

fullness of joys in your presence,

the delights at your right hand forever.

R. You are my inheritance, O Lord.

Alleluia – Matthew 11:25

R. Alleluia, alleluia.

25 Blessed are you, Father, Lord of heaven and earth; you have revealed to little ones the mysteries of the Kingdom.

R. Alleluia, alleluia.

Gospel – Matthew 19:13-15

[13]Children were brought to Jesus that he might lay his hands
on them and pray. The disciples rebuked them, [14]but Jesus
said, "Let the children come to me, and do not prevent them;
for the Kingdom of heaven belongs to such as these." [15]After
he placed his hands on them, he went away.

Sunday August 20, 2023

Twentieth Sunday in Ordinary Time, Year A

First Reading – Isaiah 56:1, 6-7

[1]Thus says the LORD: Observe what is right, do what is just;
for my salvation is about to come, my justice, about to be
revealed. [6]The foreigners who join themselves to the LORD,
ministering to him, loving the name of the LORD, and
becoming his servants all who keep the Sabbath free from
profanation and hold to my covenant, [7]them I will bring to my
holy mountain and make joyful in my house of prayer; their
burnt offerings and sacrifices will be acceptable on my altar,
for my house shall be called a house of prayer for all peoples.

Responsorial Psalm – Psalms 67:2-3, 5, 6, 8

R. (4) O God, let all the nations praise you!

[2] May God have pity on us and bless us;

may he let his face shine upon us.

[3] So may your way be known upon earth;

among all nations, your salvation.

R. O God, let all the nations praise you!

[5] May the nations be glad and exult

because you rule the peoples in equity;

the nations on the earth you guide.

R. O God, let all the nations praise you!

[6] May the peoples praise you, O God;

may all the peoples praise you!

[8] May God bless us,

and may all the ends of the earth fear him!

R. O God, let all the nations praise you!

Second Reading – Romans 11:13-15, 29-32

Brothers and sisters: [13]I am speaking to you Gentiles. Inasmuch as I am the apostle to the Gentiles, I glory in my ministry [14]in order to make my race jealous and thus save some of them. [15]For if their rejection is the reconciliation of the world, what will their acceptance be but life from the dead? [29]For the gifts and the call of God are irrevocable. [30]Just as you once disobeyed God but have now received mercy because of their disobedience, [31]so they have now disobeyed in order that, by virtue of the mercy shown to you, they too may now receive mercy. [32]For God delivered all to disobedience, that he might have mercy upon all.

Alleluia – Matthew 4:23

R. Alleluia, alleluia.

[23] Jesus proclaimed the Gospel of the kingdom and cured every disease among the people.

R. Alleluia, alleluia.

Gospel – Matthew 15:21-28

[21]At that time, Jesus withdrew to the region of Tyre and Sidon. [22]And behold, a Canaanite woman of that district came and called out, "Have pity on me, Lord, Son of David! My daughter is tormented by a demon." [23]But Jesus did not say a word in answer to her. Jesus' disciples came and asked him, "Send her away, for she keeps calling out after us." [24]He said in reply, "I was sent only to the lost sheep of the house of Israel." [25]But the woman came and did Jesus homage, saying, "Lord, help me." [26]He said in reply, "It is not right to take the food of the children and throw it to the dogs." [27]She said, "Please, Lord, for even the dogs eat the scraps that fall from the table of their masters." [28]Then Jesus said to her in reply, "O woman, great is your faith! Let it be done for you as you wish." And the woman's daughter was healed from that hour.

Monday August 21, 2023

Memorial of Saint Pius X - Pope

First Reading – Judges 2:11-19

[11]The children of Israel offended the LORD by serving the
Baals. [12]Abandoning the LORD, the God of their fathers, who
led them out of the land of Egypt, they followed the other gods
of the various nations around them, and by their worship of
these gods provoked the LORD. [13]Because they had thus
abandoned him and served Baal and the Ashtaroth, [14]the
anger of the LORD flared up against Israel, and he delivered
them over to plunderers who despoiled them. He allowed them
to fall into the power of their enemies round about whom they
were no longer able to withstand. [15]Whatever they undertook,
the LORD turned into disaster for them, as in his warning he
had sworn he would do, till they were in great distress. [16]Even
when the LORD raised up judges to deliver them from the
power of their despoilers, [17]they did not listen to their judges,
but abandoned themselves to the worship of other gods. They
were quick to stray from the way their fathers had taken, and
did not follow their example of obedience to the
commandments of the LORD. [18]Whenever the LORD raised
up judges for them, he would be with the judge and save them
from the power of their enemies as long as the judge lived; it
was thus the LORD took pity on their distressful cries of
affliction under their oppressors. [19]But when the judge died,
they would relapse and do worse than their ancestors,
following other gods in service and worship, relinquishing none
of their evil practices or stubborn conduct.

Responsorial Psalm – Psalms 106:34-35, 36-37, 39-40, 43AB AND 44

R. [(4a)] Remember us, O Lord, as you favor your people.

[34] They did not exterminate the peoples,

as the LORD had commanded them,

[35] But mingled with the nations

and learned their works.

R. Remember us, O Lord, as you favor your people.

36 They served their idols,

which became a snare for them.

37 They sacrificed their sons

and their daughters to demons.

R. Remember us, O Lord, as you favor your people.

39 They became defiled by their works,

and wanton in their crimes.

40 And the LORD grew angry with his people,

and abhorred his inheritance.

R. Remember us, O Lord, as you favor your people.

43AB Many times did he rescue them,

but they embittered him with their counsels.

44 Yet he had regard for their affliction

when he heard their cry.

R. Remember us, O Lord, as you favor your people.

Alleluia – Matthew 5:3

R. Alleluia, alleluia.

3 Blessed are the poor in spirit; for theirs is the Kingdom of heaven.

R. Alleluia, alleluia.

Gospel – Matthew 19:16-22

16A young man approached Jesus and said, “Teacher, what
good must I do to gain eternal life?” 17He answered him, “Why
do you ask me about the good? There is only One who is
good. If you wish to enter into life, keep the commandments.”
18He asked him, “Which ones?” And Jesus replied, *“You shall
not kill; you shall not commit adultery; you shall not steal; you
shall not bear false witness;* 19*honor your father and your
mother; and you shall love your neighbor as yourself.”* 20The
young man said to him, “All of these I have observed. What do
I still lack?” 21Jesus said to him, “If you wish to be perfect, go,
sell what you have and give to the poor, and you will have
treasure in heaven. Then come, follow me.” 22When the young

man heard this statement, he went away sad, for he had many
possessions.

Tuesday August 22, 2023

Memorial of Our Lady, Mother and Queen

First Reading – Judges 6:11-24A

[11]The angel of the LORD came and sat under the terebinth in
Ophrah that belonged to Joash the Abiezrite. While his son
Gideon was beating out wheat in the wine press to save it
from the Midianites, [12]the angel of the LORD appeared to him
and said, “The LORD is with you, O champion!” [13]Gideon said
to him, “My Lord, if the LORD is with us, why has all this
happened to us? Where are his wondrous deeds of which our
fathers told us when they said, ‘Did not the LORD bring us up
from Egypt?’ For now the LORD has abandoned us and has
delivered us into the power of Midian.” [14]The LORD turned to
him and said, “Go with the strength you have and save Israel
from the power of Midian. It is I who send you.” [15]But Gideon
answered him, “Please, my lord, how can I save Israel? My
family is the lowliest in Manasseh, and I am the most
insignificant in my father’s house.” [16]“I shall be with you,” the
LORD said to him, “and you will cut down Midian to the last
man.” [17]Gideon answered him, “If I find favor with you, give me
a sign that you are speaking with me. [18]Do not depart from
here, I pray you, until I come back to you and bring out my
offering and set it before you.” He answered, “I will await your
return.” [19]So Gideon went off and prepared a kid and a
measure of flour in the form of unleavened cakes. Putting the
meat in a basket and the broth in a pot, he brought them out to
him under the terebinth and presented them. [20]The angel of
God said to him, “Take the meat and unleavened cakes and
lay them on this rock; then pour out the broth.” When he had
done so, [21]the angel of the LORD stretched out the tip of the
staff he held, and touched the meat and unleavened cakes.
Thereupon a fire came up from the rock that consumed the
meat and unleavened cakes, and the angel of the LORD
disappeared from sight. [22]Gideon, now aware that it had been
the angel of the LORD, said, “Alas, Lord GOD, that I have
seen the angel of the LORD face to face!” [23]The LORD
answered him, “Be calm, do not fear. You shall not die.” [24A]So

Gideon built there an altar to the LORD and called it Yahweh-shalom.

Responsorial Psalm – Psalms 85:9, 11-12, 13-14

R. (see 9b) The Lord speaks of peace to his people.

9 I will hear what God proclaims;

the LORD–for he proclaims peace

To his people, and to his faithful ones,

and to those who put in him their hope.

R. The Lord speaks of peace to his people.

11 Kindness and truth shall meet;

justice and peace shall kiss.

12 Truth shall spring out of the earth,

and justice shall look down from heaven.

R. The Lord speaks of peace to his people.

13 The LORD himself will give his benefits;

our land shall yield its increase.

14 Justice shall walk before him,

and salvation, along the way of his steps.

R. The Lord speaks of peace to his people.

Alleluia – 2 Corinthians 8:9

R. Alleluia, alleluia.

9 Jesus Christ became poor although he was rich so that by his poverty you might become rich.

R. Alleluia, alleluia.

Gospel – Matthew 19:23-30

23Jesus said to his disciples: "Amen, I say to you, it will be hard for one who is rich to enter the Kingdom of heaven.
24Again I say to you, it is easier for a camel to pass through the eye of a needle than for one who is rich to enter the Kingdom of God." 25When the disciples heard this, they were greatly astonished and said, "Who then can be saved?"

26Jesus looked at them and said, “For men this is impossible,
but for God all things are possible.” 27Then Peter said to him in
reply, “We have given up everything and followed you. What
will there be for us?” 28Jesus said to them, “Amen, I say to you
that you who have followed me, in the new age, when the Son
of Man is seated on his throne of glory, will yourselves sit on
twelve thrones, judging the twelve tribes of Israel. 29And
everyone who has given up houses or brothers or sisters or
father or mother or children or lands for the sake of my name
will receive a hundred times more, and will inherit eternal life.
30But many who are first will be last, and the last will be first.”

Wednesday August 23, 2023

Wednesday of Twentieth Week in Ordinary Time

First Reading – Judges 9:6-15

6All the citizens of Shechem and all Beth-millo came together
and proceeded to make Abimelech king by the terebinth at the
memorial pillar in Shechem. 7When this was reported to him,
Jotham went to the top of Mount Gerizim and, standing there,
cried out to them in a loud voice: “Hear me, citizens of
Shechem, that God may then hear you! 8Once the trees went
to anoint a king over themselves. So they said to the olive
tree, ‘Reign over us.’ 9But the olive tree answered them, ‘Must
I give up my rich oil, whereby men and gods are honored, and
go to wave over the trees?’ 10Then the trees said to the fig
tree, ‘Come; you reign over us!’ 11But the fig tree answered
them, ‘Must I give up my sweetness and my good fruit, and go
to wave over the trees?’ 12Then the trees said to the vine,
‘Come you, and reign over us.’ 13But the vine answered them,
‘Must I give up my wine that cheers gods and men, and go to
wave over the trees?’ 14Then all the trees said to the
buckthorn, ‘Come; you reign over us!’ 15But the buckthorn
replied to the trees, ‘If you wish to anoint me king over you in
good faith, come and take refuge in my shadow. Otherwise, let
fire come from the buckthorn and devour the cedars of
Lebanon.’”

Responsorial Psalm – Psalms 21:2-3, 4-5, 6-7

R.(2a) Lord, in your strength the king is glad.

2 O LORD, in your strength the king is glad;

in your victory how greatly he rejoices!

[3] You have granted him his heart's desire;

you refused not the wish of his lips.

R. Lord, in your strength the king is glad.

[4] For you welcomed him with goodly blessings,

you placed on his head a crown of pure gold.

[5] He asked life of you: you gave him

length of days forever and ever.

R. Lord, in your strength the king is glad.

[6] Great is his glory in your victory;

majesty and splendor you conferred upon him.

[7] You made him a blessing forever,

you gladdened him with the joy of your face.

R. Lord, in your strength the king is glad.

Alleluia – Hebrews 4:12

R. Alleluia, alleluia.

[12] The word of God is living and effective, able to discern the reflections and thoughts of the heart.

R. Alleluia, alleluia.

Gospel – Matthew 20:1-16

Jesus told his disciples this parable: [1]"The Kingdom of heaven
is like a landowner who went out at dawn to hire laborers for
his vineyard. [2]After agreeing with them for the usual daily
wage, he sent them into his vineyard. [3]Going out about nine
o'clock, he saw others standing idle in the marketplace, [4]and
he said to them, 'You too go into my vineyard, and I will give
you what is just.' [5]So they went off. And he went out again
around noon, and around three o'clock, and did likewise.
[6]Going out about five o'clock, he found others standing
around, and said to them, 'Why do you stand here idle all
day?' [7]They answered, 'Because no one has hired us.' He
said to them, 'You too go into my vineyard.' [8]When it was
evening the owner of the vineyard said to his foreman,

'Summon the laborers and give them their pay, beginning with
the last and ending with the first.' 9When those who had
started about five o'clock came, each received the usual daily
wage. 10So when the first came, they thought that they would
receive more, but each of them also got the usual wage. 11And
on receiving it they grumbled against the landowner, 12saying,
'These last ones worked only one hour, and you have made
them equal to us, who bore the day's burden and the heat.'
13He said to one of them in reply, 'My friend, I am not cheating
you. Did you not agree with me for the usual daily wage?
14Take what is yours and go. What if I wish to give this last one
the same as you? 15Or am I not free to do as I wish with my
own money? Are you envious because I am generous?'
16Thus, the last will be first, and the first will be last."

Thursday August 24, 2023

Feast of Saint Bartholomew, Apostle

First Reading – Revelation 21:9B-14

9BThe angel spoke to me, saying, "Come here. I will show you
the bride, the wife of the Lamb." 10He took me in spirit to a
great, high mountain and showed me the holy city Jerusalem
coming down out of heaven from God. 11It gleamed with the
splendor of God. Its radiance was like that of a precious stone,
like jasper, clear as crystal. 12It had a massive, high wall, with
twelve gates where twelve angels were stationed and on
which names were inscribed, the names of the twelve tribes of
the children of Israel. 13There were three gates facing east,
three north, three south, and three west. 14The wall of the city
had twelve courses of stones as its foundation, on which were
inscribed the twelve names of the twelve Apostles of the
Lamb.

Responsorial Psalm – Psalms 145:10-11, 12-13, 17-18

R. (12) Your friends make known, O Lord, the glorious splendor of your Kingdom.

10 Let all your works give you thanks, O LORD,

and let your faithful ones bless you.

11 Let them discourse of the glory of your Kingdom

and speak of your might.

R. Your friends make known, O Lord, the glorious splendor of your Kingdom.

12 Making known to men your might

and the glorious splendor of your Kingdom.

13 Your Kingdom is a Kingdom for all ages,

and your dominion endures through all generations.

R. Your friends make known, O Lord, the glorious splendor of your Kingdom.

17 The LORD is just in all his ways

and holy in all his works.

18 The LORD is near to all who call upon him,

to all who call upon him in truth.

R. Your friends make known, O Lord, the glorious splendor of your Kingdom.

Alleluia – John 1:49B

R. Alleluia, alleluia.

49B Rabbi, you are the Son of God; you are the King of Israel.

R. Alleluia, alleluia.

Gospel – John 1:45-51

45 Philip found Nathanael and told him, “We have found the one
about whom Moses wrote in the law, and also the prophets,
Jesus son of Joseph, from Nazareth.” 46 But Nathanael said to
him, “Can anything good come from Nazareth?” Philip said to
him, “Come and see.” 47 Jesus saw Nathanael coming toward
him and said of him, “Here is a true child of Israel. There is no
duplicity in him.” 48 Nathanael said to him, “How do you know
me?” Jesus answered and said to him, “Before Philip called
you, I saw you under the fig tree.” 49 Nathanael answered him,
“Rabbi, you are the Son of God; you are the King of Israel.”
50 Jesus answered and said to him, “Do you believe because I
told you that I saw you under the fig tree? You will see greater
things than this.” 51 And he said to him, “Amen, amen, I say to
you, you will see heaven opened and the angels of God
ascending and descending on the Son of Man.”

Friday August 25, 2023

Friday of Twentieth Week in Ordinary Time

First Reading – Ruth 1:1, 3-6, 14B-16, 22

1 Once in the time of the judges there was a famine in the land;
so a man from Bethlehem of Judah departed with his wife and
two sons to reside on the plateau of Moab. 3 Elimelech, the
husband of Naomi, died, and she was left with her two sons,
4 who married Moabite women, one named Orpah, the other
Ruth. When they had lived there about ten years, 5 both
Mahlon and Chilion died also, and the woman was left with
neither her two sons nor her husband. 6 She then made ready
to go back from the plateau of Moab because word reached
her there that the LORD had visited his people and given them
food. 14B Orpah kissed her mother-in-law good-bye, but Ruth
stayed with her. 15 Naomi said, "See now! Your sister-in-law
has gone back to her people and her god. Go back after your
sister-in-law!" 16 But Ruth said, "Do not ask me to abandon or
forsake you! For wherever you go, I will go, wherever you
lodge I will lodge, your people shall be my people, and your
God my God." 22 Thus it was that Naomi returned with the
Moabite daughter-in-law, Ruth, who accompanied her back
from the plateau of Moab. They arrived in Bethlehem at the
beginning of the barley harvest.

Responsorial Psalm – Psalms 146:5-6AB, 6C-7, 8-9A, 9BC-10

R. (1b) Praise the Lord, my soul!

5 Blessed is he whose help is the God of Jacob,

whose hope is in the LORD, his God,

6AB Who made heaven and earth,

the sea and all that is in them.

R. Praise the Lord, my soul!

6C The LORD keeps faith forever,

7 secures justice for the oppressed,

gives food to the hungry.

The LORD sets captives free.

R. Praise the Lord, my soul!

[8] The LORD gives sight to the blind.

The LORD raises up those who were bowed down;

The LORD loves the just.

[9A] The LORD protects strangers.

R. Praise the Lord, my soul!

[9BC] The fatherless and the widow he sustains,

but the way of the wicked he thwarts.

[10] The LORD shall reign forever;

your God, O Zion, through all generations. Alleluia.

R. Praise the Lord, my soul!

Alleluia – Psalms 25:4B, 5A

R. Alleluia, alleluia.

[4B] Teach me your paths, my God, [5A] guide me in your truth.

R. Alleluia, alleluia.

Gospel – Matthew 22:34-40

[34]When the Pharisees heard that Jesus had silenced the Sadducees, they gathered together, [35]and one of them, a scholar of the law, tested him by asking, [36]"Teacher, which commandment in the law is the greatest?" [37]He said to him, "You shall love the Lord, your God, with all your heart, with all your soul, and with all your mind. [38]This is the greatest and the first commandment. [39]The second is like it: You shall love your neighbor as yourself. [40]The whole law and the prophets depend on these two commandments."

Saturday August 26, 2023

Saturday of Twentieth Week in Ordinary Time

First Reading – Ruth 2:1-3, 8-11; 4:13-17

[1]Naomi had a prominent kinsman named Boaz, of the clan of her husband Elimelech. [2]Ruth the Moabite said to Naomi, "Let me go and glean ears of grain in the field of anyone who will allow me that favor." Naomi said to her, "Go, my daughter,"

and she went. [3]The field she entered to glean after the
harvesters happened to be the section belonging to Boaz of
the clan of Elimelech. [8]Boaz said to Ruth, "Listen, my
daughter! Do not go to glean in anyone else's field; you are
not to leave here. Stay here with my women servants. [9]Watch
to see which field is to be harvested, and follow them; I have
commanded the young men to do you no harm. When you are
thirsty, you may go and drink from the vessels the young men
have filled." [10]Casting herself prostrate upon the ground, Ruth
said to him, "Why should I, a foreigner, be favored with your
notice?" [11]Boaz answered her: "I have had a complete account
of what you have done for your mother-in-law after your
husband's death; you have left your father and your mother
and the land of your birth, and have come to a people whom
you did not know previously." [13]Boaz took Ruth. When they
came together as man and wife, the LORD enabled her to
conceive and she bore a son. [14]Then the women said to
Naomi, "Blessed is the LORD who has not failed to provide
you today with an heir! May he become famous in Israel! [15]He
will be your comfort and the support of your old age, for his
mother is the daughter-in-law who loves you. She is worth
more to you than seven sons!" [16]Naomi took the child, placed
him on her lap, and became his nurse. [17]And the neighbor
women gave him his name, at the news that a grandson had
been born to Naomi. They called him Obed. He was the father
of Jesse, the father of David.

Responsorial Psalm – Psalms 128:1B-2, 3, 4, 5

R. (4) See how the Lord blesses those who fear him.

1B Blessed are you who fear the LORD,

who walk in his ways!

2 For you shall eat the fruit of your handiwork;

blessed shall you be, and favored.

R. See how the Lord blesses those who fear him.

3 You wife shall be like a fruitful vine

in the recesses of your home;

Your children like olive plants

around your table.

R. See how the Lord blesses those who fear him.

[4] Behold, thus is the man blessed

who fears the LORD.

R. See how the Lord blesses those who fear him.

[5] The LORD bless you from Zion:

may you see the prosperity of Jerusalem

all the days of your life.

R. See how the Lord blesses those who fear him.

Alleluia – Matthew 23:9B, 10B

R. Alleluia, alleluia.

[9B] You have but one Father in heaven; [10B] you have but one master, the Christ.

R. Alleluia, alleluia.

Gospel – Matthew 23:1-12

[1]Jesus spoke to the crowds and to his disciples, [2]saying, "The
scribes and the Pharisees have taken their seat on the chair of
Moses. [3]Therefore, do and observe all things whatsoever they
tell you, but do not follow their example. For they preach but
they do not practice. [4]They tie up heavy burdens hard to carry
and lay them on people's shoulders, but they will not lift a
finger to move them. [5]All their works are performed to be
seen. They widen their phylacteries and lengthen their tassels.
[6]They love places of honor at banquets, seats of honor in
synagogues, [7]greetings in marketplaces, and the salutation
'Rabbi.' [8]As for you, do not be called 'Rabbi.' You have but
one teacher, and you are all brothers. [9]Call no one on earth
your father; you have but one Father in heaven. [10]Do not be
called 'Master'; you have but one master, the Christ. [11]The
greatest among you must be your servant. [12]Whoever exalts
himself will be humbled; but whoever humbles himself will be
exalted."

Sunday August 27, 2023

Twenty-first Sunday in Ordinary Time, Year A

First Reading – Isaiah 22:19-23

Thus says the LORD to Shebna, master of the palace: [19]"I will
thrust you from your office and pull you down from your
station. [20]On that day I will summon my servant Eliakim, son of
Hilkiah; [21]I will clothe him with your robe, and gird him with
your sash, and give over to him your authority. He shall be a
father to the inhabitants of Jerusalem, and to the house of
Judah. [22]I will place the key of the House of David on Eliakim's
shoulder; when he opens, no one shall shut when he shuts, no
one shall open. [23]I will fix him like a peg in a sure spot, to be a
place of honor for his family."

Responsorial Psalm – Psalms 138:1-2, 2-3, 6, 8

R. (8bc) **Lord, your love is eternal; do not forsake the work of your hands.**

[1] I will give thanks to you, O LORD, with all my heart,

for you have heard the words of my mouth;

in the presence of the angels I will sing your praise;

[2A] I will worship at your holy temple.

R. Lord, your love is eternal; do not forsake the work of your hands.

[2B] I will give thanks to your name,

because of your kindness and your truth:

[3] When I called, you answered me;

you built up strength within me.

R. Lord, your love is eternal; do not forsake the work of your hands.

[6] The LORD is exalted, yet the lowly he sees,

and the proud he knows from afar.

[8] Your kindness, O LORD, endures forever;

forsake not the work of your hands.

R. Lord, your love is eternal; do not forsake the work of your hands.

Second Reading – Romans 11:33-36

[33]Oh, the depth of the riches and wisdom and knowledge of God! How inscrutable are his judgments and how unsearchable his ways! [34]For who has known the mind of the Lord or who has been his counselor? [35]Or who has given the Lord anything that he may be repaid? [36]For from him and through him and for him are all things. To him be glory forever. Amen.

Alleluia – Matthew 16:18

R. Alleluia, alleluia.

[18] You are Peter and upon this rock I will build my Church and the gates of the netherworld shall not prevail against it.

R. Alleluia, alleluia.

Gospel – Matthew 16:13-20

[13]Jesus went into the region of Caesarea Philippi and he asked his disciples, "Who do people say that the Son of Man is?" [14]They replied, "Some say John the Baptist, others Elijah, still others Jeremiah or one of the prophets." [15]He said to them, "But who do you say that I am?" [16]Simon Peter said in reply, "You are the Christ, the Son of the living God." [17]Jesus said to him in reply, "Blessed are you, Simon son of Jonah. For flesh and blood has not revealed this to you, but my heavenly Father. [18]And so I say to you, you are Peter, and upon this rock I will build my church, and the gates of the netherworld shall not prevail against it. [19]I will give you the keys to the kingdom of heaven. Whatever you bind on earth shall be bound in heaven; and whatever you loose on earth shall be loosed in heaven." [20]Then he strictly ordered his disciples to tell no one that he was the Christ.

Monday August 28, 2023

Memorial of Saint Augustine – Bishop & Doctor

First Reading – 1 Thessalonians 1:1-5, 8B-10

[1]Paul, Silvanus, and Timothy to the Church of the Thessalonians in God the Father and the Lord Jesus Christ:

grace to you and peace. [2]We give thanks to God always for all
of you, remembering you in our prayers, [3]unceasingly calling
to mind your work of faith and labor of love and endurance in
hope of our Lord Jesus Christ, before our God and Father,
[4]knowing, brothers and sisters loved by God, how you were
chosen. [5]For our Gospel did not come to you in word alone,
but also in power and in the Holy Spirit and with much
conviction. You know what sort of people we were among you
for your sake. [8B]In every place your faith in God has gone
forth, so that we have no need to say anything. [9]For they
themselves openly declare about us what sort of reception we
had among you, and how you turned to God from idols to
serve the living and true God and [10]to await his Son from
heaven, whom he raised from the dead, Jesus, who delivers
us from the coming wrath.

Responsorial Psalm – Psalms 149:1B-2, 3-4, 5-6A AND 9B

R. [(see 4a)] **The Lord takes delight in his people.** or: **R. Alleluia.**

[1B] Sing to the LORD a new song

of praise in the assembly of the faithful.

[2] Let Israel be glad in their maker,

let the children of Zion rejoice in their king.

R. The Lord takes delight in his people. or: **R. Alleluia.**

[3] Let them praise his name in the festive dance,

let them sing praise to him with timbrel and harp.

[4] For the LORD loves his people,

and he adorns the lowly with victory.

R. The Lord takes delight in his people. or: **R. Alleluia.**

[5] Let the faithful exult in glory;

let them sing for joy upon their couches;

[6A] Let the high praises of God be in their throats.

[9B] This is the glory of all his faithful. Alleluia.

R. The Lord takes delight in his people. or: **R. Alleluia.**

Alleluia – John 10:27

R. Alleluia, alleluia.

[27] My sheep hear my voice, says the Lord; I know them, and they follow me.

R. Alleluia, alleluia.

Gospel – Matthew 23:13-22

Jesus said to the crowds and to his disciples: [13]"Woe to you, scribes and Pharisees, you hypocrites. You lock the Kingdom of heaven before men. You do not enter yourselves, nor do you allow entrance to those trying to enter. [15]"Woe to you, scribes and Pharisees, you hypocrites. You traverse sea and land to make one convert, and when that happens you make him a child of Gehenna twice as much as yourselves. [16]"Woe to you, blind guides, who say, 'If one swears by the temple, it means nothing, but if one swears by the gold of the temple, one is obligated.' [17]Blind fools, which is greater, the gold, or the temple that made the gold sacred? [18]And you say, 'If one swears by the altar, it means nothing, but if one swears by the gift on the altar, one is obligated.' [19]You blind ones, which is greater, the gift, or the altar that makes the gift sacred? [20]One who swears by the altar swears by it and all that is upon it; [21]one who swears by the temple swears by it and by him who dwells in it; [22]one who swears by heaven swears by the throne of God and by him who is seated on it."

Tuesday August 29, 2023

Martyrdom of John the Baptist

First Reading – 1 Thessalonians 2:1-8

[1]You yourselves know, brothers and sisters, that our reception among you was not without effect. [2]Rather, after we had suffered and been insolently treated, as you know, in Philippi, we drew courage through our God to speak to you the Gospel of God with much struggle. [3]Our exhortation was not from delusion or impure motives, nor did it work through deception. [4]But as we were judged worthy by God to be entrusted with the Gospel, that is how we speak, not as trying to please men, but rather God, who judges our hearts. [5]Nor, indeed, did we ever appear with flattering speech, as you know, or with a

pretext for greed-God is witness– [6]nor did we seek praise from men, either from you or from others, [7]although we were able to impose our weight as Apostles of Christ. Rather, we were gentle among you, as a nursing mother cares for her children. [8]With such affection for you, we were determined to share with you not only the Gospel of God, but our very selves as well, so dearly beloved had you become to us.

Responsorial Psalm – Psalms 139:1-3, 4-6

R. (1) You have searched me and you know me, Lord.

1 O LORD, you have probed me and you know me;

2 you know when I sit and when I stand;

you understand my thoughts from afar.

3 My journeys and my rest you scrutinize,

with all my ways you are familiar.

R. You have searched me and you know me, Lord.

4 Even before a word is on my tongue,

behold, O LORD, you know the whole of it.

5 Behind me and before, you hem me in

and rest your hand upon me.

6 Such knowledge is too wonderful for me;

too lofty for me to attain.

R. You have searched me and you know me, Lord.

Alleluia – Hebrews 4:12

R. Alleluia, alleluia.

12 The word of God is living and effective, able to discern reflections and thoughts of the heart.

R. Alleluia, alleluia.

Gospel – Matthew 23:23-26

Jesus said: [23]"Woe to you, scribes and Pharisees, you hypocrites. You pay tithes of mint and dill and cummin, and have neglected the weightier things of the law: judgment and mercy and fidelity. But these you should have done, without neglecting the others. 24Blind guides, who strain out the gnat and swallow the camel! 25"Woe to you, scribes and Pharisees, you hypocrites. You cleanse the outside of cup and dish, but inside they are full of plunder and self-indulgence. 26Blind Pharisee, cleanse first the inside of the cup, so that the outside also may be clean."

Wednesday August 30, 2023

Wednesday of Twenty-first Week in Ordinary Time

First Reading – 1 Thessalonians 2:9-13

9You recall, brothers and sisters, our toil and drudgery. Working night and day in order not to burden any of you, we proclaimed to you the Gospel of God. 10You are witnesses, and so is God, how devoutly and justly and blamelessly we behaved toward you believers. 11As you know, we treated each one of you as a father treats his children, 12exhorting and encouraging you and insisting that you walk in a manner worthy of the God who calls you into his Kingdom and glory. 13And for this reason we too give thanks to God unceasingly, that, in receiving the word of God from hearing us, you received it not as the word of men, but as it truly is, the word of God, which is now at work in you who believe.

Responsorial Psalm – Psalms 139:7-8, 9-10, 11-12AB

R.(1) You have searched me and you know me, Lord.

7 Where can I go from your spirit?

From your presence where can I flee?

8 If I go up to the heavens, you are there;

if I sink to the nether world, you are present there.

R. You have searched me and you know me, Lord.

9 If I take the wings of the dawn,

if I settle at the farthest limits of the sea,

10 Even there your hand shall guide me,

and your right hand hold me fast.

R. You have searched me and you know me, Lord.

[11] If I say, "Surely the darkness shall hide me,

and night shall be my light"–

[12A] For you darkness itself is not dark,

and night shines as the day.

R. You have searched me and you know me, Lord.

Alleluia – 1 John 2:5

R. Alleluia, alleluia.

[5] Whoever keeps the word of Christ, the love of God is truly perfected in him.

R. Alleluia, alleluia.

Gospel – Matthew 23:27-32

Jesus said, [27]"Woe to you, scribes and Pharisees, you
hypocrites. You are like whitewashed tombs, which appear
beautiful on the outside, but inside are full of dead men's
bones and every kind of filth. [28]Even so, on the outside you
appear righteous, but inside you are filled with hypocrisy and
evildoing. [29]"Woe to you, scribes and Pharisees, you
hypocrites. You build the tombs of the prophets and adorn the
memorials of the righteous, [30]and you say, 'If we had lived in
the days of our ancestors, we would not have joined them in
shedding the prophets' blood.' [31]Thus you bear witness
against yourselves that you are the children of those who
murdered the prophets; [32]now fill up what your ancestors
measured out!"

Thursday August 31, 2023

Thursday of Twenty-first Week in Ordinary Time

First Reading – 1 Thessalonians 3:7-13

[7]We have been reassured about you, brothers and sisters, in
our every distress and affliction, through your faith. [8]For we
now live, if you stand firm in the Lord. [9]What thanksgiving,
then, can we render to God for you, for all the joy we feel on
your account before our God? [10]Night and day we pray
beyond measure to see you in person and to remedy the
deficiencies of your faith. [11]Now may God himself, our Father,
and our Lord Jesus direct our way to you, [12]and may the Lord

make you increase and abound in love for one another and for all, just as we have for you, [13]so as to strengthen your hearts, to be blameless in holiness before our God and Father at the coming of our Lord Jesus with all his holy ones. Amen.

Responsorial Psalm – Psalms 90:3-5A, 12-13, 14 AND 17

R. (14) Fill us with your love, O Lord, and we will sing for joy!

3 You turn man back to dust,

saying, "Return, O children of men."

4 For a thousand years in your sight

are as yesterday, now that it is past,

5A or as a watch of the night.

R. Fill us with your love, O Lord, and we will sing for joy!

12 Teach us to number our days aright,

that we may gain wisdom of heart.

13 Return, O LORD! How long?

Have pity on your servants!

R. Fill us with your love, O Lord, and we will sing for joy!

14 Fill us at daybreak with your kindness,

that we may shout for joy and gladness all our days.

17 And may the gracious care of the LORD our God be ours;

prosper the work of our hands for us!

Prosper the work of our hands!

R. Fill us with your love, O Lord, and we will sing for joy!

Alleluia – Matthew 24:42A, 44

R. Alleluia, alleluia.

42A Stay awake! 44 For you do not know when the Son of Man will come.

R. Alleluia, alleluia.

Gospel – Matthew 24:42-51

Jesus said to his disciples: [42]"Stay awake! For you do not know on which day your Lord will come. [43]Be sure of this: if the master of the house had known the hour of night when the thief was coming, he would have stayed awake and not let his house be broken into. [44]So too, you also must be prepared, for at an hour you do not expect, the Son of Man will come. [45]"Who, then, is the faithful and prudent servant, whom the master has put in charge of his household to distribute to them their food at the proper time? [46]Blessed is that servant whom his master on his arrival finds doing so. [47]Amen, I say to you, he will put him in charge of all his property. [48]But if that wicked servant says to himself, 'My master is long delayed,' [49]and begins to beat his fellow servants, and eat and drink with drunkards, [50]the servant's master will come on an unexpected day and at an unknown hour [51]and will punish him severely and assign him a place with the hypocrites, where there will be wailing and grinding of teeth."

SEPTEMBER 2023

Friday September 1, 2023

Friday of the Twenty-first Week in Ordinary Time

First Reading – 1 Thessalonians 4:1-8

Brothers and sisters, [1]we earnestly ask and exhort you in the Lord Jesus that, as you received from us how you should conduct yourselves to please God – and as you are conducting yourselves – you do so even more. [2] For you know what instructions we gave you through the Lord Jesus. [3]This is the will of God, your holiness: that you refrain from immorality, [4]that each of you know how to acquire a wife for himself in holiness and honor, [5]not in lustful passion as do the Gentiles who do not know God; [6]not to take advantage of or exploit a brother or sister in this matter, for the Lord is an avenger in all these things, as we told you before and solemnly affirmed. [7]For God did not call us to impurity but to holiness. [8]Therefore, whoever disregards this, disregards not a human being but God, who also gives his Holy Spirit to you.

Responsorial Psalm – Psalms 97:1 AND 2B, 5-6, 10, 11-12

R. (12a) Rejoice in the Lord, you just!

1 The LORD is king; let the earth rejoice; let the many isles be glad.

2B Justice and judgment are the foundation of his throne.

R. Rejoice in the Lord, you just!

5 The mountains melt like wax before the LORD, before the LORD of all the earth.

6 The heavens proclaim his justice, and all peoples see his glory.

R. Rejoice in the Lord, you just!

10 The LORD loves those who hate evil; he guards the lives of his faithful ones; from the hand of the wicked he delivers them.

R. Rejoice in the Lord, you just!

11 Light dawns for the just; and gladness, for the upright of heart.

12 Be glad in the LORD, you just, and give thanks to his holy name.

R. Rejoice in the Lord, you just!

Alleluia – Luke 21:36

R. Alleluia, alleluia.

36 Be vigilant at all times and pray, that you may have the strength to stand before the Son of Man.

R. Alleluia, alleluia.

Gospel – Matthew 25:1-13

Jesus told his disciples this parable: 1 "The Kingdom of heaven
will be like ten virgins who took their lamps and went out to
meet the bridegroom. 2 Five of them were foolish and five were
wise. 3 The foolish ones, when taking their lamps, brought no
oil with them, 4 but the wise brought flasks of oil with their
lamps. 5 Since the bridegroom was long delayed, they all
became drowsy and fell asleep. 6 At midnight, there was a cry,

'Behold, the bridegroom! Come out to meet him!' [7]Then all those virgins got up and trimmed their lamps. [8]The foolish ones said to the wise, 'Give us some of your oil, for our lamps are going out.' [9]But the wise ones replied, 'No, for there may not be enough for us and you. Go instead to the merchants and buy some for yourselves.' [10]While they went off to buy it, the bridegroom came and those who were ready went into the wedding feast with him. Then the door was locked. [11]Afterwards, the other virgins came and said, 'Lord, Lord, open the door for us!' [12]But he said in reply, 'Amen, I say to you, I do not know you.' [13]Therefore, stay awake, for you know neither the day nor the hour."

Saturday September 2, 2023

Saturday of Twenty-first Week in Ordinary Time

First Reading – 1 Thessalonians 4:9-11

Brothers and sisters: [9]On the subject of fraternal charity you have no need for anyone to write you, for you yourselves have been taught by God to love one another. [10]Indeed, you do this for all the brothers throughout Macedonia. Nevertheless we urge you, brothers and sisters, to progress even more, [11]and to aspire to live a tranquil life, to mind your own affairs, and to work with your own hands, as we instructed you.

Responsorial Psalm – Psalms 98:1, 7-8, 9

R. (9) The Lord comes to rule the earth with justice.

[1] Sing to the LORD a new song,

for he has done wondrous deeds;

His right hand has won victory for him,

his holy arm.

R. The Lord comes to rule the earth with justice.

[7] Let the sea and what fills it resound,

the world and those who dwell in it;

[8] Let the rivers clap their hands,

the mountains shout with them for joy.

R. The Lord comes to rule the earth with justice.

9 Before the LORD, for he comes,

for he comes to rule the earth;

He will rule the world with justice

and the peoples with equity.

R. The Lord comes to rule the earth with justice.

Alleluia – John 13:34

R. Alleluia, alleluia.

34 I give you a new commandment: love one another as I have loved you.

R. Alleluia, alleluia.

Gospel – Matthew 25:14-30

Jesus told his disciples this parable: 14"A man going on a
journey called in his servants and entrusted his possessions to
them. 15To one he gave five talents; to another, two; to a third,
one – to each according to his ability. Then he went away.
16Immediately the one who received five talents went and
traded with them, and made another five. 17Likewise, the one
who received two made another two. 18But the man who
received one went off and dug a hole in the ground and buried
his master's money. 19After a long time the master of those
servants came back and settled accounts with them. 20The
one who had received five talents came forward bringing the
additional five. He said, 'Master, you gave me five talents.
See, I have made five more.' 21His master said to him, 'Well
done, my good and faithful servant. Since you were faithful in
small matters, I will give you great responsibilities. Come,
share your master's joy.' 22Then the one who had received two
talents also came forward and said, 'Master, you gave me two
talents. See, I have made two more.' 23His master said to him,
'Well done, my good and faithful servant. Since you were
faithful in small matters, I will give you great responsibilities.
Come, share your master's joy.' 24Then the one who had
received the one talent came forward and said, 'Master, I
knew you were a demanding person, harvesting where you did
not plant and gathering where you did not scatter; 25so out of
fear I went off and buried your talent in the ground. Here it is
back.' 26His master said to him in reply, 'You wicked, lazy
servant! So you knew that I harvest where I did not plant and

gather where I did not scatter? [27]Should you not then have put
my money in the bank so that I could have got it back with
interest on my return? [28]Now then! Take the talent from him
and give it to the one with ten. [29]For to everyone who has,
more will be given and he will grow rich; but from the one who
has not, even what he has will be taken away. [30]And throw this
useless servant into the darkness outside, where there will be
wailing and grinding of teeth.'"

Sunday September 3, 2023

Twenty-second Sunday in Ordinary, Time Year A

First Reading – Jeremiah 20:7-9

[7]You duped me, O LORD, and I let myself be duped; you were
too strong for me, and you triumphed. All the day I am an
object of laughter; everyone mocks me. [8]Whenever I speak, I
must cry out, violence and outrage is my message; the word of
the LORD has brought me derision and reproach all the day. [9]I
say to myself, I will not mention him, I will speak in his name
no more. But then it becomes like fire burning in my heart,
imprisoned in my bones; I grow weary holding it in, I cannot
endure it.

Responsorial Psalm – Psalms 63:2, 3-4, 5-6, 8-9

R. (2b) My soul is thirsting for you, O Lord my God.

[2] O God, you are my God whom I seek;

for you my flesh pines and my soul thirsts

like the earth, parched, lifeless and without water.

R. My soul is thirsting for you, O Lord my God.

[3] Thus have I gazed toward you in the sanctuary

to see your power and your glory,

[4] for your kindness is a greater good than life;

my lips shall glorify you.

R. My soul is thirsting for you, O Lord my God.

[5] Thus will I bless you while I live;

lifting up my hands, I will call upon your name.

6 As with the riches of a banquet shall my soul be satisfied,

and with exultant lips my mouth shall praise you.

R. My soul is thirsting for you, O Lord my God.

8 You are my help,

and in the shadow of your wings I shout for joy.

9 My soul clings fast to you;

your right hand upholds me.

R. My soul is thirsting for you, O Lord my God.

Second Reading – Romans 12:1-2

1I urge you, brothers and sisters, by the mercies of God, to
offer your bodies as a living sacrifice, holy and pleasing to
God, your spiritual worship. 2Do not conform yourselves to this
age but be transformed by the renewal of your mind, that you
may discern what is the will of God, what is good and pleasing
and perfect.

Alleluia – Ephesians 1:17-18

R. Alleluia, alleluia.

17 May the Father of our Lord Jesus Christ enlighten the eyes
of our hearts, 18 that we may know what is the hope that
belongs to our call.

R. Alleluia, alleluia.

Gospel – Matthew 16:21-27

21Jesus began to show his disciples that he must go to
Jerusalem and suffer greatly from the elders, the chief priests,
and the scribes, and be killed and on the third day be raised.
22Then Peter took Jesus aside and began to rebuke him, "God
forbid, Lord! No such thing shall ever happen to you." 23He
turned and said to Peter, "Get behind me, Satan! You are an
obstacle to me. You are thinking not as God does, but as
human beings do." 24Then Jesus said to his disciples,
"Whoever wishes to come after me must deny himself, take up
his cross, and follow me. 25For whoever wishes to save his life
will lose it, but whoever loses his life for my sake will find it.
26What profit would there be for one to gain the whole world
and forfeit his life? Or what can one give in exchange for his

life? [27]For the Son of Man will come with his angels in his
Father's glory, and then he will repay all according to his
conduct."

Monday September 4, 2023

Monday of Twenty-second Week in Ordinary Time

First Reading – 1 Thessalonians 4:13-18

[13]We do not want you to be unaware, brothers and sisters,
about those who have fallen asleep, so that you may not
grieve like the rest, who have no hope. [14]For if we believe that
Jesus died and rose, so too will God, through Jesus, bring with
him those who have fallen asleep. [15]Indeed, we tell you this,
on the word of the Lord, that we who are alive, who are left
until the coming of the Lord, will surely not precede those who
have fallen asleep. [16]For the Lord himself, with a word of
command, with the voice of an archangel and with the trumpet
of God, will come down from heaven and the dead in Christ
will rise first. [17]Then we who are alive, who are left, will be
caught up together with them in the clouds to meet the Lord in
the air. Thus we shall always be with the Lord. [18]Therefore,
console one another with these words.

Responsorial Psalm – Psalms 96:1 AND 3, 4-5, 11-12, 13

R. (13b) The Lord comes to judge the earth.

[1] Sing to the LORD a new song;

sing to the LORD, all you lands.

[3] Tell his glory among the nations;

among all peoples, his wondrous deeds.

R. The Lord comes to judge the earth.

[4] For great is the LORD and highly to be praised;

awesome is he, beyond all gods.

[5] For all the gods of the nations are things of nought,

but the LORD made the heavens.

R. The Lord comes to judge the earth.

[11] Let the heavens be glad and the earth rejoice;

let the sea and what fills it resound;

12 let the plains be joyful and all that is in them!

Then shall all the trees of the forest exult.

R. The Lord comes to judge the earth.

13 Before the LORD, for he comes;

for he comes to rule the earth.

He shall rule the world with justice

and the peoples with his constancy.

R. The Lord comes to judge the earth.

Alleluia – Luke 4:18

R. Alleluia, alleluia.

18 The Spirit of the Lord is upon me; he has sent me to bring glad tidings to the poor.

R. Alleluia, alleluia.

Gospel – Luke 4:16-30

16 Jesus came to Nazareth, where he had grown up, and went
according to his custom into the synagogue on the Sabbath
day. He stood up to read 17 and was handed a scroll of the
prophet Isaiah. He unrolled the scroll and found the passage
where it was written: 18 The Spirit of the Lord is upon me,
because he has anointed me to bring glad tidings to the poor.
He has sent me to proclaim liberty to captives and recovery of
sight to the blind, to let the oppressed go free, 19 and to
proclaim a year acceptable to the Lord. 20 Rolling up the scroll,
he handed it back to the attendant and sat down, and the eyes
of all in the synagogue looked intently at him. 21 He said to
them, "Today this Scripture passage is fulfilled in your
hearing." 22 And all spoke highly of him and were amazed at
the gracious words that came from his mouth. They also
asked, "Is this not the son of Joseph?" 23 He said to them,
"Surely you will quote me this proverb, 'Physician, cure
yourself,' and say, 'Do here in your native place the things that
we heard were done in Capernaum.'" 24 And he said, "Amen, I
say to you, no prophet is accepted in his own native place.
25 Indeed, I tell you, there were many widows in Israel in the
days of Elijah when the sky was closed for three and a half

years and a severe famine spread over the entire land. [26]It
was to none of these that Elijah was sent, but only to a widow
in Zarephath in the land of Sidon. [27]Again, there were many
lepers in Israel during the time of Elisha the prophet; yet not
one of them was cleansed, but only Naaman the Syrian."
[28]When the people in the synagogue heard this, they were all
filled with fury. [29]They rose up, drove him out of the town, and
led him to the brow of the hill on which their town had been
built, to hurl him down headlong. [30]But he passed through the
midst of them and went away.

Tuesday September 5, 2023

Tuesday of Twenty-second Week in Ordinary Time

First Reading – 1 Thessalonians 5:1-6, 9-11

[1]Concerning times and seasons, brothers and sisters, you
have no need for anything to be written to you. [2]For you
yourselves know very well that the day of the Lord will come
like a thief at night. [3]When people are saying, "Peace and
security," then sudden disaster comes upon them, like labor
pains upon a pregnant woman, and they will not escape. [4]But
you, brothers and sisters, are not in darkness, for that day to
overtake you like a thief. [5]For all of you are children of the light
and children of the day. We are not of the night or of darkness.
[6]Therefore, let us not sleep as the rest do, but let us stay alert
and sober. [9]For God did not destine us for wrath, but to gain
salvation through our Lord Jesus Christ, [10]who died for us, so
that whether we are awake or asleep we may live together
with him. [11]Therefore, encourage one another and build one
another up, as indeed you do.

Responsorial Psalm – Psalms 27:1, 4, 13-14

R. (13) I believe that I shall see the good things of the Lord in the land of the living.

[1] The LORD is my light and my salvation;

whom should I fear?

The LORD is my life's refuge;

of whom should I be afraid?

R. I believe that I shall see the good things of the Lord in the land of the living.

[4] One thing I ask of the LORD;

this I seek:

To dwell in the house of the LORD

all the days of my life,

That I may gaze on the loveliness of the LORD

and contemplate his temple.

R. I believe that I shall see the good things of the Lord in the land of the living.

[13] I believe that I shall see the bounty of the LORD

in the land of the living.

[14] Wait for the LORD with courage;

be stouthearted, and wait for the LORD.

R. I believe that I shall see the good things of the Lord in the land of the living.

Alleluia – Luke 7:16

R. Alleluia, alleluia.

[16] A great prophet has arisen in our midst and God has visited his people.

R. Alleluia, alleluia.

Gospel – Luke 4:31-37

[31]Jesus went down to Capernaum, a town of Galilee. He
taught them on the Sabbath, [32]and they were astonished at his
teaching because he spoke with authority. [33]In the synagogue
there was a man with the spirit of an unclean demon, and he
cried out in a loud voice, [34]"What have you to do with us,
Jesus of Nazareth? Have you come to destroy us? I know who
you are–the Holy One of God!" [35]Jesus rebuked him and said,
"Be quiet! Come out of him!" Then the demon threw the man
down in front of them and came out of him without doing him
any harm. [36]They were all amazed and said to one another,
"What is there about his word? For with authority and power
he commands the unclean spirits, and they come out." [37]And
news of him spread everywhere in the surrounding region.

Wednesday September 6, 2023

Wednesday of Twenty-second Week in Ordinary Time

First Reading – Colosians 1:1-8

1 Paul, an Apostle of Christ Jesus by the will of God, and
Timothy our brother, 2 to the holy ones and faithful brothers
and sisters in Christ in Colossae: grace to you and peace from
God our Father. 3 We always give thanks to God, the Father of
our Lord Jesus Christ, when we pray for you, 4 for we have
heard of your faith in Christ Jesus and the love that you have
for all the holy ones 5 because of the hope reserved for you in
heaven. Of this you have already heard through the word of
truth, the Gospel, 6 that has come to you. Just as in the whole
world it is bearing fruit and growing, so also among you, from
the day you heard it and came to know the grace of God in
truth, 7 as you learned it from Epaphras our beloved fellow
slave, who is a trustworthy minister of Christ on your behalf
8 and who also told us of your love in the Spirit.

Responsorial Psalm – Psalms 52:10, 11

R. (10) I trust in the mercy of God for ever.

10 I, like a green olive tree

in the house of God,

Trust in the mercy of God

forever and ever.

R. I trust in the mercy of God for ever.

11 I will thank you always for what you have done,

and proclaim the goodness of your name

before your faithful ones.

R. I trust in the mercy of God for ever.

Alleluia – Luke 4:18

R. Alleluia, alleluia.

18 The Lord sent me to bring glad tidings to the poor and to proclaim liberty to captives.

R. Alleluia, alleluia.

Gospel – Luke 4:38-44

38After Jesus left the synagogue, he entered the house of Simon. Simon's mother-in-law was afflicted with a severe fever, and they interceded with him about her. 39He stood over her, rebuked the fever, and it left her. She got up immediately and waited on them. 40At sunset, all who had people sick with various diseases brought them to him. He laid his hands on each of them and cured them. 41And demons also came out from many, shouting, "You are the Son of God." But he rebuked them and did not allow them to speak because they knew that he was the Christ. 42At daybreak, Jesus left and went to a deserted place. The crowds went looking for him, and when they came to him, they tried to prevent him from leaving them. 43But he said to them, "To the other towns also I must proclaim the good news of the Kingdom of God, because for this purpose I have been sent." 44And he was preaching in the synagogues of Judea.

Thursday September 7, 2023

Thursday of Twenty-second Week in Ordinary Time

First Reading – Colosians 1:9-14

Brothers and sisters: 9From the day we heard about you, we do not cease praying for you and asking that you may be filled with the knowledge of God's will through all spiritual wisdom and understanding 10to walk in a manner worthy of the Lord, so as to be fully pleasing, in every good work bearing fruit and growing in the knowledge of God,11strengthened with every power, in accord with his glorious might, for all endurance and patience, 12with joy giving thanks to the Father, who has made you fit to share in the inheritance of the holy ones in light. 13He delivered us from the power of darkness and transferred us to the Kingdom of his beloved Son, 14in whom we have redemption, the forgiveness of sins.

Responsorial Psalm – Psalms 98:2-3AB, 3CD-4, 5-6

R. (2) The Lord has made known his salvation.

2 The LORD has made his salvation known:

in the sight of the nations he has revealed his justice.

3AB He has remembered his kindness and his faithfulness

toward the house of Israel.

R. The Lord has made known his salvation.

3CD All the ends of the earth have seen

the salvation by our God.

4 Sing joyfully to the LORD, all you lands;

break into song; sing praise.

R. The Lord has made known his salvation.

5 Sing praise to the LORD with the harp,

with the harp and melodious song.

6 With trumpets and the sound of the horn

sing joyfully before the King, the LORD.

R. The Lord has made known his salvation.

Alleluia – Matthew 4:19

R. Alleluia, alleluia.

19 Come after me, says the Lord, and I will make you fishers of men.

R. Alleluia, alleluia.

Gospel – Luke 5:1-11

1While the crowd was pressing in on Jesus and listening to the
word of God, he was standing by the Lake of Gennesaret. 2He
saw two boats there alongside the lake; the fishermen had
disembarked and were washing their nets. 3Getting into one of
the boats, the one belonging to Simon, he asked him to put
out a short distance from the shore. Then he sat down and
taught the crowds from the boat. 4After he had finished
speaking, he said to Simon, "Put out into deep water and
lower your nets for a catch." 5Simon said in reply, "Master, we
have worked hard all night and have caught nothing, but at
your command I will lower the nets." 6When they had done
this, they caught a great number of fish and their nets were
tearing. 7They signaled to their partners in the other boat to
come to help them. They came and filled both boats so that
the boats were in danger of sinking. 8When Simon Peter saw
this, he fell at the knees of Jesus and said, "Depart from me,

Lord, for I am a sinful man." [9]For astonishment at the catch of fish they had made seized him and all those with him, [10]and likewise James and John, the sons of Zebedee, who were partners of Simon. Jesus said to Simon, "Do not be afraid; from now on you will be catching men." [11]When they brought their boats to the shore, they left everything and followed him.

Friday September 8, 2023

Feast of Nativity of the Blessed Virgin Mary

First Reading – Micah 5:1-4A

The LORD says: [1]You, Bethlehem-Ephrathah, too small to be among the clans of Judah, From you shall come forth for me one who is to be ruler in Israel; Whose origin is from of old, from ancient times. [2](Therefore the Lord will give them up, until the time when she who is to give birth has borne, And the rest of his brethren shall return to the children of Israel.) [3]He shall stand firm and shepherd his flock by the strength of the LORD, in the majestic name of the LORD, his God; And they shall remain, for now his greatness shall reach to the ends of the earth; [4A]he shall be peace.

Or Romans 8:28-30

Brothers and sisters: [28]We know that all things work for good for those who love God, who are called according to his purpose. [29]For those he foreknew he also predestined to be conformed to the image of his Son, so that he might be the firstborn among many brothers. [30]And those he predestined he also called; and those he called he also justified; and those he justified he also glorified.

Responsorial Psalm – Psalms 13:6AB, 6C

R. (Isaiah 61:10) **With delight I rejoice in the Lord.**

[6AB] Though I trusted in your mercy,

let my heart rejoice in your salvation.

R. With delight I rejoice in the Lord.

[6C] Let me sing of the LORD, "He has been good to me."

R. With delight I rejoice in the Lord.

Alleluia

R. Alleluia, alleluia.

Blessed are you, holy Virgin Mary, deserving of all praise; from you rose the sun of justice, Christ our God.

R. Alleluia, alleluia.

Gospel – Matthew 1:1-16, 18-23

1The book of the genealogy of Jesus Christ, the son of David,
the son of Abraham. 2Abraham became the father of Isaac,
Isaac the father of Jacob, Jacob the father of Judah and his
brothers. 3Judah became the father of Perez and Zerah,
whose mother was Tamar. Perez became the father of
Hezron, Hezron the father of Ram, 4Ram the father of
Amminadab. Amminadab became the father of Nahshon,
Nahshon the father of Salmon, 5Salmon the father of Boaz,
whose mother was Rahab. Boaz became the father of Obed,
whose mother was Ruth. Obed became the father of Jesse,
6Jesse the father of David the king. David became the father
of Solomon, whose mother had been the wife of Uriah.
7Solomon became the father of Rehoboam, Rehoboam the
father of Abijah, Abijah the father of Asaph. 8Asaph became
the father of Jehoshaphat, Jehoshaphat the father of Joram,
Joram the father of Uzziah. 9Uzziah became the father of
Jotham, Jotham the father of Ahaz, Ahaz the father of
Hezekiah. 10Hezekiah became the father of Manasseh,
Manasseh the father of Amos, Amos the father of Josiah.
11Josiah became the father of Jechoniah and his brothers at
the time of the Babylonian exile. 12After the Babylonian exile,
Jechoniah became the father of Shealtiel, Shealtiel the father
of Zerubbabel, 13Zerubbabel the father of Abiud. Abiud
became the father of Eliakim, Eliakim the father of Azor, 14Azor
the father of Zadok. Zadok became the father of Achim, Achim
the father of Eliud, 15Eliud the father of Eleazar. Eleazar
became the father of Matthan, Matthan the father of Jacob,
16Jacob the father of Joseph, the husband of Mary. Of her was
born Jesus who is called the Christ. 18Now this is how the birth
of Jesus Christ came about. When his mother Mary was
betrothed to Joseph, but before they lived together, she was
found with child through the Holy Spirit. 19Joseph her husband,
since he was a righteous man, yet unwilling to expose her to
shame, decided to divorce her quietly. 20Such was his
intention when, behold, the angel of the Lord appeared to him
in a dream and said, “Joseph, son of David, do not be afraid to

take Mary your wife into your home. For it is through the Holy
Spirit that this child has been conceived in her. [21]She will bear
a son and you are to name him Jesus, because he will save
his people from their sins." [22]All this took place to fulfill what
the Lord had said through the prophet: [23]Behold, the virgin
shall conceive and bear a son, and they shall name him
Emmanuel, which means "God is with us."

Or Matthew 1:18-23

[18]Now this is how the birth of Jesus Christ came about. When
his mother Mary was betrothed to Joseph, but before they
lived together, she was found with child through the Holy
Spirit. [19]Joseph her husband, since he was a righteous man,
yet unwilling to expose her to shame, decided to divorce her
quietly. [20]Such was his intention when, behold, the angel of
the Lord appeared to him in a dream and said, "Joseph, son of
David, do not be afraid to take Mary your wife into your home.
For it is through the Holy Spirit that this child has been
conceived in her. [21]She will bear a son and you are to name
him Jesus, because he will save his people from their sins."
[22]All this took place to fulfill what the Lord had said through the
prophet: [23]Behold, the virgin shall conceive and bear a son,
and they shall name him Emmanuel, which means "God is
with us."

Saturday September 9, 2023

Memorial of Saint Peter Claver, Priest

First Reading – Colosians 1:21-23

Brothers and sisters: [21]You once were alienated and hostile in
mind because of evil deeds; [22]God has now reconciled you in
the fleshly Body of Christ through his death, to present you
holy, without blemish, and irreproachable before him,
[23]provided that you persevere in the faith, firmly grounded,
stable, and not shifting from the hope of the Gospel that you
heard, which has been preached to every creature under
heaven, of which I, Paul, am a minister.

Responsorial Psalm – Psalms 54:3-4, 6 AND 8

R. (6) God himself is my help.

[3] O God, by your name save me,

and by your might defend my cause.

4 O God, hear my prayer;

hearken to the words of my mouth.

R. God himself is my help.

6 Behold, God is my helper;

the Lord sustains my life.

8 Freely will I offer you sacrifice;

I will praise your name, O LORD, for its goodness.

R. God himself is my help.

Alleluia – John 14:6

R. Alleluia, alleluia.

6 I am the way and the truth and the life, says the Lord; no one comes to the Father except through me.

R. Alleluia, alleluia.

Gospel – Luke 6:1-5

1While Jesus was going through a field of grain on a Sabbath,
his disciples were picking the heads of grain, rubbing them in
their hands, and eating them. 2Some Pharisees said, "Why are
you doing what is unlawful on the Sabbath?" 3Jesus said to
them in reply, "Have you not read what David did when he and
those who were with him were hungry? 4How he went into the
house of God, took the bread of offering, which only the priests could lawfully eat, ate of it, and shared it with his
companions?" 5Then he said to them, "The Son of Man is lord of the Sabbath."

Sunday September 10, 2023

Twenty-third Sunday in Ordinary Time,Year A

First Reading – Ezekiel 33:7-9

Thus says the LORD: 7You, son of man, I have appointed
watchman for the house of Israel; when you hear me say anything, you shall warn them for me. 8If I tell the wicked, "O
wicked one, you shall surely die, " and you do not speak out to dissuade the wicked from his way, the wicked shall die for his

guilt, but I will hold you responsible for his death. [9]But if you warn the wicked, trying to turn him from his way, and he refuses to turn from his way, he shall die for his guilt, but you shall save yourself.

Responsorial Psalm – Psalms 95:1-2, 6-7, 8-9

R. (8) If today you hear his voice, harden not your hearts.

1 Come, let us sing joyfully to the LORD;

let us acclaim the rock of our salvation.

2 Let us come into his presence with thanksgiving;

let us joyfully sing psalms to him.

R. If today you hear his voice, harden not your hearts.

6 Come, let us bow down in worship;

let us kneel before the LORD who made us.

7 For he is our God,

and we are the people he shepherds, the flock he guides.

R. If today you hear his voice, harden not your hearts.

8 Oh, that today you would hear his voice:

"Harden not your hearts as at Meribah,

as in the day of Massah in the desert,

9 where your fathers tempted me;

they tested me though they had seen my works."

R. If today you hear his voice, harden not your hearts.

Second Reading – Romans 13:8-10

Brothers and sisters: [8]Owe nothing to anyone, except to love one another; for the one who loves another has fulfilled the law. [9]The commandments, "You shall not commit adultery; you shall not kill; you shall not steal; you shall not covet," and whatever other commandment there may be, are summed up in this saying, namely, "You shall love your neighbor as yourself." [10]Love does no evil to the neighbor; hence, love is the fulfillment of the law.

Alleluia – 2 Corinthians 5:19

R. Alleluia, alleluia.

[19] God was reconciling the world to himself in Christ and entrusting to us the message of reconciliation.

R. Alleluia, alleluia.

Gospel – Matthew 18:15-20

Jesus said to his disciples: [15]"If your brother sins against you, go and tell him his fault between you and him alone. If he listens to you, you have won over your brother. [16]If he does not listen, take one or two others along with you, so that 'every fact may be established on the testimony of two or three witnesses.' [17]If he refuses to listen to them, tell the church. If he refuses to listen even to the church, then treat him as you would a Gentile or a tax collector. [18]Amen, I say to you, whatever you bind on earth shall be bound in heaven, and whatever you loose on earth shall be loosed in heaven. [19]Again, amen, I say to you, if two of you agree on earth about anything for which they are to pray, it shall be granted to them by my heavenly Father. [20]For where two or three are gathered together in my name, there am I in the midst of them."

Monday September 11, 2023

Monday of Twenty-third Week Ordinary Time

First Reading – Colosians 1:24-2:3

Brothers and sisters: [24]I rejoice in my sufferings for your sake, and in my flesh I am filling up what is lacking in the afflictions of Christ on behalf of his Body, which is the Church, [25]of which I am a minister in accordance with God's stewardship given to me to bring to completion for you the word of God, [26]the mystery hidden from ages and from generations past. But now it has been manifested to his holy ones, [27]to whom God chose to make known the riches of the glory of this mystery among the Gentiles; it is Christ in you, the hope for glory. [28]It is he whom we proclaim, admonishing everyone and teaching everyone with all wisdom, that we may present everyone perfect in Christ. [29]For this I labor and struggle, in accord with the exercise of his power working within me. [1]For I want you to know how great a struggle I am having for you and for those in

Laodicea and all who have not seen me face to face, [2]that
their hearts may be encouraged as they are brought together
in love, to have all the richness of assured understanding, for
the knowledge of the mystery of God, Christ, [3]in whom are
hidden all the treasures of wisdom and knowledge.

Responsorial Psalm – Psalms 62:6-7, 9

R.(8) In God is my safety and my glory.

[6] Only in God be at rest, my soul,

for from him comes my hope.

[7] He only is my rock and my salvation,

my stronghold; I shall not be disturbed.

R. In God is my safety and my glory.

[9] Trust in him at all times, O my people!

Pour out your hearts before him;

God is our refuge!

R. In God is my safety and my glory.

Alleluia – John 10:27

R. Alleluia, alleluia.

[27]My sheep hear my voice, says the Lord; I know them, and they follow me.

R. Alleluia, alleluia.

Gospel – Luke 6:6-11

[6]On a certain Sabbath Jesus went into the synagogue and
taught, and there was a man there whose right hand was
withered. [7]The scribes and the Pharisees watched him closely
to see if he would cure on the Sabbath so that they might
discover a reason to accuse him. [8]But he realized their
intentions and said to the man with the withered hand, “Come
up and stand before us.” And he rose and stood there. [9]Then
Jesus said to them, “I ask you, is it lawful to do good on the
Sabbath rather than to do evil, to save life rather than to
destroy it?” [10]Looking around at them all, he then said to him,
“Stretch out your hand.” He did so and his hand was restored.

[11]But they became enraged and discussed together what they
might do to Jesus.

Tuesday September 12, 2023

Tuesday of Twenty-third Week in Ordinary Time

First Reading – Colosians 2:6-15

Brothers and sisters: [6]As you received Christ Jesus the Lord,
walk in him, [7]rooted in him and built upon him and established
in the faith as you were taught, abounding in thanksgiving.
[8]See to it that no one captivate you with an empty, seductive
philosophy according to the tradition of men, according to the
elemental powers of the world and not according to Christ.
[9]For in him dwells the whole fullness of the deity bodily, [10]and
you share in this fullness in him, who is the head of every
principality and power. [11]In him you were also circumcised with
a circumcision not administered by hand, by stripping off the
carnal body, with the circumcision of Christ. [12]You were buried
with him in baptism, in which you were also raised with him
through faith in the power of God, who raised him from the
dead. [13]And even when you were dead in transgressions and
the uncircumcision of your flesh, he brought you to life along
with him, having forgiven us all our transgressions;
[14]obliterating the bond against us, with its legal claims, which
was opposed to us, he also removed it from our midst, nailing
it to the cross; [15] despoiling the principalities and the powers,
he made a public spectacle of them, leading them away in
triumph by it.

Responsorial Psalm – Psalms 145:1B-2, 8-9, 10-11

R.[(9)] The Lord is compassionate toward all his works.

[1B] I will extol you, O my God and King,

and I will bless your name forever and ever.

[2] Every day will I bless you,

and I will praise your name forever and ever.

R. The Lord is compassionate toward all his works.

[8] The LORD is gracious and merciful,

slow to anger and of great kindness.

[9] The LORD is good to all

and compassionate toward all his works.

R. The Lord is compassionate toward all his works.

[10] Let all your works give you thanks, O LORD,

and let your faithful ones bless you.

[11] Let them discourse of the glory of your Kingdom

and speak of your might.

R. The Lord is compassionate toward all his works.

Alleluia – John 15:16

R. Alleluia, alleluia.

[16] I chose you from the world, that you may go and bear fruit that will last, says the Lord.

R. Alleluia, alleluia.

Gospel – Luke 6:12-19

[12]Jesus departed to the mountain to pray, and he spent the
night in prayer to God. [13]When day came, he called his
disciples to himself, and from them he chose Twelve, whom
he also named Apostles: [14]Simon, whom he named Peter, and
his brother Andrew, James, John, Philip, Bartholomew,
[15]Matthew, Thomas, James the son of Alphaeus, Simon who
was called a Zealot, [16]and Judas the son of James, and Judas
Iscariot, who became a traitor. [17]And he came down with them
and stood on a stretch of level ground. A great crowd of his
disciples and a large number of the people from all Judea and
Jerusalem and the coastal region of Tyre and Sidon [18]came to
hear him and to be healed of their diseases; and even those
who were tormented by unclean spirits were cured.
[19]Everyone in the crowd sought to touch him because power
came forth from him and healed them all.

Wednesday September 13, 2023

Memorial of Saint John Chrysostom, Bishop & Doctor

First Reading – Colossians 3:1-11

Brothers and sisters: [1]If you were raised with Christ, seek what is above, where Christ is seated at the right hand of God.

2Think of what is above, not of what is on earth. 3For you have
died, and your life is hidden with Christ in God. 4When Christ
your life appears, then you too will appear with him in glory.
5Put to death, then, the parts of you that are earthly:
immorality, impurity, passion, evil desire, and the greed that is
idolatry. 6Because of these the wrath of God is coming upon
the disobedient. 7By these you too once conducted
yourselves, when you lived in that way. 8But now you must put
them all away: anger, fury, malice, slander, and obscene
language out of your mouths. 9Stop lying to one another, since
you have taken off the old self with its practices 10and have put
on the new self, which is being renewed, for knowledge, in the
image of its creator. 11Here there is not Greek and Jew,
circumcision and uncircumcision, barbarian, Scythian, slave,
free; but Christ is all and in all.

Responsorial Psalm – Psalms 145:2-3, 10-11, 12-13AB

R. (9) The Lord is compassionate toward all his works.

2 Every day will I bless you,

and I will praise your name forever and ever.

3 Great is the LORD and highly to be praised;

his greatness is unsearchable.

R. The Lord is compassionate toward all his works.

10 Let all your works give you thanks, O LORD,

and let your faithful ones bless you.

11 Let them discourse of the glory of your Kingdom

and speak of your might.

R. The Lord is compassionate toward all his works.

12 Making known to men your might

and the glorious splendor of your Kingdom.

13AB Your Kingdom is a Kingdom for all ages,

and your dominion endures through all generations.

R. The Lord is compassionate toward all his works.

Alleluia – Luke 6:23AB

R. Alleluia, alleluia.

[23AB] Rejoice and leap for joy! Your reward will be great in heaven.

R. Alleluia, alleluia.

Gospel – Luke 6:20-26

[20]Raising his eyes toward his disciples Jesus said: "Blessed are you who are poor, for the Kingdom of God is yours. [21]Blessed are you who are now hungry, for you will be satisfied. Blessed are you who are now weeping, for you will laugh. [22]Blessed are you when people hate you, and when they exclude and insult you, and denounce your name as evil on account of the Son of Man. [23]"Rejoice and leap for joy on that day! Behold, your reward will be great in heaven. For their ancestors treated the prophets in the same way. [24]But woe to you who are rich, for you have received your consolation. [25]But woe to you who are filled now, for you will be hungry. Woe to you who laugh now, for you will grieve and weep. [26]Woe to you when all speak well of you, for their ancestors treated the false prophets in this way."

Thursday September 14, 2023

Feast of the Exaltation of the Holy Cross

First Reading – Numbers 21:4B-9

[4B]With their patience worn out by the journey, [5]the people complained against God and Moses, "Why have you brought us up from Egypt to die in this desert, where there is no food or water? We are disgusted with this wretched food!" [6]In punishment the LORD sent among the people saraph serpents, which bit the people so that many of them died. [7]Then the people came to Moses and said, "We have sinned in complaining against the LORD and you. Pray the LORD to take the serpents from us." So Moses prayed for the people, [8]and the LORD said to Moses, "Make a saraph and mount it on a pole, and if any who have been bitten look at it, they will live." [9]Moses accordingly made a bronze serpent and mounted it on a pole, and whenever anyone who had been bitten by a serpent looked at the bronze serpent, he lived.

Responsorial Psalm – Psalms 78:1BC-2, 34-35, 36-37, 38

R. (See 7b) Do not forget the works of the Lord!

1BC Hearken, my people, to my teaching;

incline your ears to the words of my mouth.

2 I will open my mouth in a parable,

I will utter mysteries from of old.

R. Do not forget the works of the Lord!

34 While he slew them they sought him

and inquired after God again,

35 Remembering that God was their rock

and the Most High God, their redeemer.

R. Do not forget the works of the Lord!

36 But they flattered him with their mouths

and lied to him with their tongues,

37 Though their hearts were not steadfast toward him,

nor were they faithful to his covenant.

R. Do not forget the works of the Lord!

38 But he, being merciful, forgave their sin

and destroyed them not;

Often he turned back his anger

and let none of his wrath be roused.

R. Do not forget the works of the Lord!

Second Reading – Philippians 2:6-11

Brothers and sisters: 6Christ Jesus, though he was in the form
of God, did not regard equality with God something to be
grasped. 7Rather, he emptied himself, taking the form of a
slave, coming in human likeness; and found human in
appearance, 8he humbled himself, becoming obedient to
death, even death on a cross. 9Because of this, God greatly
exalted him and bestowed on him the name that is above

every name, [10]that at the name of Jesus every knee should bend, of those in heaven and on earth and under the earth, [11]and every tongue confess that Jesus Christ is Lord, to the glory of God the Father.

Alleluia

R. Alleluia, alleluia.

We adore you, O Christ, and we bless you, because by your Cross you have redeemed the world.

R. Alleluia, alleluia.

Gospel – John 3:13-17

Jesus said to Nicodemus: [13]"No one has gone up to heaven except the one who has come down from heaven, the Son of Man. [14]And just as Moses lifted up the serpent in the desert, so must the Son of Man be lifted up, [15]so that everyone who believes in him may have eternal life." [16]For God so loved the world that he gave his only Son, so that everyone who believes in him might not perish but might have eternal life. [17]For God did not send his Son into the world to condemn the world, but that the world might be saved through him.

Friday September 15, 2023

Memorial of Our Lady of Sorrows

First Reading – 1 Timothy 1:1-2, 12-14

[1]Paul, an Apostle of Christ Jesus by command of God our savior and of Christ Jesus our hope, [2]to Timothy, my true child in faith: grace, mercy, and peace from God the Father and Christ Jesus our Lord. [12]I am grateful to him who has strengthened me, Christ Jesus our Lord, because he considered me trustworthy in appointing me to the ministry. [13]I was once a blasphemer and a persecutor and an arrogant man, but I have been mercifully treated because I acted out of ignorance in my unbelief. [14]Indeed, the grace of our Lord has been abundant, along with the faith and love that are in Christ Jesus.

Responsorial Psalm – Psalms 16:1B-2A AND 5, 7-8, 11

R.(see 5) You are my inheritance, O Lord.

[1B] Keep me, O God, for in you I take refuge;

[2A] I say to the LORD, "My Lord are you."

[5] O LORD, my allotted portion and my cup,

you it is who hold fast my lot.

R. You are my inheritance, O Lord.

[7] I bless the LORD who counsels me;

even in the night my heart exhorts me.

[8] I set the LORD ever before me;

with him at my right hand I shall not be disturbed.

R. You are my inheritance, O Lord.

[11] You will show me the path to life,

fullness of joys in your presence,

the delights at your right hand forever.

R. You are my inheritance, O Lord.

Alleluia – John 17:17B, 17A

R. Alleluia, alleluia.

[17B] Your word, O Lord, is truth; [17A] consecrate us in the truth.

R. Alleluia, alleluia.

Gospel – Luke 6:39-42

[39]Jesus told his disciples a parable: "Can a blind person guide
a blind person? Will not both fall into a pit? [40]No disciple is
superior to the teacher; but when fully trained, every disciple
will be like his teacher. [41]Why do you notice the splinter in your
brother's eye, but do not perceive the wooden beam in your
own? [42]How can you say to your brother, 'Brother, let me
remove that splinter in your eye,' when you do not even notice
the wooden beam in your own eye? You hypocrite! Remove
the wooden beam from your eye first; then you will see clearly
to remove the splinter in your brother's eye."

Saturday September 16, 2023

Memorial of Saints Cornelius and Saint Cyprian

First Reading – 1 Timothy 1:15-17

Beloved: [15]This saying is trustworthy and deserves full acceptance: Christ Jesus came into the world to save sinners. Of these I am the foremost. [16]But for that reason I was mercifully treated, so that in me, as the foremost, Christ Jesus might display all his patience as an example for those who would come to believe in him for everlasting life. [17]To the king of ages, incorruptible, invisible, the only God, honor and glory forever and ever. Amen.

Responsorial Psalm – Psalms 113:1B-2, 3-4, 5 AND 6-7

R. (2) Blessed be the name of the Lord for ever.

1B Praise, you servants of the LORD,

praise the name of the LORD.

2 Blessed be the name of the LORD

both now and forever.

R. Blessed be the name of the Lord for ever.

3 From the rising to the setting of the sun

is the name of the LORD to be praised.

4 High above all nations is the LORD;

above the heavens is his glory.

R. Blessed be the name of the Lord for ever.

5 Who is like the LORD, our God,

6 and looks upon the heavens and the earth below?

7 He raises up the lowly from the dust;

from the dunghill he lifts up the poor.

R. Blessed be the name of the Lord for ever.

Alleluia – John 14:23

R. Alleluia, alleluia.

23 Whoever loves me will keep my word, and my Father will love him, and we will come to him.

R. Alleluia, alleluia.

Gospel – Luke 6:43-49

Jesus said to his disciples: 43“A good tree does not bear rotten
fruit, nor does a rotten tree bear good fruit. 44For every tree is
known by its own fruit. For people do not pick figs from thorn
bushes, nor do they gather grapes from brambles. 45A good
person out of the store of goodness in his heart produces
good, but an evil person out of a store of evil produces evil; for
from the fullness of the heart the mouth speaks. 46“Why do you
call me, ‘Lord, Lord,’ but not do what I command? 47I will show
you what someone is like who comes to me, listens to my
words, and acts on them. 48That one is like a man building a
house, who dug deeply and laid the foundation on rock; when
the flood came, the river burst against that house but could not
shake it because it had been well built. 49But the one who
listens and does not act is like a person who built a house on
the ground without a foundation. When the river burst against
it, it collapsed at once and was completely destroyed.”

Sunday September 17, 2023

Twenty-fourth Sunday in Ordinary Time, Year A

First Reading – Sirach 27:30-28:7

30Wrath and anger are hateful things, yet the sinner hugs them
tight. 1The vengeful will suffer the LORD’s vengeance, for he
remembers their sins in detail. 2Forgive your neighbor’s
injustice; then when you pray, your own sins will be forgiven.
3Could anyone nourish anger against another and expect
healing from the LORD? 4Could anyone refuse mercy to
another like himself, can he seek pardon for his own sins? 5If
one who is but flesh cherishes wrath, who will forgive his sins?
6Remember your last days, set enmity aside; remember death
and decay, and cease from sin! 7Think of the commandments,
hate not your neighbor; remember the Most High’s covenant,
and overlook faults.

Responsorial Psalm – Psalms 103:1-2, 3-4, 9-10, 11-12

R. (8) The Lord is kind and merciful, slow to anger, and rich in compassion.

1 Bless the LORD, O my soul;

and all my being, bless his holy name.

2 Bless the LORD, O my soul,

and forget not all his benefits.

R. The Lord is kind and merciful, slow to anger, and rich in compassion.

3 He pardons all your iniquities,

heals all your ills.

4 He redeems your life from destruction,

crowns you with kindness and compassion.

R. The Lord is kind and merciful, slow to anger, and rich in compassion.

9 He will not always chide,

nor does he keep his wrath forever.

10 Not according to our sins does he deal with us,

nor does he requite us according to our crimes.

R. The Lord is kind and merciful, slow to anger, and rich in compassion.

11 For as the heavens are high above the earth,

so surpassing is his kindness toward those who fear him.

12 As far as the east is from the west,

so far has he put our transgressions from us.

R. The Lord is kind and merciful, slow to anger, and rich in compassion.

Second Reading – Romans 14:7-9

Brothers and sisters: 7None of us lives for oneself, and no one
dies for oneself. 8For if we live, we live for the Lord, and if we

die, we die for the Lord; so then, whether we live or die, we
are the Lord's. 9For this is why Christ died and came to life,
that he might be Lord of both the dead and the living.

Alleluia – John 13:34

R. Alleluia, alleluia.

34I give you a new commandment, says the Lord; love one
another as I have loved you.

R. Alleluia, alleluia.

Gospel – Matthew 18:21-35

21Peter approached Jesus and asked him, "Lord, if my brother
sins against me, how often must I forgive? As many as seven
times?" 22Jesus answered, "I say to you, not seven times but
seventy-seven times. 23That is why the kingdom of heaven
may be likened to a king who decided to settle accounts with
his servants. 24When he began the accounting, a debtor was
brought before him who owed him a huge amount. 25Since he
had no way of paying it back, his master ordered him to be
sold, along with his wife, his children, and all his property, in
payment of the debt. 26At that, the servant fell down, did him
homage, and said, 'Be patient with me, and I will pay you back
in full.' 27Moved with compassion the master of that servant let
him go and forgave him the loan. 28When that servant had left,
he found one of his fellow servants who owed him a much
smaller amount. He seized him and started to choke him,
demanding, 'Pay back what you owe.' 29Falling to his knees,
his fellow servant begged him, 'Be patient with me, and I will
pay you back.' 30But he refused. Instead, he had the fellow
servant put in prison until he paid back the debt. 31Now when
his fellow servants saw what had happened, they were deeply
disturbed, and went to their master and reported the whole
affair. 32His master summoned him and said to him, 'You
wicked servant! I forgave you your entire debt because you
begged me to. 33Should you not have had pity on your fellow
servant, as I had pity on you?' 34Then in anger his master
handed him over to the torturers until he should pay back the
whole debt. 35So will my heavenly Father do to you, unless
each of you forgives your brother from your heart."

Monday September 18, 2023

Monday of Twenty-fourth Week in Ordinary Time

First Reading – 1 Timothy 2:1-8

Beloved: [1]First of all, I ask that supplications, prayers, petitions, and thanksgivings be offered for everyone, [2]for kings and for all in authority, that we may lead a quiet and tranquil life in all devotion and dignity. [3]This is good and pleasing to God our savior, [4]who wills everyone to be saved and to come to knowledge of the truth. [5]For there is one God. There is also one mediator between God and men, the man Christ Jesus, [6]who gave himself as ransom for all. This was the testimony at the proper time. [7]For this I was appointed preacher and Apostle (I am speaking the truth, I am not lying), teacher of the Gentiles in faith and truth. [8]It is my wish, then, that in every place the men should pray, lifting up holy hands, without anger or argument.

Responsorial Psalm – Psalms 28:2, 7, 8-9

R. (6) Blessed be the Lord, for he has heard my prayer.

[2] Hear the sound of my pleading, when I cry to you,

lifting up my hands toward your holy shrine.

R. Blessed be the Lord, for he has heard my prayer.

[7] The LORD is my strength and my shield.

In him my heart trusts, and I find help;

then my heart exults, and with my song I give him thanks.

R. Blessed be the Lord, for he has heard my prayer.

[8] The LORD is the strength of his people,

the saving refuge of his anointed.

[9] Save your people, and bless your inheritance;

feed them, and carry them forever!

R. Blessed be the Lord, for he has heard my prayer.

Alleluia – John 3:16

R. Alleluia, alleluia.

[16]God so loved the world that he gave his only-begotten Son,
so that everyone who believes in him might have eternal life.

R. Alleluia, alleluia.

Gospel – Luke 7:1-10

[1]When Jesus had finished all his words to the people, he
entered Capernaum. [2]A centurion there had a slave who was
ill and about to die, and he was valuable to him. [3]When he
heard about Jesus, he sent elders of the Jews to him, asking
him to come and save the life of his slave. [4]They approached
Jesus and strongly urged him to come, saying, “He deserves
to have you do this for him, [5]for he loves our nation and he
built the synagogue for us.” [6]And Jesus went with them, but
when he was only a short distance from the house, the
centurion sent friends to tell him, “Lord, do not trouble yourself,
for I am not worthy to have you enter under my roof.
[7]Therefore, I did not consider myself worthy to come to you;
but say the word and let my servant be healed. [8]For I too am a
person subject to authority, with soldiers subject to me. And I
say to one, Go, and he goes; and to another, Come here, and
he comes; and to my slave, Do this, and he does it.” [9]When
Jesus heard this he was amazed at him and, turning, said to
the crowd following him, “I tell you, not even in Israel have I
found such faith.” [10]When the messengers returned to the
house, they found the slave in good health.

Tuesday September 19, 2023

Tuesday of Twenty-fourth Week in Ordinary Time

First Reading – 1 Timothy 3:1-13

[1]Beloved, this saying is trustworthy: whoever aspires to the
office of bishop desires a noble task. [2]Therefore, a bishop
must be irreproachable, married only once, temperate, self-
controlled, decent, hospitable, able to teach, [3]not a drunkard,
not aggressive, but gentle, not contentious, not a lover of
money. [4]He must manage his own household well, keeping his
children under control with perfect dignity; [5]for if a man does
not know how to manage his own household, how can he take
care of the Church of God? [6]He should not be a recent

convert, so that he may not become conceited and thus incur
the Devil's punishment. 7He must also have a good reputation
among outsiders, so that he may not fall into disgrace, the
Devil's trap. 8Similarly, deacons must be dignified, not
deceitful, not addicted to drink, not greedy for sordid gain,
9holding fast to the mystery of the faith with a clear
conscience. 10Moreover, they should be tested first; then, if
there is nothing against them, let them serve as deacons.
11Women, similarly, should be dignified, not slanderers, but
temperate and faithful in everything. 12Deacons may be
married only once and must manage their children and their
households well. 13Thus those who serve well as deacons gain
good standing and much confidence in their faith in Christ
Jesus.

Responsorial Psalm – Psalms 101:1B-2AB, 2CD-3AB, 5, 6

R. (2) I will walk with blameless heart.

1B Of mercy and judgment I will sing;

to you, O LORD, I will sing praise.

2AB I will persevere in the way of integrity;

when will you come to me?

R. I will walk with blameless heart.

2CD I will walk with blameless heart,

within my house;

3AB I will not set before my eyes

any base thing.

R. I will walk with blameless heart.

5 Whoever slanders his neighbour in secret,

him will I destroy.

The man of haughty eyes and puffed up heart

I will not endure.

R. I will walk with blameless heart.

6 My eyes are upon the faithful of the land,

that they may dwell with me.

He who walks in the way of integrity

shall be in my service.

R. I will walk with blameless heart.

Alleluia – Luke 7:16

R. Alleluia, alleluia.

16 A great prophet has arisen in our midst and God has visited his people.

R. Alleluia, alleluia.

Gospel – Luke 7:11-17

11Jesus journeyed to a city called Nain, and his disciples and a
large crowd accompanied him. 12As he drew near to the gate
of the city, a man who had died was being carried out, the only
son of his mother, and she was a widow. A large crowd from
the city was with her. 13When the Lord saw her, he was moved
with pity for her and said to her, "Do not weep." 14He stepped
forward and touched the coffin; at this the bearers halted, and
he said, "Young man, I tell you, arise!" 15The dead man sat up
and began to speak, and Jesus gave him to his mother. 16Fear
seized them all, and they glorified God, exclaiming, "A great
prophet has arisen in our midst," and "God has visited his
people." 17This report about him spread through the whole of
Judea and in all the surrounding region.

Wednesday September 20, 2023

Memorial of Saints Andrew Kim Taegon & Paul Chong Hasang, and their Companions - Martyrs

First Reading – 1 Timothy 3:14-16

Beloved: 14I am writing you, although I hope to visit you soon.
15But if I should be delayed, you should know how to behave
in the household of God, which is the Church of the living God,
the pillar and foundation of truth. 16Undeniably great is the
mystery of devotion, Who was manifested in the flesh,
vindicated in the spirit, seen by angels, proclaimed to the
Gentiles, believed in throughout the world, taken up in glory.

Responsorial Psalm – Psalms 111:1-2, 3-4, 5-6

R.(2) How great are the works of the Lord!

1 I will give thanks to the LORD with all my heart

in the company and assembly of the just.

2 Great are the works of the LORD,

exquisite in all their delights.

R. How great are the works of the Lord!

3 Majesty and glory are his work,

and his justice endures forever.

4 He has won renown for his wondrous deeds;

gracious and merciful is the LORD.

R. How great are the works of the Lord!

5 He has given food to those who fear him;

he will forever be mindful of his covenant.

6 He has made known to his people the power of his works,

giving them the inheritance of the nations.

R. How great are the works of the Lord!

Alleluia – John 6:63C, 68C

R. Alleluia, alleluia.

63C Your words, Lord, are Spirit and life, 68C you have the words of everlasting life.

R. Alleluia, alleluia.

Gospel – Luke 7:31-35

Jesus said to the crowds: 31 "To what shall I compare the
people of this generation? What are they like? 32 They are like
children who sit in the marketplace and call to one another,
'We played the flute for you, but you did not dance. We sang a
dirge, but you did not weep.' 33 For John the Baptist came
neither eating food nor drinking wine, and you said, 'He is
possessed by a demon.' 34 The Son of Man came eating and
drinking and you said, 'Look, he is a glutton and a drunkard, a

friend of tax collectors and sinners.' [35]But wisdom is vindicated by all her children."

Thursday September 21, 2023

Feast of Saint Matthew, Apostle and Evangelist

First Reading – Ephesians 4:1-7, 11-13

Brothers and sisters: [1]I, a prisoner for the Lord, urge you to live in a manner worthy of the call you have received, [2]with all humility and gentleness, with patience, bearing with one another through love, [3]striving to preserve the unity of the Spirit through the bond of peace: [4]one Body and one Spirit, as you were also called to the one hope of your call; [5]one Lord, one faith, one baptism; [6]one God and Father of all, who is over all and through all and in all. [7]But grace was given to each of us according to the measure of Christ's gift.[11]And he gave some as Apostles, others as prophets, others as evangelists, others as pastors and teachers, [12]to equip the holy ones for the work of ministry, for building up the Body of Christ,[13]until we all attain to the unity of faith and knowledge of the Son of God, to mature manhood, to the extent of the full stature of Christ.

Responsorial Psalm – Psalms 19:2-3, 4-5

R. (5) Their message goes out through all the earth.

[2] The heavens declare the glory of God;

and the firmament proclaims his handiwork.

[3] Day pours out the word to day,

and night to night imparts knowledge.

R. Their message goes out through all the earth.

[4] Not a word nor a discourse

whose voice is not heard;

[5] Through all the earth their voice resounds,

and to the ends of the world, their message.

R. Their message goes out through all the earth.

Alleluia – cf. Te Deum

R. Alleluia, alleluia.

We praise you, O God, we acclaim you as Lord; the glorious company of Apostles praise you.

R. Alleluia, alleluia.

Gospel – Matthew 9:9-13

9As Jesus passed by, he saw a man named Matthew sitting at
the customs post. He said to him, "Follow me." And he got up
and followed him. 10While he was at table in his house, many
tax collectors and sinners came and sat with Jesus and his
disciples. 11The Pharisees saw this and said to his disciples,
"Why does your teacher eat with tax collectors and sinners?"
12He heard this and said, "Those who are well do not need a
physician, but the sick do. 13Go and learn the meaning of the
words, I desire mercy, not sacrifice. I did not come to call the
righteous but sinners."

Friday September 22, 2023

Friday of Twenty-fourth Week Ordinary Time

First Reading – 1 Timothy 6:2C-12

Beloved: 2CTeach and urge these things. 3Whoever teaches
something different and does not agree with the sound words
of our Lord Jesus Christ and the religious teaching 4is
conceited, understanding nothing, and has a morbid
disposition for arguments and verbal disputes. From these
come envy, rivalry, insults, evil suspicions, 5and mutual friction
among people with corrupted minds, who are deprived of the
truth, supposing religion to be a means of gain. 6Indeed,
religion with contentment is a great gain. 7For we brought
nothing into the world, just as we shall not be able to take
anything out of it. 8If we have food and clothing, we shall be
content with that. 9Those who want to be rich are falling into
temptation and into a trap and into many foolish and harmful
desires, which plunge them into ruin and destruction. 10For the
love of money is the root of all evils, and some people in their
desire for it have strayed from the faith and have pierced
themselves with many pains. 11But you, man of God, avoid all
this. Instead, pursue righteousness, devotion, faith, love,

patience, and gentleness. 12Compete well for the faith. Lay hold of eternal life, to which you were called when you made the noble confession in the presence of many witnesses.

Responsorial Psalm – Psalms 49:6-7, 8-10, 17-18, 19-20

R. Blessed the poor in spirit; the Kingdom of heaven is theirs!

6 Why should I fear in evil days

when my wicked ensnarers ring me round?

7 They trust in their wealth;

the abundance of their riches is their boast.

R. Blessed the poor in spirit; the Kingdom of heaven is theirs!

8 Yet in no way can a man redeem himself,

or pay his own ransom to God;

9 Too high is the price to redeem one's life;

10 he would never have enough

to remain alive always and not see destruction.

R. Blessed the poor in spirit; the Kingdom of heaven is theirs!

17 Fear not when a man grows rich,

when the wealth of his house becomes great,

18 For when he dies, he shall take none of it;

his wealth shall not follow him down.

R. Blessed the poor in spirit; the Kingdom of heaven is theirs!

19 Though in his lifetime he counted himself blessed,

"They will praise you for doing well for yourself,"

20 He shall join the circle of his forebears

who shall never more see light.

R. Blessed the poor in spirit; the Kingdom of heaven is theirs!

Alleluia – Matthew 11:25

R. Alleluia, alleluia.

25 Blessed are you, Father, Lord of heaven and earth; you have revealed to little ones the mysteries of the Kingdom.

R. Alleluia, alleluia.

Gospel – Luke 8:1-3

1Jesus journeyed from one town and village to another, preaching and proclaiming the good news of the Kingdom of God. Accompanying him were the Twelve
2and some women who had been cured of evil spirits and infirmities, Mary, called Magdalene, from whom seven demons had gone out,
3Joanna, the wife of Herod's steward Chuza, Susanna, and many others who provided for them out of their resources.

Saturday September 23, 2023

Memorial of Saint Pius of Pietrelcina, Priest

First Reading – 1 Timothy 6:13-16

Beloved:
13I charge you before God, who gives life to all things, and before Christ Jesus, who gave testimony under Pontius Pilate for the noble confession,
14to keep the commandment without stain or reproach until the appearance of our Lord Jesus Christ
15that the blessed and only ruler will make manifest at the proper time, the King of kings and Lord of lords,
16who alone has immortality, who dwells in unapproachable light, and whom no human being has seen or can see. To him be honor and eternal power. Amen.

Responsorial Psalm – Psalms 100:1B-2, 3, 4, 5

R. (2) Come with joy into the presence of the Lord.

1B Sing joyfully to the LORD all you lands;

2 serve the LORD with gladness;

come before him with joyful song.

R. Come with joy into the presence of the Lord.

3 Know that the LORD is God;

he made us, his we are;

his people, the flock he tends.

R. Come with joy into the presence of the Lord.

4 Enter his gates with thanksgiving,

his courts with praise;

Give thanks to him; bless his name.

R. Come with joy into the presence of the Lord.

5 For he is good:

the LORD, whose kindness endures forever,

and his faithfulness, to all generations.

R. Come with joy into the presence of the Lord.

Alleluia – Luke 8:15

R. Alleluia, alleluia.

15 Blessed are they who have kept the word with a generous heart and yield a harvest through perseverance.

R. Alleluia, alleluia.

Gospel – Luke 8:4-15

4 When a large crowd gathered, with people from one town
after another journeying to Jesus, he spoke in a parable. 5 “A
sower went out to sow his seed. And as he sowed, some seed
fell on the path and was trampled, and the birds of the sky ate
it up. 6 Some seed fell on rocky ground, and when it grew, it
withered for lack of moisture. 7 Some seed fell among thorns,
and the thorns grew with it and choked it. 8 And some seed fell
on good soil, and when it grew, it produced fruit a
hundredfold.” After saying this, he called out, “Whoever has
ears to hear ought to hear.” 9 Then his disciples asked him
what the meaning of this parable might be. 10 He answered,
“Knowledge of the mysteries of the Kingdom of God has been
granted to you; but to the rest, they are made known through
parables so that they may look but not see, and hear but not
understand. 11 “This is the meaning of the parable. The seed is
the word of God. 12 Those on the path are the ones who have

heard, but the Devil comes and takes away the word from their
hearts that they may not believe and be saved. 13Those on
rocky ground are the ones who, when they hear, receive the
word with joy, but they have no root; they believe only for a
time and fall away in time of temptation. 14As for the seed that
fell among thorns, they are the ones who have heard, but as
they go along, they are choked by the anxieties and riches
and pleasures of life, and they fail to produce mature fruit.
15But as for the seed that fell on rich soil, they are the ones
who, when they have heard the word, embrace it with a
generous and good heart, and bear fruit through
perseverance."

Sunday September 24, 2023

Twenty-fifth Sunday in Ordinary Time, Year A

First Reading – Isaiah 55:6-9

6Seek the LORD while he may be found, call him while he is
near. 7Let the scoundrel forsake his way, and the wicked his
thoughts; let him turn to the LORD for mercy; to our God, who
is generous in forgiving. 8For my thoughts are not your
thoughts, nor are your ways my ways, says the LORD. 9As
high as the heavens are above the earth, so high are my ways
above your ways and my thoughts above your thoughts.

Responsorial Psalm – Psalms 145:2-3, 8-9, 17-18

R. (18a) The Lord is near to all who call upon him.

2 Every day will I bless you,

and I will praise your name forever and ever.

3 Great is the LORD and highly to be praised;

his greatness is unsearchable.

R. The Lord is near to all who call upon him.

8 The LORD is gracious and merciful,

slow to anger and of great kindness.

9 The LORD is good to all

and compassionate toward all his works.

R. The Lord is near to all who call upon him.

[17] The LORD is just in all his ways

and holy in all his works.

[18] The LORD is near to all who call upon him,

to all who call upon him in truth.

R. The Lord is near to all who call upon him.

Second Reading – Philippians 1:20C-24, 27A

Brothers and sisters: [20C]Christ will be magnified in my body, whether by life or by death. [21]For to me life is Christ, and death is gain. [22]If I go on living in the flesh, that means fruitful labor for me. And I do not know which I shall choose. [23]I am caught between the two. I long to depart this life and be with Christ, for that is far better. [24]Yet that I remain in the flesh is more necessary for your benefit. [27A]Only, conduct yourselves in a way worthy of the gospel of Christ.

Alleluia – Acts 16:14B

R. Alleluia, alleluia.

[14B] Open our hearts, O Lord, to listen to the words of your Son.

R. Alleluia, alleluia.

Gospel – Matthew 20:1-16A

Jesus told his disciples this parable: [1]"The kingdom of heaven is like a landowner who went out at dawn to hire laborers for his vineyard. [2]After agreeing with them for the usual daily wage, he sent them into his vineyard. [3]Going out about nine o'clock, the landowner saw others standing idle in the marketplace, [4]and he said to them, 'You too go into my vineyard, and I will give you what is just.' [5]So they went off. And he went out again around noon, and around three o'clock, and did likewise. [6]Going out about five o'clock, the landowner found others standing around, and said to them, 'Why do you stand here idle all day?' [7]They answered, 'Because no one has hired us.' He said to them, 'You too go into my vineyard.' [8]When it was evening the owner of the vineyard said to his foreman, 'Summon the laborers and give them their pay, beginning with the last and ending with the first.' [9]When those who had started about five o'clock came, each received the usual daily wage. [10]So when the first came, they thought that they would receive more, but each of them also got the usual wage. [11]And on receiving it they grumbled against the landowner, [12]saying, 'These last ones worked only one hour, and you have made them equal to us, who bore the day's burden and the heat.' [13]He said to one of them in reply, 'My friend, I am not cheating you. Did you not agree with me for the usual daily wage? [14]Take what is yours and go. What if I wish to give this last one the same as you? [15]Or am I not free to do as I wish with my own money? Are you envious because I am generous?' [16A]Thus, the last will be first, and the first will be last."

Monday September 25, 2023

Monday of Twenty-fifth Week Ordinary Time

First Reading – Ezra 1:1-6

[1]In the first year of Cyrus, king of Persia, in order to fulfill the word of the LORD spoken by Jeremiah, the LORD inspired King Cyrus of Persia to issue this proclamation throughout his kingdom, both by word of mouth and in writing: [2]"Thus says Cyrus, king of Persia: 'All the kingdoms of the earth the LORD, the God of heaven, has given to me, and he has also charged me to build him a house in Jerusalem, which is in Judah. [3]Therefore, whoever among you belongs to any part of his people, let him go up, and may his God be with him! [4]Let everyone who has survived, in whatever place he may have dwelt, be assisted by the people of that place with silver, gold, goods, and cattle, together with free-will offerings for the house of God in Jerusalem.'" [5]Then the family heads of Judah and Benjamin and the priests and Levites– everyone, that is, whom God had inspired to do so– prepared to go up to build the house of the LORD in Jerusalem. [6]All their neighbors gave them help in every way, with silver, gold, goods, and cattle, and with many precious gifts besides all their free-will offerings.

Responsorial Psalm – Psalms 126:1B-2AB, 2CD-3, 4-5, 6

R. (3) The Lord has done marvels for us.

[1B] When the LORD brought back the captives of Zion,

we were like men dreaming.

[2AB] Then our mouth was filled with laughter,

and our tongue with rejoicing.

R. The Lord has done marvels for us.

[2CD] Then they said among the nations,

[3] "The LORD has done great things for them."

The LORD has done great things for us;

we are glad indeed.

R. The Lord has done marvels for us.

[4] Restore our fortunes, O LORD,

like the torrents in the southern desert.

[5] Those that sow in tears

shall reap rejoicing.

R. The Lord has done marvels for us.

[6] Although they go forth weeping,

carrying the seed to be sown,

They shall come back rejoicing,

carrying their sheaves.

R. The Lord has done marvels for us.

Alleluia – Matthew 5:16

R. Alleluia, alleluia.

[16] Let your light shine before others, that they may see your good deeds and glorify your heavenly Father.

R. Alleluia, alleluia.

Gospel – Luke 8:16-18

Jesus said to the crowd: [16]"No one who lights a lamp conceals
it with a vessel or sets it under a bed; rather, he places it on a
lampstand so that those who enter may see the light. [17]For
there is nothing hidden that will not become visible, and
nothing secret that will not be known and come to light. [18]Take
care, then, how you hear. To anyone who has, more will be

given, and from the one who has not, even what he seems to have will be taken away."

Tuesday September 26, 2023

Tuesday of Twenty-fifth Week Ordinary Time

First Reading – Ezra 6:7-8, 12B, 14-20

King Darius issued an order to the officials of West-of-Euphrates: [7]"Let the governor and the elders of the Jews continue the work on that house of God; they are to rebuild it on its former site. [8]I also issue this decree concerning your dealing with these elders of the Jews in the rebuilding of that house of God: From the royal revenue, the taxes of West-of-Euphrates, let these men be repaid for their expenses, in full and without delay. [12B]I, Darius, have issued this decree; let it be carefully executed." [14]The elders of the Jews continued to make progress in the building, supported by the message of the prophets, Haggai and Zechariah, son of Iddo. They finished the building according to the command of the God of Israel and the decrees of Cyrus and Darius and of Artaxerxes, king of Persia. [15]They completed this house on the third day of the month Adar, in the sixth year of the reign of King Darius. [16]The children of Israel–priests, Levites, and the other returned exiles– celebrated the dedication of this house of God with joy. [17]For the dedication of this house of God, they offered one hundred bulls, two hundred rams, and four hundred lambs, together with twelve he-goats as a sin-offering for all Israel, in keeping with the number of the tribes of Israel. [18]Finally, they set up the priests in their classes and the Levites in their divisions for the service of God in Jerusalem, as is prescribed in the book of Moses. [19]The exiles kept the Passover on the fourteenth day of the first month. [20]The Levites, every one of whom had purified himself for the occasion, sacrificed the Passover for the rest of the exiles, for their brethren the priests, and for themselves.

Responsorial Psalm – Psalms 122:1-2, 3-4AB, 4CD-5

R. (1) Let us go rejoicing to the house of the Lord.

[1] I rejoiced because they said to me,

"We will go up to the house of the LORD."

[2] And now we have set foot

within your gates, O Jerusalem.

R. Let us go rejoicing to the house of the Lord.

[3] Jerusalem, built as a city

with compact unity.

4AB To it the tribes go up,

the tribes of the LORD.

R. Let us go rejoicing to the house of the Lord.

[4CD] According to the decree for Israel,

to give thanks to the name of the LORD.

[5] In it are set up judgment seats,

seats for the house of David.

R. Let us go rejoicing to the house of the Lord.

Alleluia – Luke 11:28

R. Alleluia, alleluia.

[28] Blessed are those who hear the word of God and observe it.

R. Alleluia, alleluia.

Gospel – Luke 8:19-21

[19]The mother of Jesus and his brothers came to him but were
unable to join him because of the crowd. [20]He was told, "Your
mother and your brothers are standing outside and they wish
to see you." [21]He said to them in reply, "My mother and my
brothers are those who hear the word of God and act on it."

Wednesday September 27, 2023

Memorial of Saint Vincent de Paul, Priest

First Reading – Ezra 9:5-9

[5]At the time of the evening sacrifice, I, Ezra, rose in my
wretchedness, and with cloak and mantle torn I fell on my
knees, stretching out my hands to the LORD, my God. [6]I said:
"My God, I am too ashamed and confounded to raise my face
to you, O my God, for our wicked deeds are heaped up above
our heads and our guilt reaches up to heaven. [7]From the time

of our fathers even to this day great has been our guilt, and for our wicked deeds we have been delivered up, we and our kings and our priests, to the will of the kings of foreign lands, to the sword, to captivity, to pillage, and to disgrace, as is the
case today. 8"And now, but a short time ago, mercy came to us from the LORD, our God, who left us a remnant and gave us a stake in his holy place; thus our God has brightened our
eyes and given us relief in our servitude. 9For slaves we are,
but in our servitude our God has not abandoned us; rather, he has turned the good will of the kings of Persia toward us. Thus he has given us new life to raise again the house of our God and restore its ruins, and has granted us a fence in Judah and Jerusalem."

Responsorial Psalm – TOBIT 13:2, 3-4A, 4BEFGHN, 7-8

R. (1b) Blessed be God, who lives for ever.

2 He scourges and then has mercy;

he casts down to the depths of the nether world,

and he brings up from the great abyss.

No one can escape his hand.

R. Blessed be God, who lives for ever.

3 Praise him, you children of Israel, before the Gentiles,

for though he has scattered you among them,

4A he has shown you his greatness even there.

R. Blessed be God, who lives for ever.

4B So now consider what he has done for you,

and praise him with full voice.

Bless the Lord of righteousness,

and exalt the King of ages.

R. Blessed be God, who lives for ever.

6 In the land of my exile I praise him

and show his power and majesty to a sinful nation.

R. Blessed be God, who lives for ever.

[7] Bless the Lord, all you his chosen ones,

and may all of you praise his majesty.

[8] Celebrate days of gladness, and give him praise.

R. Blessed be God, who lives for ever.

Alleluia – Mark 1:15

R. Alleluia, alleluia.

[15] The Kingdom of God is at hand; repent and believe in the Gospel.

R. Alleluia, alleluia.

Gospel – Luke 9:1-6

[1]Jesus summoned the Twelve and gave them power and
authority over all demons and to cure diseases,[2]and he sent
them to proclaim the Kingdom of God and to heal the sick. [3]He
said to them, "Take nothing for the journey, neither walking
stick, nor sack, nor food, nor money, and let no one take a
second tunic. [4]Whatever house you enter, stay there and
leave from there. [5]And as for those who do not welcome you,
when you leave that town, shake the dust from your feet in
testimony against them." [6]Then they set out and went from
village to village proclaiming the good news and curing
diseases everywhere.

Thursday September 28, 2023

Thursday of Twenty-fifth Week in Ordinary Time

First Reading – Haggai 1:1-8

[1]On the first day of the sixth month in the second year of King
Darius, The word of the LORD came through the prophet
Haggai to the governor of Judah, Zerubbabel, son of Shealtiel,
and to the high priest Joshua, son of Jehozadak: [2]Thus says
the LORD of hosts: This people says: "The time has not yet
come to rebuild the house of the LORD." [3](Then this word of
the LORD came through Haggai, the prophet:) [4]Is it time for
you to dwell in your own paneled houses, while this house lies
in ruins? [5]Now thus says the LORD of hosts: Consider your
ways! [6]You have sown much, but have brought in little; you
have eaten, but have not been satisfied; You have drunk, but
have not been exhilarated; have clothed yourselves, but not

been warmed; And whoever earned wages earned them for a bag with holes in it. 7Thus says the LORD of hosts: Consider your ways! 8Go up into the hill country; bring timber, and build the house That I may take pleasure in it and receive my glory, says the LORD.

Responsorial Psalm – Psalms 149:1B-2, 3-4, 5-6A AND 9B

R. (see 4a) **The Lord takes delight in his people.**

1B Sing to the LORD a new song

of praise in the assembly of the faithful.

2 Let Israel be glad in their maker,

let the children of Zion rejoice in their king.

R. The Lord takes delight in his people.

3 Let them praise his name in the festive dance,

let them sing praise to him with timbrel and harp.

4 For the LORD loves his people,

and he adorns the lowly with victory.

R. The Lord takes delight in his people.

5 Let the faithful exult in glory;

let them sing for joy upon their couches;

6A Let the high praises of God be in their throats.

9B This is the glory of all his faithful. Alleluia.

R. The Lord takes delight in his people.

Alleluia – John 14:6

R. Alleluia, alleluia.

6 I am the way and the truth and the life, says the Lord; no one comes to the Father except through me.

R. Alleluia, alleluia.

Gospel – Luke 9:7-9

7Herod the tetrarch heard about all that was happening, and he was greatly perplexed because some were saying, "John has been raised from the dead"; [8]others were saying, "Elijah has appeared"; still others, "One of the ancient prophets has arisen." [9]But Herod said, "John I beheaded. Who then is this about whom I hear such things?" And he kept trying to see him.

Friday September 29, 2023

Feast of Saints Michael, Gabriel, Raphael - Archangels

First Reading – Daniel 7:9-10, 13-14

[9]As I watched: Thrones were set up and the Ancient One took his throne. His clothing was bright as snow, and the hair on his head as white as wool; His throne was flames of fire, with wheels of burning fire. [10]A surging stream of fire flowed out from where he sat; Thousands upon thousands were ministering to him, and myriads upon myriads attended him. The court was convened, and the books were opened. [13]As the visions during the night continued, I saw One like a son of man coming, on the clouds of heaven; When he reached the Ancient One and was presented before him, [14]He received dominion, glory, and kingship; nations and peoples of every language serve him. His dominion is an everlasting dominion that shall not be taken away, his kingship shall not be destroyed.

Or Revelation 12:7-12AB

[7]War broke out in heaven; Michael and his angels battled against the dragon. The dragon and its angels fought back, [8]but they did not prevail and there was no longer any place for them in heaven. [9]The huge dragon, the ancient serpent, who is called the Devil and Satan, who deceived the whole world, was thrown down to earth, and its angels were thrown down with it. [10]Then I heard a loud voice in heaven say: "Now have salvation and power come, and the Kingdom of our God and the authority of his Anointed. For the accuser of our brothers is cast out, who accuses them before our God day and night. [11]They conquered him by the Blood of the Lamb and by the word of their testimony; love for life did not deter them from death. [12AB]Therefore, rejoice, you heavens, and you who dwell in them."

Responsorial Psalm – Psalms 138:1-2AB, 2CDE-3, 4-5

R. (1) In the sight of the angels I will sing your praises, Lord.

1 I will give thanks to you, O LORD, with all my heart,

for you have heard the words of my mouth;

in the presence of the angels I will sing your praise;

2AB I will worship at your holy temple

and give thanks to your name.

R. In the sight of the angels I will sing your praises, Lord.

2CDE Because of your kindness and your truth;

for you have made great above all things

your name and your promise.

3 When I called, you answered me;

you built up strength within me.

R. In the sight of the angels I will sing your praises, Lord.

4 All the kings of the earth shall give thanks to you, O LORD

when they hear the words of your mouth;

5 And they shall sing of the ways of the LORD

"Great is the glory of the LORD

R. In the sight of the angels I will sing your praises, Lord.

Alleluia – Psalms 103:21

R. Alleluia, alleluia.

21 Bless the LORD, all you angels, you ministers, who do his will.

R. Alleluia, alleluia.

Gospel – John 1:47-51

47Jesus saw Nathanael coming toward him and said of him,
"Here is a true child of Israel. There is no duplicity in him."
48Nathanael said to him, "How do you know me?" Jesus
answered and said to him, "Before Philip called you, I saw you
under the fig tree." 49Nathanael answered him, "Rabbi, you are

the Son of God; you are the King of Israel." [50]Jesus answered and said to him, "Do you believe because I told you that I saw you under the fig tree? You will see greater things than this."
[51]And he said to him, "Amen, amen, I say to you, you will see heaven opened and the angels of God ascending and descending on the Son of Man."

Saturday September 30, 2023

Memorial of Saint Jerome, Priest and Doctor

First Reading – Zechariah 2:5-9, 14-15A

[5]I, Zechariah, raised my eyes and looked: there was a man with a measuring line in his hand. [6]I asked, "Where are you going?" He answered, "To measure Jerusalem, to see how great is its width and how great its length." [7]Then the angel who spoke with me advanced, and another angel came out to meet him [8]and said to him, "Run, tell this to that young man: People will live in Jerusalem as though in open country, because of the multitude of men and beasts in her midst. [9]But I will be for her an encircling wall of fire, says the LORD, and I will be the glory in her midst." [14]Sing and rejoice, O daughter Zion! See, I am coming to dwell among you, says the LORD.
[15A]Many nations shall join themselves to the LORD on that day, and they shall be his people and he will dwell among you.

Responsorial Psalm – Jeremiah 31:10, 11-12AB, 13

R. (see 10d) The Lord will guard us as a shepherd guards his flock.

[10] Hear the word of the LORD, O nations,

proclaim it on distant isles, and say:

He who scattered Israel, now gathers them together,

he guards them as a shepherd guards his flock.

R. The Lord will guard us as a shepherd guards his flock.

[11] The LORD shall ransom Jacob,

he shall redeem him from the hand of his conqueror.

[12AB] Shouting, they shall mount the heights of Zion,

they shall come streaming to the LORD's blessings.

R. The Lord will guard us as a shepherd guards his flock.

[13] Then the virgins shall make merry and dance,

and young men and old as well.

I will turn their mourning into joy,

I will console and gladden them after their sorrows.

R. The Lord will guard us as a shepherd guards his flock.

Alleluia – 2 Timothy 1:10

R. Alleluia, alleluia.

[10] Our Savior Jesus Christ destroyed death and brought life to light through the Gospel.

R. Alleluia, alleluia.

Gospel – Luke 9:43B-45

[43B]While they were all amazed at his every deed, Jesus said to
his disciples, [44]"Pay attention to what I am telling you. The Son
of Man is to be handed over to men." [45]But they did not
understand this saying; its meaning was hidden from them so that they should not understand it, and they were afraid to ask him about this saying.

OCTOBER 2023

Sunday October 1, 2023

Twenty-sixth Sunday in Ordinary Time, Year A

First Reading – Ezekiel 18:25-28

Thus says the LORD: [25]You say, "The LORD's way is not fair!"
Hear now, house of Israel: Is it my way that is unfair, or rather,
are not your ways unfair? [26]When someone virtuous turns
away from virtue to commit iniquity, and dies, it is because of
the iniquity he committed that he must die. [27]But if he turns
from the wickedness he has committed, he does what is right
and just, he shall preserve his life; [28]since he has turned away
from all the sins that he has committed, he shall surely live, he shall not die.

Responsorial Psalm – Psalms 25:4-5, 6-7, 8-9

R. (6a) Remember your mercies, O Lord.

4 Your ways, O LORD, make known to me;

teach me your paths,

5 guide me in your truth and teach me,

for you are God my savior.

R. Remember your mercies, O Lord.

6 Remember that your compassion, O LORD,

and your love are from of old.

7 The sins of my youth and my frailties remember not;

in your kindness remember me,

because of your goodness, O LORD.

R. Remember your mercies, O Lord.

8 Good and upright is the LORD;

thus he shows sinners the way.

9 He guides the humble to justice,

and teaches the humble his way.

R. Remember your mercies, O Lord.

Second Reading – Philippians 2:1-11

Brothers and sisters: 1 If there is any encouragement in Christ,
any solace in love, any participation in the Spirit, any
compassion and mercy, 2 complete my joy by being of the
same mind, with the same love, united in heart, thinking one
thing. 3 Do nothing out of selfishness or out of vainglory; rather,
humbly regard others as more important than
yourselves, 4 each looking out not for his own interests, but also
for those of others. 5 Have in you the same attitude that is also
in Christ Jesus, 6 Who, though he was in the form of God, did
not regard equality with God something to be grasped.
7 Rather, he emptied himself, taking the form of a slave,
coming in human likeness; and found human in appearance,
8 he humbled himself, becoming obedient to the point of death,
even death on a cross. 9 Because of this, God greatly exalted

him and bestowed on him the name which is above every name, [10]that at the name of Jesus every knee should bend, of those in heaven and on earth and under the earth, [11]and every tongue confess that Jesus Christ is Lord, to the glory of God the Father.

Or Philippians 2:1-5

Brothers and sisters: [1]If there is any encouragement in Christ, any solace in love, any participation in the Spirit, any compassion and mercy,[2]complete my joy by being of the same mind, with the same love, united in heart, thinking one thing.[3]Do nothing out of selfishness or out of vainglory; rather, humbly regard others as more important than yourselves,[4]each looking out not for his own interests, but also for those of others.[5]Have in you the same attitude that is also in Christ Jesus,

Alleluia – John 10:27

R. Alleluia, alleluia.

[27]My sheep hear my voice, says the Lord; I know them, and they follow me.

R. Alleluia, alleluia.

Gospel – Matthew 21:28-32

Jesus said to the chief priests and elders of the people: [28]"What is your opinion? A man had two sons. He came to the first and said, 'Son, go out and work in the vineyard today.' [29]He said in reply, 'I will not, ' but afterwards changed his mind and went.[30]The man came to the other son and gave the same order. He said in reply, 'Yes, sir, 'but did not go.[31]Which of the two did his father's will?" They answered, "The first." Jesus said to them, "Amen, I say to you, tax collectors and prostitutes are entering the kingdom of God before you.[32]When John came to you in the way of righteousness, you did not believe him; but tax collectors and prostitutes did. Yet even when you saw that, you did not later change your minds and believe him."

Monday October 2, 2023

The Holy Guardian Angels

First Reading – Zechariah 8:1-8

[1]This word of the LORD of hosts came: [2]Thus says the LORD
of hosts: I am intensely jealous for Zion, stirred to jealous
wrath for her. [3]Thus says the LORD: I will return to Zion, and I
will dwell within Jerusalem; Jerusalem shall be called the
faithful city, and the mountain of the LORD of hosts, the holy
mountain. [4]Thus says the LORD of hosts: Old men and old
women, each with staff in hand because of old age, shall
again sit in the streets of Jerusalem. [5]The city shall be filled
with boys and girls playing in its streets. [6]Thus says the LORD
of hosts: Even if this should seem impossible in the eyes of
the remnant of this people, shall it in those days be impossible
in my eyes also, says the LORD of hosts? [7]Thus says the
LORD of hosts: Lo, I will rescue my people from the land of
the rising sun, and from the land of the setting sun. [8]I will bring
them back to dwell within Jerusalem. They shall be my people,
and I will be their God, with faithfulness and justice.

Responsorial Psalm – Psalms 102:16-18, 19-21, 29 AND 22-23

R. (17) The Lord will build up Zion again, and appear in all his glory.

[16] The nations shall revere your name, O LORD,

and all the kings of the earth your glory,

[17] When the LORD has rebuilt Zion

and appeared in his glory;

[18] When he has regarded the prayer of the destitute,

and not despised their prayer.

R. The Lord will build up Zion again, and appear in all his glory.

[19] Let this be written for the generation to come,

and let his future creatures praise the LORD:

[20] "The LORD looked down from his holy height,

from heaven he beheld the earth,

21 To hear the groaning of the prisoners,

to release those doomed to die.”

R. The Lord will build up Zion again, and appear in all his glory.

29 The children of your servants shall abide,

and their posterity shall continue in your presence.

22 That the name of the LORD may be declared in Zion;

and his praise, in Jerusalem,

23 When the peoples gather together,

and the kingdoms, to serve the LORD.

R. The Lord will build up Zion again, and appear in all his glory.

Alleluia – Mark 10:45

R. Alleluia, alleluia.

45 The Son of Man came to serve and to give his life as a ransom for many.

R. Alleluia, alleluia.

Gospel – Luke 9:46-50

46 An argument arose among the disciples about which of them
was the greatest. 47 Jesus realized the intention of their hearts
and took a child and placed it by his side 48 and said to them,
“Whoever receives this child in my name receives me, and
whoever receives me receives the one who sent me. For the
one who is least among all of you is the one who is the
greatest.” 49 Then John said in reply, “Master, we saw
someone casting out demons in your name and we tried to
prevent him because he does not follow in our
company.” 50 Jesus said to him, “Do not prevent him, for
whoever is not against you is for you.”

Tuesday October 3, 2023

Tuesday of Twenty-sixth Week in Ordinary Time

First Reading – Zechariah 8:20-23

20Thus says the LORD of hosts: There shall yet come peoples,
the inhabitants of many cities; 21and the inhabitants of one city
shall approach those of another, and say, "Come! let us go to
implore the favor of the LORD"; and, "I too will go to seek the
LORD." 22Many peoples and strong nations shall come to seek
the LORD of hosts in Jerusalem and to implore the favor of the
LORD. 23Thus says the LORD of hosts: In those days ten men
of every nationality, speaking different tongues, shall take
hold, yes, take hold of every Jew by the edge of his garment
and say, "Let us go with you, for we have heard that God is
with you."

Responsorial Psalm – Psalms 87:1B-3, 4-5, 6-7

R. (Zechariah 8:23) **God is with us.**

1B His foundation upon the holy mountains

the LORD loves:

2 The gates of Zion,

more than any dwelling of Jacob.

3 Glorious things are said of you,

O city of God!

R. God is with us.

4 I tell of Egypt and Babylon

among those that know the LORD;

Of Philistia, Tyre, Ethiopia:

"This man was born there."

5 And of Zion they shall say:

"One and all were born in her;

And he who has established her

is the Most High LORD."

R. God is with us.

6 They shall note, when the peoples are enrolled:

"This man was born there."

7 And all shall sing, in their festive dance:

"My home is within you."

R. God is with us.

Alleluia – Mark 10:45

R. Alleluia, alleluia.

45 The Son of Man came to serve and to give his life as a ransom for many.

R. Alleluia, alleluia.

Gospel – Luke 9:51-56

51When the days for Jesus to be taken up were fulfilled, he
resolutely determined to journey to Jerusalem, 52and he sent
messengers ahead of him. On the way they entered a
Samaritan village to prepare for his reception there, 53but they
would not welcome him because the destination of his journey
was Jerusalem. 54When the disciples James and John saw
this they asked, "Lord, do you want us to call down fire from
heaven to consume them?" 55Jesus turned and rebuked them,
and they journeyed to another village.

Wednesday October 4, 2023

Memorial of Saint Francis of Assisi

First Reading – Nehemiah 2:1-8

1In the month Nisan of the twentieth year of King Artaxerxes,
when the wine was in my charge, I took some and offered it to
the king. As I had never before been sad in his presence, 2the
king asked me, "Why do you look sad? If you are not sick, you
must be sad at heart." Though I was seized with great fear, 3I
answered the king: "May the king live forever! How could I not
look sad when the city where my ancestors are buried lies in
ruins, and its gates have been eaten out by fire?" 4The king
asked me, "What is it, then, that you wish?" I prayed to the
God of heaven 5and then answered the king: "If it please the
king, and if your servant is deserving of your favor, send me to
Judah, to the city of my ancestors' graves, to rebuild it." 6Then

the king, and the queen seated beside him, asked me how long my journey would take and when I would return. I set a date that was acceptable to him, and the king agreed that I might go.
7I asked the king further: “If it please the king, let letters be given to me for the governors of West-of-Euphrates, that they may afford me safe-conduct until I arrive in Judah;
8also a letter for Asaph, the keeper of the royal park, that he may give me wood for timbering the gates of the temple-citadel and for the city wall and the house that I shall occupy.” The king granted my requests, for the favoring hand of my God was upon me.

Responsorial Psalm – Psalms 137:1-2, 3, 4-5, 6

R. (6ab) Let my tongue be silenced if I ever forget you!

1 By the streams of Babylon

we sat and wept

when we remembered Zion.

2 On the aspens of that land

we hung up our harps.

R. Let my tongue be silenced if I ever forget you!

3 Though there our captors asked of us

the lyrics of our songs,

And our despoilers urged us to be joyous:

“Sing for us the songs of Zion!”

R. Let my tongue be silenced if I ever forget you!

4 How could we sing a song of the LORD

in a foreign land?

5 If I forget you, Jerusalem,

may my right hand be forgotten!

R. Let my tongue be silenced if I ever forget you!

6 May my tongue cleave to my palate

if I remember you not,

If I place not Jerusalem

ahead of my joy.

R. Let my tongue be silenced if I ever forget you!

Alleluia – Philippians 3:8-9

R. Alleluia, alleluia.

8 I consider all things so much rubbish 9 that I may gain Christ
and be found in him.

R. Alleluia, alleluia.

Gospel – Luke 9:57-62

57 As Jesus and his disciples were proceeding on their journey,
someone said to him, "I will follow you wherever you go."
58 Jesus answered him, "Foxes have dens and birds of the sky
have nests, but the Son of Man has nowhere to rest his head."
59 And to another he said, "Follow me." But he replied, "Lord,
let me go first and bury my father." 60 But he answered him,
"Let the dead bury their dead. But you, go and proclaim the
Kingdom of God." 61 And another said, "I will follow you, Lord,
but first let me say farewell to my family at home." 62 Jesus
answered him, "No one who sets a hand to the plow and looks
to what was left behind is fit for the Kingdom of God."

Thursday October 5, 2023

Thursday of Twenty-sixth Week in Ordinary Time

First Reading – Nehemiah 8:1-4A, 5-6, 7B-12

1 The whole people gathered as one in the open space before
the Water Gate, and they called upon Ezra the scribe to bring
forth the book of the law of Moses which the LORD prescribed
for Israel. 2 On the first day of the seventh month, therefore,
Ezra the priest brought the law before the assembly, which
consisted of men, women, and those children old enough to
understand. 3 Standing at one end of the open place that was
before the Water Gate, he read out of the book from daybreak
until midday, in the presence of the men, the women, and
those children old enough to understand; and all the people
listened attentively to the book of the law. 4A Ezra the scribe
stood on a wooden platform that had been made for the
occasion. 5 He opened the scroll so that all the people might
see it (for he was standing higher up than any of the people);
and, as he opened it, all the people rose. 6 Ezra blessed the

LORD, the great God, and all the people, their hands raised
high, answered, "Amen, amen!" Then they bowed down and
prostrated themselves before the LORD, their faces to the
ground. 7B As the people remained in their places, 8 Ezra read
plainly from the book of the law of God, interpreting it so that
all could understand what was read. 9 Then Nehemiah, that is,
His Excellency, and Ezra the priest-scribe and the Levites who
were instructing the people said to all the people: "Today is
holy to the LORD your God. Do not be sad, and do not weep"–
for all the people were weeping as they heard the words of the
law. 10 He said further: "Go, eat rich foods and drink sweet
drinks, and allot portions to those who had nothing prepared;
for today is holy to our LORD. Do not be saddened this day,
for rejoicing in the LORD must be your strength!" 11 And the
Levites quieted all the people, saying, "Hush, for today is holy,
and you must not be saddened." 12 Then all the people went to
eat and drink, to distribute portions, and to celebrate with great
joy, for they understood the words that had been expounded
to them.

Responsorial Psalm – Psalms 19:8, 9, 10, 11

R. (9ab) The precepts of the Lord give joy to the heart.

8 The law of the LORD is perfect,

refreshing the soul;

The decree of the LORD is trustworthy,

giving wisdom to the simple.

R. The precepts of the Lord give joy to the heart.

9 The precepts of the LORD are right,

rejoicing the heart;

The command of the LORD is clear,

enlightening the eye;

R. The precepts of the Lord give joy to the heart.

10 The fear of the LORD is pure,

enduring forever;

The ordinances of the LORD are true,

all of them just.

R. The precepts of the Lord give joy to the heart.

[11] They are more precious than gold,

than a heap of purest gold;

Sweeter also than syrup

or honey from the comb.

R. The precepts of the Lord give joy to the heart.

Alleluia – Mark 1:15

R. Alleluia, alleluia.

[15] The Kingdom of God is at hand; repent and believe in the Gospel.

R. Alleluia, alleluia.

Gospel – Luke 10:1-12

[1]Jesus appointed seventy-two other disciples whom he sent ahead of him in pairs to every town and place he intended to
visit. [2]He said to them, "The harvest is abundant but the laborers are few; so ask the master of the harvest to send out laborers for his harvest. [3]Go on your way; behold, I am
sending you like lambs among wolves. [4]Carry no money bag,
no sack, no sandals; and greet no one along the way. [5]Into
whatever house you enter, first say, 'Peace to this household.'
[6]If a peaceful person lives there, your peace will rest on him;
but if not, it will return to you. [7]Stay in the same house and eat and drink what is offered to you, for the laborer deserves his payment. Do not move about from one house to another.
[8]Whatever town you enter and they welcome you, eat what is
set before you, [9]cure the sick in it and say to them, 'The
Kingdom of God is at hand for you.' [10]Whatever town you enter and they do not receive you, go out into the streets and
say, [11]'The dust of your town that clings to our feet, even that we shake off against you.' Yet know this: the Kingdom of God
is at hand. [12]I tell you, it will be more tolerable for Sodom on that day than for that town."

Friday October 6, 2023

Friday of Twenty-sixth Week Ordinary Time

First Reading – Baruch 1:15-22

During the Babylonian captivity, the exiles prayed: 15“Justice is
with the Lord, our God; and we today are flushed with shame,
we men of Judah and citizens of Jerusalem,16that we, with our
kings and rulers and priests and prophets, and with our
ancestors, 17have sinned in the Lord’s sight 18and disobeyed
him. We have neither heeded the voice of the Lord, our God,
nor followed the precepts which the Lord set before us. 19From
the time the Lord led our ancestors out of the land of Egypt
until the present day, we have been disobedient to the Lord,
our God, and only too ready to disregard his voice. 20And the
evils and the curse that the Lord enjoined upon Moses, his
servant, at the time he led our ancestors forth from the land of
Egypt to give us the land flowing with milk and honey, cling to
us even today. 21For we did not heed the voice of the Lord, our
God, in all the words of the prophets whom he sent us, 22but
each one of us went off after the devices of his own wicked
heart, served other gods, and did evil in the sight of the Lord,
our God.”

Responsorial Psalm – Psalms 79:1B-2, 3-5, 8, 9

R. (9) For the glory of your name, O Lord, deliver us.

1B O God, the nations have come into your inheritance;

they have defiled your holy temple,

they have laid Jerusalem in ruins.

2 They have given the corpses of your servants

as food to the birds of heaven,

the flesh of your faithful ones to the beasts of the earth.

R. For the glory of your name, O Lord, deliver us.

3 They have poured out their blood like water

round about Jerusalem,

and there is no one to bury them.

4 We have become the reproach of our neighbors,

the scorn and derision of those around us.

[5] O LORD, how long? Will you be angry forever?

Will your jealousy burn like fire?

R. For the glory of your name, O Lord, deliver us.

[8] Remember not against us the iniquities of the past;

may your compassion quickly come to us,

for we are brought very low.

R. For the glory of your name, O Lord, deliver us.

[9] Help us, O God our savior,

because of the glory of your name;

Deliver us and pardon our sins

for your name's sake.

R. For the glory of your name, O Lord, deliver us.

Alleluia – Psalms 95:8

R. Alleluia, alleluia.

[8] If today you hear his voice, harden not your hearts.

R. Alleluia, alleluia.

Gospel – Luke 10:13-16

Jesus said to them, [13]"Woe to you, Chorazin! Woe to you, Bethsaida! For if the mighty deeds done in your midst had been done in Tyre and Sidon, they would long ago have repented, sitting in sackcloth and ashes. [14]But it will be more tolerable for Tyre and Sidon at the judgment than for you. [15]And as for you, Capernaum, 'Will you be exalted to heaven? You will go down to the netherworld.' [16]Whoever listens to you listens to me. Whoever rejects you rejects me. And whoever rejects me rejects the one who sent me."

Saturday October 7, 2023

Memorial of Our Lady of the Rosary

First Reading – Baruch 4:5-12, 27-29

[5]Fear not, my people! Remember, Israel, [6]You were sold to the nations not for your destruction; It was because you angered God that you were handed over to your foes. [7]For you provoked your Maker with sacrifices to demons, to no-gods; [8]You forsook the Eternal God who nourished you, and you grieved Jerusalem who fostered you. [9]She indeed saw coming upon you the anger of God; and she said: “Hear, you neighbors of Zion! God has brought great mourning upon me, [10]For I have seen the captivity that the Eternal God has brought upon my sons and daughters. [11]With joy I fostered them; but with mourning and lament I let them go. [12]Let no one gloat over me, a widow, bereft of many: For the sins of my children I am left desolate, because they turned from the law of God. [27]Fear not, my children; call out to God! He who brought this upon you will remember you. [28]As your hearts have been disposed to stray from God, turn now ten times the more to seek him; [29]For he who has brought disaster upon you will, in saving you, bring you back enduring joy.”

Responsorial Psalm – Psalms 69:33-35, 36-37

R. (34) The Lord listens to the poor.

33 “See, you lowly ones, and be glad;

you who seek God, may your hearts revive!

34 For the LORD hears the poor,

and his own who are in bonds he spurns not.

35 Let the heavens and the earth praise him,

the seas and whatever moves in them!”

R. The Lord listens to the poor.

36 For God will save Zion

and rebuild the cities of Judah.

37 They shall dwell in the land and own it,

and the descendants of his servants shall inherit it,

and those who love his name shall inhabit it.

R. The Lord listens to the poor.

Alleluia – Matthew 11:25

R. Alleluia, alleluia.

[25] Blessed are you, Father, Lord of heaven and earth; you have revealed to little ones the mysteries of the Kingdom.

R. Alleluia, alleluia.

Gospel – Luke 10:17-24

[17]The seventy-two disciples returned rejoicing and said to Jesus, “Lord, even the demons are subject to us because of your name.” [18]Jesus said, “I have observed Satan fall like lightning from the sky. [19]Behold, I have given you the power ‘to tread upon serpents’ and scorpions and upon the full force of the enemy and nothing will harm you. [20]Nevertheless, do not rejoice because the spirits are subject to you, but rejoice because your names are written in heaven.” [21]At that very moment he rejoiced in the Holy Spirit and said, “I give you praise, Father, Lord of heaven and earth, for although you have hidden these things from the wise and the learned you have revealed them to the childlike. Yes, Father, such has been your gracious will. [22]All things have been handed over to me by my Father. No one knows who the Son is except the Father, and who the Father is except the Son and anyone to whom the Son wishes to reveal him.” [23]Turning to the disciples in private he said, “Blessed are the eyes that see what you see. [24]For I say to you, many prophets and kings desired to see what you see, but did not see it, and to hear what you hear, but did not hear it.”

Sunday October 8, 2023

Twenty-seventh Sunday in Ordinary Time, Year A

First Reading – Isaiah 5:1-7

[1]Let me now sing of my friend, my friend’s song concerning his vineyard. My friend had a vineyard on a fertile hillside; [2]he spaded it, cleared it of stones, and planted the choicest vines; within it he built a watchtower, and hewed out a wine press. Then he looked for the crop of grapes, but what it yielded was wild grapes. [3]Now, inhabitants of Jerusalem and people of

Judah, judge between me and my vineyard: [4]What more was there to do for my vineyard that I had not done? Why, when I looked for the crop of grapes, did it bring forth wild grapes?
[5]Now, I will let you know what I mean to do with my vineyard: take away its hedge, give it to grazing, break through its wall, let it be trampled! [6]Yes, I will make it a ruin: it shall not be pruned or hoed, but overgrown with thorns and briers; I will command the clouds not to send rain upon it. [7]The vineyard of the LORD of hosts is the house of Israel, and the people of Judah are his cherished plant; he looked for judgment, but see, bloodshed! for justice, but hark, the outcry!

Responsorial Psalm – Psalms 80:9, 12, 13-14, 15-16, 19-20

R. (Is 5:7a) **The vineyard of the Lord is the house of Israel.**

9 A vine from Egypt you transplanted;

you drove away the nations and planted it.

12 It put forth its foliage to the Sea,

its shoots as far as the River.

R. The vineyard of the Lord is the house of Israel.

13 Why have you broken down its walls,

so that every passer-by plucks its fruit,

14 The boar from the forest lays it waste,

and the beasts of the field feed upon it?

R. The vineyard of the Lord is the house of Israel.

15 Once again, O LORD of hosts,

look down from heaven, and see;

take care of this vine,

16 and protect what your right hand has planted

the son of man whom you yourself made strong.

R. The vineyard of the Lord is the house of Israel.

19 Then we will no more withdraw from you;

give us new life, and we will call upon your name.

[20] O LORD, God of hosts, restore us;

if your face shine upon us, then we shall be saved.

R. The vineyard of the Lord is the house of Israel.

Second Reading – Philippians 4:6-9

Brothers and sisters: [6]Have no anxiety at all, but in everything,
by prayer and petition, with thanksgiving, make your requests
known to God. [7]Then the peace of God that surpasses all
understanding will guard your hearts and minds in Christ
Jesus. [8]Finally, brothers and sisters, whatever is true,
whatever is honorable, whatever is just, whatever is pure,
whatever is lovely, whatever is gracious, if there is any
excellence and if there is anything worthy of praise, think
about these things. [9]Keep on doing what you have learned
and received and heard and seen in me. Then the God of
peace will be with you.

Alleluia – John 15:16

R. Alleluia, alleluia.

[16] I have chosen you from the world, says the Lord, to go and bear fruit that will remain.

R. Alleluia, alleluia.

Gospel – Matthew 21:33-43

Jesus said to the chief priests and the elders of the people:
[33]"Hear another parable. There was a landowner who planted
a vineyard, put a hedge around it, dug a wine press in it, and
built a tower. Then he leased it to tenants and went on a
journey. [34]When vintage time drew near, he sent his servants
to the tenants to obtain his produce. [35]But the tenants seized
the servants and one they beat, another they killed, and a third
they stoned. [36]Again he sent other servants, more numerous
than the first ones, but they treated them in the same way.
[37]Finally, he sent his son to them, thinking, 'They will respect
my son.' [38]But when the tenants saw the son, they said to one
another, 'This is the heir. Come, let us kill him and acquire his
inheritance.' [39]They seized him, threw him out of the vineyard,
and killed him. [40]What will the owner of the vineyard do to
those tenants when he comes?" [41]They answered him, "He will
put those wretched men to a wretched death and lease his

vineyard to other tenants who will give him the produce at the proper times." [42]Jesus said to them, "Did you never read in the Scriptures: The stone that the builders rejected has become the cornerstone; by the Lord has this been done, and it is wonderful in our eyes? [43]Therefore, I say to you, the kingdom of God will be taken away from you and given to a people that will produce its fruit."

Monday October 9, 2023

Monday of Twenty-seventh Week in Ordinary Time

First Reading – Jonah 1:1-2:1-2, 11

[1]This is the word of the LORD that came to Jonah, son of Amittai: [2]"Set out for the great city of Nineveh, and preach against it; their wickedness has come up before me." [3]But Jonah made ready to flee to Tarshish away from the LORD. He went down to Joppa, found a ship going to Tarshish, paid the fare, and went aboard to journey with them to Tarshish, away from the LORD. [4]The LORD, however, hurled a violent wind upon the sea, and in the furious tempest that arose the ship was on the point of breaking up. [5]Then the mariners became frightened and each one cried to his god. To lighten the ship for themselves, they threw its cargo into the sea. Meanwhile, Jonah had gone down into the hold of the ship, and lay there fast asleep. [6]The captain came to him and said, "What are you doing asleep? Rise up, call upon your God! Perhaps God will be mindful of us so that we may not perish." [7]Then they said to one another, "Come, let us cast lots to find out on whose account we have met with this misfortune." So they cast lots, and thus singled out Jonah. [8]"Tell us," they said, "what is your business? Where do you come from What is your country, and to what people do you belong?" [9]Jonah answered them, "I am a Hebrew, I worship the LORD, the God of heaven, who made the sea and the dry land." [10]Now the men were seized with great fear and said to him, "How could you do such a thing! They knew that he was fleeing from the LORD, because he had told them. [11]They asked, "What shall we do with you, that the sea may quiet down for us?" For the sea was growing more and more turbulent. [12]Jonah said to them, "Pick me up and throw me into the sea, that it may quiet down for you; since I know it is because of me that this violent storm has come upon you." [13]Still the men rowed hard to

regain the land, but they could not, for the sea grew ever more
turbulent. 14Then they cried to the LORD: "We beseech you, O
LORD, let us not perish for taking this man's life; do not
charge us with shedding innocent blood, for you, LORD, have
done as you saw fit." 15Then they took Jonah and threw him
into the sea, and the sea's raging abated. Struck with great
fear of the LORD, the men offered sacrifice and made vows to
him. 1But the LORD sent a large fish, that swallowed Jonah;
and Jonah remained in the belly of the fish three days and
three nights. 2From the belly of the fish Jonah prayed to the
LORD, his God.11Then the LORD commanded the fish to
spew Jonah upon the shore.

Responsorial Psalm – Jonah 2:3, 4, 5, 8

R. (cf. 7) **You will rescue my life from the pit, O Lord.**

3 Out of my distress I called to the LORD,

and he answered me;

From the midst of the nether world I cried for help,

and you heard my voice.

R. You will rescue my life from the pit, O Lord.

4 For you cast me into the deep, into the heart of the sea,

and the flood enveloped me;

All your breakers and your billows

passed over me.

R. You will rescue my life from the pit, O Lord.

5 Then I said, "I am banished from your sight!

yet would I again look upon your holy temple."

R. You will rescue my life from the pit, O Lord.

8 When my soul fainted within me,

I remembered the LORD;

My prayer reached you

in your holy temple.

R. You will rescue my life from the pit, O Lord.

Alleluia – John 13:34

R. Alleluia, alleluia.

[34] I give you a new commandment: love one another as I have loved you.

R. Alleluia, alleluia.

Gospel – Luke 10:25-37

[25]There was a scholar of the law who stood up to test Jesus
and said, “Teacher, what must I do to inherit eternal life?”
[26]Jesus said to him, “What is written in the law? How do you
read it?” [27]He said in reply, “You shall love the Lord, your God,
with all your heart, with all your being, with all your strength,
and with all your mind, and your neighbor as yourself.” [28]He
replied to him, “You have answered correctly; do this and you
will live.” [29]But because he wished to justify himself, he said to
Jesus, “And who is my neighbor?” [30]Jesus replied, “A man fell
victim to robbers as he went down from Jerusalem to Jericho.
They stripped and beat him and went off leaving him half-
dead. [31]A priest happened to be going down that road, but
when he saw him, he passed by on the opposite side.
[32]Likewise a Levite came to the place, and when he saw him,
he passed by on the opposite side. [33]But a Samaritan traveler
who came upon him was moved with compassion at the sight.
[34]He approached the victim, poured oil and wine over his
wounds and bandaged them. Then he lifted him up on his own
animal, took him to an inn, and cared for him. [35]The next day
he took out two silver coins and gave them to the innkeeper
with the instruction, ‘Take care of him. If you spend more than
what I have given you, I shall repay you on my way back.’
[36]Which of these three, in your opinion, was neighbor to the
robbers’ victim?” [37]He answered, “The one who treated him
with mercy.” Jesus said to him, “Go and do likewise.”

Tuesday October 10, 2023

Tuesday of Twenty-seventh Week in Ordinary Time

First Reading – Jonah 3:1-10

[1]The word of the LORD came to Jonah a second time: [2]“Set
out for the great city of Nineveh, and announce to it the
message that I will tell you.” [3]So Jonah made ready and went
to Nineveh, according to the LORD’s bidding. Now Nineveh

was an enormously large city; it took three days to go through
it. [4]Jonah began his journey through the city, and had gone
but a single day's walk announcing, "Forty days more and
Nineveh shall be destroyed," [5]when the people of Nineveh
believed God; they proclaimed a fast and all of them, great
and small, put on sackcloth. [6]When the news reached the king
of Nineveh, he rose from his throne, laid aside his robe,
covered himself with sackcloth, and sat in the ashes. [7]Then he
had this proclaimed throughout Nineveh, by decree of the king
and his nobles: "Neither man nor beast, neither cattle nor
sheep, shall taste anything; they shall not eat, nor shall they
drink water. [8]Man and beast shall be covered with sackcloth
and call loudly to God; every man shall turn from his evil way
and from the violence he has in hand. [9]Who knows, God may
relent and forgive, and withhold his blazing wrath, so that we
shall not perish." [10]When God saw by their actions how they
turned from their evil way, he repented of the evil that he had
threatened to do to them; he did not carry it out.

Responsorial Psalm – Psalms 130:1B-2, 3-4AB, 7-8

R. (3) If you, O Lord, mark iniquities, who can stand?

[1B] Out of the depths I cry to you, O LORD

LORD, hear my voice!

[2] Let your ears be attentive

to my voice in supplication.

R. If you, O Lord, mark iniquities, who can stand?

[3] If you, O LORD, mark iniquities,

LORD, who can stand?

[4AB] But with you is forgiveness,

that you may be revered.

R. If you, O Lord, mark iniquities, who can stand?

[7] Let Israel wait for the LORD,

For with the LORD is kindness

and with him is plenteous redemption;

[8] And he will redeem Israel

from all their iniquities.

R. If you, O Lord, mark iniquities, who can stand?

Alleluia – Luke 11:28

R. Alleluia, alleluia.

28 Blessed are those who hear the word of God and observe it.

R. Alleluia, alleluia.

Gospel – Luke 10:38-42

38Jesus entered a village where a woman whose name was
Martha welcomed him. 39She had a sister named Mary who
sat beside the Lord at his feet listening to him speak. 40Martha,
burdened with much serving, came to him and said, "Lord, do
you not care that my sister has left me by myself to do the
serving? Tell her to help me." 41The Lord said to her in reply,
"Martha, Martha, you are anxious and worried about many
things. 42There is need of only one thing. Mary has chosen the
better part and it will not be taken from her."

Wednesday October 11, 2023

Wednesday of Twenty-seventh Week in Ordinary Time

First Reading – Jonah 4:1-11

1Jonah was greatly displeased and became angry that God
did not carry out the evil he threatened against Nineveh. 2He
prayed, "I beseech you, LORD, is not this what I said while I
was still in my own country? This is why I fled at first to
Tarshish. I knew that you are a gracious and merciful God,
slow to anger, rich in clemency, loath to punish. 3And now,
LORD, please take my life from me; for it is better for me to die
than to live." 4But the LORD asked, "Have you reason to be
angry?" 5Jonah then left the city for a place to the east of it,
where he built himself a hut and waited under it in the shade,
to see what would happen to the city. 6And when the LORD
God provided a gourd plant that grew up over Jonah's head,
giving shade that relieved him of any discomfort, Jonah was
very happy over the plant. 7But the next morning at dawn God
sent a worm that attacked the plant, so that it withered. 8And
when the sun arose, God sent a burning east wind; and the
sun beat upon Jonah's head till he became faint. Then Jonah
asked for death, saying, "I would be better off dead than alive."

9But God said to Jonah, "Have you reason to be angry over the plant?" "I have reason to be angry," Jonah answered, "angry enough to die." 10Then the LORD said, "You are concerned over the plant which cost you no labor and which you did not raise; it came up in one night and in one night it perished. 11And should I not be concerned over Nineveh, the great city, in which there are more than a hundred and twenty thousand persons who cannot distinguish their right hand from their left, not to mention the many cattle?"

Responsorial Psalm – Psalms 86:3-4, 5-6, 9-10

R. (15) Lord, you are merciful and gracious.

3 Have mercy on me, O Lord,

for to you I call all the day.

4 Gladden the soul of your servant,

for to you, O Lord, I lift up my soul.

R. Lord, you are merciful and gracious.

5 For you, O Lord, are good and forgiving,

abounding in kindness to all who call upon you.

6 Hearken, O LORD, to my prayer

and attend to the sound of my pleading.

R. Lord, you are merciful and gracious.

9 All the nations you have made shall come

and worship you, O Lord,

and glorify your name.

10 For you are great, and you do wondrous deeds;

you alone are God.

R. Lord, you are merciful and gracious.

Alleluia – Romans 8:15BC

R. Alleluia, alleluia.

15BC You have received a spirit of adoption as sons through which we cry: Abba! Father!

R. Alleluia, alleluia.

Gospel – Luke 11:1-4

[1]Jesus was praying in a certain place, and when he had
finished, one of his disciples said to him, "Lord, teach us to
pray just as John taught his disciples." [2]He said to them,
"When you pray, say: Father, hallowed be your name, your
Kingdom come. [3]Give us each day our daily bread [4]and
forgive us our sins for we ourselves forgive everyone in debt to
us, and do not subject us to the final test."

Thursday October 12, 2023

Thursday of Twenty-seventh Week in Ordinary Time

First Reading – Malachi 3:13-20B

[13]You have defied me in word, says the LORD, yet you ask,
"What have we spoken against you?" [14]You have said, "It is
vain to serve God, and what do we profit by keeping his
command, And going about in penitential dress in awe of the
LORD of hosts? [15]Rather must we call the proud blessed; for
indeed evildoers prosper, and even tempt God with impunity."
[16]Then they who fear the LORD spoke with one another, and
the LORD listened attentively; And a record book was written
before him of those who fear the LORD and trust in his name.
[17]And they shall be mine, says the LORD of hosts, my own
special possession, on the day I take action. And I will have
compassion on them, as a man has compassion on his son
who serves him. [18]Then you will again see the distinction
between the just and the wicked; Between the one who serves
God, and the one who does not serve him. [19]For lo, the day is
coming, blazing like an oven, when all the proud and all
evildoers will be stubble, And the day that is coming will set
them on fire, leaving them neither root nor branch, says the
LORD of hosts. [20AB]But for you who fear my name, there will
arise the sun of justice with its healing rays.

Responsorial Psalm – Psalms 1:1-2, 3, 4 AND 6

R. (Ps 40:5a) **Blessed are they who hope in the Lord.**

[1] Blessed the man who follows not

the counsel of the wicked

Nor walks in the way of sinners,

nor sits in the company of the insolent,

2 But delights in the law of the LORD

and meditates on his law day and night.

R. Blessed are they who hope in the Lord.

3 He is like a tree

planted near running water,

That yields its fruit in due season,

and whose leaves never fade.

Whatever he does, prospers.

R. Blessed are they who hope in the Lord.

4 Not so the wicked, not so;

they are like chaff which the wind drives away.

6 For the LORD watches over the way of the just,

but the way of the wicked vanishes.

R. Blessed are they who hope in the Lord.

Alleluia – Acts 16:14B

R. Alleluia, alleluia.

14B Open our hearts, O Lord, to listen to the words of your Son.

R. Alleluia, alleluia.

Gospel – Luke 11:5-13

Jesus said to his disciples: 5“Suppose one of you has a friend
to whom he goes at midnight and says, ‘Friend, lend me three
loaves of bread, 6for a friend of mine has arrived at my house
from a journey and I have nothing to offer him,’ 7and he says
in reply from within, ‘Do not bother me; the door has already
been locked and my children and I are already in bed. I cannot
get up to give you anything.’ 8I tell you, if he does not get up to
give him the loaves because of their friendship, he will get up
to give him whatever he needs because of his persistence.
9“And I tell you, ask and you will receive; seek and you will
find; knock and the door will be opened to you. 10For everyone
who asks, receives; and the one who seeks, finds; and to the
one who knocks, the door will be opened. 11What father
among you would hand his son a snake when he asks for a

fish? [12]Or hand him a scorpion when he asks for an egg? [13]If you then, who are wicked, know how to give good gifts to your children, how much more will the Father in heaven give the Holy Spirit to those who ask him?"

Friday October 13, 2023

Friday of Twenty-seventh Week in Ordinary Time

First Reading – Joel 1:13-15; 2:1-2

[13]Gird yourselves and weep, O priests! wail, O ministers of the altar! Come, spend the night in sackcloth, O ministers of my God! The house of your God is deprived of offering and
libation. [14]Proclaim a fast, call an assembly; Gather the elders, all who dwell in the land, Into the house of the LORD, your
God, and cry to the LORD! [15]Alas, the day! for near is the day
of the LORD, and it comes as ruin from the Almighty. [1]Blow
the trumpet in Zion, sound the alarm on my holy mountain! Let all who dwell in the land tremble, for the day of the LORD is
coming; Yes, it is near, a day of darkness and of gloom, [2]a day
of clouds and somberness! Like dawn spreading over the mountains, a people numerous and mighty! Their like has not been from of old, nor will it be after them, even to the years of distant generations.

Responsorial Psalm – Psalms 9:2-3, 6 AND 16, 8-9

R. (9) The Lord will judge the world with justice.

[2] I will give thanks to you, O LORD, with all my heart;

I will declare all your wondrous deeds.

[3] I will be glad and exult in you;

I will sing praise to your name, Most High.

R. The Lord will judge the world with justice.

[6] You rebuked the nations and destroyed the wicked;

their name you blotted out forever and ever.

[16] The nations are sunk in the pit they have made;

in the snare they set, their foot is caught.

R. The Lord will judge the world with justice.

[8] But the LORD sits enthroned forever;

he has set up his throne for judgment.

[9] He judges the world with justice;

he governs the peoples with equity.

R. The Lord will judge the world with justice.

Alleluia – John 12:31B-32

R. Alleluia, alleluia.

The prince of this world will now be cast out, and when I am lifted up from the earth I will draw all to myself, says the Lord.

R. Alleluia, alleluia.

Gospel – Luke 11:15-26

[15]When Jesus had driven out a demon, some of the crowd
said: "By the power of Beelzebul, the prince of demons, he
drives out demons." [16]Others, to test him, asked him for a sign
from heaven. [17]But he knew their thoughts and said to them,
"Every kingdom divided against itself will be laid waste and
house will fall against house. [18]And if Satan is divided against
himself, how will his kingdom stand? For you say that it is by
Beelzebul that I drive out demons. [19]If I, then, drive out
demons by Beelzebul, by whom do your own people drive
them out? Therefore they will be your judges. [20]But if it is by
the finger of God that I drive out demons, then the Kingdom of
God has come upon you. [21]When a strong man fully armed
guards his palace, his possessions are safe. [22]But when one
stronger than he attacks and overcomes him, he takes away
the armor on which he relied and distributes the spoils.
[23]Whoever is not with me is against me, and whoever does not
gather with me scatters. [24]"When an unclean spirit goes out of
someone, it roams through arid regions searching for rest but,
finding none, it says, 'I shall return to my home from which I
came.' [25]But upon returning, it finds it swept clean and put in
order. [26]Then it goes and brings back seven other spirits more
wicked than itself who move in and dwell there, and the last
condition of that man is worse than the first."

Saturday October 14, 2023

Saturday of Twenty-seventh Week in Ordinary Time

First Reading – Joel 4:12-21

Thus says the LORD: [12]Let the nations bestir themselves and
come up to the Valley of Jehoshaphat; For there will I sit in
judgment upon all the neighboring nations. [13]Apply the sickle,
for the harvest is ripe; Come and tread, for the wine press is
full; The vats overflow, for great is their malice. [14]Crowd upon
crowd in the valley of decision; For near is the day of the
LORD in the valley of decision. [15]Sun and moon are darkened,
and the stars withhold their brightness. [16]The LORD roars from
Zion, and from Jerusalem raises his voice; The heavens and
the earth quake, but the LORD is a refuge to his people, a
stronghold to the children of Israel. [17]Then shall you know that
I, the LORD, am your God, dwelling on Zion, my holy
mountain; Jerusalem shall be holy, and strangers shall pass
through her no more. [18]And then, on that day, the mountains
shall drip new wine, and the hills shall flow with milk; And the
channels of Judah shall flow with water: A fountain shall issue
from the house of the LORD, to water the Valley of Shittim.
[19]Egypt shall be a waste, and Edom a desert waste, Because
of violence done to the people of Judah, because they shed
innocent blood in their land. [20]But Judah shall abide forever,
and Jerusalem for all generations. [21]I will avenge their blood,
and not leave it unpunished. The LORD dwells in Zion.

Responsorial Psalm – Psalms 97:1-2, 5-6, 11-12

R. (12a) **Rejoice in the Lord, you just!**

[1] The LORD is king; let the earth rejoice;

let the many isles be glad.

[2] Clouds and darkness are round about him,

justice and judgment are the foundation of his throne.

R. Rejoice in the Lord, you just!

[5] The mountains melt like wax before the LORD,

before the LORD of all the earth.

[6] The heavens proclaim his justice,

and all peoples see his glory.

R. Rejoice in the Lord, you just!

11 Light dawns for the just;

and gladness, for the upright of heart.

12 Be glad in the LORD, you just,

and give thanks to his holy name.

R. Rejoice in the Lord, you just!

Alleluia – Luke 11:28

R. Alleluia, alleluia.

28 Blessed are those who hear the word of God and observe it.

R. Alleluia, alleluia.

Gospel – Luke 11:27-28

27 While Jesus was speaking, a woman from the crowd called
out and said to him, “Blessed is the womb that carried you and
the breasts at which you nursed.” 28 He replied, “Rather,
blessed are those who hear the word of God and observe it.”

Sunday October 15, 2023

Twenty-eighth Sunday in Ordinary Time, Year A

First Reading – Isaiah 25:6-10A

6 On this mountain the LORD of hosts will provide for all
peoples a feast of rich food and choice wines, juicy, rich food
and pure, choice wines. 7 On this mountain he will destroy the
veil that veils all peoples, the web that is woven over all
nations; 8 he will destroy death forever. The Lord GOD will
wipe away the tears from every face; the reproach of his
people he will remove from the whole earth; for the LORD has
spoken. 9 On that day it will be said: “Behold our God, to whom
we looked to save us! This is the LORD for whom we looked;
let us rejoice and be glad that he has saved us!” 10A For the
hand of the LORD will rest on this mountain.

Responsorial Psalm – Psalms 23:1-3A, 3B-4, 5, 6

R. (6cd) I shall live in the house of the Lord all the days of my life.

1 The LORD is my shepherd; I shall not want.

2 In verdant pastures he gives me repose;

beside restful waters he leads me;

3A he refreshes my soul.

R. I shall live in the house of the Lord all the days of my life.

3B He guides me in right paths

for his name's sake.

4 Even though I walk in the dark valley

I fear no evil; for you are at my side

with your rod and your staff

that give me courage.

R. I shall live in the house of the Lord all the days of my life.

5 You spread the table before me

in the sight of my foes;

you anoint my head with oil;

my cup overflows.

R. I shall live in the house of the Lord all the days of my life.

6 Only goodness and kindness follow me

all the days of my life;

and I shall dwell in the house of the LORD

for years to come.

R. I shall live in the house of the Lord all the days of my life.

Second Reading – Philippians 4:12-14, 19-20

Brothers and sisters: 12I know how to live in humble circumstances; I know also how to live with abundance. In every circumstance and in all things I have learned the secret of being well fed and of going hungry, of living in abundance and of being in need. [13]I can do all things in him who strengthens me. [14]Still, it was kind of you to share in my distress. [19]My God will fully supply whatever you need, in accord with his glorious riches in Christ Jesus. [20]To our God and Father, glory forever and ever. Amen.

Alleluia – Ephesians 1:17-18

R. Alleluia, alleluia.

[17] May the Father of our Lord Jesus Christ enlighten the eyes of our hearts, [18]so that we may know what is the hope that belongs to our call.

R. Alleluia, alleluia.

Gospel – Matthew 22:1-14

[1]Jesus again in reply spoke to the chief priests and elders of the people in parables, saying, [2]"The kingdom of heaven may be likened to a king who gave a wedding feast for his son. [3]He dispatched his servants to summon the invited guests to the feast, but they refused to come. [4]A second time he sent other servants, saying, 'Tell those invited: "Behold, I have prepared my banquet, my calves and fattened cattle are killed, and everything is ready; come to the feast."' [5]Some ignored the invitation and went away, one to his farm, another to his business. [6]The rest laid hold of his servants, mistreated them, and killed them. [7]The king was enraged and sent his troops, destroyed those murderers, and burned their city.n[8]Then he said to his servants, 'The feast is ready, but those who were invited were not worthy to come. [9]Go out, therefore, into the main roads and invite to the feast whomever you find.' [10]The servants went out into the streets and gathered all they found, bad and good alike, and the hall was filled with guests. [11]But when the king came in to meet the guests, he saw a man there not dressed in a wedding garment. [12]The king said to him, 'My friend, how is it that you came in here without a wedding garment?' But he was reduced to silence. [13]Then the king said to his attendants, 'Bind his hands and feet, and cast him into the darkness outside, where there will be wailing and grinding of teeth.' [14]Many are invited, but few are chosen."

Or Matthew 22:1-10

[1]Jesus again in reply spoke to the chief priests and elders of the people in parables, saying, [2]"The kingdom of heaven may be likened to a king who gave a wedding feast for his son. [3]He dispatched his servants to summon the invited guests to the feast, but they refused to come. [4]A second time he sent other servants, saying, 'Tell those invited: "Behold, I have prepared my banquet, my calves and fattened cattle are killed, and everything is ready; come to the feast."' [5]Some ignored the invitation and went away, one to his farm, another to his business. [6]The rest laid hold of his servants, mistreated them, and killed them. [7]The king was enraged and sent his troops, destroyed those murderers, and burned their city. [8]Then he said to his servants, 'The feast is ready, but those who were invited were not worthy to come. [9]Go out, therefore, into the main roads and invite to the feast whomever you find.' [10]The servants went out into the streets and gathered all they found, bad and good alike, and the hall was filled with guests.

Monday October 16, 2023

Monday of Twenty-eighth Week in Ordinary Time

First Reading – Romans 1:1-7

[1]Paul, a slave of Christ Jesus, called to be an Apostle and set apart for the Gospel of God, [2]which he promised previously through his prophets in the holy Scriptures, [3]the Gospel about his Son, descended from David according to the flesh, [4]but established as Son of God in power according to the Spirit of holiness through resurrection from the dead, Jesus Christ our Lord. [5]Through him we have received the grace of apostleship, to bring about the obedience of faith, for the sake of his name, among all the Gentiles, [6]among whom are you also, who are called to belong to Jesus Christ; [7]to all the beloved of God in Rome, called to be holy. Grace to you and peace from God our Father and the Lord Jesus Christ.

Responsorial Psalm – Psalms 98:1BCDE, 2-3AB, 3CD-4

R. (2a) The Lord has made known his salvation.

1BCDE Sing to the LORD a new song,

for he has done wondrous deeds;

His right hand has won victory for him,

his holy arm.

R. The Lord has made known his salvation.

2 The LORD has made his salvation known:

in the sight of the nations he has revealed his justice.

3AB He has remembered his kindness and his faithfulness

toward the house of Israel.

R. The Lord has made known his salvation.

3CB All the ends of the earth have seen

the salvation by our God.

4 Sing joyfully to the LORD, all you lands;

break into song; sing praise.

R. The Lord has made known his salvation.

Alleluia – Psalms 95:8

R. Alleluia, alleluia.

8 If today you hear his voice, harden not your hearts.

R. Alleluia, alleluia.

Gospel – Luke 11:29-32

29While still more people gathered in the crowd, Jesus said to
them, "This generation is an evil generation; it seeks a sign,
but no sign will be given it, except the sign of Jonah.
30Just as
Jonah became a sign to the Ninevites, so will the Son of Man
be to this generation.
31At the judgment the queen of the south
will rise with the men of this generation and she will condemn
them, because she came from the ends of the earth to hear
the wisdom of Solomon, and there is something greater than
Solomon here.
32At the judgment the men of Nineveh will arise
with this generation and condemn it, because at the preaching
of Jonah they repented, and there is something greater than
Jonah here."

Tuesday October 17, 2023

Memorial of St Ignatius of Antioch, Bishop & Martyr

First Reading – Romans 1:16-25

Brothers and sisters: [16]I am not ashamed of the Gospel. It is the power of God for the salvation of everyone who believes: for Jew first, and then Greek. [17]For in it is revealed the righteousness of God from faith to faith; as it is written, "The one who is righteous by faith will live." [18]The wrath of God is indeed being revealed from heaven against every impiety and wickedness of those who suppress the truth by their wickedness. [19]For what can be known about God is evident to them, because God made it evident to them. [20]Ever since the creation of the world, his invisible attributes of eternal power and divinity have been able to be understood and perceived in what he has made. As a result, they have no excuse; [21]for although they knew God they did not accord him glory as God or give him thanks. Instead, they became vain in their reasoning, and their senseless minds were darkened. [22]While claiming to be wise, they became fools [23]and exchanged the glory of the immortal God for the likeness of an image of mortal man or of birds or of four-legged animals or of snakes. [24]Therefore, God handed them over to impurity through the lusts of their hearts for the mutual degradation of their bodies. [25]They exchanged the truth of God for a lie and revered and worshiped the creature rather than the creator, who is blessed forever. Amen.

Responsorial Psalm – Psalms 19:2-3, 4-5

R. (2a) **The heavens proclaim the glory of God.**

2 The heavens declare the glory of God,

and the firmament proclaims his handiwork.

3 Day pours out the word to day,

and night to night imparts knowledge.

R. The heavens proclaim the glory of God.

4 Not a word nor a discourse

whose voice is not heard;

5 Through all the earth their voice resounds,

and to the ends of the world, their message.

R. The heavens proclaim the glory of God.

Alleluia – Hebrews 4:12

R. Alleluia, alleluia.

12 The word of God is living and effective, able to discern reflections and thoughts of the heart.

R. Alleluia, alleluia.

Gospel – Luke 11:37-41

37 After Jesus had spoken, a Pharisee invited him to dine at his
home. He entered and reclined at table to eat. 38 The Pharisee
was amazed to see that he did not observe the prescribed
washing before the meal. 39 The Lord said to him, “Oh you
Pharisees! Although you cleanse the outside of the cup and
the dish, inside you are filled with plunder and evil. 40 You fools!
Did not the maker of the outside also make the inside? 41 But
as to what is within, give alms, and behold, everything will be
clean for you.”

Wednesday October 18, 2023

Feast of Saint Luke, Evangelist

First Reading – 2 Timothy 4:10-17B

Beloved: 10 Demas, enamoured of the present world, deserted
me and went to Thessalonica, Crescens to Galatia, and Titus
to Dalmatia. 11 Luke is the only one with me. Get Mark and
bring him with you, for he is helpful to me in the ministry. 12 I
have sent Tychicus to Ephesus. 13 When you come, bring the
cloak I left with Carpus in Troas, the papyrus rolls, and
especially the parchments. 14 Alexander the coppersmith did
me a great deal of harm; the Lord will repay him according to
his deeds. 15 You too be on guard against him, for he has
strongly resisted our preaching. 16 At my first defence no one
appeared on my behalf, but everyone deserted me. May it not
be held against them! 17 But the Lord stood by me and gave
me strength so that through me the proclamation might be
completed and all the Gentiles might hear it.

Responsorial Psalm – Psalms 145:10-11, 12-13, 17-18

R. (12) Your friends make known, O Lord, the glorious splendour of your Kingdom.

10 Let all your works give you thanks, O LORD,

and let your faithful ones bless you.

11 Let them discourse of the glory of your Kingdom

and speak of your might.

R. Your friends make known, O Lord, the glorious splendour of your Kingdom.

12 Making known to men your might

and the glorious splendour of your Kingdom.

13 Your Kingdom is a Kingdom for all ages,

and your dominion endures through all generations.

R. Your friends make known, O Lord, the glorious splendour of your Kingdom.

17 The LORD is just in all his ways

and holy in all his works.

18 The LORD is near to all who call upon him,

to all who call upon him in truth.

R. Your friends make known, O Lord, the glorious splendour of your Kingdom.

Alleluia – cf. John 15:16

R. Alleluia, alleluia.

16 I chose you from the world, to go and bear fruit that will last, says the Lord.

R. Alleluia, alleluia.

Gospel – Luke 10:1-9

1 The Lord Jesus appointed seventy-two disciples whom he
sent ahead of him in pairs to every town and place he
intended to visit. 2 He said to them, "The harvest is abundant
but the labourers are few; so ask the master of the harvest to
send out labourers for his harvest. 3 Go on your way; behold, I

am sending you like lambs among wolves. [4]Carry no money bag, no sack, no sandals; and greet no one along the way. [5]Into whatever house you enter, first say, ‘Peace to this household.’ [6]If a peaceful person lives there, your peace will rest on him; but if not, it will return to you. [7]Stay in the same house and eat and drink what is offered to you, for the labourer deserves payment. Do not move about from one house to another. [8]Whatever town you enter and they welcome you, eat what is set before you, [9]cure the sick in it and say to them, ‘The Kingdom of God is at hand for you.’”

Thursday October 19, 2023

Memorial of Saints John de Brebeuf and Isaac Jogues, Priests, and Companions, Martyrs

First Reading – Romans 3:21-30

Brothers and sisters: [21]Now the righteousness of God has been manifested apart from the law, though testified to by the law and the prophets, [22]the righteousness of God through faith in Jesus Christ for all who believe. For there is no distinction; [23]all have sinned and are deprived of the glory of God. [24]They are justified freely by his grace through the redemption in Christ Jesus, [25]whom God set forth as an expiation, through faith, by his Blood, to prove his righteousness because of the forgiveness of sins previously committed, [26]through the forbearance of God– to prove his righteousness in the present time, that he might be righteous and justify the one who has faith in Jesus. [27]What occasion is there then for boasting? It is ruled out. On what principle, that of works? No, rather on the principle of faith. [28]For we consider that a person is justified by faith apart from works of the law. [29]Does God belong to Jews alone? Does he not belong to Gentiles, too? Yes, also to Gentiles, [30]for God is one and will justify the circumcised on the basis of faith and the uncircumcised through faith.

Responsorial Psalm – Psalms 130:1B-2, 3-4, 5-6AB

R. [(7)] With the Lord there is mercy, and fullness of redemption.

[1B] Out of the depths I cry to you, O LORD;

[2] LORD, hear my voice!

Let your ears be attentive

to my voice in supplication.

R. With the Lord there is mercy, and fullness of redemption.

3 If you, O LORD, mark iniquities,

Lord, who can stand?

4 But with you is forgiveness,

that you may be revered.

R. With the Lord there is mercy, and fullness of redemption.

5 I trust in the LORD;

my soul trusts in his word.

6AB My soul waits for the LORD

more than sentinels wait for the dawn.

R. With the Lord there is mercy, and fullness of redemption.

Alleluia – John 14:6

R. Alleluia, alleluia.

6 I am the way and the truth and the life, says the Lord; no one comes to the Father except through me.

R. Alleluia, alleluia.

Gospel – Luke 11:47-54

The Lord said: 47"Woe to you who build the memorials of the
prophets whom your fathers killed. 48Consequently, you bear
witness and give consent to the deeds of your ancestors, for
they killed them and you do the building. 49Therefore, the
wisdom of God said, 'I will send to them prophets and
Apostles; some of them they will kill and persecute' 50in order
that this generation might be charged with the blood of all the
prophets shed since the foundation of the world, 51from the
blood of Abel to the blood of Zechariah who died between the
altar and the temple building. Yes, I tell you, this generation
will be charged with their blood! 52Woe to you, scholars of the
law! You have taken away the key of knowledge. You
yourselves did not enter and you stopped those trying to

enter." [53]When Jesus left, the scribes and Pharisees began to
act with hostility toward him and to interrogate him about many
things, [54]for they were plotting to catch him at something he
might say.

Friday October 20, 2023

Friday of Twenty-eighth Week Ordinary Time

First Reading – Romans 4:1-8

Brothers and sisters: [1]What can we say that Abraham found,
our ancestor according to the flesh? [2]Indeed, if Abraham was
justified on the basis of his works, he has reason to boast; but
this was not so in the sight of God. [3]For what does the
Scripture say? Abraham believed God, and it was credited to
him as righteousness. [4]A worker's wage is credited not as a
gift, but as something due. [5]But when one does not work, yet
believes in the one who justifies the ungodly, his faith is
credited as righteousness. [6]So also David declares the
blessedness of the person to whom God credits righteousness
apart from works: [7]Blessed are they whose iniquities are
forgiven and whose sins are covered. [8]Blessed is the man
whose sin the Lord does not record.

Responsorial Psalm – Psalms 32:1B-2, 5, 11

R. (see 7) I turn to you, Lord, in time of trouble, and you fill me with the joy of salvation.

[1B] Blessed is he whose fault is taken away,

whose sin is covered.

[2] Blessed the man to whom the LORD imputes not guilt,

in whose spirit there is no guile.

R. I turn to you, Lord, in time of trouble, and you fill me with the joy of salvation.

[5] Then I acknowledged my sin to you,

my guilt I covered not.

I said, "I confess my faults to the LORD,"

and you took away the guilt of my sin.

R. I turn to you, Lord, in time of trouble, and you fill me with the joy of salvation.

11 Be glad in the LORD and rejoice, you just;

exult, all you upright of heart.

R. I turn to you, Lord, in time of trouble, and you fill me with the joy of salvation.

Alleluia – Psalms 33:22

R. Alleluia, alleluia.

22 May your kindness, O LORD, be upon us; who have put our hope in you.

R. Alleluia, alleluia.

Gospel – Luke 12:1-7

1At that time: So many people were crowding together that
they were trampling one another underfoot. Jesus began to
speak, first to his disciples, "Beware of the leaven–that is, the
hypocrisy–of the Pharisees. 2"There is nothing concealed that
will not be revealed, nor secret that will not be known.
3Therefore whatever you have said in the darkness will be
heard in the light, and what you have whispered behind closed
doors will be proclaimed on the housetops. 4I tell you, my
friends, do not be afraid of those who kill the body but after
that can do no more. 5I shall show you whom to fear. Be afraid
of the one who after killing has the power to cast into
Gehenna; yes, I tell you, be afraid of that one. 6Are not five
sparrows sold for two small coins? Yet not one of them has
escaped the notice of God. 7Even the hairs of your head have
all been counted. Do not be afraid. You are worth more than
many sparrows."

Saturday October 21, 2023

Saturday of Twenty-eighth Week in Ordinary Time

First Reading – Romans 4:13, 16-18

Brothers and sisters: 13It was not through the law that the
promise was made to Abraham and his descendants that he
would inherit the world, but through the righteousness that
comes from faith. 16For this reason, it depends on faith, so that
it may be a gift, and the promise may be guaranteed to all his

descendants, not to those who only adhere to the law but to those who follow the faith of Abraham, who is the father of all of us,
[17]as it is written, I have made you father of many nations. He is our father in the sight of God, in whom he believed, who gives life to the dead and calls into being what does not exist.
[18]He believed, hoping against hope, that he would become the father of many nations, according to what was said, Thus shall your descendants be.

Responsorial Psalm – Psalms 105:6-7, 8-9, 42-43

R. (8a) The Lord remembers his covenant for ever.

6 You descendants of Abraham, his servants,

sons of Jacob, his chosen ones!

7 He, the LORD, is our God;

throughout the earth his judgments prevail.

R. The Lord remembers his covenant for ever.

8 He remembers forever his covenant

which he made binding for a thousand generations –

9 Which he entered into with Abraham

and by his oath to Isaac.

R. The Lord remembers his covenant for ever.

42 For he remembered his holy word

to his servant Abraham.

43 And he led forth his people with joy;

with shouts of joy, his chosen ones.

R. The Lord remembers his covenant for ever.

Alleluia – John 15:26B, 27A

R. Alleluia, alleluia.

26B The Spirit of truth will testify to me, says the Lord, 27A and you also will testify.

R. Alleluia, alleluia.

Gospel – Luke 12:8-12

Jesus said to his disciples: [8]"I tell you, everyone who acknowledges me before others the Son of Man will acknowledge before the angels of God. [9]But whoever denies me before others will be denied before the angels of God. [10]"Everyone who speaks a word against the Son of Man will be forgiven, but the one who blasphemes against the Holy Spirit will not be forgiven. [11]When they take you before synagogues and before rulers and authorities, do not worry about how or what your defense will be or about what you are to say. [12]For the Holy Spirit will teach you at that moment what you should say."

Sunday October 22, 2023

Twenty-ninth Sunday in Ordinary Time, Year A

First Reading – Isaiah 45:1, 4-6

[1]Thus says the LORD to his anointed, Cyrus, whose right hand I grasp, subduing nations before him, and making kings run in his service, opening doors before him and leaving the gates unbarred: [4]For the sake of Jacob, my servant, of Israel, my chosen one, I have called you by your name, giving you a title, though you knew me not. [5]I am the LORD and there is no other, there is no God besides me. It is I who arm you, though you know me not, [6]so that toward the rising and the setting of the sun people may know that there is none besides me. I am the LORD, there is no other.

Responsorial Psalm – Psalms 96:1, 3, 4-5, 7-8, 9-10

R. (7b) Give the Lord glory and honor.

[1] Sing to the LORD a new song;

sing to the LORD, all you lands.

[3] Tell his glory among the nations;

among all peoples, his wondrous deeds.

R. Give the Lord glory and honor.

[4] For great is the LORD and highly to be praised;

awesome is he, beyond all gods.

[5] For all the gods of the nations are things of nought,

but the LORD made the heavens.

R. Give the Lord glory and honor.

[7] Give to the LORD, you families of nations,

give to the LORD glory and praise;

[8] give to the LORD the glory due his name!

Bring gifts, and enter his courts.

R. Give the Lord glory and honor.

[9] Worship the LORD, in holy attire;

tremble before him, all the earth;

[10] say among the nations: The LORD is king,

he governs the peoples with equity.

R. Give the Lord glory and honor.

Second Reading – 1 Thessalonians 1:1-5B

[1]Paul, Silvanus, and Timothy to the church of the
Thessalonians in God the Father and the Lord Jesus Christ:
grace to you and peace. [2]We give thanks to God always for all
of you, remembering you in our prayers, unceasingly [3]calling
to mind your work of faith and labor of love and endurance in
hope of our Lord Jesus Christ, before our God and Father,
[4]knowing, brothers and sisters loved by God, how you were
chosen. [5AB]For our gospel did not come to you in word alone,
but also in power and in the Holy Spirit and with much
conviction.

Alleluia – Philippians 2:15D, 16A

R. Alleluia, alleluia.

[15D] Shine like lights in the world [16A] as you hold on to the word of life.

R. Alleluia, alleluia.

Gospel – Matthew 22:15-21

[15]The Pharisees went off and plotted how they might entrap
Jesus in speech. [16]They sent their disciples to him, with the

Herodians, saying, "Teacher, we know that you are a truthful man and that you teach the way of God in accordance with the truth. And you are not concerned with anyone's opinion, for you do not regard a person's status. [17]Tell us, then, what is your opinion: Is it lawful to pay the census tax to Caesar or not?" [18]Knowing their malice, Jesus said, "Why are you testing me, you hypocrites? [19]Show me the coin that pays the census tax." Then they handed him the Roman coin. [20]He said to them, "Whose image is this and whose inscription?" [21]They replied, "Caesar's." At that he said to them, "Then repay to Caesar what belongs to Caesar and to God what belongs to God.

Monday October 23, 2023

Monday of Twenty-ninth Week in Ordinary Time

First Reading – Romans 4:20-25

Brothers and sisters: [20]Abraham did not doubt God's promise in unbelief; rather, he was empowered by faith and gave glory to God [21]and was fully convinced that what God had promised he was also able to do. [22]That is why it was credited to him as righteousness. [23]But it was not for him alone that it was written that it was credited to him; [24]it was also for us, to whom it will be credited, who believe in the one who raised Jesus our Lord from the dead, [25]who was handed over for our transgressions and was raised for our justification.

Responsorial Psalm – Luke 1:69-70, 71-72, 73-75

R. (see 68) **Blessed be the Lord, the God of Israel; he has come to his people.**

[69] He has come to his people and set them free.

[70] He has raised up for us a mighty savior,

born of the house of his servant David.

R. Blessed be the Lord, the God of Israel; he has come to his people.

[71] Through his holy prophets he promised of old

that he would save us from our enemies,

from the hands of all who hate us.

72 He promised to show mercy to our fathers

and to remember his holy covenant.

R. Blessed be the Lord, the God of Israel; he has come to his people.

73 This was the oath he swore to our father Abraham:

74 to set us free from the hands of our enemies,

free to worship him without fear,

75 holy and righteous in his sight all the days of our life.

R. Blessed be the Lord, the God of Israel; he has come to his people.

Alleluia – Matthew 5:3

R. Alleluia, alleluia.

3 Blessed are the poor in spirit; for theirs is the Kingdom of heaven.

R. Alleluia, alleluia.

Gospel – Luke 12:13-21

13 Someone in the crowd said to Jesus, “Teacher, tell my
brother to share the inheritance with me.” 14 He replied to him,
“Friend, who appointed me as your judge and arbitrator?”
15 Then he said to the crowd, “Take care to guard against all
greed, for though one may be rich, one’s life does not consist
of possessions.” 16 Then he told them a parable. “There was a
rich man whose land produced a bountiful harvest. 17 He asked
himself, ‘What shall I do, for I do not have space to store my
harvest?’ 18 And he said, ‘This is what I shall do: I shall tear
down my barns and build larger ones. There I shall store all
my grain and other goods 19 and I shall say to myself, “Now as
for you, you have so many good things stored up for many
years, rest, eat, drink, be merry!”‘ 20 But God said to him, ‘You
fool, this night your life will be demanded of you; and the
things you have prepared, to whom will they belong?’ 21 Thus
will it be for the one who stores up treasure for himself but is
not rich in what matters to God.”

Tuesday October 24, 2023

Tuesday of Twenty-ninth Week in Ordinary Time

First Reading – Romans 5:12, 15B, 17-19, 20B-21

Brothers and sisters:12Through one man sin entered the world,
and through sin, death, and thus death came to all men,
inasmuch as all sinned. 15BIf by that one person's
transgression the many died, how much more did the grace of
God and the gracious gift of the one man Jesus Christ
overflow for the many. 17For if, by the transgression of the one,
death came to reign through that one, how much more will
those who receive the abundance of grace and the gift of
justification come to reign in life through the one Jesus Christ.
18In conclusion, just as through one transgression
condemnation came upon all, so, through one righteous act
acquittal and life came to all. 19For just as through the
disobedience of one man the many were made sinners, so,
through the obedience of the one the many will be made
righteous.20BWhere sin increased, grace overflowed all the
more, 21so that, as sin reigned in death, grace also might reign
through justification for eternal life through Jesus Christ our
Lord.

Responsorial Psalm – Psalms 40:7-8A, 8B-9, 10, 17

R. (8a and 9a) **Here I am, Lord; I come to do your will.**

7 Sacrifice or oblation you wished not,

but ears open to obedience you gave me.

8A Burnt offerings or sin offerings you sought not;

then said I, "Behold I come."

R. Here I am, Lord; I come to do your will.

8B "In the written scroll it is prescribed for me,

9 To do your will, O my God, is my delight,

and your law is within my heart!"

R. Here I am, Lord; I come to do your will.

10 I announced your justice in the vast assembly;

I did not restrain my lips, as you, O LORD, know.

R. Here I am, Lord; I come to do your will.

17 May all who seek you

exult and be glad in you,

And may those who love your salvation

say ever, “The LORD be glorified.”

R. Here I am, Lord; I come to do your will.

Alleluia – Luke 21:36

R. Alleluia, alleluia.

36 Be vigilant at all times and pray that you may have the strength to stand before the Son of Man.

R. Alleluia, alleluia.

Gospel – Luke 12:35-38

Jesus said to his disciples: 35“Gird your loins and light your lamps 36and be like servants who await their master’s return from a wedding, ready to open immediately when he comes and knocks. 37Blessed are those servants whom the master finds vigilant on his arrival. Amen, I say to you, he will gird himself, have them recline at table, and proceed to wait on them. 38And should he come in the second or third watch and find them prepared in this way, blessed are those servants.”

Wednesday October 25, 2023

Wednesday of Twenty-ninth Week in Ordinary Time

First Reading – Romans 6:12-18

Brothers and sisters: 12Sin must not reign over your mortal bodies so that you obey their desires. 13And do not present the parts of your bodies to sin as weapons for wickedness, but present yourselves to God as raised from the dead to life and the parts of your bodies to God as weapons for righteousness. 14For sin is not to have any power over you, since you are not under the law but under grace. 15What then? Shall we sin because we are not under the law but under grace? Of course not! 16Do you not know that if you present yourselves to someone as obedient slaves, you are slaves of the one you obey, either of sin, which leads to death, or of obedience, which leads to righteousness? 17But thanks be to God that, although you were once slaves of sin, you have become obedient from the heart to the pattern of teaching to which you were entrusted. [18]Freed from sin, you have become slaves of righteousness.

Responsorial Psalm – Psalms 124:1B-3, 4-6, 7-8

R. (8a) Our help is in the name of the Lord.

1B Had not the LORD been with us,

let Israel say, had not the LORD been with us–

2 When men rose up against us,

then would they have swallowed us alive;

3 When their fury was inflamed against us.

R. Our help is in the name of the Lord.

4 Then would the waters have overwhelmed us;

5 The torrent would have swept over us;

over us then would have swept the raging waters.

6 Blessed be the LORD, who did not leave us

a prey to their teeth.

R. Our help is in the name of the Lord.

7 We were rescued like a bird

from the fowlers' snare;

Broken was the snare,

and we were freed.

8 Our help is in the name of the LORD,

who made heaven and earth.

R. Our help is in the name of the Lord.

Alleluia – Matthew 24:42A, 44

R. Alleluia, alleluia.

42A Stay awake! 44 For you do not know when the Son of Man will come.

R. Alleluia, alleluia.

Gospel – Luke 12:39-48

Jesus said to his disciples: [39]"Be sure of this: if the master of the house had known the hour when the thief was coming, he would not have let his house be broken into. [40]You also must be prepared, for at an hour you do not expect, the Son of Man will come." [41]Then Peter said, "Lord, is this parable meant for us or for everyone?" [42]And the Lord replied, "Who, then, is the faithful and prudent steward whom the master will put in charge of his servants to distribute the food allowance at the proper time? [43]Blessed is that servant whom his master on arrival finds doing so. [44]Truly, I say to you, he will put him in charge of all his property. [45]But if that servant says to himself, 'My master is delayed in coming,' and begins to beat the menservants and the maidservants, to eat and drink and get drunk, [46]then that servant's master will come on an unexpected day and at an unknown hour and will punish the servant severely and assign him a place with the unfaithful. [47]That servant who knew his master's will but did not make preparations nor act in accord with his will shall be beaten severely; [48]and the servant who was ignorant of his master's will but acted in a way deserving of a severe beating shall be beaten only lightly. Much will be required of the person entrusted with much, and still more will be demanded of the person entrusted with more."

Thursday October 26, 2023

Thursday of Twenty-ninth Week in Ordinary Time

First Reading – Romans 6:19-23

Brothers and sisters: [19]I am speaking in human terms because of the weakness of your nature. For just as you presented the parts of your bodies as slaves to impurity and to lawlessness for lawlessness, so now present them as slaves to righteousness for sanctification. [20]For when you were slaves of sin, you were free from righteousness. [21]But what profit did you get then from the things of which you are now ashamed? For the end of those things is death. [22]But now that you have been freed from sin and have become slaves of God, the benefit that you have leads to sanctification, and its end is eternal life. [23]For the wages of sin is death, but the gift of God is eternal life in Christ Jesus our Lord.

Responsorial Psalm – Psalms 1:1-2, 3, 4 AND 6

R. (Ps 40:5) Blessed are they who hope in the Lord.

1 Blessed the man who follows not
the counsel of the wicked
Nor walks in the way of sinners,
nor sits in the company of the insolent,
2 But delights in the law of the LORD
and meditates on his law day and night.

R. Blessed are they who hope in the Lord.

3 He is like a tree
planted near running water,
That yields its fruit in due season,
and whose leaves never fade.
Whatever he does, prospers.

R. Blessed are they who hope in the Lord.

4 Not so the wicked, not so;
they are like chaff which the wind drives away.
6 For the LORD watches over the way of the just,
but the way of the wicked vanishes.

R. Blessed are they who hope in the Lord.

Alleluia – Philippians 3:8-9

R. Alleluia, alleluia.

8 I consider all things so much rubbish 9 that I may gain Christ and be found in him.

R. Alleluia, alleluia.

Gospel – Luke 12:49-53

Jesus said to his disciples: 49"I have come to set the earth on fire, and how I wish it were already blazing! 50There is a baptism with which I must be baptized, and how great is my anguish until it is accomplished! 51Do you think that I have

come to establish peace on the earth? No, I tell you, but rather
division. 52From now on a household of five will be divided,
three against two and two against three; 53a father will be
divided against his son and a son against his father, a mother
against her daughter and a daughter against her mother, a
mother-in-law against her daughter-in-law and a daughter-in-
law against her mother-in-law."

Friday October 27, 2023

Friday of Twenty-ninth Week Ordinary Time

First Reading – Romans 7:18-25A

Brothers and sisters:18I know that good does not dwell in me,
that is, in my flesh. The willing is ready at hand, but doing the
good is not. 19For I do not do the good I want, but I do the evil I
do not want. 20Now if I do what I do not want, it is no longer I
who do it, but sin that dwells in me. 21So, then, I discover the
principle that when I want to do right, evil is at hand. 22For I
take delight in the law of God, in my inner self,23but I see in my
members another principle at war with the law of my mind,
taking me captive to the law of sin that dwells in my
members.24Miserable one that I am! Who will deliver me from
this mortal body?25AThanks be to God through Jesus Christ
our Lord.

Responsorial Psalm – Psalms 119:66, 68, 76, 77, 93, 94

R. (68b) Lord, teach me your statutes.

66 Teach me wisdom and knowledge,

for in your commands I trust.

R. Lord, teach me your statutes.

68 You are good and bountiful;

teach me your statutes.

R. Lord, teach me your statutes.

76 Let your kindness comfort me

according to your promise to your servants.

R. Lord, teach me your statutes.

[77] Let your compassion come to me that I may live,

for your law is my delight.

R. Lord, teach me your statutes.

[93] Never will I forget your precepts,

for through them you give me life.

R. Lord, teach me your statutes.

[94] I am yours; save me,

for I have sought your precepts.

R. Lord, teach me your statutes.

Alleluia – Matthew 11:25

R. Alleluia, alleluia.

[25] Blessed are you, Father, Lord of heaven and earth; you have revealed to little ones the mysteries of the Kingdom.

R. Alleluia, alleluia.

Gospel – Luke 12:54-59

[54]Jesus said to the crowds, "When you see a cloud rising in the west you say immediately that it is going to rain–and so it
does; [55]and when you notice that the wind is blowing from the
south you say that it is going to be hot–and so it is. [56]You
hypocrites! You know how to interpret the appearance of the earth and the sky; why do you not know how to interpret the
present time? [57]"Why do you not judge for yourselves what is
right? [58]If you are to go with your opponent before a magistrate, make an effort to settle the matter on the way; otherwise your opponent will turn you over to the judge, and the judge hand you over to the constable, and the constable
throw you into prison.[59]I say to you, you will not be released until you have paid the last penny."

Saturday October 28, 2023

Feast of Saints Simon and Jude, Apostles

First Reading – Ephesians 2:19-22

Brothers and sisters: [19]You are no longer strangers and sojourners, but you are fellow citizens with the holy ones and members of the household of God,[20]built upon the foundation of the Apostles and prophets, with Christ Jesus himself as the capstone.[21]Through him the whole structure is held together and grows into a temple sacred in the Lord;[22]in him you also are being built together into a dwelling place of God in the Spirit.

Responsorial Psalm – Psalms 19:2-3, 4-5

R. (5a) Their message goes out through all the earth.

2 The heavens declare the glory of God,

and the firmament proclaims his handiwork.

3 Day pours out the word to day,

and night to night imparts knowledge.

R. Their message goes out through all the earth.

4 Not a word nor a discourse

whose voice is not heard;

5 Through all the earth their voice resounds,

and to the ends of the world, their message.

R. Their message goes out through all the earth.

Alleluia – cf. Te Deum

R. Alleluia, alleluia.

We praise you, O God, we acclaim you as Lord; the glorious company of Apostles praise you.

R. Alleluia, alleluia.

Gospel – Luke 6:12-16

12 Jesus went up to the mountain to pray, and he spent the
night in prayer to God. 13 When day came, he called his
disciples to himself, and from them he chose Twelve, whom
he also named Apostles: 14 Simon, whom he named Peter, and
his brother Andrew, James, John, Philip, Bartholomew,
15 Matthew, Thomas, James the son of Alphaeus, Simon who
was called a Zealot, 16 and Judas the son of James, and Judas
Iscariot, who became a traitor.

Sunday October 29, 2023

Thirtieth Sunday in Ordinary Time, Year A

First Reading – Exodus 22:20-26

Thus says the LORD: [20]“You shall not molest or oppress an
alien, for you were once aliens yourselves in the land of Egypt.
[21]You shall not wrong any widow or orphan. [22]If ever you
wrong them and they cry out to me, I will surely hear their
cry.[23]My wrath will flare up, and I will kill you with the sword;
then your own wives will be widows, and your children
orphans. [24]“If you lend money to one of your poor neighbors
among my people, you shall not act like an extortioner toward
him by demanding interest from him. [25]If you take your
neighbor’s cloak as a pledge, you shall return it to him before
sunset;[26]for this cloak of his is the only covering he has for his
body. What else has he to sleep in? If he cries out to me, I will
hear him; for I am compassionate.”

Responsorial Psalm – Psalms 18:2-3, 3-4, 47, 51

R. [(2)] I love you, Lord, my strength.

[2] I love you, O LORD, my strength,

[3AB] O LORD, my rock, my fortress, my deliverer.

R. I love you, Lord, my strength.

[3CD] My God, my rock of refuge,

my shield, the horn of my salvation, my stronghold!

[4] Praised be the LORD, I exclaim,

and I am safe from my enemies.

R. I love you, Lord, my strength.

[47] The LORD lives and blessed be my rock!

Extolled be God my savior.

[51] You who gave great victories to your king

and showed kindness to your anointed.

R. I love you, Lord, my strength.

Second Reading – 1 Thessalonians 1:5C-10

Brothers and sisters: [5C]You know what sort of people we were among you for your sake. [6]And you became imitators of us and of the Lord, receiving the word in great affliction, with joy from the Holy Spirit, [7]so that you became a model for all the believers in Macedonia and in Achaia. [8]For from you the word of the Lord has sounded forth not only in Macedonia and in Achaia, but in every place your faith in God has gone forth, so that we have no need to say anything. [9]For they themselves openly declare about us what sort of reception we had among you, and how you turned to God from idols to serve the living and true God [10]and to await his Son from heaven, whom he raised from the dead, Jesus, who delivers us from the coming wrath.

Alleluia – John 14:23

R. Alleluia, alleluia.

[23] Whoever loves me will keep my word, says the Lord, and my Father will love him and we will come to him.

R. Alleluia, alleluia.

Gospel – Matthew 22:34-40

[34]When the Pharisees heard that Jesus had silenced the Sadducees, they gathered together, [35]and one of them, a scholar of the law tested him by asking, [36]"Teacher, which commandment in the law is the greatest?" [37]He said to him, "You shall love the Lord, your God, with all your heart, with all your soul, and with all your mind. [38]This is the greatest and the first commandment. [39]The second is like it: You shall love your neighbor as yourself. [40]The whole law and the prophets depend on these two commandments."

Monday October 30, 2023

Monday of Thirtieth Week in Ordinary Time

First Reading – Romans 8:12-17

[12]Brothers and sisters, we are not debtors to the flesh, to live according to the flesh. [13]For if you live according to the flesh, you will die, but if by the spirit you put to death the deeds of the body, you will live. [14]For those who are led by the Spirit of

God are sons of God. [15]For you did not receive a spirit of slavery to fall back into fear, but you received a spirit of adoption, through which we cry, “Abba, Father!” [16]The Spirit himself bears witness with our spirit that we are children of God, [17]and if children, then heirs, heirs of God and joint heirs with Christ, if only we suffer with him so that we may also be glorified with him.

Responsorial Psalm – Psalms 68:2 AND 4, 6-7AB, 20-21

R. [(21a)] **Our God is the God of salvation.**

[2] God arises; his enemies are scattered,

and those who hate him flee before him.

[4] But the just rejoice and exult before God;

they are glad and rejoice.

R. Our God is the God of salvation.

[6] The father of orphans and the defender of widows

is God in his holy dwelling.

[7AB] God gives a home to the forsaken;

he leads forth prisoners to prosperity.

R. Our God is the God of salvation.

[20] Blessed day by day be the Lord,

who bears our burdens; God, who is our salvation.

[21] God is a saving God for us;

the LORD, my Lord, controls the passageways of death.

R. Our God is the God of salvation.

Alleluia – John 17:17B, 17A

R. Alleluia, alleluia.

[17B] Your word, O Lord, is truth; [17A] consecrate us in the truth.

R. Alleluia, alleluia.

Gospel – Luke 13:10-17

[10]Jesus was teaching in a synagogue on the Sabbath. [11]And a woman was there who for eighteen years had been crippled by a spirit; she was bent over, completely incapable of standing erect.[12]When Jesus saw her, he called to her and said, “Woman, you are set free of your infirmity.” [13]He laid his hands on her, and she at once stood up straight and glorified God. [14]But the leader of the synagogue, indignant that Jesus had cured on the Sabbath, said to the crowd in reply, “There are six days when work should be done. Come on those days to be cured, not on the Sabbath day.” [15]The Lord said to him in reply, “Hypocrites! Does not each one of you on the Sabbath untie his ox or his ass from the manger and lead it out for watering? [16]This daughter of Abraham, whom Satan has bound for eighteen years now, ought she not to have been set free on the Sabbath day from this bondage?” [17]When he said this, all his adversaries were humiliated; and the whole crowd rejoiced at all the splendid deeds done by him.

Tuesday October 31, 2023

Tuesday of Thirtieth Week in Ordinary Time

First Reading – Romans 8:18-25

Brothers and sisters:[18]I consider that the sufferings of this present time are as nothing compared with the glory to be revealed for us.[19]For creation awaits with eager expectation the revelation of the children of God; [20]for creation was made subject to futility, not of its own accord but because of the one who subjected it, in hope [21]that creation itself would be set free from slavery to corruption and share in the glorious freedom of the children of God.[22]We know that all creation is groaning in labor pains even until now; [23]and not only that, but we ourselves, who have the first fruits of the Spirit, we also groan within ourselves as we wait for adoption, the redemption of our bodies.[24]For in hope we were saved. Now hope that sees for itself is not hope. For who hopes for what one sees? [25]But if we hope for what we do not see, we wait with endurance.

Responsorial Psalm – Psalms 126:1B-2AB, 2CD-3, 4-5, 6

R. (3a) The Lord has done marvels for us.

[1B] When the LORD brought back the captives of Zion,

we were like men dreaming.

[2AB] Then our mouth was filled with laughter,

and our tongue with rejoicing.

R. The Lord has done marvels for us.

[2CD] Then they said among the nations,

"The LORD has done great things for them."

[3] The LORD has done great things for us;

we are glad indeed.

R. The Lord has done marvels for us.

[4] Restore our fortunes, O LORD,

like the torrents in the southern desert.

[5] Those that sow in tears

shall reap rejoicing.

R. The Lord has done marvels for us.

[6] Although they go forth weeping,

carrying the seed to be sown,

They shall come back rejoicing,

carrying their sheaves.

R. The Lord has done marvels for us.

Alleluia – Matthew 11:25

R. Alleluia, alleluia.

[25] Blessed are you, Father, Lord of heaven and earth; you have revealed to little ones the mysteries of the Kingdom.

R. Alleluia, alleluia.

Gospel – Luke 13:18-21

[18]Jesus said, "What is the Kingdom of God like? To what can I
compare it? [19]It is like a mustard seed that a man took and
planted in the garden. When it was fully grown, it became a
large bush and 'the birds of the sky dwelt in its branches.'"

20Again he said, “To what shall I compare the Kingdom of
God? 21It is like yeast that a woman took and mixed in with
three measures of wheat flour until the whole batch of dough
was leavened.”

NOVEMBER 2023

Wednesday November 1, 2023

Solemnity of All Saints (All Saints Day)

First Reading – Revelation 7:2-4, 9-14

2I, John, saw another angel come up from the East, holding
the seal of the living God. He cried out in a loud voice to the
four angels who were given power to damage the land and the
sea,3“Do not damage the land or the sea or the trees until we
put the seal on the foreheads of the servants of our God.” 4I
heard the number of those who had been marked with the
seal, one hundred and forty-four thousand marked from every
tribe of the children of Israel.9After this I had a vision of a great
multitude, which no one could count, from every nation, race,
people, and tongue. They stood before the throne and before
the Lamb, wearing white robes and holding palm branches in
their hands.10They cried out in a loud voice: “Salvation comes
from our God, who is seated on the throne, and from the
Lamb.” 11All the angels stood around the throne and around
the elders and the four living creatures. They prostrated
themselves before the throne, worshiped God,12and
exclaimed: “Amen. Blessing and glory, wisdom and
thanksgiving, honor, power, and might be to our God forever
and ever. Amen.” 13Then one of the elders spoke up and said
to me, “Who are these wearing white robes, and where did
they come from?” 14I said to him, “My lord, you are the one
who knows.” He said to me, “These are the ones who have
survived the time of great distress; they have washed their
robes and made them white in the Blood of the Lamb.”

Responsorial Psalm – Psalms 24:1BC-2, 3-4AB, 5-6

R. (see 6) Lord, this is the people that longs to see your face.

1BC The LORD’s are the earth and its fullness;

the world and those who dwell in it.

2 For he founded it upon the seas

and established it upon the rivers.

R. Lord, this is the people that longs to see your face.

3 Who can ascend the mountain of the LORD?

or who may stand in his holy place?

4AB One whose hands are sinless, whose heart is clean,

who desires not what is vain.

R. Lord, this is the people that longs to see your face.

5 He shall receive a blessing from the LORD,

a reward from God his savior.

6 Such is the race that seeks him,

that seeks the face of the God of Jacob.

R. Lord, this is the people that longs to see your face.

Second Reading – 1 John 3:1-3

Beloved:1See what love the Father has bestowed on us that
we may be called the children of God. Yet so we are. The
reason the world does not know us is that it did not know
him.2Beloved, we are God's children now; what we shall be
has not yet been revealed. We do know that when it is
revealed we shall be like him, for we shall see him as he is.
3Everyone who has this hope based on him makes himself
pure, as he is pure.

Alleluia – Matthew 11:28

R. Alleluia, alleluia.

28Come to me, all you who labor and are burdened, And I will give you rest, says the Lord.

R. Alleluia, alleluia.

Gospel – Matthew 5:1-12A

1When Jesus saw the crowds, he went up the mountain, and
after he had sat down, his disciples came to him. 2He began to
teach them, saying: 3"Blessed are the poor in spirit, for theirs
is the Kingdom of heaven. 4Blessed are they who mourn, for
they will be comforted. 5Blessed are the meek, for they will
inherit the land. 6Blessed are they who hunger and thirst for

righteousness, for they will be satisfied. [7]Blessed are the merciful, for they will be shown mercy. [8]Blessed are the clean of heart, for they will see God. [9]Blessed are the peacemakers, for they will be called children of God. [10]Blessed are they who are persecuted for the sake of righteousness, for theirs is the Kingdom of heaven. [11]Blessed are you when they insult you and persecute you and utter every kind of evil against you falsely because of me. [12A]Rejoice and be glad, for your reward will be great in heaven."

Thursday November 2, 2023

Commemoration of All the Faithful Departed - All Souls Day

First Reading – Wisdom 3:1-9

[1]The souls of the just are in the hand of God, and no torment shall touch them.[2]They seemed, in the view of the foolish, to be dead; and their passing away was thought an affliction [3]and their going forth from us, utter destruction. But they are in peace.[4]For if before men, indeed, they be punished, yet is their hope full of immortality; [5]chastised a little, they shall be greatly blessed, because God tried them and found them worthy of himself.[6]As gold in the furnace, he proved them, and as sacrificial offerings he took them to himself. [7]In the time of their visitation they shall shine, and shall dart about as sparks through stubble; [8]they shall judge nations and rule over peoples, and the LORD shall be their King forever. [9]Those who trust in him shall understand truth, and the faithful shall abide with him in love: because grace and mercy are with his holy ones, and his care is with his elect.

Responsorial Psalm – Psalms 23:1-3A, 3B-4, 5, 6

R. (1) The Lord is my shepherd; there is nothing I shall want. or: **R. Though I walk in the valley of darkness, I fear no evil, for you are with me.**

[1] The LORD is my shepherd; I shall not want.

[2] In verdant pastures he gives me repose;

beside restful waters he leads me;

[3A] he refreshes my soul.

R. The Lord is my shepherd; there is nothing I shall want. or: **R. Though I walk in the valley of darkness, I fear no evil, for you are with me.**

3B He guides me in right paths

for his name's sake.

4 Even though I walk in the dark valley

I fear no evil; for you are at my side

with your rod and your staff

that give me courage.

R. The Lord is my shepherd; there is nothing I shall want. or: **R. Though I walk in the valley of darkness, I fear no evil, for you are with me.**

5 You spread the table before me

in the sight of my foes;

You anoint my head with oil;

my cup overflows.

R. The Lord is my shepherd; there is nothing I shall want. or: **R. Though I walk in the valley of darkness, I fear no evil, for you are with me.**

6 Only goodness and kindness follow me

all the days of my life;

and I shall dwell in the house of the LORD

for years to come.

R. The Lord is my shepherd; there is nothing I shall want. or: **R. Though I walk in the valley of darkness, I fear no evil, for you are with me.**

Second Reading – Romans 5:5-11

Brothers and sisters: 5Hope does not disappoint, because the
love of God has been poured out into our hearts through the
Holy Spirit that has been given to us. 6For Christ, while we
were still helpless, died at the appointed time for the ungodly.
7Indeed, only with difficulty does one die for a just person,
though perhaps for a good person one might even find

courage to die. [8]But God proves his love for us in that while
we were still sinners Christ died for us. [9]How much more then,
since we are now justified by his Blood, will we be saved
through him from the wrath.[10]Indeed, if, while we were
enemies, we were reconciled to God through the death of his
Son, how much more, once reconciled, will we be saved by his
life. [11]Not only that, but we also boast of God through our Lord
Jesus Christ, through whom we have now received
reconciliation.

Or Romans 6:3-9

Brothers and sisters:[3]Are you unaware that we who were
baptized into Christ Jesus were baptized into his death? [4]We
were indeed buried with him through baptism into death, so
that, just as Christ was raised from the dead by the glory of the
Father, we too might live in newness of life.[5]For if we have
grown into union with him through a death like his, we shall
also be united with him in the resurrection.[6]We know that our
old self was crucified with him, so that our sinful body might be
done away with, that we might no longer be in slavery to
sin.[7]For a dead person has been absolved from sin.[8]If, then,
we have died with Christ, we believe that we shall also live
with him.[9]We know that Christ, raised from the dead, dies no
more; death no longer has power over him.

Alleluia – Matthew 25:34

R. Alleluia, alleluia.

[34]Come, you who are blessed by my Father; inherit the
kingdom prepared for you from the foundation of the world.

R. Alleluia, alleluia.

Gospel – John 6:37-40

Jesus said to the crowds:[37]“Everything that the Father gives
me will come to me, and I will not reject anyone who comes to
me,[38]because I came down from heaven not to do my own will
but the will of the one who sent me.[39]And this is the will of the
one who sent me, that I should not lose anything of what he
gave me, but that I should raise it on the last day.[40]For this is
the will of my Father, that everyone who sees the Son and
believes in him may have eternal life, and I shall raise him on
the last day.”

Friday November 3, 2023

Friday of the Thirtieth Week in Ordinary Time

First Reading – Romans 9:1-5

Brothers and sisters:1I speak the truth in Christ, I do not lie; my
conscience joins with the Holy Spirit in bearing me witness
2that I have great sorrow and constant anguish in my heart.
3For I could wish that I myself were accursed and cut off from
Christ for the sake of my own people, my kindred according to
the flesh. 4They are children of Israel; theirs the adoption, the
glory, the covenants, the giving of the law, the worship, and
the promises; 5theirs the patriarchs, and from them, according
to the flesh, is the Christ, who is over all, God blessed forever.
Amen.

Responsorial Psalm – Psalms 147:12-13, 14-15, 19-20

R. Praise the Lord, Jerusalem.

12 Glorify the LORD, O Jerusalem;

praise your God, O Zion.

13 For he has strengthened the bars of your gates;

he has blessed your children within you.

R. Praise the Lord, Jerusalem.

14 He has granted peace in your borders;

with the best of wheat he fills you.

15 He sends forth his command to the earth;

swiftly runs his word!

R. Praise the Lord, Jerusalem.

19 He has proclaimed his word to Jacob,

his statutes and his ordinances to Israel.

20 He has not done thus for any other nation;

his ordinances he has not made known to them. Alleluia.

R. Praise the Lord, Jerusalem.

Alleluia – John 10:27

R. Alleluia, alleluia.

27 My sheep hear my voice, says the Lord; I know them, and they follow me.

R. Alleluia, alleluia.

Gospel – Luke 14:1-6

1 On a Sabbath Jesus went to dine at the home of one of the leading Pharisees, and the people there were observing him carefully. 2 In front of him there was a man suffering from dropsy. 3 Jesus spoke to the scholars of the law and Pharisees in reply, asking, "Is it lawful to cure on the Sabbath or not?" 4 But they kept silent; so he took the man and, after he had healed him, dismissed him. 5 Then he said to them "Who among you, if your son or ox falls into a cistern, would not immediately pull him out on the sabbath day?" 6 But they were unable to answer his question.

Saturday November 4, 2023

Memorial of Saint Charles Borromeo - Bishop

First Reading – Romans 11:1-2A, 11-12, 25-29

Brothers and sisters: 1 I ask, then, has God rejected his people? Of course not! For I too am a child of Israel, a descendant of Abraham, of the tribe of Benjamin. 2A God has not rejected his people whom he foreknew. Do you not know what the Scripture says about Elijah, how he pleads with God against Israel? 11 Hence I ask, did they stumble so as to fall? Of course not! But through their transgression salvation has come to the Gentiles, so as to make them jealous. 12 Now if their transgression is enrichment for the world, and if their diminished number is enrichment for the Gentiles, how much more their full number. 25 I do not want you to be unaware of this mystery, brothers and sisters, so that you will not become wise in your own estimation: a hardening has come upon Israel in part, until the full number of the Gentiles comes in, 26 and thus all Israel will be saved, as it is written: The deliverer will come out of Zion, he will turn away godlessness from Jacob; 27 and this is my covenant with them when I take away their sins. 28 In respect to the Gospel, they are enemies on your account; but in respect to election, they are beloved because of the patriarch.[29]For the gifts and the call of God are irrevocable.

Responsorial Psalm – Psalms 94:12-13A, 14-15, 17-18

R. (14a) The Lord will not abandon his people.

12 Blessed the man whom you instruct, O LORD,

whom by your law you teach,

13A Giving him rest from evil days.

R. The Lord will not abandon his people.

14 For the LORD will not cast off his people,

nor abandon his inheritance;

15 But judgment shall again be with justice,

and all the upright of heart shall follow it.

R. The Lord will not abandon his people.

17 Were not the LORD my help,

my soul would soon dwell in the silent grave.

18 When I say, "My foot is slipping,"

your mercy, O LORD, sustains me.

R. The Lord will not abandon his people.

Alleluia – Matthew 11:29AB

R. Alleluia, alleluia.

29AB Take my yoke upon you and learn from me, For I am meek and humble of heart.

R. Alleluia, alleluia.

Gospel – Luke 14:1, 7-11

1On a Sabbath Jesus went to dine at the home of one of the leading Pharisees, and the people there were observing him
carefully.7He told a parable to those who had been invited, noticing how they were choosing the places of honor at the
table.8"When you are invited by someone to a wedding banquet, do not recline at table in the place of honor. A more

distinguished guest than you may have been invited by him,[9]and the host who invited both of you may approach you and say, 'Give your place to this man,' and then you would proceed with embarrassment to take the lowest place.[10]Rather, when you are invited, go and take the lowest place so that when the host comes to you he may say, 'My friend, move up to a higher position.' Then you will enjoy the esteem of your companions at the table. [11]For everyone who exalts himself will be humbled, but the one who humbles himself will be exalted."

Sunday November 5, 2023

Thirty-first Sunday in Ordinary Time, Year A

First Reading – Malachi 1:14B-2:2B, 8-10

[14B]A great King am I, says the LORD of hosts, and my name will be feared among the nations.[1]And now, O priests, this commandment is for you: If you do not listen,[2AB]if you do not lay it to heart, to give glory to my name, says the LORD of hosts, I will send a curse upon you and of your blessing I will make a curse.[8]You have turned aside from the way, and have caused many to falter by your instruction; you have made void the covenant of Levi, says the LORD of hosts.[9]I, therefore, have made you contemptible and base before all the people, since you do not keep my ways, but show partiality in your decisions.[10]Have we not all the one father? Has not the one God created us? Why then do we break faith with one another, violating the covenant of our fathers?

Responsorial Psalm – Psalms 131:1, 2, 3

R. In you, Lord, I have found my peace.

[1] O LORD, my heart is not proud,

nor are my eyes haughty;

I busy not myself with great things,

nor with things too sublime for me.

R. In you, Lord, I have found my peace.

[2] Nay rather, I have stilled and quieted

my soul like a weaned child.

Like a weaned child on its mother's lap,

so is my soul within me.

R. In you, Lord, I have found my peace.

3 O Israel, hope in the LORD,

both now and forever.

R. In you, Lord, I have found my peace.

Second Reading – 1 Thessalonians 2:7B-9, 13

Brothers and sisters: 7B We were gentle among you, as a nursing mother cares for her children. 8 With such affection for you, we were determined to share with you not only the gospel of God, but our very selves as well, so dearly beloved had you become to us. 9 You recall, brothers and sisters, our toil and drudgery. Working night and day in order not to burden any of you, we proclaimed to you the gospel of God. 13 And for this reason we too give thanks to God unceasingly, that, in receiving the word of God from hearing us, you received not a human word but, as it truly is, the word of God, which is now at work in you who believe.

Alleluia – Matthew 23:9B, 10B

R. Alleluia, alleluia.

9B You have but one Father in heaven 10B and one master, the Christ.

R. Alleluia, alleluia.

Gospel – Matthew 23:1-12

1 Jesus spoke to the crowds and to his disciples, 2 saying, "The scribes and the Pharisees have taken their seat on the chair of Moses. 3 Therefore, do and observe all things whatsoever they tell you, but do not follow their example. For they preach but they do not practice. 4 They tie up heavy burdens hard to carry and lay them on people's shoulders, but they will not lift a finger to move them. 5 All their works are performed to be seen. They widen their phylacteries and lengthen their tassels. 6 They love places of honor at banquets, seats of honor in synagogues, 7 greetings in marketplaces, and the salutation 'Rabbi.' 8 As for you, do not be called 'Rabbi.' You have but one teacher, and you are all brothers. 9 Call no one on earth

your father; you have but one Father in heaven.[10]Do not be called ‘Master’; you have but one master, the Christ.[11]The greatest among you must be your servant.[12]Whoever exalts himself will be humbled; but whoever humbles himself will be exalted.”

Monday November 6, 2023

Monday of Thirty-first Week in Ordinary Time

First Reading – Romans 11:29-36

Brothers and sisters: [29]The gifts and the call of God are
irrevocable. [30]Just as you once disobeyed God but have now
received mercy because of their disobedience, [31]so they have
now disobeyed in order that, by virtue of the mercy shown to
you, they too may now receive mercy. [32]For God delivered all
to disobedience, that he might have mercy upon all. [33]Oh, the
depth of the riches and wisdom and knowledge of God! How
inscrutable are his judgments and how unsearchable his ways!
[34]For who has known the mind of the Lord or who has been
his counselor? [35]Or who has given him anything that he may
be repaid? [36]For from him and through him and for him are all
things. To God be glory forever. Amen.

Responsorial Psalm – Psalms 69:30-31, 33-34, 36

R. (14c) Lord, in your great love, answer me.

30 But I am afflicted and in pain;

let your saving help, O God, protect me.

31 I will praise the name of God in song,

and I will glorify him with thanksgiving.

R. Lord, in your great love, answer me.

33 “See, you lowly ones, and be glad;

you who seek God, may your hearts revive!

34 For the LORD hears the poor,

and his own who are in bonds he spurns not.”

R. Lord, in your great love, answer me.

36 For God will save Zion

and rebuild the cities of Judah.

They shall dwell in the land and own it,

and the descendants of his servants shall inherit it,

and those who love his name shall inhabit it.

R. Lord, in your great love, answer me.

Alleluia – John 8:31B-32

R. Alleluia, alleluia.

[31B]If you remain in my word, you will truly be my disciples, [32]
and you will know the truth, says the Lord.

R. Alleluia, alleluia.

Gospel – Luke 14:12-14

On a Sabbath Jesus went to dine at the home of one of the
leading Pharisees.[12]He said to the host who invited him,
"When you hold a lunch or a dinner, do not invite your friends
or your brothers or sisters or your relatives or your wealthy
neighbors, in case they may invite you back and you have
repayment. [13]Rather, when you hold a banquet, invite the
poor, the crippled, the lame, the blind; [14]blessed indeed will
you be because of their inability to repay you. For you will be
repaid at the resurrection of the righteous."

Tuesday November 7, 2023

Tuesday of Thirty-first Week Ordinary Time

First Reading – Romans 12:5-16AB

Brothers and sisters: [5]We, though many, are one Body in
Christ and individually parts of one another.[6]Since we have
gifts that differ according to the grace given to us, let us
exercise them: if prophecy, in proportion to the faith; [7]if
ministry, in ministering; if one is a teacher, in teaching; [8]if one
exhorts, in exhortation; if one contributes, in generosity; if one
is over others, with diligence; if one does acts of mercy, with
cheerfulness. [9]Let love be sincere; hate what is evil, hold on to
what is good; [10]love one another with mutual affection;
anticipate one another in showing honor. [11]Do not grow slack
in zeal, be fervent in spirit, serve the Lord. [12]Rejoice in hope,
endure in affliction, persevere in prayer. [13]Contribute to the

needs of the holy ones, exercise hospitality. [14]Bless those who
persecute you, bless and do not curse them. [15]Rejoice with
those who rejoice, weep with those who weep.[16AB]Have the
same regard for one another; do not be haughty but associate
with the lowly.

Responsorial Psalm – Psalms 131:1BCDE, 2, 3

R. In you, O Lord, I have found my peace.

[1] O LORD, my heart is not proud,

nor are my eyes haughty;

I busy not myself with great things,

nor with things too sublime for me.

R. In you, O Lord, I have found my peace.

[2] Nay rather, I have stilled and quieted

my soul like a weaned child.

Like a weaned child on its mother's lap,

so is my soul within me.

R. In you, O Lord, I have found my peace.

[3] O Israel, hope in the LORD,

both now and forever.

R. In you, O Lord, I have found my peace.

Alleluia – Matthew 11:28

R. Alleluia, alleluia.

[28] Come to me, all you who labor and are burdened, and I will give you rest, says the Lord.

R. Alleluia, alleluia.

Gospel – Luke 14:15-24

[15]One of those at table with Jesus said to him, "Blessed is the
one who will dine in the Kingdom of God." He replied to him,
[16]"A man gave a great dinner to which he invited many.
[17]When the time for the dinner came, he dispatched his
servant to say to those invited, 'Come, everything is now
ready.' [18]But one by one, they all began to excuse themselves.

The first said to him, 'I have purchased a field and must go to examine it; I ask you, consider me excused.' [19]And another said, 'I have purchased five yoke of oxen and am on my way to evaluate them; I ask you, consider me excused.' [20]And another said, 'I have just married a woman, and therefore I cannot come.' [21]The servant went and reported this to his master. Then the master of the house in a rage commanded his servant, 'Go out quickly into the streets and alleys of the town and bring in here the poor and the crippled, the blind and the lame.' [22]The servant reported, 'Sir, your orders have been carried out and still there is room.' [23]The master then ordered the servant, 'Go out to the highways and hedgerows and make people come in that my home may be filled. [24]For, I tell you, none of those men who were invited will taste my dinner.'"

Wednesday November 8, 2023

Wednesday of Thirty-first Week in Ordinary Time

First Reading – Romans 13:8-10

Brothers and sisters: [8]Owe nothing to anyone, except to love one another; for the one who loves another has fulfilled the law.[9]The commandments, You shall not commit adultery; you shall not kill; you shall not steal; you shall not covet, and whatever other commandment there may be, are summed up in this saying, namely, You shall love your neighbor as yourself. [10]Love does no evil to the neighbor; hence, love is the fulfillment of the law.

Responsorial Psalm – Psalms 112:1B-2, 4-5, 9

R. (5a) **Blessed the man who is gracious and lends to those in need.** or: **R. Alleluia.**

[1B] Blessed the man who fears the LORD,

who greatly delights in his commands.

[2] His posterity shall be mighty upon the earth;

the upright generation shall be blessed.

R. Blessed the man who is gracious and lends to those in need. or: **R. Alleluia.**

[4] He dawns through the darkness, a light for the upright;

he is gracious and merciful and just.

[5] Well for the man who is gracious and lends,

who conducts his affairs with justice.

R. Blessed the man who is gracious and lends to those in need. or: **R. Alleluia.**

[9] Lavishly he gives to the poor;

his generosity shall endure forever;

his horn shall be exalted in glory.

R. Blessed the man who is gracious and lends to those in need. or: **R. Alleluia.**

Alleluia – 1 Peter 4:14

R. Alleluia, alleluia.

[14] If you are insulted for the name of Christ, blessed are you, for the Spirit of God rests upon you.

R. Alleluia, alleluia.

Gospel – Luke 14:25-33

[25]Great crowds were traveling with Jesus, and he turned and
addressed them, [26]"If anyone comes to me without hating his
father and mother, wife and children, brothers and sisters, and
even his own life, he cannot be my disciple. [27]Whoever does
not carry his own cross and come after me cannot be my
disciple.[28]Which of you wishing to construct a tower does not
first sit down and calculate the cost to see if there is enough
for its completion? [29]Otherwise, after laying the foundation and
finding himself unable to finish the work the onlookers should
laugh at him [30]and say, 'This one began to build but did not
have the resources to finish.' [31]Or what king marching into
battle would not first sit down and decide whether with ten
thousand troops he can successfully oppose another king
advancing upon him with twenty thousand troops? [32]But if not,
while he is still far away, he will send a delegation to ask for
peace terms. [33]In the same way, everyone of you who does
not renounce all his possessions cannot be my disciple."

Thursday November 9, 2023

Feast of Dedication of Lateran Basilica Rome

First Reading – Ezekiel 47:1-2, 8-9, 12

1The angel brought me back to the entrance of the temple, and I saw water flowing out from beneath the threshold of the temple toward the east, for the façade of the temple was toward the east; the water flowed down from the southern side of the temple, south of the altar.
2He led me outside by the north gate, and around to the outer gate facing the east, where I saw water trickling from the southern side.
8He said to me, "This water flows into the eastern district down upon the Arabah, and empties into the sea, the salt waters, which it makes fresh.
9Wherever the river flows, every sort of living creature that can multiply shall live, and there shall be abundant fish, for wherever this water comes the sea shall be made fresh.
12Along both banks of the river, fruit trees of every kind shall grow; their leaves shall not fade, nor their fruit fail. Every month they shall bear fresh fruit, for they shall be watered by the flow from the sanctuary. Their fruit shall serve for food, and their leaves for medicine."

Responsorial Psalm – Psalms 46:2-3, 5-6, 8-9

R. (5) The waters of the river gladden the city of God, the holy dwelling of the Most High!

2 God is our refuge and our strength,

an ever-present help in distress.

3 Therefore, we fear not, though the earth be shaken

and mountains plunge into the depths of the sea.

R. The waters of the river gladden the city of God, the holy dwelling of the Most High!

5 There is a stream whose runlets gladden the city of God,

the holy dwelling of the Most High.

6 God is in its midst; it shall not be disturbed;

God will help it at the break of dawn.

R. The waters of the river gladden the city of God, the holy dwelling of the Most High!

8 The LORD of hosts is with us;

our stronghold is the God of Jacob.

9 Come! behold the deeds of the LORD,

the astounding things he has wrought on earth.

R. The waters of the river gladden the city of God, the holy dwelling of the Most High!

Second Reading – 1 Corinthians 3:9C-11, 16-17

Brothers and sisters: 9CYou are God's building. 10According to the grace of God given to me, like a wise master builder I laid a foundation, and another is building upon it. But each one must be careful how he builds upon it, 11for no one can lay a foundation other than the one that is there, namely, Jesus Christ. 16Do you not know that you are the temple of God, and that the Spirit of God dwells in you? 17If anyone destroys God's temple, God will destroy that person; for the temple of God, which you are, is holy.

Alleluia 2 Chronicles 7:16

R. Alleluia, alleluia.

16 I have chosen and consecrated this house, says the Lord, that my name may be there forever.

R. Alleluia, alleluia.

Gospel – John 2:13-22

13Since the Passover of the Jews was near, Jesus went up to Jerusalem. 14He found in the temple area those who sold oxen, sheep, and doves, as well as the money-changers seated there. 15He made a whip out of cords and drove them all out of the temple area, with the sheep and oxen, and spilled the coins of the money-changers and overturned their tables, 16and to those who sold doves he said, "Take these out of here, and stop making my Father's house a marketplace." 17His disciples recalled the words of Scripture, Zeal for your house will consume me. 18At this the Jews answered and said to him, "What sign can you show us for doing this?" 19Jesus answered and said to them, "Destroy this temple and in three

days I will raise it up.” 20The Jews said, “This temple has been
under construction for forty-six years, and you will raise it up in
three days?” 21But he was speaking about the temple of his
Body. 22Therefore, when he was raised from the dead, his
disciples remembered that he had said this, and they came to
believe the Scripture and the word Jesus had spoken.

Friday November 10, 2023

Memorial of Saint Leo the Great, Pope and Doctor

First Reading – Romans 15:14-21

14I myself am convinced about you, my brothers and sisters,
that you yourselves are full of goodness, filled with all
knowledge, and able to admonish one another. 15But I have
written to you rather boldly in some respects to remind you,
because of the grace given me by God 16to be a minister of
Christ Jesus to the Gentiles in performing the priestly service
of the Gospel of God, so that the offering up of the Gentiles
may be acceptable, sanctified by the Holy Spirit.17In Christ
Jesus, then, I have reason to boast in what pertains to
God.18For I will not dare to speak of anything except what
Christ has accomplished through me to lead the Gentiles to
obedience by word and deed,19by the power of signs and
wonders, by the power of the Spirit of God, so that from
Jerusalem all the way around to Illyricum I have finished
preaching the Gospel of Christ.20Thus I aspire to proclaim the
Gospel not where Christ has already been named, so that I do
not build on another’s foundation,21but as it is written: “Those
who have never been told of him shall see, and those who
have never heard of him shall understand.”

Responsorial Psalm – Psalms 98:1, 2-3AB, 3CD-4

R. (see 2b) **The Lord has revealed to the nations his saving power.**

1 Sing to the LORD a new song,

for he has done wondrous deeds;

His right hand has won victory for him,

his holy arm.

R. The Lord has revealed to the nations his saving power.

2 The LORD has made his salvation known:

in the sight of the nations he has revealed his justice.

3AB He has remembered his kindness and his faithfulness

toward the house of Israel.

R. The Lord has revealed to the nations his saving power.

3CD All the ends of the earth have seen

the salvation by our God.

4 Sing joyfully to the LORD, all you lands;

break into song; sing praise.

R. The Lord has revealed to the nations his saving power.

Alleluia – 1 John 2:5

R. Alleluia, alleluia.

5 Whoever keeps the word of Christ, the love of God is truly perfected in him.

R. Alleluia, alleluia.

Gospel – Luke 16:1-8

1Jesus said to his disciples, “A rich man had a steward who
was reported to him for squandering his property. 2He
summoned him and said, ‘What is this I hear about you?
Prepare a full account of your stewardship, because you can
no longer be my steward.’ 3The steward said to himself, ‘What
shall I do, now that my master is taking the position of steward
away from me? I am not strong enough to dig and I am
ashamed to beg. 4I know what I shall do so that, when I am
removed from the stewardship, they may welcome me into
their homes.’ 5He called in his master’s debtors one by one.
To the first he said, ‘How much do you owe my master?’ 6He
replied, ‘One hundred measures of olive oil.’ He said to him,
‘Here is your promissory note. Sit down and quickly write one
for fifty.’ 7Then to another he said, ‘And you, how much do you
owe?’ He replied, ‘One hundred measures of wheat.’ He said
to him, ‘Here is your promissory note; write one for eighty.’
8And the master commended that dishonest steward for acting
prudently. For the children of this world are more prudent in
dealing with their own generation than the children of light.”

Saturday November 11, 2023

Saint Martin of Tours, Bishop

First Reading – Romans 16:3-9, 16, 22-27

Brothers and sisters: [3]Greet Prisca and Aquila, my co-workers in Christ Jesus,[4]who risked their necks for my life, to whom not only I am grateful but also all the churches of the Gentiles; [5]greet also the Church at their house. Greet my beloved Epaenetus, who was the first fruits in Asia for Christ. [6]Greet Mary, who has worked hard for you. [7]Greet Andronicus and Junia, my relatives and my fellow prisoners; they are prominent among the Apostles and they were in Christ before me.[8]Greet Ampliatus, my beloved in the Lord.[9]Greet Urbanus, our co-worker in Christ, and my beloved Stachys.[16]Greet one another with a holy kiss. All the churches of Christ greet you.[22]I, Tertius, the writer of this letter, greet you in the Lord.[23]Gaius, who is host to me and to the whole Church, greets you. Erastus, the city treasurer, and our brother Quartus greet you.[25]Now to him who can strengthen you, according to my Gospel and the proclamation of Jesus Christ, according to the revelation of the mystery kept secret for long ages [26]but now manifested through the prophetic writings and, according to the command of the eternal God, made known to all nations to bring about the obedience of faith,[27]to the only wise God, through Jesus Christ be glory forever and ever. Amen.

Responsorial Psalm – Psalms 145:2-3, 4-5, 10-11

R. (1b) I will praise your name for ever, Lord.

[2] Every day will I bless you,

and I will praise your name forever and ever.

[3] Great is the LORD and highly to be praised;

his greatness is unsearchable.

R. I will praise your name for ever, Lord.

[4] Generation after generation praises your works

and proclaims your might.

5 They speak of the splendor of your glorious majesty

and tell of your wondrous works.

R. I will praise your name for ever, Lord.

10 Let all your works give you thanks, O LORD,

and let your faithful ones bless you.

11 Let them discourse of the glory of your Kingdom

and speak of your might.

R. I will praise your name for ever, Lord.

Alleluia – 2 Corinthians 8:9

R. Alleluia, alleluia.

9 Jesus Christ became poor although he was rich, so that by his poverty you might become rich.

R. Alleluia, alleluia.

Gospel – Luke 16:9-15

Jesus said to his disciples: 9"I tell you, make friends for
yourselves with dishonest wealth, so that when it fails, you will
be welcomed into eternal dwellings. 10The person who is
trustworthy in very small matters is also trustworthy in great
ones; and the person who is dishonest in very small matters is
also dishonest in great ones. 11If, therefore, you are not
trustworthy with dishonest wealth, who will trust you with true
wealth? 12If you are not trustworthy with what belongs to
another, who will give you what is yours? 13No servant can
serve two masters. He will either hate one and love the other,
or be devoted to one and despise the other. You cannot serve
God and mammon." 14The Pharisees, who loved money,
heard all these things and sneered at him. 15And he said to
them, "You justify yourselves in the sight of others, but God
knows your hearts; for what is of human esteem is an
abomination in the sight of God."

Sunday November 12, 2023

Thirty-second Sunday in Ordinary Time, Year A

First Reading – Wisdom 6:12-16

12Resplendent and unfading is wisdom, and she is readily
perceived by those who love her, and found by those who
seek her. 13She hastens to make herself known in anticipation
of their desire;14Whoever watches for her at dawn shall not be
disappointed, for he shall find her sitting by his gate.15For
taking thought of wisdom is the perfection of prudence, and
whoever for her sake keeps vigil shall quickly be free from
care;16because she makes her own rounds, seeking those
worthy of her, and graciously appears to them in the ways,
and meets them with all solicitude.

Responsorial Psalm – Psalms 63:2, 3-4, 5-6, 7-8

R. (2b) **My soul is thirsting for you, O Lord my God.**

2 O God, you are my God whom I seek;

for you my flesh pines and my soul thirsts

like the earth, parched, lifeless and without water.

R. My soul is thirsting for you, O Lord my God.

3 Thus have I gazed toward you in the sanctuary

to see your power and your glory,

4 For your kindness is a greater good than life;

my lips shall glorify you.

R. My soul is thirsting for you, O Lord my God.

5 Thus will I bless you while I live;

lifting up my hands, I will call upon your name.

6 As with the riches of a banquet shall my soul be satisfied,

and with exultant lips my mouth shall praise you.

R. My soul is thirsting for you, O Lord my God.

7 I will remember you upon my couch,

and through the night-watches I will meditate on you:

8 You are my help,

and in the shadow of your wings I shout for joy.

R. My soul is thirsting for you, O Lord my God.

Second Reading – 1 Thessalonians 4:13-18

[13]We do not want you to be unaware, brothers and sisters,
about those who have fallen asleep, so that you may not
grieve like the rest, who have no hope. [14]For if we believe that
Jesus died and rose, so too will God, through Jesus, bring with
him those who have fallen asleep.[15]Indeed, we tell you this, on
the word of the Lord, that we who are alive, who are left until
the coming of the Lord, will surely not precede those who have
fallen asleep. [16]For the Lord himself, with a word of command,
with the voice of an archangel and with the trumpet of God,
will come down from heaven, and the dead in Christ will rise
first.[17]Then we who are alive, who are left, will be caught up
together with them in the clouds to meet the Lord in the air.
Thus we shall always be with the Lord. [18]Therefore, console
one another with these words.

Or 1 Thessalonians 4:13-14

[13]We do not want you to be unaware, brothers and sisters,
about those who have fallen asleep, so that you may not
grieve like the rest, who have no hope. [14]For if we believe that
Jesus died and rose, so too will God, through Jesus, bring with
him those who have fallen asleep.

Alleluia – Matthew 24:42A, 44

R. Alleluia, alleluia.

[42A] Stay awake and be ready! [44] For you do not know on what
day your Lord will come.

R. Alleluia, alleluia.

Gospel – Matthew 25:1-13

Jesus told his disciples this parable: [1]"The kingdom of heaven
will be like ten virgins who took their lamps and went out to
meet the bridegroom. [2]Five of them were foolish and five were
wise.[3]The foolish ones, when taking their lamps, brought no oil
with them, [4]but the wise brought flasks of oil with their
lamps.[5]Since the bridegroom was long delayed, they all
became drowsy and fell asleep.[6]At midnight, there was a cry,
'Behold, the bridegroom! Come out to meet him!' [7]Then all

those virgins got up and trimmed their lamps.8The foolish ones
said to the wise, ‘Give us some of your oil, for our lamps are
going out.’ 9But the wise ones replied, ‘No, for there may not
be enough for us and you. Go instead to the merchants and
buy some for yourselves.’ 10While they went off to buy it, the
bridegroom came and those who were ready went into the
wedding feast with him. Then the door was
locked.11Afterwards the other virgins came and said, ‘Lord,
Lord, open the door for us!’ 12But he said in reply, ‘Amen, I say
to you, I do not know you.’13Therefore, stay awake, for you
know neither the day nor the hour.”

Monday November 13, 2023

Memorial of Saint Frances Xavier Cabrini

First Reading – Wisdom 1:1-7

1Love justice, you who judge the earth; think of the Lord in
goodness, and seek him in integrity of heart; 2Because he is
found by those who test him not, and he manifests himself to
those who do not disbelieve him. 3For perverse counsels
separate a man from God, and his power, put to the proof,
rebukes the foolhardy; 4Because into a soul that plots evil,
wisdom enters not, nor dwells she in a body under debt of sin.
5For the holy Spirit of discipline flees deceit and withdraws
from senseless counsels; and when injustice occurs it is
rebuked. 6For wisdom is a kindly spirit, yet she acquits not the
blasphemer of his guilty lips; Because God is the witness of
his inmost self and the sure observer of his heart and the
listener to his tongue. 7For the Spirit of the Lord fills the world,
is all-embracing, and knows what man says.

Responsorial Psalm – Psalms 139:1B-3, 4-6, 7-8, 9-10

R. (24b) Guide me, Lord, along the everlasting way.

1B O LORD, you have probed me and you know me;

2 you know when I sit and when I stand;

you understand my thoughts from afar.

3 My journeys and my rest you scrutinize,

with all my ways you are familiar.

R. Guide me, Lord, along the everlasting way.

4 Even before a word is on my tongue,

behold, O LORD, you know the whole of it.

5 Behind me and before, you hem me in

and rest your hand upon me.

6 Such knowledge is too wonderful for me;

too lofty for me to attain.

R. Guide me, Lord, along the everlasting way.

7 Where can I go from your spirit?

From your presence where can I flee?

8 If I go up to the heavens, you are there;

if I sink to the nether world, you are present there.

R. Guide me, Lord, along the everlasting way.

9 If I take the wings of the dawn,

if I settle at the farthest limits of the sea,

10 Even there your hand shall guide me,

and your right hand hold me fast.

R. Guide me, Lord, along the everlasting way.

Alleluia – Philippians 2:15D, 16A

R. Alleluia, alleluia.

15D Shine like lights in the world, 16A as you hold on to the word of life.

R. Alleluia, alleluia.

Gospel – Luke 17:1-6

1Jesus said to his disciples, "Things that cause sin will inevitably occur, but woe to the one through whom they occur.
2It would be better for him if a millstone were put around his neck and he be thrown into the sea than for him to cause one of these little ones to sin.
3Be on your guard! If your brother sins, rebuke him; and if he repents, forgive him.
4And if he wrongs you seven times in one day and returns to you seven

times saying, 'I am sorry,' you should forgive him." [5]And the Apostles said to the Lord, "Increase our faith." [6]The Lord replied, "If you have faith the size of a mustard seed, you would say to this mulberry tree, 'Be uprooted and planted in the sea,' and it would obey you."

Tuesday November 14, 2023

Tuesday of Thirty-second Week in Ordinary Time

First Reading – Wisdom 2:23-3:9

[23]God formed man to be imperishable; the image of his own nature he made them.[24]But by the envy of the Devil, death entered the world, and they who are in his possession experience it.[1]But the souls of the just are in the hand of God, and no torment shall touch them.[2]They seemed, in the view of the foolish, to be dead; and their passing away was thought an affliction [3]and their going forth from us, utter destruction. But they are in peace.[4]For if before men, indeed, they be punished, yet is their hope full of immortality; [5]Chastised a little, they shall be greatly blessed, because God tried them and found them worthy of himself.[6]As gold in the furnace, he proved them, and as sacrificial offerings he took them to himself. [7]In the time of their visitation they shall shine, and shall dart about as sparks through stubble; [8]They shall judge nations and rule over peoples, and the Lord shall be their King forever. [9]Those who trust in him shall understand truth, and the faithful shall abide with him in love: Because grace and mercy are with his holy ones, and his care is with his elect.

Responsorial Psalm – Psalms 34:2-3, 16-17, 18-19

R.(2a) I will bless the Lord at all times.

[2] I will bless the LORD at all times;

his praise shall be ever in my mouth.

[3] Let my soul glory in the LORD;

the lowly will hear me and be glad.

R. I will bless the Lord at all times.

[16] The LORD has eyes for the just,

and ears for their cry.

[17] The LORD confronts the evildoers,

to destroy remembrance of them from the earth.

R. I will bless the Lord at all times.

[18] When the just cry out, the LORD hears them,

and from all their distress he rescues them.

[19] The LORD is close to the brokenhearted;

and those who are crushed in spirit he saves.

R. I will bless the Lord at all times.

Alleluia – John 14:23

R. Alleluia, alleluia.

[23] Whoever loves me will keep my word, and my Father will
love him, and we will come to him.

R. Alleluia, alleluia.

Gospel – Luke 17:7-10

Jesus said to the Apostles: [7]"Who among you would say to
your servant who has just come in from plowing or tending
sheep in the field, 'Come here immediately and take your
place at table'? [8]Would he not rather say to him, 'Prepare
something for me to eat. Put on your apron and wait on me
while I eat and drink. You may eat and drink when I am
finished'? [9]Is he grateful to that servant because he did what
was commanded? [10]So should it be with you. When you have
done all you have been commanded, say, 'We are
unprofitable servants; we have done what we were obliged to
do.'"

Wednesday November 15, 2023

Wednesday of Thirty-second Week in Ordinary Time

First Reading – Wisdom 6:1-11

[1]Hear, O kings, and understand; learn, you magistrates of the
earth's expanse! [2]Hearken, you who are in power over the
multitude and lord it over throngs of peoples! [3]Because
authority was given you by the Lord and sovereignty by the
Most High, who shall probe your works and scrutinize your
counsels. [4]Because, though you were ministers of his

kingdom, you judged not rightly, and did not keep the law, nor walk according to the will of God, [5]Terribly and swiftly shall he come against you, because judgment is stern for the exalted– [6]For the lowly may be pardoned out of mercy but the mighty shall be mightily put to the test. [7]For the Lord of all shows no partiality, nor does he fear greatness, Because he himself made the great as well as the small, and he provides for all alike; [8]but for those in power a rigorous scrutiny impends. [9]To you, therefore, O princes, are my words addressed that you may learn wisdom and that you may not sin. [10]For those who keep the holy precepts hallowed shall be found holy, and those learned in them will have ready a response. [11]Desire therefore my words; long for them and you shall be instructed.

Responsorial Psalm – Psalms 82:3-4, 6-7

R. (8a) Rise up, O God, bring judgment to the earth.

3 Defend the lowly and the fatherless;

render justice to the afflicted and the destitute.

4 Rescue the lowly and the poor;

from the hand of the wicked deliver them.

R. Rise up, O God, bring judgment to the earth.

6 I said: "You are gods,

all of you sons of the Most High;

7 yet like men you shall die,

and fall like any prince."

R. Rise up, O God, bring judgment to the earth.

Alleluia – 1 Thessalonians 5:18

R. Alleluia, alleluia.

18 In all circumstances, give thanks, for this is the will of God for you in Christ Jesus.

R. Alleluia, alleluia.

Gospel – Luke 17:11-19

[11]As Jesus continued his journey to Jerusalem, he traveled through Samaria and Galilee. [12]As he was entering a village,

ten lepers met him. They stood at a distance from him [13]and raised their voice, saying, “Jesus, Master! Have pity on us!” [14]And when he saw them, he said, “Go show yourselves to the priests.” As they were going they were cleansed. [15]And one of them, realizing he had been healed, returned, glorifying God in a loud voice; [16]and he fell at the feet of Jesus and thanked him. He was a Samaritan. [17]Jesus said in reply, “Ten were cleansed, were they not? Where are the other nine? [18]Has none but this foreigner returned to give thanks to God?” [19]Then he said to him, “Stand up and go; your faith has saved you.”

Thursday November 16, 2023

Thursday of Thirty-second Week in Ordinary Time

First Reading – Wisdom 7:22B-8:1

[22]In Wisdom is a spirit intelligent, holy, unique, Manifold, subtle, agile, clear, unstained, certain, Not baneful, loving the good, keen, [23]unhampered, beneficent, kindly, Firm, secure, tranquil, all-powerful, all-seeing, And pervading all spirits, though they be intelligent, pure and very subtle. [24]For Wisdom is mobile beyond all motion, and she penetrates and pervades all things by reason of her purity. [25]For she is an aura of the might of God and a pure effusion of the glory of the Almighty; therefore nought that is sullied enters into her. [26]For she is the refulgence of eternal light, the spotless mirror of the power of God, the image of his goodness. [27]And she, who is one, can do all things, and renews everything while herself perduring; And passing into holy souls from age to age, she produces friends of God and prophets. [28]For there is nought God loves, be it not one who dwells with Wisdom. [29]For she is fairer than the sun and surpasses every constellation of the stars. Compared to light, she takes precedence; [30]for that, indeed, night supplants, but wickedness prevails not over Wisdom. [1]Indeed, she reaches from end to end mightily and governs all things well.

Responsorial Psalm – Psalms 119:89, 90, 91, 130, 135, 175

R. (89a) Your word is for ever, O Lord.

[89] Your word, O LORD, endures forever;

it is firm as the heavens.

R. Your word is for ever, O Lord.

90 Through all generations your truth endures;

you have established the earth, and it stands firm.

R. Your word is for ever, O Lord.

91 According to your ordinances they still stand firm:

all things serve you.

R. Your word is for ever, O Lord.

130 The revelation of your words sheds light,

giving understanding to the simple.

R. Your word is for ever, O Lord.

135 Let your countenance shine upon your servant,

and teach me your statutes.

R. Your word is for ever, O Lord.

175 Let my soul live to praise you,

and may your ordinances help me.

R. Your word is for ever, O Lord.

Alleluia – John 15:5

R. Alleluia, alleluia.

5 I am the vine, you are the branches, says the Lord: whoever remains in me and I in him will bear much fruit.

R. Alleluia, alleluia.

Gospel – Luke 17:20-25

20Asked by the Pharisees when the Kingdom of God would
come, Jesus said in reply, “The coming of the Kingdom of God
cannot be observed, 21and no one will announce, ‘Look, here it
is,’ or, ‘There it is.’ For behold, the Kingdom of God is among
you.” 22Then he said to his disciples, “The days will come
when you will long to see one of the days of the Son of Man,
but you will not see it. 23There will be those who will say to
you, ‘Look, there he is,’ or ‘Look, here he is.’ Do not go off, do
not run in pursuit. 24For just as lightning flashes and lights up

the sky from one side to the other, so will the Son of Man be in
his day. [25]But first he must suffer greatly and be rejected by
this generation."

Friday November 17, 2023

Memorial of Saint Elizabeth of Hungary, Religious

First Reading – Wisdom 13:1-9

[1]All men were by nature foolish who were in ignorance of God,
and who from the good things seen did not succeed in
knowing him who is, and from studying the works did not
discern the artisan; [2]But either fire, or wind, or the swift air, or
the circuit of the stars, or the mighty water, or the luminaries of
heaven, the governors of the world, they considered gods.
[3]Now if out of joy in their beauty they thought them gods, let
them know how far more excellent is the Lord than these; for
the original source of beauty fashioned them. [4]Or if they were
struck by their might and energy, let them from these things
realize how much more powerful is he who made them. [5]For
from the greatness and the beauty of created things their
original author, by analogy, is seen. [6]But yet, for these the
blame is less; For they indeed have gone astray perhaps,
though they seek God and wish to find him. [7]For they search
busily among his works, but are distracted by what they see,
because the things seen are fair. [8]But again, not even these
are pardonable. [9]For if they so far succeeded in knowledge
that they could speculate about the world, how did they not
more quickly find its Lord?

Responsorial Psalm – Psalms 19:2-3, 4-5AB

R. (2a) The heavens proclaim the glory of God.

[2] The heavens declare the glory of God,

and the firmament proclaims his handiwork.

[3] Day pours out the word to day,

and night to night imparts knowledge.

R. The heavens proclaim the glory of God.

[4] Not a word nor a discourse

whose voice is not heard;

5AB Through all the earth their voice resounds,

and to the ends of the world, their message.

R. The heavens proclaim the glory of God.

Alleluia – Luke 21:28

R. Alleluia, alleluia.

28 Stand erect and raise your heads because your redemption is at hand.

R. Alleluia, alleluia.

Gospel – Luke 17:26-37

Jesus said to his disciples: 26“As it was in the days of Noah, so
it will be in the days of the Son of Man; 27they were eating and
drinking, marrying and giving in marriage up to the day that
Noah entered the ark, and the flood came and destroyed them
all. 28Similarly, as it was in the days of Lot: they were eating,
drinking, buying, selling, planting, building; 29on the day when
Lot left Sodom, fire and brimstone rained from the sky to
destroy them all. 30So it will be on the day the Son of Man is
revealed. 31On that day, someone who is on the housetop and
whose belongings are in the house must not go down to get
them, and likewise one in the field must not return to what was
left behind. 32Remember the wife of Lot. 33Whoever seeks to
preserve his life will lose it, but whoever loses it will save it. 34I
tell you, on that night there will be two people in one bed; one
will be taken, the other left. 35And there will be two women
grinding meal together; one will be taken, the other left.”
37They said to him in reply, “Where, Lord?” He said to them,
“Where the body is, there also the vultures will gather.”

Saturday November 18, 2023

Saturday of Thirty-third Week in Ordinary Time

First Reading – Wisdom 18:14-16; 19:6-9

14When peaceful stillness compassed everything and the night
in its swift course was half spent, 15Your all-powerful word,
from heaven’s royal throne bounded, 16a fierce warrior, into the
doomed land, bearing the sharp sword of your inexorable
decree. And as he alighted, he filled every place with death;
he still reached to heaven, while he stood upon the earth. 6For

all creation, in its several kinds, was being made over anew, serving its natural laws, that your children might be preserved unharmed.
7The cloud overshadowed their camp; and out of what had before been water, dry land was seen emerging: Out of the Red Sea an unimpeded road, and a grassy plain out of the mighty flood.
8Over this crossed the whole nation sheltered by your hand, after they beheld stupendous wonders.
9For they ranged about like horses, and bounded about like lambs, praising you, O Lord! their deliverer.

Responsorial Psalm – Psalms 105:2-3, 36-37, 42-43

R. (5a) Remember the marvels the Lord has done! or: **R. Alleluia.**

2 Sing to him, sing his praise,

proclaim all his wondrous deeds.

3 Glory in his holy name;

rejoice, O hearts that seek the LORD!

R. Remember the marvels the Lord has done! or: **R. Alleluia.**

36 Then he struck every first born throughout their land,

the first fruits of all their manhood.

37 And he led them forth laden with silver and gold,

with not a weakling among their tribes.

R. Remember the marvels the Lord has done! or: **R. Alleluia.**

42 For he remembered his holy word

to his servant Abraham.

43 And he led forth his people with joy;

with shouts of joy, his chosen ones.

R. Remember the marvels the Lord has done! or: **R. Alleluia.**

Alleluia – 2 Thessalonians 2:14

R. Alleluia, alleluia.

14 God has called us through the Gospel, to possess the glory
of our Lord Jesus Christ.

R. Alleluia, alleluia.

Gospel – Luke 18:1-8

1 Jesus told his disciples a parable about the necessity for
them to pray always without becoming weary. 2 He said, “There
was a judge in a certain town who neither feared God nor
respected any human being. 3 And a widow in that town used
to come to him and say, ‘Render a just decision for me against
my adversary.’ 4 For a long time the judge was unwilling, but
eventually he thought, ‘While it is true that I neither fear God
nor respect any human being, 5 because this widow keeps
bothering me I shall deliver a just decision for her lest she
finally come and strike me.’” 6 The Lord said, “Pay attention to
what the dishonest judge says. 7 Will not God then secure the
rights of his chosen ones who call out to him day and night?
Will he be slow to answer them? 8 I tell you, he will see to it
that justice is done for them speedily. But when the Son of
Man comes, will he find faith on earth?”

Sunday November 19, 2023

Thirty-third Sunday in Ordinary Time, Year A

First Reading – Proverbs 31:10-13, 19-20, 30-31

10 When one finds a worthy wife, her value is far beyond pearls.
11 Her husband, entrusting his heart to her, has an unfailing
prize. 12 She brings him good, and not evil, all the days of her
life. 13 She obtains wool and flax and works with loving hands.
19 She puts her hands to the distaff, and her fingers ply the
spindle. 20 She reaches out her hands to the poor, and extends
her arms to the needy. 30 Charm is deceptive and beauty
fleeting; the woman who fears the LORD is to be praised.
31 Give her a reward for her labors, and let her works praise her
at the city gates.

Responsorial Psalm – Psalms 128:1-2, 3, 4-5

R. (cf. 1a) **Blessed are those who fear the Lord.**

1 Blessed are you who fear the LORD,

who walk in his ways!

2 For you shall eat the fruit of your handiwork;

blessed shall you be, and favored.

R. Blessed are those who fear the Lord.

3 Your wife shall be like a fruitful vine

in the recesses of your home;

Your children like olive plants

around your table.

R. Blessed are those who fear the Lord.

4 Behold, thus is the man blessed

who fears the LORD.

5 The LORD bless you from Zion:

may you see the prosperity of Jerusalem

all the days of your life.

R. Blessed are those who fear the Lord.

Second Reading – 1 Thessalonians 5:1-6

1Concerning times and seasons, brothers and sisters, you
have no need for anything to be written to you. 2For you
yourselves know very well that the day of the Lord will come
like a thief at night. 3When people are saying, "Peace and
security, " then sudden disaster comes upon them, like labor
pains upon a pregnant woman, and they will not escape. 4But
you, brothers and sisters, are not in darkness, for that day to
overtake you like a thief. 5For all of you are children of the light
and children of the day. We are not of the night or of darkness.
6Therefore, let us not sleep as the rest do, but let us stay alert
and sober.

Alleluia – John 15:4A, 5B

R. Alleluia, alleluia.

4A Remain in me as I remain in you, says the Lord. 5B Whoever remains in me bears much fruit.

R. Alleluia, alleluia.

Gospel – Matthew 25:14-30

Jesus told his disciples this parable: [14]“A man going on a
journey called in his servants and entrusted his possessions to
them. [15]To one he gave five talents; to another, two; to a third,
one to each according to his ability. Then he went away.
Immediately [16]the one who received five talents went and
traded with them, and made another five. [17]Likewise, the one
who received two made another two. [18]But the man who
received one went off and dug a hole in the ground and buried
his master’s money. [19]After a long time the master of those
servants came back and settled accounts with them. [20]The
one who had received five talents came forward bringing the
additional five. He said, ‘Master, you gave me five talents.
See, I have made five more.’ [21]His master said to him, ‘Well
done, my good and faithful servant. Since you were faithful in
small matters, I will give you great responsibilities. Come,
share your master’s joy.’ [22]Then the one who had received two
talents also came forward and said, ‘Master, you gave me two
talents. See, I have made two more.’ [23]His master said to him,
‘Well done, my good and faithful servant. Since you were
faithful in small matters, I will give you great responsibilities.
Come, share your master’s joy.’ [24]Then the one who had
received the one talent came forward and said, ‘Master, I
knew you were a demanding person, harvesting where you did
not plant and gathering where you did not scatter; [25]so out of
fear I went off and buried your talent in the ground. Here it is
back.’ [26]His master said to him in reply, ‘You wicked, lazy
servant! So you knew that I harvest where I did not plant and
gather where I did not scatter? [27]Should you not then have put
my money in the bank so that I could have got it back with
interest on my return? [28]Now then! Take the talent from him
and give it to the one with ten. [29]For to everyone who has,
more will be given and he will grow rich; but from the one who
has not, even what he has will be taken away. [30]And throw this
useless servant into the darkness outside, where there will be
wailing and grinding of teeth.'”

Or Matthew 25:14-15, 19-21

Jesus told his disciples this parable: [14]“A man going on a
journey called in his servants and entrusted his possessions to
them. [15]To one he gave five talents; to another, two; to a third,
one to each according to his ability. Then he went away.

19After a long time the master of those servants came back and settled accounts with them. 20The one who had received five talents came forward bringing the additional five. He said, 'Master, you gave me five talents. See, I have made five more.' 21His master said to him, 'Well done, my good and faithful servant. Since you were faithful in small matters, I will give you great responsibilities. Come, share your master's joy.'

Monday November 20, 2023

Monday of Thirty-third Week Ordinary Time

First Reading – 1 Maccabees 1:10-15, 41-43, 54-57, 62-63

[From the descendants of Alexander's officers] 10there sprang a sinful offshoot, Antiochus Epiphanes, son of King Antiochus, once a hostage at Rome. He became king in the year one hundred and thirty seven of the kingdom of the Greeks. 11In those days there appeared in Israel men who were breakers of the law, and they seduced many people, saying: "Let us go and make an alliance with the Gentiles all around us; since we separated from them, many evils have come upon us." 12The proposal was agreeable; 13some from among the people promptly went to the king, and he authorized them to introduce the way of living of the Gentiles. 14Thereupon they built a gymnasium in Jerusalem according to the Gentile custom. 15They covered over the mark of their circumcision and abandoned the holy covenant; they allied themselves with the Gentiles and sold themselves to wrongdoing. 41Then the king wrote to his whole kingdom that all should be one people, 42each abandoning his particular customs. All the Gentiles conformed to the command of the king, 43and many children of Israel were in favor of his religion; they sacrificed to idols and profaned the Sabbath. 54On the fifteenth day of the month Chislev, in the year one hundred and forty-five, the king erected the horrible abomination upon the altar of burnt offerings and in the surrounding cities of Judah they built pagan altars. 55They also burned incense at the doors of the houses and in the streets.56Any scrolls of the law which they found they tore up and burnt. 57Whoever was found with a scroll of the covenant, and whoever observed the law, was condemned to death by royal decree. 62But many in Israel were determined and resolved in their hearts not to eat anything unclean; 63they preferred to die rather than to be defiled with unclean food or to profane the holy covenant; and they did die. 64Terrible affliction was upon Israel.

Responsorial Psalm – Psalms 119:53, 61, 134, 150, 155, 158

R. (see 88) **Give me life, O Lord, and I will do your commands.**

53 Indignation seizes me because of the wicked

who forsake your law.

R. Give me life, O Lord, and I will do your commands.

61 Though the snares of the wicked are twined about me,

your law I have not forgotten.

R. Give me life, O Lord, and I will do your commands.

134 Redeem me from the oppression of men,

that I may keep your precepts.

R. Give me life, O Lord, and I will do your commands.

150 I am attacked by malicious persecutors

who are far from your law.

R. Give me life, O Lord, and I will do your commands.

155 Far from sinners is salvation,

because they seek not your statutes.

R. Give me life, O Lord, and I will do your commands.

158 I beheld the apostates with loathing,

because they kept not to your promise.

R. Give me life, O Lord, and I will do your commands.

Alleluia – John 8:12

R. Alleluia, alleluia.

12I am the light of the world, says the Lord; whoever follows me will have the light of life.

R. Alleluia, alleluia.

Gospel – Luke 18:35-43

35As Jesus approached Jericho a blind man was sitting by the
roadside begging, 36and hearing a crowd going by, he inquired
what was happening. 37They told him, “Jesus of Nazareth is
passing by.” 38He shouted, “Jesus, Son of David, have pity on
me!” 39The people walking in front rebuked him, telling him to
be silent, but he kept calling out all the more, “Son of David,
have pity on me!” 40Then Jesus stopped and ordered that he
be brought to him; and when he came near, Jesus asked him,
41“What do you want me to do for you?” He replied, “Lord,
please let me see.” 42Jesus told him, “Have sight; your faith
has saved you.” 43He immediately received his sight and
followed him, giving glory to God. When they saw this, all the
people gave praise to God.

Tuesday November 21, 2023

The Presentation of the Blessed Virgin Mary

First Reading – 2 Maccabees 6:18-31

18Eleazar, one of the foremost scribes, a man of advanced age
and noble appearance, was being forced to open his mouth to
eat pork. 19But preferring a glorious death to a life of
defilement, 20he spat out the meat, and went forward of his
own accord to the instrument of torture, as people ought to do
who have the courage to reject the food which it is unlawful to
taste even for love of life. 21Those in charge of that unlawful
ritual meal took the man aside privately, because of their long
acquaintance with him, and urged him to bring meat of his own
providing, such as he could legitimately eat, and to pretend to
be eating some of the meat of the sacrifice prescribed by the
king; 22in this way he would escape the death penalty, and be
treated kindly because of their old friendship with him. 23But
Eleazar made up his mind in a noble manner, worthy of his
years, the dignity of his advanced age, the merited distinction
of his gray hair, and of the admirable life he had lived from
childhood; and so he declared that above all he would be loyal
to the holy laws given by God. He told them to send him at
once to the abode of the dead, explaining: 24“At our age it
would be unbecoming to make such a pretense; many young
people would think the ninety-year-old Eleazar had gone over
to an alien religion. 25Should I thus pretend for the sake of a
brief moment of life, they would be led astray by me, while I

would bring shame and dishonor on my old age. [26]Even if, for the time being, I avoid the punishment of men, I shall never, whether alive or dead, escape the hands of the Almighty.
[27]Therefore, by manfully giving up my life now, I will prove myself worthy of my old age, [28]and I will leave to the young a noble example of how to die willingly and generously for the revered and holy laws." Eleazar spoke thus, and went immediately to the instrument of torture. [29]Those who shortly before had been kindly disposed, now became hostile toward him because what he had said seemed to them utter madness. [30]When he was about to die under the blows, he groaned and said: "The Lord in his holy knowledge knows full well that, although I could have escaped death, I am not only enduring terrible pain in my body from this scourging, but also suffering it with joy in my soul because of my devotion to him."
[31]This is how he died, leaving in his death a model of courage and an unforgettable example of virtue not only for the young but for the whole nation.

Responsorial Psalm – Psalms 3:2-3, 4-5, 6-7

R. (6b) The Lord upholds me.

2 O LORD, how many are my adversaries!

Many rise up against me!

3 Many are saying of me,

"There is no salvation for him in God."

R. The Lord upholds me.

4 But you, O LORD, are my shield;

my glory, you lift up my head!

5 When I call out to the LORD,

he answers me from his holy mountain.

R. The Lord upholds me.

6 When I lie down in sleep,

I wake again, for the LORD sustains me.

7 I fear not the myriads of people

arrayed against me on every side.

R. The Lord upholds me.

Alleluia – 1 John 4:10B

R. Alleluia, alleluia.

[10B] God loved us, and sent his Son as expiation for our sins.

R. Alleluia, alleluia.

Gospel – Luke 19:1-10

[1]At that time Jesus came to Jericho and intended to pass
through the town. [2]Now a man there named Zacchaeus, who
was a chief tax collector and also a wealthy man, [3]was
seeking to see who Jesus was; but he could not see him
because of the crowd, for he was short in stature. [4]So he ran
ahead and climbed a sycamore tree in order to see Jesus,
who was about to pass that way. [5]When he reached the place,
Jesus looked up and said, "Zacchaeus, come down quickly,
for today I must stay at your house." [6]And he came down
quickly and received him with joy. [7]When they saw this, they
began to grumble, saying, "He has gone to stay at the house
of a sinner." [8]But Zacchaeus stood there and said to the Lord,
"Behold, half of my possessions, Lord, I shall give to the poor,
and if I have extorted anything from anyone I shall repay it four
times over." [9]And Jesus said to him, "Today salvation has
come to this house because this man too is a descendant of
Abraham. [10]For the Son of Man has come to seek and to save
what was lost."

Wednesday November 22, 2023

Memorial of Saint Cecilia, Virgin and Martyr

First Reading – 2 Maccabees 7:1, 20-31

[1]It happened that seven brothers with their mother were
arrested and tortured with whips and scourges by the king, to
force them to eat pork in violation of God's law.[20]Most
admirable and worthy of everlasting remembrance was the
mother, who saw her seven sons perish in a single day, yet
bore it courageously because of her hope in the Lord.[21]Filled
with a noble spirit that stirred her womanly heart with manly
courage, she exhorted each of them in the language of their

ancestors with these words: [22]"I do not know how you came
into existence in my womb; it was not I who gave you the
breath of life, nor was it I who set in order the elements of
which each of you is composed.[23]Therefore, since it is the
Creator of the universe who shapes each man's beginning, as
he brings about the origin of everything, he, in his mercy, will
give you back both breath and life, because you now
disregard yourselves for the sake of his law."[24]Antiochus,
suspecting insult in her words, thought he was being ridiculed.
As the youngest brother was still alive, the king appealed to
him, not with mere words, but with promises on oath, to make
him rich and happy if he would abandon his ancestral
customs: he would make him his Friend and entrust him with
high office.[25]When the youth paid no attention to him at all, the
king appealed to the mother, urging her to advise her boy to
save his life. [26]After he had urged her for a long time, she went
through the motions of persuading her son. In derision of the
cruel tyrant, [27]she leaned over close to her son and said in
their native language: "Son, have pity on me, who carried you
in my womb for nine months, nursed you for three years,
brought you up, educated and supported you to your present
age. [28]I beg you, child, to look at the heavens and the earth
and see all that is in them; then you will know that God did not
make them out of existing things; and in the same way the
human race came into existence. [29]Do not be afraid of this
executioner, but be worthy of your brothers and accept death,
so that in the time of mercy I may receive you again with
them." [30]She had scarcely finished speaking when the youth
said: "What are you waiting for? I will not obey the king's
command. I obey the command of the law given to our fathers
through Moses. [31]But you, who have contrived every kind of
affliction for the Hebrews, will not escape the hands of God."

Responsorial Psalm – Psalms 17:1BCD, 5-6, 8B AND 15

R. (15b) Lord, when your glory appears, my joy will be full.

[1BCD] Hear, O LORD, a just suit;

attend to my outcry;

hearken to my prayer from lips without deceit.

R. Lord, when your glory appears, my joy will be full.

5 My steps have been steadfast in your paths,

my feet have not faltered.

6 I call upon you, for you will answer me, O God;

incline your ear to me; hear my word.

R. Lord, when your glory appears, my joy will be full.

8B Keep me as the apple of your eye;

hide me in the shadow of your wings.

15 But I in justice shall behold your face;

on waking, I shall be content in your presence.

R. Lord, when your glory appears, my joy will be full.

Alleluia – John 15:16

R. Alleluia, alleluia.

16 I chose you from the world, to go and bear fruit that will last, says the Lord.

R. Alleluia, alleluia.

Gospel – Luke 19:11-28

11 While people were listening to Jesus speak, he proceeded to
tell a parable because he was near Jerusalem and they
thought that the Kingdom of God would appear there
immediately. 12 So he said, "A nobleman went off to a distant
country to obtain the kingship for himself and then to
return. 13 He called ten of his servants and gave them ten gold
coins and told them, 'Engage in trade with these until I return.'
14 His fellow citizens, however, despised him and sent a
delegation after him to announce, 'We do not want this man to
be our king.' 15 But when he returned after obtaining the
kingship, he had the servants called, to whom he had given
the money, to learn what they had gained by trading. 16 The first
came forward and said, 'Sir, your gold coin has earned ten
additional ones.' 17 He replied, 'Well done, good servant! You
have been faithful in this very small matter; take charge of ten
cities.' 18 Then the second came and reported, 'Your gold coin,
sir, has earned five more.' 19 And to this servant too he said,
'You, take charge of five cities.' 20 Then the other servant came
and said, 'Sir, here is your gold coin; I kept it stored away in a

handkerchief, 21for I was afraid of you, because you are a
demanding man; you take up what you did not lay down and
you harvest what you did not plant.’ 22He said to him, ‘With
your own words I shall condemn you, you wicked servant. You
knew I was a demanding man, taking up what I did not lay
down and harvesting what I did not plant; 23why did you not
put my money in a bank? Then on my return I would have
collected it with interest.’ 24And to those standing by he said,
‘Take the gold coin from him and give it to the servant who has
ten.’ 25But they said to him, ‘Sir, he has ten gold coins.’ 26He
replied, ‘I tell you, to everyone who has, more will be given,
but from the one who has not, even what he has will be taken
away. 27Now as for those enemies of mine who did not want
me as their king, bring them here and slay them before me.’”
28After he had said this, he proceeded on his journey up to
Jerusalem.

Thursday November 23, 2023

Thursday of Thirty-third Week in Ordinary Time

First Reading – 1 Maccabees 2:15-29

15The officers of the king in charge of enforcing the apostasy
came to the city of Modein to organize the sacrifices. 16Many
of Israel joined them, but Mattathias and his sons gathered in
a group apart. 17Then the officers of the king addressed
Mattathias: “You are a leader, an honorable and great man in
this city, supported by sons and kin. 18Come now, be the first
to obey the king’s command, as all the Gentiles and the men
of Judah and those who are left in Jerusalem have done. Then
you and your sons shall be numbered among the King’s
Friends, and shall be enriched with silver and gold and many
gifts.” 19But Mattathias answered in a loud voice: “Although all
the Gentiles in the king’s realm obey him, so that each
forsakes the religion of his fathers and consents to the king’s
orders, 20yet I and my sons and my kin will keep to the
covenant of our fathers. 21God forbid that we should forsake
the law and the commandments. 22We will not obey the words
of the king nor depart from our religion in the slightest degree.”
23As he finished saying these words, a certain Jew came
forward in the sight of all to offer sacrifice on the altar in
Modein according to the king’s order. 24When Mattathias saw
him, he was filled with zeal; his heart was moved and his just

fury was aroused; he sprang forward and killed him upon the
altar. [25]At the same time, he also killed the messenger of the
king who was forcing them to sacrifice, and he tore down the
altar. [26]Thus he showed his zeal for the law, just as Phinehas
did with Zimri, son of Salu. [27]Then Mattathias went through the
city shouting, "Let everyone who is zealous for the law and
who stands by the covenant follow after me!" [28]Thereupon he
fled to the mountains with his sons, leaving behind in the city
all their possessions. [29]Many who sought to live according to
righteousness and religious custom went out into the desert to
settle there.

Responsorial Psalm – Psalms 50:1B-2, 5-6, 14-15

R. (23b) To the upright I will show the saving power of God.

[1B] God the LORD has spoken and summoned the earth,

from the rising of the sun to its setting.

[2] From Zion, perfect in beauty,

God shines forth.

R. To the upright I will show the saving power of God.

[5] "Gather my faithful ones before me,

those who have made a covenant with me by sacrifice."

[6] And the heavens proclaim his justice;

for God himself is the judge.

R. To the upright I will show the saving power of God.

[14] "Offer to God praise as your sacrifice

and fulfill your vows to the Most High;

[15] Then call upon me in time of distress;

I will rescue you, and you shall glorify me."

R. To the upright I will show the saving power of God.

Alleluia – Psalms 95:8

R. Alleluia, alleluia.

[8] If today you hear his voice, harden not your hearts.

R. Alleluia, alleluia.

Gospel – Luke 19:41-44

[41]As Jesus drew near Jerusalem, he saw the city and wept over it, [42]saying, "If this day you only knew what makes for peace – but now it is hidden from your eyes.[43]For the days are coming upon you when your enemies will raise a palisade against you; they will encircle you and hem you in on all sides. [44]They will smash you to the ground and your children within you, and they will not leave one stone upon another within you because you did not recognize the time of your visitation."

Friday November 24, 2023

Friday of Thirty-third Week in Ordinary Time

First Reading – 1 Maccabees 4:36-37, 52-59

[36]Judas and his brothers said, "Now that our enemies have been crushed, let us go up to purify the sanctuary and rededicate it." [37] So the whole army assembled, and went up to Mount Zion. [52]Early in the morning on the twenty-fifth day of the ninth month, that is, the month of Chislev, in the year one hundred and forty-eight, they arose [53]and offered sacrifice according to the law on the new altar of burnt offerings that they had made. [54]On the anniversary of the day on which the Gentiles had defiled it, on that very day it was reconsecrated with songs, harps, flutes, and cymbals. [55]All the people prostrated themselves and adored and praised Heaven, who had given them success. [56]For eight days they celebrated the dedication of the altar and joyfully offered burnt offerings and sacrifices of deliverance and praise. [57]They ornamented the facade of the temple with gold crowns and shields; they repaired the gates and the priests' chambers and furnished them with doors. [58]There was great joy among the people now that the disgrace of the Gentiles was removed. [59]Then Judas and his brothers and the entire congregation of Israel decreed that the days of the dedication of the altar should be observed with joy and gladness on the anniversary every year for eight days, from the twenty-fifth day of the month Chislev.

Responsorial Psalm – 1 Chronicles 29:10BCD, 11ABC, 11D-12A, 12BCD

R. [13b] **We praise your glorious name, O mighty God.**

10BCD "Blessed may you be, O LORD,

God of Israel our father,

from eternity to eternity."

R. We praise your glorious name, O mighty God.

11ABC "Yours, O LORD, are grandeur and power,

majesty, splendor, and glory.

For all in heaven and on earth is yours."

R. We praise your glorious name, O mighty God.

11D "Yours, O LORD, is the sovereignty;

you are exalted as head over all.

12A Riches and honor are from you."

R. We praise your glorious name, O mighty God.

12BCD "You have dominion over all,

In your hand are power and might;

it is yours to give grandeur and strength to all."

R. We praise your glorious name, O mighty God.

Alleluia – John 10:27

R. Alleluia, alleluia.

27My sheep hear my voice, says the Lord; I know them, and they follow me.

R. Alleluia, alleluia.

Gospel – Luke 19:45-48

45Jesus entered the temple area and proceeded to drive out those who were selling things, 46saying to them, "It is written, My house shall be a house of prayer, but you have made it a den of thieves." 47And every day he was teaching in the temple area. The chief priests, the scribes, and the leaders of the people, meanwhile, were seeking to put him to death, 48but they could find no way to accomplish their purpose because all the people were hanging on his words.

Saturday November 25, 2023

Saturday of Thirty-third Week Ordinary Time

First Reading – 1 Maccabees 6:1-13

1As King Antiochus was traversing the inland provinces, he
heard that in Persia there was a city called Elymais, famous
for its wealth in silver and gold, 2and that its temple was very
rich, containing gold helmets, breastplates, and weapons left
there by Alexander, son of Philip, king of Macedon, the first
king of the Greeks.3He went therefore and tried to capture and
pillage the city. But he could not do so, because his plan
became known to the people of the city 4who rose up in battle
against him. So he retreated and in great dismay withdrew
from there to return to Babylon. 5While he was in Persia, a
messenger brought him news that the armies sent into the
land of Judah had been put to flight; 6that Lysias had gone at
first with a strong army and been driven back by the children
of Israel; that they had grown strong by reason of the arms,
men, and abundant possessions taken from the armies they
had destroyed; 7that they had pulled down the Abomination
which he had built upon the altar in Jerusalem; and that they
had surrounded with high walls both the sanctuary, as it had
been before, and his city of Beth-zur. 8When the king heard
this news, he was struck with fear and very much shaken. Sick
with grief because his designs had failed, he took to his bed.
9There he remained many days, overwhelmed with sorrow, for
he knew he was going to die.10So he called in all his Friends
and said to them: "Sleep has departed from my eyes, for my
heart is sinking with anxiety.11I said to myself: 'Into what
tribulation have I come, and in what floods of sorrow am I now!
Yet I was kindly and beloved in my rule.' 12But I now recall the
evils I did in Jerusalem, when I carried away all the vessels of
gold and silver that were in it, and for no cause gave orders
that the inhabitants of Judah be destroyed.13I know that this is
why these evils have overtaken me; and now I am dying, in
bitter grief, in a foreign land."

Responsorial Psalm – Psalms 9:2-3, 4 AND 6, 16 AND 19

R. (see 16a) **I will rejoice in your salvation, O Lord.**

2 I will give thanks to you, O LORD, with all my heart;

I will declare all your wondrous deeds.

3 I will be glad and exult in you;

I will sing praise to your name, Most High.

R. I will rejoice in your salvation, O Lord.

4 Because my enemies are turned back,

overthrown and destroyed before you.

6 You rebuked the nations and destroyed the wicked;

their name you blotted out forever and ever.

R. I will rejoice in your salvation, O Lord.

16 The nations are sunk in the pit they have made;

in the snare they set, their foot is caught.

19 For the needy shall not always be forgotten,

nor shall the hope of the afflicted forever perish.

R. I will rejoice in your salvation, O Lord.

Alleluia – 2 Timothy 1:10

R. Alleluia, alleluia.

10 Our Savior Jesus Christ has destroyed death and brought life to light through the Gospel.

R. Alleluia, alleluia.

Gospel – Luke 20:27-40

27Some Sadducees, those who deny that there is a
resurrection, came forward and put this question to Jesus,
28saying, "Teacher, Moses wrote for us, If someone's brother
dies leaving a wife but no child, his brother must take the wife
and raise up descendants for his brother. 29Now there were
seven brothers; the first married a woman but died
childless.30Then the second 31and the third married her, and
likewise all the seven died childless.32Finally the woman also
died.33Now at the resurrection whose wife will that woman be?
For all seven had been married to her." 34Jesus said to them,

"The children of this age marry and remarry; [35]but those who are deemed worthy to attain to the coming age and to the resurrection of the dead neither marry nor are given in marriage. [36]They can no longer die, for they are like angels; and they are the children of God because they are the ones who will rise.[37]That the dead will rise even Moses made known in the passage about the bush, when he called 'Lord' the God of Abraham, the God of Isaac, and the God of Jacob;[38]and he is not God of the dead, but of the living, for to him all are alive." [39]Some of the scribes said in reply, "Teacher, you have answered well." [40]And they no longer dared to ask him anything.

Sunday November 26, 2023

Feast of Christ the Universal King, Year A

First Reading – Ezekiel 34:11-12, 15-17

[11]Thus says the Lord GOD: I myself will look after and tend my sheep.[12]As a shepherd tends his flock when he finds himself among his scattered sheep, so will I tend my sheep. I will rescue them from every place where they were scattered when it was cloudy and dark. [15]I myself will pasture my sheep; I myself will give them rest, says the Lord GOD.[16]The lost I will seek out, the strayed I will bring back, the injured I will bind up, the sick I will heal, but the sleek and the strong I will destroy, shepherding them rightly.[17]As for you, my sheep, says the Lord GOD, I will judge between one sheep and another, between rams and goats.

Responsorial Psalm – Psalms 23:1-2, 2-3, 5-6

R. (1) The Lord is my shepherd; there is nothing I shall want.

[1] The LORD is my shepherd; I shall not want.

[2AB] In verdant pastures he gives me repose.

R. The Lord is my shepherd; there is nothing I shall want.

[2C] Beside restful waters he leads me;

[3] he refreshes my soul.

He guides me in right paths

for his name's sake.

R. The Lord is my shepherd; there is nothing I shall want.

[5] You spread the table before me

in the sight of my foes;

you anoint my head with oil;

my cup overflows.

R. The Lord is my shepherd; there is nothing I shall want.

[6] Only goodness and kindness follow me

all the days of my life;

and I shall dwell in the house of the LORD

for years to come.

R. The Lord is my shepherd; there is nothing I shall want.

Second Reading – 1 Corinthians 15:20-26, 28

Brothers and sisters: [20]Christ has been raised from the dead,
the firstfruits of those who have fallen asleep. [21]For since
death came through man, the resurrection of the dead came
also through man. [22]For just as in Adam all die, so too in Christ
shall all be brought to life, [23]but each one in proper order:
Christ the first fruits; then, at his coming, those who belong to
Christ; [24]then comes the end, when he hands over the
kingdom to his God and Father, when he has destroyed every
sovereignty and every authority and power.[25]For he must reign
until he has put all his enemies under his feet.[26]The last
enemy to be destroyed is death.[28]When everything is
subjected to him, then the Son himself will also be subjected
to the one who subjected everything to him, so that God may
be all in all.

Alleluia – Mark 11:9, 10

R. Alleluia, alleluia.

[9] Blessed is he who comes in the name of the Lord! [10] Blessed
is the kingdom of our father David that is to come!

R. Alleluia, alleluia.

Gospel – Matthew 25:31-46

Jesus said to his disciples: [31]“When the Son of Man comes in
his glory, and all the angels with him, he will sit upon his
glorious throne,[32]and all the nations will be assembled before
him. And he will separate them one from another, as a
shepherd separates the sheep from the goats.[33]He will place
the sheep on his right and the goats on his left.[34]Then the king
will say to those on his right, ‘Come, you who are blessed by
my Father. Inherit the kingdom prepared for you from the
foundation of the world. [35]For I was hungry and you gave me
food, I was thirsty and you gave me drink, a stranger and you
welcomed me, [36]naked and you clothed me, ill and you cared
for me, in prison and you visited me.’ [37]Then the righteous will
answer him and say, ‘Lord, when did we see you hungry and
feed you, or thirsty and give you drink? [38]When did we see you
a stranger and welcome you, or naked and clothe you?
[39]When did we see you ill or in prison, and visit you?’ [40]And
the king will say to them in reply, ‘Amen, I say to you,
whatever you did for one of the least brothers of mine, you did
for me.’ [41]Then he will say to those on his left, ‘Depart from
me, you accursed, into the eternal fire prepared for the devil
and his angels. [42]For I was hungry and you gave me no food, I
was thirsty and you gave me no drink, [43]a stranger and you
gave me no welcome, naked and you gave me no clothing, ill
and in prison, and you did not care for me.’ [44]Then they will
answer and say, ‘Lord, when did we see you hungry or thirsty
or a stranger or naked or ill or in prison, and not minister to
your needs?’ [45]He will answer them, ‘Amen, I say to you, what
you did not do for one of these least ones, you did not do for
me.’ [46]And these will go off to eternal punishment, but the
righteous to eternal life.”

Monday November 27, 2023

Monday of Thirty-fourth Week Ordinary Time

First Reading – Daniel 1:1-6, 8-20

[1]In the third year of the reign of Jehoiakim, king of Judah, King
Nebuchadnezzar of Babylon came and laid siege to
Jerusalem. [2]The Lord handed over to him Jehoiakim, king of
Judah, and some of the vessels of the temple of God; he
carried them off to the land of Shinar, and placed the vessels
in the temple treasury of his god. [3]The king told Ashpenaz, his
chief chamberlain, to bring in some of the children of Israel of

royal blood and of the nobility, [4]young men without any defect, handsome, intelligent and wise, quick to learn, and prudent in judgment, such as could take their place in the king's palace; they were to be taught the language and literature of the Chaldeans; after three years' training they were to enter the king's service. [5]The king allotted them a daily portion of food and wine from the royal table.[6]Among these were men of Judah: Daniel, Hananiah, Mishael, and Azariah. [8]But Daniel was resolved not to defile himself with the king's food or wine; so he begged the chief chamberlain to spare him this defilement. [9]Though God had given Daniel the favor and sympathy of the chief chamberlain, [10]he nevertheless said to Daniel, "I am afraid of my lord the king; it is he who allotted your food and drink. If he sees that you look wretched by comparison with the other young men of your age, you will endanger my life with the king." [11]Then Daniel said to the steward whom the chief chamberlain had put in charge of Daniel, Hananiah, Mishael, and Azariah, [12]"Please test your servants for ten days. Give us vegetables to eat and water to drink.[13]Then see how we look in comparison with the other young men who eat from the royal table, and treat your servants according to what you see." [14]He acceded to this request, and tested them for ten days;[15]after ten days they looked healthier and better fed than any of the young men who ate from the royal table.[16]So the steward continued to take away the food and wine they were to receive, and gave them vegetables.[17]To these four young men God gave knowledge and proficiency in all literature and science, and to Daniel the understanding of all visions and dreams.[18]At the end of the time the king had specified for their preparation, the chief chamberlain brought them before Nebuchadnezzar.[19]When the king had spoken with all of them, none was found equal to Daniel, Hananiah, Mishael, and Azariah; and so they entered the king's service.[20]In any question of wisdom or prudence which the king put to them, he found them ten times better than all the magicians and enchanters in his kingdom.

Responsorial Psalm – Daniel 3:52, 53, 54, 55, 56

R. (52b) Glory and praise for ever!

[52] "Blessed are you, O Lord, the God of our fathers,

praiseworthy and exalted above all forever;

And blessed is your holy and glorious name,

praiseworthy and exalted above all for all ages."

R. Glory and praise for ever!

53 "Blessed are you in the temple of your holy glory,

praiseworthy and glorious above all forever."

R. Glory and praise for ever!

54 "Blessed are you on the throne of your Kingdom,

praiseworthy and exalted above all forever."

R. Glory and praise for ever!

55 "Blessed are you who look into the depths

from your throne upon the cherubim,

praiseworthy and exalted above all forever."

R. Glory and praise for ever!

56 "Blessed are you in the firmament of heaven,

praiseworthy and glorious forever."

R. Glory and praise for ever!

Alleluia – Matthew 24:42A, 44

R. Alleluia, alleluia.

42A Stay awake! 44 For you do not know when the Son of Man will come.

R. Alleluia, alleluia.

Gospel – Luke 21:1-4

1When Jesus looked up he saw some wealthy people putting their offerings into the treasury 2and he noticed a poor widow putting in two small coins. 3He said, "I tell you truly, this poor widow put in more than all the rest; 4for those others have all made offerings from their surplus wealth, but she, from her poverty, has offered her whole livelihood."

Tuesday November 28, 2023

Tuesday of Thirty-fourth Week in Ordinary Time

First Reading – Daniel 2:31-45

Daniel said to Nebuchadnezzar: 31“In your vision, O king, you
saw a statue, very large and exceedingly bright, terrifying in
appearance as it stood before you. 32The head of the statue
was pure gold, its chest and arms were silver, its belly and
thighs bronze, 33the legs iron, its feet partly iron and partly tile.
34While you looked at the statue, a stone which was hewn
from a mountain without a hand being put to it, struck its iron
and tile feet, breaking them in pieces.35The iron, tile, bronze,
silver, and gold all crumbled at once, fine as the chaff on the
threshing floor in summer, and the wind blew them away
without leaving a trace. But the stone that struck the statue
became a great mountain and filled the whole earth. 36“This
was the dream; the interpretation we shall also give in the
king’s presence. 37You, O king, are the king of kings; to you
the God of heaven has given dominion and strength, power
and glory; 38men, wild beasts, and birds of the air, wherever
they may dwell, he has handed over to you, making you ruler
over them all; you are the head of gold. 39Another kingdom
shall take your place, inferior to yours, then a third kingdom, of
bronze, which shall rule over the whole earth. 40There shall be
a fourth kingdom, strong as iron; it shall break in pieces and
subdue all these others, just as iron breaks in pieces and
crushes everything else.41The feet and toes you saw, partly of
potter’s tile and partly of iron, mean that it shall be a divided
kingdom, but yet have some of the hardness of iron. As you
saw the iron mixed with clay tile,42and the toes partly iron and
partly tile, the kingdom shall be partly strong and partly
fragile.43The iron mixed with clay tile means that they shall
seal their alliances by intermarriage, but they shall not stay
united, any more than iron mixes with clay.44In the lifetime of
those kings the God of heaven will set up a kingdom that shall
never be destroyed or delivered up to another people; rather,
it shall break in pieces all these kingdoms and put an end to
them, and it shall stand forever. 45That is the meaning of the
stone you saw hewn from the mountain without a hand being
put to it, which broke in pieces the tile, iron, bronze, silver, and
gold. The great God has revealed to the king what shall be in
the future; this is exactly what you dreamed, and its meaning
is sure.”

Responsorial Psalm – Daniel 3:57, 58, 59, 60, 61

R. (59b) Give glory and eternal praise to him.

57 “Bless the Lord, all you works of the Lord,

praise and exalt him above all forever.”

R. Give glory and eternal praise to him.

58 “Angels of the Lord, bless the Lord,

praise and exalt him above all forever.”

R. Give glory and eternal praise to him.

59 “You heavens, bless the Lord,

praise and exalt him above all forever.”

R. Give glory and eternal praise to him.

60 “All you waters above the heavens, bless the Lord,

praise and exalt him above all forever.”

R. Give glory and eternal praise to him.

61 “All you hosts of the Lord, bless the Lord;

praise and exalt him above all forever.”

R. Give glory and eternal praise to him.

Alleluia – Revelation 2:10C

R. Alleluia, alleluia.

10C Remain faithful until death, and I will give you the crown of life.

R. Alleluia, alleluia.

Gospel – Luke 21:5-11

5While some people were speaking about how the temple was
adorned with costly stones and votive offerings, Jesus
said,6“All that you see here – the days will come when there
will not be left a stone upon another stone that will not be
thrown down.” 7Then they asked him, “Teacher, when will this
happen? And what sign will there be when all these things are
about to happen?” 8He answered, “See that you not be
deceived, for many will come in my name, saying, ‘I am he,’
and ‘The time has come.’ Do not follow them! 9When you hear
of wars and insurrections, do not be terrified; for such things

must happen first, but it will not immediately be the end." [10]Then he said to them, "Nation will rise against nation, and kingdom against kingdom.[11]There will be powerful earthquakes, famines, and plagues from place to place; and awesome sights and mighty signs will come from the sky."

Wednesday November 29, 2023

Wednesday of Thirty-fourth Week in Ordinary Time

First Reading – Daniel 5:1-6, 13-14, 16-17, 23-28

[1]King Belshazzar gave a great banquet for a thousand of his lords, with whom he drank.[2]Under the influence of the wine, he ordered the gold and silver vessels which Nebuchadnezzar, his father, had taken from the temple in Jerusalem, to be brought in so that the king, his lords, his wives and his entertainers might drink from them.[3]When the gold and silver vessels taken from the house of God in Jerusalem had been brought in, and while the king, his lords, his wives and his entertainers were drinking [4]wine from them, they praised their gods of gold and silver, bronze and iron, wood and stone. [5]Suddenly, opposite the lampstand, the fingers of a human hand appeared, writing on the plaster of the wall in the king's palace. When the king saw the wrist and hand that wrote, [6]his face blanched; his thoughts terrified him, his hip joints shook, and his knees knocked.[13]Then Daniel was brought into the presence of the king. The king asked him, "Are you the Daniel, the Jewish exile, whom my father, the king, brought from Judah? [14]I have heard that the Spirit of God is in you, that you possess brilliant knowledge and extraordinary wisdom. [16]I have heard that you can interpret dreams and solve difficulties; if you are able to read the writing and tell me what it means, you shall be clothed in purple, wear a gold collar about your neck, and be third in the government of the kingdom." [17]Daniel answered the king: "You may keep your gifts, or give your presents to someone else; but the writing I will read for you, O king, and tell you what it means.[23]You have rebelled against the Lord of heaven. You had the vessels of his temple brought before you, so that you and your nobles, your wives and your entertainers, might drink wine from them; and you praised the gods of silver and gold, bronze and iron, wood and stone, that neither see nor hear nor have intelligence. But the God in whose hand is your life breath and

the whole course of your life, you did not glorify. [24]By him were the wrist and hand sent, and the writing set down. [25]"This is the writing that was inscribed: **MENE**, **TEKEL**, and **PERES**. These words mean: [26]MENE, God has numbered your kingdom and put an end to it; [27]TEKEL, you have been weighed on the scales and found wanting; [28]PERES, your kingdom has been divided and given to the Medes and Persians."

Responsorial Psalm – Daniel 3:62, 63, 64, 65, 66, 67

R. (59b) **Give glory and eternal praise to him.**

62 "Sun and moon, bless the Lord;

praise and exalt him above all forever."

R. Give glory and eternal praise to him.

63 "Stars of heaven, bless the Lord;

praise and exalt him above all forever."

R. Give glory and eternal praise to him.

64 "Every shower and dew, bless the Lord;

praise and exalt him above all forever."

R. Give glory and eternal praise to him.

65 "All you winds, bless the Lord;

praise and exalt him above all forever."

R. Give glory and eternal praise to him.

66 "Fire and heat, bless the Lord;

praise and exalt him above all forever."

R. Give glory and eternal praise to him.

67 "Cold and chill, bless the Lord;

praise and exalt him above all forever."

R. Give glory and eternal praise to him.

Alleluia – Revelation 2:10C

R. Alleluia, alleluia.

[10C] Remain faithful until death, and I will give you the crown of life.

R. Alleluia, alleluia.

Gospel – Luke 21:12-19

Jesus said to the crowd: [12]"They will seize and persecute you, they will hand you over to the synagogues and to prisons, and they will have you led before kings and governors because of my name. [13]It will lead to your giving testimony.[14]Remember, you are not to prepare your defense beforehand,[15]for I myself shall give you a wisdom in speaking that all your adversaries will be powerless to resist or refute.[16]You will even be handed over by parents, brothers, relatives, and friends, and they will put some of you to death.[17]You will be hated by all because of my name,[18]but not a hair on your head will be destroyed.[19]By your perseverance you will secure your lives."

Thursday November 30, 2023

Feast of Saint Andrew - Apostle

First Reading – Romans 10:9-18

Brothers and sisters:[9]If you confess with your mouth that Jesus is Lord and believe in your heart that God raised him from the dead, you will be saved. [10]For one believes with the heart and so is justified, and one confesses with the mouth and so is saved.[11]The Scripture says, No one who believes in him will be put to shame.[12]There is no distinction between Jew and Greek; the same Lord is Lord of all, enriching all who call upon him.[13]For everyone who calls on the name of the Lord will be saved.[14]But how can they call on him in whom they have not believed? And how can they believe in him of whom they have not heard? And how can they hear without someone to preach? [15]And how can people preach unless they are sent? As it is written, How beautiful are the feet of those who bring the good news! [16]But not everyone has heeded the good news; for Isaiah says, Lord, who has believed what was heard from us? [17]Thus faith comes from what is heard, and what is heard comes through the word of Christ. [18]But I ask, did they not hear? Certainly they did; for

Their voice has gone forth to all the earth, and their words to the ends of the world.

Responsorial Psalm – Psalms 19:8, 9, 10, 11

R. (10) The judgments of the Lord are true, and all of them are just. or: **R. (John 6:63) Your words, Lord, are Spirit and life.**

8 The law of the LORD is perfect,

refreshing the soul;

The decree of the LORD is trustworthy,

giving wisdom to the simple.

R. The judgments of the Lord are true, and all of them are just. or: **R. Your words, Lord, are Spirit and life.**

9 The precepts of the LORD are right,

rejoicing the heart;

The command of the LORD is clear,

enlightening the eye.

R. The judgments of the Lord are true, and all of them are just. or: **R. Your words, Lord, are Spirit and life.**

10 The fear of the LORD is pure,

enduring forever;

The ordinances of the LORD are true,

all of them just.

R. The judgments of the Lord are true, and all of them are just. or: **R. Your words, Lord, are Spirit and life.**

11 They are more precious than gold,

than a heap of purest gold;

Sweeter also than syrup

or honey from the comb.

R. The judgments of the Lord are true, and all of them are just. or: **R. Your words, Lord, are Spirit and life.**

Alleluia – Matthew 4:19

R. Alleluia, alleluia.

19 Come after me, says the Lord, and I will make you fishers of men.

R. Alleluia, alleluia.

Gospel – Matthew 4:18-22

18 As Jesus was walking by the Sea of Galilee, he saw two
brothers, Simon who is called Peter, and his brother Andrew,
casting a net into the sea; they were fishermen. 19 He said to
them, "Come after me, and I will make you fishers of men."
20 At once they left their nets and followed him. 21 He walked
along from there and saw two other brothers, James, the son
of Zebedee, and his brother John. They were in a boat, with
their father Zebedee, mending their nets. He called them,
22 and immediately they left their boat and their father and
followed him.

DECEMBER 2023

Friday December 1, 2023

Friday of Thirty-fourth Week Ordinary Time

First Reading – Daniel 7:2-14

2 In a vision I, Daniel, saw during the night, the four winds of
heaven stirred up the great sea, 3 from which emerged four
immense beasts, each different from the others. 4 The first was
like a lion, but with eagle's wings. While I watched, the wings
were plucked; it was raised from the ground to stand on two
feet like a man, and given a human mind. 5 The second was like
a bear; it was raised up on one side, and among the teeth in
its mouth were three tusks. It was given the order, "Up, devour
much flesh." 6 After this I looked and saw another beast, like a
leopard; on its back were four wings like those of a bird, and it
had four heads. To this beast dominion was given. 7 After this,
in the visions of the night I saw the fourth beast, different from
all the others, terrifying, horrible, and of extraordinary strength;
it had great iron teeth with which it devoured and crushed, and
what was left it trampled with its feet. 8 I was considering the ten
horns it had, when suddenly another, a little horn, sprang out
of their midst, and three of the previous horns were torn away
to make room for it. This horn had eyes like a man, and a

mouth that spoke arrogantly.[9]As I watched, Thrones were set up and the Ancient One took his throne. His clothing was snow bright, and the hair on his head as white as wool; His throne was flames of fire, with wheels of burning fire. [10]A surging stream of fire flowed out from where he sat; Thousands upon thousands were ministering to him, and myriads upon myriads attended him. The court was convened, and the books were opened.[11]I watched, then, from the first of the arrogant words which the horn spoke, until the beast was slain and its body thrown into the fire to be burnt up.[12]The other beasts, which also lost their dominion, were granted a prolongation of life for a time and a season.[13]As the visions during the night continued, I saw One like a son of man coming, on the clouds of heaven; When he reached the Ancient One and was presented before him,[14]He received dominion, glory, and kingship; nations and peoples of every language serve him. His dominion is an everlasting dominion that shall not be taken away, his kingship shall not be destroyed.

Responsorial Psalm – Daniel 3:75, 76, 77, 78, 79, 80, 81

R. Give glory and eternal praise to him!

75 “Mountains and hills, bless the Lord;

praise and exalt him above all forever.”

R. Give glory and eternal praise to him!

76 “Everything growing from the earth, bless the Lord;

praise and exalt him above all forever.

R. Give glory and eternal praise to him!”

77 “You springs, bless the Lord;

praise and exalt him above all forever.”

R. Give glory and eternal praise to him!

78 “Seas and rivers, bless the Lord;

praise and exalt him above all forever.”

R. Give glory and eternal praise to him!

79 “You dolphins and all water creatures, bless the Lord;

praise and exalt him above all forever.”

R. Give glory and eternal praise to him!

80 "All you birds of the air, bless the Lord;

praise and exalt him above all forever."

R. Give glory and eternal praise to him!

81 "All you beasts, wild and tame, bless the Lord;

praise and exalt him above all forever."

R. Give glory and eternal praise to him!

Alleluia – Luke 21:28

R. Alleluia, alleluia.

28 Stand erect and raise your heads because your redemption is at hand.

R. Alleluia, alleluia.

Gospel – Luke 21:29-33

29Jesus told his disciples a parable. "Consider the fig tree and
all the other trees.
30When their buds burst open, you see for
yourselves and know that summer is now near;
31in the same
way, when you see these things happening, know that the
Kingdom of God is near.
32Amen, I say to you, this generation
will not pass away until all these things have taken place.
33Heaven and earth will pass away, but my words will not pass
away."

Saturday December 2, 2023

Saturday of Thirty-fourth Week in Ordinary Time

First Reading – Daniel 7:15-27

15I, Daniel, found my spirit anguished within its covering of
flesh, and I was terrified by the visions of my mind.
16I
approached one of those present and asked him what all this
meant in truth; in answer, he made known to me the meaning
of the things:
17"These four great beasts stand for four
kingdoms which shall arise on the earth.
18But the holy ones of
the Most High shall receive the kingship, to possess it forever
and ever."
19But I wished to make certain about the fourth
beast, so very terrible and different from the others, devouring
and crushing with its iron teeth and bronze claws, and

trampling with its feet what was left; [20]about the ten horns on
its head, and the other one that sprang up, before which three
horns fell; about the horn with the eyes and the mouth that
spoke arrogantly, which appeared greater than its fellows.
[21]For, as I watched, that horn made war against the holy ones
and was victorious [22]until the Ancient One arrived; judgment
was pronounced in favor of the holy ones of the Most High,
and the time came when the holy ones possessed the
kingdom.[23]He answered me thus: "The fourth beast shall be a
fourth kingdom on earth different from all the others; It shall
devour the whole earth, beat it down, and crush it.[24]The ten
horns shall be ten kings rising out of that kingdom; another
shall rise up after them, Different from those before him, who
shall lay low three kings.[25]He shall speak against the Most
High and oppress the holy ones of the Most High, thinking to
change the feast days and the law. They shall be handed over
to him for a year, two years, and a half-year.[26]But when the
court is convened, and his power is taken away by final and
absolute destruction, [27]Then the kingship and dominion and
majesty of all the kingdoms under the heavens shall be given
to the holy people of the Most High, Whose Kingdom shall be
everlasting: all dominions shall serve and obey him."

Responsorial Psalm – Daniel 3:82, 83, 84, 85, 86, 87

R. Give glory and eternal praise to him.

[82] "You sons of men, bless the Lord;

praise and exalt him above all forever."

R. Give glory and eternal praise to him.

[83] "O Israel, bless the Lord;

praise and exalt him above all forever."

R. Give glory and eternal praise to him.

[84] "Priests of the Lord, bless the Lord;

praise and exalt him above all forever."

R. Give glory and eternal praise to him.

[85] "Servants of the Lord, bless the Lord;

praise and exalt him above all forever."

R. Give glory and eternal praise to him.

[86] "Spirits and souls of the just, bless the Lord;

praise and exalt him above all forever."

R. Give glory and eternal praise to him.

[87] "Holy men of humble heart, bless the Lord;

praise and exalt him above all forever."

R. Give glory and eternal praise to him.

Alleluia – Luke 21:36

R. Alleluia, alleluia.

[36] Be vigilant at all times and pray, That you may have the strength to stand before the Son of Man.

R. Alleluia, alleluia.

Gospel – Luke 21:34-36

[34]Jesus said to his disciples: "Beware that your hearts do not become drowsy from carousing and drunkenness and the anxieties of daily life, and that day catch you by surprise [35] like
a trap. For that day will assault everyone who lives on the face of the earth. [36]Be vigilant at all times and pray that you have the strength to escape the tribulations that are imminent and to stand before the Son of Man."

Sunday December 3, 2023

First Sunday of Advent, Year B

First Reading – Isaiah 63:16B-17, 19B; 64:2-7

[16B]You, LORD, are our father, our redeemer you are named
forever. [17]Why do you let us wander, O LORD, from your ways, and harden our hearts so that we fear you not? Return for the sake of your servants, the tribes of your heritage.[19B]Oh, that you would rend the heavens and come down, with the
mountains quaking before you,[2]while you wrought awesome
deeds we could not hope for, [3]such as they had not heard of from of old. No ear has ever heard, no eye ever seen, any God but you doing such deeds for those who wait for
him.[4]Would that you might meet us doing right, that we were mindful of you in our ways! Behold, you are angry, and we are

sinful; 5all of us have become like unclean people, all our good
deeds are like polluted rags; we have all withered like leaves,
and our guilt carries us away like the wind. 6There is none who
calls upon your name, who rouses himself to cling to you; for
you have hidden your face from us and have delivered us up
to our guilt. 7Yet, O LORD, you are our father; we are the clay
and you the potter: we are all the work of your hands.

Responsorial Psalm – Psalms 80:2-3, 15-16, 18-19

R. (4) Lord, make us turn to you; let us see your face and we shall be saved.

2 O shepherd of Israel, hearken,

from your throne upon the cherubim, shine forth.

3 Rouse your power,

and come to save us.

R. Lord, make us turn to you; let us see your face and we shall be saved.

15 Once again, O LORD of hosts,

look down from heaven, and see;

take care of this vine,

16 and protect what your right hand has planted

the son of man whom you yourself made strong.

R. Lord, make us turn to you; let us see your face and we shall be saved.

18 May your help be with the man of your right hand,

with the son of man whom you yourself made strong.

19 Then we will no more withdraw from you;

give us new life, and we will call upon your name.

R. Lord, make us turn to you; let us see your face and we shall be saved.

Second Reading – 1 Corinthians 1:3-9

Brothers and sisters: 3Grace to you and peace from God our
Father and the Lord Jesus Christ. 4I give thanks to my God
always on your account for the grace of God bestowed on you

in Christ Jesus, [5]that in him you were enriched in every way, with all discourse and all knowledge, [6]as the testimony to Christ was confirmed among you, [7]so that you are not lacking in any spiritual gift as you wait for the revelation of our Lord Jesus Christ. [8]He will keep you firm to the end, irreproachable on the day of our Lord Jesus Christ. [9]God is faithful, and by him you were called to fellowship with his Son, Jesus Christ our Lord.

Alleluia – Psalms 85:8

R. Alleluia, alleluia.

[8] Show us Lord, your love; and grant us your salvation.

R. Alleluia, alleluia.

Gospel – Mark 13:33-37

Jesus said to his disciples: [33]"Be watchful! Be alert! You do not know when the time will come.[34]It is like a man traveling abroad. He leaves home and places his servants in charge, each with his own work, and orders the gatekeeper to be on the watch.[35]Watch, therefore; you do not know when the Lord of the house is coming, whether in the evening, or at midnight, or at cockcrow, or in the morning. [36]May he not come suddenly and find you sleeping. [37]What I say to you, I say to all: 'Watch!'"

Monday December 4, 2023

Monday of the First Week of Advent

First Reading – Isaiah 2:1-5

[1]This is what Isaiah, son of Amoz, saw concerning Judah and Jerusalem. [2]In days to come, The mountain of the LORD's house shall be established as the highest mountain and raised above the hills. All nations shall stream toward it; [3]many peoples shall come and say: "Come, let us climb the LORD's mountain, to the house of the God of Jacob, That he may instruct us in his ways, and we may walk in his paths." For from Zion shall go forth instruction, and the word of the LORD from Jerusalem. [4]He shall judge between the nations, and impose terms on many peoples. They shall beat their swords into plowshares and their spears into pruning hooks; One nation shall not raise the sword against another, nor shall they

train for war again.[5]O house of Jacob, come, let us walk in the light of the LORD!

Responsorial Psalm – Psalms 122:1-2, 3-4B, 4CD-5, 6-7, 8-9

R. Let us go rejoicing to the house of the Lord.

1 I rejoiced because they said to me,

"We will go up to the house of the LORD."

2 And now we have set foot

within your gates, O Jerusalem.

R. Let us go rejoicing to the house of the Lord.

3 Jerusalem, built as a city

with compact unity.

4AB To it the tribes go up,

the tribes of the LORD.

R. Let us go rejoicing to the house of the Lord.

4CD According to the decree for Israel,

to give thanks to the name of the LORD.

5 In it are set up judgment seats,

seats for the house of David.

R. Let us go rejoicing to the house of the Lord.

6 Pray for the peace of Jerusalem!

May those who love you prosper!

7 May peace be within your walls,

prosperity in your buildings.

R. Let us go rejoicing to the house of the Lord.

8 Because of my relatives and friends

I will say, "Peace be within you!"

9 Because of the house of the LORD, our God,

I will pray for your good.

R. Let us go rejoicing to the house of the Lord.

Alleluia – cf. Psalms 80:4

R. Alleluia, alleluia.

4 Come and save us, LORD our God; let your face shine upon us, that we may be saved.

R. Alleluia, alleluia.

Gospel – Matthew 8:5-11

5When Jesus entered Capernaum, a centurion approached
him and appealed to him, 6saying, "Lord, my servant is lying at
home paralyzed, suffering dreadfully." 7He said to him, "I will
come and cure him." 8The centurion said in reply, "Lord, I am
not worthy to have you enter under my roof; only say the word
and my servant will be healed. 9For I too am a man subject to
authority, with soldiers subject to me. And I say to one, 'Go,'
and he goes; and to another, 'Come here,' and he comes; and
to my slave, 'Do this,' and he does it." 10When Jesus heard
this, he was amazed and said to those following him, "Amen, I
say to you, in no one in Israel have I found such faith. 11I say
to you, many will come from the east and the west, and will
recline with Abraham, Isaac, and Jacob at the banquet in the
Kingdom of heaven."

Tuesday December 5, 2023

Tuesday of the First Week of Advent

First Reading – Isaiah 11:1-10

1On that day, A shoot shall sprout from the stump of Jesse,
and from his roots a bud shall blossom.2The Spirit of the
LORD shall rest upon him: a Spirit of wisdom and of
understanding, A Spirit of counsel and of strength, a Spirit of
knowledge and of fear of the LORD,3and his delight shall be
the fear of the LORD. Not by appearance shall he judge, nor
by hearsay shall he decide,4But he shall judge the poor with
justice, and decide aright for the land's afflicted. He shall strike
the ruthless with the rod of his mouth, and with the breath of
his lips he shall slay the wicked.5Justice shall be the band

around his waist, and faithfulness a belt upon his hips. 6 Then
the wolf shall be a guest of the lamb, and the leopard shall lie
down with the kid; The calf and the young lion shall browse
together, with a little child to guide them. 7 The cow and the
bear shall be neighbors, together their young shall rest; the
lion shall eat hay like the ox. 8 The baby shall play by the
cobra's den, and the child lay his hand on the adder's
lair. 9 There shall be no harm or ruin on all my holy mountain;
for the earth shall be filled with knowledge of the LORD, as
water covers the sea. 10 On that day, The root of Jesse, set up
as a signal for the nations, The Gentiles shall seek out, for his
dwelling shall be glorious.

Responsorial Psalm – Psalms 72:1-2, 7-8, 12-13, 17

R. (see 7) **Justice shall flourish in his time, and fullness of peace for ever.**

1 O God, with your judgment endow the king,

and with your justice, the king's son;

2 He shall govern your people with justice

and your afflicted ones with judgment.

R. Justice shall flourish in his time, and fullness of peace for ever.

7 Justice shall flower in his days,

and profound peace, till the moon be no more.

8 May he rule from sea to sea,

and from the River to the ends of the earth.

R. Justice shall flourish in his time, and fullness of peace for ever.

12 He shall rescue the poor when he cries out,

and the afflicted when he has no one to help him.

13 He shall have pity for the lowly and the poor;

the lives of the poor he shall save.

R. Justice shall flourish in his time, and fullness of peace for ever.

17 May his name be blessed forever;

as long as the sun his name shall remain.

In him shall all the tribes of the earth be blessed;

all the nations shall proclaim his happiness.

R. Justice shall flourish in his time, and fullness of peace for ever.

Alleluia

R. Alleluia, alleluia.

Behold, our Lord shall come with power; he will enlighten the eyes of his servants.

R. Alleluia, alleluia.

Gospel – Luke 10:21-24

21Jesus rejoiced in the Holy Spirit and said, "I give you praise, Father, Lord of heaven and earth, for although you have hidden these things from the wise and the learned you have revealed them to the childlike. Yes, Father, such has been your gracious will.
22All things have been handed over to me by my Father. No one knows who the Son is except the Father, and who the Father is except the Son and anyone to whom the Son wishes to reveal him."
23Turning to the disciples in private he said, "Blessed are the eyes that see what you see.
24For I say to you, many prophets and kings desired to see what you see, but did not see it, and to hear what you hear, but did not hear it."

Wednesday December 6, 2023

Wednesday of the First Week of Advent

First Reading – Isaiah 25:6-10A

6On this mountain the LORD of hosts will provide for all peoples A feast of rich food and choice wines, juicy, rich food and pure, choice wines.
7On this mountain he will destroy the veil that veils all peoples, The web that is woven over all nations;
8he will destroy death forever. The Lord GOD will wipe away the tears from all faces; The reproach of his people he will remove from the whole earth; for the LORD has spoken.
9On that day it will be said: "Behold our God, to whom we looked to save us! This is the LORD for whom we looked;

let us rejoice and be glad that he has saved us!" [10A]For the hand of the LORD will rest on this mountain.

Responsorial Psalm – Psalms 23:1-3A, 3B-4, 5, 6

R. (6cd) I shall live in the house of the Lord all the days of my life.

1 The LORD is my shepherd; I shall not want.

2 In verdant pastures he gives me repose;

Beside restful waters he leads me;

3A he refreshes my soul.

R. I shall live in the house of the Lord all the days of my life.

3B He guides me in right paths

for his name's sake.

4 Even though I walk in the dark valley

I fear no evil; for you are at my side

With your rod and your staff

that give me courage.

R. I shall live in the house of the Lord all the days of my life.

5 You spread the table before me

in the sight of my foes;

You anoint my head with oil;

my cup overflows.

R. I shall live in the house of the Lord all the days of my life.

6 Only goodness and kindness follow me

all the days of my life;

And I shall dwell in the house of the LORD

for years to come.

R. I shall live in the house of the Lord all the days of my life.

Alleluia

R. Alleluia, alleluia.

Behold, the Lord comes to save his people; blessed are those prepared to meet him.

R. Alleluia, alleluia.

Gospel – Matthew 15:29-37

At that time: [29]Jesus walked by the Sea of Galilee, went up on the mountain, and sat down there. [30]Great crowds came to him, having with them the lame, the blind, the deformed, the mute, and many others. They placed them at his feet, and he cured them. [31]The crowds were amazed when they saw the mute speaking, the deformed made whole, the lame walking, and the blind able to see, and they glorified the God of Israel. [32]Jesus summoned his disciples and said, "My heart is moved with pity for the crowd, for they have been with me now for three days and have nothing to eat. I do not want to send them away hungry, for fear they may collapse on the way." [33]The disciples said to him, "Where could we ever get enough bread in this deserted place to satisfy such a crowd?" [34]Jesus said to them, "How many loaves do you have?" "Seven," they replied, "and a few fish." [35]He ordered the crowd to sit down on the ground. [36]Then he took the seven loaves and the fish, gave thanks, broke the loaves, and gave them to the disciples, who in turn gave them to the crowds. [37]They all ate and were satisfied. They picked up the fragments left over seven baskets full.

Thursday December 7, 2023

Commemoration of Saint Ambrose – Bishop & Doctor

First Reading – Isaiah 26:1-6

[1]On that day they will sing this song in the land of Judah: "A strong city have we; he sets up walls and ramparts to protect us.[2]Open up the gates to let in a nation that is just, one that keeps faith.[3]A nation of firm purpose you keep in peace; in peace, for its trust in you." [4]Trust in the LORD forever! For the

LORD is an eternal Rock.[5]He humbles those in high places, and the lofty city he brings down; He tumbles it to the ground, levels it with the dust.[6]It is trampled underfoot by the needy, by the footsteps of the poor.

Responsorial Psalm – Psalms 118:1 and 8-9, 19-21, 25-27A

R. (26a) **Blessed is he who comes in the name of the Lord.** or: **R. Alleluia.**

1 Give thanks to the LORD, for he is good,

for his mercy endures forever.

8 It is better to take refuge in the LORD

than to trust in man.

9 It is better to take refuge in the LORD

than to trust in princes.

R. Blessed is he who comes in the name of the Lord. or: **R. Alleluia.**

19 Open to me the gates of justice;

I will enter them and give thanks to the LORD.

20 This gate is the LORD's;

the just shall enter it.

21 I will give thanks to you, for you have answered me

and have been my savior.

R. Blessed is he who comes in the name of the Lord. or: **R. Alleluia.**

25 O LORD, grant salvation!

O LORD, grant prosperity!

26 Blessed is he who comes in the name of the LORD;

we bless you from the house of the LORD.

27A The LORD is God, and he has given us light.

R. Blessed is he who comes in the name of the Lord. or: **R. Alleluia.**

Alleluia – Isaiah 55:6

R. Alleluia, alleluia.

6 Seek the LORD while he may be found; call him while he is near.

R. Alleluia, alleluia.

Gospel – Matthew 7:21, 24-27

Jesus said to his disciples: 21“Not everyone who says to me,
‘Lord, Lord,’ will enter the Kingdom of heaven, but only the
one who does the will of my Father in heaven. 24“Everyone
who listens to these words of mine and acts on them will be
like a wise man who built his house on rock. 25The rain fell, the
floods came, and the winds blew and buffeted the house. But
it did not collapse; it had been set solidly on rock. 26And
everyone who listens to these words of mine but does not act
on them will be like a fool who built his house on sand. 27The
rain fell, the floods came, and the winds blew and buffeted the
house. And it collapsed and was completely ruined.”

Friday December 8, 2023

Immaculate Conception of the Blessed Virgin Mary

First Reading – Genesis 3:9-15, 20

9After the man, Adam, had eaten of the tree, the LORD God
called to the man and asked him, “Where are you?” 10He
answered, “I heard you in the garden; but I was afraid,
because I was naked, so I hid myself.” 11Then he asked, “Who
told you that you were naked? You have eaten, then, from the
tree of which I had forbidden you to eat!” 12The man replied,
“The woman whom you put here with me she gave me fruit
from the tree, and so I ate it.” 13The LORD God then asked the
woman, “Why did you do such a thing?” The woman
answered, “The serpent tricked me into it, so I ate it.” 14Then
the LORD God said to the serpent: “Because you have done
this, you shall be banned from all the animals and from all the
wild creatures; on your belly shall you crawl, and dirt shall you

eat all the days of your life. [15]I will put enmity between you and the woman, and between your offspring and hers; he will strike at your head, while you strike at his heel." [20]The man called his wife Eve, because she became the mother of all the living.

Responsorial Psalm – Psalms 98:1, 2-3AB, 3CD-4

R. (1) Sing to the Lord a new song, for he has done marvelous deeds.

1 Sing to the LORD a new song,

for he has done wondrous deeds;

His right hand has won victory for him,

his holy arm.

R. Sing to the Lord a new song, for he has done marvelous deeds.

2 The LORD has made his salvation known:

in the sight of the nations he has revealed his justice.

3AB He has remembered his kindness and his faithfulness

toward the house of Israel.

R. Sing to the Lord a new song, for he has done marvelous deeds.

3CD All the ends of the earth have seen

the salvation by our God.

4 Sing joyfully to the LORD, all you lands;

break into song; sing praise.

R. Sing to the Lord a new song, for he has done marvelous deeds.

Second Reading – Ephesians 1:3-6, 11-12

Brothers and sisters: [3]Blessed be the God and Father of our Lord Jesus Christ, who has blessed us in Christ with every spiritual blessing in the heavens, [4]as he chose us in him, before the foundation of the world, to be holy and without blemish before him. In love [5]he destined us for adoption to himself through Jesus Christ, in accord with the favor of his will, [6]for the praise of the glory of his grace that he granted us in the beloved. [11]In him we were also chosen, destined in accord with the purpose of the One who accomplishes all things according to the intention of his will, [12]so that we might exist for the praise of his glory, we who first hoped in Christ.

Alleluia – cf. Luke 1:28

R. Alleluia, alleluia.

[28] Hail, Mary, full of grace, the Lord is with you; blessed are you among women.

R. Alleluia, alleluia.

Gospel – Luke 1:26-38

[26]The angel Gabriel was sent from God to a town of Galilee called Nazareth,[27]to a virgin betrothed to a man named Joseph, of the house of David, and the virgin's name was Mary. [28]And coming to her, he said, "Hail, full of grace! The Lord is with you." [29]But she was greatly troubled at what was said and pondered what sort of greeting this might be.[30]Then the angel said to her, "Do not be afraid, Mary, for you have found favor with God.[31]Behold, you will conceive in your womb and bear a son, and you shall name him Jesus.[32]He will be great and will be called Son of the Most High, and the Lord God will give him the throne of David his father, [33]and he will rule over the house of Jacob forever, and of his Kingdom there will be no end." [34]But Mary said to the angel, "How can this be, since I have no relations with a man?" [35]And the angel said to her in reply, "The Holy Spirit will come upon you, and the power of the Most High will overshadow you. Therefore the child to be born will be called holy, the Son of God. [36]And behold, Elizabeth, your relative, has also conceived a son in her old age, and this is the sixth month for her who was called barren; [37]for nothing will be impossible for God." [38]Mary said, "Behold, I am the handmaid of the Lord. May it be done to me according to your word." Then the angel departed from her.

Saturday December 9, 2023

Saturday of the First Week of Advent

First Reading – Isaiah 30:19-21, 23-26

Thus says the Lord GOD,[19]the Holy One of Israel: O people of Zion, who dwell in Jerusalem, no more will you weep; He will be gracious to you when you cry out, as soon as he hears he will answer you.[20]The Lord will give you the bread you need and the water for which you thirst. No longer will your Teacher hide himself, but with your own eyes you shall see your Teacher,[21]While from behind, a voice shall sound in your ears: "This is the way; walk in it," when you would turn to the right or to the left.[23]He will give rain for the seed that you sow in the ground, And the wheat that the soil produces will be rich and abundant. On that day your flock will be given pasture and the lamb will graze in spacious meadows; [24]The oxen and the asses that till the ground will eat silage tossed to them with shovel and pitchfork.[25]Upon every high mountain and lofty hill there will be streams of running water. On the day of the great slaughter, when the towers fall, [26]The light of the moon will be like that of the sun and the light of the sun will be seven times greater like the light of seven days. On the day the LORD binds up the wounds of his people, he will heal the bruises left by his blows.

Responsorial Psalm – Psalms 147:1-2, 3-4, 5-6

R. (See Isaiah 30:18d) **Blessed are all who wait for the Lord.**

[1] Praise the LORD, for he is good;

sing praise to our God, for he is gracious;

it is fitting to praise him.

[2] The LORD rebuilds Jerusalem;

the dispersed of Israel he gathers.

R. Blessed are all who wait for the Lord.

[3] He heals the brokenhearted

and binds up their wounds.

[4] He tells the number of the stars;

he calls each by name.

R. Blessed are all who wait for the Lord.

[5] Great is our LORD and mighty in power:

to his wisdom there is no limit.

[6] The LORD sustains the lowly;

the wicked he casts to the ground.

R. Blessed are all who wait for the Lord.

Alleluia – Isaiah 33:22

R. Alleluia, alleluia.

[22] The LORD is our Judge, our Lawgiver, our King; he it is who will save us.

R. Alleluia, alleluia.

Gospel – Matthew 9:35-10:1, 5A, 6-8

[35]Jesus went around to all the towns and villages, teaching in their synagogues, proclaiming the Gospel of the Kingdom, and
curing every disease and illness.[36]At the sight of the crowds, his heart was moved with pity for them because they were troubled and abandoned, like sheep without a
shepherd.[37]Then he said to his disciples, "The harvest is
abundant but the laborers are few; [38]so ask the master of the
harvest to send out laborers for his harvest." [1]Then he summoned his Twelve disciples and gave them authority over unclean spirits to drive them out and to cure every disease
and every illness.[5A]Jesus sent out these Twelve after
instructing them thus,[6]"Go to the lost sheep of the house of
Israel. [7]As you go, make this proclamation: 'The Kingdom of
heaven is at hand.' [8]Cure the sick, raise the dead, cleanse lepers, drive out demons. Without cost you have received; without cost you are to give."

Sunday December 10, 2023

Second Sunday of Advent, Year B

First Reading – Isaiah 40:1-5, 9-11

[1]Comfort, give comfort to my people, says your God. [2]Speak
tenderly to Jerusalem, and proclaim to her that her service is at an end, her guilt is expiated; indeed, she has received from
the hand of the LORD double for all her sins.[3]A voice cries
out: In the desert prepare the way of the LORD! Make straight
in the wasteland a highway for our God! [4]Every valley shall be
filled in, every mountain and hill shall be made low; the rugged land shall be made a plain, the rough country, a broad valley.

[5]Then the glory of the LORD shall be revealed, and all people
shall see it together; for the mouth of the LORD has
spoken.[9]Go up on to a high mountain, Zion, herald of glad
tidings; cry out at the top of your voice, Jerusalem, herald of
good news! Fear not to cry out and say to the cities of Judah:
Here is your God! [10]Here comes with power the Lord GOD,
who rules by his strong arm; here is his reward with him, his
recompense before him. [11]Like a shepherd he feeds his flock;
in his arms he gathers the lambs, carrying them in his bosom,
and leading the ewes with care.

Responsorial Psalm – Psalms 85:9-10, 11-12, 13-14

R. [(8)] Lord, let us see your kindness, and grant us your salvation.

[9] I will hear what God proclaims;

the LORD, for he proclaims peace to his people.

[10] Near indeed is his salvation to those who fear him,

glory dwelling in our land.

R. Lord, let us see your kindness, and grant us your salvation.

[11] Kindness and truth shall meet;

justice and peace shall kiss.

[12] Truth shall spring out of the earth,

and justice shall look down from heaven.

R. Lord, let us see your kindness, and grant us your salvation.

[13] The LORD himself will give his benefits;

our land shall yield its increase.

[14] Justice shall walk before him,

and prepare the way of his steps.

R. Lord, let us see your kindness, and grant us your salvation.

Second Reading – 2 Peter 3:8-14

[8]Do not ignore this one fact, beloved, that with the Lord one
day is like a thousand years and a thousand years like one
day.[9]The Lord does not delay his promise, as some regard
“delay,” but he is patient with you, not wishing that any should
perish but that all should come to repentance. [10]But the day of
the Lord will come like a thief, and then the heavens will pass
away with a mighty roar and the elements will be dissolved by
fire, and the earth and everything done on it will be found
out.[11]Since everything is to be dissolved in this way, what sort
of persons ought you to be, conducting yourselves in holiness
and devotion,[12]waiting for and hastening the coming of the day
of God, because of which the heavens will be dissolved in
flames and the elements melted by fire.[13]But according to his
promise we await new heavens and a new earth in which
righteousness dwells. [14]Therefore, beloved, since you await
these things, be eager to be found without spot or blemish
before him, at peace.

Alleluia – Luke 3:4, 6

R. Alleluia, alleluia.

[4] Prepare the way of the Lord, make straight his paths: [6] All
flesh shall see the salvation of God.

R. Alleluia, alleluia.

Gospel – Mark 1:1-8

[1]The beginning of the gospel of Jesus Christ the Son of God.
[2]As it is written in Isaiah the prophet: Behold, I am sending my
messenger ahead of you; he will prepare your way. [3]A voice of
one crying out in the desert: “Prepare the way of the Lord,
make straight his paths.” [4]John the Baptist appeared in the
desert proclaiming a baptism of repentance for the forgiveness
of sins.[5]People of the whole Judean countryside and all the
inhabitants of Jerusalem were going out to him and were
being baptized by him in the Jordan River as they
acknowledged their sins.[6]John was clothed in camel’s hair,
with a leather belt around his waist. He fed on locusts and wild
honey.[7]And this is what he proclaimed: “One mightier than I is
coming after me. I am not worthy to stoop and loosen the
thongs of his sandals. [8]I have baptized you with water; he will
baptize you with the Holy Spirit.”

Monday December 11, 2023

Monday of the Second Week of Advent

First Reading – Isaiah 35:1-10

1 The desert and the parched land will exult; the steppe will rejoice and bloom. 2 They will bloom with abundant flowers, and rejoice with joyful song. The glory of Lebanon will be given to them, the splendor of Carmel and Sharon; They will see the glory of the LORD, the splendor of our God. 3 Strengthen the hands that are feeble, make firm the knees that are weak, 4 Say to those whose hearts are frightened: Be strong, fear not! Here is your God, he comes with vindication; With divine recompense he comes to save you. 5 Then will the eyes of the blind be opened, the ears of the deaf be cleared; 6 Then will the lame leap like a stag, then the tongue of the mute will sing. Streams will burst forth in the desert, and rivers in the steppe. 7 The burning sands will become pools, and the thirsty ground, springs of water; The abode where jackals lurk will be a marsh for the reed and papyrus. 8 A highway will be there, called the holy way; No one unclean may pass over it, nor fools go astray on it. 9 No lion will be there, nor beast of prey go up to be met upon it. It is for those with a journey to make, and on it the redeemed will walk. 10 Those whom the LORD has ransomed will return and enter Zion singing, crowned with everlasting joy; They will meet with joy and gladness, sorrow and mourning will flee.

Responsorial Psalm – Psalms 85:9AB AND 10, 11-12, 13-14

R. (Isaiah 35:4f) **Our God will come to save us!**

9AB I will hear what God proclaims;

the LORD –for he proclaims peace to his people.

10 Near indeed is his salvation to those who fear him,

glory dwelling in our land.

R. Our God will come to save us!

11 Kindness and truth shall meet;

justice and peace shall kiss.

12 Truth shall spring out of the earth,

and justice shall look down from heaven.

R. Our God will come to save us!

13 The LORD himself will give his benefits;

our land shall yield its increase.

14 Justice shall walk before him,

and salvation, along the way of his steps.

R. Our God will come to save us!

Alleluia

R. Alleluia, alleluia.

Behold the king will come, the Lord of the earth, and he himself will lift the yoke of our captivity.

R. Alleluia, alleluia.

Gospel – Luke 5:17-26

17One day as Jesus was teaching, Pharisees and teachers of the law, who had come from every village of Galilee and Judea and Jerusalem, were sitting there, and the power of the Lord was with him for healing. 18And some men brought on a stretcher a man who was paralyzed; they were trying to bring him in and set him in his presence. 19But not finding a way to bring him in because of the crowd, they went up on the roof and lowered him on the stretcher through the tiles into the middle in front of Jesus. 20When Jesus saw their faith, he said, "As for you, your sins are forgiven." 21Then the scribes and Pharisees began to ask themselves, "Who is this who speaks blasphemies? Who but God alone can forgive sins?" 22Jesus knew their thoughts and said to them in reply, "What are you thinking in your hearts? 23Which is easier, to say, 'Your sins are forgiven,' or to say, 'Rise and walk'? 24But that you may know that the Son of Man has authority on earth to forgive sins" he said to the one who was paralyzed, "I say to you, rise, pick up your stretcher, and go home." 25He stood up immediately before them, picked up what he had been lying on, and went home, glorifying God. [26]Then astonishment seized them all and they glorified God, and, struck with awe, they said, "We have seen incredible things today."

Tuesday December 12, 2023

Feast of Our Lady of Guadalupe

First Reading – Zechariah 2:14-17

[14]Sing and rejoice, O daughter Zion! See, I am coming to dwell among you, says the LORD.[15]Many nations shall join themselves to the LORD on that day, and they shall be his people, and he will dwell among you, and you shall know that the LORD of hosts has sent me to you.[16]The LORD will possess Judah as his portion in the holy land, and he will again choose Jerusalem.[17]Silence, all mankind, in the presence of the LORD! For he stirs forth from his holy dwelling.

Or Revelation 11:19A; 12:1-6A, 10AB

[19A]God's temple in heaven was opened, and the ark of his covenant could be seen in the temple.[1]A great sign appeared in the sky, a woman clothed with the sun, with the moon under her feet, and on her head a crown of twelve stars.[2]She was with child and wailed aloud in pain as she labored to give birth.[3]Then another sign appeared in the sky; it was a huge red dragon, with seven heads and ten horns, and on its heads were seven diadems.[4]Its tail swept away a third of the stars in the sky and hurled them down to the earth. Then the dragon stood before the woman about to give birth, to devour her child when she gave birth.[5]She gave birth to a son, a male child, destined to rule all the nations with an iron rod. Her child was caught up to God and his throne.[6A]The woman herself fled into the desert where she had a place prepared by God.[10AB]Then I heard a loud voice in heaven say: "Now have salvation and power come, and the Kingdom of our God and the authority of his Anointed."

Responsorial Psalm – Judith 13:18BCDE, 19

R. [(15:9d)] **You are the highest honor of our race.**

[18BCDE] Blessed are you, daughter, by the Most High God,

above all the women on earth;

and blessed be the LORD God,

the creator of heaven and earth.

R. You are the highest honor of our race.

19 Your deed of hope will never be forgotten

by those who tell of the might of God.

R. You are the highest honor of our race.

Alleluia

R. Alleluia, alleluia.

Blessed are you, holy Virgin Mary, deserving of all praise; From you rose the sun of justice, Christ our Lord.

R. Alleluia, alleluia.

Gospel – Luke 1:26-38

26 The angel Gabriel was sent from God to a town of Galilee
called Nazareth, 27 to a virgin betrothed to a man named
Joseph, of the house of David, and the virgin's name was
Mary. 28 And coming to her, he said, "Hail, full of grace! The
Lord is with you." 29 But she was greatly troubled at what was
said and pondered what sort of greeting this might be. 30 Then
the angel said to her, "Do not be afraid, Mary, for you have
found favor with God. 31 Behold, you will conceive in your
womb and bear a son, and you shall name him Jesus. 32 He will
be great and will be called Son of the Most High, and the Lord
God will give him the throne of David his father, 33 and he will
rule over the house of Jacob forever, and of his Kingdom there
will be no end." 34 But Mary said to the angel, "How can this be,
since I have no relations with a man?" 35 And the angel said to
her in reply, "The Holy Spirit will come upon you, and the
power of the Most High will overshadow you. Therefore the
child to be born will be called holy, the Son of God. 36 And
behold, Elizabeth, your relative, has also conceived a son in
her old age, and this is the sixth month for her who was called
barren; 37 for nothing will be impossible for God." 38 Mary said,
"Behold, I am the handmaid of the Lord. May it be done to me
according to your word." Then the angel departed from her.

Or Luke 1:39-47

[39]Mary set out and traveled to the hill country in haste to a
town of Judah, [40]where she entered the house of Zechariah
and greeted Elizabeth. [41]When Elizabeth heard Mary's
greeting, the infant leaped in her womb, and Elizabeth, filled
with the Holy Spirit, [42]cried out in a loud voice and said, "Most
blessed are you among women, and blessed is the fruit of
your womb.[43]And how does this happen to me, that the mother
of my Lord should come to me? [44]For at the moment the
sound of your greeting reached my ears, the infant in my
womb leaped for joy. [45]Blessed are you who believed that
what was spoken to you by the Lord would be fulfilled." [46]And
Mary said: "My soul proclaims the greatness of the Lord; [47]my
spirit rejoices in God my savior."

Wednesday December 13, 2023

Memorial of Saint Lucy – Virgin & Martyr

First Reading – Isaiah 40:25-31

[25]To whom can you liken me as an equal? says the Holy One.
[26]Lift up your eyes on high and see who has created these
things: He leads out their army and numbers them, calling
them all by name. By his great might and the strength of his
power not one of them is missing! [27]Why, O Jacob, do you
say, and declare, O Israel, "My way is hidden from the LORD,
and my right is disregarded by my God"? [28]Do you not know or
have you not heard? The LORD is the eternal God, creator of
the ends of the earth. He does not faint nor grow weary, and
his knowledge is beyond scrutiny. [29]He gives strength to the
fainting; for the weak he makes vigor abound. [30]Though young
men faint and grow weary, and youths stagger and fall, [31]They
that hope in the LORD will renew their strength, they will soar
as with eagles' wings; They will run and not grow weary, walk
and not grow faint.

Responsorial Psalm – Psalms 103:1-2, 3-4, 8 & 10

R. (1) O bless the Lord, my soul!

[1] Bless the LORD, O my soul;

and all my being, bless his holy name.

[2] Bless the LORD, O my soul,

and forget not all his benefits.

R. O bless the Lord, my soul!

[3] He pardons all your iniquities,

he heals all your ills.

[4] He redeems your life from destruction,

he crowns you with kindness and compassion.

R. O bless the Lord, my soul!

[8] Merciful and gracious is the LORD,

slow to anger and abounding in kindness.

[10] Not according to our sins does he deal with us,

nor does he requite us according to our crimes.

R. O bless the Lord, my soul!

Alleluia

R. Alleluia, alleluia.

Behold, the Lord comes to save his people; blessed are those prepared to meet him.

R. Alleluia, alleluia.

Gospel – Matthew 11:28-30

Jesus said to the crowds: [28]"Come to me, all you who labor
and are burdened, and I will give you rest. [29]Take my yoke
upon you and learn from me, for I am meek and humble of
heart; and you will find rest for yourselves. [30]For my yoke is
easy, and my burden light."

Thursday December 14, 2023

Memorial of St John of the Cross – Priest & Doctor

First Reading – Isaiah 41:13-20

[13]I am the LORD, your God, who grasp your right hand; It is I
who say to you, "Fear not, I will help you." [14]Fear not, O worm
Jacob, O maggot Israel; I will help you, says the LORD; your
redeemer is the Holy One of Israel. [15]I will make of you a
threshing sledge, sharp, new, and double-edged, To thresh
the mountains and crush them, to make the hills like chaff.
[16]When you winnow them, the wind shall carry them off and

the storm shall scatter them. But you shall rejoice in the LORD, and glory in the Holy One of Israel.
17The afflicted and the needy seek water in vain, their tongues are parched with thirst. I, the LORD, will answer them; I, the God of Israel, will not forsake them.
18I will open up rivers on the bare heights, and fountains in the broad valleys; I will turn the desert into a marshland, and the dry ground into springs of water.
19I will plant in the desert the cedar, acacia, myrtle, and olive; I will set in the wasteland the cypress, together with the plane tree and the pine,
20That all may see and know, observe and understand, That the hand of the LORD has done this, the Holy One of Israel has created it.

Responsorial Psalm – Psalms 145:1 AND 9, 10-11, 12-13AB

R. (8) The Lord is gracious and merciful; slow to anger, and of great kindness.

1 I will extol you, O my God and King,

and I will bless your name forever and ever.

9 The LORD is good to all

and compassionate toward all his works.

R. The Lord is gracious and merciful; slow to anger, and of great kindness.

10 Let all your works give you thanks, O LORD,

and let your faithful ones bless you.

11 Let them discourse of the glory of your Kingdom

and speak of your might.

R. The Lord is gracious and merciful; slow to anger, and of great kindness.

12 Let them make known to men your might

and the glorious splendor of your Kingdom.

13AB Your Kingdom is a Kingdom for all ages,

and your dominion endures through all generations.

R. The Lord is gracious and merciful; slow to anger, and of great kindness.

Alleluia – Isaiah 45:8

R. Alleluia, alleluia.

8 Let the clouds rain down the Just One, and the earth bring forth a Savior.

R. Alleluia, alleluia.

Gospel – Matthew 11:11-15

Jesus said to the crowds:
11"Amen, I say to you, among those born of women there has been none greater than John the Baptist; yet the least in the Kingdom of heaven is greater than he.
12From the days of John the Baptist until now, the Kingdom of heaven suffers violence, and the violent are taking it by force.
13All the prophets and the law prophesied up to the time of John. And if you are willing to accept it, he is Elijah, the one who is to come. Whoever has ears ought to hear."

Friday December 15, 2023

Friday of the Second Week of Advent

First Reading – Isaiah 48:17-19

17Thus says the LORD, your redeemer, the Holy One of Israel: I, the LORD, your God, teach you what is for your good, and lead you on the way you should go.
18If you would hearken to my commandments, your prosperity would be like a river, and your vindication like the waves of the sea;
19Your descendants would be like the sand, and those born of your stock like its grains, Their name never cut off or blotted out from my presence.

Responsorial Psalm – Psalms 1:1-2, 3, 4 AND 6

R. (see John 8:12) **Those who follow you, Lord, will have the light of life.**

1 Blessed the man who follows not

the counsel of the wicked

Nor walks in the way of sinners,

nor sits in the company of the insolent,

2 But delights in the law of the LORD

and meditates on his law day and night.

R. Those who follow you, Lord, will have the light of life.

3 He is like a tree

planted near running water,

That yields its fruit in due season,

and whose leaves never fade.

Whatever he does, prospers.

R. Those who follow you, Lord, will have the light of life.

4 Not so the wicked, not so;

they are like chaff which the wind drives away.

6 For the LORD watches over the way of the just,

but the way of the wicked vanishes.

R. Those who follow you, Lord, will have the light of life.

Alleluia

R. Alleluia, alleluia.

The Lord will come; go out to meet him! He is the prince of peace.

R. Alleluia, alleluia.

Gospel – Matthew 11:16-19

Jesus said to the crowds: 16"To what shall I compare this
generation? It is like children who sit in marketplaces and call
to one another,17'We played the flute for you, but you did not
dance, we sang a dirge but you did not mourn.' 18For John
came neither eating nor drinking, and they said, 'He is
possessed by a demon.' 19The Son of Man came eating and
drinking and they said, 'Look, he is a glutton and a drunkard, a
friend of tax collectors and sinners.' But wisdom is vindicated
by her works."

Saturday December 16, 2023

Saturday of the Second Week of Advent

First Reading – Sirach 48:1-4, 9-11

[1]In those days, like a fire there appeared the prophet Elijah whose words were as a flaming furnace.[2]Their staff of bread he shattered, in his zeal he reduced them to straits;[3]By the Lord's word he shut up the heavens and three times brought down fire.[4]How awesome are you, Elijah, in your wondrous deeds! Whose glory is equal to yours? [9]You were taken aloft in a whirlwind of fire, in a chariot with fiery horses.[10]You were destined, it is written, in time to come to put an end to wrath before the day of the LORD, To turn back the hearts of fathers toward their sons, and to re-establish the tribes of Jacob.[11]Blessed is he who shall have seen you and who falls asleep in your friendship.

Responsorial Psalm – Psalms 80:2AC AND 3B, 15-16, 18-19

R. (4) Lord, make us turn to you; let us see your face and we shall be saved.

[2AC] O shepherd of Israel, hearken,

From your throne upon the cherubim, shine forth.

[3B] Rouse your power.

R. Lord, make us turn to you; let us see your face and we shall be saved.

[15] Once again, O LORD of hosts,

look down from heaven, and see;

[16] Take care of this vine,

and protect what your right hand has planted

the son of man whom you yourself made strong.

R. Lord, make us turn to you; let us see your face and we shall be saved.

[18] May your help be with the man of your right hand,

with the son of man whom you yourself made strong.

[19] Then we will no more withdraw from you;

give us new life, and we will call upon your name.

R. Lord, make us turn to you; let us see your face and we shall be saved.

Alleluia – Luke 3:4, 6

R. Alleluia, alleluia.

[4] Prepare the way of the Lord, make straight his paths: [6] All flesh shall see the salvation of God.

R. Alleluia, alleluia.

Gospel – Matthew 17:9A, 10-13

[9A]As they were coming down from the mountain,[10]the disciples
asked Jesus, "Why do the scribes say that Elijah must come
first?" [11]He said in reply, "Elijah will indeed come and restore
all things;[12]but I tell you that Elijah has already come, and they
did not recognize him but did to him whatever they pleased.
So also will the Son of Man suffer at their hands." [13]Then the
disciples understood that he was speaking to them of John the
Baptist.

Sunday December 17, 2023

Third Sunday of Advent, Year B

First Reading – Isaiah 61:1-2A, 10-11

[1]The spirit of the Lord GOD is upon me, because the LORD
has anointed me; he has sent me to bring glad tidings to the
poor, to heal the brokenhearted, to proclaim liberty to the
captives and release to the prisoners, [2A]to announce a year of
favor from the LORD and a day of vindication by our God.[10]I
rejoice heartily in the LORD, in my God is the joy of my soul;
for he has clothed me with a robe of salvation and wrapped
me in a mantle of justice, like a bridegroom adorned with a
diadem, like a bride bedecked with her jewels.[11]As the earth
brings forth its plants, and a garden makes its growth spring
up, so will the Lord GOD make justice and praise spring up
before all the nations.

Responsorial Psalm – Luke 1:46-48, 49-50, 53-54

R. (Isaiah 61:10b) **My soul rejoices in my God.**

46 My soul proclaims the greatness of the Lord;

47 my spirit rejoices in God my Savior,

48 for he has looked upon his lowly servant.

From this day all generations will call me blessed:

R. My soul rejoices in my God.

49 the Almighty has done great things for me,

and holy is his Name.

50 He has mercy on those who fear him

in every generation.

R. My soul rejoices in my God.

53 He has filled the hungry with good things,

and the rich he has sent away empty.

54 He has come to the help of his servant Israel

for he has remembered his promise of mercy,

R. My soul rejoices in my God.

Second Reading – 1 Thessalonians 5:16-24

Brothers and sisters: 16Rejoice always. 17Pray without ceasing.
18In all circumstances give thanks, for this is the will of God for
you in Christ Jesus. 19Do not quench the Spirit. 20Do not
despise prophetic utterances. 21Test everything; retain what is
good. 22Refrain from every kind of evil. 23May the God of
peace make you perfectly holy and may you entirely, spirit,
soul, and body, be preserved blameless for the coming of our
Lord Jesus Christ. 24The one who calls you is faithful, and he
will also accomplish it.

Alleluia – Isaiah 61:1 (CITED IN Luke 4:18)

R. Alleluia, alleluia.

1The Spirit of the Lord is upon me, because he has anointed me to bring glad tidings to the poor.

R. Alleluia, alleluia.

Gospel – John 1:6-8, 19-28

[6]A man named John was sent from God. [7]He came for
testimony, to testify to the light, so that all might believe
through him. [8]He was not the light, but came to testify to the
light. [19]And this is the testimony of John. When the Jews from
Jerusalem sent priests and Levites to him to ask him, "Who
are you?" [20]He admitted and did not deny it, but admitted, "I
am not the Christ." [21]So they asked him, "What are you then?
Are you Elijah?" And he said, "I am not." "Are you the
Prophet?" He answered, "No." [22]So they said to him, "Who are
you, so we can give an answer to those who sent us? What do
you have to say for yourself?" [23]He said: "I am the voice of one
crying out in the desert, 'make straight the way of the Lord,'"
as Isaiah the prophet said." [24]Some Pharisees were also sent.
[25]They asked him, "Why then do you baptize if you are not the
Christ or Elijah or the Prophet?" [26]John answered them, "I
baptize with water; but there is one among you whom you do
not recognize, [27]the one who is coming after me, whose
sandal strap I am not worthy to untie." [28]This happened in
Bethany across the Jordan, where John was baptizing.

Monday December 18, 2023

Monday of the Third Week of Advent

First Reading – Jeremiah 23:5-8

[5]Behold, the days are coming, says the LORD, when I will
raise up a righteous shoot to David; As king he shall reign and
govern wisely, he shall do what is just and right in the land. [6]In
his days Judah shall be saved, Israel shall dwell in security.
This is the name they give him: "The LORD our justice."
[7]Therefore, the days will come, says the LORD, when they
shall no longer say, "As the LORD lives, who brought the
children of Israel out of the land of Egypt"; [8]but rather, "As the
LORD lives, who brought the descendants of the house of
Israel up from the land of the north" – and from all the lands to
which I banished them; they shall again live on their own land.

Responsorial Psalm – Psalms 72:1-2, 12-13, 18-19

R.(see 7) Justice shall flourish in his time, and fullness of peace for ever.

1 O God, with your judgment endow the king,

and with your justice, the king's son;

2 He shall govern your people with justice

and your afflicted ones with judgment.

R. Justice shall flourish in his time, and fullness of peace for ever.

12 For he shall rescue the poor when he cries out,

and the afflicted when he has no one to help him.

12 He shall have pity for the lowly and the poor;

the lives of the poor he shall save.

R. Justice shall flourish in his time, and fullness of peace for ever.

18 Blessed be the LORD, the God of Israel,

who alone does wondrous deeds.

19 And blessed forever be his glorious name;

may the whole earth be filled with his glory.

R. Justice shall flourish in his time, and fullness of peace for ever.

Alleluia

R. Alleluia, alleluia.

O Leader of the House of Israel, giver of the Law to Moses on Sinai: come to rescue us with your mighty power!

R. Alleluia, alleluia.

Gospel – Matthew 1:18-25

18This is how the birth of Jesus Christ came about. When his mother Mary was betrothed to Joseph, but before they lived together, she was found with child through the Holy Spirit.
19Joseph her husband, since he was a righteous man, yet unwilling to expose her to shame, decided to divorce her quietly.20Such was his intention when, behold, the angel of the

Lord appeared to him in a dream and said, "Joseph, son of David, do not be afraid to take Mary your wife into your home. For it is through the Holy Spirit that this child has been conceived in her.[21]She will bear a son and you are to name him Jesus, because he will save his people from their sins." [22]All this took place to fulfill what the Lord had said through the prophet: [23]Behold, the virgin shall be with child and bear a son, and they shall name him Emmanuel, which means "God is with us." [24]When Joseph awoke, he did as the angel of the Lord had commanded him and took his wife into his home. [25]He had no relations with her until she bore a son, and he named him Jesus.

Tuesday December 19, 2023

Tuesday of the Third Week of Advent

First Reading – Judges 13:2-7, 24-25A

[2]There was a certain man from Zorah, of the clan of the Danites, whose name was Manoah. His wife was barren and had borne no children. [3]An angel of the LORD appeared to the woman and said to her, "Though you are barren and have had no children, yet you will conceive and bear a son. [4]Now, then, be careful to take no wine or strong drink and to eat nothing unclean.[5]As for the son you will conceive and bear, no razor shall touch his head, for this boy is to be consecrated to God from the womb. It is he who will begin the deliverance of Israel from the power of the Philistines." [6]The woman went and told her husband, "A man of God came to me; he had the appearance of an angel of God, terrible indeed. I did not ask him where he came from, nor did he tell me his name.[7]But he said to me, 'You will be with child and will bear a son. So take neither wine nor strong drink, and eat nothing unclean. For the boy shall be consecrated to God from the womb, until the day of his death.'" [24]The woman bore a son and named him Samson. The boy grew up and the LORD blessed him; [25A]the Spirit of the LORD stirred him.

Responsorial Psalm – Psalms 71:3-4A, 5-6AB, 16-17

R. (See 8) **My mouth shall be filled with your praise, and I will sing your glory!**

3 Be my rock of refuge,

a stronghold to give me safety,

for you are my rock and my fortress.

4A O my God, rescue me from the hand of the wicked.

R. My mouth shall be filled with your praise, and I will sing your glory!

5 For you are my hope, O LORD;

my trust, O God, from my youth.

6AB On you I depend from birth;

from my mother's womb you are my strength.

R. My mouth shall be filled with your praise, and I will sing your glory!

16 I will treat of the mighty works of the LORD;

O God, I will tell of your singular justice.

17 O God, you have taught me from my youth,

and till the present I proclaim your wondrous deeds.

R. My mouth shall be filled with your praise, and I will sing your glory!

Alleluia

R. Alleluia, alleluia.

O Root of Jesse's stem, sign of God's love for all his people: come to save us without delay!

R. Alleluia, alleluia.

Gospel – Luke 1:5-25

5In the days of Herod, King of Judea, there was a priest named Zechariah of the priestly division of Abijah; his wife was from the daughters of Aaron, and her name was Elizabeth.
6Both were righteous in the eyes of God, observing all the commandments and ordinances of the Lord blamelessly. 7But they had no child, because Elizabeth was barren and both were advanced in years. 8Once when he was serving as priest in his division's turn before God, 9according to the practice of the priestly service, he was chosen by lot to enter the

sanctuary of the Lord to burn incense. 10Then, when the whole
assembly of the people was praying outside at the hour of the
incense offering, 11the angel of the Lord appeared to him,
standing at the right of the altar of incense. 12Zechariah was
troubled by what he saw, and fear came upon him. 13But the
angel said to him, “Do not be afraid, Zechariah, because your
prayer has been heard. Your wife Elizabeth will bear you a
son, and you shall name him John. 14And you will have joy and
gladness, and many will rejoice at his birth, 15for he will be
great in the sight of the Lord. He will drink neither wine nor
strong drink. He will be filled with the Holy Spirit even from his
mother’s womb, 16and he will turn many of the children of
Israel to the Lord their God. 17He will go before him in the spirit
and power of Elijah to turn the hearts of fathers toward
children and the disobedient to the understanding of the
righteous, to prepare a people fit for the Lord.” 18Then
Zechariah said to the angel, “How shall I know this? For I am
an old man, and my wife is advanced in years.” 19And the
angel said to him in reply, “I am Gabriel, who stand before
God. I was sent to speak to you and to announce to you this
good news. 20But now you will be speechless and unable to
talk until the day these things take place, because you did not
believe my words, which will be fulfilled at their proper time.”
21Meanwhile the people were waiting for Zechariah and were
amazed that he stayed so long in the sanctuary. 22But when
he came out, he was unable to speak to them, and they
realized that he had seen a vision in the sanctuary. He was
gesturing to them but remained mute. 23Then, when his days
of ministry were completed, he went home. 24After this time his
wife Elizabeth conceived, and she went into seclusion for five
months, saying, 25“So has the Lord done for me at a time
when he has seen fit to take away my disgrace before others.”

Wednesday December 20, 2023

Wednesday of the Third Week of Advent

First Reading – Isaiah 7:10-14

10The LORD spoke to Ahaz: 11Ask for a sign from the LORD,
your God; let it be deep as the nether world, or high as the
sky! 12But Ahaz answered, “I will not ask! I will not tempt the
LORD!” 13Then Isaiah said: Listen, O house of David! Is it not
enough for you to weary men, must you also weary my God?

14Therefore the Lord himself will give you this sign: the virgin
shall conceive and bear a son, and shall name him
Emmanuel.

Responsorial Psalm – Psalms 24:1-2, 3-4AB, 5-6

R. (See 7c and 10b) **Let the Lord enter; he is the king of glory.**

1 The LORD's are the earth and its fullness;

the world and those who dwell in it.

2 For he founded it upon the seas

and established it upon the rivers.

R. Let the Lord enter; he is the king of glory.

3 Who can ascend the mountain of the LORD?

or who may stand in his holy place?

4AB He whose hands are sinless, whose heart is clean,

who desires not what is vain.

R. Let the Lord enter; he is the king of glory.

5 He shall receive a blessing from the LORD,

a reward from God his savior.

6 Such is the race that seeks for him,

that seeks the face of the God of Jacob.

R. Let the Lord enter; he is the king of glory.

Alleluia

R. Alleluia, alleluia.

O Key of David, opening the gates of God's eternal Kingdom: come and free the prisoners of darkness!

R. Alleluia, alleluia.

Gospel – Luke 1:26-38

26In the sixth month, the angel Gabriel was sent from God to a
town of Galilee called Nazareth, 27to a virgin betrothed to a
man named Joseph, of the house of David, and the virgin's

name was Mary. 28And coming to her, he said, "Hail, full of
grace! The Lord is with you." 29But she was greatly troubled at
what was said and pondered what sort of greeting this might
be. 30Then the angel said to her, "Do not be afraid, Mary, for
you have found favor with God. 31Behold, you will conceive in
your womb and bear a son, and you shall name him Jesus.
32He will be great and will be called Son of the Most High, and
the Lord God will give him the throne of David his father,33and
he will rule over the house of Jacob forever, and of his
Kingdom there will be no end." 34But Mary said to the angel,
"How can this be, since I have no relations with a man?" 35And
the angel said to her in reply, "The Holy Spirit will come upon
you, and the power of the Most High will overshadow you.
Therefore the child to be born will be called holy, the Son of
God. 36And behold, Elizabeth, your relative, has also
conceived a son in her old age, and this is the sixth month for
her who was called barren; 37for nothing will be impossible for
God." 38Mary said, "Behold, I am the handmaid of the Lord.
May it be done to me according to your word." Then the angel
departed from her.

Thursday December 21, 2023

Thursday of the Third Week of Advent

First Reading – Songs of Songs 2:8-14

8Hark! my lover–here he comes springing across the
mountains, leaping across the hills.9My lover is like a gazelle
or a young stag. Here he stands behind our wall, gazing
through the windows, peering through the lattices. 10My lover
speaks; he says to me, "Arise, my beloved, my dove, my
beautiful one, and come! 11"For see, the winter is past, the
rains are over and gone. 12The flowers appear on the earth,
the time of pruning the vines has come, and the song of the
dove is heard in our land. 13The fig tree puts forth its figs, and
the vines, in bloom, give forth fragrance. Arise, my beloved,
my beautiful one, and come! 14"O my dove in the clefts of the
rock, in the secret recesses of the cliff, Let me see you, let me
hear your voice, For your voice is sweet, and you are lovely."

Or Zephaniah 3:14-18A

14Shout for joy, O daughter Zion! Sing joyfully, O Israel! Be
glad and exult with all your heart, O daughter Jerusalem!

[15]The LORD has removed the judgment against you, he has
turned away your enemies; The King of Israel, the LORD, is in
your midst, you have no further misfortune to fear. [16]On that
day, it shall be said to Jerusalem: Fear not, O Zion, be not
discouraged! [17]The LORD, your God, is in your midst, a mighty
savior; He will rejoice over you with gladness, and renew you
in his love, He will sing joyfully because of you, [18A]as one
sings at festivals.

Responsorial Psalm – Psalms 33:2-3, 11-12, 20-21

R. (1a; 3a) Exult, you just, in the Lord! Sing to him a new song.

2 Give thanks to the LORD on the harp;

with the ten-stringed lyre chant his praises.

3 Sing to him a new song;

pluck the strings skillfully, with shouts of gladness.

R. Exult, you just, in the Lord! Sing to him a new song.

11 But the plan of the LORD stands forever;

the design of his heart, through all generations.

12 Blessed the nation whose God is the LORD,

the people he has chosen for his own inheritance.

R. Exult, you just, in the Lord! Sing to him a new song.

20 Our soul waits for the LORD,

who is our help and our shield,

21 For in him our hearts rejoice;

in his holy name we trust.

R. Exult, you just, in the Lord! Sing to him a new song.

Alleluia

R. Alleluia, alleluia.

O Emmanuel, our King and Giver of Law: come to save us, Lord our God!

R. Alleluia, alleluia.

Gospel – Luke 1:39-45

[39]Mary set out in those days and traveled to the hill country in
haste to a town of Judah,[40]where she entered the house of
Zechariah and greeted Elizabeth. [41]When Elizabeth heard
Mary's greeting, the infant leaped in her womb, and Elizabeth,
filled with the Holy Spirit, [42]cried out in a loud voice and said,
"Most blessed are you among women, and blessed is the fruit
of your womb. [43]And how does this happen to me, that the
mother of my Lord should come to me? [44]For at the moment
the sound of your greeting reached my ears, the infant in my
womb leaped for joy. [45]Blessed are you who believed that
what was spoken to you by the Lord would be fulfilled."

Friday December 22, 2023

Friday of the Third Week of Advent

First Reading – 1 Samuel 1:24-28

In those days,[24]Hannah brought Samuel with her, along with a
three-year-old bull, an ephah of flour, and a skin of wine, and
presented him at the temple of the LORD in Shiloh.[25]After the
boy's father had sacrificed the young bull,[26]Hannah, his
mother, approached Eli and said: "Pardon, my lord! As you
live, my lord, I am the woman who stood near you here,
praying to the LORD.[27]I prayed for this child, and the LORD
granted my request.[28]Now I, in turn, give him to the LORD; as
long as he lives, he shall be dedicated to the LORD." She left
Samuel there.

Responsorial Psalm – 1 Samuel 2:1, 4-5, 6-7, 8ABCD

R. (see 1a) **My heart exults in the Lord, my Savior.**

[1] "My heart exults in the LORD,

my horn is exalted in my God.

I have swallowed up my enemies;

I rejoice in my victory."

R. My heart exults in the Lord, my Savior.

[4] "The bows of the mighty are broken,

while the tottering gird on strength.

5 The well-fed hire themselves out for bread,

while the hungry batten on spoil.

The barren wife bears seven sons,

while the mother of many languishes."

R. My heart exults in the Lord, my Savior.

6 "The LORD puts to death and gives life;

he casts down to the nether world;

he raises up again.

7 The LORD makes poor and makes rich,

he humbles, he also exalts."

R. My heart exults in the Lord, my Savior.

8ABCD "He raises the needy from the dust;

from the dung heap he lifts up the poor,

To seat them with nobles

and make a glorious throne their heritage."

R. My heart exults in the Lord, my Savior.

Alleluia

R. Alleluia, alleluia.

O King of all nations and keystone of the Church: come and save man, whom you formed from the dust!

R. Alleluia, alleluia.

Gospel – Luke 1:46-56

46 Mary said: "My soul proclaims the greatness of the Lord;
47 my spirit rejoices in God my savior. 48 for he has looked upon
his lowly servant. From this day all generations will call me
blessed: 49 the Almighty has done great things for me, and holy
is his Name. 50 He has mercy on those who fear him in every
generation. 51 He has shown the strength of his arm, and has
scattered the proud in their conceit. 52 He has cast down the
mighty from their thrones and has lifted up the lowly. 53 He has
filled the hungry with good things, and the rich he has sent
away empty. 54 He has come to the help of his servant Israel for

he remembered his promise of mercy,[55]the promise he made to our fathers, to Abraham and his children for ever."[56]Mary remained with Elizabeth about three months and then returned to her home.

Saturday December 23, 2023

Saturday of the Third Week of Advent

First Reading – Malachi 3:1-4, 23-24

[1]Thus says the Lord GOD: Lo, I am sending my messenger to prepare the way before me; And suddenly there will come to the temple the LORD whom you seek, And the messenger of the covenant whom you desire. Yes, he is coming, says the
LORD of hosts.[2]But who will endure the day of his coming? And who can stand when he appears? For he is like the
refiner's fire, or like the fuller's lye.[3]He will sit refining and purifying silver, and he will purify the sons of Levi, Refining them like gold or like silver that they may offer due sacrifice to
the LORD.[4]Then the sacrifice of Judah and Jerusalem will please the LORD, as in the days of old, as in years gone by.
[23]Lo, I will send you Elijah, the prophet, Before the day of the
LORD comes, the great and terrible day,[24]To turn the hearts of the fathers to their children, and the hearts of the children to their fathers, Lest I come and strike the land with doom.

Responsorial Psalm – Psalms 25:4-5AB, 8-9, 10 AND 14

R. (see Luke 21:28) **Lift up your heads and see; your redemption is near at hand.**

[4] Your ways, O LORD, make known to me;

teach me your paths,

[5AB] Guide me in your truth and teach me,

for you are God my savior.

R. Lift up your heads and see; your redemption is near at hand.

[8] Good and upright is the LORD;

thus he shows sinners the way.

[9] He guides the humble to justice,

he teaches the humble his way.

R. Lift up your heads and see; your redemption is near at hand.

[10] All the paths of the LORD are kindness and constancy

toward those who keep his covenant and his decrees.

[14] The friendship of the LORD is with those who fear him,

and his covenant, for their instruction.

R. Lift up your heads and see; your redemption is near at hand.

Alleluia

R. Alleluia, alleluia.

O King of all nations and keystone of the Church: come and save man, whom you formed from the dust!

R. Alleluia, alleluia.

Gospel – Luke 1:57-66

[57]When the time arrived for Elizabeth to have her child she
gave birth to a son.[58]Her neighbors and relatives heard that
the Lord had shown his great mercy toward her, and they
rejoiced with her.[59]When they came on the eighth day to
circumcise the child, they were going to call him Zechariah
after his father,[60]but his mother said in reply, "No. He will be
called John." [61]But they answered her, "There is no one
among your relatives who has this name." [62]So they made
signs, asking his father what he wished him to be called.[63]He
asked for a tablet and wrote, "John is his name," and all were
amazed.[64]Immediately his mouth was opened, his tongue
freed, and he spoke blessing God.[65]Then fear came upon all
their neighbors, and all these matters were discussed
throughout the hill country of Judea.[66]All who heard these
things took them to heart, saying, "What, then, will this child
be? For surely the hand of the Lord was with him."

Sunday December 24, 2023

Fourth Sunday of Advent, Year B

First Reading – 2 Samuel 7:1-5, 8B-12, 14A, 16

[1]When King David was settled in his palace, and the LORD
had given him rest from his enemies on every side,[2]he said to
Nathan the prophet, “Here I am living in a house of cedar,
while the ark of God dwells in a tent!” [3]Nathan answered the
king, “Go, do whatever you have in mind, for the LORD is with
you.” [4]But that night the LORD spoke to Nathan and said:
[5]“Go, tell my servant David, ‘Thus says the LORD: Should you
build me a house to dwell in?’ [8B]“It was I who took you from
the pasture and from the care of the flock to be commander of
my people Israel. [9]I have been with you wherever you went,
and I have destroyed all your enemies before you. And I will
make you famous like the great ones of the earth. [10]I will fix a
place for my people Israel; I will plant them so that they may
dwell in their place without further disturbance. Neither shall
the wicked continue to afflict them as they did of old,[11]since
the time I first appointed judges over my people Israel. I will
give you rest from all your enemies. The LORD also reveals to
you that he will establish a house for you.[12]And when your
time comes and you rest with your ancestors, I will raise up
your heir after you, sprung from your loins, and I will make his
kingdom firm.[14A]I will be a father to him, and he shall be a son
to me.[16]Your house and your kingdom shall endure forever
before me; your throne shall stand firm forever.”

Responsorial Psalm – Psalms 89:2-3, 4-5, 27, 29

R. (2a) For ever I will sing the goodness of the Lord.

[2] The promises of the LORD I will sing forever;

through all generations my mouth shall proclaim your faithfulness.

[3] For you have said, “My kindness is established forever”;

in heaven you have confirmed your faithfulness.

R. For ever I will sing the goodness of the Lord.

[4] “I have made a covenant with my chosen one,

I have sworn to David my servant:

[5] Forever will I confirm your posterity

and establish your throne for all generations.”

R. For ever I will sing the goodness of the Lord.

27 “He shall say of me, ‘You are my father,

my God, the Rock, my savior.’

29 Forever I will maintain my kindness toward him,

and my covenant with him stands firm.”

R. For ever I will sing the goodness of the Lord.

Second Reading – Romans 16:25-27

Brothers and sisters: 25To him who can strengthen you,
according to my gospel and the proclamation of Jesus Christ,
according to the revelation of the mystery kept secret for long
ages 26but now manifested through the prophetic writings and,
according to the command of the eternal God, made known to
all nations to bring about the obedience of faith, 27to the only
wise God, through Jesus Christ be glory forever and ever.
Amen.

Alleluia – Luke 1:38

R. Alleluia, alleluia.

38Behold, I am the handmaid of the Lord. May it be done to me
according to your word.

R. Alleluia, alleluia.

Gospel – Luke 1:26-38

26The angel Gabriel was sent from God to a town of Galilee
called Nazareth,27to a virgin betrothed to a man named
Joseph, of the house of David, and the virgin’s name was
Mary.28And coming to her, he said, “Hail, full of grace! The
Lord is with you.” 29But she was greatly troubled at what was
said and pondered what sort of greeting this might be.30Then
the angel said to her, “Do not be afraid, Mary, for you have
found favor with God. 31“Behold, you will conceive in your
womb and bear a son, and you shall name him Jesus.32He will
be great and will be called Son of the Most High, and the Lord
God will give him the throne of David his father,33and he will
rule over the house of Jacob forever, and of his kingdom there
will be no end.” 34But Mary said to the angel, “How can this be,
since I have no relations with a man?” 35And the angel said to
her in reply, “The Holy Spirit will come upon you, and the
power of the Most High will overshadow you. Therefore the

child to be born will be called holy, the Son of God. [36]And behold, Elizabeth, your relative, has also conceived a son in her old age, and this is the sixth month for her who was called barren; [37]for nothing will be impossible for God." [38]Mary said, "Behold, I am the handmaid of the Lord. May it be done to me according to your word." Then the angel departed from her.

Sunday December 24, 2023

Christmas Vigil Mass – The Nativity of the Lord

First Reading – Isaiah 62:1-5

[1]For Zion's sake I will not be silent, for Jerusalem's sake I will not be quiet, until her vindication shines forth like the dawn and her victory like a burning torch.[2]Nations shall behold your vindication, and all the kings your glory; you shall be called by a new name pronounced by the mouth of the LORD. [3]You shall be a glorious crown in the hand of the LORD, a royal diadem held by your God. [4]No more shall people call you "Forsaken," or your land "Desolate," but you shall be called "My Delight," and your land "Espoused." For the LORD delights in you and makes your land his spouse. [5]As a young man marries a virgin, your Builder shall marry you; and as a bridegroom rejoices in his bride so shall your God rejoice in you.

Responsorial Psalm – Psalms 89:4-5, 16-17, 27, 29

R. (2a) For ever I will sing the goodness of the Lord.

[4] I have made a covenant with my chosen one,

I have sworn to David my servant:

[5] Forever will I confirm your posterity

and establish your throne for all generations.

R. For ever I will sing the goodness of the Lord.

[16] Blessed the people who know the joyful shout;

in the light of your countenance, O LORD, they walk.

[17] At your name they rejoice all the day,

and through your justice they are exalted.

R. For ever I will sing the goodness of the Lord.

[27] He shall say of me, "You are my father,

my God, the rock, my savior."

[29] Forever I will maintain my kindness toward him,

and my covenant with him stands firm.

R. For ever I will sing the goodness of the Lord.

Second Reading – Acts 13:16-17, 22-25

[16]When Paul reached Antioch in Pisidia and entered the
synagogue, he stood up, motioned with his hand, and said,
"Fellow Israelites and you others who are God-fearing, listen.
[17]The God of this people Israel chose our ancestors and
exalted the people during their sojourn in the land of Egypt.
With uplifted arm he led them out of it. [22]Then he removed
Saul and raised up David as king; of him he testified, 'I have
found David, son of Jesse, a man after my own heart; he will
carry out my every wish.' [23]From this man's descendants God,
according to his promise, has brought to Israel a savior, Jesus.
[24]John heralded his coming by proclaiming a baptism of
repentance to all the people of Israel; [25]and as John was
completing his course, he would say, 'What do you suppose
that I am? I am not he. Behold, one is coming after me; I am
not worthy to unfasten the sandals of his feet.'"

Alleluia

R. Alleluia, alleluia.

Tomorrow the wickedness of the earth will be destroyed: the Savior of the world will reign over us.

R. Alleluia, alleluia.

Gospel – Matthew 1:1-25

[1]The book of the genealogy of Jesus Christ, the son of David,
the son of Abraham. [2]Abraham became the father of Isaac,
Isaac the father of Jacob, Jacob the father of Judah and his
brothers. [3]Judah became the father of Perez and Zerah,
whose mother was Tamar. Perez became the father of
Hezron, Hezron the father of Ram, [4]Ram the father of
Amminadab. Amminadab became the father of Nahshon,
Nahshon the father of Salmon, [5]Salmon the father of Boaz,
whose mother was Rahab. Boaz became the father of Obed,

whose mother was Ruth. Obed became the father of Jesse,
6Jesse the father of David the king. David became the father
of Solomon, whose mother had been the wife of Uriah.
7Solomon became the father of Rehoboam, Rehoboam the
father of Abijah,Abijah the father of Asaph. 8Asaph became
the father of Jehoshaphat, Jehoshaphat the father of Joram,
Joram the father of Uzziah. 9Uzziah became the father of
Jotham, Jotham the father of Ahaz, Ahaz the father of
Hezekiah. 10Hezekiah became the father of Manasseh,
Manasseh the father of Amos, Amos the father of Josiah.
11Josiah became the father of Jechoniah and his brothers at
the time of the Babylonian exile. 12After the Babylonian exile,
Jechoniah became the father of Shealtiel, Shealtiel the father
of Zerubbabel, 13Zerubbabel the father of Abiud. Abiud
became the father of Eliakim, Eliakim the father of Azor, 14Azor
the father of Zadok. Zadok became the father of Achim, Achim
the father of Eliud, 15Eliud the father of Eleazar. Eleazar
became the father of Matthan, Matthan the father of Jacob,
16Jacob the father of Joseph, the husband of Mary. Of her was
born Jesus who is called the Christ. 17Thus the total number of
generations from Abraham to David is fourteen generations;
from David to the Babylonian exile, fourteen generations; from
the Babylonian exile to the Christ, fourteen generations. 18Now
this is how the birth of Jesus Christ came about. When his
mother Mary was betrothed to Joseph, but before they lived
together, she was found with child through the Holy Spirit.
19Joseph her husband, since he was a righteous man, yet
unwilling to expose her to shame, decided to divorce her
quietly. 20Such was his intention when, behold, the angel of the
Lord appeared to him in a dream and said, “Joseph, son of
David, do not be afraid to take Mary your wife into your home.
For it is through the Holy Spirit that this child has been
conceived in her. 21She will bear a son and you are to name
him Jesus, because he will save his people from their sins.”
22All this took place to fulfill what the Lord had said through the
prophet: 23Behold, the virgin shall conceive and bear a son,
and they shall name him Emmanuel, which means “God is
with us.” 24When Joseph awoke, he did as the angel of the
Lord had commanded him and took his wife into his home.
25He had no relations with her until she bore a son, and he
named him Jesus.

Or Matthew 1:18-25

[18]Now this is how the birth of Jesus Christ came about. When
his mother Mary was betrothed to Joseph, but before they
lived together, she was found with child through the Holy
Spirit. [19]Joseph her husband, since he was a righteous man,
yet unwilling to expose her to shame, decided to divorce her
quietly. [20]Such was his intention when, behold, the angel of
the Lord appeared to him in a dream and said, "Joseph, son of
David, do not be afraid to take Mary your wife into your home.
For it is through the Holy Spirit that this child has been
conceived in her. [21]She will bear a son and you are to name
him Jesus, because he will save his people from their sins."
[22]All this took place to fulfill what the Lord had said through the
prophet: [23]Behold, the virgin shall conceive and bear a son,
and they shall name him Emmanuel, which means "God is
with us." [24]When Joseph awoke, he did as the angel of the
Lord had commanded him and took his wife into his home. [25]
He had no relations with her until she bore a son, and he
named him Jesus.

Sunday December 24, 2023

Nativity of the Lord – Mid Night Mass Readings

First Reading – Isaiah 9:1-6

[1]The people who walked in darkness have seen a great light;
upon those who dwelt in the land of gloom a light has shone.
[2]You have brought them abundant joy and great rejoicing, as
they rejoice before you as at the harvest, as people make
merry when dividing spoils. [3]For the yoke that burdened them,
the pole on their shoulder, and the rod of their taskmaster you
have smashed, as on the day of Midian. [4]For every boot that
tramped in battle, every cloak rolled in blood, will be burned as
fuel for flames. [5]For a child is born to us, a son is given us;
upon his shoulder dominion rests. They name him Wonder-
Counselor, God-Hero, Father-Forever, Prince of Peace. [6]His
dominion is vast and forever peaceful, from David's throne,
and over his kingdom, which he confirms and sustains by
judgment and justice, both now and forever. The zeal of the
LORD of hosts will do this!

Responsorial Psalm – Psalms 96: 1-2, 2-3, 11-12, 13

R. (Luke 2:11) **Today is born our Savior, Christ the Lord.**

[1] Sing to the LORD a new song;

sing to the LORD, all you lands.

2A Sing to the LORD; bless his name.

R. Today is born our Savior, Christ the Lord.

2B Announce his salvation, day after day.

3 Tell his glory among the nations;

among all peoples, his wondrous deeds.

R. Today is born our Savior, Christ the Lord.

11 Let the heavens be glad and the earth rejoice;

let the sea and what fills it resound;

12 let the plains be joyful and all that is in them!

Then shall all the trees of the forest exult.

R. Today is born our Savior, Christ the Lord.

13 They shall exult before the LORD, for he comes;

for he comes to rule the earth.

He shall rule the world with justice

and the peoples with his constancy.

R. Today is born our Savior, Christ the Lord.

Second Reading – Titus 2:11-14

Beloved: 11The grace of God has appeared, saving all 12and
training us to reject godless ways and worldly desires and to
live temperately, justly, and devoutly in this age, 13as we await
the blessed hope, the appearance of the glory of our great
God and savior Jesus Christ, 14who gave himself for us to
deliver us from all lawlessness and to cleanse for himself a
people as his own, eager to do what is good.

Alleluia – Luke 2:10-11

R. Alleluia, alleluia.

10 I proclaim to you good news of great joy: 11 today a Savior is
born for us, Christ the Lord.

R. Alleluia, alleluia.

Gospel – Luke 2:1-14

[1]In those days a decree went out from Caesar Augustus that
the whole world should be enrolled. [2]This was the first
enrollment, when Quirinius was governor of Syria. [3]So all went
to be enrolled, each to his own town. [4]And Joseph too went up
from Galilee from the town of Nazareth to Judea, to the city of
David that is called Bethlehem, because he was of the house
and family of David, [5]to be enrolled with Mary, his betrothed,
who was with child. [6]While they were there, the time came for
her to have her child, [7]and she gave birth to her firstborn son.
She wrapped him in swaddling clothes and laid him in a
manger, because there was no room for them in the inn. [8]Now
there were shepherds in that region living in the fields and
keeping the night watch over their flock. [9]The angel of the Lord
appeared to them and the glory of the Lord shone around
them, and they were struck with great fear. [10]The angel said to
them, "Do not be afraid; for behold, I proclaim to you good
news of great joy that will be for all the people. [11]For today in
the city of David a savior has been born for you who is Christ
and Lord. [12]And this will be a sign for you: you will find an
infant wrapped in swaddling clothes and lying in a manger."
[13]And suddenly there was a multitude of the heavenly host
with the angel, praising God and saying: [14]"Glory to God in the
highest and on earth peace to those on whom his favor rests."

Monday December 25, 2023

The Nativity of the Lord - Mass Readings at Dawn

First Reading – Isaiah 62:11-12

[11]See, the LORD proclaims to the ends of the earth: say to
daughter Zion, your savior comes! Here is his reward with him,
his recompense before him. [12]They shall be called the holy
people, the redeemed of the LORD, and you shall be called
"Frequented," a city that is not forsaken.

Responsorial Psalm – Psalms 97:1, 6, 11-12

R. A light will shine on us this day: the Lord is born for us.

[1] The LORD is king; let the earth rejoice;

let the many isles be glad.

[6] The heavens proclaim his justice,

and all peoples see his glory.

R. A light will shine on us this day: the Lord is born for us.

11 Light dawns for the just;

and gladness, for the upright of heart.

12 Be glad in the LORD, you just,

and give thanks to his holy name.

R. A light will shine on us this day: the Lord is born for us.

Second Reading – Titus 3:4-7

Beloved: 4When the kindness and generous love of God our
savior appeared, 5 not because of any righteous deeds we had
done but because of his mercy, He saved us through the bath
of rebirth and renewal by the Holy Spirit, 6whom he richly
poured out on us through Jesus Christ our savior, 7so that we
might be justified by his grace and become heirs in hope of
eternal life.

Alleluia – Luke 2:14

R. Alleluia, alleluia.

14Glory to God in the highest, and on earth peace to those on whom his favor rests.

R. Alleluia, alleluia.

Gospel – Luke 2:15-20

15When the angels went away from them to heaven, the
shepherds said to one another, "Let us go, then, to Bethlehem
to see this thing that has taken place, which the Lord has
made known to us." 16So they went in haste and found Mary
and Joseph, and the infant lying in the manger. 17When they
saw this, they made known the message that had been told
them about this child. 18All who heard it were amazed by what
had been told them by the shepherds. 19And Mary kept all
these things, reflecting on them in her heart. 20Then the
shepherds returned, glorifying and praising God for all they
had heard and seen, just as it had been told to them.

Monday December 25, 2023

The Nativity of the Lord – Mass During the Day

First Reading – Isaiah 52:7-10

[7]How beautiful upon the mountains are the feet of him who
brings glad tidings, announcing peace, bearing good news,
announcing salvation, and saying to Zion, "Your God is King!"
[8]Hark! Your sentinels raise a cry, together they shout for joy,
for they see directly, before their eyes, the LORD restoring
Zion. [9]Break out together in song, O ruins of Jerusalem! For
the LORD comforts his people, he redeems Jerusalem. [10]The
LORD has bared his holy arm in the sight of all the nations; all
the ends of the earth will behold the salvation of our God.

Responsorial Psalm – Psalms 98:1, 2-3, 3-4, 5-6

R. (3c) All the ends of the earth have seen the saving power of God.

[1] Sing to the LORD a new song,

for he has done wondrous deeds;

his right hand has won victory for him,

his holy arm.

R. All the ends of the earth have seen the saving power of God.

[2] The LORD has made his salvation known:

in the sight of the nations he has revealed his justice.

[3] He has remembered his kindness and his faithfulness

toward the house of Israel.

R. All the ends of the earth have seen the saving power of God.

[3] All the ends of the earth have seen

the salvation by our God.

[4] Sing joyfully to the LORD, all you lands;

break into song; sing praise.

R. All the ends of the earth have seen the saving power of God.

[5] Sing praise to the LORD with the harp,

with the harp and melodious song.

[6] With trumpets and the sound of the horn

sing joyfully before the King, the LORD.

R. All the ends of the earth have seen the saving power of God.

Second Reading – Hebrews 1:1-6

Brothers and sisters: [1]In times past, God spoke in partial and
various ways to our ancestors through the prophets; [2]in these
last days, he has spoken to us through the Son, whom he
made heir of all things and through whom he created the
universe, [3]who is the refulgence of his glory, the very imprint of
his being, and who sustains all things by his mighty word.
When he had accomplished purification from sins, he took his
seat at the right hand of the Majesty on high, [4]as far superior
to the angels as the name he has inherited is more excellent
than theirs. [5]For to which of the angels did God ever say: You
are my son; this day I have begotten you? Or again: I will be a
father to him, and he shall be a son to me? [6]And again, when
he leads the firstborn into the world, he says: Let all the angels
of God worship him.

Alleluia

R. Alleluia, alleluia.

A holy day has dawned upon us. Come, you nations, and adore the Lord. For today a great light has come upon the earth.

R. Alleluia, alleluia.

Gospel – John 1:1-18

[1]In the beginning was the Word, and the Word was with God,
and the Word was God. [2]He was in the beginning with God.
[3]All things came to be through him, and without him nothing
came to be. What came to be [4]through him was life, and this
life was the light of the human race; [5]the light shines in the
darkness, and the darkness has not overcome it. [6]A man
named John was sent from God. [7]He came for testimony, to
testify to the light, so that all might believe through him. [8]He
was not the light, but came to testify to the light. [9]The true
light, which enlightens everyone, was coming into the world.
[10]He was in the world, and the world came to be through him,
but the world did not know him. [11]He came to what was his
own, but his own people did not accept him. [12]But to those

who did accept him he gave power to become children of God, to those who believe in his name, [13]who were born not by natural generation nor by human choice nor by a man's decision but of God. [14]And the Word became flesh and made his dwelling among us, and we saw his glory, the glory as of the Father's only Son, full of grace and truth. [15]John testified to him and cried out, saying, "This was he of whom I said, 'The one who is coming after me ranks ahead of me because he existed before me.'" [16]From his fullness we have all received, grace in place of grace, [17]because while the law was given through Moses, grace and truth came through Jesus Christ. [18]No one has ever seen God. The only Son, God, who is at the Father's side, has revealed him.

Or John 1:1-5, 9-14

[1]In the beginning was the Word, and the Word was with God, and the Word was God. [2]He was in the beginning with God. [3]All things came to be through him, and without him nothing came to be. What came to be [4]through him was life, and this life was the light of the human race; [5]the light shines in the darkness, and the darkness has not overcome it. [9]The true light, which enlightens everyone, was coming into the world. [10]He was in the world, and the world came to be through him, but the world did not know him. [11]He came to what was his own, but his own people did not accept him. [12]But to those who did accept him he gave power to become children of God, to those who believe in his name, [13]who were born not by natural generation nor by human choice nor by a man's decision but of God. [14]And the Word became flesh and made his dwelling among us, and we saw his glory, the glory as of the Father's only Son, full of grace and truth.

Tuesday December 26, 2023

Feast of Saint Stephen, First Martyr

First Reading – Acts 6:8-10; 7:54-59

[8]Stephen, filled with grace and power, was working great wonders and signs among the people. [9]Certain members of the so-called Synagogue of Freedmen, Cyrenians, and Alexandrians, and people from Cilicia and Asia, came forward and debated with Stephen, [10]but they could not withstand the wisdom and the spirit with which he spoke. [54]When they heard

this, they were infuriated, and they ground their teeth at him.
55But he, filled with the Holy Spirit, looked up intently to
heaven and saw the glory of God and Jesus standing at the
right hand of God, 56and he said, “Behold, I see the heavens
opened and the Son of Man standing at the right hand of
God.” 57But they cried out in a loud voice, covered their ears,
and rushed upon him together. 58They threw him out of the
city, and began to stone him. The witnesses laid down their
cloaks at the feet of a young man named Saul. 59 As they were
stoning Stephen, he called out “Lord Jesus, receive my spirit.”

Responsorial Psalm – Psalms 31:3CD-4, 6 AND 8AB, 16BC AND 17

R. (6) Into your hands, O Lord, I commend my spirit.

3CD Be my rock of refuge,

a stronghold to give me safety.

4 You are my rock and my fortress;

for your name’s sake you will lead and guide me.

R. Into your hands, O Lord, I commend my spirit.

6 Into your hands I commend my spirit;

you will redeem me, O LORD, O faithful God.

8AB I will rejoice and be glad because of your mercy.

R. Into your hands, O Lord, I commend my spirit.

16BC Rescue me from the clutches of my enemies and my persecutors.

17 Let your face shine upon your servant;

save me in your kindness.

R. Into your hands, O Lord, I commend my spirit.

Alleluia – Psalms 118:26A, 27A

R. Alleluia, alleluia.

26A Blessed is he who comes in the name of the LORD: 27A the LORD is God and has given us light.

R. Alleluia, alleluia.

Gospel – Matthew 10:17-22

Jesus said to his disciples: [17]"Beware of men, for they will
hand you over to courts and scourge you in their synagogues,
[18]and you will be led before governors and kings for my sake
as a witness before them and the pagans. [19]When they hand
you over, do not worry about how you are to speak or what
you are to say. You will be given at that moment what you are
to say. [20]For it will not be you who speak but the Spirit of your
Father speaking through you. [21]Brother will hand over brother
to death, and the father his child; children will rise up against
parents and have them put to death. [22]You will be hated by all
because of my name, but whoever endures to the end will be
saved."

Wednesday December 27, 2023

Feast of Saint John, Apostle and Evangelist

First Reading – 1 John 1:1-4

Beloved: [1]What was from the beginning, what we have heard,
what we have seen with our eyes, what we looked upon and
touched with our hands concerns the Word of life [2]for the life
was made visible; we have seen it and testify to it and
proclaim to you the eternal life that was with the Father and
was made visible to us [3]what we have seen and heard we
proclaim now to you, so that you too may have fellowship with
us; for our fellowship is with the Father and with his Son,
Jesus Christ. [4]We are writing this so that our joy may be
complete.

Responsorial Psalm – Psalms 97:1-2, 5-6, 11-12

R. (12) Rejoice in the Lord, you just!

[1]The LORD is king; let the earth rejoice;

let the many isles be glad.

[2] Clouds and darkness are around him,

justice and judgment are the foundation of his throne.

R. Rejoice in the Lord, you just!

[5]The mountains melt like wax before the LORD,

before the LORD of all the earth.

6 The heavens proclaim his justice,

and all peoples see his glory.

R. Rejoice in the Lord, you just!

11 Light dawns for the just;

and gladness, for the upright of heart.

12 Be glad in the LORD, you just,

and give thanks to his holy name.

R. Rejoice in the Lord, you just!

Alleluia – Te Deum

R. Alleluia, alleluia.

We praise you, O God, we acclaim you as Lord; the glorious company of Apostles praise you.

R. Alleluia, alleluia.

Gospel – John 20:1A AND 2-8

1A On the first day of the week, 2 Mary Magdalene ran and went
to Simon Peter and to the other disciple whom Jesus loved,
and told them, “They have taken the Lord from the tomb, and
we do not know where they put him.” 3 So Peter and the other
disciple went out and came to the tomb. 4 They both ran, but
the other disciple ran faster than Peter and arrived at the tomb
first; 5 he bent down and saw the burial cloths there, but did not
go in. 6 When Simon Peter arrived after him, he went into the
tomb and saw the burial cloths there, 7 and the cloth that had
covered his head, not with the burial cloths but rolled up in a
separate place. 8 Then the other disciple also went in, the one
who had arrived at the tomb first, and he saw and believed.

Thursday December 28, 2023

Feast of the Holy Innocents, Martyrs

First Reading – 1 John 1:5-2:2

Beloved: 5 This is the message that we have heard from Jesus
Christ and proclaim to you: God is light, and in him there is no
darkness at all. 6 If we say, “We have fellowship with him,”
while we continue to walk in darkness, we lie and do not act in

truth. 7But if we walk in the light as he is in the light, then we
have fellowship with one another, and the Blood of his Son
Jesus cleanses us from all sin. 8If we say, “We are without
sin,” we deceive ourselves, and the truth is not in us. 9If we
acknowledge our sins, he is faithful and just and will forgive
our sins and cleanse us from every wrongdoing. 10If we say,
“We have not sinned,” we make him a liar, and his word is not
in us. 1My children, I am writing this to you so that you may not
commit sin. But if anyone does sin, we have an Advocate with
the Father, Jesus Christ the righteous one. 2He is expiation for
our sins, and not for our sins only but for those of the whole
world.

Responsorial Psalm – Psalms 124:2-3, 4-5, 7CD-8

R. (7) Our soul has been rescued like a bird from the fowler’s snare.

2 Had not the LORD been with us

When men rose up against us,

3 then would they have swallowed us alive,

When their fury was inflamed against us.

R. Our soul has been rescued like a bird from the fowler’s snare.

4 Then would the waters have overwhelmed us;

The torrent would have swept over us;

5 over us then would have swept the raging waters.

R. Our soul has been rescued like a bird from the fowler’s snare.

7CD Broken was the snare,

and we were freed.

8 Our help is in the name of the LORD,

who made heaven and earth.

R. Our soul has been rescued like a bird from the fowler’s snare.

Alleluia – cf. Te Deum

R. Alleluia, alleluia.

We praise you, O God, we acclaim you as Lord; the white robed army of martyrs praise you.

R. Alleluia, alleluia.

Gospel – Matthew 2:13-18

[13]When the magi had departed, behold, the angel of the Lord appeared to Joseph in a dream and said, "Rise, take the child and his mother, flee to Egypt, and stay there until I tell you. Herod is going to search for the child to destroy him." [14]Joseph rose and took the child and his mother by night and departed for Egypt. [15]He stayed there until the death of Herod, that what the Lord had said through the prophet might be fulfilled, Out of Egypt I called my son. [16]When Herod realized that he had been deceived by the magi, he became furious. He ordered the massacre of all the boys in Bethlehem and its vicinity two years old and under, in accordance with the time he had ascertained from the magi. [17]Then was fulfilled what had been said through Jeremiah the prophet: [18]A voice was heard in Ramah, sobbing and loud lamentation; Rachel weeping for her children, and she would not be consoled, since they were no more.

Friday December 29, 2023

Fifth Day in the Octave of Christmas

First Reading – 1 John 2:3-11

Beloved: [3]The way we may be sure that we know Jesus is to keep his commandments. [4]Whoever says, "I know him," but does not keep his commandments is a liar, and the truth is not in him. [5]But whoever keeps his word, the love of God is truly perfected in him. This is the way we may know that we are in union with him: [6]whoever claims to abide in him ought to walk just as he walked. [7]Beloved, I am writing no new commandment to you but an old commandment that you had from the beginning. The old commandment is the word that you have heard. [8]And yet I do write a new commandment to you, which holds true in him and among you, for the darkness is passing away, and the true light is already shining. [9]Whoever says he is in the light, yet hates his brother, is still in the darkness.[10]Whoever loves his brother remains in the light, and there is nothing in him to cause a fall. [11]Whoever hates his brother is in darkness; he walks in darkness and does not know where he is going because the darkness has blinded his eyes.

Responsorial Psalm – Psalms 96:1-2A, 2B-3, 5B-6

R. (11a) Let the heavens be glad and the earth rejoice!

1 Sing to the LORD a new song;

sing to the LORD, all you lands.

2A Sing to the LORD; bless his name.

R. Let the heavens be glad and the earth rejoice!

2B Announce his salvation, day after day.

3 Tell his glory among the nations;

among all peoples, his wondrous deeds.

R. Let the heavens be glad and the earth rejoice!

5B The LORD made the heavens.

6 Splendor and majesty go before him;

praise and grandeur are in his sanctuary.

R. Let the heavens be glad and the earth rejoice!

Alleluia – Luke 2:32

R. Alleluia, alleluia.

32 A light of revelation to the Gentiles and glory for your people Israel.

R. Alleluia, alleluia.

Gospel – Luke 2:22-35

22When the days were completed for their purification
according to the law of Moses, They took him up to Jerusalem
to present him to the Lord, 23just as it is written in the law of
the Lord, Every male that opens the womb shall be
consecrated to the Lord, 24and to offer the sacrifice of a pair of
turtledoves or two young pigeons, in accordance with the
dictate in the law of the Lord. 25Now there was a man in
Jerusalem whose name was Simeon. This man was righteous
and devout, awaiting the consolation of Israel, and the Holy

Spirit was upon him. 26It had been revealed to him by the Holy
Spirit that he should not see death before he had seen the
Christ of the Lord. 27He came in the Spirit into the temple; and
when the parents brought in the child Jesus to perform the
custom of the law in regard to him, 28He took him into his arms
and blessed God, saying: 29"Now, Master, you may let your
servant go in peace, according to your word, 30for my eyes
have seen your salvation, 31which you prepared in sight of all
the peoples, 32a light for revelation to the Gentiles, and glory
for your people Israel." 33The child's father and mother were
amazed at what was said about him; 34and Simeon blessed
them and said to Mary his mother, "Behold, this child is
destined for the fall and rise of many in Israel, and to be a sign
that will be contradicted 35and you yourself a sword will pierce
so that the thoughts of many hearts may be revealed."

Saturday December 30, 2023

Sixth Day in the Octave of Christmas

First Reading – 1 John 2:12-17

12I am writing to you, children, because your sins have been
forgiven for his name's sake.13I am writing to you, fathers,
because you know him who is from the beginning. I am writing
to you, young men, because you have conquered the Evil
One.14I write to you, children, because you know the Father. I
write to you, fathers, because you know him who is from the
beginning. I write to you, young men, because you are strong
and the word of God remains in you, and you have conquered
the Evil One.15Do not love the world or the things of the world.
If anyone loves the world, the love of the Father is not in
him.16For all that is in the world, sensual lust, enticement for
the eyes, and a pretentious life, is not from the Father but is
from the world.17Yet the world and its enticement are passing
away. But whoever does the will of God remains forever.

Responsorial Psalm – Psalms 96:7-8A, 8B-9, 10

R. (11a) Let the heavens be glad and the earth rejoice!

7 Give to the LORD, you families of nations,

give to the LORD glory and praise;

8A give to the LORD the glory due his name!

R. Let the heavens be glad and the earth rejoice!

8B Bring gifts, and enter his courts;

9 worship the LORD in holy attire.

Tremble before him, all the earth.

R. Let the heavens be glad and the earth rejoice!

10 Say among the nations: The LORD is king.

He has made the world firm, not to be moved;

he governs the peoples with equity.

R. Let the heavens be glad and the earth rejoice!

Alleluia

R. Alleluia, alleluia.

A holy day has dawned upon us. Come, you nations, and adore the Lord. Today a great light has come upon the earth.

R. Alleluia, alleluia.

Gospel – Luke 2:36-40

36There was a prophetess, Anna, the daughter of Phanuel, of
the tribe of Asher. She was advanced in years, having lived
seven years with her husband after her marriage,
37and then as
a widow until she was eighty-four. She never left the temple,
but worshiped night and day with fasting and prayer.
38And
coming forward at that very time, she gave thanks to God and
spoke about the child to all who were awaiting the redemption
of Jerusalem.
39When they had fulfilled all the prescriptions of
the law of the Lord, they returned to Galilee, to their own town
of Nazareth.
40The child grew and became strong, filled with
wisdom; and the favor of God was upon him.

Sunday December 31, 2023

Feast of Holy Family of Jesus, Mary & Joseph

First Reading – Sirach 3:2-6, 12-14

2God sets a father in honor over his children; a mother's
authority he confirms over her sons.
3Whoever honors his
father atones for sins, and preserves himself from them. When
he prays, he is heard;
4he stores up riches who reveres his

mother.[5]Whoever honors his father is gladdened by children, and, when he prays, is heard.[6]Whoever reveres his father will live a long life; he who obeys his father brings comfort to his mother.[12]My son, take care of your father when he is old; grieve him not as long as he lives. [13]Even if his mind fail, be considerate of him; revile him not all the days of his life; [14]kindness to a father will not be forgotten, firmly planted against the debt of your sins a house raised in justice to you.

Or Genesis 15:1-6; 21:1-3

[1]The word of the LORD came to Abram in a vision, saying: "Fear not, Abram! I am your shield; I will make your reward very great." [2]But Abram said, "O Lord GOD, what good will your gifts be, if I keep on being childless and have as my heir the steward of my house, Eliezer?" [3]Abram continued, "See, you have given me no offspring, and so one of my servants will be my heir." [4]Then the word of the LORD came to him: "No, that one shall not be your heir; your own issue shall be your heir." [5]The Lord took Abram outside and said, "Look up at the sky and count the stars, if you can. Just so," he added, "shall your descendants be." [6]Abram put his faith in the LORD, who credited it to him as an act of righteousness.[1]The LORD took note of Sarah as he had said he would; he did for her as he had promised. [2]Sarah became pregnant and bore Abraham a son in his old age, at the set time that God had stated.[3]Abraham gave the name Isaac to this son of his whom Sarah bore him.

Responsorial Psalm – Psalms 128:1-2, 3, 4-5

R. (cf. 1) **Blessed are those who fear the Lord and walk in his ways.**

[1] Blessed is everyone who fears the LORD,

who walks in his ways!

[2] For you shall eat the fruit of your handiwork;

blessed shall you be, and favored.

R. Blessed are those who fear the Lord and walk in his ways.

[3] Your wife shall be like a fruitful vine

in the recesses of your home;

your children like olive plants

around your table.

R. Blessed are those who fear the Lord and walk in his ways.

4 Behold, thus is the man blessed

who fears the LORD.

5 The LORD bless you from Zion:

may you see the prosperity of Jerusalem

all the days of your life.

R. Blessed are those who fear the Lord and walk in his ways.

Or Psalms 105:1-2, 3-4, 5-6, 8-9

R. (7a, 8a) The Lord remembers his covenant for ever.

1 Give thanks to the LORD, invoke his name;

make known among the nations his deeds.

2 Sing to him, sing his praise,

proclaim all his wondrous deeds.

R. The Lord remembers his covenant for ever.

3 Glory in his holy name;

rejoice, O hearts that seek the LORD!

4 Look to the LORD in his strength;

constantly seek his face.

R. The Lord remembers his covenant for ever.

5 You descendants of Abraham, his servants,

sons of Jacob, his chosen ones!

6 He, the LORD, is our God;

throughout the earth his judgments prevail.

R. The Lord remembers his covenant for ever.

8 He remembers forever his covenant

which he made binding for a thousand generations

9 which he entered into with Abraham

and by his oath to Isaac.

R. The Lord remembers his covenant for ever.

Second Reading – Colossians 3:12-21

Brothers and sisters: 12Put on, as God's chosen ones, holy
and beloved, heartfelt compassion, kindness, humility,
gentleness, and patience, 13bearing with one another and
forgiving one another, if one has a grievance against another;
as the Lord has forgiven you, so must you also do.14And over
all these put on love, that is, the bond of perfection. 15And let
the peace of Christ control your hearts, the peace into which
you were also called in one body. And be thankful. 16Let the
word of Christ dwell in you richly, as in all wisdom you teach
and admonish one another, singing psalms, hymns, and
spiritual songs with gratitude in your hearts to God. 17And
whatever you do, in word or in deed, do everything in the
name of the Lord Jesus, giving thanks to God the Father
through him. 18Wives, be subordinate to your husbands, as is
proper in the Lord. 19Husbands, love your wives, and avoid
any bitterness toward them. 20Children, obey your parents in
everything, for this is pleasing to the Lord. 21Fathers, do not
provoke your children, so they may not become discouraged.

Or Colossians 3:12-17

Brothers and sisters: 12Put on, as God's chosen ones, holy
and beloved, heartfelt compassion, kindness, humility,
gentleness, and patience, 13bearing with one another and
forgiving one another, if one has a grievance against another;
as the Lord has forgiven you, so must you also do. 14And over
all these put on love, that is, the bond of perfection. 15And let
the peace of Christ control your hearts, the peace into which
you were also called in one body. And be thankful. 16Let the
word of Christ dwell in you richly, as in all wisdom you teach
and admonish one another, singing psalms, hymns, and
spiritual songs with gratitude in your hearts to God. 17And
whatever you do, in word or in deed, do everything in the
name of the Lord Jesus, giving thanks to God the Father
through him.

Or Hebrews 11:8, 11-12, 17-19

Brothers and sisters: 8By faith Abraham obeyed when he was
called to go out to a place that he was to receive as an
inheritance; he went out, not knowing where he was to go.
11By faith he received power to generate, even though he was
past the normal age – and Sarah herself was sterile – for he
thought that the one who had made the promise was
trustworthy.12So it was that there came forth from one man,
himself as good as dead, descendants as numerous as the
stars in the sky and as countless as the sands on the
seashore.17By faith Abraham, when put to the test, offered up
Isaac, and he who had received the promises was ready to
offer his only son,18of whom it was said, "Through Isaac
descendants shall bear your name." 19He reasoned that God
was able to raise even from the dead, and he received Isaac
back as a symbol.

Alleluia – Colossians 3:15A, 16A

R. Alleluia, alleluia.

15A Let the peace of Christ control your hearts; 16A let the word
of Christ dwell in you richly.

R. Alleluia, alleluia.

Or Hebrews 1:1-2

R. Alleluia, alleluia.

1 In the past God spoke to our ancestors through the prophets;
2 in these last days, he has spoken to us through the Son.

R. Alleluia, alleluia.

Gospel – Luke 2:22-40

22When the days were completed for their purification
according to the law of Moses, They took him up to Jerusalem
to present him to the Lord, 23just as it is written in the law of
the Lord, Every male that opens the womb shall be
consecrated to the Lord, 24and to offer the sacrifice of a pair of
turtledoves or two young pigeons, in accordance with the
dictate in the law of the Lord. 25Now there was a man in
Jerusalem whose name was Simeon. This man was righteous
and devout, awaiting the consolation of Israel, and the Holy
Spirit was upon him. 26It had been revealed to him by the Holy

Spirit that he should not see death before he had seen the
Christ of the Lord.[27]He came in the Spirit into the temple; and
when the parents brought in the child Jesus to perform the
custom of the law in regard to him, [28]He took him into his arms
and blessed God, saying: [29]"Now, Master, you may let your
servant go in peace, according to your word, [30]for my eyes
have seen your salvation, [31]which you prepared in sight of all
the peoples, [32]a light for revelation to the Gentiles, and glory
for your people Israel." [33]The child's father and mother were
amazed at what was said about him; [34]and Simeon blessed
them and said to Mary his mother, "Behold, this child is
destined for the fall and rise of many in Israel, and to be a sign
that will be contradicted [35]and you yourself a sword will pierce
so that the thoughts of many hearts may be revealed." [36]There
was also a prophetess, Anna, the daughter of Phanuel, of the
tribe of Asher. She was advanced in years, having lived seven
years with her husband after her marriage, [37]and then as a
widow until she was eighty-four. She never left the temple, but
worshiped night and day with fasting and prayer. [38]And coming
forward at that very time, she gave thanks to God and spoke
about the child to all who were awaiting the redemption of
Jerusalem. [39]When they had fulfilled all the prescriptions of the
law of the Lord, they returned to Galilee, to their own town of
Nazareth. [40]The child grew and became strong, filled with
wisdom; and the favor of God was upon him.

Or Luke 2:22, 39-40

[22]When the days were completed for their purification
according to the law of Moses, They took him up to Jerusalem
to present him to the Lord, [39]When they had fulfilled all the
prescriptions of the law of the Lord, they returned to Galilee, to
their own town of Nazareth. [40]The child grew and became
strong, filled with wisdom; and the favor of God was upon him.

For comments, corrections, requests and other pieces of information that may help us serve you better, please contact:

Email: info@catholiclectionary.com

Website: www.catholiclectionary.com

Facebook: www.facebook.com/catholiclectionary

Twitter: https://twitter.com/catholiclector

Thanks and God Bless You!

Printed in Great Britain
by Amazon

19353937R00443